ON THE ROAD

YOUR COMPLETE DESTINATION GUIDE

D0372460

SURVIVAL GUIDE

VITAL PRACTICAL INFORMATION TO HELP YOU HAVE A SMOOTH TRIP

Directory
A–Z

THIS EDITION WRITTEN AND RESEARCHED BY

Brendan Sainsbury

John Noble, Josephine Quintero, Daniel Schechter

welcome to Andalucía

Land of Many Mysteries

Andalucía has multiple faces: a parched region fertile with culture, a conquered land that went on to conquer, a fiercely traditional place that has accepted rapid modernisation. Here, in the cradle of quintessential Spain, the questions are often as intriguing as the answers. Who first concocted flamenco? How did tapas become a national obsession? Could Cádiz be Europe's oldest settlement? Are those *really* Christopher Columbus' bones inside Seville's cathedral? And, where on earth did the audacious builders of the Alhambra get their divine inspiration from? Putting together the missing pieces of the puzzle is what makes travel in Andalucía the glori-

ous adventure it is, a never-ending mystery trail that will deposit you in places where you can peel off the checkered history in dusty layers. There's edgy Granada, arty Málaga, vivacious Seville, sleepy Setenil de las Bodegas, rugged Ronda, brassy Marbella, and even a rocky rump of the British Empire named after an erstwhile Berber warlord called Tariq.

A Cultural Marinade

The fascination of Andalucía springs from its peculiar history, Christianity and Islam. For centuries the region stood on the porous frontier between two different faiths and ideologies. Left to slowly ferment like a barrel of the bone dry local sherry, these

The smell of orange blossom, the lilt of a flamenco guitar, the flash of the matador's cape; memories of Andalucía stay with you like collected souvenirs, begging you to return

(left) Balcón de Europa beach, Nerja (p178), Málaga province
(below) Tapas bar in Sanlúcar de Barrameda (p116), Cádiz province

sometimes peaceful, sometimes battling kingdoms threw up a slew of esoteric cultural colossi: ancient mosques masquerading as churches, vast palace complexes strafed with stucco, a passionate musical genre bizarrely called flamenco, and a chain of lofty white towns that still dominates the arid, craggy landscape. This visually and viscerally compelling legacy can be found all over the region in places such as Córdoba's Mezquita, Jerez' music venues and the hilltop settlements of Cádiz province.

Beyond the Coast

It takes more than a few ugly Costa del Sol condo towers to steamroller 3000 years of illustrious history. Indeed, large tracts of Andalucía's coast remain relatively unblemished, while inland, you'll stumble into sun-bleached white villages where life doesn't seem to have changed much since playwright Federico Lorca envisioned *Bodas de Sangre* (Blood Wedding). The local bar is where it all happens. The noisy farmers in flat caps playing dominoes, the faded photo of a long dead flamenco singer taped clumsily to the wall, the ruined Moorish castle winking through the open doorway, and those ubiquitous Andalucian aromas – lemon trees, church incense, frying garlic – that work on your senses, making you wonder that just perhaps, in a previous life, you were Andalucian too.

› Andalucía

ELEVATION

2000m
1500m
1000m
500m
200m
100m
0

N

| 0 | | 80 km |
| 0 | | 40 miles |

Córdoba
Western and Islamic architecture
spanning 1000 years (p183)

Seville
Gothic church meets
Mudéjar palace (p46)

SPAIN

EXTREMADURA

Santa
Eufemia

Badajoz

Mérida

Pozoblan

CÓRDOBA

Peñarroya-
Pueblonuevo

Río Guadiato

La Capitana
(959m)

Guadalcanal

**Parque Natural
Sierra de Aracena
y Picos de Aroche**

Jabugo

Aracena

**Parque
Natural Sierra
Norte**

Constantina

**Parque Natural
Sierra de
Hornachuelos**

Córdoba

Beja

PORTUGAL

Rosal
de la
Frontera

Castaño
(966m)

Zalamea la Real

Río Odiel

HUELA

Palma
del Río

Lora
del Río

Écija

Río Huesna

Río Genil

SEVILLA

Carmona

Marchena

Osuna

Seville

Monte
Francisco

Lepe

Huelva

Almonte

Coria del Río

Utrera

Río Guadalquivir

Ayamonte

Isla
Cristina

Punta
Umbría

**Parque
Nacional
de Doñana**

Coripe

Corbones

MÁLA

El Chorro

Matalascañas

*Golfo
di Cádiz*

Trebujena

Villamartín

*Embalse de
Bornos*

El Torreón
(1654m)

Olvera

Ronda

El Bur

37°N

Sanlúcar de
Barrameda

Jerez
de la Frontera

**Arcos de la
Frontera**

Grazalema

Ubrique

Torreci
(1918m)

Parque
Natural Sie
de las Niev

Parque Nacional de Doñana
Island of biodiversity in the
Río Guadalquivir delta (p117)

*Bahía
de Cádiz*

CÁDIZ

**Parque Natural
Sierra de
Grazalema**

Gaucín

Mar

Cádiz

San Fernando

Medina
Sidonia

San Pedro
de Alcántara

Cádiz
Dive into the riotous fun of
Europe's oldest city (p103)

Conil de la Frontera

Los Caños de Meca

Costa de la Luz

Barbate

**Parque
Natural del
Estrecho**

Gibraltar (UK)

36°N

Zahara
de los Atunes

Bolonia

Algeciras

Costa de la Luz
Room to loaf on broad
yellow-sand beaches (p131)

Tarifa

Strait of Gibraltar

Ceuta

*ATLANTIC
OCEAN*

Tangier

MOROCCO

6°W

5°W

7°W

Tarifa
Andalucía's windsurfing and
kiteboarding capital (p133)

Ronda
Clifftop town in brawny
mountain setting (p165)

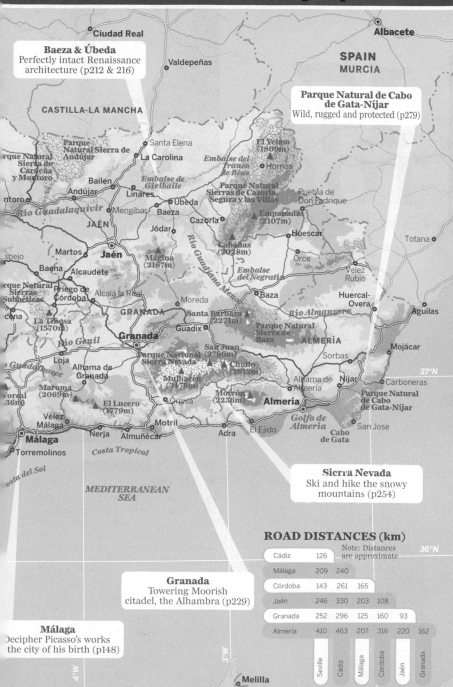

Baeza & Úbeda
Perfectly intact Renaissance
architecture (p212 & 216)

SPAIN
MURCIA

**Parque Natural de Cabo
de Gata-Níjar**
Wild, rugged and protected (p279)

CASTILLA-LA MANCHA

Sierra Nevada
Ski and hike the snowy
mountains (p254)

Granada
Towering Moorish
citadel, the Alhambra (p229)

Málaga
Decipher Picasso's works
the city of his birth (p148)

ROAD DISTANCES (km)

	Cádiz	Málaga	Córdoba	Jaén	Granada	
Cádiz	126	Note: Distances are approximate				
Málaga	209	240				
Córdoba	143	261	165			
Jaén	246	330	203	108		
Granada	252	296	125	160	93	
Almería	410	463	207	316	220	162
	Seville	Cádiz	Málaga	Córdoba	Jaén	Granada

17
TOP
EXPERIENCES

Alhambra

1 What is there to say? If the Nasrid builders of the Alhambra (p229) proved one thing, it was that – given the right blend of talent and foresight – art and architecture can speak far more eloquently than words. Perched on a hill with the snow-dusted Sierra Nevada as a backdrop, Granada's towering Moorish citadel has been rendering visitors speechless for nigh on 1000 years. The reason: a harmonious architectural balance between humankind and the natural environment. Fear not the dense crowds and the snaking queues; this is an essential pilgrimage.

Seville's Cathedral & Alcázar

2 The 13th-century builders of Seville's cathedral (p49) wanted to construct a church so big that future generations would think they were mad. They gloriously succeeded. Only a bunch of loco architectural geniuses could have built a Gothic masterpiece this humongous. Offering greater subtlety and more intricate beauty is the adjacent Alcázar (p53), still a palace for the Spanish Royals and an identikit of Mudéjar architecture. The two buildings sit side by side across from the Plaza del Triunfo in ironic juxtaposition.

Ronda

3 For Ronda (p165), read 'rugged'. First, there's the brawny mountain setting in the Serranía de Ronda where the town sits atop sheer cliffs. Second, there's the embattled history infested with bandits, smugglers, warriors and rebels. Third, there's the local penchant for bullfighting – Spain's modern bullfighting tradition was carved out here by the hard-bitten Romero and Ordóñez families. And fourth, there are the famous artistic connections with self-styled 'rugged' Hollywood types, namely Ernest Hemingway and Orson Welles. Dust off your mountain boots and pay it a visit.

Córdoba's Mezquita

4 A church that became a mosque before reverting to a church, Córdoba's Mezquita (p186) charts the evolution of Western and Islamic architecture over a 1000-year trajectory. Its most innovative features include some early horseshoe arches, an intricate mihrab (prayer niche), and a veritable 'forest' of 856 columns, many of them recycled from Roman ruins. The sheer scale of the Mezquita reflects Córdoba's erstwhile power as the most cultured city in 10th-century Europe. It was also inspiration for even greater buildings to come, most notably in Seville and Granada.

Sherry Tasting

5 A very Spanish product made for very British tastes, sherry is often considered a drink for mildly inebriated English grannies sitting down to discuss blue rinses before Sunday lunch. But wine·lovers can dig deeper. Here in the sun-dappled vineyards of Cádiz province, fortified white wine has been produced since Phoenician times and enjoyed by everyone from Christopher Columbus to Francis Drake. To get a sniff of its oaky essence, head to the historic 'sherry triangle' towns of Jerez de la Frontera (p118), El Puerto de Santa María (p112) and Sanlúcar de Barrameda (p116).

Sierra Nevada & Las Alpujarras

6 Snow in Andalucía is a rarity, which adds more exoticism to the Sierra Nevada (p254; literally 'snowy mountains'), the mountain range that forms a lofty backdrop to one of the most striking cityscapes in Spain, nay, Europe – Moorish Granada. Other rarities here include Andalucía's only ski station and a chance to scale mainland Spain's highest peak. The scattered white villages on the mountain's southern slopes are known communally as Las Alpujarras and are well known for their ancient craft-making and agricultural fertility.

Flamenco

7 Like all great anguished music, flamenco has the power to lift you out of the doldrums and stir your soul. It's as if by sharing in the pain of innumerable generations of dispossessed misfits you open a door to a secret world of musical ghosts and ancient Andalucian spirits. On the other side of the coin, flamenco culture can also be surprisingly jolly, jokey and tongue-in-cheek. There's only one real proviso: you have to hear it live, preferably in its Seville-Jerez-Cádiz heartland.

6

7

Cabo de Gata

8 For a cherished memory of what the Spanish coastline used to look like before mega-resorts gatecrashed the Costa del Sol, come to Cabo de Gata (p280) in Almería province, a wild, rugged, golfcourse-free zone where fishing boats still reel in the day's catch and bold cliffs clash with the azure Mediterranean. Considering it's one of the driest areas of Europe, the Cabo is abundant with feathered fauna and scrubby vegetation. It's also a protected area, so you can wave goodbye to your car; biking and hiking are the best means of transport.

Tapas

9 Spanish cuisine might have gone molecular in recent years but there's no getting away from the basics. Tapas define Spain's *style* of eating as much as its *type* of cuisine, a long drawn-out smorgasbord of tasting and savouring that can go on well into the night. Seville claims the most creative *platillos*, although *malagueños* might agree to differ. Granada is one of few places in Spain that still serves up recession-busting free tapas with every drink you order at the bar.

Cádiz

10 The *gaditanos* (citizens of Cádiz) are Spain's great laughers and jokers. Here in the city of ancient *barrios* (districts) and the nation's greatest Carnaval (p109), nothing is taken too seriously. Even the locally concocted brand of flamenco, known as *alegrías*, is uncharacteristically joyful and upbeat. Sitting like a great unlaunched ship on a peninsula that juts into the Atlantic, Cádiz (p103) also sports the region's most romantic sea drive, its most expansive municipal beaches and an unbelievable stash of sights that are free to visit.

Parque Nacional de Doñana

11 A figurative 'island' of biodiversity in the delta of the Río Guadalquivir, Parque Nacional de Doñana (p82) is one of Europe's most important wetland sites, and one of only two national parks in Andalucía. Offering multiple nature excursions, the region is a precious landfall for migrating waterfowl and home to the rare Iberian lynx. Long a blueprint for ecomanagement, the park's assertive environmental policies have set precedents on how to balance the wonders of the natural world with the demands of tourism and agriculture. Iberian lynx

Beaches of Costa de la Luz

12 Habitual Costa del Sol–goers may not have heard of Barbate, Zahara de los Atunes or El Palmar, as Andalucía's less known west-facing Atlantic coast is wilder and windier than the southern Mediterranean beaches. But it's also far less crowded, and for those in the know, what the Costa de la Luz (p131) lacks – theme parks, fish-and-chip shops, and a massive hotel infrastructure – is actually its main draw. Beach loafers are outnumbered by windsurfers, horse-riders and happy wanderers, though there's plenty of room to loaf on broad sweeps of fine yellow sand should you desire.

11

12

WITOLD SKRYPCZAK / GETTY IMAGES ©

13

HILARY MORGAN / ALAMY ©

Málaga's Picasso Museum

13 Aside from being the font of Renaissance art during Spain's Siglo de Oro (Golden Century), Andalucía also produced one of the most famous and influential artists of the 20th century, Pablo Picasso. A son of Málaga and grandfather of Cubism who ultimately went on to make a bigger name for himself in Barcelona and Paris, the modernist master, nonetheless, posthumously bequeathed the city of his birth with a fine museum. Opened in 2003, the Museo Picasso Málaga (p148) displays a fascinating cross-section of nearly 300 of the artist's works.

Semana Santa in Seville

14 Only the *sevillanos* could take the themes of grief and death and make them into a jaw-dropping spectacle. Many cities around the world mark the Catholic feast of Holy Week (p65), but none approach it with the verve and outright passion of Seville. Watch ancient processions led by various *hermanadades* (brotherhoods; the oldest dating back to 1340) shoulder elaborately decorated floats through the city streets in an atmosphere doused in emotion and religious significance.

Renaissance Baeza & Úbeda

15 These two little-visited outposts etched in the olive groves of Jaén province look more Italian than Spanish. It's the perfectly intact Renaissance architecture that deceives you. Remodelled by urban planners in the 16th century, the monumental palaces and symmetrical civic buildings introduced Renaissance ideas to Spain and ultimately provoked its assimilation into Latin America. In 2003 Baeza (p212) and Úbeda (p216) joined the Alhambra, Córdoba's Mezquita and Seville's cathedral as an Andalucian Unesco World Heritage Site, yet they get far less foot traffic. Baeza

DAVID C TOMLINSON / GETTY IMAGES ©

BEN WELSH / GETTY IMAGES ©

Touring the White Villages

16 Choosing your favourite white village is like choosing your favourite Beatles album. They're all so good it's hard to make a definitive decision. Pressured for an answer, most people tend to look out for the classic calling cards: a thrillingly sited location, a soporific old town, a fancy *parador* hotel, and a volatile frontier history. The best examples lie dotted all over the region with two heavy concentrations: one in eastern Cádiz province (p124) and the other in the mountainous Alpujarras (p254). Tour them by bike, foot, car or bus. Vélez Blanco

Windsurfing in Tarifa

17 If Andalucía has a hallmark outdoor activity, it is windsurfing, a daring white-knuckle sport given extra oomph by the stiff winds that enliven the choppy waters off the Straits of Gibraltar. The activity, along with its riskier sporting cousin, kiteboarding, has lent a hip vibe to the Costa de la Luz and its windy southern nexus Tarifa (p133), a whitewashed coastal town that often feels more Moroccan than Spanish. Cool windsurfing and kiteboarding outlets proliferate along the nearby beachfronts providing a refreshing antidote to the kitsch of the Costa del Sol.

need to know

Currency
» Euro (€);
Gibraltar pound (£)

Language
» Spanish (Castellano);
English in Gibraltar

When to Go

Córdoba
GO Oct–May

Seville
GO Oct–Apr

Granada
GO Sep–Jun

Almería
GO Oct–Apr

Málaga
GO year-round

Dry climate
Warm to hot summers; cold winters

High Season
(Jun–Aug)

» The sun is boiling hot in the summer and the climate very dry.

» Most Spaniards holiday in July and, in particular, August; expect traffic jams and heavy crowds.

» Hotels hike up their prices.

Shoulder
(Mar–May, Sep–Oct)

» Hotel prices can triple during Semana Santa and the various city and town ferias.

» Ideal weather – warm, but not too hot.

» In spring there is a colourful cavalcade of Andalucian festivals to choose from.

Low Season
(Nov–Feb)

» Climate remains warm and relatively dry on the Costa del Sol, but cooler and wetter inland.

» Skiing is possible in the Sierra Nevada.

» The best time for hotel bargains, but some sights close up for the winter.

Your Daily Budget

Budget less than
€65

» *Hostales* and *pensiones* €25–50

» Tapas and shared *ración* plates

» Make the most of free sights

Midrange
€65–140

» Room at a midrange hotel €65–120

» Main meal at lunch or dinner, some cheap evening entertainment

» Use buses to get around

Top end over
€140

» Stay at *paradores* or boutique hotels

» Regular meals in good restaurants

» Take in evening dinner and a show; use taxis and AVE trains

Visas

» Generally not required for stays of up to 90 days (not at all for members of EU or Schengen countries); some nationalities need a Schengen visa.

Money

» ATMs widely available. Credit cards accepted in most hotels, restaurants and shops.

Mobile Phones

» Local SIM cards widely available and can be used in European and Australian mobile phones.

Accommodation

» Huge range of accommodation options from historic *paradores* and luxury boutique hotels to quaint rural homestays and humble hostels.

Websites

» **Turismo Andalucía** (www.andalucia.org) Encyclopedic official tourism site.

» **Holiday in Spain** (www.spain.info) Useful official site.

» **Andalucia.com** (www.andalucia.com) One of the most interesting and comprehensive guides to the region.

» **Lonely Planet** (lonelyplanet.com /spain/andalucia) Build your own itinerary.

» **Iberianature** (www.iberianature.com) Devoted to Spain's natural world.

Exchange Rates

Australia	A$1	€0.78
Canada	C$1	€0.75
Japan	¥100	€0.91
Morocco	Dh1	€0.09
New Zealand	NZ$1	€0.62
UK	UK£1	€1.20
US	US$1	€0.75

For current exchange rates see www.xe.com

Important Numbers

Telephone numbers in Spain don't use area codes; simply dial the nine-digit numbers as they appear in this guide.

Country code	☎ +34
International access code	☎ +00
Ambulance	☎ +061
Emergency	☎ +112
National police	☎ +091

Arriving in Andalucía

» **Seville Airport**
Bus – €2.40; leaves every 15 minutes at peak times to the city centre; every 30 minutes off-peak and Sundays
Taxi – €21–25; takes about 15 to 20 minutes

» **Málaga Airport**
Train – €1.20–1.30; leaves every 20 minutes; takes 15 minutes to city centre
Bus – €1.20; number 75 leaves for city centre (20 minutes) every 20 to 30 minutes from outside main arrivals hall at Terminal 3
Taxi – €15–19

Driving in Andalucía

Andalucía has an excellent road system. Though public transportation provision is good, some visitors elect to opt for the greater freedom offered with a hire (or private) car. If you're renting, you'll save time organising the details before you leave. Bank on paying €120 to €150 for a four-door economy car. Málaga Airport firms have some good deals. Traffic is rarely heavy on country roads, but cities are a different matter. Metro areas such as Seville have introduced many traffic restrictions in recent years; once you've located your city accommodation and parked, you may want to spend the rest of your urban time exploring by foot, bike or public transport. Parking in cities can be sporadic. Pay car parks aren't always cheap (approximately €1 per hour), but they are generally secure. Drive on the right.

what's new

For this new edition of Andalucía, our authors have hunted down the fresh, the transformed, the hot and the happening. These are some of our favourites. For up-to-the-minute recommendations, see lonelyplanet.com/andalucia.

Metropol Parasol, Seville

1 Seville's giant 'flying waffle' has injected a dose of modernism into the city's traditional urban core. Sparking predictable controversy, the jury's still out on its architectural merits. (p59)

Museo Carmen Thyssen, Málaga

2 Look out for Málaga! Andalucía's emerging art capital has just added a new string to its bow in this showcase of 19th-century Spanish and Andalucian art. (p149)

Hammam Aíre de Almería, Almería

3 A new luxury *hammam* in an old Arab souq (marketplace) has added a touch of cool class to hot Almería. (p275)

El Pabellon de la Navegación, Seville

4 Another new architectural icon on the banks of Seville's Río Guadalquivir; this museum and exhibition space focuses on the city's longstanding relationship with the sea. (p63)

Smurf Town, Júcar

5 The white village of Júcar in Málaga province was painted blue in 2011 when a big-grossing Smurf film was shot there. It has since become a big, blue tourist attraction. (p169)

Unesco Listings

6 In 2010, Unesco added two cornerstones of Andalucian culture to its list of Intangible Cultural Heritages: 'Flamenco' and the 'Mediterranean diet'.

Hotel Casa 1800, Seville

7 Seville's historic new Santa Cruz hotel puts service and all-round friendliness on par with its plush new interior. Highlights are the rooftop penthouses and the free afternoon *merienda* (a 5pm snack). (p290)

Medina Azahara, Córdoba

8 The sleek new museum on this Cordoban archaeological site has cleverly blended in with the ruins of Abd ar-Rahman III's legendary palace-city. (p192)

Francisco Bernis Birdwatching Centre, El Rocío

9 A window over the Parque Nacional de Doñana marshes in Huelva province with ornithological experts on hand to identify the multitude of bird species. (p85)

Museo de Nerja, Nerja

10 Pretty coastal Nerja in Málaga province has gained a history museum with an ethnological vent filled with artefacts found in the famous caves nearby. (p178)

Gibraltar Expansion

11 Making the most of its diminutive size, the British territory has continued to expand, completing the plush Ocean Village marina and a new airport terminal. (p139)

if you like...

Hiking

A mountainous region with a long coastline, bags of historical diversions and a balmy climate, Andalucía ought to be higher up on the list of the world's great hiking destinations. Get out and discover what few have yet to cotton on to.

Grazalema Guided-only hikes or vigorous solo stints through brawny mountain ruggedness among flying vultures and delicate orchids. (p125)

Parque Natural Sierra Nevada The lost world of Huelva province is a mystery to many, a jigsaw of pastoral paths punctuated by tiny time-warped villages. (p254)

Cabo de Gata Sixty kilometres of wild coastal paths ought to be enough to prove that 'spoiled' isn't the only adjective to describe Andalucía's much maligned *costas* (coasts). (p280)

Sierra Nevada Tick off mainland Spain's highest peak, Mulhacén or the easier and slighter Veleta, both possible as day hikes for the physically fit. (p254)

Parque Natural Sierra de Hornachuelos Some little-known easy walks west of Córdoba in an untrampled natural park. (p200)

Beaches

Beaches may well have saved Andalucía's economy in the 1960s and '70s by luring in pallid Brits and Germans. These days the best ones are often the least frequented strips of sand, wedged between lairy coastal resorts.

Cabo de Gata You can pretend you're still living in the 1950s in the sheltered sandy coves of the Costa de Almería's protected littoral. (p280)

Cádiz The grand Playa de la Victoria is large enough to accommodate most of Cádiz' population on hot weekends in summer. (p109)

Nerja A cute Málaga province beach town that has found the right balance between tourism and authenticity. (p178)

Zahara de los Atunes Run marathons on the wide empty beaches of the Costa de la Luz with the continent of Africa shimmering on the horizon. (p132)

Almuñécar Welcome to the Costa Tropical. Never heard of it? Head east out of Málaga and keep going until you hit tourist-free serenity. (p263)

Moorish Architecture

Andalucía exhibits plenty of fine genres of architecture, but it is Moorish that turns the most heads. To many the style marks the high-watermark of artistic expression in Europe. Doubters should head to Seville and Granada to be converted.

Alhambra In a thousand years of history it never got any better than this. The high point of Moorish (nay, all!) architecture was reached in the 1350s under Sultan Muhammad V. (p229)

Alcázar (Seville) Only the Alhambra could overshadow the Alcázar, which is only a few smidgeons down on the brilliance scale. (p53)

Mezquita One of the greatest mosques ever built is today a Christian church and a historical manual of early Al-Andalus architecture. (p186)

Alcazaba (Almería) A magnificent fort in an equally magnificent coastal setting from where it once rivalled the Alhambra. (p267)

Giralda Formerly a minaret, now a bell tower; this Moorish remnant blends with surprising harmony into the Gothic mass of Seville's cathedral. (p49)

» Tapas, Granada

Great Local Food

Guarding Spain's culinary tradition while the rest of the nation samples foamed beetroot and frozen air of parmesan, Andalucian menus star fish dishes, with meat stews offering a good supporting role. Then there's the never-ending pot-luck of tapas.

Sanlúcar de Barrameda Fantastic fish moulded into highly inventive tapas and all washed down with a glass of that subtly salty manzanilla sherry. (p116)

Jabugo Created from black pigs fattened on acorns from the Parque Natural Sierra de Aracena y Picos de Aroche, Spain's luxury ham is best sampled in this Huelva town. (p91)

Granada Free tapas, Moroccan-influenced food, endless bars and cafes, and fresh vegetables plucked straight out of the nearby *vega* (agricultural land). (p243)

Málaga *Pescaito frito* (fried fish) is Andalucía's stand-out offering and it's ubiquitous here where you can enjoy it within sight of the sea with a glass of local wine. (p154)

Hilltop Towns

Going to Andalucía and not visiting a hilltop town is like going to Rome and not eating pizza. Dozens of these white cubist fantasies dot the region's rugged landscape like sparkling sentinels from another era.

Arcos de la Frontera The quintessential white town with all the classic features: ruined castle, mysterious church and dazzling Moorish houses, all clinging to a steep crag. (p129)

Vejer de la Frontera You'll fall in love here with cavernous Moorish restaurants, ornate tiled fountains, esoteric festivals, luxury boutique hotels and an indescribable timelessness. (p131)

Olvera A Grazalema province white town from which you can gain immediate access to others, preferably by plying the Vía Verde de la Sierra (a public greenway) on a bicycle. (p125)

Capileira A different kind of white village clinging to a steep-sided valley in Las Alpujarras where crafts are hewn and hikers strike out for the Sierra Nevada. (p259)

Fine Arts

Great Spanish art crawls don't have to end in Madrid's Prado. Andalucía famously directed the art world during El Siglo de Oro (the Golden Century), spearheaded by local artists Velázquez, Murillo and Zurbarán. Not surprisingly, their legacy is painted all over the region.

Málaga Pablo Picasso ought to ring a bell even with the most lukewarm gallery-goers. The great master was born in Málaga and the city is keen to brag about him in the Museo Picasso Málaga. (p148)

Seville The Museo de Bellas Artes is the obvious draw, but there are also fine works by Murillo and Zurbarán hanging in Seville's cathedral. (p58)

Cádiz Great art can be seen for free upstairs at the Museo de Cádiz including important work by the Andalucian masters. (p103)

Granada Lots of art hides in Granada's holy buildings including the Capilla Real museum by the cathedral and the intricately painted Monasterio de San Jerónimo. (p239)

month by month

January

The year starts quietly, but it's a relative quiet. Various romerías (religious pilgrimages and celebrations) and saints' days have upped the ante by the end of the month, including San Sebastián Day (20 January). Average temperatures in Málaga remain an unfrigid 12°C.

Día de los Reyes Magos

To celebrate the Feast of the Epiphany on 6 January, effigies of the three kings are carried through myriad Andalucian towns and villages. The accompanying bearers traditionally throw sweets into the amassed crowds, a practice largely aimed at children.

Festival de Jerez

The self-styled *cuna* (cradle) of flamenco hosts what is claimed to be the world's most esteemed flamenco festival (www.festivalde jerez.com) with every great artist this side of Camarón de la Isla stepping up to perform. Unlike Seville's biennial, it's an annual fixture spread over two weeks.

Carnaval

February is carnival season around the globe and Cádiz hosts mainland Spain's biggest with a spectacle that draws more on humour and satire than Rio de Janeiro–style grandeur. The party continues for 10 days. Anyone left standing can pitch into the Festival de Jerez.

Festival Internacional de Tango

International tango performances and dancing in the streets of Granada from mid to late March makes this one of Andalucía's best music/dance festivals (www .eltango.com). NB: this is tango as in the Argentine dance as opposed to the tango flamenco style.

Semana Santa (Holy Week)

The calm before the storm, the woe before the re-birth; there are few more elaborate manifestations of Catholic Holy Week than in Seville (p65), where hooded *nazarenos* (penitents) carry huge floats through the streets in ghostly solemnity. Other cities share in the grief and grandiosity.

February

Enter the big guns. Cádiz' carnival and Jerez' flamenco festival lure people from far and wide in February. It's also the best month for skiing in the Sierra Nevada, while the coast gauges a balmy 13°C.

March

The best time to visit Andalucía starts now, especially in years when Easter falls early. Sombre Semana Santa parades usher in a season of ebullient festivals that heat up as the weather gets warmer.

April

Possibly the best month of all to visit, April promises fine (but not boiling) weather and exuberant festivals headlined by the big one in Seville. Hotel prices can go through the roof, but rooms still fill up early.

Feria de Abril

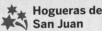

Seville's legendary spring fair (p66) proceeds something like this: drink sherry, ride a horse, dance *sevillanas*, hit the bumper cars, drink more sherry, and stumble home at 2am-ish. It's the blueprint for all spring fairs everywhere and a full bullfighting program runs alongside it.

Moto GP

Jerez' horse, flamenco and sherry aficionados also harbour a subtler motorcycle obsession: the yearly Spanish Motorcycle Grand Prix (p121) takes place here. Supporters arrive in convoy from all over Spain and many camp near the circuit in scenes resembling a giant HOG get-together.

May

The mountain slopes are strewn with wild blooms, the sunflowers are out, and everyone in Andalucía seems to be getting on their horses to take part in romerías or summer fiestas.

Feria del Caballo

Jerez hogs many of the region's best festivals including the famous horse fair (p122) that dates back to medieval times and involves plenty of parades, bullfights, fair rides and make-shift bars serving the best local sherry.

Romería del Rocío

The mother of all pilgrimages (p86) attracts over one million people annually to the obscure village of El Rocío in Huelva province to venerate the Virgin of El Rocío. They come from all directions by foot, horseback, carriage and boat. Date changes according to Easter.

Concurso de Patios Cordobeses

Everything happens in Córdoba in May from a flower festival to a spring fair. Sandwiched in between is this homage (p192) to the city's gorgeous patios where home owners open up their courtyards to compete for the title of 'best patio'.

June

The summer fiesta season is in full swing with every town and village in Andalucía hosting their own particular shindig. If Easter's late, Penteco Mojácar Pueblo st and the Romería del Rocio (second day of Pentecost) can fall in June.

Festival Internacional de la Guitarra

Flamenco is the focus of this two-week guitar festival (p193) held in late June or early July in the (by then) sizzling city of Córdoba, but you'll also hear live classical, rock and blues performances.

Corpus Christi

Another moveable Catholic feast celebrated eight-and-a-half weeks after Easter, Corpus Christi is particularly significant in Granada (p243) where, despite the underlying solemnity, it has long been fused with the annual feria.

Lush greenery traditionally carpets the streets.

Hogueras de San Juan

Bonfires and fireworks, especially on beaches, are the heart of this midsummer celebration held on 23 June. Known as St John's Eve in English, the day celebrates the supposed birthday of St John the Baptist. Many people camp overnight along Andalucía's beaches.

July

Exiles from Northern Europe hit the Mediterranean beaches. You can stay and converse with them, or escape to the hiking trails in the mountainous interior for some fresh, cloud-free hikes.

Virgen del Carmen

The patron saint of fishermen and seafarers is venerated in Andalucía every 16 July in a multitude of coastal towns (including Estepona, Barbate, Cádiz and Málaga), where her effigy is paraded around the littoral on a flower-adorned boat amid music and fireworks.

August

It's hot. Seriously hot. Hit the beaches for some sea breezes and Málaga's fiesta-ing answer to Seville. If you're on the costas, bear in mind that half of Spain will be joining you. Book ahead!

Feria de Málaga

Trying hard to emulate Seville's festival

and nearly succeeding, Málaga hosts Andalucía's second-most famous party (p153) and is awash with all of the usual calling cards: sherry, lights, dancing and fireworks. Mysteriously, relatively few Costa del Sol tourists show up.

September

At last, some relief from the heat. September promises good hiking weather, and it is harvest time for grapes. Jerez and Montilla both have wine festivals.

 Bienal de Flamenco

Seville (p66) shares this biennial flamenco festival with Málaga – the former city hosting it in even-numbered years. Top-notch artists have been gracing the stages since 1980 to perform at the 30-day event.

Feria de Pedro Romero

More costumes and more bulls, this time in the mountain town of Ronda (p167) where elaborate Goya-era attire is donned in an attempt to add historical significance to the 'ballet' of

bullfighting. A full program of events ensues.

Fiestas de Otoño

Jerez again! Even extravagant rock stars would have a tough time keeping pace in this fiesta-packed city. This shindig (p122) uses the grape harvest as an excuse to tread on grapes, drink sherry and play *bulerías*-orientated flamenco.

October

Autumn brings the harvest and an alluring stash of food festivals. Look out for cheese tastings, soup days and ham cutting contests.

Feria de la Tapa

Head to unheralded Sanlúcar de Barrameda for some alfresco tapa tasting in this great fish-biased culinary town. You can wash down the best plates with *copas* (glasses) of the local manzanilla sherry.

November

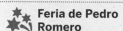 **A big month for agriculture with pig slaughters and the peak of the olive tree harvest. It's also the start**

of low season, though weather-wise Seville still registers nearly 200 hours of sunshine.

La Matanza

Rivalling the Feria de Pedro Romero as Andalucía's most macabre spectacle is November's pig slaughter, known as *la matanza*, which traditionally starts on 11 November – St Martin's Day. It's an upbeat affair held in many mountain villages with plenty of eating and drinking.

December

You think they'd be wiped out after a year of nonstop merry-making, but the Andalucians save enough energy for one last hurrah – Christmas. Otherwise December is low-key unless you're going skiing.

Fiesta Mayor de Verdiales

On 28 December the village of Almogia in Málaga province organises a competition of fandango-like folk dances known as *verdiales*. Groups of singers and dancers called *pandas* dress in ribboned costumes and play an obscure type of flamenco with guitars and violins.

itineraries

Whether you've got six days or 60, these itineraries provide a starting point for the trip of a lifetime. Want more inspiration? Head online to lonelyplanet.com /thorntree to chat with other travellers.

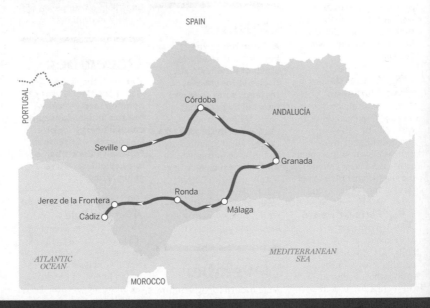

Two Weeks
Highlights

> You'll need months to poke into every corner of Andalucía, but two weeks can bag you the highlights. The best starting point is unmissable **Seville**, deserving of three days, where the famous cathedral and Alcázar stand side by side in surreal juxtaposition. Head 150km east by train and a few centuries back in time to explore **Córdoba**, site of the ancient Mezquita and guarder of hidden patios. Free tapas, shadowy tea-rooms and the incomparable Alhambra beckon in **Granada**, where you could fill at least three days reclining in Moorish bathhouses and deciphering the Lorca paraphernalia. Easily reached by bus, **Málaga** is understated by comparison. Spend a day absorbing the Picasso museum and sample fresh-from-the-Med seafood. **Ronda** is a dramatic contrast, surrounded by mountains and doused in bullfighting and rebel-rousing history. You'll be unlucky to hit **Jerez de la Frontera** and not take in a festival; the city is also famous for its horses, sherry bodegas and flamenco. Forty minutes away by train, **Cádiz** has an abundance of free sights including a fine city museum and an aficionado's flamenco club. You can contemplate your trip's achievements while walking its romantic *malecón* (sea drive).

SPAIN

PORTUGAL

Aracena

Córdoba

Baeza Úbeda
Cazorla

Carmona

Seville

ANDALUCÍA

Granada

Arcos
de la
Frontera

Olvera

Almería

Jerez de la Frontera

Ronda

Cádiz

Ubrique Grazalema

Málaga Almuñécar

ATLANTIC
OCEAN

MEDITERRANEAN
SEA

MOROCCO

One Month
Grand Tour

Lucky devils with a month to spare can linger a few days in **Seville**, visiting the obvious sights (the cathedral, Alcázar and some festivals) and the less obvious ones (Casa de Pilatos, Triana, and some quirkier flamenco haunts). Sorties to the west lead to Huelva province, which is prime hiking country if you head to the north where the gentle pastoral hills around **Aracena** promise legendary walks between sleepy villages. Passing back through Seville, head east, stopping for a day in gentle **Carmona** before a serendipitous escape to the serially overlooked Sierra Norte. On week two, head to **Córdoba**, long a historical foil to Seville, where you can map Andalucian history in its whitewashed streets, Roman relics and Islamic architecture. Tracking east to Jaén province delivers you to the land of olive oil and weighty Renaissance architecture. The former can be seen pretty much everywhere you look. The latter is concentrated in the twin towns of **Baeza** and **Úbeda**. Further east, **Cazorla** is the gateway to Andalucía's largest protected area, but one visited only by a small minority. **Granada** is a more mainstream sight at the start of week three, but loaded with exotic majesty. Checking all the provinces you'll need to circumnavigate the Sierra Nevada to **Almería**, the dry east that once hosted Spaghetti Western films. Hit the coast at the unadulterated Spanish town of **Almuñécar** and follow it west through ever-growing resorts to **Málaga**, the Costa del Sol city that is actually nothing like the Costa del Sol. Start your last week in **Ronda**, which has been on most itineraries since Hemingway visited, and for good reason – a bullfighting museum that contains work by Goya, plunging gorges and premier white-town status lure the masses. The white towns continue across the border in Cádiz province; pick and choose between **Olvera**, **Grazalema** and **Ubrique** and enjoy the surrounding natural parks. Attempts to bypass **Arcos de la Frontera** are normally futile – the sight of the spectacular hilltop settlement practically drags you off the bus. Your final week can be spent tying up the threads of Andalucía's culture in **Jerez de la Frontera** and **Cádiz**, two ancient yet quintessential cities that contain all the ingredients that have made this region so great.

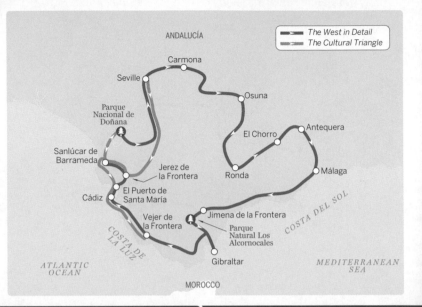

ANDALUCÍA

The West in Detail
The Cultural Triangle

Carmona

Seville

Osuna

Parque
Nacional de
Doñana

Antequera

El Chorro

Sanlúcar de
Barrameda

Jerez de
la Frontera

Ronda

Málaga

Cádiz

El Puerto de
Santa María

Vejer de
la Frontera

Jimena de la Frontera

COSTA DEL SOL

COSTA DE
LA LUZ

Parque
Natural Los
Alcornocales

ATLANTIC
OCEAN

Gibraltar

MEDITERRANEAN
SEA

MOROCCO

Two Weeks
The West in Detail

Start in Huelva province's **Parque Nacional de Doñana**, possibly Andalucía's finest natural attraction and a rare European wetland replete with birdlife. **Seville** broadcasts a litany of well-known sights, but its provincial hinterland is less heralded. Visit the tranquil towns of **Carmona** (with its Alcázar) and **Osuna** (with its grand palaces). Rugged **Ronda** is well on the tourist trail, though if you stay overnight you'll wave goodbye to 80% of them. Recommended stops on the way to Málaga include **El Chorro** gorge and ancient **Antequera**. **Málaga** is a ballsy yet arty city that offers great seafood and a decent August feria. With time to linger you can visit some of Cádiz province's less trodden jewels: **Jimena de la Frontera** demands a detour, as does hiking in the **Parque Natural Los Alcornocales**. **Gibraltar** lures expat Brits missing roast beef and warm beer. Ply the Costa de la Luz next, spending at least one night in the white village of **Vejer de la Frontera**. A final few days can be devoted to the culturally intense quartet of **Cádiz**, **El Puerto de Santa María**, **Jerez de la Frontera** and **Sanlúcar de Barrameda**, enjoying a mixture of sherry, flamenco and seafood.

One Week
The Cultural Triangle

If you have to pick a smaller region-within-a-region that best sums up Andalucía's essence, head west to the triangle of territory between Seville, Cádiz and Jerez de la Frontera. With excellent air, rail and bus connections, **Seville** is the best starting point for this sojourn. Lap up the Moorish-meets-Gothic architecture and seemingly limitless festivals for a day or two. Fast trains now forge south to **Jerez de la Frontera**, first stop on the 'sherry triangle' where you can spend two days mixing bodega tours with horse shows, authentic flamenco and perhaps a *hammam*. Continuing west by bus to **Sanlúcar de Barrameda** gives you the option to compare *fino* with *manzanilla* and bag some of the best seafood tapas in Spain. This is also a good base for forays into the bio-diverse **Parque Nacional de Doñana**. Spend the evening in **El Puerto de Santa María**, home of more bodegas, festivals and fish restaurants. Surrounded by sea, **Cádiz** feels like the edge of Europe and the home of something mystical and old. The beaches here are famously broad and they continue south along the Costa de la Luz. Explore them from a base in **Vejer de la Frontera**, a dramatically perched white town with a refined air.

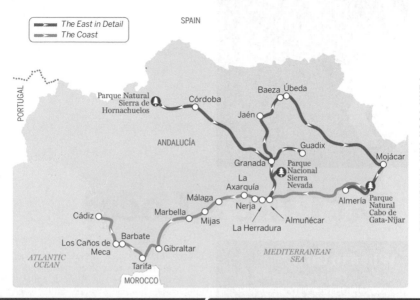

Three Weeks
The Coast

The coast looms large in Andalucía, lapping five of its eight provinces with most towns linked by bus. Empires were once built here, although more recently resorts have colonised the littoral. Start in underdeveloped **Cabo de Gata**, a spectacular combination of cliffs and salt flats. Tracking west you'll dock in **Almería**, worth a stop for its Moorish Alcazaba and winding streets. Granada's Costa Tropical is precipitous and authentic; **Almuñécar** is a great base for exploring and **La Herradura** offers good diving. A short bus ride west, **Nerja** has tempered its development better than other resorts while excellent hiking beckons in **La Axarquía**. **Málaga** deserves three days of this trip; its international reputation has sky-rocketed in recent years thanks to its fine art and inventive gastronomy. **Marbella** is possibly the most interesting stop on the busy Costa del Sol, though **Mijas** merits a day trip. Further west, **Gibraltar** guards the jaws of Europe with British pubs and fascinating military history. Starting in windsurfing mecca **Tarifa**, the Costa de la Luz harbours a variety of flavours and different food. While away three days in **Barbate** and **Los Caños de Meca** with a grand two-day finale in **Cádiz**.

Two Weeks
The East in Detail

The east is Andalucía's less obvious itinerary filled with more esoteric attractions. Spend three days each in the two big-hitter cities. **Córdoba** is a must-see, the one-time Iberian capital with one of the finest Islamic mosques ever built. **Granada** showcases the later Nasrid era, in its Alhambra, Albayzín and Moorish-style bathhouses. You can use both cities as base for rural forays into nearby mountainous regions. Córdoba province's ample wilderness includes the **Parque Natural Sierra de Hornachuelos**. Granada has the **Parque Nacional Sierra Nevada** and Las Alpujarras, the valleys that embellish their southern slopes. Detours from here can include **Guadix**, with its unusual inhabited caves, and coastal **Almuñécar**, a bit of domestic seaside bliss detached from the Costa resorts. **Jaén** is olive-oil heaven and guard of fine tapas bars, while **Baeza** and **Úbeda** are unique for their Renaissance architecture. Almería province is Andalucía's far east: **Mojácar** promises a sometimes boho, sometimes glitzy taste of the Levante; **Cabo de Gata** is the region's most unspoiled coastal enclave; while **Almería**, the city, is a kind of Granada-on-the-sea with plenty of mystic Moorish relics.

Eat Like a Local

When to Go

Andalucía is unusual in Europe in that, due to the balmy climate and exceptionally fertile soil, fruit and vegetables can be grown year-round, especially in Almería province and on the Costa Tropical.

April–August Spring and summer mean gazpacho, Andalucía's signature chilled soup, which is accompanied by its regional variations such as *salmorejo* (Córdoba) and *ajoblanco* (Málaga).

August–September The grape harvest ushers in a number of wine festivals, most notably Jerez de la Frontera's Vendimia incorporated into the Fiestas de Otoño in September – an excellent opportunity to pair your finos and manzanillas with tapas.

November–January November is the start of the pig *matanza* (slaughter) and its accompanying feasts which are heavy on pork. The olive tree harvest is also underway. Winter is the time for hot roast chestnuts plied by street vendors, especially in the more mountainous areas.

Eating like a local in Andalucía will not only keep you in rude good health but it will also pass as a valid form of cultural immersion, especially since 2010 when Unesco recognised the Mediterranean diet – of which Andalucía is a primary proponent – as an Intangible Cultural Heritage.

Food-wise, tradition still rules in this part of Spain. You'll find a few of the gastro-boffins of the Basque and Catalonia regions setting up their chemistry labs here as well as plenty of fresh fish, legendary cured ham, year-round tomatoes and bitter-sweet olive oil.

Food culture in Andalucía isn't just about *what* you eat; it's also about *how* you eat. Typically, Andalucians enjoy savoury snacks for breakfast, graze regularly in small amounts, take their sweets at 5pm and eat dinner late. Don't resist while you're there – join them!

Food Experiences
Cheap Treats

» **Free tapas** That old adage about there being no such thing as a free lunch comes a cropper in Granada and Almería, two of Spain's last bastions of free tapas. Watch as small gratis snack plates arrive with every drink that you order.

» **Chiringuitos** Semipermanent beach shacks/restaurants that specialise in fried seafood. The staples – *espeto de sardinas* (sardine skewers) and *boquerones fritos* (fried anchovies) – are

VEGETARIANS & VEGANS

Throughout Andalucía fruit and vegetables are delicious and fresh, and eaten in season, but unfortunately there are only a handful of avowedly vegetarian restaurants in the region. A word of warning: 'vegetable' dishes may contain more than just vegetables (eg beans with bits of ham). Vegetarians will find that salads in most restaurants are a good bet, as are gazpacho (chilled tomato soup) and *ajoblanco* (a white gazpacho made from a blend of almonds, garlic and grapes). Another reliable dish is *pisto* (ratatouille), especially good when eaten with bread dipped in the sauce; or try *espárragos trigueros* (thin wild asparagus), either grilled or in *revueltos* (scrambled eggs cooked with slices of fried garlic). Tapas without meat include *pimientos asados* (roasted red peppers), *alcachofas* (artichokes), *garbanzos con espinacas* (chickpeas with spinach) and, of course, *queso* (cheese). A plate of Andalucian *aceitunas* (olives) is another staple of the region's tapas.

best washed down with a bottle of beer. Most *chiringuitos* only operate during the summer months.

» **Casetas** Temporary tents set up at Andalucía's seemingly endless round of festivals and parties. Many of them sell cheap snack-orientated food and drink.

» **Churros** Crunchy deep-fried doughnut-like strips that are best bought from street vendors or in small cafes. They're impossibly addictive when dipped in cups of thick hot chocolate.

» **Menú del día** A three-course lunchtime restaurant meal that's usually served with bread and wine. Prices start at €10, all included. It's not likely to be nouveau cuisine, but if you're on a budget...

Dare to Try Something Different

» **Rabo de toro** Stewed bull's tail that's cut from the toppled bull from the local *corrida de toros* (bullfight), preferably eaten on the same day.

» **Mollete** Toasted bread roll drizzled with olive oil and topped with raw garlic (and sometimes tomato). All very well, but you're supposed to eat it for breakfast!

» **Ortiguillas** Croquette-sized sea anemone deep-fried in olive oil. Their intense seafood flavour is considered a delicacy in the Cádiz area.

» **Partridge** Game meat best enjoyed in mountain villages in areas such as the Sierra de Grazalema and the Sierra de Cazorla.

» **Tripe stew** Just one of the many esoteric menu items at Ángel León's cutting-edge El Puerto de Santa María restaurant, Aponiente (p115).

» **Fish... with their heads on** Some visitors shirk at the sight of a fish's head on their – urgh – fish. Others see it as confirmation of the fish's freshness and authenticity. Whatever the case, you'll learn to live with it, as it's the Andalucian way.

Famous Chefs

» **Ángel León** The fish master from Andalucía applies some of Ferran Adrià's kooky creativity to seafood in the improbable culinary hotbed of El Puerto de Santa María. In 2011, his restaurant Aponiente (p115) was listed in the *New York Times* as one of 10 restaurants in the world that were 'worth a plane ride'.

» **Martín Berasategui** The well-known Basque chef/food scientist has seven Michelin stars to his name; his latest earned in 2011 for Santo Restaurante (p68) at Seville's EME Catedral Hotel.

» **Dani García** Formerly of Restaurant Tragabuches in Ronda, Garcia now oversees Calima (p160), a two-Michelin-star restaurant in Marbella where he experiments with his favourite ingredient – fish. He also juggles a seven-strong chain of tapas bars: La Moraga.

» **Pablo Grosso** Grosso presides over four restaurants in Cádiz and El Puerto de Santa María including Japanese- and Italian-influenced outlets, but his finest moments come in the old world–new world fusion of El Aljibe (p109) using fresh-from-the-market *gaditano* products.

Meals of a Lifetime

» **Vinería San Telmo** (p66) Seville's best tapas bar, bar none.

» **Ruta del Azafrán** (p243) Ambitious east-west fusion hits the spot at this trendy Granada eatery.

» **Casa El Padrino** (p91) Country cooking and a rustic Huelva province setting make for a memorable eating experience.

» **Casa Curro** (p96) Tradition meets modernity at this dreamy Osuna tapas bar.

» **Sabores** (p122) Flavours you won't forget are part of the furniture at this creative Jerez de la Frontera nook.

» **Calima** (p160) Dani García proves why he is Andalucía's top homegrown chef with his Marbella fish extravaganza.

» **El Aljibe** (p109) Cádiz' answer to the celebrity chefs of the north; Pablo Grosso makes cooking a work of art.

Cooking Courses

» **All Ways Spain** (www.allwaysspain.com) Cookery and food appreciation near Granada.

» **Finca Buen Vino** (www.fincabuenvino.com) Cookery classes in Huelva province.

» **On the Menu** (www.holidayonthemenu.com) Week-long or weekend course.

» **Cooking Holiday Spain** (637 80 27 43; www.cookingholidayspain.com) Fun, week-long Ronda-based cooking classes.

» **L'Atelier** (p260) Vegetarian cooking courses in Las Alpujarras.

» **Al-Andalus Spanish School** (www.alandalustarifa.com) Combines Spanish classes with cooking classes at a language school in Tarifa.

Local Specialities

Sevilla Province

As well as its extraordinarily varied tapas, Seville also produces some excellent sweets. *Polvorones* are small crumbly shortbreads that traditionally come from the town of Estepa. *Tortas de aceite* are sweet biscuits made from olive oil. *Huevos a la flamenco* is an ancient savoury dish made with morcilla sausage, garlic, onions and tomatoes topped with baked eggs. Seville's bitter oranges are primarily used to make marmalade, the breakfast spread so loved by the English.

Huelva Province

Two gastronomic words define Huelva province: strawberries (the region grows 90% of the Spanish crop) and *jamón ibérico*. The famous *jamón* (ham) is the champagne of Spain's cured meats and is produced from black Iberian pigs that roam freely in the Sierra de Aracena feeding mainly on acorns. Sweeter and nuttier than the more ubiquitous *jamón serrano*, it is served sliced wafer thin and is notoriously expensive.

Cádiz Province

Cádiz' Atlantic coast and river estuaries support different types of fish from the Mediterranean. Tuna headlines on the Costa de la Luz with the village of Barbate claiming the best catches. Prawns are similarly fabulous along the coast. In Sanlúcar de Barrameda they are put in fried pancakes called *tortillitas de camerones* and served as tapas. Cádiz is also the home of sherry (fortified wine). Jerez de la Frontera and El Puerto de Santa María produce the best *fino* (dry) and *oloroso* (dark and less dry) varieties. Sanlúcar de Barremeda makes its own unique manzanilla.

Málaga Province

The Med is all about fish, most notably the *boquerones* (anchovies) and *sardinas* (sardines) from Málaga. *Espeto de sardinas* are sardines grilled on a skewer. Eat 'em on the beach at a *chiringuito*. *Ajoblanco* is Málaga's take on cold gazpacho soup. It's the same basic recipe but with the tomatoes replaced by almonds, giving it a creamy white colour, and fresh grapes float on top. The local grapes also have a long history of producing sweet dessert wines (white and red), which have recently come back into fashion.

Córdoba Province

Landlocked Córdoba grows copious chickpeas and olives, while its grapes are made into Montilla wines from which comes the name *amontillado,* an unfortified sherry. Pedroches is a strong semicured sheep's milk cheese from the Pedroches-Alcudia Valley. Córdoba menu specialities include *salmorejo* (a thick gazpacho-like soup usually topped with boiled eggs and cured ham) and *flamenquín* (a pork loin wrapped in *jamón serrano,* then coated in breadcrumbs and deep-fried).

Granada Province

Few cuts of *jamón serrano* are better than those left to mature in the fresh mountain air of the village of Trevélez in Las Alpujarras.

» (above) Tapas at El Rinconcillo (p69),
  the oldest bar in Seville
» (left) Bodegas Castañeda (p247)
  in Granada

The mountains are also home to rabbit stews and goat *con ajo* (with garlic). Meanwhile, down on the flat plains of La Vega, beans and asparagus grow in abundance. Granada is Spain's most strongly Arabic-influenced city with some fine tagines, couscous and *teterías* (Moroccan-style teahouses).

Jaén Province

Jaén is the olive oil capital of the world, the province alone accounting for 10% of global production. Quality is understandably high; classic Jaén oils are bitter but fruity. The mountainous area of Parque Natural Sierras de Cazorla, Segura y Las Villas has a strong hunting fraternity and is famous for its game, in particular partridge.

Almería Province

There are more coastal fish here but rather than deep-frying them, Almerians tend to cook theirs *a la plancha* (on a metal grill). Then there's those ubiquitous greenhouses filled with fruit and vegetables soaking up the equally ubiquitous sun-rays. Almería is rightly famous for its plump year-round tomatoes.

How to Eat Like a Local

In Andalucía it's easy to spot an unversed tourist. They're that dog-tired, confused-looking, hypoglycaemic street wanderer who rolls into the local tapas bar at 6pm and tries to order full roast chicken with a two-litre jug of sangria. It doesn't have to be this way. Like a lot of things in life, eating in Andalucía is all about timing, etiquette and a little insider knowledge. Read on...

When to Eat

Tip number one: get into the groove and feast on Spanish time. A typical Andalucian eating day transpires something like this. Wake-up to a strong coffee accompanied by a light, sweet pastry, preferably taken standing up in a cafe. A more substantial *desayuno* (breakfast) can be procured at 10am-ish; the standard is a *mollete* (a bread roll, sliced in half, lightly toast, drizzled with olive oil and topped with fresh garlic and tomatoes). Your first tapa window comes at 1pm when you can *picar* (graze) your way through a few small plates as a prelude to a larger *almuerzo* (lunch) at 2pm-ish. Some favour a full-blown meal with starter and main, others just up the ante at the bar and order a selection of larger *media raciones* or *raciones*.

Next comes the siesta. Find somewhere you can lie down for an hour or two and close your eyes – you'll feel a lot better for it. If you're back vertical by 5pm consider having a revitalising *merienda*, a quick round of coffee and cakes (preferably in a cafe) to fill the hole between lunch and dinner. It is not impolite to start tapa-ing again around 7pm, or closer to 8pm in the summer. Elbow your way to the bar and claim your *platillos* as you sip on a beer or perhaps a *tinto de verano* (red wine, fizzy lemonade and ice). Remember: sangria is for tourists. *Cena* (dinner) never happens before 9pm and is usually less substantial than lunch, especially if you've warmed up with some tapas first. It's almost a faux pas to hit the sack before midnight. At weekends many party until dawn. Enterprising *churros* (long doughnuts) vendors ply their sweet treats to insomniacs in the small hours. Why resist?

Etiquette

» Andalucians can't understand drinking without eating; and they don't get the Northern European habit of knocking back pint after pint of beer. Slow down, order a tapa and soak up the sultry Mediterranean atmosphere.

» When ordering beer you can order it in a bottle, or if you prefer draft beer, in a glass. A *caña* is a 250ml glass, a *tubo* is a longer 330ml glass. If you ask for a *cerveza*, you may only get a bottle.

» Spain avoids the coffee snobbery of Italy. It's no crime to drink a cappuccino after 10am. *Café con leche* is a latte, a *cortado* is a macchiato and a *sólo* is an espresso.

» Spanish waitstaff are hardworking and dexterous, but not as effusive as in North America. Don't expect so many 'How are you enjoying your meal?' interjections here.

» There's no real tipping culture – a bit of loose change on the table should suffice.

» Kids are welcome pretty much everywhere and few are tucked up in bed by 8pm. Instead, expect little Juan and María to be running between the tables well into the night.

ORDERING TAPAS

In Andalucía, tapas are more than just a way of eating – they're a way of life. *Tapeando* (going out for tapas) is a favourite Andalucian pastime and while it may serve as the prelude to lunch, it's often the main event in the evening when Andalucians drag out their evening meal through a combination of tapas and drink. It's an ideal way to sample a range of tastes.

Bars sometimes display a range of tapas on the counter – if they do, you can either take a small plate and help yourself or point to the morsel you want. If you do this, it's customary to keep track of what you eat (by holding on to the toothpicks for example) and then tell the bar person when it comes time to pay.

Tapas can draw on the culinary peculiarities of the region. In Huelva, it would be a culinary crime to order anything but the local *jamón ibérico*, while in Granada, North African tagine tapas reflect the city's days as the historical capital of Islamic Al-Andalus. In Cádiz province, the real luxury is seafood tapas, whether marinated, fried or fresh.

Here are a few more tapa bar tips:

» Tapas bars are often situated in clusters enabling you to go bar-hopping between drinks.

» Ordering tapas is a physical contact sport; be prepared to elbow your way to the bar.

» That massive crowd at the bar usually means something. Good tapas places aren't always fancy, but they're invariably crowded.

» Don't worry about all those discarded serviettes on the floor – it's the Andalucian way to brush them off the table.

» The best tapa time-spots are from 1pm to 3pm and 7pm to 9pm (slightly later in the summer).

Menu Advice

» Always ask for the house special tapa.

» *Media raciones* are a step up from tapas. They are small plates of food that are ideal for sharing between a couple or group, and are usually enjoyed in a more leisurely fashion sitting down.

» *Raciones* are a step up from *media raciones*, ie full plates that are great for sharing if you're particularly hungry.

» Andalucian paella is often made with almonds, sherry, chicken and sausages, as well as seafood.

» Olives and a bread basket accompany most meals. Olives are nearly always served green as opposed to black.

» Gazpacho is usually only available in spring and summer and usually comes in a glass.

» Sangria isn't ubiquitous, but *tinto de verano* is a good sub during spring and summer.

» Andalucians rarely drink sweet sherry; they prefer fino or manzanilla, especially with tapas.

Choosing a Restaurant

Like elsewhere in Spain, bars are places to eat and socialise as much as they are for drinking, but they do come in many guises. These include bodegas (traditional wine bars), *cervecerías* (beer bars), *tascas* (bars specialising in tapas), *tabernas* (taverns) and even pubs (especially where's there's an English influence). In many of them you'll be able to eat tapas at the bar but there will usually be a *comedor* (dining room) too, for a sit-down meal. You'll often save 10% to 20% by eating at the bar rather than a table.

Restaurantes are usually more formal places where you sit down to eat. A *mesón* is a simple restaurant attached to a bar with homestyle cooking. A *venta* is a roadside inn – the food can be delicious and inexpensive. A *marisquería* is a seafood restaurant, while a *chiringuito* is a small open-air bar or kiosk, usually fronting onto the beach.

Outdoor Activities

Walking Highlights

Mountain hikes Sierra Nevada; Parque Natural Sierra de Grazalema

Peak baggers Mulhacén (Sierra Nevada); El Torreón (Grazalema)

Hikes for wildlife spotting Parque Natural Sierras de Cazorla, Segura y Las Villas

Hikes for birdwatching Parque Nacional de Doñana

Pastoral hikes Sierra de Aracena; Parque Natural Los Alcornocales

Coastal hikes Parque Naturel Cabo de Gata-Níjar; Parque Natural de la Breña y Marismas de Barbate

Long-distance hike GR7 trail in Las Alpujarras

Hikes for splendid isolation Parque Natural Sierra Norte (Sevilla province)

Urban hike Around the seawall and *malecón* (sea drive) in the city of Cádiz

One of the more epiphanic experiences in Andalucía is discovering that, contrary to popular opinion, the bulk of the region remains uncommercialised, traditional and loaded with outdoor possibilities. OD'd on Granada's free tapas? *No problema.* Head 27km southeast to the Sierra Nevada ski slopes. Feeling claustrophobic in that kitschy Torremolinos resort? Fear not. Escape on a bicycle along a vía verde. And if none of this swings it for you, try scuba diving, rock climbing, horse riding, kiteboarding, or even hang-gliding.

Not that going on an outdoor adventure means you necessarily leave the culture behind. Old walking trails lead to time-worn villages where flat-capped farmers sink dry sherry while playing dominoes. Cycling paths meander past ruined castles. Divers explore old shipwrecks. Spain's great outdoors is as much a history lesson as it is a tonic for your health.

Walking

Walking in Andalucía gets you to where 95% of the annual visitors never go. So if you desire a bit of alone time, a rustic history lesson, or the feeling that you're strolling like a latter-day Byron or Richard Ford through unblemished rural bliss, this is your bag.

Footpaths are plentiful in the region; maps and signage less so. The best markers are in the natural and national parks and on major routes such as the GR7 (p136) where splashes of red and white paint mark the way. In some areas you can string together day walks into a trek of several days, sleeping along the way in a variety of hotels, *hostales* (budget hotels), camping grounds or occasionally mountain refuges. For about half the year the climate is ideal, and in most areas the best months for walking are May, June, September and October.

The two main categories of marked walking routes in Spain (even so, not always well marked) are *senderos de gran recorrido* (GRs; long-distance footpaths) and *senderos de pequeño recorrido* (PRs; shorter routes of a few hours or one or two days).

Many organisations run walking holidays in Andalucía including UK-based **Exodus** (www.exodus.co.uk); self-guided trips are also possible. Tourist offices are an excellent starting point for trail information, and city bookshops stock good maps and guides. Lonely Planet's *Hiking in Spain* guide lists some of the region's more popular walking routes.

Birdwatching

Situated at the jaws of the Mediterranean, a stepping stone between Africa and Northern Europe, Andalucía is a natural fly-by for approximately 360 species of bird. And where there are birds, there are birdwatchers. Raptors and water-birds are Andalucía's ornithological highlights. The former are best seen on the craggy outcrops that lie scattered throughout Andalucía's interior. The latter congregate in winter in their thousands in Parque Nacional de Doñana, lured by dunes, lagoons and marshes. Species to look out for include avocets, marbled teal and one of the largest heronries in the Mediterranean. For birds of prey, count on seeing black vultures, red kites, kestrels and various types of eagle.

Peñon de Zaframagón is a distinctive crag and bird sanctuary near Olvera in Cádiz province that can be accessed from the Vía Verde de la Sierra (a public greenway). It supports Europe's largest colony of Griffon vultures. Cabo de Gata in Almería province is another excellent birdwatching area (it has been nominated a Special Bird Protection Area by the EU). Flamingos famously reside on the coastal salt flats. Nearby on the arid steppe you'll find larks, bustards and seabirds such as razorbills. The 'special access areas' within Parque Natural Sierra de Grazalema support small numbers of rare Egyptian vultures, and larger numbers of Griffon vultures and golden eagles.

Birdwatching outfits, often run by expat Brits, abound. The following ply the best areas.

Andalucian Guides ($\boxtimes$956 43 29 49; www .andalucianguides.com) Run out of the Costa de la Luz coastal village of Barbate by an expat Brit. Day trips to the Costa de la Luz, Alcornocales and Doñana from €55.

Birdwatch Alpujarras (www.birdwatchalpujarras.com) Based in Lanjarón in the province of Granada, this outfit offers numerous trips in and around the Sierra Nevada including El Torcal and some nearby wetlands from €75 per day.

Horse Riding

Horses define Andalucía as much as flamenco and bullfighting – no spring festival is complete without them. The best centre for horse culture in the region is Jerez de la Frontera, home of the Feria del Caballo (p122) in May and the famous **Real Escuela Andaluza del Arte Ecuestre** (Royal Andalusian School of Equestrian Art; $\boxtimes$956 31 80 08; www .realescuela.org; Avenida Duque de Abrantes; adult/child €10/7; ⊙10am-2pm Mon, Wed & Fri Sep-Jul, 10am-2pm Mon & Wed Aug). The nearby Yeguada de la Cartuja – Hierro del Bocado (p124) breeding centre is also fascinating to visit.

Excellent riding tracks criss-cross the region's marvellous landscapes, and an ever-growing number of *picaderos* (stables) are ready to take you on a guided ride for any duration, or give you classes. Many of the mounts are Andalucians or Andalucian-Arab crosses – medium-sized, intelligent, good in traffic, and usually easy to handle and sure-footed.

Typical prices for a ride or lesson are €25 to €30 for one hour, €60 to €70 for a half day and around €100 for a full day. Most stables cater for all levels of experience, from lessons for beginners or children to trail rides for more competent riders. The ideal months to ride in Andalucía are May, June, September and October.

The provinces of Sevilla and Cádiz have perhaps the highest horse populations and concentrations of stables, but there are riding opportunities throughout the region. **Andalucía Te Quiere** (www.andalucia.com) has a directory of over 100 stables and other equestrian establishments.

Among the many highlights of riding experiences in Andalucía are trail rides around Ronda and the Sierra Nevada, and beach and dune riding just out of Tarifa on Cádiz' Costa de la Luz.

Other Activities

Whale-Watching

Whales and dolphins congregate around the Straits of Gibraltar where they are pushed into the middle of the narrow 20km-wide channel in order to enter/exit the Mediterranean. The best of the whale- and dolphin-watching trips are run out of the British colony of Gibraltar (p135).

Diving

Let's be honest, Andalucía isn't a world-class diving nirvana, but there are some worthwhile spots for underwater exploration should the heat on land get too much. The Atlantic coast with its strong currents is best avoided (aside from some interesting wrecks around Gibraltar) and the western Mediterranean, with its shallow, sandy coastal waters, is of similarly limited interest for aspiring divers. This leaves the eastern Med, more specifically the Costa Tropical in Granada province (especially around La Herradura) and, even better, Cabo de Gata in Almería province, a protected area with a varied seabed of sea grass, sand and rock flecked with caves, crevices or passages. The snorkelling quality follows a similar pattern, ie it's better the further east you travel.

Most establishments offer courses under the aegis of international diving organisations such as PADI or NAUI, as well as dives for qualified divers and 'baptism' dives. A single dive with full equipment costs around €50. Introductory courses for up to three hours run from about €75.

Skiing & Snowboarding

Unless you're Spanish, skiing and snowboarding in the Sierra Nevada, Europe's most southerly ski area, has a certain novelty value. Traditionally, Andalucía is better known for its heat than its snow, and ski snobs more attuned to the glitterati of St Moritz or Klosters tend to look down on it. Yet, although the Sierra Nevada slopes lack the mega-steep, off-piste action of Switzerland and France, it would be foolish to un-derestimate their skiing potential. These are the highest mountains in Europe outside the Alps and Caucasus with a top skiing elevation of 3300m and 100km of runs. Furthermore, snow can fall as early as November and linger on the ski slopes until early May. Other pros are the lack of lift queues (there are two cable-cars and numerous chair-lifts) and the abundance of winter sunshine – this, lest we forget, is Mediterranean Spain. The small settlement of Pradollano at the base (2100m) is a rather ugly, purpose-built ski resort, but it's linked to the much mightier attractions of Granada, 27km away, by regular bus.

A day ski pass plus equipment rental costs between €60 and €70, depending on when you go. Peak season is between Christmas and New Year and from early February to early March. Six hours of group classes at a ski school are €65.

Hang-Gliding

The little-known white town of Algodonales, perched on the edge of Parque Natural de la Sierra de Grazalema, is the improbable HQ of hang-gliding and paragliding in Andalucía, with a local paragliding school and enough stiff wind to have attracted the World Hang-Gliding Championships in 2001. The views ought to be good as well, as you drift like one of the local Griffin vultures over innumerable lakes, white towns and craggy mountains. **Zero Gravity** (☎615 372554; www.paraglidingspain.co.uk; one-week guided holidays from €500) are based locally. One-week learn-to-fly courses start at €900.

Cycling

In a country that has amassed ten Tour de France wins since 1991, pro cycling is a serious business, but there's a decent infrastructure for amateurs as well. Andalucía has widespread bike hire opportunities, prescribed bike trails, and a growing number of urban bike-sharing schemes (p67). Pockets of the cycling fraternity have even embraced that heretical American invention, mountain biking. Off-road bikes are well suited to the region's rugged terrain. Hot-spots include the El Chorro region, Parque Natural Sierras de Cazorla, Segura y Las Villas, and Las Alpujarras.

The safest, flattest and most family-friendly thoroughfares for cyclists are the vía verdes (p126), though rural roads are

GREENWAYS, HERE WE COME

Spain's best environmental idea in the last 20 years could well be its vía verdes (greenways), old disused railway lines that have been transformed into designated paths for walkers, cyclists and other forms of non-motorised transport, including wheelchairs. Hard though it is to believe, Spain has 7500km of disused railway tracks, and since 1993, 1800km of it has been torn up and made into vía verdes. There are currently 17 of them in Andalucía (a total of 450km) and each has its own unique story and character.

Aside from their natural attractions (bird reserves, olive groves, natural parks etc), the greenways also guard uncommon chapters of human history. The **Vía Verde del Aceite** in Jaén province once carried trains loaded with olive oil to the coast for export, while the **Vía Verde Riotinto** in Huelva province ferried miners to the famous opencast Rio Tinto mines. Many of the engineering features of the old train lines have been preserved including bridges, viaducts, tunnels and numerous old stations, some of which have been converted into shops, cafes or rural hotels (that hire bikes).

An obvious advantage of vía verdes is their relatively slight gradients (these, after all, are ex-railway lines). Additionally, thanks to their comparatively recent overhaul, they are well-marked with kilometre posts and equipped with maps, lookouts and picnic areas.

Andalucía's finest greenway is often considered to be the **Vía Verde de la Sierra** in Cádiz province. Two more leading lights are the **Vía Verde del Aceite** in Jaén province and the **Vía Verde Subbética** in Córdoba province, which join up at the spectacular Guadajoz viaduct to form an unbroken 111km path.

also usually well maintained and not too jammed with traffic away from the population areas. Aspiring cyclists should beware of hot weather. The Río Guadalquivir valley – nicknamed the *sarten* or 'frying pan' of Andalucía for good reason – is a heat trap that you may want to avoid in July and August.

Rock Climbing

Mention Andalucía to anyone versed in rock climbing and they'll probably reply 'El Chorro'. This sheer limestone gorge above the Río Guadalhorce that lies 50km north of the city of Málaga contains well over one thousand climbing routes from easy to ultra-difficult, many of which start from the infamous Camino del Rey, a three-foot wide (currently decrepit) path that literally hangs off the side of the rock-face.

The climbing fraternity is based in the tiny village of El Chorro (p171), with experts congregating at the **Finca La Campana** (☎626 96 39 42; www.fincalacampana. com), which also offers accommodation. You can organise rock-climbing trips through La Campana or Andalucia Aventura (p171). Andalucía has other limestone crags, most notably El Torcal de Antequera in Málaga province and Los Cahorros in the Sierra Nevada.

The climbing season is October to April. A good climbing guidebook on the area is *Andalucía* by David Munilla (2007).

Windsurfing & Kiteboarding

Windsurfing and Tarifa go together like Wimbledon and tennis. The scene was first ignited in the early 1980s and the subsequent influx of boarding enthusiasts into the small town has given it a hip, outdoorsy character. The primary draw for windsurfers is the stiff winds that lap the Straits of Gibraltar. Rental of a board, sail and wetsuit costs around €35 per hour or €75 per day, with a six-hour beginner's course starting at around €120.

Kiteboarding, windsurfing's newer and more dangerous younger sibling, is a more extreme sport with all the adrenalin-spikes and latent risks that go with it. A six-hour beginner's course should cost about €120. Windsurfing and kiteboarding schools are two a penny in Tarifa (p134) these days and the area also hosts a number of annual competitions and festivals. Be warned: the strong winds and choppy seas off the Costa de la Luz aren't always beginner's territory.

Travel with Children

Best Regions for Kids

Málaga Province
Parents may balk, but the theme parks around Torremolinos and Benalmádena on the Costa del Sol have undeniable appeal for children, while beaches with shallow waters and boat rides should have the whole family smiling.

Almería Province
And now for something completely different... the Wild West shoot 'em up shows in Tabernas are bound to blow their little socks off (not literally you understand...).

Seville
Seville has a great leafy park, horse-drawn carriage rides, boat trips and an amusement park on the former Expo site.

Cádiz Province & Gibraltar
Older kids will love the kite- and windsurfing in Tarifa – one of the major destinations for the sport in Europe. You can also hop on a ferry to Morocco for the day – something different for their show-and-tell back home.

Spain is a family-friendly destination. The culture revolves around the (extended) family, and children are adored. Any child whose hair is less than jet black will get called *rubia* (blonde) if she is a girl, *rubio* if he is a boy. Children accompanied by adults are welcome at all kinds of accommodation and in virtually every cafe, bar and restaurant.

Local children stay up late, and at fiestas it's commonplace to see even tiny ones toddling the streets at 2am. Visiting children invariably warm to this idea, but can't always cope with it quite so readily.

It may seem obvious but always make a point of asking staff at tourist offices for a list of family activities, including traditional fiestas, plus suggestions on hotels that cater for children.

For further general information about travelling with children see Lonely Planet's *Travel with Children* or visit the websites www.travelwithyourkids.com, www.oddizzi.com and www.familytravelnetwork.com.

Andalucía for Kids
Stripped back to Andalucian basics, the beaches and fabulous climate here are pretty good raw ingredients. Add to this water sports, museums, parks, boat rides and loads of ice cream and it becomes serious spoil-them-rotten time. Note that the majority of theme parks and entertainment for children is in Málaga province, especially along the Costa del Sol.

Away from the coast, you may not find so many dedicated kiddie attractions, but every town will have at least one good-sized children's playground. Public spaces, such as town and village plazas, also morph into informal play spaces with children kicking a ball around, riding bikes and playing, while parents enjoy a drink and tapa in one of the surrounding terrace bars. Many Andalucian towns also have municipal swimming pools, which are ideal in summer.

Eating & Drinking

Whole families, often including several generations, sitting around a restaurant or bar table eating and chatting is a fundamental element of the lifestyle here, and it is rare to find a restaurant where children are not made welcome. Even if restaurants do not advertise children's menus (and few do), they will still normally be willing to prepare a small portion for your child or suggest a suitable tapa or two.

Note that high chairs in restaurants are increasingly common but they're by no means universal.

Favourite Foods

Perhaps not the healthiest of snacks, but you can't go wrong with ordering your child a *churro* (or two), these thick tubular doughnuts are irresistible to children – and children at heart.

Discerning young diners may like to ease themselves into Andalucian cuisine by tasting various tapas which will allow them to sample new flavours gradually and on a small scale. *Tortilla de patatas* (potato omelette), *albondigas* (meatballs), salted almonds and, of course, chips (or French fries) are a good bet. You can also find kebabs or *shwarmas* in places with a large North African population – they are essentially a hot chicken wrap and suitably tasty (and messy) to be a big hit with most youngsters.

Aside from the normal selection of soft drinks on offer, you can generally find freshly squeezed orange juice in most bars. Another popular choice for children is *Cola Cao* (chocolate drink) served hot or cold with milk.

Discounts

Children pay two thirds on the high-speed AVE train, but full price on most bus and ferries. There are generally discounts for admissions to sights and those under four generally go free.

> ### CHILD-FRIENDLY ICON
>
> A child-friendly icon (🚼) has been added to sights, eating and sleeping options in this book that seem to be particularly appropriate for children or go out of their way to welcome kids. This does not imply that other places in the book are not child-friendly.

Children's Highlights

Theme Parks

» **Tivoli World, Arroyo de la Miel** As well as various rides and slides, there are daily dance, musical and children's events.

» **Isla Mágica, Seville** Plenty of rides, including a roller coaster, plus pirate shows, bird-of-prey displays and more.

» **Crocodile Park, Torremolinos** Experienced guides provide lots of fascinating info about the various types of crocodile on view here – over 300 at last count.

» **Oasys/Mini Hollywood, Desierto de Tabernas** Wild West shows, stagecoaches, can-can dancers and a zoo at this former film set for Westerns.

» **Parque Acuático Mijas, Mijas Costa** – Plenty of chutes and slides, plus a separate minipark for toddlers.

Museums

» **Parque de las Ciencias, Granada** – A fun modern science museum with plenty of hands-on exhibits and displays for children, plus a planetarium.

» **Museo Lara, Ronda** – Vast private museum, includes an exhibition on witchcraft and torture instruments which little boys (in particular) will doubtless enjoy...!

» **Cueva Museo Municipal, Guadix** – Cave museum recreating typical cave life for a family.

» **Casa Museo de Mijas, Mijas** – Folk-themed museum with models, artefacts and a donkey made from esparto grass.

» **Museo del Bandolero, Ronda** – Dedicated to the local bandits with lots of photos, exhibits, weapons, plus a gift shop.

» **Museo del Baile Flamenco, Seville** – Includes daily flamenco performances at the family-friendly time of 7pm.

BEFORE YOU GO

» You can hire car seats for infants and children from most car-rental firms, but you should always book them in advance.

» No particular health precautions are necessary, but don't forget the sun protection essentials although they can be purchased here.

» Avoid tears and tantrums by planning which theme parks, museums and leisure pursuits you want to opt for and, more importantly, can afford early on in the holiday.

» English books can be hard to find here, so if your child enjoys reading or you have a story at bedtime routine, be sure to pack a couple to bring along.

Caves & Caverns

» **Cueva de Nerja, Nerja** Full of spooky stalactites and stalagmites.

» **St Michael's Cave, Gibraltar** A huge natural grotto with a lake and atmospheric auditorium.

» **Gruta de las Maravillas, Aracena, Seville** Explore 12 caverns here including stunning underground pools.

» **Cueva de la Pileta, Benaojan, Ronda** Fascinating uncommercial caves with narrow low walkways, lakes and cave paintings.

Wildlife

» **Biopark, Fuengirola** Animal-friendly and enclosure-free zoo in the centre of the town.

» **Zoo Jerez, Jerez de la Frontera** Over a thousand animals and two hundred species at this spacious Cádiz province zoo.

» **Selwo Aventura, Estepona** Wild animal park with an African theme and animals including rhinos, giraffes, hippos, and cheetahs.

» **Selwo Marina, Benalmádena** Aquariums, penguins, and dolphin (and other) shows.

» **Dolphin-watching, Gibraltar** The strait of Gibraltar is home to several different species of dolphin. Whales can be occasionally spotted, as well.

» **Parque Ornitológico Loro-Sexi, Almuñécar** Vast aviary with thousands of birds, plus parrot and birds-of-prey shows.

Other Sights & Activities

» **Hop-On Hop-Off City Sightseeing Buses** Open-top sightseeing bus in Seville, Granada, Cádiz, Benalmádena and Málaga.

» **Horse-Drawn Carriage Rides** Children can enjoy a clip clop around the city in Córdoba, Huelva, Málaga and Seville, as well as some smaller towns and resorts, including Marbella.

» **Fairs & Fiestas** Annual fairs are held in every Andalucian town and village and always include a fun fair with rides for kids.

» **Rowing Boats** Rent a rowing boat to paddle along the moat at Seville's Plaza de España or a four-wheel bike to explore the park further.

» **Windsurfing & Kiteboarding** Older children can take courses in both sports at Tarifa on the Cádiz coast.

» **Trip to Morocco** Take the speedy ferry from Tarifa to Tangier, Morocco for the day.

Planning

This is an easy-going, child-friendly destination with precious little advance planning necessary.

When to Go

July and August can be very busy with Spanish families as well as foreign tourists in the main tourist resorts, and some hotels are block-booked by tour companies. May to June and September to October are good for travelling with young children as it's still warm enough for paddling in the sea but has not yet reached serious sizzle factor. Theme parks and attractions are also not too crowded – aside from the Easter holidays, that is.

Accommodation

Most hotels and even *hostales* will be able to provide an extra bed or cot for a child or baby. However, always check and reserve in advance as there will be a limited number available. You will also be charged a supplement for this. When selecting a hotel, check whether it has a kids club, activities geared for youngsters and/or babysitting facilities.

Some top-end hotels may be able to help arrange childcare.

What's Available

Buy baby formula in powder or liquid form, and sterilising solutions, at *farmacias* (pharmacies). Disposable nappies are widely available at supermarkets and *farmacias*.

regions at a glance

Seville

Festivals ✓✓✓
Architecture ✓✓
Music ✓✓✓

Spring Events

No other city changes its personality so radically in the space of just one week as Seville when the constrained mourning of Semana Santa erupts into the carefree celebrations of the Feria de Abril. Springtime is the best time for festivals in Seville (check when Easter falls for exact dates), but realistically the party never stops.

p46

Cathedral & Alcázar

You can walk from bright geometric Mudéjar to dark atmospheric Gothic in less than 200 paces in central Seville, where the Alcázar and the Cathedral sit ambiguously side by side. The cathedral itself is something of a Moorish-Christian hybrid with its three-quarter Moorish Giralda bell tower. The architectural diversity is replicated to a lesser extent throughout the city in places such as the Torre del Oro and Casa de Pilatos.

Flamenco

Forget who invented it, Seville has the largest and most varied stash of flamenco venues in Andalucía. Triana is the best haunt for intimate *peñas* (small flamenco clubs) where you can hear *soleares* (a sad yet sometimes ironic piece), Barrio de Santa Cruz hosts some authentic *tablaos,* while during the raucous Feria de Abril folksy *sevillanas* (a form of Andalucian folk dance) are de rigueur. New on the block is an interesting flamenco museum.

Huelva & Sevilla Provinces

Wildlife ✓✓✓
Walking ✓✓
History ✓

Delta Birds

Parque Nacional de Doñana is surely one of Spain's – and Europe's – finest protected areas. Located in Huelva and Sevilla provinces in the Río Guadalquivir delta, the national park continues to treat visitors to sightings of rare birds and mammals.

Pastoral Trails

Guided and unguided walks are an obvious draw in Parque Nacional de Doñana, but Huelva province's north harbours the contrasting topography of the Parque Natural Sierra de Aracena y Picos de Aroche, an ancient pastoral region crisscrossed with easy walking trails.

Columbus et al

Huelva and Sevilla provinces are often bracketed as being 'on the way to Portugal', but they hide some surprising historical heirlooms, including Christopher Columbus paraphernalia, baroque Osuna, the old Almohad walled town of Niebla and the Moorish Almonaster La Real.

p74

Cádiz Province & Gibraltar

Food ✓✓
White Towns ✓✓✓
Music ✓✓✓

Fish & Sherry
Where the Atlantic meets the Mediterranean you're bound to find good fish, traditionally deep fried in olive oil to create *pescaito frito*. Then there's the sherry made from grapes that grow near the coast – a perfect complement.

Hilltop Settlements
They're all here, the famous white towns, with ruined hilltop castles, geranium-filled flower boxes and small somnolent churches. Arcos, Jimena, Castellar, Vejer... the ancient sentinels on a once volatile frontier that divided two different cultures.

Font de Flamenco
With a little help from Seville, the towns of Cádiz province pretty much created modern flamenco. Look no further than the *bulerías* of Jerez or the *alegrías* of Cádiz – all of them still performed in local *tablaos* and *peñas*.

p101

Málaga Province

Beaches ✓✓
Art ✓✓✓
Food ✓✓

Coastal Resorts
Málaga's beaches are an industry, bagging more tourist euros than the rest of the region put together. Choose according to your budget and hipster-rating between Estepona, Marbella, Fuengirola, Torremolinos, Málaga and Nerja.

Picasso & Beyond
So what if Picasso left town when he was still only 10 years old? The birthplace of the great master has branched out of late, launching two new art museums in as many years and proving that it may have just pipped Seville and Granada as Andalucía's 'art capital'.

Regional Dishes
On the coast, simple beachside *chiringuitos* (beach shack eateries) stand next to two-Michelin-star restaurants that specialise in fish. Inland, Antequera has some fine soups and desserts, while Ronda is home to mountain stews and meat dishes.

p144

Córdoba Province

Moorish Buildings ✓✓✓
Castles ✓
Natural Areas ✓✓

Córdoba Caliphate
Córdoba, the 10th-century caliphate, pretty much defined Islamic architecture 1000 years ago. You can still see it in all its glory, intact, in the famous Mezquita (Great Mosque) or – elegantly ruined – at the Medina Azahara just outside the city limits.

Border Fortifications
In Córdoba province's north, bordering the Castile region, numerous castles stand sentinel over the craggy landscape crowned by the sinister but dramatic Almodóvar del Río, a kind of Andalucian version of Harry Potter's Hogwarts.

Off the Beaten Track
Córdoba province has three little-visited natural parks including the wooded Sierra de Hornachuelos and the mountainous Sierras Subbéticas. North of the provincial capital lies the Sierra Morena, one of Andalucía's most remote regions.

p181

Jaén Province

Natural Areas ✓✓
Wildlife ✓
Architecture ✓✓

Andalucian Wilderness
Jaén province safeguards one of Europe's largest protected areas, the Parque Natural Sierras de Cazorla, Segura y Las Villas, as well as some lesser known, but no less beautiful, wild tracts such as the unsullied Parque Natural Sierra de Andújar.

Rare Fauna
Lynx, wolves, wild boar and mouflon are hardly ubiquitous in Andalucía. Your best chance of seeing these rare animals is probably in the quieter corners of Jaén province where protected parks and mountains break the monotony of the olive groves.

Renaissance Towns
Renaissance architecture makes a cameo appearance in Andalucía courtesy of Jaén province's two Unesco-listed pearls: Úbeda and Baeza, plus its less heralded provincial capital Jaén (the city) whose grandiose cathedral is befitting of a Granada or Seville.

p203

Granada Province

Architecture ✓✓✓
White Towns ✓✓
Culture ✓✓

Historical Eras
A celebrated Nasrid palace-fortress, a hilltop Moorish quarter, the charming Jewish 'Realejo' (a district of the city adjacent to the Alhambra that was the old Jewish quarter) and a baroque-Renaissance cathedral: Granada is a magnificent 'mess' of just about every architectural style known to European building.

Alpujarras Villages
Matching Cádiz province's white towns for spectacular beauty, Granada's *pueblos* are certainly higher, perched above the steep valleys of Las Alpujarras. They're notable for their artisan crafts, hearty mountain food and large communities of British expats.

Entertainment Scene
A university town with an arty vent and a strong literary tradition, Granada directs what happens next in Andalucía's social life these days. Seville might have the best festivals, but this city ultimately has the most varied entertainment scene.

p227

Almería Province

Coastal Scenery ✓✓✓
Film Sets ✓
History ✓✓

Resort-Free Coast
Forgotten, lucky or perhaps just too arid to develop, Cabo de Gata has escaped the Costa del Sol bulldozer treatment and lived to fight another day. Now protected as a natural park, it guards the most precious wildlife in the southern Mediterranean.

Mini-Hollywood
Mmm... that dusty desert backdrop looks familiar. Hang on. Isn't that where Sergio Leone shot Clint Eastwood in the Spaghetti Westerns and where Charles Bronson got shot in *The Magnificent Seven?* Come to mini-Hollywood and relive the Wild West.

Moorish Heritage
Often overlooked by Alhambra pilgrims, the city of Almería has plenty of stories to tell, many of them hailing from the pre-Christian era. Check out the old *medina* (old Moorish town) and Alcazaba (Moorish fort) before heading east for more Moorish mystery in Mojácar.

p265

> **Every listing is recommended by our authors, and their favourite places are listed first**

> **Look out for these icons:**

 Our author's top recommendation

 A green or sustainable option

 No payment required

See the Index for a full list of destinations covered in this book.

On the Road

Seville

POP 703,000 / ELEV 30M

Best Places to Eat

» Vinería San Telmo (p66)

» Los Coloniales (p68)

» Bar-Restaurante Eslava (p70)

» Restaurante Egaña Oriza (p66)

Best Places to Stay

» Hotel Casa 1800 (p290)

» Hotel Amadeus (p290)

» Hotel San Gil (p292)

» Hotel Sacristía de Santa Ana (p292)

Why Go?

Some cities have looks, others have personality. The *sevillanos* – lucky devils – get both, courtesy of their flamboyant, charismatic, ever-evolving Andalucian metropolis founded, according to myth, 3000 years ago by the Greek god Hercules. Doused in never-ending sunlight, Seville's beauty is relatively easy to uncover; pretty girls in polka-dot dresses riding in carriages to the Feria de Abril provides one of the more quintessential images. Its soul is a darker and more complex force, however. Flamenco's history is partially rooted here in the dusty taverns of Triana, and greedy conquistadors once roamed the sinuous streets of El Arenal counting their colonial gold. Tugged by the pull of both forces, it is Seville's capriciousness that leaves the heaviest impression. Come here in April and watch as haunting Semana Santa (Holy Week) metamorphoses into the cacophony of Feria de Abril (spring fair) and you'll wonder whether Bizet's Carmen wasn't more real than imagined.

When to Go

March to May is the best time to visit Seville when its two major festivals – Semana Santa and the Feria de Abril – run back to back. This is when the city wears its personality on its sleeve and is alive with colour, warm weather, orange blossom and that famous *pasión* (passion). The obvious downsides for spring visitors are the bigger crowds and elevated prices (rooms rates can triple). September and October are good quieter options, after the extreme heat of summer has diminished.

Getting Around

Seville offers a multitude of ways to get around, though walking still has to be the best option, especially in the centre. The Sevici bike-sharing scheme has made cycling easy and bike lanes are now almost as ubiquitous as pavements. The tram has recently been extended to the station of San Bernardo but its routes are still limited. Buses are more useful than the metro to link the main tourist sights. The recent 'greening' of the city has made driving increasingly difficult as whole roads in the city centre are now permanently closed to traffic; park on the periphery.

THREE PERFECT DAYS

Day 1: Lay of the Land

The joy of any new city is in those initial few hours when you're roaming the streets for the first time, sussing out the lay of the land. In Seville, you can get moving in the **Barrio de Santa Cruz**, contemplating intimate squares and narrow alleys. Come up for air in El Centro and brave a crowded tapas bar near **Plaza de la Alfalfa**. Admire (or not) the whimsical **Metropol Parasol** and the shopping chaos of **Calle Sierpes**. Then roll up for night-time drinks in the **Alameda de Hércules**.

Day 2: Big Hitters

The bell tower is calling you (literally). Take breakfast in the vicinity of Plaza Nueva and buy your ticket for the **cathedral**, which deserves at least two hours. Have lunch in the *barrio* (district) of **El Arenal** and stroll the river banks down to **Parque de María Luisa**. Two excellent museums will delay you here. Return to Santa Cruz, take tea at the **Baños Árabes** and book a ticket for a musical performance at the **Museo del Baile Flamenco**. Browse the exhibits until showtime at 7pm.

Day 3: Arty Seville

Go early to the **Alcázar** and take your time absorbing the palaces and gardens. Outside its walls you can lunch at **Catalina** or next door at **Vinería San Telmo**. Rent a Sevici bike and follow the cycle lanes to the **Museo de Bellas Artes**. After a dose of Murillo and Zurbarán, cross the river to **Triana** where ceramics shops beckon. Finish day three cruising the vivacious riverside strip of **Calle del Betis** for evening drinks and tapas.

Accommodation

Seville has boundless accommodation options in all categories, but it is still best to book well ahead during Semana Santa and Feria de Abril, when prices can treble. New top-bracket places include EME Catedral Hotel, Hotel Casa 1800 and Hotel Palacio Alcázar. Central bargains include Pensión San Pancracio and Hotel Simón. Read all about hotel choices in our dedicated Accommodation chapter (p288).

DON'T MISS

Reopened in 2012, El Pabellon de la Navegación (p64) explores Seville's history-defining relationship with the sea. It is the latest architectural icon in a city that stubbornly refuses to live in the past.

Best Places to See Flamenco

» Museo del Baile Flamenco (p58)

» Casa de la Memoria de Al-Andalus (p70)

» Tablao El Arenal (p70)

» Casa Anselma (p70)

Best Viewpoints

» Giralda (p49)

» Torre del Oro (p67)

» Schindler Tower at El Pabellon de la Navegación (p64)

» Panoramic walkway at Metropol Parasol (p59)

Resources

» **Explore Seville** (www .exploreseville.com) Covers everything from dining etiquette to safety.

» **Turismo de Sevilla** (www.visitasevilla.es) The city's official tourism site; its 'Accessible Guide' is useful for travellers with disabilities.

» **Guía Flama** (www .guiaflama.com) Who's flamencoing where and when? Find out here.

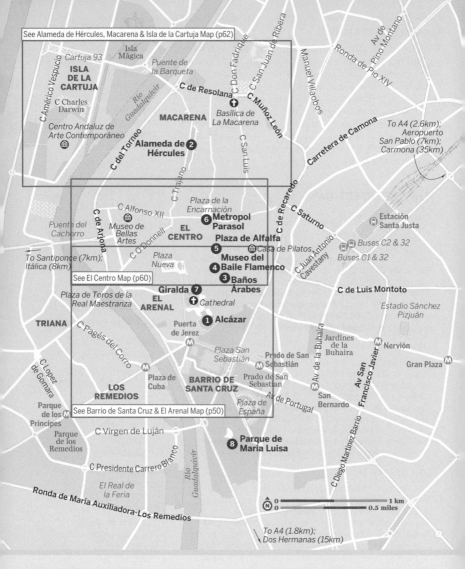

See Alameda de Hércules, Macarena & Isla de la Cartuja Map (p62)

ISLA DE LA CARTUJA

Cartuja 93

Isla Mágica

C Américo Vespucio

C Charles Darwin

Centro Andaluz de Arte Contemporáneo

Puente de la Barqueta

C de Resolana

C Don Fadrique

C San Juan de Ribera

C Muñoz León

Manuel Villalobos

Ronda de Pío Montano

Av de Pino Montano

MACARENA

Basílica de La Macarena

Alameda de Hércules ❷

Río Guadalquivir

C del Torneo

C San Luis

C de Arjona

Carretera de Camona

To A4 (2.6km); Aeropuerto San Pablo (7km); Carmona (35km)

Ronda de Pío XIV

Puente del Cachorro

C Alfonso XII

C Trajano

Plaza de la Encarnación

Metropol Parasol ❻

Plaza de Alfalfa

C de Recaredo

C Saturno

Estación Santa Justa

Museo de Bellas Artes

C O'Donnell

EL CENTRO

Museo del Baile Flamenco ❹

Casa de Pilatos ❺

Buses C2 & 32

C Juan Antonio Cavestany

Buses C1 & 32

To Santiponce (7km); Itálica (8km)

Plaza Nueva

Baños Árabes ❸

See El Centro Map (p60)

Giralda ❼

Cathedral

C de Luis Montoto

Plaza de Toros de la Real Maestranza

EL ARENAL

Alcázar ❶

Estadio Sánchez Pizjuán

TRIANA

C Pagés del Corro

Puerta de Jerez

Plaza San Sebastián

Prado de San Sebastián

Jardines de la Buhaira

Av de la Buhaira

Nervión

Gran Plaza

C López de Gomara

Plaza de Cuba

BARRIO DE SANTA CRUZ

Prado de San Sebastián

Av de Portugal

San Bernardo

Av San Francisco Javier

LOS REMEDIOS

See Barrio de Santa Cruz & El Arenal Map (p50)

Plaza de España

C Diego Martínez Barrio

Parque de los Príncipes

Parque de los Remedios

C Virgen de Luján

Parque de María Luisa ❽

C Presidente Carrero Blanco

Río Guadalquivir

El Real de la Feria

Ronda de María Auxiliadora-Los Remedios

N 0 — 1 km
0 — 0.5 miles

To A4 (1.8km); Dos Hermanas (15km)

Seville Highlights

❶ Picking up expensive interior-design and gardening tips at the exquisite **Alcázar** (p53)

❷ Enjoying an early evening glass of something alcoholic in the **Alameda de Hércules** (p70)

❸ Taking tea and a bath (or a bath and tea) at the moody **Baños Árabes** (p58)

❹ Attending an aficionados' concert at the **Museo del Baile Flamenco** (p58)

❺ Going tapa-ing in and around **Plaza de la Alfalfa** (p68)

❻ Strolling the panoramic walkway at the new **Metropol Parasol** (p59)

❼ Looking down on the Gothic Seville cathedral from the top of the **Giralda** (p49)

❽ Inhaling orange blossom while cycling a Sevici bike around **Parque de María Luisa** (p63)

History

Founded by the Romans, the city of Seville didn't really flower until the Moorish Almoravid period, which began in 1085. They were replaced by the Almohads in the 12th century, and Caliph Yacub Yusuf made Seville capital of the Almohad realm and built a great mosque where Seville's cathedral now stands. But as Almohad power dwindled after the disastrous defeat of Las Navas de Tolosa in 1212, Castile's Fernando III (El Santo; the Saint) went on to capture Seville in 1248.

Fernando brought 24,000 settlers to Seville and by the 14th century it was the most important Castilian city. Seville's biggest break was Columbus' discovery of the Americas in 1492. In 1503 the city was awarded an official monopoly on Spanish trade with the new-found continent. It rapidly became one of the biggest, richest and most cosmopolitan cities on earth.

But it was not to last. A plague in 1649 caused the death of half the city's population, and as the 17th century wore on, the Río Guadalquivir became more silted and less navigable. In 1717 the Casa de la Contratación (Contracting House; the government office controlling commerce with the Americas) was transferred to Cádiz.

The beginnings of industry in the mid-19th century saw the first bridge across the Guadalquivir, the Puente de Triana (or Puente de Isabel II), built in 1852, and the old Almohad walls were knocked down in 1869 to let the city expand. In 1936 Seville fell very quickly to the Nationalists at the start of the Spanish Civil War, despite resistance in working-class areas (which brought savage reprisals).

More recently, things have been looking up since the 1980s when Seville was named capital of the newly autonomous Andalucía (over the last quarter of a century a number of provinces in Spain have been given a certain amount of autonomy from Madrid). Seville's economy was steadily improving with a mix of tourism, commerce, technology and industry in the early 2000s. Then, in 2008, the financial crisis hit the city with a sharp jolt, as it did the rest of Andalucía. Although big metropolitan projects, such as the Metropol Parasol, have continued, the economic situation has remained dire with unemployment affecting one in four adults by 2012. Despite all this, the *sevillanos* (residents of Seville) have demonstrated remarkable social cohesion, pulling together to counter the crisis.

◉ Sights & Activities

Cathedral & Giralda   CHURCH

(Map p50; adult/child €8/free; ◷11am-5.30pm Mon-Sat, 2.30-6.30pm Sun Sep-Jun, 9.30am-4.30pm Mon-Sat, 2.30-6.30pm Sun Jul & Aug) Seville's immense cathedral, officially the biggest in the world (by volume), is awe-inspiring in its scale and sheer majesty. It stands on the site of the great 12th-century Almohad mosque, with the mosque's minaret (the Giralda) still towering beside it.

After Seville fell to the Christians in 1248, the mosque was used as a church until 1401. Then, in view of its decaying state, the church authorities decided to knock it down and start again. 'Let's construct a church so large future generations will think we were mad,' they decided (or so legend has it). The result is a cathedral measuring 126m long and 83m wide.

The entry system and timetable for visiting Seville's cathedral change frequently. Current regulations are usually displayed fairly clearly.

Exterior

From close up, the bulky exterior of the cathedral gives few hints of the treasures within. But have a look at the **Puerta del Perdón** on Calle Alemanes (a legacy of the Islamic mosque).

The Giralda, the 104m decorative brick tower on the northeastern side of the cathedral, was the minaret of the mosque, constructed between 1184 and 1198 at the height of Almohad power. Its proportions, delicate brick-pattern decoration and colour, which changes with the light, make it perhaps Spain's most perfect Islamic building. The top-most parts of the Giralda – from the bell level up – were added in the 16th century, when Spanish Christians were busy 'improving on' surviving Islamic buildings. At the very top is **El Giraldillo**, a 16th-century bronze weathervane representing 'faith' that has become a symbol of Seville. The entrance to the Giralda is inside the cathedral.

Sala del Pabellón

Selected treasures from the cathedral's art collection are exhibited in this room, the first after the ticket office. Much of what's displayed here, as elsewhere in the cathedral, is the work of masters from Seville's 17th-century artistic golden age.

Barrio de Santa Cruz & El Arenal

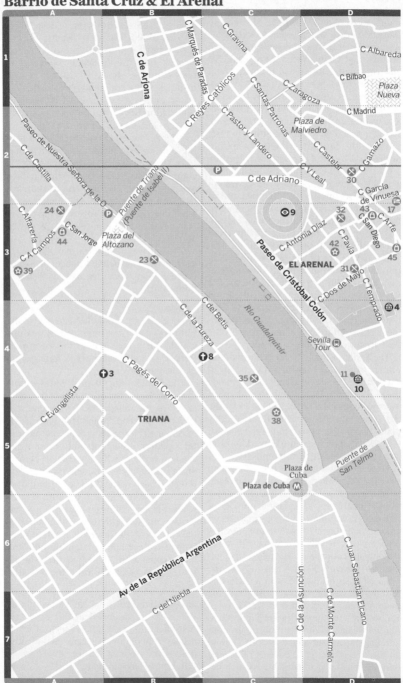

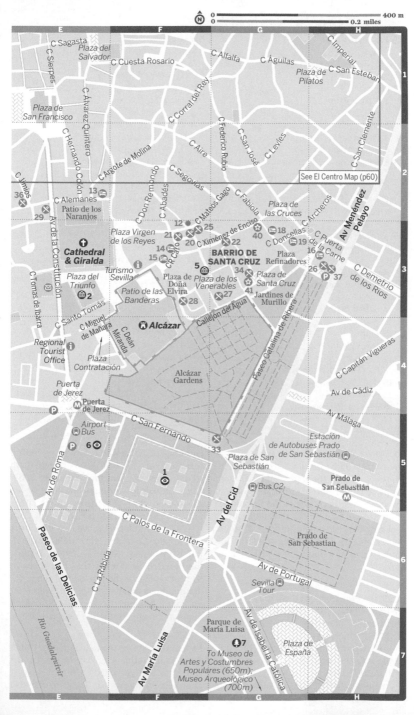

0 ___ 400 m
0 ___ 0.2 miles

C Sagasta
Plaza del Salvador
C Cuesta Rosario
C Alfalfa
C Águilas
C Imperial
C San Esteban
Plaza de Pilatos
C Sierpes
C Álvarez Quintero
C Corral del Rey
C Federico Rubio
C San José
C Leyies
C San Clemente
Plaza de San Francisco
C Hernando Colón
C Argote de Molina
C Aire
See El Centro Map (p60)
C Vinios
36
13
C Alemanes
Patio de los Naranjos
Av de la Constitución
29
C Don Remondo
C Abadés
C Segovias
C Mateos Gago
C Fabiola
Plaza de las Cruces
C Archeros
Av Menéndez Pelayo
12
25
21
20
22
Plaza Virgen de los Reyes
14
15
C Ximénez de Enciso
40
18
C Doncellas
19
C Puerta de la Carne
16
26
37
Cathedral & Giralda
Turismo Sevilla
BARRIO DE SANTA CRUZ
Plaza Refinadores
C Demetrio de los Ríos
C Tomás de Ibarra
Plaza del Triunfo
2
Plaza de Doña Elvira
5
34
Plaza de los Venerables
Plaza de Santa Cruz
Patio de las Banderas
27
41
28
Jardines de Murillo
Alcázar
Callejón del Agua
C Santo Tomás
C Miguel de Mañara
C Deán Miranda
Regional Tourist Office
Plaza Contratación
C Capitán Vigueras
Puerta de Jerez
Alcázar Gardens
Paseo Catalina de Ribera
Av de Cádiz
Puerta de Jerez
Av Málaga
Airport Bus
6
C San Fernando
Estación de Autobuses Prado de San Sebastián
33
Av de Roma
Plaza de San Sebastián
1
Bus C2
Prado de San Sebastián
Av del Cid
C Palos de la Frontera
Prado de San Sebastián
Paseo de las Delicias
C La Rábida
Av de Portugal
Sevilla Tour
Río Guadalquivir
Av María Luisa
Parque de María Luisa
7
To Museo de Artes y Costumbres Populares (650m); Museo Arqueológico (700m)
Av de Isabel la Católica
Plaza de España

Barrio de Santa Cruz & El Arenal

◎ Top Sights

Alcázar		F4
Cathedral & Giralda		E3

◎ Sights

1	Antigua Fábrica de Tabacos	F5
2	Archivo de Indias	E3
3	Capilla del Rocío	B4
4	Hospital de la Caridad	D4
5	Hospital de los Venerables Sacerdotes	F3
6	Hotel Alfonso XIII	E5
7	Parque de María Luisa	G7
8	Parroquia de Santa Ana	C4
9	Plaza de Toros de la Real Maestranza	C3
10	Torre del Oro	D4

◎ Activities, Courses & Tours

11	Cruceros Turísticos Torre del Oro	D4
12	Giralda Center	F3

◎ Sleeping

13	EME Catedral Hotel	E2
14	Hotel Casa 1800	F3
15	Hotel Palacio Alcázar	F3
16	Hotel Puerta de Sevilla	H3
17	Hotel Simón	D2
18	Pensión San Pancracio	G3
19	Un Patio en Santa Cruz	G3

◎ Eating

20	Álvaro Peregil	F3
21	Bodega Santa Cruz	F3
22	Café Bar Las Teresas	G3
23	Café de la Prensa	B3
24	Casa Cuesta	A3
25	Casa Tomate	F3
26	Catalina	H3
27	Corral del Agua	G3
28	Extraverde	F3
29	Horno de San Buenaventura	E2
30	Mesón Cinco Jotas	D2
31	Mesón de la Infanta	D3
32	Mesón Serranito	D3
33	Restaurante Egaña Oriza	G5
34	Restaurante La Albahaca	G3
35	Ristorante Cosa Nostra	C4
36	Taberna Los Coloniales	E2
37	Vinería San Telmo	H3

◎ Entertainment

38	Boss	C5
39	Casa Anselma	A3
40	Casa de la Memoria de Al-Andalus	G3
41	Los Gallos	G3
42	Tablao El Arenal	D3

◎ Shopping

43	Baco	D3
44	Cerámica Santa Ana	A3
45	El Postigo	D3

Southern & Northern Chapels

The chapels along the southern and northern sides of the cathedral hold riches of sculpture and painting. Near the western end of the northern side is the **Capilla de San Antonio**, housing Murillo's 1666 canvas depicting the vision of St Anthony of Padua; thieves cut out the kneeling saint in 1874 but he was later found in New York and put back.

Tomb of Christopher Columbus

Inside the **Puerta de los Príncipes** (Door of the Princes) stands the monumental tomb of Christopher Columbus (Cristóbal Colón in Spanish) – the subject of a continuous riddle – containing what were long believed to be the great explorer's bones, brought here from Cuba in 1898.

Columbus died in 1506 in Valladolid, in northern Spain. His remains lay at La Cartuja monastery in Seville before being moved to Hispaniola in 1536. Even though there were suggestions that the bones kept in Seville's cathedral were possibly those of his son Diego (who was buried with his father in Santo Domingo, Hispaniola), recent DNA tests seemed to finally prove that it really is Christopher Columbus lying in that box. Yet, unfortunately, to confuse matters further, the researchers also say that the bones in Santo Domingo could also be real, since Columbus' body was moved several times after his death. It seems that even death couldn't dampen the great explorer's urge to travel.

Capilla Mayor

East of the choir is the Capilla Mayor (Main Chapel). Its Gothic retable is the jewel of the cathedral and reckoned to be the biggest altarpiece in the world. Begun by Flemish sculptor Pieter Dancart in 1482 and finished by others in 1564, this sea of gilt and poly-chromed wood holds over 1000 carved biblical figures. At the centre of the lowest level is the tiny 13th-century silver-plated cedar image of the Virgen de la Sede (Virgin of the See), patron of the cathedral.

Sacristía de los Cálices

South of the Capilla Mayor are rooms containing some of the cathedral's main art treasures. The westernmost of these is the Sacristy of the Chalices, where Francisco de Goya's painting of the Seville martyrs, *Santas Justa y Rufina* (1817), hangs above the altar.

Sacristía Mayor

This large room with a finely carved stone dome was created between 1528 and 1547: the arch over its portal has carvings of 16th-century foods. Pedro de Campaña's 1547 *Descendimiento* (Descent from the Cross), above the central altar at the southern end, and Francisco de Zurbarán's *Santa Teresa*, to its right, are two of the cathedral's most precious paintings. The room's centrepiece is the **Custodia de Juan de Arfe**, a huge 475kg silver monstrance made in the 1580s by Renaissance metalsmith Juan de Arfe.

Cabildo

The beautifully domed chapter house, also called the Sala Capitular, in the southeastern corner, was originally built between 1558 and 1592 as a venue for meetings of the cathedral hierarchy. Hanging high above the archbishop's throne at the southern end is a Murillo masterpiece, *La Inmaculada*.

Giralda

In the northeastern corner of the cathedral you'll find the passage for the climb up to the belfry of the Giralda. The ascent is quite easy, as a series of ramps goes all the way up to the top, built so that the guards could ride up on horseback.

Patio de los Naranjos

Outside the cathedral's northern side, this patio was originally the courtyard of the mosque. It's planted with 66 *naranjos* (orange trees), and a Visigothic fountain sits in the centre. Hanging from the ceiling in the patio's southeastern corner is a replica stuffed crocodile – the original was a gift to Alfonso X from the Sultan of Egypt.

Alcázar CASTLE

(Map p50; adult/child €7.50/free; ☉9.30am-7pm Apr-Sep, to 6pm Oct-Mar) If heaven really *does* exist, then let's hope it looks a little bit like the inside of Seville's Alcázar. Built primarily in the 1300s during the so-called 'dark ages' in Europe, the architecture is anything but dark. Indeed, compared to our modern-day shopping malls and throw-away apartment blocks, it could be argued that the Alcázar marked one of history's architectural high points. Unesco agreed, making it a World Heritage Site in 1987.

Originally founded as a fort for the Cordoban governors of Seville in 913, the Alcázar has been expanded or reconstructed many times in its 11 centuries of existence. In the 11th century Seville's prosperous Muslim *taifa* (small kingdom) rulers developed the original fort by building a palace called Al-Muwarak (the Blessed) in what's now the western part of the Alcázar. The 12th-century Almohad rulers added another palace east of this, around what's now the Patio del Crucero. Christian Fernando III moved into the Alcázar when he captured Seville in 1248, and several later Christian monarchs used it as their main residence. Fernando's son Alfonso X replaced much of the Almohad palace with a Gothic one. Between 1364 and 1366 Pedro I created the Alcázar's crown jewel, the sumptuous Mudéjar Palacio de Don Pedro.

Patio del León

From the ticket office inside the **Puerta del León** (Lion Gate) you emerge into the Patio del León (Lion Patio), which was the garrison yard of the original Al-Muwarak palace. Just off here is the **Sala de la Justicia** (Hall of Justice), with beautiful Mudéjar plaster work and an *artesonado* (ceiling of interlaced beams with decorative insertions). This room was built in the 1340s by Christian King Alfonso XI, who disported here with one of his mistresses, Leonor de Guzmán, reputedly the most beautiful woman in Spain. It leads on to the pretty **Patio del Yeso**, which is part of the 12th-century Almohad palace reconstructed in the 19th century.

Patio de la Montería

The rooms on the western side of this patio were part of the **Casa de la Contratación** (Contracting House), founded by the Catholic Monarchs in 1503 to control trade with

Seville Cathedral

WHAT TO LOOK FOR

'We're going to construct a church so large, future generations will think we were mad' declared the inspired architects of Seville in 1402 at the beginning of one of the most grandiose building projects in medieval history. Just over a century later their madness was triumphantly confirmed.

To avoid getting lost, orientate yourself by the main highlights. Directly inside the southern (main) entrance is the grand **mausoleum of Christopher Columbus 1**. Turn right here and head into the south-eastern corner to uncover some major art treasures: a Goya in the Sacristía de los Cálices, a Zurbarán in the **Sacristía Mayor 2**, and Murillo's shining Immaculada in the Sala Capitular. Skirt the cathedral's eastern wall taking a look inside the **Capilla Real 3** with its important royal tombs. By now it's impossible to avoid the lure of **Capilla Mayor 4** with its fantastical altarpiece. Hidden over in the northwest corner is the **Capilla de San Antonio 5** with a legendary Murillo. That huge doorway almost in front of you is rarely opened **Puerta de la Asunción 6**. Make for the **Giralda 7** next, stealing admiring looks at the high, vaulted ceiling on the way. After looking down on the cathedral's immense footprint, descend and depart via the **Patio de los Naranjos 8**.

Capilla Mayor
Behold! The cathedral's main focal point contains its greatest treasure, a magnificent gold-plated altarpiece depicting various scenes in the life of Christ. It constitutes the life's work of one man, Flemish artist Pieter Dancart.

Patio de los Naranjos
Inhale the perfume of 60 Sevillan orange trees in a cool patio bordered by fortress-like walls – a surviving remnant of the original 12th-century mosque. Exit is gained via the horseshoe-shaped Puerta del Perdón.

Puerta del Perdón

Iglesia del Sagrario

Puerta del Bautismo

Puerta de la Asunción
Located on the western side of the cathedral and also known as the Puerta Mayor, these huge, rarely opened doors are pushed back during Semana Santa to allow solemn processions of Catholic *hermanadades* (brotherhoods) to pass through.

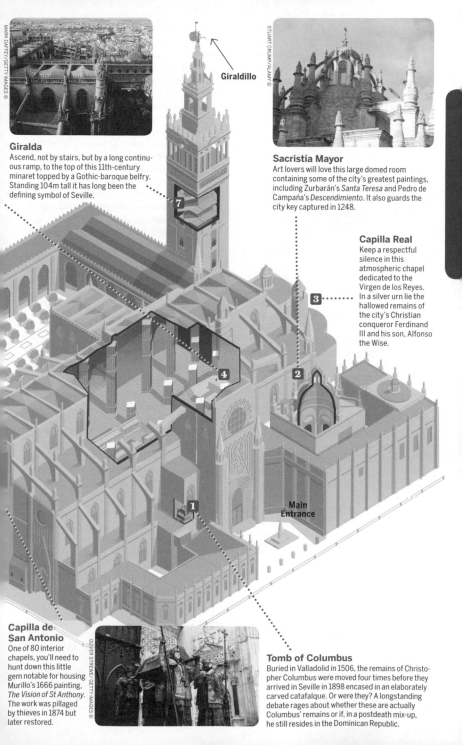

Giraldillo

Giralda
Ascend, not by stairs, but by a long continuous ramp, to the top of this 11th-century minaret topped by a Gothic-baroque belfry. Standing 104m tall it has long been the defining symbol of Seville.

Sacristía Mayor
Art lovers will love this large domed room containing some of the city's greatest paintings, including Zurbarán's *Santa Teresa* and Pedro de Campaña's *Descendimiento*. It also guards the city key captured in 1248.

Capilla Real
Keep a respectful silence in this atmospheric chapel dedicated to the Virgen de los Reyes. In a silver urn lie the hallowed remains of the city's Christian conqueror Ferdinand III and his son, Alfonso the Wise.

Main Entrance

Capilla de San Antonio
One of 80 interior chapels, you'll need to hunt down this little gem notable for housing Murillo's 1666 painting, *The Vision of St Anthony*. The work was pillaged by thieves in 1874 but later restored.

Tomb of Columbus
Buried in Valladolid in 1506, the remains of Christopher Columbus were moved four times before they arrived in Seville in 1898 encased in an elaborately carved catafalque. Or were they? A longstanding debate rages about whether these are actually Columbus' remains or if, in a postdeath mix-up, he still resides in the Dominican Republic.

Spain's American colonies. The **Salón del Almirante** (Admiral's Hall) houses 19th- and 20th-century paintings showing historical events and personages associated with Seville. The room off its northern end has an international collection of beautiful, elaborate fans. The **Sala de Audiencias** (Audience Hall) is hung with tapestry representations of the shields of Spanish admirals and Alejo Fernández' 1530s painting *Virgen de los Mareantes* (Virgin of the Sailors), the earliest known painting about the discovery of the Americas.

Cuarto Real Alto

The Alcázar is still a royal palace. In 1995 it staged the wedding feast of Infanta Elena, daughter of King Juan Carlos I, after her marriage in Seville's cathedral. The **Cuarto Real Alto** (Upper Royal Quarters), the rooms used by the Spanish royal family on their visits to Seville, are open for (heavily subscribed) tours several times a day, some in Spanish, some in English. It's essential to book ahead (954 50 23 24; tour €4.50). Highlights of the tour include the 14th-century **Salón de Audiencias**, still the monarch's reception room, and Pedro I's bedroom, with marvellous Mudéjar tiles and plasterwork.

Palacio de Don Pedro

Posterity owes Pedro I a big thank you for creating this palace (also called the Palacio Mudéjar), the single most stunning architectural feature in Seville.

Though at odds with many of his fellow Christians, Pedro had a long-standing alliance with the Muslim emir of Granada, Mohammed V, the man responsible for much of the Alhambra's finest decoration. So in 1364, when Pedro decided to build a new palace within the Alcázar, Mohammed sent along many of his best artisans. These were joined by others from Seville and Toledo. Their work, drawing on the Islamic traditions of the Almohads and caliphal Córdoba, is a unique synthesis of Iberian Islamic art.

Inscriptions on the palace's facade, facing the Patio de la Montería, encapsulate the collaborative nature of the enterprise. While one announces in Spanish that the building's creator was 'the very high, noble and conquering Don Pedro, by the grace of God king of Castila and León,' another proclaims repeatedly in Arabic that 'there is no conqueror but Allah.'

At the heart of the palace is the wonderful **Patio de las Doncellas** (Patio of the Maidens), surrounded by beautiful arches, plasterwork and tiling. The sunken garden in the centre was uncovered by archaeologists in 2004 from beneath a 16th-century marble covering.

The **Cámara Regia** (King's Quarters), on the northern side of the patio, has stunningly beautiful ceilings and wonderful plaster- and tile-work. Its rear room was probably the monarch's summer bedroom.

From here you can move west into the little **Patio de las Muñecas** (Patio of the Dolls), the heart of the palace's private quarters, featuring delicate Granada-style decoration; indeed, plasterwork was actually brought here from the Alhambra in the 19th century when the mezzanine and top gallery were added for Queen Isabel II. The **Cuarto del Príncipe** (Prince's Room), to its north, has a superb wooden cupola ceiling trying to re-create a starlit night sky.

The spectacular **Salón de Embajadores** (Hall of Ambassadors), at the western end of the Patio de las Doncellas, was the throne room of Pedro I's palace. The room's fabulous wooden dome of multiple star patterns, symbolising the universe, was added in 1427. The dome's shape gives the room its alternative name, **Sala de la Media Naranja** (Hall of the Half Orange).

On the western side of the Salón de Embajadores, the beautiful Arco de Pavones, named after its peacock motifs, leads into the **Salón del Techo de Felipe II**, with a Renaissance ceiling (1589–91).

Salones de Carlos V

Reached via a staircase at the southeastern corner of the Patio de las Doncellas, these are the much-remodelled rooms of Alfonso X's 13th-century Gothic palace. The rooms are now named after the 16th-century Spanish king Carlos I, using his title as Holy Roman Emperor, Charles V.

Patio del Crucero

This patio outside the Salones de Carlos V was originally the upper storey of the patio of the 12th-century Almohad palace. Originally it consisted only of raised walkways along the four sides and two cross-walkways that met in the middle. Below grew orange trees, the fruit of which could be plucked at hand height by the lucky folk strolling along the walkways.

The patio's lower level was built over in the 18th century after earthquake damage.

Gardens & Exit

From the Salones de Carlos V you can go out into the Alcázar's large and sleepy gardens. Immediately in front of the building is a series of small linked gardens, some with pools and fountains. From one, the **Jardín de las Danzas** (Garden of the Dances), a passage runs beneath the Salones de Carlos V to the **Baños de Doña María de Padilla** (María de Padilla Baths). These are the vaults beneath the Patio del Crucero – originally that patio's lower level – with a grotto that replaced the patio's original pool.

Concerts are sometimes held in the gardens in the summer; see www.actidea.com (in Spanish) for more information. There is also a fun hedge maze, which will delight children. The gardens to the east, beyond a long wall, are 20th-century creations, but don't hold that against them – they are heavenly indeed.

FREE **Archivo de Indias** MUSEUM
(Map p50; Calle Santo Tomás; ⊙10am-4pm Mon-Sat, to 2pm Sun & holidays) On the western side of Plaza del Triunfo, the Archivo de Indias is the main archive on Spain's American empire, with 80 million pages of documents dating from 1492 through to the end of the empire in the 19th century – a most effective statement of Spain's power and influence

during its Golden Age. A short film inside tells the full story of the building along with some fascinating original colonial maps and documents. The building was refurbished between 2003 and 2005.

Barrio de Santa Cruz

Seville's medieval *judería* (Jewish quarter), east of the cathedral and Alcázar, is today a tangle of atmospheric, winding streets and lovely plant-decked plazas perfumed with orange blossom. Among its most characteristic plazas is Plaza de Santa Cruz, which gives the *barrio* its name. Plaza de Doña Elvira is perhaps the most romantic small square in Andalucía, especially in the evening.

Hospital de los Venerables Sacerdotes GALLERY
(Map p50; ☑954 56 26 96; Plaza de los Venerables 8; adult/child €4.75/2.40, Sun afternoon free; ⊙10am-2pm & 4-8pm) Once a residence for aged priests, this 17th-century baroque mansion guards what is perhaps Seville's most typical *sevillano* patio – it's intimate, plant embellished and spirit-reviving. The building's other highlights are its 17th-century church, with rich religious murals, and the celebrated painting *Santa Rufina* by Diego Velázquez, which was procured for a hefty €12.5 million by the on-site Centro Velázquez foundation in 2007. Other roving art exhibitions provide an excellent support act.

THE NEW GOLDEN AGE?

It would be easy for a city of Seville's stature to rest on its historical laurels, but in a metropolis not averse to ambitious projects (remember *that* cathedral?), the desire to re-create the spirit of El Siglo de Oro (the Golden Century) is never far from the surface. Seville's 'new golden age' was first ignited two decades ago at Expo '92, held on the 500th anniversary of Columbus' first voyage to the Americas. on the Isla de la Cartuja, an island in the Río Guadalaquivir that city planners masterfully connected to the river's west bank in a massive rejuvenation project. The sharp modernism of Expo '92 was reflected in its giant international exhibits and the infrastructure projects that were built to support them, including the spectacular river-spanning Alamillo and Barqueta bridges.

Keen to keep the ball rolling, Seville continued its march into the 21st century under the auspices of proactive city mayor Alfredo Sánchez Monteseirín (1999–2011), who reacted to the challenges of climate change and urban renewal with fiery aplomb. In the space of just five years, Monteseirín oversaw the opening of an overland tram, a subterranean metro, a bike-sharing scheme and an electric car-sharing project. At the same time, he helped launch two architectural icons that would rival the Gothic cathedral in their audacity: the controversial Metropol Parasol and the carefully revived El Pabellon de la Navegación. What next? Locals ask.

As 2012 dawned, the home of flamenco and the spring feria was putting the finishing touches to its first skyscraper, the 180m **Cajasol Tower** – a new controversy and a prickly new talking point in a city that has always refused to stand still.

Baños Árabes   HAMMAM

(Map p60; ☎955 01 00 25; www.airedesevilla.com; Calle Aire 15; admission from €20; ⊙every 2hr from 10am-midnight) Jumping on the *hammam* bandwagon, Seville wins prizes for tranquil atmosphere, historic setting (in the Barrio de Santa Cruz), and Moroccan riad–style decor – living proof that those Moors knew a thing or two about how to relax. For an excellent postbath pick-me-up, hit the on-site *tetería* (teahouse; p70) for a silver pot of mint tea.

El Arenal

A short walk west from Avenida de la Constitución brings you to the Río Guadalquivir and the El Arenal district. The name comes from the word for the sand *(arena)* that used to pile up on the river bank. Until the 17th century this was the centre of the city's shipyards and maritime operations. Today, a pleasant footpath runs along the waterfront from where you can board boats for a river tour.

Torre del Oro   MUSEUM

(Map p50; Paseo de Cristóbal Colón; admission €2; ⊙10am-1.30pm Tue-Sun) This 13th-century Almohad watchtower by the river supposedly had a dome covered in golden tiles, hence its name, 'Tower of Gold'. It was also once used to store the booty siphoned off the colonial coffers by the returning conquistadors from Mexico and Peru. Since then it has become one of the most recognisable architectural symbols of Seville.

Inside is a small **maritime museum** spread over two floors and a rooftop viewing platform.

Hospital de la Caridad   GALLERY

(Map p50; Calle Temprado 3; admission €5; ⊙9.30am-1pm & 3.30-7pm Mon-Sat, 9am-12.30pm Sun) The Hospital de la Caridad, a block east of the river, is an art gallery that was once a hospice for the elderly, which was founded by Miguel de Mañara, who, according to legend, was a notorious libertine who changed his ways after seeing a vision of his own funeral procession.

In the 1670s Mañara commissioned a series of works on the theme of death and redemption from Seville's three finest artists of the day – Bartolomé Esteban Murillo, Juan de Valdés Leal and Pedro Roldán – for the church here. The result is a marvellous example of *sevillano* art of El Siglo de Oro (the Golden Century).

Plaza de Toros de la Real Maestranza   BULLRING, MUSEUM

(Map p50; ☎954 22 45 77; www.realmaestranza.es; Paseo de Cristóbal Colón 12; tours adult/child €6.50/2.50; ⊙tours half-hourly 9.30am-8pm, 9.30am-3pm bullfight days) In the world of bullfighting, Seville's bullring is the Old Trafford and Camp Nou of bullfighting. In other words, if you're selected to fight here then you've made it. In addition to being regarded as a building of almost religious significance to fans, it's also the oldest ring in Spain (building began in 1758) and it was here, along with the bullring in Ronda, that bullfighting on foot began in the 18th century. Interesting guided visits, in English and Spanish, take you into the ring and its museum.

El Centro

As the name suggests, this is Seville's centre, and the densely packed zone of narrow streets and squares north of the cathedral is the heart of the Seville shopping world as well as the home of some excellent bars and restaurants.

Museo del Baile Flamenco   MUSEUM

(Map p60; www.museoflamenco.com; Calle Manuel Rojas Marcos 3; adult/child €10/6; ⊙9.30am-7pm) The brainchild of *sevillana* flamenco dancer Cristina Hoyos this museum spread over three floors of an 18th-century palace makes a noble effort to showcase the mysterious art, although at €10 a pop it is more than a little overpriced. Exhibits include sketches, paintings, photos of erstwhile (and contemporary) flamenco greats, plus a collection of dresses and shawls.

Classes, workshops and fantastic concerts are regular occurrences here and there's the obligatory shop.

Museo de Bellas Artes   GALLERY

(Fine Arts Museum; Map p60; Plaza del Museo 9; admission €1.50; ⊙9am-8.30pm Tue-Sat, to 2.30pm Sun & holidays) Housed in the beautiful former Convento de la Merced, Seville's Museo de Bellas Artes does full justice to Seville's leading role in Spain's 17th-century artistic Siglo de Oro. Much of the work here is of the dark, brooding religious type.

Featured work on the ground floors includes Pedro Millán's terracotta sculptures, Alonso Vázquez' large *Sagrada Cena* (Last Supper) and the grisly head of St John the Baptist (*Cabeza de San Juan Bautista;* 1591) by Gaspar Núñez Delgado. The most visually startling room is that of the convent church,

METROPOL PARASOL

Some call him the Ferran Adriá of modern architecture, and it's true, German architect Jurgen Mayer H possesses a strange kind of artistic genius. Who else would have dreamt of constructing a 'flying waffle' in the middle of one of Seville's most traditional shopping squares? Smarting with the audacity of a modern-day Eiffel Tower, the opinion-dividing **Metropol Parasol** (Map p60; Plaza de la Encarnación), which opened in March 2011 in the Plaza de la Encarnación ,claims to be the largest wooden building in the world. Its undulating honeycombed roof is held up by giant five mushroom-like pillars, earning it the local nickname *Las Setas de la Encarnación*.

Six years in the making, the construction covers a former dead zone in Seville's central district once filled with an ugly car park. Roman ruins discovered during the building's conception have been cleverly incorporated into the foundations at the **Museo Antiquarium** (Map p60; Plaza de la Encarnación; admission €2; ⊙11am-2pm & 3-8pm), while upstairs on level 2 you can pay €1.20 to stroll along a surreal panoramic walkway with killer city views. The Metropol also houses the plaza's former market, a restaurant and a concert space. Though costly and controversial, Mayer's daring creation has slotted into Seville's ancient core with a weird kind of harmony, turning (and tilting) the heads of all who pass.

which is hung with paintings by masters of *sevillano* baroque, above all Murillo. His *Inmaculada Concepción Grande* at the head of the church displays all the curving, twisting movement so central to baroque art. Upstairs, highlights include José de Ribera's very Spanish-looking *Santiago Apóstol* (St James the Apostle) and Zurbarán's deeply sombre *Cristo Crucificado* (Christ Crucified).

Casa de Pilatos
PALACE, MUSEUM
(Map p60; ☑954 22 52 98; www.fundacionmedina celi.org; Plaza de Pilatos; admission ground fl only €5, whole house €8; ⊙9am-7pm Apr-Oct, to 6pm Nov-Mar) The haunting Casa de Pilatos, which is still occupied by the ducal Medinaceli family, is one of the city's most glorious mansions. It's a mixture of Mudéjar, Gothic and Renaissance styles, with some beautiful tile work and *artesonado*. The overall effect is like a poor-man's Alcázar.

The staircase to the upper floor has the most magnificent tiles in the building, and a great golden *artesonado* dome above. Visits to the upper floor itself, still partly inhabited by the Medinacelis, are guided. Of interest are the several centuries' worth of Medinaceli portraits and a small Goya bullfighting painting.

Palacio de la Condesa de Lebrija
MUSEUM, PALACE
(Map p60; Calle de la Cuna 8; admission whole bldg/ ground fl only €8/5, admission ground fl 9am-noon Wed free; ⊙10.30am-7.30pm Mon-Fri, 10am-2pm & 4-6pm Sat, 10am-2pm Sun) The Palacio de la Condesa de Lebrija, a block east of Calle Si-

erpes, is a 16th-century mansion with a rich collection of art and artisanry and a beautiful Renaissance-Mudéjar courtyard. The late Countess of Lebrija was an archaeologist, and she remodelled the house in 1914, filling many of the rooms with treasures from her travels.

Ancient Rome was the countess' speciality, so the library is full of books on antiquity and there are plenty of remains from Roman Itálica, including some marvellous mosaics. If you want to see the top floor, with its Arabic, baroque and Spanish rooms, you must wait for the guided tour, but it's worth it.

Plaza de San Francisco
SQUARE
(Map p60) Plaza de San Francisco has been Seville's main public square since the 16th century. The southern end of the *ayuntamiento* (town hall) here is encrusted with lovely Renaissance carving from the 1520s and '30s.

Calle Sierpes
STREET
(Map p60) Pedestrianised Calle Sierpes, heading north from the Plaza de San Francisco, and the parallel Calle Tetuán/Velázquez are the hub of Seville's fanciest shopping zone. Between the two streets is the 18th-century **Capilla de San José** (Map p60; Calle Jovellanos; ⊙8am-12.30pm & 6.30-8.30pm), with breathtakingly intense baroque ornamentation.

Plaza Salvador
SQUARE
(Map p60) This plaza, which has a few popular bars, was once the forum of Roman Hispalis. It's dominated by the **Parroquia del Divino Salvador**, a big baroque church built between 1674 and 1712 on the site of Muslim

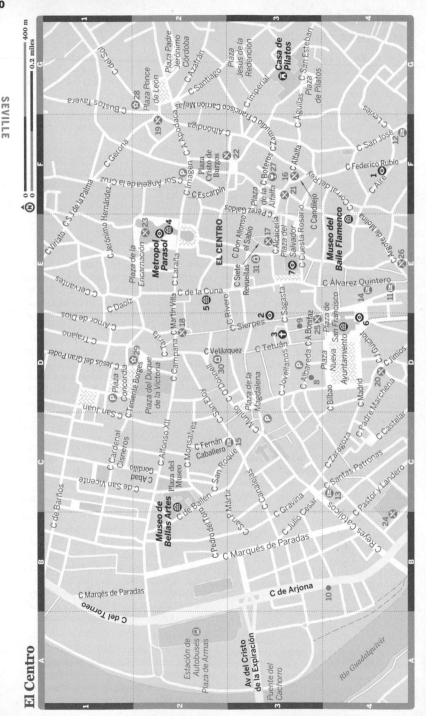

SEVILLE

El Centro

El Centro

SEVILLE SIGHTS & ACTIVITIES

Ishbiliya's main mosque. The interior reveals a fantastic richness of carving and gilding. At sunset, colour from stained-glass windows plays on the carvings to enhance their surreal beauty.

Triana

The legendary *barrio* of Triana, across the Río Guadalquivir from central Seville, used to be the quarter of the city's *gitanos* (Roma people) and was one of the birthplaces of flamenco. The neighbourhood's name is often heard in flamenco songs, nostalgically remembered by the singers over many generations.

Triana's 'main street' is the riverside Calle del Bétis, popular for both lunchtime tapas and late-night drinking sessions.

Parroquia de Santa Ana   CHURCH
(Map p50; Calle de la Pureza 80) The Parroquia de Santa Ana, dating from 1280, has a wealth of antique religious imagery.

A strange tradition has it that every woman who kicks 'El Negro,' a 16th-century tomb that has tiles depicting a recumbent knight, will find a husband. Poor El Negro has been protected by benches and other obstacles to prevent damage to this precious artwork, but women still want husbands so El Negro keeps getting a stiletto where it hurts.

Capilla del Rocío   CHURCH
(Map p50; Calle Evangelista 23) In the southern part of Triana, the Capilla del Rocío is home to the Hermandad del Rocío de Triana. The departure of this brotherhood's procession of horses and covered wagons to El Rocío on the Thursday before Pentecost is one of the most colourful and emotive events on the Seville calendar.

South of the Centre

South of Santa Cruz and El Centro, the city opens out into expansive parks and broad streets recently reclaimed by trams, bikes and strollers.

Parque de María Luisa   PARK
(Map p50; ⊙8am-10pm Sep-Jun, to midnight Jul & Aug; ⊞) The lungs of central Seville are the dreamy Parque de María Luisa, which is a delightful place to escape from the noise of

Alameda de Hércules, Macarena & Isla de la Cartuja

0.25 miles
500 m

C San Juan de Ribera

Complejo Hospitalario Virgen Macarena

Parlamento de Andalucía

C Don Fadrique

C de Resolana

Buses C2 & C4

C Andueza

C Muñoz León

Old City Wall

Basílica de La Macarena

MACARENA

C San Luis

2

C Arrayán

C Castellar

C Bustos Tavera

Buses C1 & C3

C Parras

7

C Bécquer

C de la Feria

13

C F Alvarez

C Relator

C Peral

C de la Feria

Plaza San Martín

4

C Viriato

C Calatrava

12

C Credito

5 **9**

Alameda de Hércules

Alameda de Hércules

10

C Amor de Dios

C Lumbreras

6

C Jesús del Gran Poder

11

C Trajano

Av de Ribera

C José Gálvez

Puente de la Barqueta

Bus C2

Bus C1

Sevilla Tour

Río Guadalquivir

C de San Vicente

C Santa Clara

C Santa Ana

Plaza San Antonio de Padua

C Eslava

8

Plaza de San Lorenzo

C Teodosio

C Miguel Cid

Isla Mágica

3

C del Torneo

C Curtidurías

C Juan Rabadán

C Pascual de Gayangos

C de Barrios

C Marie Curie

C Marie Curie

C Albert Einstein

C Albert Einstein

C Charles Darwin

C Leonardo da Vinci

ISLA DE LA CARTUJA

C Américo Vespucio

Auditorio de la Cartuja

Camino de los Descubrimientos

Centro Andaluz de Arte Contemporáneo

1

Puente de la Cartuja (Footbridge sometimes closed)

Bus C1

Bus C2

Sevilla Tour

To Pabellón de la Navegación (150m)

Alameda de Hércules, Macarena & Isla de la Cartuja

SEVILLE SIGHTS & ACTIVITIES

the city, with its duck ponds, snoozing *sevillanos* and paths snaking underneath the trees.

If you'd rather continue your cultural education than commune with the flowers, then the park contains a couple of sites that'll keep you smiling. Curving round the **Plaza de España**, with its fountains and mini-canals, is the most grandiose of the buildings built for the 1929 Exposición Iberoamericana, a brick-and-tile confection featuring Seville tile work at its gaudiest, with a map and historical scene for each Spanish province. You can hire row boats to ply the canals from only €5.

The **Museo Arqueológico** (adult/child €1.50/free; ⊙9am-8.30pm Tue-Sat, to 2.30pm Sun & holidays), at the southern end of the park, is an unexpected depository of Roman sculptures, mosaics and statues – much of it gathered from Itálica. There is also a room of gold jewellery from the mysterious Tartessos culture.

Opposite is the **Museo de Artes y Costumbres Populares** (✆954 23 25 76; admission €1.50; ⊙9am-8.30pm Tue-Sat, to 2.30pm Sun & holidays), with a spotlight on the ceramic tiles produced in a factory founded by Englishman Carlos Pickman in the former Monsatery of Cartuja in 1840.

The park is a great place for children to run off some steam; they'll enjoy feeding the doves in the plaza by the museum at the southern end of the park. Four-person quad bikes are available to rent for €12 per half-hour.

FREE **Antigua Fábrica de Tabacos**   UNIVERSITY
(Map p50; Calle San Fernando; ⊙8am-9.30pm Mon-Fri, to 2pm Sat) Seville's massive former tobacco factory – workplace of Bizet's passionate operatic heroine, Carmen – was built in the 18th century and is the second-largest building in Spain after El Escorial. It's now a university and is wheelchair accessible.

Hotel Alfonso XIII   LANDMARK
(Map p50; Calle San Fernando 2) As much a monument as it is an accommodation option, and certainly more affordable if you come for a cup of coffee as opposed to a room, this striking hotel – conceived as the most luxurious in Europe when it was built in 1928 – was constructed in tandem with the Plaza de España for the 1929 world fair

The style is classic neo-Mudéjar with glazed tiles and terracotta bricks.

Isla de la Cartuja

This former island on the Río Guadalquivir takes its name from the on-site Cartuja monastery. It was connected to Seville's west river bank in 1992 to incorporate the city's Expo '92 site.

El Pabellon de la Navegación   MUSEUM
(www.pabellondelanavegacion.es; Camino de los Descubrimientos 2; adult/child €4.90/3.50; ⊙to 3pm Sun; ♿) Seville's 'other' futuristic new building may have been overshadowed by its precocious cousin, the Metropol Parasol, but its ultramodern museum and

exhibition space which opened in January 2012, is equally thought-provoking. The architecturally impressive pavillion, which has revived a previous navigation museum that lasted from the 1992 Expo until 1999, resides on the banks of the Río Guadalquivir on the Isla de la Cartuja.

Its permanent collection is split into four parts – navigation, mariners, shipboard life and historical views of Seville - and many exhibits are interactive and kid-friendly. As a bonus, your ticket allows you to ascend the adjacent Schindler Tower for some fine contemporary views.

Conjunto Monumental
de la Cartuja
MONASTERY, ART

(Cartuja Monastery; Map p62; ☑955 03 70 70; www .caac.es; admission complete visit/monument or temporary exhibitions €3/1.80, free 7-9pm Tue-Fri & all day Sat; ☉11am-9pm Tue-Sat, to 3pm Sun) Founded in 1399, this monastery is today home of the superb **Centro Andaluz de Arte Contemporáneo** (Andalusian Contemporary Art Centre; Map p62) which has a collection of modern Andalucian art and frequent temporary exhibitions. The Conjunto Monumental de la Cartuja became the favourite *sevillano* lodging place for Columbus, who prayed in its chapel before his trip to the Americas and whose remains lay here for more than two decades in the 1530s and 40s.

In 1839 the complex was bought by an enterprising Englishman, Charles Pickman, who turned it into a porcelain factory, building the tall bottle-shaped kilns that stand incongruously beside the monastery buildings. The factory ceased production in the 1980s and in 1992 the building was the Royal Pavillion during the Expo.

Isla Mágica
AMUSEMENT PARK

(Map p62; ☑902 16 17 16; www.islamagica.es; adult/ child €29/20; ☉around 11am-10pm high season, closed Dec-Mar; ☝) This Disney-goes-Spanish-colonial amusement park provides a great if expensive day out for kids and all lovers of white-knuckle rides. Confirm times before going as hours vary by season – see the website. Both buses C1 and C2 run to Isla Mágica.

Alameda de Hércules & Around
While the Barrio de Santa Cruz and cathedral area are where things once happened in Seville, it's the Alameda de Hércules area where the young are making things happen today.

Alameda de Hércules was once a no-go area – reserved only for the city's 'painted ladies', pimps and a wide range of shady characters – but the parklike strip has undergone the 'Soho makeover' and is now crammed with trendy bars, chic shops and the popular **Teatro Alameda** (Map p62; ☑954 90 01 64; Calle Crédito 11; admission around €8), which is one of the city's best experimental theatres.

The two distinct columns at the south end of the square are Roman originals.

Basílica de La Macarena
CHURCH, MUSEUM

(Map p62; ☑954 90 18 00; Calle Bécquer 1; museum admission €5; ☉9.30am-2pm & 5-9pm) This basilica is the home of Seville's most revered Virgin and will give you a whiff of the fervour inspired by Semana Santa. The *Virgen de la Esperanza Macarena* (Macarena Virgin of Hope), a magnificent statue adorned with a golden crown, lavish vestments, and five diamond-and-emerald brooches donated by famous 20th-century matador Joselito El Gallo, stands in splendour behind the main altarpiece.

La Macarena, as she is commonly known, is the patron of bullfighters and Seville's supreme representation of the grieving, yet hopeful, mother of Christ. The power of this fragile, beautiful statue is most evident in the small hours of the *madrugá* (Good Friday) Semana Santa procession. Where she passes, a rain of rose petals falls, and crazed *sevillanos* shout: 'Macarena guapa' (Beautiful Macarena). To top it all off a *saeta* (sacred Andalucian song) is sung, praising the Virgin's beauty. The church also has a recently refurbished museum containing some of the iconography. Across the street is the longest surviving stretch of Seville's 12th-century Almohad walls.

Iglesia de San Luis
CHURCH

(Map p62; ☑954 55 02 07; Calle San Luis; ☉9am-2pm Tue-Thu, 9am-2pm & 6-9pm Fri & Sat, closed Aug) One of Seville's most impressive churches, Iglesia de San Luis stands 500m south of the Basílica de La Macarena. Designed for the Jesuits by Leonardo de Figueroa in 1731, the baroque San Luis has an unusual equal-armed cross plan, 16 twisting stone pillars and a superb soaring dome. Look out for the human skulls with crowns of flowers on the altar of San Francisco de Borja.

🎓 Courses

Seville is a great city in which to hang around for a while and learn a new skill. Many visitors from overseas join a Spanish language course and there are dozens of schools offering courses.

If learning a language is just too scholarly, then how about learning how to shimmy with the best of them? Seville has many dance and flamenco schools open to visitors staying a while.

CLIC   LANGUAGE COURSE
(Map p60; 📞954 50 21 31; www.clic.es; Calle Albareda 19) CLIC is a well-established language centre with a good social scene; courses in business Spanish and Hispanic studies available.

Giralda Center   LANGUAGE COURSE
(Map p50; 📞954 22 13 46, 954 21 31 65; www.giralda center.com; Calle Mateos Gago 17) Has a friendly atmosphere, plenty of excursions and a reputation for good teaching.

Lenguaviva   LANGUAGE COURSE
(Map p62; 📞954 90 51 31; www.lenguaviva.net; Calle Viriato 24) Good on spare-time activities like tapas tours and social drinks; courses in business Spanish available.

Linc   LANGUAGE COURSE
(Map p60; 📞954 50 04 59; www.linc.es; Calle General Polavieja 13) Linc is a small, popular school, which is good on cultural activities and excursions.

Fundación Cristina Heeren de Arte Flamenco   FLAMENCO
(Map p60; 📞954 21 70 58; www.flamencoheeren .com; Avenida de Jerez 2) This is by far the best-known flamenco school and offers long-term courses in all flamenco arts; also one-month intensive summer courses.

✺ Festivals & Events

Semana Santa   HOLY WEEK
(www.semana-santa.org) Every day from Palm Sunday to Easter Sunday, large, life-sized *pasos* (sculptural representations of events from Christ's Passion) are carried from Seville's churches through the streets to the cathedral, accompanied by processions that may take more than an hour to pass. The processions are organised by over 50 different *hermandades* or *cofradías* (brotherhoods, some of which include women).

The climax of the week is the *madrugada* (early hours) of Good Friday, when some of the most-respected brotherhoods file through the city. The costume worn by the marching penitents consists of a full robe and a conical hat with slits cut for the eyes. The regalia was incongruously copied by America's Ku Klux Klan.

Procession schedules are widely available during Semana Santa, or see the Semana Santa website. Arrive near the cathedral in the early evening for a better view.

AZULEJOS TILES

Seville's emblematic *azulejos* tiles were popularised in a factory founded in an abandoned 14th-century monastery on the Isla de la Cartuja in 1841. Ironically, the factory's instigator was neither a monk nor a Spaniard, but an Englishman from Liverpool called Charles Pickman. Pickman had first arrived in Andalucía via Cádiz in 1822 during a time when refined English ceramics were in vogue in Spain. Sensing a lucrative business opportunity he gravitated to Seville, where he set up shop in the disused Cartuja monastery recently vacated by Napoleon's retreating army (who had used it as a barracks).

Pickman's genius was to combine advanced British industrial savvy with centuries-old *sevilliano* tradition. *Azulejos* tiles (the name comes from the Arabic word *zellige*, meaning 'polished stone') were first introduced into Spain by the Moors. The Englishman used printing presses and innovative moulds to shape and paint his ceramics – a stash that included tiles, porcelain and crockery – and his products quickly went on to define *sevilliano* fashion and architecture.

The company hit a high-water mark in the late 19th and early 20th centuries when the Pickman brand gained royal commissions and was used to dramatic effect in spectacular neo-Mudéjar buildings including Plaza de España and Hotel Alfonso XIII. It ceased operations at the Cartuja site in 1982 and moved to new premises in the suburb of Santiponce.

Feria de Abril
SPRING FAIR

The April fair, held in the second half of the month (sometimes edging into May), is the jolly counterpart to the sombre Semana Santa. The biggest and most colourful of all Andalucía's ferias is less invasive (and also less inclusive) than the Easter celebration. It takes place on El Real de la Feria, in the Los Remedios area west of the Río Guadalquivir.

The ceremonial lighting-up of the fair grounds on the opening Monday night is the starting gun for six nights of *sevillanos'* favourite activities: eating, drinking, dressing up and dancing till dawn.

Corpus Christi
RELIGIOUS

An important early-morning procession of the Custodia de Juan de Arfe, along with accompanying images from the cathedral. It's a moveable feast held anytime between late May and late June, always on a Thursday.

Bienal de Flamenco
FLAMENCO

(www.bienal-flamenco.org) Most of the big names of the flamenco world participate in this major flamenco festival. Held in the September of even-numbered years.

✖ Eating

Seville has hundreds of decent salt-of-the-earth tapas bars, but it has also pushed the boat out with what are undoubtedly Andalucía's most inventive tapas.

Mercado del Arenal (Map p60; Calle Pastor y Landero) and **Mercado de la Encarnación** (Map p60; Plaza de la Encarnación) are central Seville's two food markets. The Encarnación, which mainly sells fruit, vegies and fish, has recently been relocated into new digs under the giant mushroom pillars of the Metropol Parasol.

Barrio de Santa Cruz, Alcázar & Cathedral

TOP
CHOICE Vinería San Telmo
TAPAS, FUSION €€

(Map p50; ☎954 41 06 00; www.vineriasantelmo .com; Paseo Catalina de Ribera 4; tapas €3.50, media raciones €10) San Telmo invented the *rascocielo* (skyscraper) tapa, an 'Empire State' of tomatoes, aubergine, goat's cheese and smoked salmon. If this – and other creative nuggets such as foie gras with quails eggs and lychees, or exquisitely cooked bricks of tuna – don't make you drool with expectation then you're probably dead.

Catalina
TAPAS €€

(Map p50; Paseo Catalina de Ribera 4; raciones €10) If your view of tapas is that they're 'glorified bar snacks', then your ideas could be blown out of the water here, with a creative mix of just about every ingredient known to Iberian cooking. Start with the cheese, eggplant and paprika special.

Restaurante Egaña Oriza
CONTEMPORARY SPANISH €€€

(Map p50; www.restauranteoriza.com; Calle San Fernando 41; mains €22-32; ⊙closed Sat lunch & Sun) Say Basque and you've got a byword for fine dining these days, so it's not surprising that Basque-run Egaña Oriza is regarded as one of the city's stand-out restaurants. Situated close to the Prado de San Sebastián bus station, this could be your first (and best) culinary treat in Seville. There's an equally posh tapas spot on the ground floor.

Café Bar Las Teresas
TAPAS €

(Map p50; Calle Santa Teresa 2; tapas €3) The hanging hams look as ancient as the bar itself, a sinuous wrap-around affair with just enough room for two stout waiters to pass carrying precariously balanced tapas plates. The atmosphere is dark but not dingy, the food highly traditional, and the crowd an integrated mix of tourists and Santa Cruz locals.

Casa Tomate
TAPAS, ANDALUCIAN €€

(Map p50; Calle Mateos Gago 24; media raciones €8-9, raciones €12) A newish place in an old building decorated with art deco feria posters, Tomate cares more about satisfying the palates of locals than making a fast buck off tourists. The waiters recommend the garlic prawns and the pork sirloin in a white-wine-and-pine-nut sauce. The waiters are right.

Corral del Agua
ANDALUCIAN €€€

(Map p50; ☎954 22 48 41; www.corraldelagua.es; Callejón del Agua 6; mains €16.50-22; ⊙lunch & dinner Mon-Sat) If you're hankering for inventive food on a hot day, then book a table at Corral del Agua. Its leafy courtyard makes a pleasant spot to sample traditional stews and Arabic-inspired desserts.

Restaurante La Albahaca
CONTEMPORARY ANDALUCIAN €€€

(Map p50; ☎954 22 07 14; Plaza de Santa Cruz 12; mains €20-25, menú €19) Gastronomic inventions are the mainstay of this swish restaurant. Housed inside an imposing building

CYCLING SEVILLE

Offsetting decades of driving chaos, the inauguration of Seville's **Sevici** (☎902 01 10 32; www.sevici.es; ☉7am-9pm) bike-sharing scheme in April 2007 was something of a godsend, even for avowed car-users. Sevici was the second bike-sharing initiative in Spain (there are now nine), opening a couple of weeks after Barcelona's Bicing program. Despite subsequent bike-sharing projects – Paris' Vélib was launched in June 2007 – it remains the fifth-largest scheme of its kind in Europe with 2500 bikes. Grab a two-wheeled machine from any one of 250 docking stations and you'll quickly discover that cycling rather suits this flat, balmy metropolis that was seemingly designed with visceral experiences in mind.

Most of Sevici's 250,000 daily users are local, but visitors can take advantage of the sharing system by purchasing a seven-day pass (€10 plus a €150 returnable deposit) online. Proceed to the nearest docking station, punch in the number from your coded receipt and hey presto. Seville has 120km of city bike lanes (all painted green and equipped with their own traffic signals) and the first 30 minutes of usage are free. Beyond that, it's €1 for the first hour and €2 an hour thereafter.

Another way of taking advantage of the new cycling infrastructure is to take a bike tour around the city's main sights. **Sevilla Bike Tour** (Map p60; www.sevillabiketour.com; adult/child €25/19) runs easy three-hour (10km) guided trips daily, starting at 10.30am and 6pm. Meet outside the Torre del Oro. Reservations aren't required and bikes are provided.

---

with massive studded doors, it looks as if a trip here may break the bank, but the lunchtime *menú del día* (daily set menu) is, in fact, a really great deal.

Try the pork trotter with mushroom, young garlic and pea mousse (essentially just a posh version of mushy peas or the rabbit stew.

🌿 Extraverde   TAPAS €
(Map p50; www.extraverde.es; Plaza de Doña Elvira 8; tapas €2.50-4; ☉10.30am-11.30pm) Recently arrived on the Santa Cruz scene, Extraverde is a unique bar-shop specialising in Andalucian products such as olive oil, cheese and wine. You can taste free samples standing up, or sit down inside and order a full tapa.

Álvaro Peregil   TAPAS €
(Map p50; 20 Calle Mateos Gago; tapas €2.50-4) In terms of decoration, this tiny bar has not much more than garlic bunches hanging overhead and a trio of wooden tables outside to rest your tapas on. It's situated near the cathedral in a row of rarely empty bars, the kitchens of which never seem to shut (good for hypoglycemic Northern Europeans unaccustomed to late dinners).

Most of the good stuff comes on a skewer, including chicken, scallops and prawns. You're encouraged to wash it all down with some local manzanilla sherry.

Bodega Santa Cruz   TAPAS €
(Map p50; Calle Mateos Gago; tapas €2) Forever crowded and with a mountain of paper on the floor, this place is usually standing room only, with tapas and drinks enjoyed alfresco as you dodge the marching army of tourists squeezing through Santa Cruz' narrow streets.

Horno de San Buenaventura   CAFE, SNACKS €
(Map p50; www.hornosanbuenaventura.com; Avenida de la Constitución; pastries from €1; ☉9am-9pm) There are actually two of these gilded pastry/coffee/snack bars in Seville, one here in Avenida de la Constitución opposite the cathedral and the other (inferior one) at the Plaza de la Alfalfa (Map p60; Plaza de Alfalfa). All kinds of fare are on show though it's probably best enjoyed for its lazy continental breakfasts (yes, the service can be slow) or a spontaneous late-night cake fix.

El Arenal

Enrique Becerra   ANDALUCIAN €€€
(Map p60; ☎954 21 30 49; www.enriquebecerra.com; Calle Gamazo 2; mains €17-25; ☉closed Sat & Sun) Squeeze in with the locals at lunchtime and enjoy some hearty Andalucian dishes. The lamb drenched in honey sauce and stuffed with spinach and pine nuts (€22) is just one of many delectable offerings, but be warned that it charges a whopping €2.50 for bread and olives!

Mesón Cinco Jotas　　　　TAPAS €€

(Map p50; www.mesoncincojotas.com; Calle
Castelar 1; tapas €3.80, media raciones €10) In
the world of *jamón* (ham) making, if you
are awarded Cinco Jotas (Five Js) for your
jamón, it's like getting an Oscar. The owner
of this place, Sánchez Romero Carvajal, is
the biggest producer of Jabugo ham, and has
a great selection on offer.

It's best to try a range of different things,
but note that the top-pig *jamones* can cost
just under €40!

Mesón de la Infanta　　　　TAPAS €

(Map p50; ✆954 56 15 54; www.infantasevilla.es;
Calle Dos de Mayo 26; tapas €3) If you like your
tapas with a touch of class and a glass of cool
sherry, indulge in innovative, well-presented
dishes at this *sevillano* favourite. While eating you can ponder the purpose of the tins of
peas and jars of jam lined up on the shelves –
see if you can solve the mystery!

Mesón Serranito　　TAPAS, ANDALUCIAN €

(Map p50; ✆954 21 12 43; Calle Antonia Díaz 11;
media raciones €7) Vegetarians steer clear: this
place is dangerously close to the bullring
and has tasty bull's tail on the menu to go
with the less tasty bulls' heads hanging on
the wall – next to pictures of the final few
seconds of their lives.

It also specialises in the *serranito,* a
Spanish gastronomic institution consisting of a slice of toasted bread heaped with
a pork fillet, roasted pepper, a nice bit of
jamón and garlic.

El Centro

Plaza de la Alfalfa is the hub of the tapas
scene and has some excellent bars.

Los Coloniales　　CONTEMPORARY ANDALUCIAN €€

(Map p60; www.tabernacoloniales.es; cnr Calle
Dormitorio & Plaza Cristo de Burgos; tapas €2.50,
raciones €10-12) The quiet ones are always
the best. It might not look like much from
the outside, but take it on trust that Los
Coloniales is something very special. The
quality plates line up like models on a cat
walk: *chorizo a la Asturiana,* a divine spicy
sausage in an onion sauce served on a bed
of lightly fried potato; eggplants in honey;
and pork tenderloin *al whiskey* (a whiskey-
flavoured sauce).

There is another inferior, more touristy
branch, **Taberna Los Coloniales** (Map p50;
Calle Jimios), near the cathedral.

Santo Restaurante　　　　FUSION €€€

(Map p60; www.emecatedralhotel.com; Calle Argote de Molina 29; mains from €34; ☒closed Sun
& Mon) Famous Basque chef Martin Berasategui won Seville its first Michelin star
at this pricey joint connected to the EME
Catedral Hotel (p291) next to the cathedral. The food is headily experimental with
a passing nod to Andalucian tradition; the
elaborately worded menu contains such
strange-sounding exoticisms as roasted
pigeon with spinach and stewed cherries.

Bar Alfalfa　　　　TAPAS €

(Map p60; cnr Calles Alfalfa & Candilejo; tapas €3)
It's amazing how many people, hams, wine
bottles and knick-knacks you can stuff into
such a small space. No matter, order through
the window when the going gets crowded.
You won't forget the tomato-tinged magnifi-
cence of the Italy-meets-Iberia *salmorejo*
(thick, garlicky gazpacho) bruschetta.

Robles Laredo　　CONTEMPORARY SPANISH €€

(Map p60; www.casa-robles.com; Plaza de San
Francisco; raciones €9-12) This small Italianate
cafe-restaurant is fairly dwarfed by its two
huge chandeliers and a vast collection of
delicate desserts displayed in glass cases.
The tapas are equally refined. Try the foie
gras, beef burgers with truffle sauce, or oysters and whitebait.

Bar Europa　　　　TAPAS €

(Map p60; ✆954 22 13 54; www.bareuropa.info;
Calle Siete Revueltas 35, cnr Calle Alcaicería; tapas
€3, media raciones €6-8) Up there with the best
of the best, this neighbourhood institution
serves tapas so exciting they've won awards
for several years in a row. The unusual, and
rather tasty, *quesadilla los balanchares
gratinada sobre manzana* was voted the
most innovative tapa in 2006. This beauty
of the menu involves turning a boring old
Granny Smith apple into a taste sensation
by covering it in goat's cheese and laying it
on a bed of strawberries.

Confitería La Campana　　CAFE, BAKERY €

(Map p60; www.confiterialacampana.com; cnr
Calles Sierpes & Martín Villa; large cakes from €7)
La Campana has been heaving with sugar
addicts since 1885, and workers and the
elite alike storm Seville's most popular bakery for a *yema* (a soft, crumbly biscuit cake
wrapped like a toffee), or a delicious *nata*
(custard cake) that quivers under the glass.

SEVILLE TOURS

A number of companies offer tours of Seville on foot, by boat, bus or even horse and cart. Check the Sevilla Card (p72) for discounts.

Cruceros Turísticos Torre del Oro (Map p50; ☎954 56 16 92; www.crucerostorre deloro.com; adult/child under 14yr €16/free) One-hour sightseeing river cruises every half-hour from 11am from the river bank by the Torre del Oro. Last departure can range from 6pm in winter to 10pm in summer.

Sevilla Tour (☎902 10 10 81; www.sevillatour.com; adult/child €17/7; ⊙7am-8pm) One-hour city tours in open-topped double-decker buses and converted trams made with earphone commentary in a choice of languages. The ticket is valid for 48 hours and you can hop on or off along Paseo de Cristóbal Colón (near the Torre del Oro), Avenida de Portugal behind Plaza de España, or the Isla de la Cartuja. Buses typically leave every 30 minutes from 7am to 8pm.

Sevilla Walking Tours (☎902 15 82 26; www.sevillawalkingtours.com; per person €12) English-language tours of the main monumental area, lasting about two hours, at 10.30am daily. The same people also offer tours of the cathedral and the Alcázar.

Horse-drawn carriages These wait around near the cathedral, Plaza de España and Puerta de Jerez, and charge €40 for a one-hour trot around the Barrio de Santa Cruz and Parque de María Luisa areas.

It's about the only business left on this road that hasn't been gobbled up by a multinational – hopefully its maturity and quality will keep it safe for a while longer.

El Rinconcillo TAPAS, ANDALUCIAN €
(Map p60; ☎954 22 31 83; www.elrinconcillo.es; Calle Gerona 40; tapas €3, raciones €12) Seville's oldest bar first opened in 1670 and has been dishing out the goods since before many countries were even a twinkle in someone's eye. Time has allowed this place to build up an impressive range of little morsels; though to be fair you do probably come here more for the sense of history than for the food. However, the *ortiguillas fritas* (fried sea anemones) are memorable for all the right reasons and it serves the biggest olives you've ever seen.

Triana

Café de la Prensa SEAFOOD €
(Map p50; Calle del Betis 8; tapas €3) Tapas were surely invented to be enjoyed next to the river on Triana's ebullient Calle del Betis with the Giralda beckoning in the background. It would be heresy to try anything but the fish here, preferably dipped in chickpea flour and briefly fried in olive oil.

Casa Cuesta CONTEMPORARY SPANISH €
(Map p50; ☎954 33 33 37; www.casacuesta.net; Calle de Castilla 3-5; mains €10) Something about the carefully buffed wooden bar and gleaming beer pumps gives a sense that the owners are proud of Casa Cuesta. Indeed they should be; it's a real find for food and wine lovers alike.

Ristorante Cosa Nostra ITALIAN €€
(Map p50; ☎954 27 07 52; Calle del Betis 52; pizzas €8.50-12; ⊙closed Mon; 🖐) Forget the Mafiosi nameplate, this is the best Italian food in Seville and well worth crossing the river for. The pizzas are spun in front of your eyes and the rich creamy risottos ought to have every paella chef in the city looking over their shoulder.

Alameda de Hércules

Duo Tapas TAPAS, FUSION €€
(Map p62; Calle Calatrava 10; tapas €3-4.50, media raciones €9-12) Missed by the masses who rarely wander north from the Alameda de Hércules, Duo Tapas is 'new school' to El Rinconcillo's 'old school.' But, what it lacks in *azulejos* tiles and illustrious past patrons, it makes up for in inventive tapas with an Asian twist. Alameda trendies swear by its green chicken with rice and spicy noodles.

Bar-Restaurante Eslava TAPAS, ANDALUCIAN €€
(Map p62; www.espacioeslava.com; Calle Eslava 3; tapas €4, media raciones €9-13) A legend in its own dinnertime, Eslava shirks the traditional tilework and bullfighting posters of tapas-bar lore and delivers where it matters: fine food backed up with equally fine service.

There's a 'nouvelle' tinge to the memorable *costillas a la miel* (pork ribs in a honey and rosemary glaze) and vegetable strudel in a cheese sauce, but there's nothing snobby about the atmosphere which is local and pretty fanatical after 9pm. An equally good restaurant (with shared kitchen) sits next door.

🍷 Drinking

Bars usually open from 6pm to 2am on weekdays and 8pm to 4am on weekends. Drinking and partying get going as late as midnight on Friday and Saturday (daily when it's hot), upping the tempo as the night goes on.

In summer dozens of *terrazas de verano* (summer terraces; temporary, open-air, late-night bars), many of them with live music and plenty of room to dance, spring up along both banks of the river. They change names and ambience from year to year.

Drinking neighbourhoods are legion here. Classic spots include drinks on the banks of the Río Guadalquivir in Triana (the wall along Calle del Betis forms a fantastic makeshift bar), Plaza de la Alfalfa (cocktail and dive bars), the Barrio de Santa Cruz and the Alameda de Hércules (*the* place for young *sevillanos* these days). The slightly rundown feeling of the Alameda adds to the exclusivity and discourages some *sevillanos*, so the boho lot get to keep the place more or less to themselves.

Many of the tapas bars listed in the Eating section also double up as great bars in their own right.

TOP CHOICE Baños Árabes Tetería   TEAHOUSE
(Map p60; Calle Aire 15) Seville's no Granada when it comes to exotically infused teahouses, but exceptions should be made for this cushioned comfort zone encased in the pindropping tranquility of the Baños Árabes in Santa Cruz. With no on-site shisha pipes or yodeling singers, the atmosphere is generated by the edgy art and murmuring intellectuals discussing Almodóvar movies.

Bulebar Café   BAR, CAFE
(Map p62; ☑954 90 19 54; Alameda de Hércules 83; ⊙4pm-late) This place gets pretty *caliente* (hot) at night but is pleasantly chilled in the early evening, with friendly staff. Don't write off its spirit-reviving alfresco breakfasts that pitch early birds with up-all-nighters.

El Garlochi   BAR
(Map p60; Calle Boteros 4) Dedicated entirely to the iconography, smells and sounds of Semana Santa, the ubercamp El Garlochi is a true marvel. A cloud of church incense hits you as you go up the stairs, and the faces of baby Jesus and the Virgin welcome you into the velvet-walled bar, decked out with more Virgins and Jesuses.

Taste the rather revolting sounding cocktails Sangre de Cristo (Blood of Christ) and Agua de Sevilla, both heavily laced with vodka, whisky and grenadine, and pray they open more bars like this.

☆ Entertainment

Tablao El Arenal   FLAMENCO
(www.tablaoelarenal.com; Calle Rodo 7; admission with 1 drink €37, with dinner €72; ⊙restaurant from 7pm, shows 8pm & 10pm) Of the three places in Seville that offer flamenco dinner shows this – ask any local – is the best. A smaller seating capacity (100 compared to 600 at the Palacio Andaluz) offers greater intimacy, although, as a big venue, it still lacks the grit and – invariably – *duende* (flamenco spirit) of the peñas (small flamenco clubs).

TOP CHOICE Casa de la Memoria de Al-Andalus   FLAMENCO
(Map p50; ☑954 56 06 70; www.casadelamemoria .es; Calle Ximénez de Enciso 28; tickets €15; ⊙9pm) This flamenco *tablao* (place that stages professional flamenco shows) in Santa Cruz is without doubt the most intimate and authentic nightly flamenco show outside the Museo del Baile Flamenco, offering a wide variety of *palos* (flamenco styles) in a courtyard of shifting shadows and overhanging plants. Space is limited to 100, so reserve tickets a day or so in advance by calling or visiting the venue.

Casa Anselma   FLAMENCO
(Map p50; Calle Pagés del Corro 49; ⊙midnight-late Mon-Sat) If you can squeeze in past the foreboding form of Anselma (a celebrated Triana flamenco dancer) at the door, you'll quickly realise that anything can happen in here. Casa Anselma is the antithesis of a tourist flamenco *tablao*, with cheek-to-jowl crowds, thick cigarette smoke, zero amplification and spontaneous outbreaks of dexterous dancing. Pure magic. (Beware: there's no sign, just a doorway embellished with *azulejos* tiles.)

SEVILLE FOR KIDS

Many of Seville's adult attractions will appeal to kids on a different level, including the cathedral and Alcázar, the latter of which has a dedicated booklet for kids available in most newsagents. For more information see the Travel with Children chapter.

» The city abounds in open spaces and parks (often with special kids' sections); head for the banks of the Río Guadalquivir, Parque de María Luisa (p63) and the **Jardines de Murrillo**, all of which have decent play areas.

» If the tapas get too sophisticated, try an ice-cream or *churros* cafe, or a good Italian restaurant; there are many in the vicinity of **Plaza de la Alfalfa**.

» Isla Mágica (p64) is a theme park specifically targeted at kids, particularly those aged 10 or above. Nearby, the brand new El Pabellon de la Navegacion (p64) is full of high-tech, interactive gadgets that will both amuse and educate your children. Tours by boat, open-top double-decker or horse-drawn carriage also prove popular.

» The best flamenco for young'uns is the excellent nightly performances at the Museo del Baile Flamenco (p58), which kick off at a reasonable hour (7pm) and last from 45 to 60 minutes.

» On Sunday morning visit the pet market at Plaza de la Alfalfa, but remember a dog's not just for Christmas in Seville.

» On a hot summer day kids will want to do nothing more than dive into a pool. The waterslides and wave pools at **Aquópolis Sevilla** (☑902 34 50 10; www.aquopolis.es; Avenida del Deporte; adult/child €18.95/13.95; ☉11am-7pm or 8pm approx late May-early Sep) will keep them happy for hours. It's located in Barrio Las Delicias in the east of the city (off the A92 towards Málaga).

Anselma is in Triana about 200m from the western side of the Puente de Isabel II.

Los Gallos FLAMENCO
(Map p50; ☑954 21 69 81; www.tablaolosgallos .com; Plaza de Santa Cruz 11; ☉8pm & 10.30pm) An above-average Santa Cruz *tablao* where some top-notch flamenco artists have trodden the boards. There are two-hour shows at 8pm and 10.30pm nightly for €30, including one drink, in a kind of old-school jazz club set-up (comfy chairs and small, low drinks tables).

Teatro Duque La Imperdible THEATRE
(Map p60; ☑954 90 54 58; www.imperdible.org; Plaza del Duque de la Victoria; admission €12) This is Seville's epicentre of experimental arts in El Centro district. Its small theatre stages lots of contemporary dance and a bit of drama and music, usually at 9pm. Wednesday night is flamenco night.

Sala Cero Teatro THEATRE
(Map p60; ☑954 22 51 65; www.salacero.com; Calle del Sol 5; admission around €10) This former flamenco haunt located 300m northeast of the Metropol Parasol has had a change of name and a change of heart and now stages art-house plays as well as a few moments of flamenco.

Boss CLUB
(Map p50; www.salaboss.es; Calle del Betis 67; admission from €12; ☉8pm-7am Tue-Sun) Make it past the two gruff bouncers and you'll find Boss a top dance spot, and relatively posh for Triana. The music is highly varied.

Naima Café Jazz BLUES, JAZZ
(Map p62; ☑954 38 24 85; Calle Trajano 47; ☉live performances from 11pm) If you're getting tired of flamenco, then you can find respite at this intimate place, which sways to the sound of mellow jazz (live at weekends).

🔒 Shopping

Shopping in Seville is a major pastime, and shopping for clothes is at the top of the list for any *sevillano*. Shoes fetishists beware: Seville possibly has the densest quota of shoe shops on the planet.

Calles Sierpes, Velázquez/Tetuán and de la Cuna have retained their charm with a host of small shops selling everything from polka-dot *trajes de flamenca* (flamenco dresses) to antique fans. Most shops open between 9am and 9pm, but expect it to be ghostly quiet between 2pm and 5pm when they close for siesta.

For a more alternative choice of shops, head for Calles Amor de Dios and Doctor Letamendi, close to Alameda de Hércules.

Tourist-oriented craft shops are dotted all around Barrio de Santa Cruz, east of the Alcázar.

Triana is famous for its pottery and tile-making. A dozen shops and workshops still sell charming and artistic ceramics on the corner of Calles Alfarería and Antillano Campos.

Cerámica Santa Ana   CERAMICS
(Map p50; ☎954 33 39 90; www.ceramicasantaana .com; Calle San Jorge 31) Cerámica Santa Ana is one of the better-regarded ceramic shops and the building itself almost qualifies as a tourist attraction.

El Jueves Market   MARKET
(Map p62; Calle de la Feria; ☺7am-2pm Thu) For a different kind of religious experience – shopping! – check out El Jueves Market, east of Alameda de Hércules, where you can find everything from hat stands to antiquated household appliances. It's as interesting for those who like people-watching as it is for those with an eye for a bargain.

Baco   FOOD
(Map p50; Calle Arfe 20) If you've enjoyed sampling the food that much (and who hasn't?), then you can take some of it home with you from this wonderful deli stocked with quality local food products such as olives and olive oil, *jamón*, cheeses and *bacalao* (salted cod).

El Postigo   MARKET
(Map p50; cnr Calles Arfe & Dos de Mayo) This covered arts and crafts market houses a few shops selling everything from pottery and textiles to silverware.

Casa del Libro   BOOKS
(Map p60; www.casadellibro.com; Calle Velázquez 8) Part of Spain's oldest bookshop chain, this

branch is spread over four floors and stocks plenty of multilingual fiction and guidebooks (including this one).

María Rosa   CLOTHING
(Map p60; Calle Linares 6) Full of flamenco flounces, polka dots and frills, this is the place to get dressed up like a flamenco queen. Blokes and children needn't feel left out as it also stocks a men's and children's range in addition to all the shiny accessories you might want.

❶ Information

Emergencies
Ambulance (☎061)
Fire (☎085)
Policía Local (☎092)
Policía Nacional (☎091)

Tourist Information
Inhfor (☎954 54 19 52; Estación Santa Justa; ☺8am-10pm, closes for lunch Sat & Sun) Independent tourist office at the Estación Santa Justa.
Regional Tourist Office (Avenida de la Constitución 21; ☺9am-7pm Mon-Fri, 10am-2pm & 3-7pm Sat, 10am-2pm Sun, closed holidays) The Constitución office is well informed but often very busy. There is also a branch at the **airport** (☎954 44 91 28; Aeropuerto San Pablo; ☺9am-8.30pm Mon-Fri, 10am-6pm Sat, 10am-2pm Sun, closed holidays).
Turismo Sevilla (www.turismosevilla.org; Plaza del Triunfo 1; ☺10.30am-7pm Mon-Fri) Information on all Sevilla province.

❶ Getting There & Away

Air
Seville's **Aeropuerto San Pablo** (SVQ; www.sevilla -airport.com; ☺24hr), 7km east of the city, is Andalucía's second-busiest airport after Málaga's. Non-Spanish destinations include London, Paris, Amsterdam, Warsaw and Geneva. It is served by various budget airlines:
Easyjet (www.easyjet.com)
Ryanair (www.ryanair.com)
Vueling Airlines (www.vueling.com)

Bus
Estación de Autobuses Plaza de Armas (Avenida del Cristo de la Expiración) Buses to/from the north of Sevilla province, Huelva province, Portugal and most other parts of Spain, including Madrid, leave from the main station, Estación de Autobuses Plaza de Armas. This is also the main station for Eurolines and international services to Germany, Belgium, France and beyond.

SEVILLA CARD

The **Sevilla Card** (☎913 60 47 72; www .sevillacard.es; ICONOS, Avenida de la Constitución 21; 24/48/72hr €33/53/71) allows discounted access to city sights, tours and some shops and restaurants.

CITY DRIVING

If you like getting hot, sweaty, frustrated, angry and sometimes frightened, then you'll enjoy driving in Seville. If you don't, then avoid picking up your hire car until after you leave the city. Car crime is rampant – never leave anything in your car. There are numerous underground car parks (many marked on the relevant maps), which cost around €18 per 24 hours. Street parking (€0.60 per hour) is metered and often limited to three hours. The most convenient car park in Barrio de Santa Cruz is on the corner of Avenida Menéndez Pelayo and the northern edge of the Jardines de Murillo.

Estación de Autobuses Prado de San Sebastián (Plaza San Sebastián) Other buses – primarily those running inside Andalucía (except Huelva) – use the Estación de Autobuses Prado de San Sebastián. Buses from here run roughly hourly to Cádiz, Córdoba, Granada, Jerez de la Frontera, Málaga and Madrid.

Train

Seville's **Estación Santa Justa** (☑902 43 23 43; Avenida Kansas City) is 1.5km northeast of the centre.

TO	FARE (€)	DURATION	FREQUENCY
Cádiz	13.25	1hr 45min	15 daily
Córdoba	33.20	42min	30 daily
Huelva	10.05	1½hr	3 daily
Granada	24.80	3hr	4 daily
Madrid	83.30	2½hr	20 daily
Málaga	38.70	2hr	11 daily

ⓘ Getting Around

To/From the Airport

AIR Seville's Aeropuerto San Pablo has a fair range of international and domestic flights.

BUS Buses (€2.40) make the trip between the airport and the city centre roughly every 15 minutes throughout the day. The service is reduced to every 30 minutes on Sundays as well as very early in the morning and late in the evening. The first bus from the airport to the city is at 5.45am and the last at 12.15am. From the city to the airport the first bus is at 5.15am and the last at 12.45am. It picks up and drops off in the city centre near the Puerta de Jerez, and also makes stops along Avenida del Cíd, Avenida de Carlos V and a number of other places.

TAXI A taxi costs a set €22 with a charge of €1 per bag from the airport to the centre, but going the other way you'll be lucky to pay less than €25. There's a €3 to €4 surcharge late at night, and on weekends and holidays.

Bus

Buses C1, C2, C3 and C4 do useful circular routes linking the main transport terminals and the city centre. The standard ticket is €1.30 but a range of passes are available (from stations and kiosks next to stops) if you're likely to use it a lot.

Car

For car hire there's **Avis** (☑902 48 03 21; www.avis.com; Avenida de Italia 107) or **National Atesa** (☑959 28 17 12; www.atesa.es) at the Santa Justa train station concourse, and all the normal brands at the airport.

Metro

First mooted some 30 years ago, Seville's **metro system** (www.sevilla21.com/metro) has finally emerged from the darkness and seen the light of day (so to speak). The first line opened in April 2009 and connects Ciudad Expo with Olivar de Quinto (this line isn't that useful for visitors). Three more lines are due for completion by 2017. The standard ticket is €1.35. A one-day travel card costs €4.50.

Taxi

Taxis are common and a journey across the city centre during daylight hours is unlikely to cost more than €5 to €7.

Tram

Tranvia (www.tussam.es) is the city's sleek tram service first introduced in 2007. Two parallel lines run in pollution-free bliss between Plaza Nueva, Avenida de la Constitucíon, Puerta de Jerez, San Sebastián and San Bernardo (the latter station was added in 2011). The standard ticket is €1.30 but a range of passes are available if you're likely to use it a lot.

Huelva & Sevilla Provinces

Why Go?

Gleaming white cities of spires and palaces, vast stretches of untrammelled coastline, fishing ports where the day's catch is served up in unpretentious restaurants, remote mountain villages and Europe's largest wetlands reserve: the western portion of Andalucía, comprising the provinces of Sevilla and Huelva, packs a matchless combination of historical interest, natural beauty, culinary wizardry and sun worship. Though the city of Seville gets all the attention, to the east stands a trio of towns with similarly enticing historic cores and tapas opportunities, yet far less touristed. Southwest of Seville lies a vast zone of protected marshes, dunes and forest, the Parque Nacional de Doñana. From there to Portugal extends the Costa de la Luz, a pristine coastline quite unlike the packaged chaos further east. Northward, towards Extremadura, rises the Sierra Morena, a sparsely visited range, criss-crossed by well-maintained trails and dotted with cobblestoned villages.

Best Places to Eat

» El Picoteo (p78)
» Casa El Padrino (p91)
» Agustina Restaurante (p98)
» Casa Curro (p96)

Best Places to Stay

» Casa de Carmona (p294)
» Las Navezuelas (p294)
» Hotel Sol y Mar (p293)
» Molino Río Alájar (p293)
» Hotel La Malvasia (p293)

Driving Distances (km)

	Aracena	Ayamonte	El Rocío	Huelva
Ayamonte	142			
El Rocío	118	107		
Huelva	101	52	60	
Niebla	87	75	35	29

Getting Around

Bus services link almost all the destinations described in this chapter to Seville and Huelva, the transport hubs for their respective provinces. It's usually possible to catch an afternoon bus back to your base after a day's hiking or beachcombing. Railroads link Huelva to Seville, and trains from either city stop in Sierra towns on their way to Extremadura. Driving almost anywhere in the region is a joy, with particularly scenic routes north to Cazalla de la Sierra and west to Portugal.

THREE PERFECT DAYS

Day 1: A Day in Doñana

Start with a morning tour of **Parque Nacional de Doñana**. The excellent tour offered by the park's guides covers the main zones: coast, dunes, marsh and forest, with plenty of opportunities to spot fallow deer, wild boar and all manner of migratory birds – and if you're lucky the endangered imperial eagle. Have a seafood lunch at one of the beachfront cafes in **Matalascañas**. Spend the afternoon enjoying the waves of Matalascañas beach.

Day 2: Over & Under

Catch a glimpse of the **Sierra de Aracena** – both above and below the ground! Starting from the village of Castaño del Robledo, hike through flowery fields to Galaroza, then return along the shady banks of the Rivera de Jabugo. Back in Castaño take a balcony table at **Maricastaña**, which puts an enticing nouveau twist on traditional country fare. Travel east to Aracena and join an afternoon tour of the **Gruta de las Maravillas**, a mesmerizing maze of underground caverns. For dinner, stop into **Rincón de Juan** and sample the ham of the legendary black pigs that roam the Sierra.

Day 3: La Campiña

Amid the rolling countryside east of Seville stands a trio of towns that are a treasure chest of Sevillan baroque, not to mention a tapas hopper's dream. Take the A-92 east to Osuna where you can tour the formidable **Colegiata de Santa María** containing a cache of baroque paintings. Cut north through the olive-dotted plains to reach **Écija**, with some incredibly preserved mosaics leftover from the Roman occupation. Then head back towards Seville, stopping in **Carmona**, the largest and most lavish of the three. In the evening sample up to a dozen bars on the town's renowned tapas trail.

Accommodation

Accommodation in the mountainous north is of the rustic variety, making for fun rural experiences, while the towns of La Campiña offer the chance to stay in historic mansions. On the Costa de la Luz, Isla Cristina has some excellent-value hotels at or near the beach. Read all about hotel choices in our dedicated Accommodation chapter (p288).

DON'T MISS

On display at Écija's history museum are half a dozen enormous and remarkably preserved stone mosaics from the period when the city loomed large in Roman Hispania. Lifted from beneath the central square and elsewhere, the richly detailed tableaux depict sea nymphs, satyrs and the 'discovery' of wine.

Best Birdwatching

» Paraje Natural Marismas del Odiel (p78)
» Sendero Charco de la Boca (p84)
» Parque Nacional de Doñana (p82)
» Dehesa de Abajo (p92)
» Sierra de Aracena (p90)

Best Beaches

» Matalascañas (p81)
» Isla Cristina (p81)
» Ayamonte (p81)
» Flecha El Rompido (p81)

Resources

» **Turismo de Huelva** (www.turismohuelva.org) Includes descriptions of beaches and an accommodation search function.

» **Sierra de Aracena** (www.sierradearacena.com) Information about the mountainous north, including downloadable directions for 16 hikes.

» **Turismo Sevilla** (www.turismosevilla.org) Information on all Sevilla province.

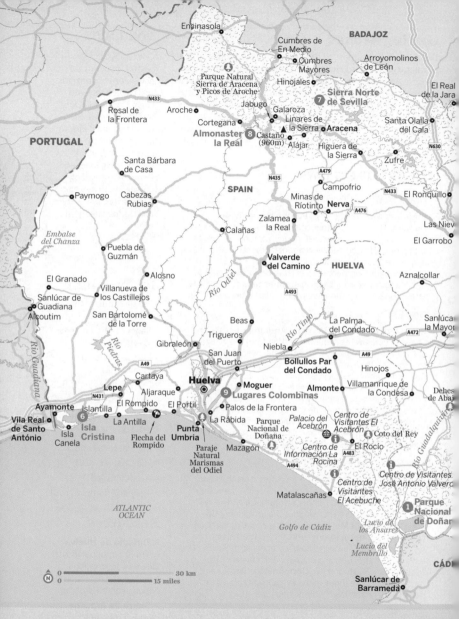

Huelva & Sevilla Provinces Highlights

1 Birdwatching in the domain of the Spanish imperial eagle, **Parque Nacional de Doñana** (p82)

2 Glimpsing the past at **Itálica** (p92), a well-preserved Roman settlement with a huge amphitheatre

3 Following the tapas trail in **Carmona** (p92), a gorgeous enclave of castles and churches

4 Viewing the riches at **Osuna** (p95), a showcase of ducal wealth and Sevillan baroque art

5 Gorging on **jamón Ibérico de bellota** (p354), product of

Guadalcanal

Alanís
San Nicolás
del Puerto

7 Sierra Norte
de Sevilla

Río Bembezar

Córdoba

El Pintado

Parque
Natural Sierra
Norte

**Cazalla de
la Sierra**

Las Navas de
la Concepción

Almadén
de la Plata

El Pedroso

Constantina

SE163

Río Huéznar

Río Guadalquivir

Villanueva del
Río y Minas

**Lora
del Río**

Río Genil

Villaverde
del Río

Cantillana

A4

Under Construction

ivera de Huelva

Alcalá
del Río

Brenes

A431

Écija

Itálica
2
Santiponce

Carmona **3**

A4

Río Corbones

Seville

Mairena
del Alcor

El Viso
del Alcor

SEVILLA

Marinaleda

Herrera

Gelves

**Alcalá de
Guadaira**

Río Guadaira

Marchena

A92 Estepa

Coria
el Río

**Dos
Hermanas**

Arahal

4
Osuna

To Málaga (85km)
Granada (121km)

La Puebla
del Río

**Los Palacios
y Villafranca**

Utrera

La Puebla
de Cazalla

lafranco del
adalquivir

AP4

A364

**Morón de
la Frontera**

NIV

A384

Lebrija

A471

Cuervo

Andalucía's famed acorn-fed
pigs

6 Enjoying the carnival
atmosphere in **Isla Cristina**
(p81), renowned for white-
sand beaches and tasty tuna

7 Walking between
enchanted villages in
the **Sierra Norte de Sevilla**
(p98)

8 Checking out the Islamic
architecture in **Almonaster**

la Real (p91), a remote,
labyrinthine village

9 Getting in touch with your
inner explorer at historic New
World departure point **Lugares
Colombinos** (p80)

HUELVA

POP 148.918

The capital of Huelva province is a modern, unpretentious industrial port that is set between the Odiel and Tinto estuaries. Despite its unpromising approaches, central Huelva is a likeable, lively place, and the city's people – called *choqueros* because of their supposed preference for the locally abundant *chocos* (cuttlefish) – are noted for their warmth.

Huelva's history dates back 3000 years to the Phoenician town of Onuba, the rivermouth location of which made it a natural base for the export of inland minerals to the Mediterranean. The town was levelled by the 1755 Lisbon earthquake but later grew after the British Río Tinto company developed the mines in the province's interior in the 1870s. Today Huelva has a sizeable fishing fleet and a heavy dose of petrochemical industry.

◉ Sights & Activities

More a scene than a collection of sights, Huelva nevertheless offers a few compelling points of interest.

FREE **Museo De Huelva**   MUSEUM
(www.museosdeandalucia.es/cultura/museos/MHU; Alameda Sundheim 13; ⊙2.30-8.30pm Tue, 9am-8.30pm Wed-Sat, 9am-2.30pm Sun) Standing on the Alameda, domain of the early-20th-century bourgeoisie, Huelva's town museum is stuffed to the gills with art and history. The permanent exhibition here concentrates on the province's impressive archaeological pedigree, with interesting items culled from its Roman and mining history. Upstairs, the changing exhibits mine the museum's substantial art collection, going all the way back to the 16th century.

FREE **Embarcadero de Mineral de Río Tinto**   HISTORIC SITE
An odd legacy of the area's mining history, this impressive iron pier curves out into the Odiel estuary about 500m south of the port. It was built for the Río Tinto company in the 1870s. Equipped with boardwalks on the upper and lower levels, it makes for a delightful stroll to admire the harbor and ships. It's about 1km southwest of the Plaza de las Monjas.

FREE **Paraje Natural Marismas del Odiel**   PROTECTED AREA
(☑959 52 43 35; ⊙10am-2pm & 4-6pm Tue-Sun) This 72-sq-km reserve across the Odiel estuary from Huelva is a uniquely productive tidal marsh system. A strategic point in the migratory flyways between Europe and Africa, it harbours a large, varied bird population, including up to 1000 blushing-pink greater flamingos in winter, plus ospreys, grey and purple herons, and many other waterfowl.

The marshes can be reached by car along the A497 Punta Umbría road west from Huelva. Cross either of the parallel bridges over Río Odiel, then follow 'PN Marismas del Odiel' signs to reach the **Centro de Visitantes Anastasio Senra** (Visitor Centre Anastasio Senra; ☑959 50 90 11; ⊙10am-2pm & 6-8pm Tue-Sun Apr-Sep, 10am-2pm & 4-6pm Tue-Sun Oct-Mar), which has an extensive exhibit on the ecology and history of the zone. Several paths to good birdwatching spots strike off the road through the reserve. Near the visitor center, the Sendero Calatilla de Bacuta is a 750m walk along the ancient salt flats, at the end of which are views to a small island harbouring the largest spoonbill nesting colony on the Iberian peninsula.

✯ Festivals & Events

Fiestas Colombinas   FESTIVAL
During the first week of August, Huelva celebrates Columbus' departure for the Americas (3 August 1492) with this six-day festival of music, dancing, funfairs, cultural events and bullfighting.

✖ Eating

In a salty city like Huelva it should come as no surprise that it's the fruits of the sea that are the stars of the menu. These items figure prominently on the menus of the numerous tapas bars lining Avenida Pablo Rada, north of the centre.

TOP CHOICE **El Picoteo**   TAPAS €
(Avenida Pablo Rada 5; raciones €9.50) On the north side of Pablo Rada is this casual tapas joint for gourmands in the know. It's usually packed but the kitchen can handle any size crowd. *Bacalao* (cod) is prepared in many ways (in lobster or Pedro Ximénez wine sauce, for example) and there are plenty of vegetarian items such as eggplant tart stuffed with Gouda cheese.

Huelva

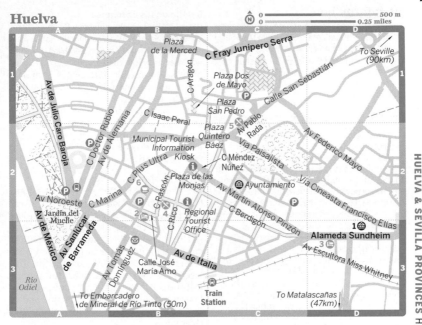

Ciquitrake TAPAS €

(www.ciquitrake.com; Calle Rascón 21; tapas €2.50, raciones €7.50; ⊘closed Sun) 'To know how to eat is to know how to live' is the motto of this innovative tapas maker, which specialises in novel variations on *choquero* mainstays, attractively presented in cool minimalist surroundings (with a glossary of Huelva slang as wallpaper). Try the *salmorejo* (thick, garlicky, tomato-based version of gazpacho, garnished with bits of ham and crumbled egg) croquettes and cuttlefish balls or ask what's new on an ever-expanding menu.

Restaurante Juan José ANDALUCIAN €

(☑959 26 38 57; Calle Villamundaka 1; tapas €2, raciones €9) It's a bit out of the way (north of the centre) but locals regularly flock to this humble establishment for the fabulously gooey *tortilla española* (drenched in mayo). You'll find the tuna (fresh from Isla Cristina) and *carne mechada* (meat stuffed with pepper and ham) are equally amazing. If you arrive after 2pm you'll have to wait for a table. It's located about 1.5km northeast of the Plaza de las Monjas. Catch bus number 6 from the city bus station and get off at Plaza Huerto Paco. Walk one block south down Avenida de

Huelva

◉ Sights
1 Museo De Huelva D3

⬛ Sleeping
2 Hotel Costa de la Luz B2
3 Hotel Familia Condes D3

⊗ Eating
4 Ciquitrake B2
5 El Picoteo C1

⊖ Drinking
6 Café Central..B2

las Adoratrices and turn left on Calle Villamundaka.

🍷 Drinking

Café Central CAFE

(Calle Duque de la Victoria 6; ⊘closed Sun) A bit of tradition amid the relentless urban renewal of the centre, the Café Central feels like it's been there forever with its steel counter, marble-top tables and super-attentive waiters. No *churros* here, but it's alright to get them at Bar Paco Perdigones across the way and tote them over.

❶ Information

Municipal Tourist Information Kiosk (Plaza de las Monjas; ⏱10am-2pm & 5-8.30pm Mon-Sat) Download a bluetooth guide of Huelva here.

Regional Tourist Office (www.turismohuelva .org; Plaza Alcalde Coto Mora 2; ⏱9am-7.30pm Mon-Fri, to 3pm Sat & Sun) Well informed and helpful.

❶ Getting There & Around

BUS Most buses from the **bus station** (☎959 25 69 00; Calle Doctor Rubio) are operated by **Damas** (☎959 25 69 00; www.damas-sa.es), with service to such destinations as Aracena, Isla Cristina, Moguer, Matalascañas and Faro (Portugal). Frequency to destinations in Huelva province is reduced on Saturday, Sunday and public holidays. **Socibus** (www.socibus.es) runs at least two buses a day to Madrid (€24, 7¼ hours).

CAR There's metered street parking (Monday to Saturday) indicated by blue lines all around downtown and a useful parking lot off Calle Duque de la Victoria by the Café Central.

TRAIN Three services daily run to Seville (€10, 1½ hours) and once a day to Córdoba and Madrid (€70, four hours) from the **train station** (☎902 43 23 43; www.renfe.com; Avenida de Italia).

AROUND HUELVA

Lugares Colombinos

The 'Columbian Sites' are the three townships of La Rábida, Palos de la Frontera and Moguer, along the eastern bank of the Tinto estuary. All three played a key role in Columbus' preparation for his journey of discovery and can be visited in an enjoyable 40km return trip from Huelva.

LA RÁBIDA

Monasterio de la Rábida   MONASTERY
(☎959 35 04 11; admission €3; ⏱10am-1pm & 4-7pm Tue-Sun) In the pretty and peaceful town of La Rábida, don't miss this 14th- and 15th-century Franciscan monastery, visited several times by Columbus before his great voyage of discovery.

Here Columbus met Abbot Juan Pérez, who took up his cause and drummed up support for his far-fetched plans to discover new lands and in the process make Spain very rich. Within the monastery is a chapel with an alabaster Virgin before which Columbus prayed, and a Mudéjar cloister, one of the few bit of the original structure that remained after the earthquake of 1755.

Muelle de las Carabelas   HISTORIC SITE
(Wharf of the Caravels; admission €3.55; ⏱10am-2pm & 5-9pm Tue-Fri, 11am-8pm Sat & Sun Jun-Aug, 10am-7pm Tue-Sun Sep-May) On the waterfront below the Monasterio de La Rábida is this pseudo 15th-century quayside, where you can board replicas of Columbus' tiny three-ship fleet.

The ships are moored behind an interesting museum, displaying instruments of navigation and providing a glimpse of the indigenous experience at the time of the Spaniards' arrival.

Parque Botánico
José Celestino Mutis   GARDENS
(☎959 53 05 35; Paraje de la Rábida; ⏱10am-2pm & 5-9pm Tue-Sun Jun-Sep, 10am-7pm Tue-Sun Oct-May) On the way back to the N-442 sits this beautifully landscaped botanical garden on a hillside with plants and trees from both the New World and the Old. The large park makes for a delightful ramble, featuring palm-lined canals, pools, a greenhouse containing tropical plants and a fine observation deck overlooking the Río Guadiana.

PALOS DE LA FRONTERA

It was from the port of Palos de la Frontera that Columbus and his merry band set sail into the unknown. The town provided the explorer with two of his ships, two captains (Martín Alonso Pinzón and Vicente Yañez Pinzón) and more than half his crew.

In town the **Casa Museo Martín Alonso Pinzón** (☎959 10 00 41; Calle Colón 24; admission free; ⏱10am-2pm Mon-Fri) is the former home of the captain of the *Pinta*. Inside is a permanent exhibit on Palos' crucial contribution to the expedition.

MOGUER

From Palos de la Frontera it's a 7km drive along the A494 to the pretty whitewashed town of Moguer. It was here that Columbus' ship, the *Niña*, was built. The main Columbus site in town is the 14th-century **Monasterio de Santa Clara** (☎959 37 01 07; www .santa-clara.tk; Plaza de las Monjas; guided tour €3; ⏱10.30am-1pm & 4.30-7pm Tue-Sat, 10.30am-1pm Sun), where Columbus spent a night of vigil and prayer after returning from his first voyage. Visit is by guided tour, offered hourly. You'll see a lovely Mudéjar cloister and an impressive collection of Renaissance religious art.

Moguer has its own charming flavour of Andalucian baroque, and its sunny beauty was fulsomely expressed by local poet laureate Juan Ramón Jiménez (1881–1958), who won the Nobel Prize for literature in 1956. The **Casa Museo Zenobia y Juan Ramón Jiménez** (Calle Juan Ramón Jiménez 10; admission €3; ◷10.15am-1pm Tue-Sun & 5.15-7pm Tue-Sat), the old home of the poet and his wife, is open for guided visits.

Right across the plaza from the monastery, **Barola** (www.barola.es; Plaza de las Monjas) is a cool, stylish tapas bar in a cavernous reconstructed building with Moorish arches.

Costa de la Luz

Extending from the mouth of the Río Guadalquivir to the Portuguese border, Huelva province's modestly developed coastline consists of broad beaches of white sands backed by dunes and pine trees. It's a world away from the 'Costa del Chaos' of Andalucía's Mediterranean coast. The main resorts east of Huelva are Matalascañas and Mazagón, while to the west the most notable beach locales are Punta Umbría, Flecha El Rompido, Isla Cristina and Ayamonte. All are unpretentious places, more popular with Spanish holidaymakers than visitors from overseas. Splashing about in the waves is the main event, but a couple of low-key attractions add to the seaside fun.

MATALASCAÑAS

Abutting the Parques Nacional and Natural de Doñana, Matalascañas is a slap-it-up-quick tourist resort. Fortunately development is confined to a 4km by 1km space and the beach here is simply gorgeous. A notable landmark partially submerged by the shoreline is the Torre de Higuera, a piece of a toppled tower dating from 1600.

Follow the road east to find a boardwalk trail leading down along the edge of the national park to the beach. From a control post near the Gran Hotel El Coto, a 1.5km boardwalk trail snakes through the dunes, here dotted with umbrella pine and maritime juniper.

At the opposite end of town, **Parque Dunar** (☑959 44 80 86; www.parquedunar.com; Avenida de las Adelfas; ◷9am-8pm) is a 1.3-sq-km expanse of high, pine-covered dunes laced with a maze of sandy pathways and boardwalk trails.

Facing the beach on the west end of town are about a half dozen seafood restaurants serving extremely fresh shrimp and cockles.

FLECHA EL ROMPIDO

Possibly the most spectacular beach along the Costa de la Luz, this 8km-long sand bar is separated from the mainland by the mouth of the Río Piedras. Its roadless expanse can be reached only by ferry, which keeps the crowds away, even in midsummer. The waters on the inland side remain calm, while the south side faces the open sea. Part of the Río Piedras wetlands reserve, it's a place of great ornithological and botanical interest, with possibilities to observe cormorants, pintail ducks and egrets as well as the odd lynx. To get there, take a bus from Huelva to El Portil or Cartaya and get off at the last stop (across from the AC Nuevo Portil hotel). Descend to the beach where you'll find a Transbordador Papalima boat (€3 round trip), which leaves whenever it fills, though you normally won't have to wait long.

ISLA CRISTINA

Isla Cristina is first and foremost a bustling fishing port with a 250-strong fleet. Aside from its tuna and sardines, the town is renowned for its vibrant Carnival celebration. If you can't make it in February, stop into the **Museo del Carnaval** (☑959 33 26 94; Calle San Francisco 12; ◷10am-2pm & 5.30-7.30pm), located above the Municipal Tourist Office, with a permanent exhibit of prize-winning costumes.

Below the town a bridge traverses a lagoon to reach the sprawling **Playa de la Gaviota**. Along the rear of the beach, a boardwalk trail heads east to **Playa Central**, the main tourism zone with a few hotels and restaurants. Further east a nature trail winds through forested marshlands, with good birdwatching opportunities.

Some of the most appealing seafood restaurants are on a square by the northwest tip of the peninsula, opposite the seafood auction market (where you can watch restaurant buyers from around Spain bid for the day's catch). These busy spots serve *chocos* (cuttlefish), *casatñuelas* (small cuttlefish) and *chipirones* (squid) – it just doesn't get any fresher.

AYAMONTE

Staring across the Río Guadiana to Portugal, Ayamonte has a cheerful border-town buzz. The old town is dotted with attractive plazas and old churches and riddled with cafes, shops and restaurants.

THE FOUR VOYAGES OF CHRISTOPHER COLUMBUS

In April 1492 Christopher Columbus (Cristóbal Colón to Spaniards) finally won Spanish royal support for his proposed westward voyage of exploration to the spice-rich Orient, a proposal that was to result in no fewer than four voyages by the great navigator and a fabulous golden age for Spain.

On 3 August 1492 Columbus embarked from Palos de la Frontera with 100 men and three ships. After a near mutiny as the crew despaired of finding land, they finally made landfall on the Bahamian island of Guanahaní on 12 October, naming it San Salvador. The expedition went on to discover Cuba and Hispaniola, where the *Santa María* sank. Its timbers were used to build a fort, Fuerte Navidad, which 33 Spaniards were left to hold. The *Niña* and the *Pinta* got back to Palos on 15 March 1493.

Columbus – with animals, plants, gold ornaments and six Caribbean Indians – received a hero's welcome on his return, as all were convinced that he had reached the fabled East Indies (in fact, his calculations were some 16,000km out).

Columbus made further voyages in 1493 and 1498, discovering Jamaica, Trinidad and the mouth of the Orinoco River. But he proved to be a disastrous colonial administrator, enslaving the indigenous people and alienating the Spanish settlers. Eventually his mishandling led to a revolt by settlers on Hispaniola and before he could suppress the uprising he was arrested by a royal emissary from Spain and sent home in chains.

In a final attempt to redeem himself and find a strait to Asia, Columbus embarked on his fourth and final voyage in April 1502. This time he reached Honduras and Panama, but then became stranded for a year in Jamaica, having lost his ships to sea worms.

Columbus died in 1506 in Valladolid, northern Spain – impoverished and apparently still believing he had reached Asia. His remains were eventually returned to the Caribbean, as he had wished, before being brought back to Seville (p52). Or were they? The story of Columbus' posthumous voyages has recently become quite a saga itself.

South of town are the broad beaches of **Isla Canela** and **Punta del Moral**, the latter more developed.

For Portugal-bound romantics, it's possible to skip the fast modern road and enjoy a slower pace on the ferry (15 minutes) across the Guadiana to Portugal's Vila Real de Santo António by **Transporte Fluvial del Guadiana** (959 47 06 17; www.rioguadi ana.net; Muelle de Portugal; Passenger/bicycle/car €1.70/1.10/5; hourly departures 9.30am-7.30pm mid-Sep–Jun, half-hourly departures 9.30am-9pm Jul–mid-Sep). The same operator runs daily cruises up the Río Guadiana, one of Spain's longest rivers, to the Portuguese village of Alcoutim (8½ hours). Purchase tickets and check departure times from the kiosks on the ferry dock.

Among the many seafood purveyors here, **Casa Luciano** (www.casaluciano.com; Calle de la Palma 1; mains €12-15; closed Sun) is among the most appealing. Everything on your plate is freshly cooked and only minutes out of the water: its version of tuna, particularly prized along this stretch of coast, is simply outstanding.

EAST OF HUELVA

Parque Nacional de Doñana

The Parque Nacional de Doñana is a place of haunting natural beauty and exotic horizons where flocks of flamingos tinge the evening skies pink, huge herds of deer and boar flit between the trees and the elusive Iberian lynx slinks ever closer to extinction. Here, in the largest roadless region in Western Europe, and Spain's most celebrated national park, you can literally taste the scent of nature at her most raw and powerful.

The 542-sq-km national park extends 30km along or close to the Atlantic coast and up to 25km inland. Much of its perimeter is bordered by the separate **Parque Natural de Doñana** (Doñana Natural Park), under less strict protection, which forms a buffer for the national park. The two *parques* together provide a refuge for 419 bird species and 39 types of mammal, including endangered species such as the Iberian lynx and Spanish imperial eagle (eight breeding pairs). It's also a crucial habitat for millions of migrating birds.

Since its inception in 1969, the national park has been under pressure from tourism, agriculture, hunters, developers and builders who oppose the restrictions on land use. Ecologists, for their part, argue that Doñana is increasingly hemmed in by tourism and agricultural schemes, roads and other infrastructure that threaten to deplete its water supplies and cut it off from other undeveloped areas. The beach resort of Matalascañas, for example, swells in population from 1000 to around 200,000 in summer, and traffic flow increases as summer residents commute to work in Seville. Some resident lynx have been run over attempting to cross the roads around Doñana. On the bright side, for the past few years the lynx population has been steady at around 60 individuals. There's also an increasingly successful captive breeding program (to find out more about these efforts and watch videos of the newborns, have a look at www.lynxexsitu.es).

TOURING THE PARK

Access to the interior of the national park is restricted, although anyone may walk along the beach between Matalascañas and the mouth of the Río Guadalquivir (which can be crossed by boats from Sanlúcar de Barrameda in Cádiz province), as long as they do not stray inland.

To visit the interior of the national park, you must book a guided tour leaving from El Acebuche visitor centre. Run by the **Cooperativa Marismas del Rocío** (☎959 43 04 32; www.donanavisitas.es; 4hr tour per person €27; ☺8.30am & 3pm Tue-Sun mid-Sep–Apr, 8.30am & 5pm Mon-Sat May–mid-Sep), these tours are in all-terrain vehicles, each holding 20 people. They traverse 70km in four hours and cover all the major ecosystems – coast, dunes, marsh and Mediterranean forest. The experience can feel like a theme-park outing but the guides have plenty of good information to share. It is usually possible to join a group with a bilingual guide. You need to book ahead by telephone – the tours can be full more than a month before in spring, summer and all holiday times. Binoculars can be hired at the visitors center. Bring mosquito repellent (except in winter) and drinking water.

These tours are fine for the interested amateur who just wants an overview of the park, but for the dedicated nature lover, private operators are the way to go. They normally spend part of their time in the national park and part in the natural park, and range through pine and oak forests and across marshlands, with a great diversity of birds and high chances of seeing deer and boar. The following operators use smallish vehicles carrying a maximum of 12 people.

HUELVA & SEVILLA PROVINCES PARQUE NACIONAL DE DOÑANA

PARQUE NACIONAL DE DOÑANA LIFE CYCLES

The many interwoven ecosystems that make up Parque Nacional de Doñana give rise to fantastic diversity. Nearly half the park is occupied by marshes. These are almost dry from July to October but in autumn they start to fill with water, eventually leaving only a few islets of dry land. Hundreds of thousands of waterbirds arrive from the north to winter here, including an estimated 80% of Western Europe's wild ducks. As the waters sink in spring, greater flamingos, spoonbills, storks, herons, avocets, hoopoes, bee-eaters, stilts and other birds arrive for the summer, many of them to nest. Fledglings flock around the *lucios* (ponds) and as these dry up in July, herons, storks and kites move in to feast on trapped perch.

Between the marshlands and the park's 35km-long beach is a band of sand dunes, pushed inland by the wind at a rate of up to 6m per year. The shallow valleys between the dunes, called *corrales*, host pines and other trees favoured as nesting sites by raptors. When dune sand eventually reaches the marshlands, rivers carry it back down to the sea, which washes it up on the beach – and the cycle begins all over again.

Elsewhere in the park, stable sands support 144 sq km of *coto*, the name given here to areas of woodland and scrub. *Coto* is the favoured habitat of many nesting birds and the park's abundant mammal population – 39 species including red and fallow deer, wild boar, mongooses and genets.

The park is also a haven for much smaller creatures, but ones that are no less spectacular. Reptiles and amphibians are abundant and include the charming spur-thighed tortoise, the less charming Lataste's viper, and the warty midwife toad.

WALKS

The walking trails near the park's visitor centres are an unmissable highlight, and are easy enough to be undertaken by most. The March–May and September–November migration seasons are overall the most exciting for birdwatchers.

» **Sendero Charco de la Boca**, at La Rocina (☉9am-3pm & 4-7pm, to 8pm or 9pm Apr-Aug, to 3pm Sun 15 Jun–14 Sep) centre, is a 3km round trip with four birdwatching hides and it takes you through a range of habitats.

» **Sendero Charco del Acebrón**, by the Centro de Visitantes El Acebrón (p84), is a 1.5km trail between the palace and the parking lot, following the banks of a creek shaded by willows, honeysuckle and buckthorn. Sections of boardwalk cross the marshier bits. Though crowded out by eucalyptus and pine, traces of endemic vegetation such as cork and mastic remain.

» **Sendero Lagunas del Acebuche**, by the Centro de Visitantes El Acebuche (p84), has good walking paths (1.5km and 3.5km round trip) leading to birdwatching hides overlooking nearby lagoons.

» The more remote **Centro de Visitantes José Antonio Valverde** (☎671 564145; ☉10am-7pm, to 8pm or 9pm Apr-Aug), on the eastern edge of the park, is generally an excellent birdwatching spot as it overlooks a year-round *lucio* (pond). The Caño de Rosalimán waterway, just west of here, is also a fine site. The easiest way to reach the Valverde centre is by taking an authorised tour from El Rocío; the alternative is to drive yourself on rough roads from Villamanrique de la Condesa or La Puebla del Río to the northeast.

» **Raya Real**, one of the most important routes used by Romería pilgrims on their journeys to and from El Rocío, can be accessed from the northeastern edge of that village, by crossing the Puente del Ajolí, and following the track into the woodland. It crosses the **Coto del Rey**, a large woodland zone where you may spot deer or boar in the early morning or late evening.

Doñana Reservas BIRDWATCHING
(☎959 44 24 74; www.donanareservas.com; Avenida La Canaliega, El Rocío; 4hr trip 4-12 people per person €35, 10hr trip 3-6 people per person €85) English-speaking guides with expertise in identification of birds, wildflowers, mushrooms and mammals. Tours focus on the marshes and woods in the northern section of the park. Binoculars, telescopes and checklists are provided.

Doñana Bird Tours BIRDWATCHING
(☎959 46 59 47; www.donanabirdtours.com; 9hr trip 1-3 people €150, each extra person €30) Top-class birdwatching tours departing from Villamanrique de la Condesa.

Doñana Nature GUIDED TOUR
(☎959 44 21 60; www.donana-nature.com; Calle Las Carretas 10; 3½hr trip per person €26) Half-day trips, at 8am and 3.30pm daily, are general interest, though specialised ornithological and photographic trips are also offered; English- and French-speaking guides available.

ℹ Information

Centro de Visitantes El Acebuche (☎959 43 96 29; ☉8am-9pm May-Sep, to 7pm Oct-Apr) Twelve kilometres south of El Rocío on the A483, then 1.6km west, El Acebuche is the national park's main visitor centre. It has an interactive exhibit on the park and paths to birdwatching hides, plus a film show of Iberian lynxes at El Acebuche – the closest visitors can get to them.

Centro de Información La Rocina (☎959 44 23 40; ☉9am-3pm & 4-7pm Sep-Mar, to 8 or 9pm Apr-Aug) Beside the A483, 1km south of El Rocío. Has an exhibition on the history of the El Rocío pilgrimage.

Centro de Visitantes El Acebrón (☉9am-3pm & 4-7pm Sep-Mar, to 8 or 9pm Apr-Aug) Six kilometres along a paved road west from La Rocina, with an ethnographic exhibition of the park inside a palatial residence.

ℹ Getting There & Away

CAR & BUS You cannot enter the park in your own vehicle. **Damas** (www.damas-sa.es) runs nine to 11 buses daily between El Rocío and Matalascañas; these will stop at the El Acebuche turn-off on the A483. Otherwise all tour companies, as well as the tours run by the national park, will pick you up from Matalascañas if you give advance notice.

El Rocío

POP 1639

El Rocío, the most significant town in the vicinity of Parque Nacional de Doñana, comes as a surprise to first-time visitors. A major pilgrimage site for a week in late spring, it remains somnolent the rest of the year.

The streets of the town, left unpaved and covered with sand, are lined with colourfully decked-out single-storey houses with sweeping verandahs. These are the well-tended properties of over 90 *hermandades* (brotherhoods), whose pilgrims converge on the town every Pentecost (Whitsuntide) for the Romería del Rocío, Spain's largest religious festival. At other times the houses are vacant, and it feels like a sandy ghost town.

Beyond its unlikely ambience, El Rocío also impresses travellers with its striking setting in front of luminous *marismas* (wetlands), where herds of deer drink at dawn and, at certain times of year, pink flocks of flamingos gather in massive numbers. Whatever way you look at it, El Rocío is one of the most exotic villages in all of Europe.

Whether it's the play of the light on the marshes in front of the town, an old woman praying to the Virgin in the church or a girl passing by in a sultry flamenco dress, there is always something of interest to catch the eye on the dusky, sand-blown streets.

◉ Sights & Activities

Ermita del Rocío   CHURCH
(☺8am-10.30pm Apr-Sep, 8.30am-8pm Oct-Mar)
In the heart of the village stands the Ermita del Rocío, built in its present form in 1964. This is the home of the celebrated **Nuestra Señora del Rocío** (Our Lady of El Rocío), a small wooden image of the Virgin dressed in long, jewelled robes, which normally stands above the main altar. People arrive to see the Virgin every day of the year and especially on weekends, when the brotherhoods of El Rocío often gather here for colourful celebrations.

Museo del Rocío   MUSEUM
(Camino de Moguer; admission €2) Located across the main road on the west end of the marsh, the museum provides an overview of El Rocío's culture, nature and economy, with sections on the Ermita, pilgrimage festivals and Doñana. There are lots of great old photos of former pilgrimages, a film about El Rocío's brotherhoods and a saddle workshop.

Wildlife-Watching
The marshlands in front of El Rocío, which have water all year round, offer some of the best bird- and beast-watching in the entire Doñana region. Deer and horses graze in the shallows and you may be lucky enough to see a flock of flamingos wheeling through the sky in a big pink cloud. Pack a pair of binoculars and stroll the waterfront promenade.

FREE Francisco Bernis
Birdwatching Centre   BIRDWATCHING
(☎959 44 23 72; ☺9am-2pm & 4-6pm Tue-Sun) About 350m east of the Ermita along the waterfront, this facility backs on to the marsh, and from here flamingos, glossy

---

RABBIT REDUCTION

To the Romans, this was the land of rabbits, Hispania, and it is the only part of Europe where rabbits were endemic rather than introduced from elsewhere. The population was traditionally controlled by natural predators such as the Iberian lynx and imperial eagle. But in the 1950s an epidemic of a virus called myxomatosis, followed in the 1990s by a plague of haemorrhagic pneumonia, almost completely eradicated Spain's rabbit population, leaving the lynx and eagles without their natural source of sustenance. The Parque Nacional de Doñana has made efforts to to reintroduce rabbits to the park environment: the habitat was reconditioned to increase their food supply, rabbits were brought in from Cádiz province, and pens were built from the stumps of cleared eucalyptus trees. Despite initial setbacks, the rabbits' numbers have grown steadily.

THE WHITE DOVE

Like most of Spain's holiest images, Nuestra Señora del Rocío (also known as La Blanca Paloma – the White Dove) has legendary origins. Back in the 13th century, a hunter from Almonte village found the effigy in a marshland tree and started to carry her home. But when he stopped for a rest, the Virgin magically returned to the tree. Before long, a chapel was built on the site of the tree (El Rocío) and it became a place of pilgrimage.

ibis, spoonbills and more can be observed through the rear windows or from the observation deck. (High-power binoculars are provided.) The experts here can help you identify species and inform you about which migratory birds are visiting and where to see them.

Festivals & Events

Romería del Rocío   RELIGIOUS
Seven weeks after Easter El Rocío turns from a quiet backwater into an explosive mess of noise, colour and passion. This is the culmination of Spain's biggest religious pilgrimage, which draws hundreds of thousands of festive pilgrims. Most belong to 106 brotherhoods, who arrive from towns all across southern Spain on foot, horseback and in gaily decorated covered wagons.

Solemn is the last word you'd apply to this quintessentially Andalucian event. Participants dress in fine Andalucian costume and sing, dance, drink, laugh and romance their way to their goal. The total number of people in the village on this special weekend can reach about a million.

The weekend reaches an ecstatic climax in the very early hours of Monday. Members of the Almonte *hermandad*, which claims the Virgin as its own, barge into the church and bear her out on a float. Violent struggles ensue as others battle for the honour of carrying La Blanca Paloma. The crush and chaos are immense, but somehow the Virgin is carried round to each of the *hermandad* buildings before finally being returned to the church in the afternoon.

A smaller, more locally oriented procession, **El Rocío Chico**, takes place on August

18 and 19 in nearby Almonte, as a commemoration of the termination of French reprisals in 1810 after the townsfolk executed a French officer. Once every seven years, the celebrants bear the Virgin of Rocío 15km north across Doñana to their town, where she resides for nine months until her return to El Rocío with great festivity a week before the Romería.

Eating

Restaurante Toruño   ANDALUCIAN €€
(☎959 44 24 22; www.toruno.es; Plaza Acebuchal 22; mains €12-20) With its traditional Andalucian atmosphere, excellent food and huge portions, this is the one must-try restaurant in town. A highlight of the menu is the free-range *mostrenca* calf, grilled to perfection. There's a formal dining room at the rear; on warm evenings dine in front of the restaurant by the 1000-year old *acebuche* tree.

Restaurante El Real   ANDALUCIAN €
(Calle Real 7; set lunch €9; ☻8am-7pm Tue-Sun) This may be a tourist-oriented place but one that seems to relish serving outsiders. The food is homemade and there's a pleasant terrace. Be sure to try the *salmorejo*, and for dessert the 'heavenly bacon' (flan with pine nuts).

ⓘ Information

Tourist office (www.turismodedonana.com; Camino de Moguer; ☻9.30am-2pm Tue-Sun) Inside the Museo del Rocío, at the southwestern corner of the village just off the A483.

ⓘ Getting There & Away

Damas (www.damas-sa.es) buses run from Seville to El Rocío and on to Matalascañas (€5.80, 1½ hours, three daily). From Huelva, take a Damas bus to Almonte, and catch another to El Rocío (10 daily).

NORTH OF HUELVA

To the north, straight highways are replaced by winding byways and you enter a more temperate zone, up to 960m higher than the coast. The rolling hills of Huelva's portion of the Sierra Morena are covered with a thick pelt of cork oak and pine and punctuated by winding river valleys, enchanting villages of stone and tile, and the bustling 'capital' of the area, Aracena.

This is a still little-discovered rural world, threaded with trails and blessed with a rich hill-country cuisine that abounds in game, local cheeses and fresh vegetables, though it's best known for its prized *jamón serrano* (dry cured mountain ham). Most of the area lies within the 1840-sq-km Parque Natural Sierra de Aracena y Picos de Aroche, Andalucía's second-largest protected zone.

Minas de Riotinto

POP 4157 / ELEV 420M

Tucked away on the southern fringe of the sierra is one of the world's oldest mining districts, so old that even King Solomon of faraway Jerusalem is said to have mined gold here for his famous temple. Though the miners clocked off for the last time in 2001, it's still a fascinating place to explore, with its superb museum and the opportunity to visit the old mines and ride the mine railway.

The Río Tinto itself rises a few kilometres northeast of town, its name ('red river') stemming from the deep red-brown hue produced by the reaction of its acidic waters with the abundant iron and copper ores.

⊙ Sights & Activities

Museo Minero   MUSEUM
(☑959 59 00 25; www.parquemineroderiotinto.com; Plaza Ernest Lluch; adult/child €4/3; ☉10.30am-3pm & 4-7pm) The mining museum is a figurative goldmine for devotees of industrial archaeology, taking you through the area's unique history from the megalithic tombs of the 3rd millennium BC to the Roman and British colonial eras and finally the closure of the mines in 2001. The tour includes an elaborate 200m-long re-creation of a Roman mine.

The museum also features a big display on the railways that served the mines. Pride of place goes to the Vagón del Maharajah, a luxurious carriage built in 1892 for a tour of India by Britain's Queen Victoria, though she never actually rode in it.

Peña de Hierro   MINE
(adult/child €8/7; ☉noon-1.30pm & 5.30-7pm) These are old copper and sulphur mines 3km north of Nerva. Here you see the source of Río Tinto, an 65m-deep open-cast mine, and are taken into a 200m-long underground mine gallery. It's essential to book ahead through the Museo Minero, and schedules may change.

Ferrocarril Turístico-Minero   TOUR
(☑959 59 00 25; www.parquemineroderiotinto .com; adult/child €10/9; ☉1pm Mon-Fri & 4.30pm Sat & Sun Mar–mid-Jun & Oct-Nov, 1.30pm & 5.30pm daily mid-Jul–Sep) A fun way to see the area (especially with children) is to ride the old mining train, running 22km (round-trip) through the surreal landscape in restored early-20th-century carriages. The train parallels the river for the entire journey, giving passengers the opportunity to appreciate its constantly shifting hues and at the end of the line to wade in its waters.

Trips start at the old railway repair workshops 4km east of Minas de Ríotinto off the road to Nerva. Commentary is in Spanish. It's mandatory to book ahead. Tickets may be purchased either at the museum or the railway station.

⊙ Getting There & Away

From Monday to Friday, **Damas** (www.damas-sa .es) runs five buses between Minas de Riotinto and Huelva (€6.30, 1¾ hours), three on weekends. There is no public transport to the Ferrocarril Turístico-Minero.

Aracena

POP 7812 / ELEV 730M

Sparkling white in its mountain bowl, the thriving old market town of Aracena is an

---

THE MARTE PROJECT

Since 2003, scientists from NASA and Spain's Centro de Astrobiología in Madrid have been conducting a research program around the Minas de Riotinto known as Marte (Mars Analog Research and Technology Experiment) in preparation for seeking life on Mars. It's thought that the high acid levels that give the Río Tinto its colour (by the action of acid on iron) are a product of underground micro-organisms comparable with those that scientists believe may exist below the surface of Mars. Experiments in locating these microbes up to 150m below ground level are being used to help develop techniques and instruments for looking for similar subterranean life on the red planet.

Aracena

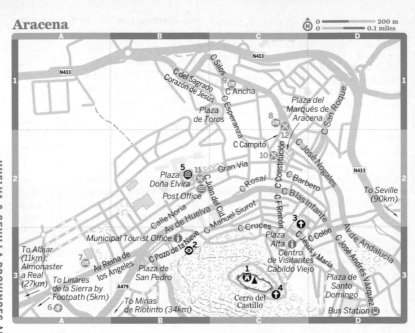

Aracena

appealingly lively place that's wrapped like a ribbon around a medieval church and ruined castle. With a stash of good places to stay and eat it makes an ideal base from which to explore this lovely area.

◉ Sights & Activities

Gruta de las Maravillas   CAVE
(Cave of Marvels; ☎663 93 78 76; Calle Pozo de la Nieve; tour adult/child €8.50/6; ☺10.30am-1.30pm & 3-6pm, tours every hour Mon-Fri, every half-hour Sat, Sun & holidays) Beneath the castle hill is a web of caves and tunnels carved from the karstic topography. An extraordinary 1km route takes you through 12 chambers and past six underground lakes, all beautifully illuminated and filled with weird and wonderful rock formations that provided a backdrop for the film *Journey to the Centre of the Earth.*

Tours are in Spanish but audioguides are available. You're not allowed to take photos but a photographer is on hand on the way in for that obligatory portrait. Tickets can sell out in the afternoons and on weekends when busloads of visitors arrive.

Museo del Jamón   MUSEUM
(Gran Vía; admission €3, discount with purchase of ticket to Gruta de las Maravillas; ☺11am-1.45pm & 3.30-6.30pm) The *jamón* for which the sierra is famed gets due recognition in this modern museum. You'll learn why the acorn-fed Iberian pig gives such succulent meat, about the importance of the native pastures in which they are reared and about

traditional and modern methods of slaughter and curing. A room near the entrance is devoted to wild mushrooms, another local delicacy.

The Old Town
Dramatically dominating the town are the tumbling, hilltop ruins of the **castillo**, an atmospheric fortification built by the kingdoms of Portugal and Castile in the 12th century. Next door is the **Iglesia Prioral de Nuestra Señora del Mayor Dolor** (⊙10am-7pm), built about a century later, a Gothic-Mudéjar hybrid that combines an interior of ribbed vaults with attractive brick tracery on the tower, noted for its distinctive Islamic influence. The castle is reached up a steep lane from Plaza Alta, a handsome, cobbled square that was originally the centre of the town. Here stands the elegant 15th-century **Cabildo Viejo**, the former town hall, with a handsome Renaissance doorway. From Plaza Alta, Calle Francisco Rincón descends the hill back towards town, passing a series of narrow streets that are attractively lined with humbler whitewashed houses, before finally entering the **Plaza del Marqués de Aracena**, a lively square fronted by a couple of decent pavement cafes.

Hiking
The hills and mountains around Aracena offer some of the most beautiful, and least known, walking country in Andalucía. Any time of year is a good time to hike here but spring, when the meadows are awash in wildflowers and carnival-coloured butterflies, is by far the best time to strike out on the trail. The tourist office can recommend a number of simple day walks and sells an excellent map with dozens of suggested hikes.

A sublime and fairly gentle ramble of about 5km can be made by leaving Aracena between the Piscina Municipal (municipal swimming pool) and the HU-8105 road at the western end of town. From there, a path descends a verdant valley to **Linares de la Sierra**, a hike of approximately two hours. The walk can be extended to the village of Alájar (5.5km, three hours), with the possibility of returning to Aracena on the 4pm bus (except Sunday).

Another trail leads east to Corteconcepción, returning via the Rebollar trail, to form a 10.5km loop. This route is regularly used for religious pilgrimages and is dotted with shrines.

Eating
The hills around Aracena have given rise to some superb cuisine. Delights include the region's mushrooms; dozens of different varieties pop up out of the ground every autumn. And then there's the ham: the *jamón serrano* of nearby Jabugo is considered the best in the entire country and as you explore these hills you won't fail to notice the providers of this bounty – contented-looking black pigs foraging in the forests for acorns.

TOP CHOICE **Rincón de Juan** TAPAS €
(☑627 33 47 66; Calle José Nogales; tapas €1.80, raciones €7-10; ⊙7am-4pm & 6.30pm-midnight Mon-Fri, 8am-midnight Sat) It's standing room only at this wedge-shaped, stone-walled corner bar, indisputably the finest tapas joint in town. Iberian ham is certainly the star attraction and forms the basis for a variety of *montaditos* (little sandwiches) and *rebanadas* (sliced loaves that feed several people). The homemade sausage, sweet or spicy, is always a good bet.

Mesón Rural las Tinajas TAPAS €€
(☑959 12 78 82; Calle Juan del Cíd López; mains €8-10) This ever-popular hang-out is managed by an affable Argentine, and it has a definite gaucho influence: try the excellent empanadas, whether warm (stuffed with chopped meat and egg) or cold (tuna).

Café-Bar Manzano TAPAS €€
(☑959 12 75 13; Calle Campito 9; raciones €9-14; ⊙9am-4:30pm & 8pm-midnight Wed-Mon) This classy terrace cafe on the main plaza is a fine spot to watch Aracena go by and enjoy varied tapas and *raciones* (large tapas servings) that celebrate wild mushrooms and other regional fare. Even out of season, it serves up such tempting toadstools as *tentullos*, *gurumelos* and *tanas*, sauteed or in enticing scrambles.

ℹ Information
Centro de Visitantes Cabildo Viejo (☑959 12 95 53; Plaza Alta; ⊙10am-2pm & 4-6pm Tue-Sun) Showcases the highlights of Parque Natural Sierra de Aracena y Picos de Aroche, with exhibits on the park's flora, fauna, culture and history.
Municipal Tourist Office (www.aracena.es; Calle Pozo de la Nieve; ⊙10am-2pm & 4-6pm) Faces the entrance to the Gruta de las Maravillas and sells some maps of the area.

❶ Getting There & Around

BUS The **bus station** (Avenida de Sevilla) is 700m southeast of the Plaza del Marqués de Aracena. Damas runs one morning and two afternoon buses from Seville (€6.80, 1¼ hours), continuing on to Cortegana via Alájar or Jabugo. From Huelva, there are two afternoon departures daily (€10, three hours). There is also local service between Aracena and Cortegana via Linares, Alájar and Almonaster la Real.

CAR Aracena has plenty of free street-side parking.

Sierra de Aracena

Stretching west of Aracena is one of Andalucía's most unexpectedly picturesque landscapes, a flower-sprinkled hill-country dotted with old stone villages and imposing castles. Woodlands alternate with expanses of *dehesa* (evergreen oak pastures where the region's famed black pigs forage for acorns). The area is threaded by an extensive network of well-maintained walking trails, with ever-changing vistas and mostly gentle ascents and descents, making for some of the most delightful rambling in Andalucía.

Great hiking routes extend over all parts of the **Parque Natural Sierra de Aracena y Picos de Aroche**, but they're particularly thick in the area between Aracena and Cortegana, making attractive villages such as Alájar, Castaño del Robledo, Galaroza and Almonaster la Real good bases from which to set forth.

Blissfully ensconced amid nature's undulating tableaus, the villages of the Sierra de Aracena are spaced within walking distance of one another, making it easy to poke your nose into hidden corners and take regular refreshment breaks.

LINARES DE LA SIERRA

Just 7km west of Aracena along the HU-8105, you'll bump into one of the cutest of the area's villages, Linares de la Sierra. Surrounded by a verdant river valley, its mosaic cobbled streets are lined with oddly angled, tiled-roof houses. In the centre, beside the parish church, a minute bullring plaza is paved with concentric rings around a shield of flowers. Nearby, sample such local snacks as *puchero* (stewpot) croquettes and *carrillera* (pig cheeks) at **El Balcón de Linares** (Calle Real 4, Linares de la Sierra; raciones €8), a welcoming bar.

ALÁJAR

Five kilometres west of Linares de la Sierra is possibly the region's most picturesque village, Alájar. Though larger than Linares, it retains its narrow cobbled streets and cubist stone houses, as well as a fine baroque church.

Above it all a rocky spur, the **Peña de Arias Montano**, provides magical views over the village. The site takes its name from Benito Arias Montano, a remarkable 16th-century polymath and humanist who made repeated visits to this spot for retreat and meditation. The peña's 16th-century chapel, the **Ermita de Nuestra Señora Reina de los Ángeles** (⊙11am-sunset), contains a small carving of the Virgin that is considered the patron of the whole Sierra de Aracena. The chapel is the focus of the area's biggest annual

Sierra de Aracena

religious event, the **Romería de la Reina de los Ángeles** (7 and 8 September), when people from all around the sierra and beyond converge here to honour their Virgin. Outside the chapel are stalls selling local cheeses and an **information hut** (☺11am-2pm & 4-6.30pm Fri-Sun) with advice for hiking in the region.

With atmospheric dining by a brick-ring fireplace or on a sunny terrace, **Casa El Padrino** (☑959 12 56 01; Plaza Miguel Moya 2; mains €10-15; ☺lunch Sat & Sun, dinner Fri & Sat) serves scrumptious country fare loosely based on old village recipes. The *pencas de acelgas* (Swiss chard stuffed with Iberian pork) is memorable, as is the *lomo ibérico* (cured pork sausage) in chestnut sauce, broiled to perfection.

CASTAÑO DEL ROBLEDO

North of Alájar on a minor road between Fuenteheridos and Jabugo, the small village of Castaño del Robledo is a truly idyllic spot, surrounded by hazy green olive and cork forests. Barely a single modern building mars the beauty of this village. Its jigsaw of tiled terracotta roofs is overlooked by two large churches, either of which could easily accommodate the entire village population.

A nice loop hike can be made by taking the PR A-38 trail from Castaño del Robledo to the village of Galaroza and returning via an alternate riverside route, the SL A-129. The walk traverses varied woodlands interspersed with long-distance panoramas. Wildflowers abound in spring and you're likely to spot some of the *pata negra* pigs of Jabugo fame rutting about for acorns. The whole loop should take about three hours, excluding stops.

Leave via the path through the shady Área Recreativa Capilla del Cristo, on the north side of the H5211 road passing along the north of the village. To the left you'll soon be able to see **Cortegana** and **Jabugo**, before you fork right at a sign attached to a yellow-striped post, 15 minutes along the track. Your path starts winding downhill until you reach the crossing with the Jabugo–Fuenteheridos trail after 10 minutes. About 50m beyond, go right at a fork. In 10 minutes Galaroza comes into view as you pass between its outlying *fincas* (rural properties). Cross a small river on a footbridge and emerge on the N433 road three minutes later. Walk left towards Galaroza, skirting the town along the N433

for around 800m until you reach some palm trees, then leave by the track on the left marked by a 'Sendero Ribera del Jabugo' route sign.

Fork right one minute out from the mentioned sign, then turn left four or five minutes later down to a footbridge that stretches over a stream. The path soon starts winding up the valley of the Río Jabugo, a particularly lovely stretch lined with poplars, willows and alders. Half an hour from the footbridge you will reach a vehicle track marked 'Camino de Jabugo a Fuenteheridos'. Head right, passing a couple of *cortijos* (country properties), to cross the river on a low bridge. Turn left 50m past the bridge, then left at a fork 30m further on. You re-cross the river, then gradually wind up and away from it. Fifteen minutes from the river, turn left at a red-tile-roofed house (Monte Blanco) and in 15 minutes (mostly upward) you're re-entering Castaño del Robledo, this time from the west.

✖ Eating

Popular with *sevillano* weekenders, **Restaurante Maricastaña** (☑654 24 85 83; Plaza del Álamo 7; mains €15-20; ☺dinner Fri & Sat, lunch Sat & Sun) puts an upscale urban spin on Sierra classics such as wild mushrooms and *jamón de bellota* (served on a bed of pickled eggplant with a balsamic vinegar reduction). Dining is in the old house or on a brilliant terrace overlooking the hill. You'll certainly need reservations on Sunday afternoon.

ALMONASTER LA REAL

Almonaster la Real is a picturesque place that harbours a fabulous gem of Islamic architecture. The little **mezquita** (Mosque; admission free; ☺approx 9am-dusk) stands above the town about five minutes' walk from the main square. The almost perfectly preserved structure is like a miniature version of the great mosque in Córdoba. Despite being Christianised in the 13th century, it retains nearly all its original Islamic features: the horseshoe arches, the semicircular mihrab, an ablutions fountain and various Arabic inscriptions. Even older are the capitals of the columns nearest the mihrab, which are Roman. The original minaret, a square tower, adjoins the building. You can climb to the upper chamber and look down on Almonaster's 19th-century bullring, but take care near the open, unprotected windows.

HUELVA & SEVILLA PROVINCES SIERRA DE ARACENA

In the village, the Mudéjar **Iglesia de San Martín** (Placeta de San Cristóbal) has a 16th-century portal in the Portuguese Manueline style, unique in the region.

The restaurant of the Casa García (p293) hotel serves gourmet versions of local fare in a cosy setting with a fireplace and brick arches.

❶ Getting There & Around

BUS Monday to Saturday, morning and afternoon buses travel the HU-8105 from Cortegana to Aracena, stopping in Almonaster La Real, Alájar and Linares de la Sierra en route. Both return in the afternoon. Four buses take the N-433 between Cortegana and Aracena, stopping in Jabugo and Galaroza.

TRAIN There are two daily trains running each way between Huelva and the stations of Almonaster-Cortegana (€8, 1¾ hours) and Jabugo-Galaroza. Almonaster-Cortegana station is 1km off the Almonaster-Cortegana road, about halfway between the two villages. Jabugo-Galaroza station is in El Repilado, on the N433, 4km west of Jabugo.

SEVILLA PROVINCE

Just northwest of Seville you'll find the Roman ruins of Itálica, at Santiponce. To the east, the flat and fertile farmlands of La Campiña stretch into the fiery distance, a land of huge agricultural estates belonging to a few landowners, dotted with scattered towns and villages.

Santiponce

The small town of Santiponce, 6km northwest of Seville, is the location of **Itálica** (📞955 62 22 66; www.juntadeandalucia.es/cultura/italica; Avenida de Extremadura 2; admission €1.50; ⏰8.30am-9pm Tue-Sat, 9am-3pm Sun & holidays Apr-Sep, 9am-6.30pm Tue-Sat, 10am-4pm Sun & holidays Oct-Mar), the most formidable Roman site in Andalucía. It makes for a superb day trip from Seville.

Itálica was the first Roman town in Spain, founded in 206 BC, and was the birthplace of the 2nd-century-AD Roman emperor Trajan, and probably of his adopted son and successor Hadrian (he of the wall across northern England).

Although emperors are fairly rare at Itálica today, what is left of those times is the incredible remains of the town that once stood here. The site includes broad paved streets and ruins of houses built around patios with beautiful mosaics. The most notable houses are the **Casa del Planetario** (House of the Planetarium), with a mosaic depicting the gods of the seven days of the week, and the **Casa de los Pájaros** (House of the Birds). Itálica also contains one of the biggest of all Roman **amphitheatres** (able to hold 20,000 spectators), and for the layperson this is probably the most impressive site. You enter the amphitheatre through what was once the main gate.

From Seville's Plaza de Armas, the M-172 bus goes to Santiponce (30 minutes) at least twice an hour, making its final stop at the entrance to the archaeological site.

Dehesa de Abajo

Toward El Rocío and the Parque Nacional de Doñana in Huelva province, the small nature reserve of Dehesa de Abajo holds a transitional spot between woodlands and wetlands, resulting in an extraordinary degree of species diversity and making for fantastic birdwatching opportunities. Walkways lead to observation hides around the Laguna La Rianzuela, where flamingos, spoonbills, herons, avocets and such exotics as the crested coot reside. Europe's largest woodland colony of white storks (400 pairs) also nests here.

To get there from Seville, head southwestward via Avenida de la República Argentina and the A3122 to Coria del Río and La Puebla del Río, from where a small sign points to the reserve, 14km to the southwest, past Venta del Cruce.

Another good place to observe white storks and more than 150 other bird species is **La Cañada de los Pájaros** (📞955 77 21 84; www.canadadelospajaros.com; Carretera Puebla del Río-Isla Mayor Km8; adult/child €9/5; ⏰10am-dusk), a former garbage dump that has been converted into a private wetland reserve/zoo. Here you can get close enough to the enormous storks to hear their wings rustle as they swoop between the umbrella pines. It's back towards Seville along the road to La Puebla del Río, about 1.75km east of the Isla Mayor turnoff.

Carmona

POP 28,679 / ELEV 250M

Perched on a low hill overlooking a wonderful *vega* (valley) that sizzles in the summer heat, dotted with old palaces and impressive monuments, Carmona is a lesser-known highlight of western Andalucía.

This strategic site was important as long ago as Carthaginian times. The Romans laid out a street plan that survives to this day: the Via Augusta, running from Rome to Cádiz, entered Carmona by the eastern Puerta de Córdoba and left by the western Puerta de Sevilla. The Muslims built a strong defensive wall around Carmona but the town fell in 1247 to Fernando III. Later on, Mudéjar and Christian artisans constructed fine churches, convents and mansions.

◉ Sights

Alcázar de la Puerta de Sevilla   GATE
(adult/child €2/1, Mon free; ⊙10am-6pm Mon-Sat, to 3pm Sun & holidays) You can walk through the best of old Carmona in an easy stroll, starting from the Puerta de Sevilla, the impressive main gate of the old town. The gate is one element of a fortification that had already been standing for five centuries when the Romans reinforced it and built a temple on top. The Islamic Almohads added an *aljibe* (cistern) to the upper patio, which remains a hawklike perch from which to admire the typically Andalucian tableau of white cubes and soaring spires.

Iglesia Prioral de Santa María   CHURCH
(☑954 19 14 82; Plaza Marqués de las Torres; admission €3; ⊙9am-2pm & 5.30-7.30pm Mon-Fri, 9am-2pm Sat) This splendid church was built mainly in the 15th and 16th centuries on the site of the former main mosque. The Patio de los Naranjos by which you enter has a Visigothic calendar carved into one of its pillars. Inside, the plateresque (richly ornamented) altar is detailed to an almost perverse degree, with 20 panels of biblical scenes framed by gilt-scrolled columns.

Upstairs, a museum of sacred art nicely displays the collection of silver objects, polychrome statuary and paintings that the church has amassed over the centuries.

Museo de la Ciudad   MUSEUM
(City History Museum; ☑954 14 01 28; www.museociudad.carmona.org; Calle San Ildefonso 1; adult/child €3/free, Tue free; ⊙11am-7pm Tue-Sun, to 2pm Mon) Explore the town's interesting history at the city museum, housed in a centuries-old palace, with pieces dating back to Paleolithic times. The sections on the the Tartessos and their Roman successors are highlights: the former includes a unique collection of large earthenware vessels with

Middle Eastern decorative motifs, the latter several excellent mosaics.

Convento de Santa Clara   CONVENT
(Calle Torno de Santa Clara; admission €2; ⊙11am-1.30pm & 4-6pm Fri-Mon) With its gothic ribbed vaulting, carved Mudéjar-style ceiling and dazzling altarpiece – a shining example of Sevillan baroque – the Santa Clara convent should appeal to both art and architecture buffs. A visit starts with a spiral ascent of the tower, a later addition, with displays of art and poetry at different levels and gorgeous views of the city from the top.

Puerta de Córdoba   GATE
(Calle de Dolores Quintanilla; admission €2; ⊙tours min 8 people 11.30am, 12.30pm & 1.30pm Tue, Sat & Sun) The Roman gate that controlled access to the city from the east is in marvellous repair, framing the fertile countryside outside it like a precious, faded rug. Guided tours of the Puerta de Córdoba can be arranged through the Museo de la Ciudad, providing at least eight participants show up at the appointed time.

FREE Necrópolis Romana   RUINS
(Roman cemetery; ☑955 62 46 15; Avenida de Jorge Bonsor; ⊙9am-6pm Tue-Fri, to 3.30pm Sat & Sun) On the southwestern edge of the city lie the remains of a Roman city of the dead. In the 1st and 2nd centuries AD, a dozen or more family tombs were hewn into the rock here, some of them elaborate and many-chambered. Most of the inhabitants were cremated, and in the tombs are wall niches for the boxlike stone urns containing the ashes.

You may enter the huge Tumba de Servilia, which was the tomb of a family of Hispano-Roman bigwigs. The site also features an interesting museum with objects found in the tombs, and across the street is a 1st-century-BC **Roman amphitheatre**, though you can't go in.

✖ Eating

Tapeando – tapas noshing – is such a pastime here that Carmona has made it official by establishing a tapas route. The Ruta de la Tapa includes 17 eateries, an impressive number for a town this size. Pick up a brochure with maps and descriptions of the bars at the tourist office and hit the trail!

Bar Goya   TAPAS €€
(Calle Prim 2; tapas €2, raciones €8; ⊙closed Tue evening & Wed) From the kitchens of this ever-crammed bar alongside Plaza San Fernando

Carmona

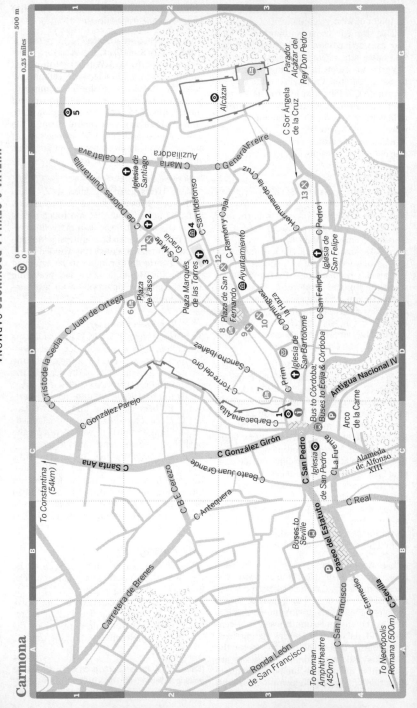

0 0.25 miles

0 500 m

Parador Alcázar del Rey Don Pedro

Alcázar

5

C de Dolores Quintanilla

C Calatrava

Iglesia de Santiago

C Sor Ángela de la Cruz

C María Auxiliadora

C General Freire

C Hermana de la Cruz

13

C Pedro I

2

11

C S M de Gracia

C San Ildefonso

4

3

12

C Ramón y Cajal

Ayuntamiento

C San Felipe

Iglesia de San Felipe

Plaza de Lasso

Plaza Marqués de las Torres

Plaza de San Fernando

C el Haza

C Domínguez

6

8

9

10

7

Iglesia de San Bartolomé

C San Felipe

C Ecija & Córdoba

C Juan de Ortega

C Cristo de la Sedia

C Torre del Oro

C Sancho Ibáñez

C Barbacana Alta

C Prim

Buses to Córdoba
Buses to Ecija & Córdoba

Antigua Nacional IV

Arco de la Carne

C González Parejo

C González Girón

C Santa Ana

C Beato Juan Grande

Iglesia de San Pedro

C San Pedro

C La Fuente

1

Alameda de Alfonso XIII

To Constantina (54km)

C Antequera

C B E Cerezo

Carretera de Brenes

Buses to Seville

Paseo del Estatuto

C Real

C Emmedio

C San Francisco

C Sevilla

Ronda León de San Francisco

To Roman Amphitheatre (450m)

To Necrópolis Romana (500m)

Carmona

Sights
1 Alcázar de la Puerta de Sevilla...........C3
2 Convento de Santa Clara...................E2
3 Iglesia Prioral de Santa María............E2
4 Museo de la Ciudad............................E2
5 Puerta de Córdoba..............................F1

Sleeping
6 Casa de Carmona................................D2
7 Hostal Comercio.................................D3
8 Posada San Fernando........................D3

Eating
9 Bar Goya...D3
10 Bar Plaza...D3
11 Casa Curro Montoya.........................E2
12 Mingalario...E3
13 Molino de la Romera........................F3

come forth a fabulous array of tasty tapas. Apart from such carnivores' faves as *carrillada* and *menudo* (tripe), chef Isabel offers vegetarian items such as *albornía*, a delicious potato and pepper stew, and an excellent version of Carmona spinach (blended with chickpeas).

Casa Curro Montoya TAPAS €€
(Calle Santa María de Gracia 13; tapas €2.50; ⊘closed Tue) This friendly, family-run joint opposite the Convento de Santa Clara occupies a narrow hall littered with memorabilia. Long-cultivated family traditions find expression in such items as fresh tuna in a luscious onion sauce, foie gras–stuffed eggplant and fried *pizcotas*, small sardinelike fish.

Mingalario TAPAS €
(Calle El Salvador; montaditos €2, raciones €2-8) This small, very old eatery with hams hanging from the rafters is big on *montaditos* – small toasted sandwiches stuffed with things like salt cod and prawns in garlic sauce. Wild mushrooms get prepared in a number of variations.

Bar Plaza TAPAS €
(Plaza de San Fernando; ⊘closed Mon evening) Overseen by the affable Don Antonio, this tile-lined, family-run joint just off the Plaza San Fernando serves tapas that seem more like main courses with huge rolls for sopping up the sumptuous sauces. Try the bull tail, so tender it falls off the bone.

Molino de la Romera ANDALUCIAN €€
(☎954 14 20 00; www.molinodelaromera.com; Calle Sor Ángela de la Cruz 8; mains €17-19; ⊘lunch only Sun & Tue-Fri, lunch & dinner Sat, closed Mon) This acclaimed restaurant serves hearty, well-prepared meals in a lovely 15th-century olive oil mill with views to the valley below. Traditional Andalucian fare rules but some novel variations (squid balls over basmati rice, fish flambéed in vodka) keep things interesting. If you fancy something lighter, there's a bar and cafe as well.

Information
Tourist office (www.turismo.carmona.org; Alcázar de la Puerta de Sevilla; ⊘10am-6pm Mon-Sat, to 3pm Sun & holidays) The helpful tourist office is inside the Puerta de Sevilla.

Getting There & Away
BUS Casal (www.autocarescasal.com) runs hourly buses, Monday to Friday, to Seville from the stop on Paseo del Estatuto, less often on weekends. Two or three buses a day go to Córdoba via Écija from the car park next to the Puerta de Sevilla.
CAR There's around-the-clock underground parking on Paseo del Estatuto (24hr €12.50). Parking in the old town is limited.

Osuna
POP 17,973 / ELEV 330M
The legacy of a fabulously wealthy line of dukes who loaned the town its name, Osuna dazzles visitors with its beautifully preserved baroque mansions and impressive Spanish Renaissance monastery filled with art treasures. This startling tableau unfolds like a mirage amid an otherwise empty landscape, as if its cache of architectural and artistic gems were no big thing.
It is 91km southeast of Seville, along the Granada–Seville A92.

Sights
Colegiata de Santa María de la Asunción MUSEUM
(☎954 81 04 44; Plaza de la Encarnación; admission by guided tour only €3; ⊘10am-1.30pm & 4-7pm Tue-Sun May-Sep, 10am-1:30pm & 3.30-6.30pm Oct-Apr) This imposing renaissance structure overlooks Osuna from the site of the ancient parish church. Its halls contain a wealth of fine art and treasure collected by the House of Osuna, among them a series of paintings by José Ribera, aka 'El Españoleto', and sculpted works by Juan de Mesa.

HUELVA & SEVILLA PROVINCES OSUNA

The guided tour (in Spanish only) also includes the lugubrious underground sepulchre, created in 1548 with its own chapel as the family vault of the Osunas, who are entombed in wall niches.

Monasterio de la Encarnación   MUSEUM
(Plaza de la Encarnación; admission €2.50; ⊘10am-1.30pm & 4-7pm Tue-Sun May-Sep, 10am-1.30pm & 3.30-6.30pm Oct-Apr) The former monastery is now Osuna's museum of religious art. Its church is decked with baroque sculpture and art, while the cloister features tiled *tableaux* depicting various biblical, hunting, bullfighting and monastic scenes that are among the most beautiful of Sevillan tilework. Entry is by guided tour only (in Spanish), led by one of the resident nuns.

Baroque Mansions
The triangle west of Plaza Mayor is sprinkled with mansions and churches and cut up by lovely little streets and passages. Calle Sevilla, which leads west off the main square, and Calle San Pedro, a few blocks north, are particularly packed with stately buildings. You can't go inside most of Osuna's mansions, but their facades are still mesmerising.

One of the most impressive is **Palacio de los Cepeda** (Calle de la Huerta 10), behind the town hall, with rows of Churrigueresque columns topped by stone halberdiers holding the Cepeda family coat of arms. The portal of the 18th-century **Palacio de Govantes y Herdara** (Calle Sevilla 44) has twisted pillars encrusted with grapes and vine leaves. At one time Osuna's courthouse, it's a couple of blocks west of Plaza Mayor. The facade of the **Cilla del Cabildo Colegial** (Calle San Pedro 16) bears a sculpted representation of Seville's Giralda.

Among the most ornate of Osuna's 18th-century mansions, the **Palacio del Marqués de La Gomera** (Calle San Pedro 20) features elaborate pillars on its facade, with the family shield at the top. It's now a hotel – step inside for a drink.

✖ Eating

⌖TOP CHOICE Casa Curro   TAPAS €€
(Plazuela Salitre 5; tapas €2, raciones €8) Here's the tapas bar of your dreams, a marvelous blend of tradition and nouvelle cuisine. Plate after plate issue from the kitchen at the locally popular hall west of the centre: eggplant in shrimp and muscatel sauce, homemade meatballs, Iberian 'secret' in a quince sauce served with wild mushrooms. You'll want to try them all.

El Mesón del Duque   ANDALUCIAN €€
(Plaza de la Duquesa; tapas €2.50, raciones €2.50) Here you can sample Osuna's signature dish, *ardoria*, a local variation on *salmorejo*, the garlicky cold soup served throughout Andalucia. In Osuna, it's garnished with tuna and chopped egg along with the usual bits of Iberian ham.

Restaurante Doña Guadalupe   ANDALUCIAN €€
(☑954 81 05 58; Plaza Guadalupe 6; 4-course menú €15, mains €17-19; ✱) To the contented murmurings of its numerous patrons, the Doña Guadalupe serves up quality Andalucian fare from partridge with rice to wild asparagus casserole. There's a good list of Spanish wines too. It opens on a courtyard between Calles Quijada and Gordillo (both off Calle Carrera).

Confitería Santo Domingo   BAKERY €
(Calle Carrera 63; pastries €1.50) This little bakery on Osuna's main street is famed for its *aldeanas*: elongated pastries filled with a sweet potato cream and dusted with confectioners' sugar. The baker recommends not eating them at once but instead letting all the ingredients ooze together.

ℹ Information

Oficina Municipal de Turismo (☑954 81 57 32; www.turismosuna.es; Calle Carrera 82; ⊘9.30am-1.30pm & 4-6pm Tue-Sat, 9.30am-1.30pm Sun) All the info you will need on the town, including some useful guides.

Écija

POP 38,771 / ELEV 110M

Probably the least visited of the towns in La Campiña, Écija for that very reason offers a genuine insight into Andalucian urban life. To the Romans, this was Colonia Augusta Firma Astigi, one of the principal cities of their Iberian realm, which struck it rich supplying its far-flung markets with olive oil. Remains of public baths and a gymnasium from the Roman era were recently found underneath Écija's main plaza. The town's many Gothic-Mudéjar palaces and churches, the towers of which glitter in the sun, have earned it the moniker *ciudad de las torres* (the city of towers). Talking of the sun, you might want to avoid visiting Écija during high summer because it's then that the town earns its other nickname, *la sartén de Andalucía* (the frying pan of Andalucía), with temperatures approaching a sweaty 45°C.

Écija lies 53km east along the A4 from Carmona.

LOCAL KNOWLEDGE

PABLO A FONTALES: OBSERVER

Philosophy prof at a local high school, Pablo has a passion for the architecture of his adopted city, Écija. Even a walk around the block is an excuse to tote his camera.

You spend a lot of time just walking around and admiring buildings? Yes, whenever I leave the house, I try to capture my own special view of the town.

But it's such a small town, you must have already seen everything, right? No, because it's been a while since I stopped trying to 'see' but instead 'feel'. Every photo I take is new, the light, the colour, my mood, my attention to new details, etc.

You're primarily interested in civic architecture, right? Yeah, anything but churches. Religious buildings bore me; they're all over the place. But in Écija there are lots of interesting palaces and old houses – civic buildings with quite beautiful architectural design.

What's so special about Écija's palaces? There aren't many cities in Spain that have 20 or 30 palaces and houses from the 16th to 18th centuries, at least not ones as small as Écija.

Why does such a small town have so many palaces? Because it was an important historic centre where a bourgeoisie developed. The buildings of the wool and silk guilds, both quite beautiful, are still intact. On Calle Platería is the silver guild, and the ribbon-makers guild. The city had a great deal of trade and craftmanship in the middle ages and the Renaissance, which left its mark.

Do these palaces have a unique style? Yes, the local version of Andalucian baroque called Écija baroque, with cast iron grilles, molded brick, sculpted adornments on the facades and so on.

Doesn't it bother you that these buildings are symbols of an entrenched elite? I can also admire the Santa Sofia basilica in Istanbul or the Sistine Chapel, or the Taj Mahal, or any other building, even if the interest and history of those who had them built was tragic, horrible or tyrannical.

◉ Sights

The centre of Écija life is the cafe-lined Plaza de España, referred to as El Salón (the parlor); before you dive into the old quarter that surrounds this square you'd be wise to drop by for a drink and a spot of people-watching.

FREE **Museo Histórico Municipal** MUSEUM (http://museo.ecija.es; Plaza de la Constitución 1; ☺10am-1.30pm & 4.30-6.30pm Tue-Sat, 10am-3pm Sun) The 18th-century Palacio de Benamejí houses the city's history museum. Pride of place goes to the best Roman finds from the area, including a sculpture of an Amazon (legendary female warrior). The upper level features a hall devoted to six fantastically preserved Roman mosaics, some unearthed beneath Écija's central square, with one tableau depicting the 'birth' of wine.

Palacio de Peñaflor PALACE (Calle Emilio Castelar 26) The huge 18th-century Palacio de Peñaflor or 'the palace of the long balconies' is Écija's most iconic image. Though the interior is closed indefinitely for

renovations, the curved, fresco-lined facade is bewitching enough, morning or evening.

Casa Museo Hermandad de San Gil MUSEUM (www.hermandadsangil.es; Calle San Marcos 3; admission €3; ☺10am-1pm Tue-Sun) The box-shaped museum, next to the church of San Gil, is a showcase for the brotherhood of San Gil. On display are the *pasos*, weighty platforms for bearing icons of Christ and the Virgin Mary. These baroque-style decorated floats are borne by as many as 40 men during Écija's Easter processions and a video monitor shows them in action.

Churches & Bell Towers

Écija's spire-studded townscape is evidence of its prosperous past though some structures toppled as a result of Lisbon's great quake in 1755. One of the finest towers belongs to the Iglesia de Santa María (Plaza Santa María), just off Plaza de España, while that of the Iglesia de San Juan (Plaza San Juan) rises like a frosted wedding cake a few blocks south. The tower of the Iglesia de San Pablo-Santo Domingo (Plaza de Santo

Domingo), east of the square, is startlingly strung with a gigantic set of rosary beads.

The **Parroquia Mayor de Santa Cruz** (Plazuela de Nuestra Señora del Valle; admission free; ⊙9am-1pm & 5-8.30pm Mon-Sat, 10am-1pm & 6-8pm Sun May-Sep, 9am-1pm & 6-8pm Mon-Sat, 10am-1pm & 6-9pm Sun Oct-Apr) was once the town's principal mosque and still has traces of Islamic features and some Arabic inscriptions. Beyond a roofless atrium is an interior crammed with sacred paraphernalia and baroque silverwork. A sarcophagus in front of the altar dates from the early Christian period, with a chiseled likeness of Daniel flanked by a pair of lions.

✖ Eating

Hispania   TAPAS €€
(www.hispaniacafe.com; Pasaje Virgen de Soterraño; tapas €2, mains €10-14) Hip, friendly and invariably packed with locals, this sidestreet operation has a bold colour scheme that matches its exuberant kitchen. The innovative chefs keep coming up with new creations that give classic Spanish fare a contemporary zing, whether they're doing tapas, *bocatas* (sandwiches) or desserts – leave room for the white chocolate soup.

Restaurante Amrita   ANDALUCIAN €€
(www.amrita.es; Calle Emilio Castelar 15; tapas €2.50-5.50, 4-course sampler €30) This modern, chic establishment has a vertical arrangement with dining on three levels. It serves tapa-sized portions of such exotic items as cheese-leek fritters in Pedro Ximénez sauce and fried *ortiguillas* (a sort of sea anemone).

❶ Information

Tourist office (www.turismoecija.com; Calle Elvira 1; ⊙9.30am-3pm Mon-Fri) On weekends, get info at the Museo Histórico Municipal.

Parque Natural Sierra Norte de Sevilla

This 1775-sq-km protected zone, stretching across the north of Seville province, presents an ever-changing landscape of green valleys and hills, woodlands, rivers and atmospheric old towns and villages with Islamic-era forts or castles. You could spend days drifting around the back roads of the sierra enjoying the numerous walking trails, with little to no competition from other foreign travellers.

At least 14 walks of a few hours each are signposted in various areas. The routes are shown on the *IGN/Junta de Andalucía* 1:10,000 map, available at **Centro de Visitantes El Robledo** (Carretera Constantina-El Pedroso Km1; ⊙10am-2pm & 4-6pm Oct-Mar, 10am-2pm & 6-8pm Apr-Sep), located 1km west of Constantina along the A452 El Pedroso road. This visitors centre has a clearly labelled botanical garden of Andalucian plants. It is divided into regional environments, with representative plants from each region, providing a useful guide to what you're likely to encounter in the Sierra Morena.

CAZALLA DE LA SIERRA
POP 5072 / ELEV 600M

This attractive little white town sits on a hilltop 85km northeast of Seville, and is the gateway for exploring the Parque Natural Sierra Norte, which stretches out to the west. Cazalla has a great little selection of places to stay and pleasant local walks through the surrounding woods.

🏃 Activities

Two tracks lead from Cazalla down to the Huéznar Valley; by combining them you can enjoy a round trip of 9km. They pass through typical Sierra Norte evergreen oak woodlands, olive groves and small cultivated plots, plus the odd chestnut wood and vineyard.

One track is the **Sendero de las Laderas**, which starts at El Chorrillo fountain on the eastern edge of Cazalla at the foot of Calle Parras. A 'Sendero de las Laderas 900m' sign on Paseo El Moro, just down from the Posada del Moro, directs you to this starting point. The path leads down to the Puente de los Tres Ojos bridge on the Río Huéznar, from where you go up the western bank of the river a short way, then head west under the Puente del Castillejo railway bridge (first take a break at the picnic area on the far bank, if you like) and return to Cazalla by the **Camino Viejo de la Estación** (Old Station Track).

✖ Eating

Agustina Restaurante   TAPAS €€
(www.agustinarestaurante.com; Plaza del Concejo; tapas €2, raciones €10) The youthful owners create traditional sierra dishes with a nod to the wider world. The *magret de pato con miel y vinagre de módena* (duck with honey and vinegar) is sensational. If you just want a tapas snack then try the speciality *queso de cabra con miel* (goats cheese with honey).

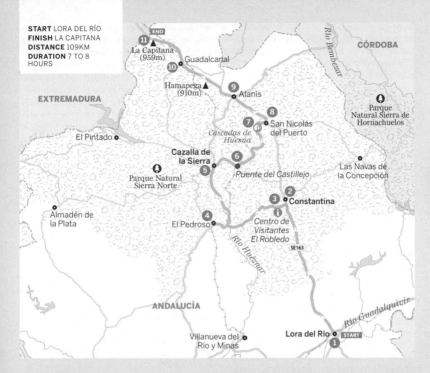

START LORA DEL RÍO
FINISH LA CAPITANA
DISTANCE 109KM
DURATION 7 TO 8 HOURS

Driving Tour
Sierra Norte de Sevilla

❯ Penetrating the Parque Natural Sierra Norte de Sevilla from the south makes for a rather startling transition and an exhilarating drive. From Seville, follow the Río Guadalquivir east along the A431 till ❶ **Lora del Río**, then strike north on the A455. The orange groves recede and you start climbing, at each bend enjoying varied vistas of green hills. Soon you enter the *parque natural* proper; continue climbing till ❷ **Constantina** and stop into one of the town's cosy cafes. Then head west along the A452, stopping at the ❸ **Centro de Visitantes El Robledo**, where you can pick up a few maps and tour the botanical garden. The road to El Pedroso winds through hilly countryside, mists clinging to the mountains as they recede into the distance. As you cross the Río Huéznar an old aqueduct appears. Then tiny ❹ **El Pedroso** comes into view, inviting you to explore its compact core. Go back east momentarily, then pick up the A432 north. It's a 15km drive through the mountains to ❺ **Cazalla de la Sierra**, the shining 'capital' of the northern

range. Make a lunch of some of the exquisite tapas found here. Leaving Cazalla, head north and pick up the A455 back towards Constantina. This road again crosses the Río Huéznar just east of the Cazalla-Constantina train station. A 1km drivable track leads downstream from here to the ❻ **Puente del Castillejo** railway bridge and a recreation area. Upstream the river is paralleled by the SE7101 road which runs 13km to the village of San Nicolas del Puerto. Two kilometres before the village are the ❼ **Cascadas de Huesna**, a series of powerful waterfalls. From ❽ **San Nicolas del Puerto**, take the SE8100 northwest. The landscape gets more dramatic as you approach ❾ **Alanís**, topped by a medieval castle surrounded by shrines. Continue northwest, along the edge of the park, to reach remote ❿ **Guadalcanal**. North of town, don your hiking boots and hit the trail: the Sendero Sierra del Viento follows a ridge to ⓫ **La Capitana**, the highest peak in the park and a suitable eyrie for the conclusion of your tour.

Bodeguita Granado　　ANDALUCIAN €
(Calle Velarde 4; tapas €2, raciones €8) A grotto-like den serving the finest country fare: wild mushrooms, homemade croquettes and Iberian ham in little casserole dishes.

Las Navezuelas　　ANDALUCIAN, ITALIAN €€
(☏954 88 47 64; www.lasnavezuelas.com; menú €19) Several nights a week this *finca* hotel prepares superb meals the old-fashioned way. In other words, they try to use only produce that's sprouted out of the farm's very own soil. The difference reveals itself in the wonderful tastes and a perfect ambience; with soft classical music playing in the background and the managers' real attention to service. It all helps to make this one of the nicest places to eat in the sierra. It's open to nonguests if you reserve in advance. It's 2km south of town along the A432.

CONSTANTINA

Constantina is the largest town in the Sierra Norte with a population of over 7,000. Cars and trucks rumble down the central Calle El Peso and townsfolk retreat into utterly traditional cafes where the purest olive oil is poured from silver ewers.

The western side of town is topped by a ruined Almoravid-era Islamic fort – worth the climb for the views alone. Below are the medieval streets and 18th-century mansions of the **Barrio de la Morería**.

The **Sendero Los Castañares**, a 5.5km loop trail, starts from the north end of Paseo de la Alameda in the north of town. It takes you up through thick chestnut woods to a hilltop viewpoint, then back into Constantina below the fort (about two hours in total).

A rustic barn often filled with families and friends, **El Mesón de la Abuela Carmen** (Paseo de la Alameda 39; raciones €8-12), near the northern end of town, serves succulent grilled meats in big combo plates or as tapas.

EL PEDROSO

A pleasant village of broad cobbled streets, El Pedroso lies 16km south of Cazalla de la Sierra on the A432 from Seville. The **Sendero del Arroyo de las Cañas**, a 10km marked walking route around the flattish country west of El Pedroso, beginning opposite Bar Triana on the western side of town, is one of the prettiest walks in the park. It goes through a landscape strewn with boulders and, in spring, gorgeous wild flowers.

❶ Information

The **tourist office** (www.cazalladelasierra .es/turismo.html; ☺10am-2pm Tue & Wed, 10am-2pm & 6-8pm Thu-Sat, 10am-1pm Sun) is on Plaza Mayor, next to the Iglesia de la Consolación.

❶ Getting There & Around

Buses wind along the mountain roads between Cazalla de la Sierra and Seville five to six times a day during the week, twice on Saturdays and three times on Sundays.

Cádiz Province & Gibraltar

Includes »

Best Places to Eat

» Sabores (p122)
» El Aljibe (p109)
» Poma (p117)
» Mandrágora (p136)

Best Places to Stay

» V... (p297)
» La Casa de la Favorita (p297)
» Hotel Argantonio (p295)
» Parador Casa del Corregidor (p297)

Why Go?

If you had to break off one part of Andalucía to demonstrate to aliens what it looked like, you'd probably choose Cádiz province. Emblematic regional highlights are part of the furniture here: thrillingly sited white towns, craggy mountains, endless olive trees, flamenco in its purest incarnation, the original (and best) fortified sherry, the font of Andalucian horse culture, festivals galore, and – just when you thought you'd half-sussed it out – that idiosyncratic British anomaly, Gibraltar. Stuffed in among all of this condensed culture are two expansive natural parks that cover an unbroken tract of land that runs from Olvera in the north to Algeciras in the south. The same line once marked the blurred frontier between Christian Spain and Moorish Granada, and the ancient border is flecked with huddled 'white towns,' many of them given a 'de la Frontera' suffix, testifying to their volatile but fascinating history.

Driving Distances (km)

	Cádiz	Jerez de la Frontera	Tarifa	Gibraltar
Jerez de la Frontera	32			
Tarifa	103	113		
Gibraltar	144	113	43	
Arcos de la Frontera	63	32	113	115

DON'T MISS

Listen out for word on the street about private flamenco clubs or *peñas* (small private clubs) – few experiences in Andalucía can equal their musical performances for authenticity, drama and raw emotion.

Best White Towns

» Vejer de la Frontera (p131)

» Grazalema (p125)

» Jimena de la Frontera (p138)

» Arcos de la Frontera (p129)

Best Hikes

» Salto del Cabrero (p128)

» Garganta del Verde (p128)

» Sendero del Acantilado (p132)

» Sendero de Río Hozgarganta (p138)

Resources

» **Cádiz Net** (www.cadiz net.com) Expansive guide to Cádiz province.

» **Cádiz Turismo** (www .cadizturismo.com) Official government overview of tourism in Cádiz province.

Getting Around

Cádiz province is served by two bus companies, Comes and Los Amarillos, which link all the major towns plus a surprising number of small villages. Fast trains from Madrid serve Jerez, El Puerto de Santa María and Cádiz. One of Spain's most scenic train lines runs from Ronda down to Algerciras. With a little advance planning it is possible to cover almost every corner of the province on public transportation. The best driving routes thread through the mountains of the northeast.

THREE PERFECT DAYS

Day 1: Seafaring Cities

Spend the morning in Cádiz getting geographically oriented with a stroll around the urban coastline. Stop-offs should include the **cathedral**, **Museo de Cádiz** and **Playa de la Caleta**. In the late afternoon take the short ferry ride to El Puerto de Santa María for some of Andalucía's best food. Warm up with tapas in the city centre before hitting **Mesón del Asador** or **Aponiente**, depending on your budget.

Day 2: Jerez Sojourn

Jump on a train for a day in underrated **Jerez de la Frontera**. Start with the **cathedral**, a Gothic-baroque masterpiece, before sidestepping to the Almohad-era Alcázar. While in the area, submit to the lure of the **Hammam Andalusi** – 90 minutes of unforgettable bliss. The afternoon is a toss-up between a horse show or a sherry bodega tour; book ahead. Jerez's most reative dinner restaurant is **Sabores**, handily placed for evening sojourns around the legendary flamenco bars of Calle Francos.

Day 3: The White Towns

Drive a car or catch a bus to the white towns. **Arcos de la Frontera**, the closest to Cádiz, is a great place for street wandering. Highlights include the town's splendid **Basíllica-Parroquia de Santa María**, and coffee and cake in the eagle's nest **Parador Casa del Corregidor**. After lunch press on via El Bosque to Grazalema, where you can stretch your legs with a couple of gentle mountain hikes. If time allows, motor back via Benaocaz and Ubrique, taking in resplendent mountain scenery.

Accommodation

The white towns sport some splendid *casas rurales* (farmstead accommodation) along with small family-run *hostales* (budget hotels) and hotels. The best boutique options lie in Cádiz, Jerez and Tarifa, while magnificent palace hotels characterise El Puerto de Santa María and Sanlúcar de Barrameda. One of Cádiz's few *paradores* (luxurious state-owned hotels) can be found in Arcos de la Frontera. Read about hotel choices in our dedicated Accommodation chapter (p288).

CÁDIZ

POP 125,000

You could write several weighty university theses about Cádiz and still fall a mile short of nailing its essence. Old age accounts for much of the complexity. Cádiz is generally considered to be the oldest continuously inhabited settlement in Europe. Now well into its fourth millennium, the ancient centre, surrounded almost entirely by water, is a romantic hodgepodge of sinuous streets where Atlantic waves crash against eroded sea walls, municipal beaches stretch for miles, and rambunctious taverns echo with the sounds of cawing gulls and frying fish.

But old as it is, Cádiz has also proved to be durable and, ultimately, influential. Spain's first liberal constitution was signed here in 1812, while the city's distinctive urban model went on to provide an identikit for fortified Spanish colonial cities in the Americas. Indeed the port with its crenellated sea walls and chunky forts is heavily reminiscent of Havana in Cuba or San Juan in Puerto Rico.

Return visitors to Cádiz talk fondly of its seafood, surfing and cache of intriguing churches and museums that inflict little, if any, damage on your wallet. More importantly, they wax lyrically about the *gaditanos*, an upfront and gregarious populace whose Carnaval is an exercise in ironic humour and whose upbeat flamenco songs (known as *alegrías*) will bring warmth to your heart.

◎ Sights & Activities

To understand Cádiz you need to first become acquainted with its *barrios* (districts). The old city can be split into classic quarters: Barrio del Pópulo, home of the cathedral, and nexus of the once prosperous medieval settlement; Barrio de Santa María, the old Roma quarter and an important fount of flamenco; Barrio de la Viña, a former vineyard that became the city's main fishing quarter; and the Barrio del Mentidero, centre of Cádiz' modern nightlife and bar scene.

Cadiz Catedral   CATHEDRAL
(✆956 28 61 54; Plaza de la Catedral; adult/child €5/3, 7-8pm & 11am-1pm Sun free; ◎10am-6.30pm Mon-Sat, 1-6.30pm Sun) Cádiz's yellow-domed cathedral is an impressively proportioned baroque-cum-neoclassical construction, but by Spanish standards is very sober in its decoration. It fronts a broad, traffic-free plaza where the cathedral's ground plan is picked out in the paving stones.

The decision to build the cathedral was taken in 1716 but the project wasn't finished until 1838, by which time neoclassical elements, such as the dome, towers and main facade, had diluted Vicente Acero's original baroque plan.

A stone's throw to the east of Cádiz cathedral, the **Museo Catedralicio** (Cathedral Museum; Map p106; Plaza de Fray Félix; admission €5; ◎10am-6.30pm Mon-Sat, 2-6.30pm Sun) has an excavated medieval street alongside cathedral treasures and assorted art.

FREE Roman Theatre   RUIN
(Campo del Sur; ◎10am-2.30pm & 5-7pm Wed-Mon) On the seaward edge of the Barrio del Pópulo, the excavated Teatro Romano is Cádiz' most easily accessible Roman site. Its ancient stage lies buried beneath the surrounding buildings, but you can walk along the gallery beneath the tiers of seating.

Casa del Obispo   MUSEUM
(Plaza de Fray Félix 5; admission €5, combined ticket with Torre de Poniente €7; ◎10am-6pm mid-Sep–mid-Jun, to 8pm mid-Jun–mid-Sep) Outside Cádiz cathedral's eastern exterior wall is the fascinating Casa del Obispo. This expansive museum of glass walkways over 1500 sq metres of excavated ruins takes you through every conceivable period of Cádiz' history, from the 8th century BC to the 18th century.

It served as a Phoenician funerary complex, Roman temple and the city's mosque, before becoming the city's Episcopal Palace in the 16th century. There are four free guided tours in Spanish daily.

Plaza de Topete   SQUARE
(◎9.30am-2pm Mon-Sat) A short walk northwest from the cathedral, this triangular plaza is one of Cádiz' most intimate, bright with flower stalls and still widely known by its old name, Plaza de las Flores (Square of the Flowers). It adjoins the large, animated Mercado Central, built in 1837 and the oldest covered market in Spain, but undergoing major renovations when we were there.

Museo de Cádiz   MUSEUM
(Plaza de Mina; admission €1.50; ◎2.30-8.30pm Tue, 9am-8.30pm Wed-Sat, 9.30am-2.30pm Sun) The Museo de Cádiz, on one of Cádiz' leafiest squares, is the best museum in the province. The ground-floor archaeology section includes two Phoenician marble sarcophagi carved in human likeness, lots of headless Roman statues, plus *continued on page 108*

CÁDIZ PROVINCE & GIBRALTAR CÁDIZ

Cádiz Province & Gibraltar Highlights

1 Walking around the perimeter of Cadiz' sea-encircled **old city** (p103) absorbing 3000 years of history

2 Searching for authentic, salt-of-the-earth flamenco in **Jerez de la Frontera** (p118)

3 Enjoying fresh-from-the-ocean fish in Sanlúcar de Barrameda's **Bajo de Guía** (p117) neighbourhood

4 Washing down tapas with a local sherry in **El Puerto de Santa María** (p112)

5 Biking the **Vía Verde de la Sierra** (p126) between Olvera and Puerto Serrano

6 Looking out at Africa from the **Castillo** (p138) in Jimena de la Frontera

7 Hiking to Los Caños de la Meca through the **Parque Natural de la Breña y Marismas de Barbate** (p132)

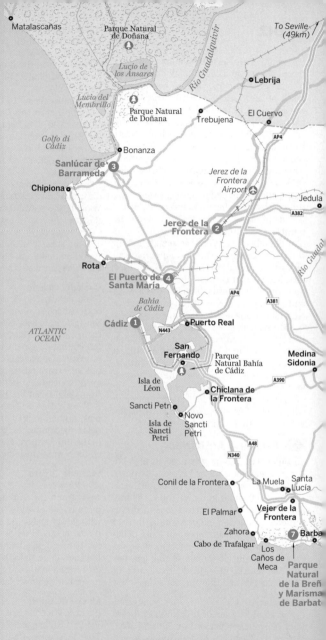

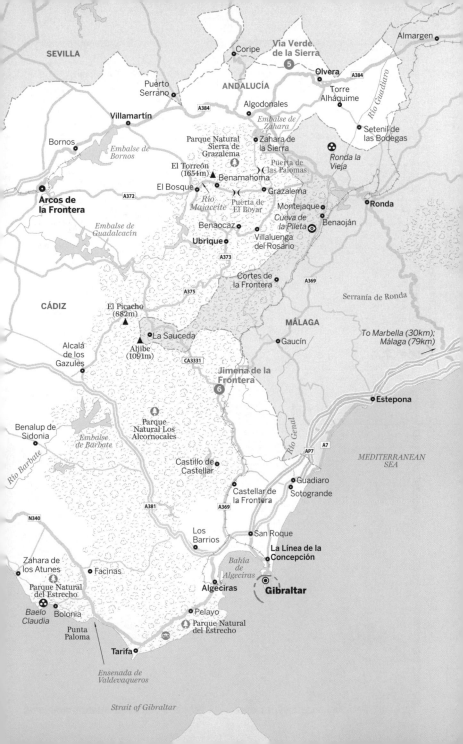

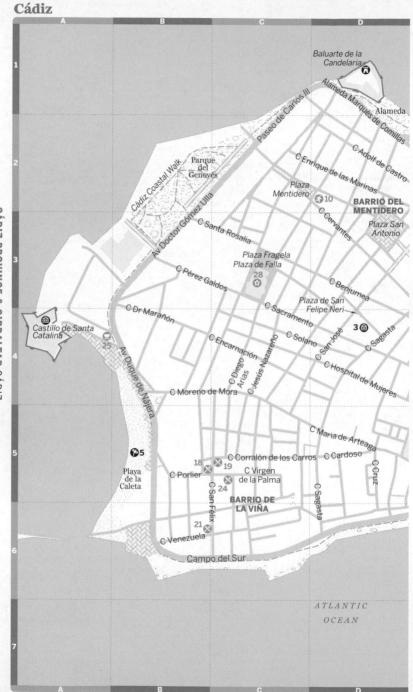

CÁDIZ PROVINCE & GIBRALTAR CÁDIZ

Baluarte de la Candelaria

Alameda Marqués de Comillas

Alameda

Paseo de Carlos III

C Adolf de Castro

C Enrique de las Marinas

Cádiz Coastal Walk

Parque del Genovés

Plaza Mentidero

10

BARRIO DEL MENTIDERO

C Cervantes

Plaza San Antonio

C Santa Rosalía

Av Doctor Gómez Ulla

Plaza Fragela
Plaza de Falla

28

C Pérez Galdos

C Benjumea

Plaza de San Felipe Neri

C Dr Marañón

C Sacramento

Castillo de Santa Catalina

25

C Encarnación

C Solano

3

C Sagasta

C San José

C Diego Arias

C Jesús Nazareno

C Hospital de Mujeres

C Moreno de Mora

C Maria de Arteaga

5

C Corralón de los Carros

C Cardoso

Playa de la Caleta

18

19

C Porlier

C Virgen de la Palma

C Cruz

24

C San Felix

BARRIO DE LA VIÑA

C Sagasta

21

C Venezuela

Campo del Sur

ATLANTIC

OCEAN

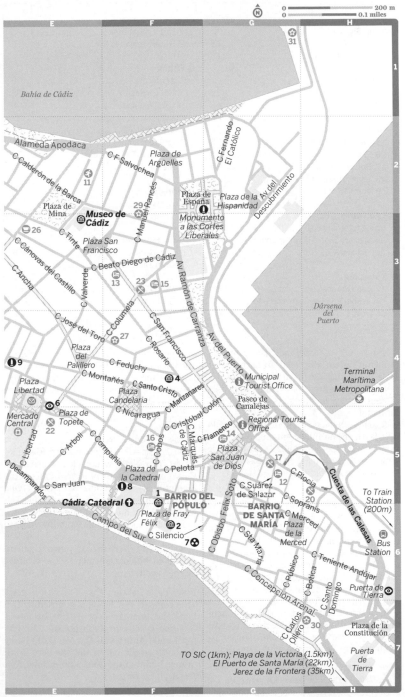

0 _____ 200 m
0 _____ 0.1 miles

CÁDIZ PROVINCE & GIBRALTAR CÁDIZ

Bahía de Cádiz

Alameda Apodaca
C Calderón de la Barca
Plaza de Mina
Museo de Cádiz
Plaza San Francisco
C F Salvochea
Plaza de Argüelles
C Fernando El Católico
Plaza de España
Plaza de la Hispanidad
Monumento a las Cortes Liberales
Av del Descubrimiento

Dársena del Puerto

Plaza del Palillero
Municipal Tourist Office
Paseo de Canalejas
Regional Tourist Office
Terminal Marítima Metropolitana

Mercado Central
Plaza de Topete
Plaza de la Catedral
Plaza San Juan de Dios
Cuesta de las Calesas
To Train Station (200m)
Bus Station

Cádiz Catedral
BARRIO DEL PÓPULO
Plaza de Fray Félix
BARRIO DE SANTA MARÍA
Plaza de la Merced
Puerta de Tierra

Plaza de la Constitución
Puerta de Tierra

TO SIC (1km); Playa de la Victoria (1.5km);
El Puerto de Santa María (22km);
Jerez de la Frontera (35km)

Cádiz

continued from page 103

Emperor Trajan, with head, from the ruins of Baelo Claudia. The fine arts collection, upstairs, features a group of 18 superb canvases of saints, angels and monks by Francisco de Zurbarán.

Also here is the painting that cost Murillo his life, the beautifully composed altarpiece from the chapel of Cádiz' Convento de Capuchinas (the artist died in 1682 after falling from the scaffolding).

Torre de Poniente   TOWER
(Western Tower; adult/child €4/3; ⊙10am-6pm, to 8pm mid-Jun–mid-Sep) Next to the main cathedral entrance on Plaza de la Catedral you can climb up inside one of its bell towers, the Torre de Poniente, for marvellous views over the old city with its many 18th-century watchtowers (built so citizens could keep an eye on shipping movements without stepping outside their front doors).

Back then Cádiz had 160 of these watchtowers: 127 still stand. There are no steps; instead you must tackle a continuously ascending ramp – easier and a lot more fun!

Torre Tavira   TOWER
(Calle Marqués del Real Tesoro 10; admission €4; ⊙10am-6pm mid-Sep–mid-Jun, to 8pm mid-Jun–

mid-Sep) Northwest of Plaza de Topete, the Torre Tavira has another dramatic panorama of Cádiz and a camera obscura that projects live, moving images of the city onto a screen (sessions start every half-hour).

FREE Museo de las Cortes de Cádiz   MUSEUM
(Calle Santa Inés 9; ⊙9am-6pm Tue-Fri, to 2pm Sat & Sun) The recently remodelled Museo de las Cortes de Cádiz is full of memorabilia of the revolutionary 1812 Cádiz parliament. One exhibit jumps out at you: the huge, marvellously detailed model of 18th-century Cádiz, made in mahogany and ivory by Alfonso Ximénez in 1777–79.

The plush overhanging viewing gallery decorated with old city maps allows a bird's-eye perspective.

Playa de la Caleta   BEACH
This compact city beach is guarded by two forts and is notable for its kitschy mock-Moorish *balneario* (bath house). Mimicking Ursula Andress in *Dr. No*, Halle Berry famously strode out of the sea here in an orange bikini in the 2002 James Bond film *Die Another Day*.

Playa de la Victoria   BEACH

This lovely, wide strip of fine Atlantic sand stretches about 4km along the peninsula from its beginning at the Puertas de Tierra. At weekends in summer almost the whole city seems to be out here. Bus 1 (Plaza España-Cortadura) from Plaza de España will get you there or you can walk along the promenade from Barrio Santa María.

Museo de Vinos y Toros   MUSEUM

(Museum of Wine & Bulls; www.vinosytoros.com; Calle Feduchy 17; admission €5; ◎10am-2pm & 4-8pm Mon-Fri, 10am-2pm Sat) The engaging Museo de Vinos y Toros is like a window on the Andalucian soul. Displays include over 1000 (mostly antique) wine bottles from Cádiz province and a host of bullfighting photos, posters and lithographs, and the entry ticket includes a glass of wine.

🎊 Festivals & Events

Carnaval   CARNIVAL

No other Spanish city celebrates Carnaval with the verve, dedication and humour of Cádiz, where it's a 10-day singing, dancing and drinking fancy-dress party spanning two weekends in February. The fun, abetted by huge quantities of alcohol, is irresistible.

Costumed groups called *murgas* tour the city on foot or on floats, dancing, singing satirical ditties or performing sketches (most of their famed verbal wit will be lost on all but fluent Spanish speakers). In addition to the 300-or-so officially recognised *murgas*, who are judged by a panel in the Gran Teatro Falla, there are also the *ilegales* – any group that fancies taking to the streets and trying to play or sing.

Some of the liveliest and most drunken scenes are in the working-class Barrio de la Viña, between the Mercado Central and Playa de la Caleta, and along Calle Ancha and around Plaza de Topete, where *ilegales* tend to congregate.

If you plan to be in Cádiz during Carnaval, book accommodation months in advance.

🐢 Courses

Cádiz is an excellent place to study Spanish language and culture. **Gadir Escuela Internacional de Español** (✆956 26 05 57; www.gadir.net; Calle Pérgolas 5) is a recommended, long-established school southeast of the Puerta de Tierra. Other good language schools include: **Melkart Centro Internacional de Idiomas** (✆956 22 22 13; www.centromelkart.com; Calle General Menacho 7); **K2 Internacional** (✆956 21 26 46; www.k2interna

cional.com; Plaza Mentidero 19); and **SIC** (✆956 25 27 24; www.spanishincadiz.com; Calle Condesa Villafuente Bermeja 7), about 1km southeast of the Puerta de Tierra. These schools also organise flamenco, salsa and even surf courses and a range of other activities, as well as accommodation.

🍴 Eating

Just as Jerez de la Frontera carries the aroma of sherry, Cádiz smells unforgettably of fresh fish. Calle Plocia is the city's gourmet eat-street with the latest creative restaurants broadcasting inflections from all parts of Spain including the Basque and Galicia regions. Barrio de la Viña – especially on Calle Virgen de la Palma – is a more earthy salt-of-the-sea specialist where alfresco tables are spread with the latest catches from nearby Playa de la Caleta.

⌜TOP⌝ El Aljibe   TAPAS €€
⌞CHOICE⌟

(www.pablogrosso.com; Calle Plocia 25; tapas €2-3.50, mains €10-15) Refined restaurant upstairs and supercool tapas bar downstairs, El Aljibe on its own is almost reason enough to come to Cádiz. The cuisine developed by *gaditano* chef Pablo Grosso is a delicious combination of the traditional and the adventurous – goat's cheese on nut bread with blueberry sauce, courgette and prawn lasagna...you get the drift?

Atxuri   BASQUE, ANDALUCIAN €€

(✆956 25 36 13; www.atxuri.es; Calle Plocia 7; mains from €12; ◎1-4.30pm daily & 9-11pm Thu-Sat) One of Cádiz' most decorated and long-standing restaurants, Atxuri fuses Basque and Andalucian influences and the result is a sophisticated range of flavours. *Bacalao* (cod) and high-quality steaks are recurring themes, as you'd expect in a place with Basque roots, but fish and meat tastes are such staples of Andalucian cooking that the boundary between Andalucía and the Basque Country is often deliciously blurred.

Bar Balneario   SEAFOOD €€

(✆636 946566; cnr Calles Virgen de la Palma & San Félix; mains €10-18; ◎closed Sun evening & Mon) Most of the eateries in the Barrio de la Viña are pretty informal places in keeping with its working-class roots, but Bar Balneario has a touch of class. Perhaps that's why it's almost always full, but it could also be the *arroz señorito* (rice with peeled seafood) or *arroz negro* (black rice, cooked in squid ink). Service is fast and friendly.

CÁDIZ PROVINCE & GIBRALTAR CÁDIZ

Casa Manteca
TAPAS €

(☎956 21 36 03; Calle Corralón de los Carros 66; tapas €1.50-2; ☺closed Sun evening & Mon) The hub of La Viña's Carnaval fun, and with almost every inch of wall covered in colourful flamenco, bullfighting and Carnaval memorabilia, Casa Manteca is inevitably one of the barrio's liveliest and best tapas bars.

Ask the amiable bar staff for a tapa of *chicharrones* – pressed pork dressed with a squeeze of lemon, served on a paper napkin and amazingly delicious.

Arrocería La Pepa
SPANISH €€

(☎956 26 38 21; Paseo Maritimo 14; paella per person €12-17) To get a decent paella you have to leave the old town behind and head for a few kilometres southeast along Playa de la Victoria, a pleasant, appetite-inducing oceanside walk along a popular jogging route or a quick ride on the No 1 bus. Either method is worth it.

The fish in La Pepa's seafood paella tastes as if it's just jumped the 100 or so metres from the Atlantic onto your plate.

El Faro
SEAFOOD €€

(www.elfarodecadiz.com; Calle San Félix 15; mains €15-25) Ask many *gaditanos* for their favourite Cádiz restaurant and there's a fair chance they'll choose El Faro. Close to the Playa de la Caleta, this place is at once crammed-to-the-rafters tapas bar and upmarket restaurant decorated with pretty ceramics. Seafood is why people come here, although the *rabo de toro* (bull's tail stew) has its devotees.

If any place in this casual city has a dress code, it's El Faro, although even here it extends only to a prohibition on swimsuits...

Freiduría Las Flores
SEAFOOD €

(☎956 22 61 12; Plaza de Topete 4; seafood per 250g €3-8) Cádiz's addiction to fried fish finds wonderful expression here. If it comes from the sea, chances are that it's been fried and served in Las Flores as either a tapa, *ración* (large tapas serving) or *media ración* (small tapas serving), or served in an improvised paper cup, fish-and-chips style. You order by weight (250g is the usual order).

If you're finding it hard to choose, order a *surtido* (mixed fry-up). Tables can be hard to come by, especially at lunchtime.

Mesón Criolla
ANDALUCIAN €

(cnr Calles Virgen de la Palma & Lubet; tapas €3, raciones €10-12) In the plethora of Barrio La Viña's fish joints, this one stands out for its prawns, fish bruschettas and individual paella (no sharing or half-hour waits here). Sit out in the street at tapas time and you'll feel as if there's a permanent carnival going on in what is Cadiz' primary Carnanval quarter.

La Gorda Te Da De Comer
FUSION €

(Calle General Luque 1; tapas €2; ☺9-11.30pm Mon, 1.30-4pm & 9-11.30pm Tue-Sat) Incredibly tasty food at incredibly low prices amid cool pop-art design. The tastes are fresh and innovative but it's almost always done with a discernibly local twist. No wonder competition for the half-dozen tables is fierce: get there at least 10 minutes before opening to avoid a long wait.

Try the curried chicken strips with Marie-Rose sauce, the deep-fried eggplants with honey or a dozen other mouth-watering concoctions.

🍷 Drinking

As you'd expect in such a seafaring and flamenco-biased city, Cádiz has raffish bars around every corner. They range from old tile-walled joints with a few locals chinwagging over a *vino tinto* (red wine) to chic music bars with a cooler younger clientele. The area around Plazas San Francisco, España and Mina is the hub of the old city's late-night bar scene. Things steam up around 11pm or midnight at these places but can be quiet in the first half of the week.

TOP CHOICE Quilla
CAFE

(www.quilla.es; Playa de la Caleta; ☺10am-midnight; 🛜) A bookish coffee bar encased in what appears to be the rusty hulk of an old ship overlooking Playa de la Caleta, with pastries, tapas, wine, art expos and free wi-fi – to say nothing of the gratis sunsets.

Tetería El Oasis
TEAROOM

(Calle San José 6) Find dark nooks under the red and orange lace curtains and sip discreetly on a Darjeeling in a state of contemplative meditation – until the belly dancers arrive!

☆ Entertainment

In case you'd forgotten, Cádiz helped invent flamenco and subtly nurtured the talent of Andalucía's finest classical composer, Manuel de Falla. The weighty musical legacy is ingrained in the city's entertainment scene.

TOP CHOICE Peña Flamenca La Perla   FLAMENCO

(✆956 25 91 01; www.laperladecadiz.es; Calle Carlos Ollero; admission free) The paint-peeled Peña La Perla, set romantically next to the crashing Atlantic surf, hosts flamenco nights at 10pm most Fridays, more so in spring and summer. It's right beside the ocean just off Calle Concepción Arenal in the Barrio de Santa María, entry is free and the audience is stuffed with aficionados. It's an unforgettable experience.

Gran Teatro Falla   THEATRE

(✆956 22 08 34; Plaza de Falla) A remarkable theatre named for a remarkable man – native son and classical composer Manuel de Falla. The building deserves a peep in its own right for its red-bricked neo-Mudéjar majesty. Its premier performances are its annual carnival competitions. The rest of the year it also hosts plays and musical concerts.

Barabass   BAR, MUSIC

(✆856 07 90 26; www.barabasscadiz.es; Calle General Muñoz Arenillas 4-6; admission incl 1 drink €10; ☺10pm-6am) The glamorous Barabass is one of the hippest bars in Cádiz' other night-time nexus: Playa de la Victoria.

Cambalache   JAZZ, BLUES

(Calle José del Toro 20; ☺closed Sun) This long, dim, jazz and blues bar often hosts live music on Thursdays around 10.30pm, but it's the sort of place that has a great atmosphere most nights of the week.

Sala Anfiteátro   CLUB

(Paseo Pascual Pery; admission €6-8) On the *punta* (Punta de San Felipe) on the northern side of the harbour, this big club is packed with an 18-to-25 crowd from around 3am to 6am.

La Cava   FLAMENCO

(www.flamencolacava.com; Calle António López 16; €22, with tapas €39; ☺shows 10pm) Cádiz's main *tablao* (organised flamenco show) happens in a rustically bedecked tavern with drinks and tapas. It's professional, if heavy with tourists (the hotels push it).

ℹ Information

Hospital Puerta del Mar (✆956 00 21 00; Avenida Ana de Viya 21) The main general hospital, 2¼km southeast of the Puerta de Tierra.

Medical Emergency (✆061)

Municipal Tourist Office (Paseo de Canalejas; ☺8.30am-6pm Mon-Fri, 9am-5pm Sat & Sun) Handily close to the bus and train stations.

Policía Nacional (✆091, 956 28 61 11; Avenida de Andalucía 28) National police, 500m southeast of the Puerta de Tierra.

Regional Tourist Office (Avenida Ramón de Carranza; ☺9am-7.30pm Mon-Fri, 10am-2pm Sat, Sun & holidays)

ℹ Getting There & Around

Boat

The **catamaran** (www.cmtbc.es; Terminal Marítima Metropolitana) leaves from the Terminal Marítima Metropolitana with 18 daily departures for El Puerto de Santa María (€2.35) Monday to Friday, but just six on Saturdays and five on Sundays.

Bus

Comes (✆956 80 70 59; www.tgcomes.es; Plaza de la Hispanidad) Has regular departures from the **bus station** (✆956 80 70 59; Plaza Sevilla) to Arcos de la Frontera (€5, one hour), El Puerto de Santa María (€1.50, 45 minutes), Granada (€33, 5½ hours), Jerez de la Frontera (€1.70, one hour), Málaga (€24, four hours), Ronda (€15, two hours), Seville (€9, 1¾ hours), Tarifa (€9, 1½ hours), and Vejer de la Frontera (€6, 1 hour 20 minutes).

Los Amarillos (www.losamarillos.es) In addition to some of the above destinations, Los Amarillos also runs buses to El Bosque, Sanlúcar de Barrameda and Ubrique from the southern end of Avenida Ramón de Carranza.

Consorcio de Transportes Bahía de Cádiz (✆956 01 21 00; www.cmtbc.com) Buses M050 and M051 travel from Jerez de la Frontera airport to Cádiz' Comes bus station, via Jerez city and El Puerto de Santa María.

Car & Motorcycle

The AP4 motorway from Seville to Puerto Real, on the eastern side of the Bahía de Cádiz, carries a toll of €5.90. From Puerto Real, a bridge crosses the neck of the bay to join the A48 entering Cádiz from the south.

Twenty-four-hour underground car parks in the old city include Campo del Sur (€17) and Paseo de Canalejas (€9).

Train

From the **train station** (✆902 24 02 02), plenty of trains run daily to/from El Puerto de Santa María (€4.10, 30 minutes, 15 daily), Jerez de la Frontera (€5, 40 minutes, 15 daily), Seville (€13.25, one hour 45 minutes, 15 daily) and Madrid (€72.20, 4½ hours, three daily). The high-speed AVE service from Madrid should reach Cádiz by the time you read this.

A VERY BRITISH DRINK

It's the names that give it away: Harvey, Sandeman, Terry, Humbert and Osborne. Andalucía's sherry industry might be Spanish in character but it was undisputedly Anglo-Irish in its genesis. You can blame Francis Drake for Britain's sherry obsession. The daring Elizabethan privateer set a precedent in 1587 when he sacked Cádiz and greedily made off with over 3000 barrels of the local vino. Before long the normally undiscerning Brits had developed an incurable taste for Spain's fortified wine – and they wanted more of it. To meet the demand, a whole new industry was inauspiciously born.

Thomas Osborne Mann, a shopkeeper from Exeter who had resettled in Cádiz, was one of the first to get in on the act. Befriending local wine-growers in El Puerto de Santa María in 1772, he set up what is today one of Spain's oldest family firms, Osborne, famous for its imposing black bull logo. George Sandeman, a Scotsman from Perth, was another early mover and shaker founding his fledgling sherry empire in Tom's Coffee House in the City of London in 1790. By now every business-minded Brit was trying their hand in the wine-producing trade, including John Harvey from Bristol, who began importing sherry from Spain in 1796 and concocted the world's first cream sherry, Harvey's Bristol Cream, in the 1860s. Another innovator was William Garvey, an Irish aristocrat from Waterford who, after being shipwrecked off Cádiz in 1780, decided to stay on and chance his arm in the wine business. The Terry family was also from southern Ireland and founded their famous bodegas in El Puerto de Santa María in 1865. Even Spain's most famous sherry dynasty Gonzalez-Byass – producers of the trademark Tío Pepe brand – was formed from a Anglo-Spanish alliance hatched in 1835 between Andaucian Manuel Maria Gonzalez and his London-based agent (and Englishman) Robert Byass.

THE SHERRY TRIANGLE

North of Cádiz, the towns of Jerez de la Frontera, Sanlúcar de Barrameda and El Puerto de Santa María form the three corners of the 'sherry triangle.' Even if Andalucía's unique, smooth wine isn't your cup of tea, you'll still find these three towns historically compelling. And don't forget the beaches, the horses, the flamenco and the environmental marvel that is Parque Nacional de Doñana.

El Puerto de Santa María

POP 89,000

When you're surrounded by such cultural luminaries as Cádiz, Jerez de la Frontera and Seville, it's easy to get lost in the small print; such is the fate of El Puerto de Santa María, despite its stash of well-known icons. Osborne sherry, with its famous bull logo (which has become the national symbol of Spain) was founded and retains its HQ here, as do half a dozen other sherry bodegas. El Puerto also claims one of Spain's great bullrings and a weighty bullfighting legacy to go with it. Gastronomy is its other *fuerte* (strength). There are more decent tapas bars per head here than almost anywhere else in Spain. El Puerto can seem like southern Andalucía in microcosm, offering an abundance of good beaches, sherry bodegas and a smattering of architectural heirlooms. Review your itinerary and try to squeeze it in.

⊙ Sights & Activities

FREE Plaza de Toros   BULLRING
(Plaza Elías Ahuja; ⊙11am-1.30pm & 6-7.30pm Tue-Sun May-Sep, 11am-1.30pm & 5.30-7pm Tue-Sun Oct-Apr) Four blocks southwest from Plaza de España is El Puerto's grand Plaza de Toros, which was built in 1880 and remains one of Andalucía's most beautiful and important bullrings, with room for 15,000 spectators. It's closed on days before and after bullfights. Entry to the bullring is from Calle Valdés.

Fundación Rafael Alberti   MUSEUM
(☑956 85 07 11; www.rafaelalberti.es; Calle Santo Domingo 25; admission €5, audioguide €1; ⊙11am-2.30pm Tue-Sun) A few blocks inland from Castillo de San Marcos, this place has interesting exhibits on Rafael Alberti (1902–99), one of the great poets of Spain's 'Generation of 27', who grew up here. The exhibits are well displayed and audioguides in English, German or Spanish (€1) are available.

Castillo San Marcos
CASTLE

(2956 85 17 51; Plaza Alfonso X El Sabio; admission Tue free, Thu & Sat €5; ⊙tours 11.30am, 12.30pm & 1.30pm Tue, 10.30am, 11.30am, 12.30pm & 1.30pm Thu & Sat) Heavily restored in the 20th century, the fine Castillo San Marcos was built over a Muslim mosque by Alfonso X of Castile after he took the town in 1260. The castle's decorated battlements are beautiful, but the old mosque inside, now converted into a church, is the highlight. The Thursday and Saturday tours include a tasting of local products.

Tours last just under an hour and the last ones each day are in English.

Beaches
BEACHES

El Puerto is one of the more popular beach escapes in southern Spain, drawing a predominantly Spanish crowd of beach lovers for its fabulous white sandy beaches. The closest to town is pine-flanked **Playa de la Puntilla**, a half-hour walk southwest (or take bus 26, heading southwest on Avenida Aramburu de Mora).

A couple of kilometres further west is a swish marina development called, of course, **Puerto Sherry**. Beyond Puerto Sherry is picturesque **Playa de la Muralla**, and the 3km **Playa de Santa Catalina**, with beach bars open in summer. Bus 35 from the centre runs out to **Playa de Fuenterrabía**, at the far end of **Playa de Santa Catalina**. If you're driving, take the 'Rota' and 'Playas' road west from the roundabout at the northwest end of Calle Valdés.

On the eastern side of the Río Guadalete is **Playa de Valdelagrana**, a fine beach backed by high-rise hotels and apartments and a strip of bars and restaurants. Bus 35 also runs there.

Sherry Bodegas

El Puerto's seven home-grown bodegas include some of the big guns, including Osborne and Terry. Most of them open their doors to the public, their guided tours taking you through the various stages of production and the bottling process, and you can visit their on-site museums and sample the final product. The bodegas customarily hide in extensive gardens fringed with tall palm trees.

Bodegas Osborne
WINERY

(2956 86 91 00; www.osborne.es; Calle Los Moros 7; tours in English/Spanish/German €6; ⊙tours 10.30am, 11am, noon & 12.30pm Mon-Fri, 11am & noon Sat) Creator of the legendary black bull logo still exhibited on life-sized billboards all over Spain (though without the name advertised these days), Osborne, the best known of El Puerto's seven sherry wineries was set up – with no intentional irony – by an Englishman, Thomas Osborne Mann (from Exeter) in 1772. It remains one of Spain's oldest companies run continuously by the same family.

The gorgeous whitewashed bodega offers weekday tours and sometimes adds extra tours, including on Saturday, in summer. It is best to phone ahead.

Bodegas Terry
WINERY

(2956 15 15 00; www.bodegasterry.com; Calle Toneleros 1; tour €8, tour & horse show €15; ⊙tours 10.30am & 12.30pm Mon-Fri, noon Sat) You can visit the Irish-founded Bodegas Terry without booking. Situated close to El Puerto's train station, the bodega is known for its summer horse spectaculars (11am Fridays; bookings required) and antique carriage museum.

THE SECRET OF SHERRY

How you get your bottle of sherry is intriguing. Once sherry grapes have been harvested, they are pressed and the resulting must is left to ferment. Within a few months a frothy veil of *flor* (yeast) appears on the surface. The wine is then transferred to the bodegas in big barrels of American oak.

Wine enters the *solera* (from *suelo*, meaning floor) process when it's a year old. The barrels, about five-sixths full, are lined up in rows at least three barrels high. The barrels on the bottom layer, called the *solera*, contain the oldest wine. From these, around three times a year, 10% of the wine is drawn off. This is replaced with the same amount from the barrels in the layer above, which is in turn replaced from the next layer. The wines age for between three and seven years. A small amount of brandy is added to stabilise the wine before bottling, bringing the alcohol content to 16% to 18%, which stops fermentation.

Jerez *coñac* (brandy), widely drunk in Spain, is also a profitable, locally made product – around 65 million bottles are produced annually.

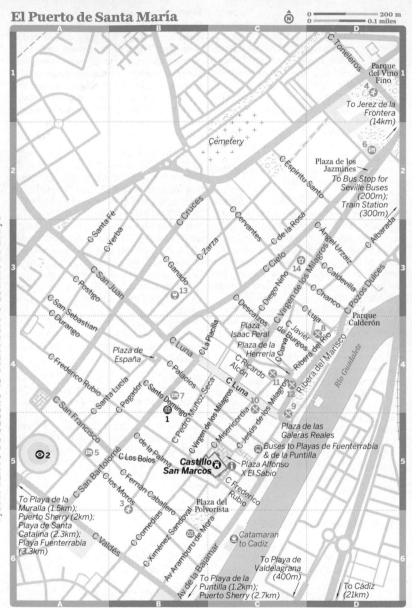

✸ Festivals & Events

**Feria de Primavera
y Fiestas del Vino Fino** WINE
This four-day fiesta (the Spring Fair) confirms that El Puerto's fino (sherry) is not just produced for export. During the fiesta, in late April or early May, around 200,000 half-bottles are drunk.

Festividad Virgen del Carmen RELIGIOUS
Fisherfolk Andalucía-wide pay homage to their patron on the evening of 16 July; in El

El Puerto de Santa María

Puerto the Virgin's image is paraded along the Río Guadalete followed by a flotilla.

🍴 Eating

El Puerto is rightly famed for its outstanding seafood, fine restaurants and terrific tapas bars. Try the local speciality *urta roteña* (sea bream cooked in white wine, tomatoes, peppers and thyme), and it would be sacrilege to wash it down with anything other than a local wine.

TOP CHOICE **Mesón del Asador**   SPANISH, GRILL €€
(www.mesondelasador.com; Calle Misericordia 2; tapas €2.20, mains €12-15) It's a measure of El Puerto's gastronomic nous that, in such a seafood orientated town, there exists a meat restaurant that could compete with any steakhouse in Buenos Aires. The power of the Mesón's delivery is in the smell that hits you as soon as you open the door – chargrilled beef and pork sizzling away on mini-barbecues that they bring to your table.

Try the chorizo and don't miss the chicken or pork bruschetta.

Aponiente   SEAFOOD, FUSION €€€
(☑956 85 18 70; www.aponiente.com; Puerto Escondido 6; 12-course tasting menu €95; ☺closed Sun dinner & Mon, closed Jan–mid Mar) Audacious is the word for the bold experimentation of leading Spanish chef Angel León, whose seafood biased *nueva cocina* menu has won a cavalcade of awards including a Michelin star and a 2011 plug from the *New York Times* citing it as one of 10 restaurants in the world 'worth a plane ride' (not particularly eco, but you get the drift).

The restaurant splits the opinion of locals in traditional El Puerto. Some snort at its prices and pretension, others salivate at the thought of tripe stew, yeast-fermented mackerel and creamy rice with micro seaweeds.

Romerijo   SEAFOOD €
(☑956 54 12 54; Plaza de la Herrería; seafood per 250g from €4.50) A huge, always-busy El Puerto institution, Romerijo has two buildings, one boiling the seafood, the other frying it. Choose from the displays and buy by the quarter-kilogram in paper cones to eat at the formica tables.

Cervecería El Puerto   SEAFOOD €€
(☑956 85 89 39; Calle Misericordia 15; tapas €3, raciones €8; ☺11.30am-4.30pm & 8-11.30pm Wed-Mon, closed Dec) In its own words this place specialises in seafood and beer, which is clearly a winning combination if the lack of room at the bar is any indication. The restaurant offers a full range of Mediterranean fish and seafood specialities, as well as plenty of dishes from Galicia, a world away to the northwest; the *navajas* (razor clams) are unrivalled along this stretch of the coast.

Bar Santa María   TAPAS €
(Plaza Galeras Reales; tapas €2-3.50) Clink your glasses and compare tapa recipes in this riverfront haven of good taste, where fish rules.

🍷 Drinking

Bodega Obregón   BAR
(Calle Zarza 51; ☺closed Mon) Think sherry's just a drink for grandmas? Come and have your illusions blown out of the water at this spit-and-sawdust-style bar where the sweet stuff is siphoned from woody barrels. Flamenco is supposed to happen Sundays between 12.30pm and 3pm.

☆ Entertainment

Peña Flamenca Tomás El Nitri   FLAMENCO
(📞956 54 32 37; Diego Niño 1) A good honest *peña* (small private club) with the air of a foot-stomping, 19th-century flamenco bar that showcases some truly amazing guitarists, singers and dancers in a club full of regular aficionados. Platefuls of tasty food appear miraculously out of a tiny back kitchen.

ℹ Information

Tourist office (📞956 54 24 13; www.turismo elpuerto.com; Plaza de Alfonso X El Sabio 9; ⊙10am-2pm & 6-8pm May-Sep) Organises guided walks of the town from €5 at 6.30pm on Tuesdays and Thursdays and noon on Saturdays.

ℹ Getting There & Around

BOAT The **catamaran** (www.cmtbc.es) leaves from in front of the Hotel Santa María bound for Cádiz' Terminal Marítima Metropolitana (€2.35) with 18 daily departures Monday to Friday, six on Saturdays and five on Sundays.

BUS Regular bus services connect El Puerto de Santa María's Plaza de Toros to Cádiz (€1.56, 45 minutes), Jerez de la Frontera (€1.60, 20 minutes) and Sanlúcar de Barrameda (€1.67, 15 minutes). Buses to Seville go daily from the train station.

CAR You shouldn't pay more than €1 per day in most supervised parking areas, including at the train station, around the Plaza de Toros and along the riverfront.

TRAIN Daily trains go to to/from Jerez de la Frontera (€2.20, 10 minutes, 15 daily) and Cádiz (€4.10, 30 minutes, 15 daily) and Seville (€11.10, 1 hour 20 minutes, 15 daily).

Sanlúcar de Barrameda

POP 67,000

Sanlúcar is one of those lesser-known Andalucian cities that you'd do well to shoehorn into your itinerary. The reasons? Firstly, there's gastronomy. Sanlúcar cooks up some of the best seafood in the region on a hallowed waterside strip called Bajo de Guía. The local *langostinos* (king prawns) are a particular speciality. Secondly, Sanlúcar sits at the northern tip of the esteemed sherry triangle and the bodegas here, nestled in the somnolent old town, retain a less commercial, earthier quality. They also produce a more delicate sherry, the esteemed manzanilla. Thirdly, situated at the mouth of the Río Guadalquivir estuary, the city provides a quieter, less trammelled entry point into the ethereal Parque Nacional de Doñana, preferably via boat.

As if that wasn't enough, Sanlúcar harbours a proud nautical history; both Columbus (on this third sojourn) and Portuguese mariner Ferdinand Magellan struck out from here on their voyages of discovery.

With excellent transport links, Sanlúcar makes an easy day trip from Cádiz or Jerez.

◉ Sights & Activities

Sanlúcar has a number of attractions, from its monument-strewn old town and numerous bodegas to wonderful seafood restaurants by the water. It's also a good base for visits to the Parque Nacional de Doñana.

TOP CHOICE ▸ Barbadillo Bodega   WINERY
(📞956 38 55 00; www.museobarbadillo.com; Calle Luis de Eguilaz 11; tour €3, museum free; ⊙tours noon & 1pm Mon-Sat, in English 11am Tue-Sat, Museo de Manzanilla 10am-3pm Mon-Sat) Sanlúcar is famous for its unique manzanilla wine and Barbadillo is easily its most famous export, not to mention the producers of one of Spain's most popular *vinos*. The Barbadillo bodega has a museum in a 19th-century building that traces the 200-year history of manzanilla wine and the history of the Barbadillo family, the first to bottle manzanilla.

The tourist office has a list of the other six or so bodegas scattered around Sanlúcar, some of which offer tours.

FREE Palacio de Orleans y Borbon   PALACE
(cnr Cuesta de Belén & Calle Caballero; ⊙10am-1.30pm Mon-Fri) From Plaza del Cabildo, cross Calle Ancha to Plaza San Roque and head up Calle Bretones, which becomes Calle Cuesta de Belén. Then dog-leg up to this beautiful neo-Mudéjar palace in the Old Town that was built as a summer home for the aristocratic Montpensier family in the 19th century and is now Sanlúcar's town hall.

Palacio de los Duques de Medina Sidonia   PALACE, MUSEUM
(📞956 36 01 61; www.fcmedinasidonia.com; Plaza Condes de Niebla 1; admission €3; ⊙tours 11am & noon Mon-Sat, by appointment Sun) Next door to the Iglesia de Nuestra Señora de la O, this was the rambling home of the aristocratic family that once owned more of Spain than anyone else. The house, mostly dating from the 17th century, bursts with antiques, and paintings by Goya, Zurbarán and other famous Spanish artists.

Iglesia de Nuestra Señora de la O   CHURCH

(Plaza de la Paz; ⊘mass 7.30pm Mon-Fri, 9am, noon & 7.30pm Sun) A block to the left from Palacio de Orleans y Borbón, along Calle Caballeros, this medieval church stands out among Sanlúcar's churches for its beautiful Gothic-Mudéjar main portal, created in the 1360s, and the richness of its interior decoration, including the Mudéjar *artesonado* (ceiling of interlaced beams with decorative insertions).

Castillo de Santiago   CASTLE

(☑956 08 83 29; www.castillodesantiago.com; Plaza del Castillo de Santiago; ⊘guided tours 11am, noon & 1pm Thu-Sun) Located amid buildings of the Barbadillo sherry company, this restored 15th-century castle has great views from its hexagonal Torre del Homenaje (keep). Entry to the Patio de Armas, the castle's central courtyard, and its restaurant is free.

Bajo de Guía   NEIGHBOURHOOD

Once a fishing village, now a gastronomic heaven of seafood restaurants that revel in their simplicity, the Guía is joined physically to Sanlúcar, though its location directly opposite Parque Doñana on the other side of the Río Guadalaquivir means you get a less hemmed-in feeling.

There are popular beaches here that are famously commandeered for sunset horse races every August. It is also the river crossing point for pilgrims on their way to the Romería del Rocío.

Parque Nacional de Doñana   PARK

The Parque Nacional de Doñana is visible just across the Guadalquivir from Sanlúcar, which serves as an excellent base for forays into the park. Before setting out, stop by the **Centro de Visitantes Fábrica de Hielo** (☑956 38 16 35; Bajo de Guía; ⊘9am 7pm), an original visitor centre run by the national-parks folk. This is also where you buy tickets for the **Real Fernando** (☑956 36 38 13; www .visitasdonana.com; adult/child €17/9; ⊘10am Nov-Feb, 10am & 4pm Mar-May & Oct, 10am & 5pm Jun-Sep), a leisurely 3½-hour boat trip around the park's fringes; it's more for day trippers than serious nature enthusiasts. Book up to a week in advance.

To delve a little deeper, **Viajes Doñana** (☑956 36 25 40; viajesdonana@hotmail.com; Calle San Juan 20; ⊘8.30am & 4.30pm Tue & Fri May-mid-Sep, 8.30am & 2.30pm Tue & Fri mid-Sep–Apr) and **Viajes Recorrecaminos** (☑956 38 20 40; Calle Ramón y Cajal 4) run fun tours in 4WD vehicles holding about 20 people, going deep into the national park through the

dunes, marshlands and pine forests. Expect to pay around €40 per person.

✫✫ Festivals & Events

Feria de la Manzanilla   WINE

The Sanlúcar summer begins with a big fair devoted to Sanlúcar's unique wine, manzanilla; held late May/early June.

Romería del Rocío   RELIGIOUS

(Pentecost) Many pilgrims and covered wagons set out for El Rocío from here; seventh weekend after Easter.

Carreras de Caballo   HORSE RACING

(www.carrerassanlucar.es) Two horse-race meets held over three to four days every August on the sands beside the Guadalquivir estuary. They've been held almost every year since 1845.

✗ Eating

Strung out along the Bajo de Guía is one of Andalucía's most famous restaurant strips, which is reason enough for visiting Sanlúcar. Most restaurants have outdoor tables and an upstairs dining area, and the undisputed speciality is *arroz caldoso a la marinera* (seafood rice), which usually costs around €9 per person and requires at least two for an order. And, of course, don't think about washing it down with anything other than a fresh local manzanilla.

TOP CHOICE Poma   SEAFOOD €€

(www.restaurantepoma.com; Avenida de Bajo de Guía 6; mains €12-18) You could kick a football on the Guía de Bajo and guarantee it'd land on a decent plate of fish. It just might be Poma, where the *plato variado* comes with about five different varieties of lightly fried species plucked out of the nearby sea and river.

Casa Bigote   SEAFOOD €€

(www.restaurantecasabigote.com; Avenida Bajo de Guía 10; fish mains €7-14; ⊘closed Sun) The most renowned of the Bajo de Guía restaurants is Casa Bigote, which has a classier air than most places and serves only fish and seafood. Its tapas bar across the small lane is always packed.

Cafetería Guzmán El Bueno   CAFE, DESSERTS €

(Plaza Condes de Niebla 1; dishes €3-8; ⊘8.30am-9pm, extended hours Sat & Jul-Aug) Sink into plump cushions surrounded by antique furnishings at the cafe in the Palacio de los

Duques de Medina Sidonia. Fare is simple – omelettes, cheese, ham – but the setting is uniquely atmospheric.

Helados Artesanos Toni
ICE CREAM €

(www.heladostoni.com; Plaza de Cabildo 2) For some of the best ice cream in Andalucía don't miss this spot, family run since 1896, with videos demonstrating the fine art of ice-cream making rolling behind the counter.

Casa Balbino
TAPAS, SEAFOOD €

(www.casabalbino.com; Plaza del Cabildo 11; tapas €3) It doesn't seem to matter when you're here, but Casa Balbino is always overflowing with people, drawn here by the fantastic seafood tapas on offer. Whether you're standing at the bar or lucky enough to have snaffled one of the outdoor tables on the plaza, you'll need to elbow your way to the bar, shout your order to a waiter who'll shout back then bring you a plate to carry to your chosen corner.

The list of possibilities is endless, but the *tortillas de camarones* (crisp shrimp fritters) and *langostinos a la plancha* (grilled king prawns; €100 per kilogram) are the best we've tasted.

ⓘ Information

Tourist office (www.turismosanlucar.com; Calzada del Ejército; ⊙10am-2pm & 6-8pm Mon-Fri, 10am-12.45pm Sat, 10am-2pm Sun) Multilingual and very helpful.

ⓘ Getting There & Away

Los Amarillos (✆956 38 50 60; www.losamarillos.es) Runs hourly buses to/from El Puerto de Santa María (€2, 15 minutes), Cádiz (€4.55, one hour) and Seville (€8, 1½ hours) from the bus station on Avenida de la Estación.

Linesur (✆956 34 10 63) Runs hourly buses to/from Jerez de la Frontera.

Jerez de la Frontera

POP 211,000

Stand down all other claimants. Jerez, as savvy Spain-o-philes know, *is* Andalucía. It just doesn't broadcast the fact the way that Seville and Granada do. As a result, few people plan their trip around a visit here, preferring instead to jump-cut to the glories of the Giralda and the Alhambra. If only they knew. Jerez is the capital of Andaluz horse culture, stop one on the famed sherry triangle and – cue the protestations from Cádiz and Seville – the cradle of Spanish flamenco. The *bulería*, Jerez's jokey, tongue-in-cheek antidote to Se-

ville's tragic *soleá* was first concocted in the legendary Roma *barrios* of Santiago and San Miguel. If you really want to unveil the eternal riddle that is Andalucía, start here.

◉ Sights & Activities

Jerez' understated sights are strung out and often creep up on you. Many are hidden behind other buildings, so you only become aware of them once you're inside. It can take a couple of days to 'get' the city. But once you're bitten, it's like *duende* (flamenco spirit) – no turning back.

Alcázar
FORTRESS

(✆956 14 99 55; Alameda Vieja; admission incl/excl camera obscura €5.40/3; ⊙10am-7.30pm Mon-Sat, to 2.30pm Sun May–mid-Sep, 10am-5.30pm Mon-Sat, to 2.30pm Sun mid-Sep–Apr) Jerez' muscular yet refined 11th- or 12th-century fortress is one of the best-preserved Almohad-era (1140–1212) relics left in Andalucía. It's noted for its octagonal tower, a classic example of Almohad defensive forts.

You enter the Alcázar via the **Patio de Armas**. On the left is the beautiful *mezquita* (mosque), which was converted to a chapel by Alfonso X in 1264. Beyond the Patio de Armas, the lovely gardens re-create the ambience of Islamic times with their geometrical plant beds and tinkling fountains, while the domed **Baños Árabes** (Arab Baths) with their shafts of light are another highlight. Back on the Patio de Armas, the 18th-century **Palacio Villavicencio**, built over the ruins of the old Islamic palace, contains works of art, but is best known for its bird's-eye view of Jerez from the summit; the palace's tower also contains a camera obscura, which provides a picturesque live panorama of Jerez.

⬆ CHOICE Catedral de San Salvador
CATHEDRAL

(Plaza de la Encarnación; admission €5; ⊙10.30am-6.30pm Mon-Sat, 12.30-3.30pm Sun) Echoes of Seville colour Jerez's wonderful cathedral, a surprisingly harmonious mix of baroque, neoclassical and gothic styles. Stand-out features are its broad flying butresses and its intricately decorated stone ceilings. In 2012 the cathedral opened as a musuem showing off its art (including works by Zurbarán and Pacheco), religious garments and silverware in a series of rooms and chapels behind the main altar.

You can enjoy an orange tree–lined patio (the church was built on the site of an old mosque) and a 'secret staircase' to nowhere. Named for San Salvador, the building only offically became a cathedral in 1980.

A couple of blocks northeast of the cathedral is Plaza de la Asunción, with the handsome 16th-century **Antiguo Cabildo** (Old Town Hall; Map p120) and lovely 15th-century Mudéjar **Iglesia de San Dionisio** (Map p120).

Real Escuela Andaluza
del Arte Ecuestre   EQUESTRIAN SHOW
(☑956 31 80 08; www.realescuela.org; Avenida Duque de Abrantes; training sessions adult/child €10/6, exhibición adult/child €19/12; ⊘training sessions 11am-1pm Mon, Wed & Fri Sep-Jul, Mon & Wed Aug, noon Tue & Thu Sep-Jul, exhibición noon Tue, Thu & Fri Aug) The famed Royal Andalucian School of Equestrian Art trains horses and riders in equestrian skills, and you can watch them going through their paces in training sessions and visit the **Horse Carriage Museum**, which includes an 18th-century Binder Hunting Break. The highlight for most is the official **exhibición** (show) where the handsome white horses show off their tricks to classical music. You can book tickets online for this – advisable for the official shows, which can sell out.

Hammam Andalusi   HAMMAM
(Arabic baths; ☑956 34 90 66; www.hammam andalusi.com; Calle Salvador 6; baths €22, with 15/30 min massage €32/50; ⊘10am-midnight) Jerez is replete with echoes of the city's Moorish past, none more evocative than Hammam Andalusi. As you enter, you're greeted by the wafting scent of incense and essential oils, and the soothing sound of tinkling water and Arab music. Once inside, you pass, depending on the package you choose, through the three pools (hot, tepid or cold); you can add a massage and/or a variety of beauty treatments. There's even a chocolate bath (€85). Numbers per session are limited to 15 people, so reserve beforehand.

FREE **Centro Andaluz**
de Flamenco   ARTS CENTRE
(Andalusian Flamenco Centre; ☑856 81 41 32; www .centroandaluzdeflamenco.es; Plaza de San Juan 1; ⊘9am-2pm Mon-Fri) At once architecturally interesting (note the original 15th-century Mudéjar *artesonado* in the entrance and the Andalucian baroque courtyard) and a fantastic flamenco resource, this centre has print and music libraries holding thousands of works.

Flamenco videos are screened at 10am, 11am, noon and 1pm, and staff can provide you with a list of 17 local *peñas,* as well as flamenco dance and singing classes in Jerez. Its website also lists upcoming performances under 'Actualidad', then the 'Festivales' tab.

Sherry Bodegas

Jerez – the word even *means* 'sherry' – has at least 20 sherry producers, including

SHERRY & FOOD PAIRINGS

Wine neophytes are in luck. Sherry, aside from being one of the world's unappreciated wines, is also one of its most versatile, particularly the fino and manzanilla varietals, so you don't need a degree in oenology to pair it. Here are some pointers:

TYPE OF SHERRY	SERVING TEMPERATURE	QUALITIES	FOOD PAIRINGS
manzanilla	well chilled	dry, fresh, delicate, slightly salty essence	tapas, almonds, sushi, olives
fino	chilled	very dry & pale	aperitif, tapas, soup, white fish, shellfish, prawns, oysters, counterpoint for cheeses
amontillado	cool, but not chilled	off dry	aperitif, blue cheeses, chicken & white meat, cured cheese, foie gras, rabbit, consommé soups
oloroso	cool, but not chilled	dry, nutty, dark	red meat & game, cheese sauces
pale cream	room temperature	sweetened fino	fresh fruit, blue cheese
cream	room temperature	sweet	dried fruit, cheesecake
Pedro Ximénez	room temperature	very sweet	dark chocolate, biscotti

Jerez de la Frontera

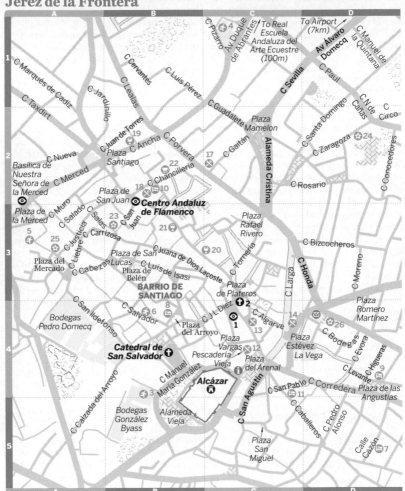

famous names such as González Byass, Williams & Humbert, Sandeman, Pedro Domecq, Garvey and Harveys. Most bodegas require you to book your visit, though a few offer tours where you can just turn up. Confirm arrangements and hours with the wineries or with the tourist office, which has the contact and tour details for 14 bodegas. Tours are in Spanish, and sometimes English, German and French. Most include sherry tasting.

Wineries where you can turn up without booking include the following:

Bodegas González Byass
WINERY

(Bodegas Tio Pepe; Map p120; ☑956 35 70 16; www .bodegastiopepe.com; Calle Manuel María González 12; tour €11, with tapas €16; ⊘tours in English & Spanish hourly 11am-6pm Mon-Sat, to 2pm Sun Oct-Apr) Home of the Tio Pepe brand and one of the biggest sherry houses, handily located just west of the Alcázar. Six or seven tours each are given daily in English and Spanish, and a few in German and French. Reservations can be made online.

Bodegas Sandeman
WINERY

(☑956 15 17 11; www.sandeman.com; Calle Pizarro 10; tour in English €7, with tasting €14; ⊘tours hourly

11.30am-2.30pm Mon, Wed & Fri, 10.30am & hourly noon-3pm Tue & Thu, 11am, 1pm & 2pm Sat) Sandeman sherries carry the black-caped 'Don' logo. Visits include an audiovisual presentation and a tasting of three sherries.

Bodegas Tradición   WINERY
(☑956 16 86 28; www.bodegastradicion.com; Plaza Cordobeses 3; tours €18; ☺9am-6.30pm Mon-Fri, 10am-2pm Sat Mar-Jun, 8am-3pm Sat Jul & Aug) An interesting bodega, not only for its extra-aged sherries (20 or more years old), but because it houses the Colección Joaquín Rivera, a private Spanish art collection that includes important works by Goya,

Velázquez and Zurbarán. Tours of the collection are given three or four times a day.

☆ Festivals & Events

Festival de Jerez   FLAMENCO
(www.festivaldejerez.com) Jerez's biggest celebration of flamenco; late February/early March.

Motorcycle Grand Prix   MOTORCYCLES
Usually in March, April or May. Jerez's **Circuito Permanente de Velocidad** (Racing Circuit; ☑956 15 11 00; www.circuitodejerez.com), on the A382 10km east of town, hosts several

motorcycle- and car-racing events each year, including one of the Grand Prix races of the World Motorcycle Championship.

Feria del Caballo   HORSES
Held in late April or the first half of May, Jerez's weeklong horse fair is one of Andalucía's grandest festivals, with music, dance and bullfights as well as all kinds of equestrian competitions and parades.

Fiestas de Otoño   FLAMENCO, WINE
The 'Autumn Fiestas' celebrate the grape harvest for two weeks or so in September, with flamenco, horse events and the traditional treading of the first grapes on Plaza de la Asunción.

✕ Eating

Jerez food combines a Moorish heritage and maritime influences with English and French touches. Not surprisingly, sherry flavours many local dishes such as *riñones al jerez* (kidneys braised in sherry) and *rabo de toro*.

In addition to the following, some fine tapas bars surround quiet little Plaza Rafael Rivero, about 500m north of Plaza del Arenal, with tables out under the sky.

TOP CHOICE Sabores   CONTEMPORARY ANDALUCIAN €€€
(☎956 32 98 35; www.restaurantesabores.es; Chancillera 21; mains from €12) Not without merit, Sabores is one of Andalucía's best restaurants and is located in what might be Jerez' best hotel, the Chancillería. When the scrambled eggs go gourmet, you know you're onto something special. In actual fact, the eggs are flambéed with cured ham, but whatever the method, the results at this restaurant are melt-in-your-mouth delicious.

You can back it up with dishes such as beef cheek, or creative fish all presented like modern art on your plate.

Cruz Blanca   TAPAS €
(www.lacruzblanca.com; Plaza de la Yerva; tapas €1.80-3) The Cruz whips up good seafood, egg, meat and salad offerings and has tables on a quiet little plaza. The marinated fish in a pesto-inflected sauce could compete for the crown for Jerez' best meal.

Bar Juanito   TAPAS €
(www.bar-juanito.com; Calle Pescadería Vieja 8-10; tapas from €2.20, media raciones €5-7) One of the best tapas bars in Jerez, 60-year-old Bar Juanito, with its outdoor tables and checked tablecloths, is like a slice of village Andalucía in the heart of the city. Its *alcachofas* (artichokes) are a past winner of the National Tapa Competition, but there's so much local cuisine to choose from here and it's all served up with the best local wines. Calle Pescadería Vieja, which runs off Plaza del Arenal, catches a refreshing breeze on a hot day.

El Gallo Azul   SPANISH €€
(Calle Larga 2; raciones from €11.50) Housed in what has become Jerez' signature building, with a circular facade emblazoned with a sherry logo, El Gallo Azul (the Blue Cockerel) has a restaurant upstairs and tapas at street level. It's also an excellent perch to enjoy an afternoon coffee and a slice of cake as the city springs back to life after the siesta.

La Carboná   ANDALUCIAN €€
(☎956 34 74 75; www.lacarbona.com; Calle San Francisco de Paula 2; mains €12.50-16.50; ☺closed Tue) This popular, cavernous restaurant with an eccentric menu occupies an old bodega with a hanging fireplace that's oh-so-cosy in winter. The specialities here include grilled meats and fresh fish, and the quirky quail with foie gras and rose petals. If you can't decide, there is a set menu with Jerez wines (€30).

Mesón El Patio   ANDALUCIAN €€
(Calle San Francisco de Paula 7; mains €8-17; ☺closed Sun evening & Mon) This place combines a touch of refinement with local conviviality. It occupies a restored sherry warehouse, which means lofty ceilings, warm tones and carved wooden chairs, but there are echoes of other eras of the city's history with Moorish-style tile work and a collection of old radios. Above all, the food (a snapshot of Andalucía's obsession with fish and meat dishes) is terrific.

Restaurante Gaitán   ANDALUCIAN €€
(☎956 16 80 21; www.restaurantegaitan.es; Calle Gaitán 3; starters from €8.50, mains from €12; ☺closed Sun) There's an intimacy to the eating experience here with a cosy dining area and walls adorned with antlers and photos of past clients. Alongside the staples of Andalucian meat and fish, there are some surprising local twists – the *cordero confitado con miel al brandy de Jerez* (lamb in a honey and Jerez brandy sauce), for example.

A stroll down nearby Calle Porvera, with its breath of lavender from the honour guard of trees, is the perfect encore to the meal.

 Drinking

To find out what's on in Jerez, check www .turismojerez.com, watch for posters and look in the newspapers *Diario de Jerez* and *Jerez Información.*

Bar Gitanería   BAR, FLAMENCO
(Calle Ancha 18) Every facet of Jerez' culture is present here: bone-dry sherry, chilled gazpacho soup, bullfighting posters, discarded serviettes on the floor and spontaneous outbreaks of flamenco pouring out of the open door. We dare you to walk on by!

Tetería La Jaima   TEAHOUSE
(Calle Chancillería 10; ☉4-11.30pm Mon-Thu, to 2am Fri & Sat, to 9pm Sun) You'll feel more like a Moorish sultan than a 21st-century computer geek reclining in this atmospherically dark tea room decked out with the best in Moroccan paraphernalia. Choose a comfy corner and imbibe one of the fruity, aromatic brews.

☆ **Entertainment**

[TOP CHOICE] **El Lagá Tio Parrilla**   FLAMENCO
(Plaza del Mercado; show plus 2 drinks €25; ☉10.30pm Mon-Sat) A high quota of Roma (both performers and clientele) ensures that this place wins most plaudits for its regular flamenco *tablaos.* Gutsy shows rarely end without rousing renditions of that old Jerez stalwart – the *bulería.*

Centro Cultural Flamenco
Don Antonio Chacón   FLAMENCO
(✆956 34 74 72; Calle Salas 2) One of the best *peñas* in town (and hence Andalucía), the Chacón, named for the great Jerez-born flamenco singer, is run by the Tota twins, who often (note: not always) host top-notch flamenco performers on Saturdays at 10pm. At other times things happen impromptu, especially during the February flamenco festival.

Teatro Villamarta   THEATRE
(✆956 35 02 72; www.villamarta.com; Plaza Romero Martínez) Stages a busy program where you can pick up Bizet, Verdi, Mozart and – of course – a dash of flamenco.

Discoteca Oxi   CLUB
(www.oxixerez.es; Calle Zaragoza 20; ☉9pm-6am Wed-Sat) Jerez' ultimate disco has four different rooms and attracts a young crowd who dance till dawn (7am) at weekends. Theme nights are popular.

ⓘ **Information**
Municipal Tourist Office (✆956 33 88 74; www.turismojerez.com; Plaza del Arenal; ☉9am-3pm & 5-7pm Mon-Fri, 9.30am-2.30pm Sat & Sun)

ⓘ **Getting There & Around**
Air
Jerez airport (✆956 15 00 00; www.aena.es), the only one serving Cádiz province, is 7km northeast of town on the NIV. Over a dozen airlines fly into Jerez from elsewhere in Europe including:

JEREZ' FERTILE FLAMENCO SCENE

Jerez' moniker as the 'cradle of flamenco' is regularly challenged by aficionados in Cádiz and Seville, but the claim has merit. This surprisingly untouristed city harbours not just one but *two* Roma quarters, **Santiago** and **San Miguel**, which, between them, have produced a glut of renowned artists including Roma singers Manuel Torre and António Chacón. Like its rival cities to the north and west, Jerez has also concocted its own flamenco *palo* (musical form), the intensely popular *bulerías*, a fast, rhythmic musical style with the same *compás* (accented beat) as the *soleá.*

Explorations of Jerez' flamenco scene ought to start at the Centro Andaluz de Flamenco (p119), Spain's only bona fide flamenco library, where you can pick up information on clubs, performances and singing/dance/guitar lessons. From here you can stroll down Calle Francos and visit legendary flamenco bars such as **Damajuana** (Map p120; www .damajuanacafebar.com; Calle Francos 18; ☉4.30pm-3am Tue-Sun) and **El Arriate** (Map p120; Calle Francos 41) where singers and dancers still congregate. To the north, in the Santiago quarter, you'll find dozens of *peñas* (small private clubs) all known for their accessibility and intimacy; entrance is normally free if you buy a drink at the bar. The *peña* scene is particularly fertile during the February flamenco festival, which is arguably Andalucía's finest.

CÁDIZ PROVINCE & GIBRALTAR JEREZ DE LA FRONTERA

Air-Berlin (www.airberlin.com) From Mallorca and Düsseldorf (seasonal).
Iberia (www.iberia.com) Daily to/from Madrid.
Ryanair (www.ryanair.com) From Barcelona and London-Stansted (seasonal).

Taxis from the airport start at €14. The local airport buses M050 and M051 (€1, 30 minutes) run 12 times daily Monday to Friday and six times daily on weekends. From Jerez this service continues to El Puerto de Santa María and Cádiz.

Bus
The **bus station** (956 33 96 66; Plaza de la Estación) is 1.3km southeast of the centre.

TO	FARE (€)	DURATION	FREQUENCY
Arcos de la Frontera	3	45min	3 daily
Cádiz	2	1hr	9 daily
El Puerto de Santa María	1.60	20min	15 daily
Ronda	1.50	3hr	3 daily
Sanlúcar de Barrameda	2	30min	7 daily
Seville	7.50	1¼hr	11 daily

Car
Parking Doña Blanca (cnr Plaza Estévez & Calle Doña Blanca; per 24hr €15)

Train
The Jerez train station is right beside the bus station. Regular trains go from here to El Puerto de Santa María (€2.20, 10 minutes, 15 daily) and Cádiz (€5, 40 minutes, 15 daily), and 10 or more trains go to Seville (€9.15, 1¼ hours) daily.

Around Jerez de la Frontera

La Cartuja Monastery   MONASTERY
(Cartuja de Santa María de la Defensión; 956 15 64 65; Carretera Jerez-Algeciras; gardens 9.30-11.15am & 12.45-6.30pm Tue-Sat, mass 8am Tue-Sat, 5.30pm Mon & Sun) This monastery is an architectural gem founded in the 15th century, set amid lovely gardens beside the A381, 9km from central Jerez. The early Carthusian monks here are credited with breeding the Cartujano at a time when the horse's popularity had declined. You can look around the gardens and admire the church's impressive baroque facade, but you can only peep inside during mass.

Yeguada de la Cartuja – Hierro del Bocado   HORSE SHOW
(956 16 28 09; www.yeguadacartuja.com; Finca Fuente del Suero; adult/child €18/13; 11am-1pm Sat) This stud farm is dedicated to improving the Cartujano stock, on land that once belonged to La Cartuja Monastery. You're allowed to take a look around, followed by a spectacular show consisting of free-running colts, demonstrations by a string of mares, and dressage. You need to book ahead.

To get here, turn off the A381 at the 'La Yeguada' sign 5km after La Cartuja, and follow the side road for 1.6km to the entrance.

THE WHITE TOWNS

Zahara de la Sierra
POP 1500
Rugged Zahara, set around a vertiginous crag at the foot of the Grazalema Mountains, hums with Moorish mystery. For over 150 years in the 14th and 15th centuries, it stood on the old medieval frontier facing off against Christian Olvera clearly visible in the distance. These days Zahara encapsulates all of the best elements of a classic white town and is popular as a result. Come during the afternoon siesta, however, and you can still hear a pin drop.

The precipitous road over the ultrasteep 1331m Puerto de los Palomas (Doves' Pass) links Zahara with Grazalema (18km) and is a spectacular ride full of white-knuckle switchbacks (try it on a bike!).

Sights & Activities
Zahara village centres on Calle San Juan, where you'll find the natural park's helpful **Punto de Información Zahara de la Sierra** (956 12 31 14; Plaza del Rey 3; 9am-2pm & 4-7pm).

Zahara's streets invite investigation, with vistas framed by tall palms and hot-pink bougainvillea. To climb to the 12th-century castle keep, take the path almost opposite the Hotel Arco de la Villa – it's a steady 10- to 15-minute climb. The castle's recapture from the Christians by Abu al-Hasan of Granada, in a night raid in 1481, provoked the Catholic Monarchs to launch the last phase of the Reconquista, which ended with the fall of Granada.

SETENIL DE LAS BODEGAS

While most white towns sought protective status atop lofty crags, the people of Setenil did the opposite and burrowed into the dark caves beneath the steep cliffs of the Río Trejo. The strategy clearly worked. It took the Christian armies a 15-day siege to dislodge the Moors from their well-defended positions in 1484. Many of the original cave-houses remain and some have been converted into bars and restaurants. Further afield, you can hike along a 6km path (the Ruta de los Molinos) past ancient mills to the next village of Alcalá del Valle.

The tourist office is near the top of the town in the 16th-century **Casa Consistorial**, which exhibits a rare wooden Mudéjar ceiling. A little higher up is the 12th-century **castle** (opening hours are sporadic; check at tourist office) captured by the Christians just eight years before the fall of Granada.

Setenil has some great tapas bars that make an ideal pit stop while you study its unique urban framework. Start in **Restaurante Palermo** in Plaza de Andalucía at the top of town and work your way down.

Olvera

POP 8500

A bandit refuge until the mid-19th century, Olvera has come in from the cold and now supports more family-run farming cooperatives than anywhere else in Spain. As a white town par excellence, it is also renowned for its olive oil, striking Renaissance church, and roller-coaster history that started with the Romans.

◉ Sights & Activities

Most come to Olvera for the Vía Verde de la Sierra, but there are other sights worth checking out if you're in town.

Built on top of an older church, the neoclassical **Iglesia Parroquial Nuestra Señora de la Encarnación** (Plaza de la Iglesia; ☉Sun Mass) was commissioned by the dukes of Osuna and completed in 1843. Perched above it is the 12th-century Nasrid **Castillo Árabe** (Plaza de la Iglesia; admission free; ☉9am-2pm Tue, Thu, Sat & Sun). Next door in **La Cilla** (Plaza de la Iglesia; ☉10.30am-2pm & 4-7pm Tue-Sun), an old grain store of the dukes of Osuna, you'll find the tourist office, the fascinating Museo La Frontera y los Castillos and the Vía Verde de la Sierra Interpretive Centre relating the natural history of the nearby bike path. All share the same opening times.

✕ Eating

Bodega La Pitarra   ANDALUCIAN €€
(www.bodegalapitarra.com; Julián Besteiro 44; media raciones €8-10) Part of a small chain of bo-

dega restaurants, most of which are based in Seville, this Olvera outpost hits all the right notes with friendly staff, football on the TV, and a memorable goat's cheese, honey and peach jam tapa that is a godsend to returning Vía Verde cyclists.

Grazalema

POP 2200

A true mountain white town, Grazalema looks like it has been dropped from a passing spaceship onto the steep rocky slopes of its eponymous mountain range. Few *pueblos blancos* are as generically perfect as this one with its spotless whitewashed houses sporting rust-tiled roofs and wrought-iron window bars. Grazalema embraces the great outdoors with hikes fanning out in all directions, but it's also an age-old producer of blankets, honey, meat-filled stews and a adrenalin-filled bull-running festival. There's an artisan textile factory in the town that still employs traditional weaving methods.

◉ Sights & Activities

The village centre is the pretty Plaza de España, overlooked by the 18th-century Iglesia de la Aurora and refreshed by a medieval fountain. A trio of good cafe-bars liven up the scene. A small information office is located down nearby Calle Mateos Gago overlooking a viewpoint. You can follow a recently restored medieval path into the valley below.

HOSTAL R.G.
\# LA Mejorana. net   58€

DON'T MISS

VÍA VERDE DE LA SIERRA

Regularly touted as the finest of Spain's prophetic *vía verdes* (greenways which have transformed old railway lines into traffic-free thoroughfares for bikers, hikers and horse-riders), the **Vía Verde de la Sierra** (www.fundacionviaverdedelasierra.com) between Olvera and Puerto Serrano is one of 17 such schemes in Andalucía. Aside from its wild, rugged scenery, the greenway is notable for four spectacular viaducts, 30 tunnels (with sensor-activated lighting), and three old stations-turned-hotels/restaurants that are spread over a 36km route. Ironically, the train line that the greenway follows was never actually completed. Constructed in the 1920s as part of the abortive Jerez to Almargen railway, the project's private backers went bankrupt during the Great Depression and the line wasn't used. After languishing for decades, it was restored in the early 2000s.

The unique **Hotel/Restaurante Estación Verde** (☑661 463207; Olvera; s/d/apt €30/50/130) just outside Olvera is the official start of the route. You can hire a multitude of bikes here, including tandems, kids' bikes and chariots, from €10 a day. Bike hire is also available at Coripe and Puerto Serrano stations. Other facilities include a kids' playground, exercise machines and the Patrulla Verde, a helpful staff of bike experts who dole out info and can help with mechanical issues.

A highlight of the Vía Verde is the **Peñon de Zaframagón**, a distinctive crag that acts as a prime breeding ground for griffon vultures. The **Centro de Interpretación y Observatorio Ornitologico** (adult/child €2/1; ☉10am-4pm), encased in the former Zaframagón station building 16km west of Olvera, allows close-up observations activated directly from a high definition camera placed up on the crag.

The Vía Verde de la Sierra is open 365 days a year. The path is well maintained and relatively flat bar a small climb into Puerto Serrano. It is suitable for all types of cyclists and extremely popular year-round. Devotee cyclists like to tackle it on hot summer nights under a full moon with head torches.

El Calvario-Corazon de Jésus WALKING
A short 40-minute return walk starting from a car park at the top of the town leads up to **El Calvario**, a hermitage ruined during the civil war, and a larger-than-life statue of Jesus called the **Corazón de Jésus**. There are fine views over the mountains and village.

🏃 **Horizon** ADVENTURE SPORTS
(☑956 13 23 63; www.horizonaventura.com; Calle Corrales Terceros 29) Horizon, a block off Plaza de España, is a highly experienced adventure firm that will take you climbing, bungee jumping, canyoning, caving, paragliding or walking, with English-speaking guides. Prices per person range from around €14 for a half-day walk to over around €60 for the 4km underground wetsuit adventure from the Cueva del Hundidero near Montejaque to the Cueva del Gato near Benaoján. Minimum group sizes apply for some activities.

✖ Eating

Restaurante El Torreón ANDALUCIAN €€
(www.restauranteeltorreongrazalema.com; mains €8-12) This friendly mountain restaurant is where you can take a break from the Cádiz fish monopoly with local chorizo, spinach, soups and the menu speciality, partridge. There's pasta for kids.

Cafeteria Rumores CAFE €
(Plaza de España) 'Rumores' is where most of the local ones start judging by the loquaciousness of the clientele. Drop by for breakfast churros. There's also an onsite pastry shop.

Parque Natural Sierra de Grazalema

Of all Andalucía's protected areas, Parque Natural Sierra de Grazalema is the most accessible and best set up for lung-stretching sorties into the countryside. Though not as lofty as the Sierra Nevada, the park's rugged

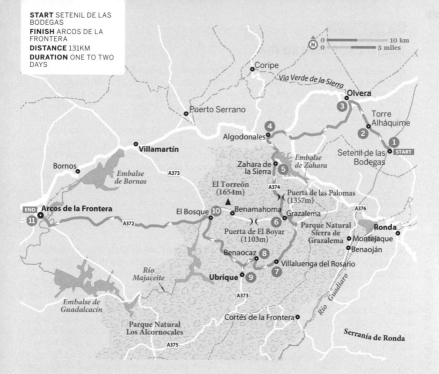

START SETENIL DE LAS BODEGAS
FINISH ARCOS DE LA FRONTERA
DISTANCE 131KM
DURATION ONE TO TWO DAYS

Coripe

Vía Verde de la Sierra

Puerto Serrano

Olvera ③

Torre Alháquime ②

④

Algodonales

Setenil de las Bodegas ① **START**

Villamartín

Bornos

Embalse de Bornos

A373

Zahara de la Sierra ⑤

Embalse de Zahara

El Torreón (1654m) ▲

A374

Puerta de las Palomas (1357m)

A376

END **Arcos de la Frontera**
⑪

El Bosque ⑩

Benamahoma

Grazalema

Ronda

A372

) (⑥
Puerta de El Boyar (1103m)

Parque Natural Sierra de Grazalema

Montejaque

Benaoján

Benaocaz ⑧

Villaluenga del Rosario ⑦

Río Majaceite

Ubrique ⑨

A373

Embalse de Guadalcacín

Cortés de la Frontera

Río Guadiaro

Parque Natural Los Alcornocales

A375

Serranía de Ronda

0 ___ 10 km
0 ___ 5 miles

Driving Tour
Sierra de Grazalema

❭ Rev up in ① **Setenil de las Bodegas** close to the border with Málaga province, a town instantly recognisable for its cave houses once used for storing wine and today offering a shady antidote to the summer heat. Winding north on CA9120 you'll pass ② **Torre Alháquime**, a little-known white town with a 13th-century Moorish castle. CA9106 takes you into ③ **Olvera**, visible for miles around thanks to its lofty neo-Renaissance church and Almohad castle, but also known for its high-quality olive oil and *vía verde* cycle path. The A384 threads west from here, passing Europe's largest griffon vulture colony at Peñón de Zaframagón, to ④ **Algodonales** on the cusp of Parque Natural de Grazalema, a white town known for its guitar-making workshop and hang-gliding/paragliding obsession. In the lee of the Grazalema Mountains above a glassy reservoir, ⑤ **Zahara de la Sierra** is a quintessential white town with a huddle of houses stretched around the skirts of a rocky crag. Count the switchbacks on steep CA9104 as you climb up to the

view-splayed Puerta de las Palomas and, beyond the village of ⑥ **Grazalema**, a red-roofed park-activity nexus also famous for its blanket-making and homemade honey. Plying the craggy western face of the Sierra on A2302 brings you to tiny ⑦ **Villaluenga del Rosario** with its artisan cheese museum. Further on is equally diminutive ⑧ **Benaocaz**, a start/finish point for numerous Grazalema park hikes and guarder of a historical museum. ⑨ **Ubrique**, close to the borders of the Grazalema and Acornocales Natural Parks, is a leather-making centre. Ply its specialist shops for bargains. You can motor more freely on to ⑩ **El Bosque**, the western gateway to Cádiz province's high country and location of the natural park's main information centre. Though the mountains quickly melt away as you track further west on A372, the drama returns at ⑪ **Arcos de la Frontera**, a Roman-turned-Moorish-turned Christian citadel perched atop a steep sandstone cliff.

DON'T MISS

SALTO DEL CABRERO HIKE

Of the park's free-access paths, the most dramatic is the 7.2km **Sendero Salto del Cabrero** that tracks between Grazalema and Benaocaz via the Puerto del Boyar traversing the western flanks of the Sierra del Endrinal. You can make this into a decent round-trip excursion starting and finishing in Grazalema village by taking the **Sendero Los Charcones** from the top of the village to the Puerta del Boyal (1.8km). From here the Sendero del Cabrero, which proceeds mainly downhill through a broad vista-laden valley, is well signposted. Look out for rare wild orchids along the way. On reaching Benaocaz grab a tapa or two in **Bar Las Vegas** (Plaza de Libertades 7) with its spectacular Sierra views. A daily bus returns from Benaocaz to Grazalema, leaving from a stop on the main road at 3.40pm. You can extend the hike by following an old Roman road from Benaocaz down to Ubrique (this is part of the E4 cross-continental path) where a return bus leaves at 3.30pm. Reserve a good five hours for the Grazalema to Benaocaz hike, or six hours with the Ubrique extension.

pillarlike peaks nonetheless rise abruptly off the plains northeast of Cádiz, revealing precipitous gorges, wild orchids and hefty rainfall (stand aside Galicia and Cantabria, this is the wettest part of Spain, logging an average 2000mm annually). Grazalema is also fine walking country (the best months are May, June, September and October). For the more intrepid there are opportunities for climbing, caving, canyoning, kayaking and paragliding.

The park, which was nominated as Spain's first Unesco Biosphere Reserve in 1977, extends into northwestern Málaga province, where it includes the Cueva de la Pileta.

🏃 Activities

Hiking, birdwatching, canyoning, caving, rock climbing and cycling; there's a lot you can do in this protected area. For the more technical stuff, it's best to go with a guide. Horizon (p126), based in Grazalema village, is probably the most respected outfit.

Hiking

The Sierra de Grazalema is criss-crossed by beautiful trails, many of which require a free permit from the **Centro de Visitantes El Bosque** (📞956 72 70 29; Calle Federico García Lorca 1; ⏰10am-2pm & 5-7pm Mon-Sat, 9am-2pm Sun). In peak season (April to June, and September to October) you'll need to contact the centre at least a week in advance of your hike.

El Torreón (1654m) is the highest peak in Cádiz province and from the summit on a clear day you can see Gibraltar, the Sierra Nevada and the Rif Mountains of Morocco. The usual route starts 100m east of the Km40 marker on the Grazalema–Benamahoma road, about 8km from Grazalema. It takes about 2½ hours of walking to reach the summit and 1½ hours back down.

The 14km **Pinsapar** walk runs between Grazalema and Benamahoma and takes around six hours. Apart from the beautiful scenery, watch out for the *pinsapo*, a dark-green Spanish fir that's a rare and beautiful relic of the great Mediterranean fir forests of the Tertiary period, and survives in significant numbers only in pockets of southwest Andalucía and northern Morocco. The trailhead is signposted off the CA531 (the road to Zahara de la Sierra), a 40-minute uphill walk from Grazalema.

The path into the **Garganta del Verde** (literally 'Green Throat'), a lushly vegetated ravine more than 100m deep, starts 3.5km from Zahara de la Sierra on the Grazalema road. It passes a large colony of enormous griffon vultures before the 300m descent to the bottom of the gorge. Allow three to four hours' walking if you drive to the start.

The information centres in El Bosque and Grazalema have general maps outlining the main walking possibilities. Far better, equip yourself with a good walking guide such as *Walking in Andalucía* by Guy Hunter-Watts or *Eight Walks from Grazalema* by RE Bradshaw. The best map is Editorial Alpina's *Sierra de Grazalema* (1:25,000), with a walking-guide booklet in English and Spanish. Some of these are sold locally, but don't count on it.

ℹ️ Getting There & Away

Los Amarillos (📞902 21 03 17; www.losamarillos.es) and **Comes** (📞902 19 92 08; www.tgcomes.es) run daily buses from Jerez de la Frontera via Arcos de la Frontera to Olvera (€8,

2¼ hours, three daily) and Setenil de las Bodegas (€9, 2½ hours, three daily). Two of these buses carry onto Málaga (€11, 2¼ hours).

Los Amarillos runs twice-daily buses either way between Zahara de la Sierra and Ronda (€3, one hour). Grazalema has buses to/from Ronda (€2.60, 45 minutes, twice daily); El Bosque (€2.35, 30 minutes, one daily), where you can change for Arcos; and Ubrique/Benaocaz (€2.20, 40 minutes, two daily).

Arcos de la Frontera

POP 31,500

Everything you imagined about a white town miraculously materialises in Arcos de la Frontera: a spectacular cliff-top location, a soporific old town, a fancy *parador,* and a volatile frontier history that meant things weren't always quite as pretty as they look today. The odd tour bus and foreign property speculator do little to dampen the drama.

For a brief period during the 11th century, Arcos was an independent Berber-ruled kingdom. In 1255 it was claimed by Christian King Alfonso X for Seville and it remained 'de la Frontera' (on the frontier) for the next 237 years until the fall of Granada in 1492.

◎ Sights & Activities

The old town captures multiple historical eras evoking the ebb and flow of the once-disputed Christian-Moorish frontier. The centre of this quarter is the Plaza del Cabildo. Close your eyes to the modern car park and focus instead on the fine surrounding buildings (all old) and a vertiginous **mirador** (lookout) with views over Río Guadalete. The 11th-century **Castillo de los Duques** (Plaza del Cabildo) is firmly closed to the public, but its outer walls frame classic Arcos views. On the eastern side, the Parador Casa del Corregidor (p297) hotel is a reconstruction of a 16th-century magistrate's house.

Basíllica-Parroquia de Santa María CHURCH
(Map p130; Plaza del Cabildo) On the north side of Plaza del Cabildo, this has to be one of Andalucía's more amazing small churches. If it's open you'll feel privileged checking out the ornate gold-leaf altarpiece (a miniature of the one in Seville cathedral) carved between 1580 and 1608, a striking painting of St Christopher, a 14th-century mural uncovered in the 1970s, an ornate wood-carved choir and some gilded side chapels.

Convento de las Mercedarías CONVENT
(Plaza Boticas; ◎8.30am-2.30pm, 5-7pm) It's not often that buying biscuits feels like going to confession, but step into the vestibule of this ancient convent, push a bell, and a concealed nun on the other side of a wooden partition will invite you to order a bag of sweet treats.

Place your money in a revolving compartment, and within a couple of minutes it will flip back round with your order on it – and no penance.

Iglesia de San Pedro CHURCH
(Calle Núñez de Prado; admission €1; ◎10.30am-2pm & 5-7pm Mon-Fri, 11am-2pm Sat) This is another of Arcos' Gothic-baroque confections, and it sports what is perhaps one of the most magnificent small-church interiors in Andalucía (and it's not depressingly dark, either).

☞ Tours

Walking Tour WALKING TOUR
Guided walking tours (€4, one hour) of the old town's monuments set out from Arcos' tourist office in Calle Cuesta de Belén at 11am Monday to Friday. For an excellent self-guided walking tour of Arcos, pick up the Walking Tour brochure from Casa Campana (p297).

🎪 Festivals & Events

Semana Santa HOLY WEEK
Arcos' Semana Santa (Holy Week) processions are among the most famous in the region and there's no finer Easter spectacle than the hooded penitents inching through the town's pretty narrow streets. The solemnity of Good Friday has its slightly manic counterpoint on Easter Sunday, when a running of the bulls takes over the streets.

Feria de San Miguel RELIGIOUS
Arcos celebrates its patron saint with a four-day fair; held around 29 September.

🍴 Eating

Arcos' restaurant scene has improved of late with old-school bars mixing with new Moroccan fusion places.

TOP CHOICE Bar La Cárcel TAPAS €€
(☏956 70 04 10; Calle Deán Espinosa 18; tapas & montaditos €2.50, raciones €8-12; ◎8am-noon Mon, to late Tue-Sun) A *cárcel* (prison) in name only, this place offers no-nonsense tapas (bank on fajitas, or eggplant with

Arcos de la Frontera

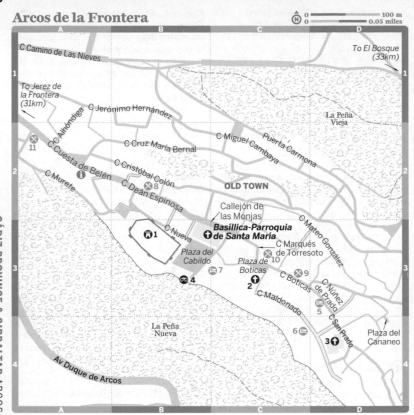

goat's cheese and honey) with ice cold *cañas* of beer for customers who sit at beer barrels doubling up as tables. It's friendly and authentic.

Restaurante-Café Babel   MOROCCAN, FUSION €€
(Calle Corredera 11; dishes €8-12) Arcos' new Moorish fusion spot has some tasteful decor (the ornate stools were shipped in from Casablanca) and some equally tasty dishes: count on tagines and couscous, or the full arabic tea treatment with silver pots and sweet pastries.

Mesón Don Fernando   ANDALUCIAN €
(Calle Boticas 5; mains €9-11; ☺closed Mon) Probably the best of several bars-cum-eateries along the old town's Calle Boticas, Don Fernando has a lively Spanish atmosphere and flamenco soundtrack. Good *montaditos* (little sandwiches) and *raciones* (large tapas serves) are served in the vaulted bar or at the outdoor tables, while the small restaurant focuses on meaty main dishes and tempting desserts.

Las Doce Campanas   CAFE, BREAKFAST €
(Calle Boticas 11; breakfast €3-5) This is the chief breakfast spot (and also a *pastelería*) for those not willing (or able) to pay premier-league prices at the *parador*. The view isn't as good, but the banter's far better.

ℹ Information

Tourist office (☎956 70 22 64; Calle Cuesta de Belén 5; ☺10am-2.30pm & 5.30-8pm Mon-Fri, 10.30am-1.30pm & 5-7pm Sat, 10.30am-1.30pm Sun) The new tourist office also doubles up as a interpretive centre with various scale models and interesting exhibits on the local history and wildlife.

ℹ Getting There & Around

BUS From the **bus station** (☎956 70 49 77), **Los Amarillos** (www.losamarillos.es) and/or **Comes** (www.tgcomes.es) have daily buses

Arcos de la Frontera

(fewer on weekends) to Cádiz (€5, one hour, eight daily), Olvera (€6, 1½ hours, three daily) and Jerez de la Frontera (€3, 45 minutes, 19 daily), Málaga (€17, 3½ hours, two daily) and Ronda (€9, two hours, two daily).

CAR Park in the underground parking on Paseo de Andalucía, then catch the half-hourly minibus (€0.95) to the top of the old town from the adjacent Plaza de España.

COSTA DE LA LUZ & THE SOUTHEAST

Arriving on the Costa de la Luz from the Costa del Sol is like opening the window and breathing in the fresh air. Bereft of tacky resorts and unplanned development, suddenly you can breathe again. More to the point, you're unequivocally back in Spain; a world of flat-capped farmers and clacking dominoes, grazing bulls and Sunday mass followed by a furtive slug of dry sherry. Don't ask why these wide yellow sandy beaches and spectacularly located white towns are so deserted. Just get out and enjoy them while you still can.

Vejer de la Frontera

POP 12,800

Vejer – the jaw drops, the eyes blink, the eloquent adjectives dry up. Looming moodily atop a rocky hill above the busy N340, 50km south of Cádiz, this placid, yet compact white town is somethin special. Yes, there's a cool labyri twisting streets, some serendipitous points and a ruined castle. But Veje sesses something else – soulfulnes_, air of mystery, an imperceptible touch of *duende*, perhaps. The details are for you to decipher.

⊙ Sights

Vejer's imposing walls date from the 15th century and enclose the 40,000-sq-metre old quarter; the ramparts peep out from the old town's perimeter all across Vejer. One of the most accessible stretches is between the Arco de la Puerta Cerrada and the Arco de la Segur, two of the four original gateways to survive; the area around the Arco de la Segur was, in the 15th century, the Judería (the Jewish Quarter).

Iglesia del Divino Salvador CHURCH
(Plaza Padre Ángel; ⊘11am-1pm & 5-7pm Mon, Wed, Fri & Sat, 11am-1pm Tue, Thu & Sun) Not far from the Arco de la Puerta Cerrada, the interior of this church is Mudéjar at the altar end and Gothic at the other. In late afternoon the sun shines surreally through the stained-glass windows, projecting multicoloured light directly above the altar.

Plaza de España SQUARE
The gorgeous palm-filled Plaza de España is many visitors' favourite Vejer corner. Its elaborate Seville-tiled fountain provides the centrepiece, while the white town hall rises up on the south side. For good views down onto the plaza, there's a small mirador above the plaza's western side (and accessible from Calle de Sancho IV).

Casa del Mayorazgo HOUSE
(Callejón de La Villa; admission by donation) If the door's open, as it often is, this 15th-century house has a pretty patio and one of just three original towers that kept watch over the city – the views from here, including down onto Plaza de España, are worth the short climb.

FREE **Castillo** CASTLE
(⊘10am-2pm & 5.30-8.30pm Jul & Aug) Vejer's much-reworked castle has great views from its battlements. Its erratically open small museum preserves one of the black cloaks that Vejer women wore until just a couple of decades ago (covering everything but the eyes).

★ Festivals & Events

Easter Sunday RELIGIOUS
Toro embolao (running of the bulls, with bandaged horns) at noon and 4pm.

Feria SPRING FAIR
Music and dancing nightly in Plaza de España, with one night devoted entirely to flamenco, from 10 to 24 August.

✖ Eating

TOP CHOICE **El Jardín de la Califa** MOROCCAN, FUSION €€
(☎956 44 77 30; Plaza de España 16; starters €6-9, mains €8.30-15; ☑) The atmosphere equals the food in La Califa, an exotically beautiful restaurant (which is also a hotel and *tetería*) buried away in the base of a truly cavernous house where even the trip to the toilets is a full-on adventure.

The menu is primarily Moroccan – tagines and couscous – and, while the presentation is fantastic, it is the Maghreb flavours (saffron, figs and almonds) and succulence of the slow-roasted meat that linger the longest.

La Vera Cruz CONTEMPORARY ANDALUCIAN €€
(☎956 45 16 83; www.restaurantelaveracruz.es; Calle Shelly 1; mains €12-18; ☑lunch Tue-Sun, dinner Thu-Sat) Situated in an old convent with slightly limited opening hours, the 'True Cross' specialises in gourmet tapas such as cold anchovy lasagne and glazed ribs with wasabi purée. Local buzz suggests it's the best in town.

La Posada ANDALUCIAN €
(Avenida Los Remedios; tapas €2-3.50, raciones €7-8; ☑closed Tue) La Posada is an old local hang-out where you can get simple tapas with zero ceremony in a bar filled with *mucho ruido* (a lot of noise). Dig in!

☆ Entertainment

Peña Cultural Flamenca 'El Aguilar de Vejer' FLAMENCO
(Calle Rosario 29; cover charge €3) Part of Vejer's magic is its genuine small-town flamenco scene, best observed in this atmospheric old-town bar/performance space. Singing and guitar lessons are offered Thursday nights.

ℹ Information

Tourist office (☎956 45 17 36; Avenida Los Remedios 2; ☑10am-2pm daily, 6-8pm Mon-Sat approx May-Oct) About 500m below the town centre. Also here is a convenient large, free car park.

ℹ Getting There & Around

Comes (☎902 19 92 08; www.tgcomes.es) buses leave from Avenida Los Remedios. Buses run to Cádiz (one hour) and Barbate (15 minutes) five or six times a day. Buses for Tarifa (45 minutes, 10 daily), Algeciras (1¼ hours, 10 daily), Jerez de la Frontera (1½ hours, two daily), Málaga (2¾ hours, two daily) and Seville (2¼ hours, four daily) stop at La Barca de Vejer, on the N340 at the bottom of the hill. It's a steep 20-minute walk up to town from here or an equally steep €6 in a taxi.

The Vejer Coast

The villages along the coast close to Vejer are some of the least pretentious *pueblos* (villages) anywhere along Spain's shoreline. Sleepy El Palmar, 10km southwest of Vejer, has a lovely 4.8km sweep of white sandy beach that draws surfers from October to May, while Los Caños de Meca, for decades a hippie hideaway, straggles along a series of gorgeous sandy coves beneath a pine-clad hill about 7km southeast of El Palmar. Further down the coast to the southeast, past the fishing port of Barbate, Zahara de los Atunes fronts onto a broad, 12km-long, west-facing sandy beach.

ℹ Getting There & Away

There are regular buses from the Plazuela in Vejer de la Frontera to Barbate – a 10-minute journey. Twice-daily buses links Los Caños de Meca with Seville.

BARBATE
POP 23,000

A newish town set on a beautiful scimitar of Costa de la Luz sand, Barbate's personality is enshrined in its fishing fleet and the way it nets its red tuna (the *almadraba* method), which dates back to Phoenician times. Though modern, Barbate is only 15 minutes by bus from Vejer and is worth visiting for its seafood and hike north to Los Caños de Meca.

⚐ Activities

TOP CHOICE **Parque Natural de la Breña y Marismas de Barbate** WALKING
This small coastal park protects important coastal marshes and pine forest from Costa del Sol–type development. Its prime entry point is the 7.2km **Sendero de Acantilado**

hike between Barbate and Los Caños de Meca along cliff-tops that rival Cabo de Gata in their serendipity.

The high point of the hike is the Torre de Tajo with its tranquil mirador (lookout) perched above the Atlantic. The path starts just west of Barbate's fishing port.

✗ Eating

El Atun Rojo SEAFOOD €€
(www.elatunrojo.com; Avenida Atlántico 21; mains €11-15) Coming to Barbate and not trying the tuna is a form of heresy. You can avoid such faux pas one block from the beach in this slick bar with mainly alfresco seating serving stuffed eggplants, meatballs and – most importantly – tuna prepared all number of ways. The *atún almadraba* with crusted peppercorns and black olives is famously delicious.

LOS CAÑOS DE MECA
POP 300

Never was a town so aptly named as Los Caños de Meca, a proverbial Mecca for many things, not least its beaches, secluded sunbathing, and kiteboarding, windsurfing or just plain old surfing opportunities. The breadth and quality of the yellow-sand beaches here will leave you wondering why Marbella even exists. Once a hippy haven, Caños these days attracts dudes of all nations and varieties. There is but one proviso. Leave your stresses at home. Tranquillity rules here, man!

◉ Sights & Activities
Cabo de Trafalgar LANDMARK
At the western end of Los Caños de Meca, a side road leads out to a lighthouse on a low spit of land, the famous Cabo de Trafalgar. It was off this cape that Spanish naval power was terminated in a few hours one day in 1805 by a British fleet under Admiral Nelson.

A plaque commemorating those who died in the battle was erected at Trafalgar on the bicentennial in October 2005.

Beaches BEACH
Wonderful beaches stretch either side of Cabo de Trafalgar. The main beach is straight in front of Avenida Trafalgar's junction with the Barbate road and is ideal for watching the highly adroit international kiteboarders (who usually launch from here). Nudist beachgoers head to the small headland at its eastern end where there are more secluded beaches, including **Playa de las Cortinas**.

✗ Eating & Drinking
El Pirata SEAFOOD €€
(Avenida Trafalgar 67; mains €9-13; year-round) Enjoying a superb beachside position, this place seems to sum up Caños' hedonism. Enjoy the excellent seafood at lunchtime and come back in the evening for music and dancing that often drifts out onto the beach.

Las Dunas CAFE, BAR
(Carretera del Faro de Trafalgar; 📞) Say hola to the ultimate relaxation spot, at least during the day when kiteboarding dudes kick back between white-knuckle sorties launched from the beach outside. There's free wi-fi, sweet *tortas* (cakes) and a laid-back, beach-shack feel.

Tarifa
POP 17,900

Tarifa's tip-of-Spain location has donned it a different climate and a different personality to the rest of Andalucía. Stiff Atlantic winds draw in surfers, wind-surfers and kiteboarders who, in turn, lend this ancient, yet deceptively small settlement a laidback internationalist image that is noticeably (some would say, refreshingly) at odds with the commercialism of the nearby Costa del Sol. While the town acts as the last stop in Spain before Morocco, it also serves as a taste of things to come. Moroccan fusion food is par for the course here, and the walled old town with its narrow whitewashed streets and ceaseless winds could pass for Chefchaouen or Essaouira on a film set.

Tarifa may be as old as Phoenician Cádiz and it was definitely a Roman settlement, but it takes its name from Tarif ibn Malik, who led a Muslim raid in AD 710, the year before the main Moorish invasion of the peninsula.

◉ Sights & Activities

Tarifa is a town with a long and distinguished history. The diminutive walled old town doesn't have many visitable sights per se, but it does have bags of atmosphere and a tangible North African feel.

Castillo de Guzmán CASTLE
(Calle Guzmán El Bueno; admission €2; 11am-4pm) Originally built in 960 on the orders of Cordoban caliph Abd ar-Rahman III, this fortress is named after the Reconquista hero Guzmán El Bueno. In 1294, when threatened

Tarifa

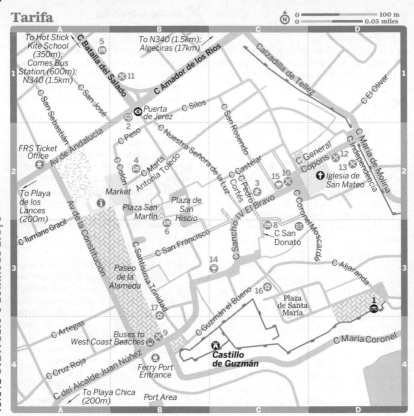

with the death of his captured son unless he surrendered the castle to attacking Islamic forces, El Bueno threw down his own dagger for the deed to be done.

Guzmán's descendants later became the Duques de Medina Sidonia, one of Spain's most powerful families. You'll need to buy tickets for the fortress at the tourist office.

Mirador El Estrecho   LOOKOUT

(Calle Aljaranda) Climb the stairs at the end of Calle Coronel Moscardó and go left on Calle Aljaranda to reach the Mirador El Estrecho atop part of the castle walls. You'll be rewarded with spectacular views across to Africa and 851m Jebel Musa, one of the so-called 'Pillars of Hercules' (Gibraltar is the other).

Beaches   BEACHES

On the isthmus leading out to Isla de las Palomas, tiny **Playa Chica** lives up to its name. Spectacular **Playa de los Lances** is a different matter, stretching northwest for

10km to the huge sand dune at **Ensenada de Valdevaqueros**.

The low dunes behind Playa de los Lances are a natural park and you can hike across them on a raised boardwalk from the end of Tarifa's concrete promenade.

Windsurfing & Kiteboarding

Occupying the spot where the Atlantic meets the Mediterranean, Tarifa's legendary winds have turned the city into one of Europe's premier windsurfing and kiteboarding destinations. The most popular strip is along the coast between Tarifa and Punta Paloma, 10km to the northwest, but you'll see kiteboarders on Tarifa's town beach as well (it's a rather good spectator sport).

Over 30 places offer equipment hire and classes (from beginners to experts, young and old). Recommended are **Club Mistral** (www.club-mistral.com) and **Spin Out** (☏956 23 63 52; www.tarifaspinout.com; El Porro Beach, N340 Km75), both of which are signposted off

Tarifa

the N340 northwest of town. Kiteboarding hire and classes are available from the same places as for windsurfing, or from **Hot Stick Kite School** (☑647 155516; www.hotsticktarifa.com; Calle Batalla del Salado 41).

Pricewise, for kiteboarding you're looking at €70 for a three hour 'baptism,' €135 for a six hour 'initiation,' €180 for a nine hour 'total course.' To hire equipment is €60 per day. You can also train in windsurfing, surfing and paddle-boarding (all €50 for two hours).

Diving

Diving is another possibility. It's generally done from boats around the Isla de las Palomas, where shipwrecks, corals, dolphins and octopuses await. Of the handful of dive companies in Tarifa, try **Aventura Marina** (☑956 05 46 26; www.aventuramarina.org; Avenida de Andalucía 1), which offers 'Discover Scuba Diving' courses (€75, three hours). One-tank dives with equipment rental and guide cost €50.

Whale-Watching

The waters off Tarifa are one of the best places in Europe to see whales and dolphins as they swim between the Atlantic and the Mediterranean between April and October; sightings of some description are almost guaranteed between these months. In addition to striped and bottlenose dolphins, long-finned pilot whales, orcas (killer whales) and sperm whales, you may also, if you're lucky, see endangered fin whales and the misleadingly named common dolphin. The best months for orcas are July and August, while sperm whales are present in the Strait of Gibraltar from April to July. Of the dozens of whale-watching outfits, not-for-profit **FIRMM** (☑956 62 70 08; www.firmm.org; Calle Pedro Cortés 4; ☉Mar-Oct) is a good bet, not least because its primary purpose is to study the whales, record data and encourage environmentally sensitive tours.

Horse Riding

Contemplating Tarifa's wind-lashed coastline (or heading off into the hilly hinterland) on horseback is a terrific way to pass an afternoon or even longer. A one-hour beach ride along Playa de los Lances costs €30, a two-hour beach and-mountain ride costs €50, while three-/five-hour rides start at €70/80. A recommended place with excellent English-speaking guides is **Aventura Ecuestre** (☑956 23 66 32; www.aventuraecuestre.com; Hotel Dos Mares, N340 Km79.5), which also has private lessons (one hour €30), pony rides for kids (half/one hour €15/30) and five-hour rides into the Parque Natural Los Alcornocales. **Molino El Mastral** (☑956 10 63 10; www.mastral.com; Carretera Sanctuario de la Luz), 5km northwest of Tarifa, is also good.

✪ Festivals & Events

Reggae Festival   MUSIC
International and Spanish reggae acts delight the crowds in Tarifa's humble bullring, one night in August.

Feria de la Virgen de la Luz   RELIGIOUS
The town fair in honour of its patron, in the first week in September, mixes religious processions, featuring the area's beautiful horses, and your typical Spanish fiesta.

CÁDIZ PROVINCE & GIBRALTAR TARIFA

GR7: SPAIN'S OTHER CAMINO

After the Camino de Santiago, the *Gran Recorrido 7* (GR7) is probably Spain's most iconic footpath, crossing the nation from Tarifa to Andorra and comprising a crucial segment of the E4 footpath that carries on for 10,000km across Europe and ends in Athens, Greece.

The Andalucian route (1000km worth), which is based on old hunting and trading paths, crosses seven natural and one national park, copious mountain ranges and vast expanses of cultivated and uncultivated land. To do the whole thing would take about 40 days, though most focus on smaller segments, most notably in Las Alpujarras and the area around Grazalema and Ronda.

After tracking northeast from Tarifa across Cádiz and Málaga provinces, the GR7 splits just east of Antequera. The more popular southern portion heads south of the Sierra Nevada through Las Alpujarras. The isolated northern route takes in Córdoba and Jaén provinces including the crinkled Cazorla highlands. The paths rejoin at Puebla de Don Fadrique, which essentially is the end of the Andalucian section of the GR7.

Waymarking (red and white makers plus signposts with distance and/or times to next destination) of the GR7 is sporadic in places. Fortunately Cicerone now produce a comprehensive guidebook detailing every section called *Walking the GR7 in Andalucía* (2007; Kirstie Shirra and Michelle Lowe).

🍴 Eating

Tarifa has an abundance of good eateries many with a strong international flavour (Italian in particular). This is also one of Andalucía's best breakfast spots, with options to break out of the *tostada* (toast) and coffee monotony. Elsewhere you can sample smoothies, gourmet burgers and ethnic fusion food.

Mandrágora MOROCCAN, MIDDLE EASTERN €€
(📞956 68 12 91; Calle Independencia 3; mains €12-18; ☺from 8pm Mon-Sat) Behind Iglesia de San Mateo, this intimate place serves Andalucian-Arabic food and does so terrifically well. It's hard to know where to start, but the options for mains include lamb with plums and almonds, prawns with *ñora* (Andalucian sweet pepper) sauce, and monkfish in a wild mushroom and sea urchin sauce.

Sitting as it does just away from the main eating hub of Tarifa, it attracts a quieter and generally more discerning crowd.

Bamboo BREAKFAST, BAR €
(Paseo de la Alameda 2; snacks from €4) The best of both worlds on the Alameda, Bamboo does great breakfasts plus shakes and smoothies in the morning, and hosts cocktails, music and DJs at night. Decor is Tarifa eclectic (sofas and pouffes) and clientele is surfer cool.

La Oca da Sergio ITALIAN €€
(www.la-oca-da-sergio.artesur.eu; Calle General Copons 6; mains €10-16) Italians rule in Tarifa, at least on the food scene. The amiable Sergio, who roams the tables Italian-style armed dexterously with loaded plates and amusing stories, resides over genuine home-country fare. Bank on homemade pasta, wood-oven thin-crust pizzas, cappuccinos and post-dinner offers of limoncello.

Bar-Restaurante Morilla TAPAS, ANDALUCIAN €€
(📞956 68 17 57; Calle Sancho IV El Bravo 2; mains from €10) One of numerous places lying in wait along Calle Sancho IV El Bravo in the heart of the old town, Morilla attracts more locals than other places. They come here for the high-quality tapas and lamb dishes, and an outstanding *cazuela de pescados y mariscos* (fish-and-seafood stew). Witty waiters scurry between the tables.

Café Azul Bar BREAKFAST €
(Calle Batalla del Salado 8; breakfast €3.50-8; ☺9am-3pm, closed Wed winter) This eccentric place with eye-catching decor has been energised by its Italian owners who prepare the best breakfasts in town. Don't miss the large muesli, fruit salad and yoghurt. There's good coffee, milkshakes, juices, *bocadillos* (filled rolls), crêpes and healthy cakes. In summer, it sometimes opens into the early evening and serves light meals with a Thai or Italian twist.

Drinking & Entertainment

A large ever-changing contingent of surfing and kiteboarding dudes ensures that Tarifa has a decent bar scene focused primarily on narrow Calle Santísima Trinidad and Calle San Francisco, just east of the Alameda.

Don't even bother going out before 11pm. The real dancing starts around 2.30am and ultimate endurance freaks keep bopping until 8am. Many places close on Sunday. Several bars line the southern end of the Alameda.

Café Central   CAFE
(Calle Sancho IV El Bravo 8) The town's best posing spot provides ample opportunities for watching other poseurs. Sweet *churros con chocolate* (fingers of doughnut dipped into a cup of hot chocolate) help pass the time.

Bear House   BAR
(Calle Sancho IV El Bravo 26; ☺2pm-2am) A sort of 'wine bar meets surf bar', the slick new Bear House has low cushioned chill-out sofas, a variety of cocktails, football on the big screen, but no bears.

Al Medina   BAR, TEAHOUSE
(☏669 639751; www.almedinacafe.net; off Plaza de Santa María; ☺10.30pm-2am Wed, 9pm-2am Thu, 10.30pm-3am Fri & Sat) On the steps just down from the Plaza de Santa María at the southern end of the old town, this cosy place stands out for many reasons, but it's the only place in town where you can consistently hear live flamenco (free); this happens on Thursday nights when people spill out onto the steps to catch a cooling evening breeze.

La Ruina   CLUB
(Calle Santísima Trinidad 2; ☺1-4am) This old town ruin with trendy new decor is Tarifa's dance capital, with a steady early-hours diet of electro and house music.

ℹ Information
Tourist office (☏956 68 09 93; www.ayto tarifa.com; Paseo de la Alameda; ☺10am-2pm daily Oct-May, 6-8pm Mon-Fri Jun-Sep) Near the north end of the palm-lined Paseo de la Alameda.

ℹ Getting There & Around
BOAT FRS (☏956 68 18 30; www.frs.es; Avenida Andalucía 16) runs a fast (35-minute) ferry between Tarifa and Tangier in Morocco (one way per adult/child/car/motorcycle €37/20/93/31) up to eight times daily. All passengers need a passport. There is also a ticket office at the Estación Marítima.

BUS Comes (☏956 68 40 38; www.tgcomes.es; Calle Batalla del Salado 13) operates from the small open lot near the petrol station at the north end of Calle Batalla del Salado. It has regular departures to Cádiz, Jerez de la Frontera, La Línea de La Concepción (for Gibraltar), Málaga, Seville and Zahara de los Atunes.

CAR There's free parking (with a guard) east of the old town off Calle El Olivar.

Around Tarifa
Baelo Claudia   RUIN
(☏956 10 67 97; admission €1.50; ☺9am-7pm Tue-Sat Mar-May & Oct, to 8pm Tue-Sat Jun-Sep, to 6pm Tue-Sat Nov-Feb, to 2pm Sun year-round) In the tiny village of Bolonia, signposted off the N340 20km northwest of Tarifa, you'll find the impressive ruins of Roman Baelo Claudia. The ruins' highlights include fine views across the water to Africa, the substantial remains of a theatre, a paved forum, the market, the marble statue and columns of the basilica, and the workshops that turned out

CÁDIZ PROVINCE & GIBRALTAR AROUND TARIFA

ALGECIRAS: GATEWAY TO MOROCCO

The major port linking Spain with Africa is an ugly industrial town and fishing port notable for producing the greatest flamenco guitarist of the modern era, Paco de Lucía, who was born here in 1947. New arrivals usually make a quick departure by catching a ferry to Morocco, or a bus to Tarifa or Gibraltar.

From the bus station on Calle San Bernardo, **Comes** (☏956 65 34 56; www.tgcomes.es) has buses for La Línea (30 minutes, every half-hour), Tarifa (30 minutes, 13 daily), Cádiz (2½ hours, 13 daily), and Seville (2½ hours, six daily).

The adjacent **train station** (☏956 63 10 05) runs services to/from Madrid (€70.90, 5½ hours, two daily) and Granada (€24.80, 4¼ hours, three daily).

The ferry crossing from Algeciras to Tangier with FRS is cheaper than departing from Tarifa, costing per adult/car one way €23/84. There are also five daily crossings to the Spanish Moroccan enclave of Ceuta €31/110.

To get from the bus station in Algeciras to the port, walk approximately 600m east along Calle San Bernardo.

the products – salted fish and *garum* (a spicy seasoning derived from fish) – that made Baelo Claudia famous in the Roman world.

The place particularly flourished in the time of Emperor Claudius (AD 41 to 54) but declined after an earthquake in the 2nd century. There are live musical performances on some July and August evenings. The bus from Tarifa to the ruins run in summer only. Otherwise it's your own wheels.

Parque Natural Los Alcornocales

Los Alcornocales is rich in archaeological, historical and natural interest, but it's well off the beaten track and sparsely populated. There are plenty of walks and opportunities for other activities in the park, but you need your own wheels to make the most of it.

This large (1700 sq km) and beautiful natural park stretches 75km north almost from the Strait of Gibraltar to the border of the Parque Natural Sierra de Grazalema. It's a spectacular jumble of sometimes rolling, sometimes rugged hills of medium height, much of it covered in Spain's most extensive *alcornocales* (cork-oak woodlands).

ℹ Information

Centro de Visitantes Cortes de la Frontera (🕾952 15 45 99; Avenida de la Democracia; ⊙10am-2pm Thu year-round, 10am-2pm & 6-8pm Fri-Sun Apr-Sep, 10am-2pm & 4-6pm Fri-Sun Oct-Mar)

Centro de Visitantes Huerta Grande (🕾956 67 91 61; Km96 N340; ⊙10am-2pm Thu year-round, 10am-2pm & 6-8pm Fri-Sun Apr-Sep, 10am-2pm & 4-6pm Fri-Sun Oct-Mar) On the Tarifa–Algeciras road.

Punto de Información Castillo de Castellar (🕾956 23 66 24; Castellar de la Frontera; ⊙11.30am-2pm & 5-7.30pm Wed-Sun May-Sep, 10am-2pm & 3-5pm Wed-Sun Oct-Apr)

Punto de Información Jimena de la Frontera (🕾956 23 68 82; Calle Misericordia; ⊙10am-2pm & 4-8pm Mon-Fri, 10am-2pm Sat & Sun)

JIMENA DE LA FRONTERA
POP 10,500

Tucked away in crinkled hills on the cusp of the Parque Natural Los Alcornocales, Jimena sits in prime cork-oak country with its blanched whiteness and crumbled castle looking out towards Gibraltar and Africa (both magnificently visible from its Nasrid-

era castle). Property-seeking Brits have discovered the town, but it has managed to keep a Spanish-village feel. The walking trails here are very special, including treks along the cross-continental E4 (GR7) path which bisects the town and forays out to Bronze Age cave paintings at Laja Alta.

◉ Sights & Activites

Castillo de Jimena CASTLE
Jimena's romantically ruined 13th-century Nasrid castle was built on Roman remains and once formed part of a line defence that stretched from Olvera down through Setenil, Zahara and Castellar to Algerciras. Features include Islamic cisterns and the remains of an ancient Mozarab church carved from rock known as **El Baño de Reina Mora**.

Sendero de Río Hozgarganta WALK
The most accessible of many hikes in the area starts at the northwest end of town where a track to the Río Hozgarganta heads left off the road soon after passing the last house. It takes about two hours.

Turn left at the river and follow a stonier path past some old mills, rustling cork oak and the remnants of the **Reales Fábricas de Artillería**, an old artillery factory from 1780s where they made the cannonballs fired at Gibraltar during the famous siege. The track follows the stone-built channels of an old canal to deposit you back in the village.

✗ Eating

TOP CHOICE **Restaurante**
El Anón INTERNATIONAL, FUSION €€
(www.hostalanon.com; Consuelo 34; mains €10-15) Walking into El Anón you'll feel you've stumbled onto one of those 'great finds'. Picture a rambling house full of interesting nooks and ample terraces, the top one of which sports a pool and Africa views. The menu is incredibly varied, with hamburgers listed alongside tagines, poached fish and nutty salads – the highlight being the memorable homemade cheesecake. It also rents rooms.

ℹ Getting There & Away

Trains run daily to Ronda (€6, one hour, three daily) and Algeciras (€4, 40 minutes, three daily) from the station in the village of Los Ángeles (1km from Jimena) or you can catch a Comes bus to the same destinations. Either way the route is incredibly scenic.

GIBRALTAR

POP 29,000

Red pillar boxes, fish-and-chip shops, bobbies on the beat and creaky seaside hotels with 1970s furnishings, Gibraltar – as British writer Laurie Lee once opined – is a piece of Portsmouth sliced off and towed 500 miles south. As with many colonial outposts, 'the Rock', as it's invariably known, tends to overstate its underlying Britishness, a bonus for lovers of pub grub and afternoon tea, but a confusing double-take for modern Brits who thought that their country had moved on since the days of stuffy naval prints and Lord Nelson memorabilia. Stuck strategically at the jaws of Europe and Africa, Gibraltar's Palladian architecture and camera-hogging Barbary apes make an interesting break from the tapas bars and white towns of Cádiz province. Playing an admirable supporting role is its swashbuckling local history; lest we forget, the Rock has been British longer than the United States has been American.

Gibraltarians speak English, Spanish and a curiously accented, singsong mix of the two, slipping back and forth from one to the other, often in mid-sentence. Signs are in English.

History

Both the Phoenicians and the ancient Greeks left traces here, but Gibraltar really entered the history books in AD 711 when Tariq ibn Ziyad, the Muslim governor of Tangier, made it the initial bridgehead for the Islamic invasion of the Iberian Peninsula, landing with an army of some 10,000 men. The name Gibraltar is derived from Jebel Tariq (Tariq's Mountain).

The Almohad Muslims founded a town here in 1159 and were usurped by the Castilians in 1462. Then in 1704 an Anglo-Dutch fleet captured Gibraltar during the War of the Spanish Succession. Spain ceded the Rock of Gibraltar to Britain by the Treaty of Utrecht in 1713, but didn't give up military attempts to regain it until the failure of the Great Siege of 1779–83.

In 1969 Francisco Franco (infuriated by a referendum in which the Gibraltarians voted by 12,138 to 44 to remain under British sovereignty) closed the Spain–Gibraltar border. The same year a new constitution committed Britain to respecting Gibraltarians' wishes over sovereignty, and gave Gibraltar domestic self-government and its own parliament, the House of Assembly. In 1985, just prior to Spain joining the European Community (now the EU) in 1986, the border was opened after 16 long years.

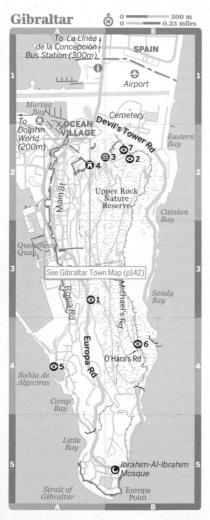

◉ Sights & Activities

Dolphin-Watching

The Bahía de Algeciras has a sizeable year-round population of dolphins and at least three companies run excellent dolphin-watching trips. From about April to September most outfits make two or more daily trips; at other times of the year they make at least one trip daily. Most of the boats go from Watergardens Quay or the adjacent Marina Bay. Trips last from 1½ to 2½ hours. The tourist office has a list of operators, which include **Dolphin World** (☏54481000; Waterport, Ferry Terminal; adult/child £20/10) and **Dolphin Adventure** (☏20050650; www .dolphin.gi; Marina Bay). Advance bookings are essential.

Upper Rock

The Rock, Gibraltar's huge pinnacle of limestone, is one of the most dramatic landforms in southern Europe. The best way to explore the Rock is to take the **cable car** (Lower Cable-Car Station; ☏20077826; Red Sands Rd; adult one way/return £6.50/8, child one way/return £4/4.50; ⊙9.30am-7.15pm Apr-Oct, to 5.15pm Nov-Mar) to the top then walk back down, perhaps catching the cable car at the middle station (if you already have a return ticket) for the final descent if the legs are weary.

DON'T MISS

THE RONDA–ALGECIRAS RAILWAY

The most spectacular train line in Spain? The **Ronda–Algeciras line** (ticket €10.20) is certainly a contender. Opened in 1892 to allow bored British military personnel bivouacked in Gibraltar access to the (then) hidden wonders of Spain, the line was engineered and financed by a couple of wealthy Brits who furnished the towns at each end with two magnificent Victorian-age hotels: the Reina Victoria (Ronda) and the Reina Cristina (Algeciras). Still running on single track, the line traverses some of Andalucía's finest scenery including cork-oak forest, Moorish white towns, boulder-strewn mountainscapes and diminutive 'Thomas the Tank Engine' stations. Trains run three times a day in either direction and take an hour and 45 minutes.

At the top station there are one-of-a-kind views over the Bahía de Algeciras and across the Strait of Gibraltar to Morocco if the weather is clear. You can also look down the sheer precipices of the Rock's eastern side.

TOP CHOICE Upper Rock Nature Reserve

NATURE RESERVE

(Map p142; adult/child incl attractions £10/5, vehicle £2, pedestrian excl attractions £0.50; ⊙9am-6.15pm, last entry 5.45pm) Most of the upper parts of the Rock (but not the main lookouts) come within the Upper Rock Nature Reserve; entry tickets include admission to St Michael's Cave, the Apes' Den, the Great Siege Tunnels, the Moorish castle, Military Heritage Centre, the 100-tonne supergun and the 'Gibraltar: A City Under Siege' exhibition. The upper Rock is home to 600 plant species and is the perfect vantage point for observing the migrations of birds between Europe and Africa.

The Rock's most famous inhabitants are the tailless Barbary macaques. Some of the 200 apes hang around the top cable-car station, while others are found at the **Apes' Den** (Map p139), near the middle cable-car station, and the **Great Siege Tunnels**. Legend has it that when the apes (which may have been introduced from North Africa in the 18th century) disappear from Gibraltar, so will the British. Summer is the ideal time to see newborn apes, but keep a safe distance to avoid their sharp teeth and short tempers, for which they're well known.

About 15 minutes' walk down St Michael's Rd from the top cable-car station, O'Hara's Rd leads up to the left to **O'Hara's Battery**, an emplacement of big guns on the Rock's summit. A few minutes further down is the extraordinary **St Michael's Cave** (Map p139; www.gibraltar.gov .gi; St Michael's Rd; ⊙9.30am-7.15pm), a spectacular natural grotto full of stalagmites and stalactites. In the past people thought the cave was a possible subterranean link with Africa. Today, apart from attracting tourists in droves, it's used for concerts, plays and even fashion shows. For a more extensive look at the cave system, the **Lower St Michael's Cave Tour** (ticket £8; ⊙6pm Wed, 2.30pm Sat) is a three-hour guided adventure into the lower cave area. Wear appropriate footwear. Children must be over 10 years old. Contact the tourist office to arrange a guide.

CÁDIZ PROVINCE & GIBRALTAR PARQUE NATURAL LOS ALCORNOCALES

MIGRATING BIRDS

One of Gibraltar's best views is right above your head. The Strait of Gibraltar is a key point of passage for migrating birds between Africa and Europe. Soaring birds such as raptors, black-and-white storks and vultures rely on thermals and updraughts, and there are just two places where the seas are narrow enough for the stork to get into Europe by this method. One is the Bosphorus between the Black Sea and the Sea of Marmara; the other is right here at the Strait of Gibraltar. White storks sometimes congregate in flocks of up to 5000 to cross the strait. In general, northward migrations occur between mid-February and early June, and southbound flights between late July and early November. When a westerly wind is blowing, Gibraltar is usually a good spot for seeing the birds. When the wind is calm or easterly, the Tarifa area is usually better.

About 30 minutes' walk north (downhill) from the top cable-car station is Princess Caroline's Battery, housing the **Military Heritage Centre** (Map p139). From here one road leads down to the Princess Royal Battery – more gun emplacements – while another leads up to the **Great Siege Tunnels** (Map p139; adult/child £8/4, price given is for admission by road - pedestrians pay less; ⊙9.30am-7pm), a complex defence system hewn out of the Rock by the British during the siege of 1779–83 to provide gun emplacements. The **WWII tunnels** (Map p139; adult/child £8/free; ⊙10am-5pm Mon-Fri) where the Allied invasion of North Africa was planned can also be visited, but this isn't included on your nature-reserve ticket. Even combined, these tunnels constitute only a tiny proportion of more than 70km of tunnels and galleries in the Rock, most of which are off limits to the public.

On Willis's Rd, the way down to the town from Princess Caroline's Battery, you'll find the 'Gibraltar: A City Under Siege' exhibition, in the first British building on the Rock, and the **Moorish Castle** (Tower of Homage; Map p139), the remains of Gibraltar's Islamic castle built in 1333.

Ginbraltar Town

Most Gibraltar sojourns start in Grand Casemates Sq, which once hosted public executions and is accessible through Landport Tunnel (once the only land entry through Gibraltar's walls), then continue along Main St, a slice of British high street with a Mediterranean lilt.

Gibraltar Museum   MUSEUM
(Map p142; Bomb House Lane; adult/child £2/1; ⊙10am-6pm Mon-Fri, to 2pm Sat) Gibraltar's history is swashbuckling to say the least and it quickly unfolds in this fine museum –

comprising a labyrinth of rooms large and small – from Neanderthal to medieval to the infamous 18th-century siege. Don't miss the well-preserved Muslim bathhouse and an intricately painted 7th-century-BC Egyptian mummy that washed up here in the late 1800s.

Trafalgar Cemetery   CEMETERY
(Map p142; Prince Edward's Rd; ⊙8.30am-sunset) Gibraltar's cemetery gives a very poignant history lesson, with its graves of British sailors who died at Gibraltar after the Battle of Trafalgar in 1805.

Nelson's Anchorage   LANDMARK
(Map p139; Rosia Rd; admission £1; ⊙9am-6.15pm) South of Trafalgar Cemetary, Nelson's Anchorage pinpoints the site where Nelson's body was brought ashore from HMS *Victory* – preserved in a rum barrel, so legend says. A 100-tonne Victorian supergun, made in Britain in 1870, commemorates the spot.

✖ Eating

Goodbye tapas, hello fish and chips. Gibraltar's food is unashamedly British. The staples are pub grub, beer and sandwiches, chips and stodgy desserts. Grand Casemates Sq has a profusion of cooler, more modern Euro-cafes, though the newest movers and shakers (including some good ethnic places) can be found in Marina Bay's spanking new Ocean Village.

TOP
CHOICE **Bistro Madeleine**   CAFE, BISTRO €
(Map p142; 256 Main St; cakes from £3; ⊙9am-11pm; 🅟🅙) If you've just polished off steak-and-ale pie in the local pub, come for your dessert to this refined, smoke-free bistro where they serve Illy coffee with big chunks of English-inspired cake. The toffee-and-date cake is outstanding.

CÁDIZ PROVINCE & GIBRALTAR PARQUE NATURAL LOS ALCORNOCALES

Gibraltar Town

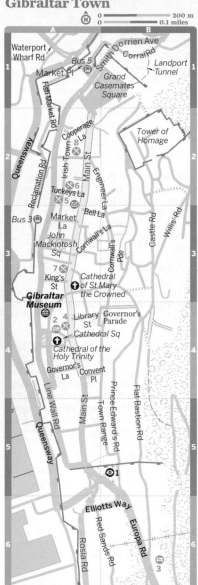

ed round the Bay of Biscay to keep the Brits happy. Full English breakfast is served from 9.30am to 11am.

Royal Calpe PUB €€
(Map p142; 176 Main St; mains £8-12) If halfway through your quintessential Gibraltar pub crawl, you get an unstoppable urge for heavily crusted meat pies, fish and chips, and a pint of Caffrey's *without* the cigarette smoke (yes, you can still smoke inside Gibraltar pubs), roll into the Royal Calpe; its non-smoking rear conservatory is popular with young mothers, health freaks and the nicotine-patch brigade. The food – classic pub grub – is none the worse for it.

House of Sacarello INTERNATIONAL €€
(Map p142; 57 Irish Town; daily specials £7-11.50; ⊙9am-7.30pm Mon-Fri, to 3pm Sat, closed Sun; 🗹) A jack of all trades and master of...well... some, House of Sacarello is located in an old coffee warehouse and serves a good range of vegetarian options and some tasty homemade soups, alongside pastas, salads and a few pub-style dishes; check out its daily specials. You can linger over afternoon tea (£3.50) between 3pm and 7.30pm. It also hosts regular art exhibitions.

Star Bar PUB €€
(Map p142; 12 Parliament Lane; breakfast £3.50-5, mains £5-11; ⊙24hr) Gibraltar's oldest bar, if the house advertising is to be believed, the Star Bar is small, smoky and – judging by the wall art – contains diehard supporters of British football team Tottenham Hotspur. If none of this puts you off, squeeze inside

Clipper BRITISH €€
(Map p142; 78B Irish Town; mains £3.50-9; 🗹) Full of that ubiquitous naval decor, the Clipper offers real pub grub, genuine atmosphere and Premier League football on big-screen TV. Picture a little piece of Portsmouth float-

GIBRALTAR PRACTICALITIES

Visas & Documents

To enter Gibraltar, you need a passport or EU national identity card. EU, American, Canadian, Australian, New Zealand and South African passport-holders are among those who do not need visas for Gibraltar. For further info contact Gibraltar's Immigration Department.

Money

The currencies are the Gibraltar pound (£) and pound sterling, which are interchangeable. You can spend euros (except in pay phones and post offices) but conversion rates are poor. Change unspent Gibraltar currency before leaving. Banks are generally open from 9am to 3.30pm weekdays. There are several on Main St.

Telephone

To phone Gibraltar from Spain, precede the eight-digit local number with the code 00350; from other countries dial the international access code, then 350 (Gibraltar's country code) and the local number. To make a call to Spain, just dial the nine-digit number. To make a call to any other country, dial the international access code (00), followed by the country code, area code and number.

for lamb chops, Irish fillet, and hake in a Spanish-style green sauce.

ℹ Information

Emergency (☎199) For police or ambulance.

Police Headquarters (☎20072500; Rosia Rd) In the south of the town at New Mole House.

St Bernard's Hospital (☎20079700; Europort) Twenty-four-hour emergency facilities.

Tourist office (Grand Casemates Sq; ☺9am-5.30pm Mon-Fri, 10am-3pm Sat, to 1pm Sun & holidays)

ℹ Getting There & Around

Air

Gibraltar's airport has a brand new terminal right next to the border which opened in November 2011.

Easyjet (www.easyjet.com) Flies daily to/from London Gatwick and three times a week from Liverpool.

Monarch Airlines (www.flymonarch.com) Flies daily to/from London Luton and Manchester.

British Airways (www.ba.com) Flies seven times a week from London Heathrow.

Boat

One **ferry** (www.frs.es) a week sails between Gibraltar and Tangier in Morocco (adult/child one-way £46/30, 70 minutes) on Fridays at 7pm. Ferries to/from Tangier are more frequent from Algeciras.

Border Crossings

The border is open 24 hours daily. Bag searches at Spanish **customs** (☎200 50762; Customs House; ☺9am-4:30pm Mon-Fri, 10am-1pm Sat) are *usually* perfunctory.

Bus

There are no cross-border bus services. Bus 5 goes from the border into town (and back) every 15 minutes on weekdays, and every 30 minutes on weekends. The fare is £1. Buses 1, 2, 3 and 4 cover the rest of Gibraltar and are free of charge. The bus station in La Línea de la Concepción is 400m from the border post. **Comes** (☎956 17 00 93; www.tgcomes.es) runs regular buses to/from Algeciras, Cádiz, Granada, Seville and Tarifa from here.

Car & Motorcycle

Gibraltar's streets are congested and vehicle queues at the border make it far less time-consuming to park in La Línea de La Concepción (on the Spanish side of the frontier), then walk across the border (1.5km from the border to Grand Casemates Sq). You do not have to pay any fee (ignore opportunists who say otherwise) to take a car into Gibraltar. In Gibraltar, driving is on the right, as in Spain.

There are car parks on Line Wall Rd and Reclamation Rd, and at the Airport Car Park on Winston Churchill Ave; the hourly charge at these car parks is 80p. Street parking meters in La Línea cost €1 for one hour or €5 for six hours and are free from 8pm until 9am Monday to Friday and from 2pm Saturday until 9am Monday.

Málaga Province

POP 1.6 MILLION

Best Places to Eat

» La Consula (p17)
» Tapeo de Cervantes (p154)
» Venta Garcia (p162)
» Oliva (p179)
» Vino Mio (p154)

Best Places to Stay

» El Molino de los Abuelos (p301)
» El Molino del Santo (p300)
» Claude (p300)
» Hostal Larios (p298)

Why Go?

Málaga is a delightful city, intrinsically Andalucian, yet with an increasingly innovative streak. It is also developing into something of a gourmet and culture capital; the historic centre has an astonishing 400-plus restaurants and bars, and is home to some world-class museums. Base yourself here and discover the equally fascinating diversity of the region, ranging from the breathtaking mountains and rural scenery of La Axarquía to the tourist-driven razzle dazzle of the Costa del Sol.

Inland are traditional *pueblos blancos* (white villages) crowned by the spectacularly situated fabled town of Ronda. Visit, too, the underappreciated, yet superbly elegant, old town of Antequera with its nearby archaeological site and fabulous *porra antequera* (garlic-laden soup).

Try to time your visit to coincide with one of the annual celebrations, when the party atmosphere is infused with flamenco, fino (sherry) and carafe-loads of fiesta spirit.

Driving Distances (km)

	Málaga	Antequera	Ronda	Mijas
Antequera	40			
Ronda	64	87		
Mijas	25	70	70	
Nerja	53	89	117	88

Getting Around

A convenient train service links Málaga and its airport with several Costa del Sol resorts, including Torremolinos and Fuengirola. There is also a reasonable bus service that links the Costa capital and several coastal towns with Ronda and Antequera, as well as trains. Interior roads in La Axarquía and the Serranía de Ronda are among the most scenic in the province so your own wheels are preferable and, overall, pretty essential, as public transport is patchy and slow.

DON'T MISS

Málaga city still gets bypassed by the vast majority of tourists here. Be sure to explore the historic quarter surrounding the cathedral; it is fabulously evocative.

THREE PERFECT DAYS

Day 1: Culture & Cuisine

Pablo Picasso is Málaga's most celebrated son so visit the **Museo Picasso** before strolling to nearby **Plaza Merced** square and the **Casa Natal de Picasso** where he was born. After enjoying tapas at one of several bars circling the square, head to the extraordinary **Museo del Vidrio y Cristal** (Museum of Glass and Crystal – you'll thank us). Afterwards take a stroll around Málaga's evocative old town, followed by Michelin-star tapas at beachfront **La Moraga Antonio Martín**.

Day 2: Explore Ronda

Make an early start to visit the one of the province's most dramatically sited towns, **Ronda**, perched over a vertiginous gorge. The town is a delight to explore with its fascinating museums, traditional tapas bars and historic sights, including the famous Puente Nuevo. Simply wandering around the town with your camera at the ready will provide plenty of evocative memories over a day, but stay overnight if you can to enjoy the surrounding countryside and national park.

Day 3: Mountain Village Tour

Wend your way past stunning scenery to explore the rural villages of La Axarquía, including mountaintop **Comares** and **Cómpeta**; the latter is famed for its local wines. Or opt for an architectural feast in **Antequera**, which is rich with cultural heritage, boasting Roman, Islamic and Spanish historic buildings, plus a fascinating archaeological site. From La Axarquía, consider returning to Málaga via the coast, with a stop at the low-key resort of **Nerja** for a plate of fried fish on the beach.

Best Beaches

» La Carihuela (Torremolinos; p158)

» Playa Burriana (Nerja; p178)

» Playa el Palo (Málaga; p153)

Best Family Attractions

» Biopark (p159)

» Tivoli World (p158)

» Selwo Aventura (safari park; p162)

» Mariposario de Benalmádena (butterfly park; p158)

Resources

» **Málaga City** (www .malaga.com) Málaga city information.

» **Turismo de Ronda** (www.turismoderonda.es) Ronda tourist board.

» **Sur in English** (www .surinenglish.com) Online English-language newspaper.

» **Costa del Sol** (www .visitcostadelsol.com) Tourist info on Costa resorts.

Accommodation

Málaga city has boosted its number of hotels over recent years, with accommodation ranging from slick business-style, with a trouser press, to homey inexpensive *hostales* (small family-run hotels). For the highest concentration, the Costa del Sol has endless choice, while the rural regions have some outstanding country hotels. Read all about hotel choices in our dedicated Accommodation chapter (p288).

Málaga Province Highlights

1 Soaking up the vibrant street life of **Málaga** (p148)

2 Following the polka dots to the **Feria de Málaga** (p153), the province's top annual fiesta

3 Marvelling at the architectural gems in the old centre of **Antequera** (p171)

4 Admiring breathtaking mountaintop views in **Comares** (p175)

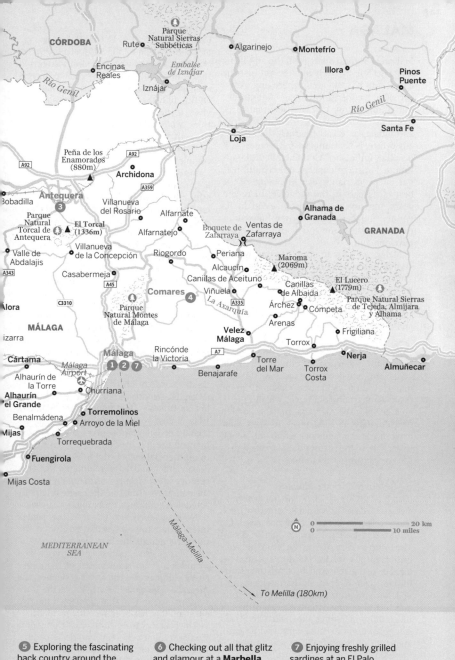

CÓRDOBA

Rute
Parque Natural Sierras Subbéticas
Algarinejo
Montefrío
Encinas Reales
Embalse de Iznájar
Illora
Pinos Puente
Río Genil
Iznájar
Río Genil
Santa Fe
Loja
Peña de los Enamorados (880m)
A92
Archidona
Alhama de Granada
Bobadilla
Antequera
Villanueva del Rosario
A359
Alfarnate
Ventas de Zafarraya
GRANADA
Parque Natural Torcal de Antequera
El Torcal (1336m)
Alfarnatejo
Boquete de Zafarraya
Maroma (2069m)
Valle de Abdalajís
Villanueva de la Concepción
Riogordo
Periana
El Lucero (1779m)
A343
Casabermeja
Alcaucín
Canillas de Aceituno
Canillas de Albaida
Parque Natural Sierras de Tejeda, Almijara y Alhama
Álora
C3310
Comares
Viñuela
La Axarquía
Árchez
Cómpeta
A45
Parque Natural Montes de Málaga
A335
MÁLAGA
izarra
Arenas
Frigiliana
Cártama
Málaga
Rincón de la Victoria
Velez Málaga
Torrox
Nerja
Alhaurín de la Torre
Málaga Airport
A7
Torre del Mar
Torrox Costa
Almuñecar
Alhaurín el Grande
Churriana
Benajarafe
Benalmádena
Torremolinos
Arroyo de la Miel
Mijas
Torrequebrada
Fuengirola
Mijas Costa

MEDITERRANEAN SEA

Málaga-Melilla

0 — 20 km
0 — 10 miles

To Melilla (180km)

⑤ Exploring the fascinating back country around the **Parque Natural Sierra de las Nieves** (p167) near Ronda

⑥ Checking out all that glitz and glamour at a **Marbella nightclub** (p161)

⑦ Enjoying freshly grilled sardines at an El Palo beachside restaurant like **El Tintero** (p155)

MÁLAGA

POP 568,507

Málaga is a world apart from the adjoining Costa del Sol; a briskly modern yet historic city, it still has the atmosphere and swagger of a Mediterranean port. Admittedly, initial impressions can be discouraging as, like most Spanish cities, the shell is drab and industrial. But the kernel, the historic city centre, is charming with its majestic, if peculiar, unfinished Gothic cathedral, surrounded by traditional balconied buildings, narrow pedestrian streets and some of the best tapas bars in the province. In recent years, the city has heavily invested in its culture and heritage with new museums, extensive restoration and a brand-new port development.

Málaga is a joy to stroll around, with a skyline that reflects the city's eclectic character; church spires jostle for space with russet-red tiled roofs and lofty apartment buildings while, like a grand old dame, the 11th-century Gibralfaro castle sits grandly and provides the best view of all.

⊙ Sights & Activities

Essentially a Renaissance city with its wide boulevards and decorative facades, Málaga's major cultural sights are clustered in or near the charming old town, which is situated beneath the Alcazaba and the Castillo de Gibralfaro. A good place to start your exploring is the landmark cathedral, which towers above the surrounding streets and is thus reassuringly easy to find.

TOP CHOICE Museo Picasso Málaga   MUSEUM
(Map p152; ☑902 44 33 77; www.museopicasso malaga.org; Calle San Agustín 8; permanent/temporary collection €6/4.50, combined ticket €8; ⊙10am-8pm Tue-Thu & Sun, to 9pm Fri & Sat) The Museo Picasso has an enviable collection of 204 works, 155 donated and 49 loaned to the museum by Christine Ruiz-Picasso (wife of Paul, Picasso's eldest son) and Bernard Ruiz-Picasso (his grandson), and includes some wonderful paintings of the family, including the heartfelt *Paulo con gorro blanco* (Paulo with a white cap), a portrait of Picasso's eldest son painted in the 1920s.

Be sure to visit the Phoenician, Islamic and Renaissance archaeological remains in the museum's basement which were discovered during construction works.

Cathedral   CATHEDRAL
(Map p152; ☑952 21 59 17; Calle Molina Lario; cathedral & museum €3.50; ⊙10am-6pm Mon-Sat, closed holidays) Málaga's cathedral was started in the 16th century when several architects set about transforming the original mosque. Of this, only the **Patio de los Naranjos** survives, a small courtyard of fragrant orange trees where the ablutions fountain used to be. It was an epic project plagued with problems and which took some 200 years to complete.

Inside, it is easy to see why it took so long. The fabulous domed ceiling soars 40m into the air, while the vast colonnaded nave houses an enormous cedar-wood choir. Aisles give access to 15 chapels with gorgeous retables and a stash of 18th-century religious art. Such was the project's cost that by 1782 it was decided that work would stop.

One of the two bell towers was left incomplete, hence the cathedral's well-worn nickname, La Manquita (the one-armed lady). The cathedral's **museum** displays a collection of religious items covering a period of 500 years. These include sacred paintings and sculptures, liturgical ornaments, and valuable pieces made of gold, silver and ivory.

Castillo de Gibralfaro   CASTLE
(Map p150; admission €2.10; ⊙9am-9pm Apr-Sep, to 6pm Oct-Mar) One remnant of Málaga's Islamic past is the craggy ramparts of the Castillo de Gibralfaro, spectacularly located high on the hill overlooking the city. Built by Abd ar-Rahman I, the 8th-century Cordoban emir, and later rebuilt in the 14th century when Málaga was the main port for the emirate of Granada, the castle originally acted as a lighthouse and military barracks.

Nothing much is original in the castle's interior, but the airy walkway around the ramparts affords the best views over Málaga. There is also a **military museum**, which includes a small scale model of the entire castle complex and the lower residence, the Alcazaba. The model clearly shows the 14th-century curtain wall that connected the two sites and that has been recently restored.

The best way to reach the castle on foot is via the scenic Paseo Don Juan de Temboury, to the south of the Alcazaba. From here a path winds pleasantly (and steeply) through lushly gardened terraces with viewpoints over the city. Alternatively, you can drive up the Camino de Gibralfaro or take bus 35 from Avenida de Cervantes.

MUSEO DEL VIDRIO Y CRISTAL

The **Museo del Vidrio y Cristal** (Museum of Glass & Crystal; Map p152; www.museovidrioy cristalmalaga.com; Plazuela Santísimo Cristo de la Sangre 2; admission €4; ⊙11am-7pm Tue-Sun) may not sound the most riveting collection in the world, but it is wonderfully historic, rich and varied. The museum is housed in an 18th-century palatial house, complete with three central patios, in a charmingly dilapidated part of town. Recently restored by aristocratic owner and historian Gonzalo Fernández-Prieto, this private collection concentrates on glass and crystal but includes antique furniture, priceless carpets, pre-Raphaelite stained-glass windows and huge 16th-century ancestral portraits.

Fascinatingly, the museum is situated on the historic site of the most important Moorish pottery districts in Spain. Exhibits include Roman glass from the 1st century AD, Byzantine glass from the 6th-7th century AD, exquisite Lalique and Venetian Murano glass, and items from the 1930s to 1980s, including Whitefriars, Jobling and George Davidson pieces.

The modest entry price includes a comprehensive tour (in English, French or Spanish), generally by the owner. The museum also hosts regular classical-music and jazz concerts.

There are plans to build a funicular railway up the hill to the Castillo but no completion date was available at the time of research.

Alcazaba
CASTLE
(Map p152; Calle Alcazabilla; admission €2.10, incl Castillo de Gibralfaro €3.40; ⊙9.30am-8pm Tue-Sun Apr-Oct) No time to visit Granada's Alhambra? Then Málaga's Alcazaba can provide a taster. The entrance is next to the **Roman ampitheatre**, from where a meandering path climbs amid lush greenery: crimson bougainvillea, lofty palms, fragrant jasmine bushes and rows of orange trees. Extensively restored, this palace-fortress dates from the 11th-century Moorish period and the caliphal horseshoe arches, courtyards and bubbling fountains are evocative of this influential period in Málaga's history. Don't miss the small **archaeological museum** located within the former servants' quarters of the Nazari palace with its exhibits of Moorish ceramics and pottery.

Museo Carmen Thyssen
MUSEUM
(Map p152; www.carmenthyssenmalaga.org; Calle Compañia 10; adult/child €6/free; ⊙10am-8pm Tue-Sun) One of the city's latest museums opened in 2011 in an aesthetically renovated 16th-century palace in the heart of the city's historic centre, the former old Moorish quarter of Málaga. The extensive collection concentrates on 19th-century Spanish and Andalucian art and includes paintings by some of the country's most exceptional painters, including Joaquín Sorolla y Bastida, Ignacio Zuloaga and Francisco de Zurbarán. Temporary exhibitions similarly focus on 19th-century art.

FREE Palacio Episcopal
PALACE
(Map p152; Plaza del Obispo; ⊙10am-2pm & 6-9pm Tue-Sun) In front of the cathedral spreads the sumptuous Plaza del Obispo, where the blood-red Bishop's Palace, the Palacio Episcopal, forms an exhibition space, generally for sculpture and paintings. This square with its central fountains and aesthetically restored buildings is one of the most beautiful in the city.

FREE Centro de Arte Contemporáneo
MUSEUM
(www.cacmalaga.org; Calle Alemania; ⊙10am-8pm Tue-Sun) The contemporary-art museum is housed in a skilfully converted 1930s wholesale market on the river estuary. The bizarre triangular floor plan of the building has been retained, with its cubist lines and shapes displaying the modern art brilliantly. Painted entirely white, windows and all, the museum exhibits works from well-known contemporary artists such as Tracey Emin and Gilbert & George.

Casa Natal de Picasso
MUSEUM
(Map p152; Plaza de la Merced 15; admission €1; ⊙9.30am-8pm) For a more intimate insight into the painter's childhood, head to the Casa Natal de Picasso, the house where Picasso was born in 1881, which now acts as a study foundation. The house has a replica 19th-century artist's studio and small quarterly exhibitions of Picasso's work. Personal

150

MÁLAGA PROVINCE

Málaga

400 m
0.2 miles

MEDITERRANEAN SEA

LA MALAGUETA

Ferry route to Melilla

OLD TOWN

See Central Málaga Map (p152)

Málaga

memorabilia of Picasso and his family make up part of the display.

Jardín Botánico La Concepción GARDENS
(http://laconcepcion.malaga.eu; adult/child €5.20/3.10; ⊘9.30am-8.30pm Tue-Sun) Four kilometres north of the city centre is this large botanical garden. Dating from the mid-19th century, it was the brainchild of a local aristocratic couple, British-born Amalia Heredia Livermore and her Spanish husband, Jorge Loring Oyarzabal. They decided to re-create a tropical forest near the shores of the Mediterranean. It is famous for its purple wisteria blooms in spring.

By car, take the A45 Antequera road north from the Málaga ring road (A7) to Km166 and follow the signs for the 'Jardín Botánico'.

Plaza de Toros BULLRING
(Paseo de Reding; admission €2; ⊘10am-1pm & 5-8pm Mon-Fri) Visit the museum of the Plaza de Toros, the busiest bullring on the coast. The museum is adequate if you want to learn more about bullfighting, but Ronda's Museo Taurino is far more comprehensive.

El Hammam HAMMAM
(Map p152; ☑952 21 23 27; www.elhammam.com; Calle Tomás de Cózar 13; bath from €20, massage €35-74; ⊘11am-9pm Sun-Thu, to 11pm Fri-Sat) A most welcome spot in Málaga is El Hammam, a perfect place to sit back and sweat it out amid the steamy semidarkness to the sound of soothing music. Unlike some Arabic baths in Andalucía, there are no pools to bathe in here, only the steam rooms. Special-

ist massages, including Ayurvedic and aromatherapy treatments, are by appointment only.

ALAMEDA PRINCIPAL & AROUND

The Alameda Principal, now a busy thoroughfare, was created in the late 18th century as a boulevard on what were then the sands of the Guadalmedina estuary. Adorned with mature trees from the Americas, the wide road is lined with 18th- and 19th-century buildings.

Paseo de España PARK
(Paseo del Parque) A palm-lined extension of the Alameda, this park was created in the 1890s on land reclaimed from the sea. The garden along its southern side is full of exotic tropical plants, making a pleasant refuge from the bustle of the city. Elderly and young *malagueños* stroll around and take shelter in the deep shade of the tall palms, and on Sundays buskers and entertainers play to the crowds.

On the northern side, the grand Palacio de la Aduana has been aesthetically restored to house the **Museo de Málaga** (originally housed in the Picasso Museum). The collection includes fine works by great artists such as Francisco de Zurbarán, Bartolomé Esteban Murillo, José de Ribera and Pedro de Mena and is scheduled to open in early 2013. Check at the tourist office for an update.

Mercado Atarazanas MARKET
(Map p150; Calle Atarazanas) North of the Alameda, in what's now the commercial district, you'll find this striking 19th-century iron-clad building which incorporates the original Moorish gate that once connected the city with the port. It has been recently restored; take a look at the magnificent stained-glass window depicting historical highlights of the city.

The daily market in here is pleasantly noisy and animated. Choose from swaying legs of ham and rolls of sausages or cheese, fish and endless varieties of olives. The fruit and veg stalls are the most colourful, selling everything that is in season, ranging from big misshapen tomatoes which are sliced and served with olive oil, chopped garlic and rough salt to large purple onions, mild-flavoured and sweet.

Muelle Uno PORT
Across from the Plaza de la Marina, enjoy a stroll under shaded structures with thickets of palms and children's playgrounds.

MÁLAGA PROVINCE MÁLAGA

Opened in November 2011, the commercial end of the new port is a tad soulless and needs some greenery. It has been designed to cater to the increase in cruise passengers to the city, with restaurants, bars and shops.

LA MALAGUETA & THE BEACHES

At the end of the Paseo del Parque lies the exclusive residential district of La Malagueta. Situated on a spit of land protruding into the sea, apartments here have frontline sea views, and some of Málaga's best restaurants are found near the **Playa**

Central Málaga

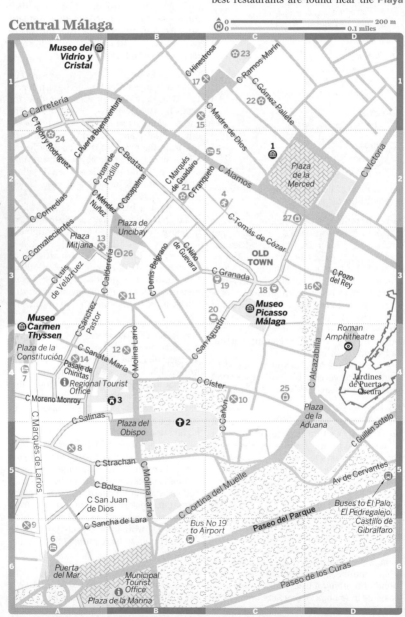

de la Malagueta (the beach closest to the city centre). Take a walk along the beach before settling down to some classy tapas at La Moraga Antonio Martín (p154).

East of Playa de la Malagueta, sandy beaches continue to line most of the waterfront for several kilometres. Next along are **Playa de Pedregalejo** and **Playa el Palo**, El Palo being the city's original, salt-of-the-earth fishing neighbourhood. This is a great place to bring children and an even better place to while away an afternoon with a cold beer and a plate of sizzling seafood. To reach either beach, take bus 11 from Paseo del Parque.

🐋 Courses

Málaga University   LANGUAGE COURSE
(www.malaga-university.org; from €383) The university here runs an excellent program of Spanish-language courses for foreign students, including one-month intensive courses held from July to September.

🎋 Festivals & Events

There's a whole host of festivals throughout the year in Málaga province, listed in the booklet ¿Qué Hacer?, available each month from the municipal tourist office.

Semana Santa   HOLY WEEK
Each night from Palm Sunday to Good Friday, six or seven *cofradías* (brotherhoods) bear their holy images for several hours through the city, watched by large crowds of onlookers.

Feria de Málaga   FAIR
Málaga's nine-day *feria* (fair), launched by a huge fireworks display on the opening Friday in mid-August, is the most ebullient of Andalucía's summer *ferias*. It resembles an exuberant Rio-style street party with plenty of flamenco and fino (sherry); head for the city centre to be in the thick of it. At night, festivities switch to large fairgrounds and nightly rock and flamenco shows at Cortijo de Torres, 3km southwest of the city centre; special buses run from all over the city.

Fiesta Mayor de Verdiales   FOLK MUSIC
Thousands congregate for a grand gathering of *verdiales* folk groups at Puerto de la Torre on 28 December. The groups perform an exhilarating brand of music and dance unique to the Málaga area. Buses 20 and 21 from the Alameda Principal go to Puerto de la Torre.

Central Málaga

TAPAS TRAIL

The pleasures of Málaga are essentially undemanding, easy to arrange and cheap. One of the best is a slow crawl around the city's numerous tapas bars and old bodegas.

El Piyayo (Map p152; Calle Granada 36; tapas €1.50-2) A popular traditionally tiled bar and restaurant, famed for its *pescaitos fritos* (fried fish) and typical local tapas, including wedges of crumbly Manchego cheese, the ideal accompaniment to a glass of hearty Rioja wine.

Rincon Chinitas (Map p152; Pasaje de Chinitas; tapas €2) Located on one of Málaga's most evocative and historic streets (Lorca used to hang out here), this tiny tapas bar dishes up the tastiest *berenjenas con miel* (fried aubergines with honey) in town. Alternatively, go for that special seafood moment with a plate of *gambas* (prawns).

La Rebaná (Map p152; www.larebana.com; Calle Molina Lario 5; tapas €4.20-8.50, raciones €7-11.50) A great, noisy and central tapas bar. The dark wood-clad interior (with its wrought-iron gallery) creates an inviting ambience. Goats cheese with cherries, foie gras and cured meats are among the offerings.

Pepa y Pepe (Map p152; Calle Calderería; tapas €1.30-1.50, raciones €3.60-5.50) A snug tapas bar that brims with young diners enjoying tapas such as *calamares fritos* (battered squid) and fried green peppers.

✘ Eating

Málaga has a staggering number of tapas bars and restaurants, particularly around the historic centre (over 400 at last count). So finding a place to eat poses no problem and the fact that this is not a tourist-driven city means that rip-off chips-with-everything places are thin on the ground and menus don't come with photos – hooray!

One local speciality to look for is *fritura malagueña* (fish, anchovies and squid quick fried in olive oil).

TOP CHOICE ▶ Vino Mio   INTERNATIONAL €€
(Map p152; www.restaurantevino.mio.com; Plaza Jeronimo Cuervo 2; mains €10-15) This Dutch-owned restaurant has a diverse and interesting menu that includes dishes like kangaroo steaks, vegetable stir-fries, duck breast with sweet chilli, pasta and several innovative salads. Tasty international tapas, like hummus and Roquefort croquettes, are also available to tantalise the tastebuds. The atmosphere is contemporary chic with regular art exhibitions and live music, including flamenco.

Casa Aranda   CAFE
(Map p152; www.casa-aranda.net; Calle Herrería del Rey; churro from €1; ♿) Casa Aranda is in a narrow alleyway next to the market and, since 1932, has been *the* place in town to enjoy chocolate and *churros* (tubular-shaped doughnuts). The cafe has taken over the whole street with several outlets all overseen by a team of mainly elderly white-shirted

waiters who welcome everyone like an old friend (most are).

Join the flat-capped men, market-stall sellers, gossiping grandmas and mothers with tots. The chocolate is rich and as thick (and sinful) as double cream. At least you can restrict your *churro* intake, just one costs €1. Or you can buy to go from cheerful Juan, who prepares the *churros* in a small and smoky streetside space.

La Moraga Antonio Martín   CONTEMPORARY ANDALUCIAN €€€
(Map p150; ☎952224153; www.lamoraga.com; Plaza Malagueta 4; tapas from €5, mains from €20) This is Michelin-star chef Dani Garcia's second Málaga-based La Moraga (the first is on Calle Fresca in the centre). The concept is based on traditional tapas given the nouvelle treatment – such as cherry gazpacho garnished with fresh cheese, anchovies and basil; king prawns wrapped in fried basil leaves; and mini-burgers created from oxtail.

The dining spaces have a cool contemporary look and overlook the beach, and the wine list is excellent, as is the service.

Tapeo de Cervantes   TAPAS €
(Map p152; www.eltapeodecervantes.com; Calle Cárcer 8; tapas €4-6; ☺Tue-Sun) This place has caught on big time, which, given its squeeze-in space, can mean a wait. Choose from traditional or more innovative tapas and *raciones* (large tapas serving) with delicious combinations and stylish presentation. Think polenta

with oyster mushrooms, chorizo and melted cheese or the more conventional *tortilla de patatas* (potato omelette), spiked with a veg or two. Portions are generous.

Terra Sana HEALTH FOOD €
(Map p152; www.restaurantesterrasana.com; Calle Alcazabilla; mains €8-10;) One of a small local chain that concentrates on healthy international cuisine. There's a great salad choice, plus wraps, with stuffings like tofu, chicken and *jamón serrano*, plus yogurt-based sundaes, Indian-style lassis and Mexican quesadillas. Children are amply catered to with a dedicated menu and the views are great, with the Roman ampitheatre and Alcazaba across the way.

El Jardín ANDALUCIAN €€
(Map p152; www.eljardinmalaga.com; Calle Cañon 1; mains €12-17) Located within confessional distance of the cathedral, this Viennese-style cafe-restaurant has an evocative feel with its lofty columns, ornate furniture and old-fashioned piano with candlesticks. The menu showcases Andalucian cuisine with the speciality being paella. Enjoy live tango and flamenco at weekends.

El Tintero SEAFOOD €€
(Plaza del Dedo, El Palo; mains €8-15) This sprawling, noisy restaurant at the far west end of the beach in El Palo can seat up to 1000 people (so not the place for a romantic dinner for two). There's no menu, waiters circle the restaurant carrying various seafood dishes and you choose whatever you fancy. The bill is totalled up according to the number and size of the plates on the table at the end of the meal.

Alumbre CONTEMPORARY ANDALUCIAN €€
(Map p152; www.alumbrebar.com; Calle Strachan 11; mains €11.50-17) Located on pedestrian street flanked by classy bars and restaurants, Alumbre dishes up arty plates of innovative Andalucian-inspired cooking with its roots in traditional 16th-century dishes. Surprises on the menu include snail croquettes, while more conservative palates may prefer the cuttlefish steak.

Drinking

The best areas to look for bars are from Plaza de la Merced in the northeast to Calle Carretería in the northwest, plus Plaza Mitjana (officially called Plaza del Marqués Vado Maestre) and Plaza de Uncibay. Plaza Mitjana heaves after midnight on Friday and Saturday.

TINTO DE VERANO

If you are visiting during the summer, consider ordering a *tinto de verano* at any local bar. This long cold drink is made with red wine, local lemonade (not too sweet), lashings of ice and a slice of lemon. Refreshing, and it shouldn't make your head reel too much on a hot day.

Bodegas El Pimpi BAR
(Map p152; www.bodegabarelpimpi.com; Calle Granada 62; 11am-2am) This rambling bar is an institution in this town. The interior encompasses a warren of rooms with a courtyard and open terrace overlooking the recently renovated Roman amphitheatre. Walls are decorated with historic *feria* posters and photos of visitors while the enormous barrels are signed by more well-known folk, including Tony Blair and Antonio Banderas. Tapas and meals also available.

Antigua Casa de Guardia BAR
(Map p150; www.antiguacasadeguardia.net; Alameda Principal 18; 11am-midnight) This atmospheric old tavern dates back to 1840 and is the oldest bar in Málaga. The peeling custard-coloured paintwork, black-and-white photographs of local boy Picasso, and elderly bar staff look fittingly antique. Try the dark brown, sherrylike *seco* (dry) Málaga wine or the romantically named *lagrima trañañejo* (very old tear).

Casa Lola BAR
(Map p152; Calle Granada 46; 11am-4pm & 7pm-midnight) Fronted by traditional blue-and-white tiles, this sophisticated spot specialises in vermouth on tap, served ice cold and costing just a couple of euros. Grab a pew on one of the tall stools and peruse the arty decor and clientele; an ideal spot to kick-start your night out on the town.

La Tetería CAFE
(Map p152; www.la-teteria.com; Calle San Agustín 9; speciality teas €2.50; 9am-midnight Mon-Sat) Serves heaps of aromatic and classic teas, herbal infusions, coffees and juices, with teas ranging from peppermint to '*antidepresivo*'. Sit outside and marvel at the beautiful church opposite or stay inside to enjoy the wafting incense and background music.

☆ Entertainment

Teatro Cervantes
THEATRE

(Map p152; www.teatrocervantes.com; Calle Ramos Marín; ⊘closed mid-Jul–Aug) The handsome art deco Cervantes has a fine program of music, theatre and dance, including some known names on the concert circuit. Rufus Wainwright called it 'the most beautiful theatre in Europe'.

Liceo
FLAMENCO

(Map p152; www.liceoflamenco.com; Calle Beatas 21; ⊘7pm-late Wed-Sun) This place is a little hard to find – especially late at night after a couple of beers - but persevere as it is well worth it. Housed in a sumptuous historical building with original tile-work, dusty chandeliers and lofty ceilings, the Liceo is a venue for live flamenco during the week but morphs into a rollicking disco from Thursday to Saturday.

Onda Pasadena
LIVE MUSIC

(Map p152; Calle Gómez Pallete 5) A congenial combination of older and younger audiences mingle on Tuesdays to listen to jazz, while handclapping is all the rage on Thursdays when flamenco gigs take over.

ZZ Pub
LIVE MUSIC

(Map p152; www.zzpub.es; Calle Tejón y Rodríguez; ⊘10pm-late Mon-Sat) Squeeze your way into this late-night club on busy Mondays and Thursdays, and dance the night away to the diverse range of regular live bands.

🔒 Shopping

Central Calle Marqués de Larios and nearby streets have glitzy boutiques and shoe shops in handsomely restored old buildings.

Ultramarinos Zoilo
FOOD

(Map p152; Calle Granada 65) This lovely deli has been a family-run business since the early 1950s. Choose from great wheels of crumbly Manchego cheese, several grades of local chorizo and the speciality: *jamón serrano*, which hang over the main counter gently curing and intensifying in flavour.

Alfajar
ARTS & CRAFTS

(Map p152; Calle Císter 3) Perfect for handcrafted Andalucian ceramics produced by local artisans. You can find traditional designs and glazes, as well as more modern, arty and individualistic pieces. A great place for presents.

Flamenka
SOUVENIRS

(Map p152; www.flamenka.com; Calle Calderería 6) This is a one-stop shop for flamenco-related goods and music.

ⓘ Information

Municipal Tourist Office (Plaza de la Marina; ⊘9am-8pm Mar-Sep, to 6pm Oct-Feb) This office offers a range of city maps and booklets. It also operates information kiosks at the Alcazaba entrance (Calle Alcazabilla), at the main train station (Explanada de la Estación), on Plaza de la Merced, in front of the main post office (Alameda Principal) and on the eastern beaches (El Palo and La Malagueta).

Regional Tourist Office (www.andalucia.org; Pasaje de Chinitas 4; ⊘9am-7.30pm Mon-Fri, 10am-7pm Sat, 10am-2pm Sun) Provides a range of information including maps of the regional cities. There's a second office at the airport.

ⓘ Getting There & Away

To/From the Airport

Málaga's **Pablo Picasso Airport** (www.aena.es) is the main international gateway to Andalucía; it is 9km southwest of the city centre and underwent a considerable expansion in 2010. It is a major hub in southern Spain, serving some top global carriers as well as budget airlines.

BUS Bus 75 to the city centre (€1.20, 20 minutes) leaves from outside the arrivals hall every 20 minutes between 7am and midnight. The bus to the airport leaves from the western end of Paseo del Parque, and from outside the bus and train stations, about every half-hour between 6.30am and 11.30pm.

CAR Numerous local and international agencies (including Avis and Hertz) have desks at the airport.

TAXI A taxi from the airport to the city centre costs around €16.

TRAIN Trains run every 20 minutes from 6.50am to 11.54pm to the **Maria Zambrano (Málaga-Renfe) station** (www.renfe.es; Explanada de la Estación) and the Málaga-Centro station beside the Río Guadalmedina. Train departures from the city to the airport are every 20 minutes between 5.30am and 10.30pm.

Bus

The **bus station** (☎952 35 00 61; www.estabus.emtsam.es; Paseo de los Tilos) is 1km southwest of the city centre, with links to all major cities in Spain.

Destinations include the following:

TO	COST (€)	DURATION	FREQUENCY
Almería	17	4¾hr	8 daily
Cádiz	24.62	4hr	3 daily
Córdoba	13.50	3½hr	4 daily
Granada	10.50	2hr	18 daily
Jaén	18.50	3¼hr	4 daily
Madrid airport	36	10hr	5 daily
Seville	30	2¾-4hr	6 daily

Train

The **Maria Zambrano (Málaga-Renfe) train station** (www.renfe.es) is near the bus station. Destinations include: Córdoba (€25.90, 2½ hours, 18 daily), Seville (€18.35, 2¾ hours, 11 daily) and Madrid (€87, 2½ hours, 10 daily). Note that for Córdoba and Seville the daily schedule includes faster trains at roughly double the cost.

❶ Getting Around

BUS Useful buses around town (€1.20 for all trips around the centre) include bus 11 to El Palo, bus 34 to El Pedregalejo and El Palo, and bus 35 to Castillo de Gibralfaro, all departing from Avenida de Cervantes. Destinations farther afield include Antequera (€6.50, one hour, nine daily) and Ronda (€11.45, 2½ hours, nine daily).

CAR There are several well-signposted underground car parks in town. The most convenient are on Avenida de Andalucía, Plaza de la Marina and Plaza de la Merced (per 24 hours €24.70).

TAXI Taxi fares typically cost around €5 per 2km to 3km. Fares within the city centre, including to the train and bus stations and Castillo de Gibralfaro, are around €7.

TRAIN There is a train from Málaga (centre) to Fuengirola running every 20 minutes from 5.30am to 10.30pm and from Fuengirola to Málaga from 6.20am to 11.20pm.

COSTA DEL SOL

It's very easy to be sniffy about the poor old Costa del Sol. It constantly gets a bad rap, especially in the UK press, with stories on crime, illegal house demolition and the escalating prices of a pint. The reality is that while, yes, of course there has been unsightly overbuilding here, there remain pockets of genuine and, dare we say, traditional charm away from the urbanisation and Sid-and-Dot-style pubs.

Torremolinos & Benalmádena
POP 128.340

Torremolinos was developed here back in the 1950s and while many of the not-so-modern blocks are Stalin-era in their grimness, there remain attractive quarters, such as the low-rise former fishing district of La Carihuela. Torremolinos has long been known as the Costa del Sol's gay capital. Spain's first gay bar opened here in 1962 and in October 2011 the resort was the fitting venue for the first annual Expo Gays symposium which attracted more than 15,000 visitors.

The adjacent resort of Benalmádena comprises a fairly bland built-up coastal stretch with the highlights being **Puerto Deportivo** (leisure port), and relatively unspoiled **Benalmádena Pueblo** (village) inland. Another resort, **Arroya de la Miel**, also falls under the Benalmádena banner and is best known as being home to the Tivoli theme park.

◉ Sights & Activities

The best beaches are **Playamar** and **La Carihuela** in Torremolinos, from where it is a pleasant walk, jog or in-line skate to Benalmádena Port, with its striking Gaudí-cum-Asian-cum-Mr Whippy architecture, and large choice of bars, restaurants and cafes overlooking the boats. The centre of

BUDDHIST STUPA

The largest **Buddhist stupa** (Benalmádena Pueblo; ☺10am-2pm & 3.30-6.30pm Tue-Sat, 10am-7.30pm Sun) in Europe is in Benalmádena Pueblo. It rises up, majestically out of place, on the outskirts of the village, surrounded by new housing and with sweeping coastal views.

The stupa is open to visitors; the lofty interior is lined with devotional, exquisitely executed paintings. Regular exhibitions are held with varied themes related to Buddhism, as well as lectures on Buddhist philosophy, plus guided meditation sessions, open to all. The gift shop sells Tibetan jewellery, Himalayan wall hangings, chimes, incense and similar, which sure make a change from straw donkey souvenirs.

MÁLAGA PROVINCE TORREMOLINOS & BENALMÁDENA

LA CONSULA

Located around 6km northwest of Torremolinos, Churriana is home to one of the coast's top professional culinary schools: **La Consula** (☎952 436 026; www.laconsula.com; Finca Consula Churriana; set menus €35-50; ☺lunch Mon-Fri, closed Aug). The setting, among mature and lush gardens, is a delight. The history of the main building has an interesting twist for literary buffs. It was owned by Americans who were apparently good pals with Ernest Hemingway, who wrote *The Dangerous Summer* while staying here in 1959, just two years before his death.

However memorable that titbit may be, it is the food that is sure to linger on your palate and in your psyche. The daily menu reflects an innovative twist on traditional Spanish dishes with beautifully crafted plates, not too much froth and drizzle, and faultless delicious flavours. The service is the best you will find anywhere – these students don't want to mess up – and the atmosphere is elegant and formal. Don't turn up in flip-flops.

Torremolinos revolves around the pedestrian shopping street of San Miguel.

Together with Mijas, Benalmádena Pueblo has maintained its traditional charm with cobbled streets, orange trees and simple, flower-festooned houses. There is a magnificent view of the coast from the tiny church at the top of the village.

Mariposario de Benalmádena
BUTTERFLY PARK

(www.mariposariodebenalmadena.com; Benalmádena Pueblo; adult/child €8.50/5; ☺10am-6pm; 🚼) Situated next to the Buddhist stupa, this butterfly park is a delight with some 1500 fluttery creatures, including exotic subtropical species, moths and cocoons (in action). There are some impressive plants, flowers, trees and a resident iguana, as well as birdlife – and a gift shop for buying those butterfly-wing earrings you always wanted.

FREE Museo Benalmádena
MUSEUM

(www.benalmadena.com; Benalmádena Pueblo; ☺10am-6pm Mon-Fri) There are two sections to this museum: one exhibiting local archaeological finds, the other, more curiously, exhibiting a fantastic collection of Mexican and Central and South American artefacts.

Costasol Cruceros
BOAT TOUR

(www.costasolcruceros.com; Benalmádena Port; adult/child €9/5) There are four daily boat cruises that leave from Benalmadena Port to Fuengirola, with a one-hour duration. The same company also arranges dolphin-spotting trips.

Tivoli World
AMUSEMENT PARK

(www.tivolicostadelsol.com; Arroya de la Miel; admission €6.95; ☺Apr-Sep; 🚼) The oldest and largest amusement park, with various rides and slides as well as daily dance, flamenco and children's events. Consider the good-value 'Supertivolino' ticket for €14; it covers admission and unlimited access to some 36 rides.

🍴 Eating & Drinking

TOP CHOICE La Alternativa
TAPAS €

(Avenida de la Constitución, Arroyo de la Miel; tapas from €2.50) Well worth seeking out, this tiny traditionally tiled place has a year-round *feria* atmosphere with its walls papered with flamenco posters, matador pics and the occasional Virgin. It's always packed and the tapas are superb. You can also have larger *raciones* like oxtail and Galician-style octopus.

Casa Juan
SEAFOOD €€

(www.losmellizos.net; Calle San Ginés 20, La Carihuela; mains €13-20) The business dates back to the 1950s but the fish is fresh daily at this, La Carihuela's most famous seafood restaurant, attracting shoals of *malagueños* on Sundays. It has been expanded into four dining spaces; you can't go wrong, provided you order carefully – some fish is sold by weight, so the bill can add up fast.

El Cordobes
ANDALUCIAN €€

(Playamar, Torremolinos; mains €12-15; 🚼) The best of the beachside *chiringuitos* (seafront restaurants), attracting a loyal Spanish clientele. Specialities include a delicious *salmorejo* (thick garlicky gazpacho), barbecued sardines, and *almejas* (clams) in a spicy paprika-based sauce. The terrace fronts onto the sand.

Kaleido
BAR
(www.kaleido.es; Darsena de Levante, Puerto Marina; ☺11am-late) This sprawling bar and terrace is in a prime spot on the marina and attracts an energetic fun-loving crowd here for the killer cocktails, regular live music (including salsa), plus DJs and theme nights.

ℹ Information
Tourist office (www.pmdt.es; Plaza de la Independencia, Torremolinos; ☺9.30am-1.30pm Mon-Fri) There are additional tourist kiosks at Playamar and La Carihuela.

ℹ Getting There & Away
Avanza (www.avanzabus.com) runs services from Málaga (€2.30, 25 minutes, 14 daily) and from Marbella (€4.50, 1¼ hours, 24 daily).

Trains (www.renfe.es) run to Torremolinos and Arroyo de la Miel-Benalmádena every 20 minutes from Málaga (€1.65, 20 minutes) from 5.30am to 10.30pm, continuing on to the final stop, Fuengirola.

Fuengirola
POP 71,783
Fuengirola is a genuine Spanish working town, as well as being firmly on the tourist circuit. It attracts mainly Northern European visitors and also has a large foreign resident population, many of who arrived here in the '60s – and stayed (yes, there are a few grey ponytails around). The beach stretches for a mighty 7km, encompassing the former fishing quarter of Los Boliches.

◉ Sights & Activities
Biopark
ZOO
(www.bioparcfuengirola; Avenida Camilo José Cela; adult/child €16.20/11.20; ☺10am-8pm; 🚻) This is a zoo that treats its animals very well with no cages or bars, but spacious enclosures, conservation and breeding programs, plus educational activities. There is no space for elephants or giraffes but you can enjoy big cats, gorillas and a range of other species. There is also a bat cave, reptile enclosure, cafes for refreshments and a large gift shop.

✖ Eating
Charolais
ANDALUCIAN €€
(www.bodegacharolais.com; Calle Larga 14; mains €12-20) This place covers three venues: a modern tapas bar, a terrace and a rustic-styled restaurant. In the latter the emphasis is on expertly prepared meat dishes, plus duck and some typical Galician plates, including *txangurro* (stuffed crab). The atmosphere is solidly traditional with not a ketchup bottle in sight and the wine list is extensive. Head to the adjoining tapas bar for lighter snacks to share.

Cafe Fresco
INTERNATIONAL €
(Las Rampas; wraps €4.20, salads €7; ☺lunch Mon-Sat) This breezy restaurant is popular with the waistline-watchers for its menu of homemade soups, selection of salads, and wraps (including Thai chicken and Greek salad), best accompanied with an energising smoothie. There is a second branch in Los Boliches.

La Picada
INTERNATIONAL €
(Calle de la Pandereta 5; tapas €3, mains €10; ☺Tue-Sat) Piles in the locals with its generously portioned tapas, including options like broccoli or fried potatoes topped with melted cheese. The main menu includes international choices such as risotto with oyster mushrooms and has several daily specials.

🍷 Drinking & Entertainment
Plenty of tacky disco-pubs line the Paseo Marítimo, and a cluster of music bars and discos can be found opposite the port.

Hipódromo Costa del Sol
HORSE RACING
(www.hipodromocostadelsol.es; admission race days €8; ☺10pm-2am Sat Jul-Sep) This well-managed horse track has several restaurants and bars, a disco, flamenco shows and a great atmosphere. To get here take the exit opposite the castle at the southwestern end of town and follow the signs. There are race nights every Saturday during the summer months.

Colón
BAR
(www.casacolon.es, Plaza de los Chinorros) Take note of the accent here...this place is one of a clutch of similar traditional Spanish bars, with sprawling terraces, behind the main post office. The wines are good, and the weekend ambience has a big-city feel and seems reassuringly Spanish despite being just a couple of blocks from the banks of sunbeds on the sand.

Pogs
LIVE MUSIC
(Calle de Lamo de Espinosa; ☺10.30pm-late Mon-Sat) This spirited Irish pub is one of the most popular places for live music in town and has a reputable line-up of local musicians, playing everything from blues to jazz, together with the perfect draught Guinness accompaniment.

MÁLAGA PROVINCE FUENGIROLA

FAIR TIME

Fuengirola has arguably the best and biggest annual *feria* (fair) on the Costa. Held from 6 to 12 October, festivities include a *romeria* (pilgrimage) when locals head to the *campo* (countryside) for flamenco, paella and pitchers of *cerveza* (beer) and a flamenco Mass (6 October), held in the main church, and followed by drinking and dancing in the street with most women dressed in their traditional flamenco frills.

❶ Information

Tourist office (www.visitfuengirola.com; Paseo Jesús Santos Rein; ⊙9.30am-1.30pm Mon-Fri) Has a wealth of information on the town.

❶ Getting There & Away

BUS Avanza (www.avanzabus.com) runs services including Fuengirola from Málaga (€3.60, 40 minutes, 15 daily) and from Estepona (€8, 1¾ hours, 11 daily).

CAR A toll road (AP-7) connects Fuengirola with Estepona (€11), providing an, albeit costly, alternative to the hazardous N340 coast road.

TRAIN Trains (www.renfe.es) run every 20 minutes to Málaga from 6.20am to 11.20pm with stops including the airport and Torremolinos.

Marbella

POP 136,322

Marbella is the Costa del Sol's classiest, and most expensive, resort. This inherent wealth glitters most brightly along the Golden Mile, a tiara of star-studded clubs, restaurants and hotels which stretches from Marbella to Puerto Banús, the flashiest marina on the Costa del Sol, where black-tinted Mercs slide along a quayside of luxury yachts. Marbella has a magnificent natural setting, sheltered by the beautiful Sierra Blanca mountains, as well as an attractive *casco antiguo* (old town).

Marbella has a long history and been home to Phoenicians, Visigoths and Romans, as well as being the most important town on the coast during Moorish times. Arab kings still own homes here, as do plenty of rich and famous people such as native *malagueño*, the actor Antonio Banderas.

◉ Sights

Casco Antiguo NEIGHBOURHOOD
The picturesque old town is chocolate-box perfect with pristine white houses, narrow, mostly traffic-free streets and geranium-filled balconies. You can easily spend an enjoyable morning or evening exploring the cafes, restaurants, bars, designer boutiques and antique and craft shops here. At the heart is pretty **Plaza de los Naranjos**, dating back to 1485, with its tropical plants, palms, orange trees and, inevitably, overpriced bars.

FREE **Museo Ralli** MUSEUM
(Urbanización Coral Beach; ⊙10am-2pm Tue-Sat) This superb private art museum exhibits paintings by primarily Latin American and European artists in bright and well-lit galleries. Part of a nonprofit foundation, its exhibits include sculptures by Henry Moore and Salvador Dali, and vibrant contemporary paintings by Argentinian surrealist Alicia Carletti and Cuban Wilfredo Lam, plus works by Joan Miró, Chagall and Chirico.

Museo del Grabado Español MUSEUM
(Calle Hospital Bazán; admission €2.50; ⊙10am-2pm & 5.30-8.30pm) This small art museum in the old town includes works by some of the great masters, including Picasso, Joan Miró and Salvador Dali, among other, primarily Spanish painters.

✖ Eating

In general the restaurants in the historic centre tend to be priced for tourists; an exception is the picturesque Calle San Lázaro near the Plaza de los Naranjos, home to several excellent tapas bars mainly frequented by locals.

Calima MODERN EUROPEAN €€€
(☑952 76 42 52; www.restaurantecalima.es; Hotel Melia Don Pepé, Calle Jose Melia; mains €22-28; ⊙7-10pm Tue-Fri, 1.30-3pm & 7.30-10pm Sat) Michelin-starred chef Dani Garcia cut his culinary teeth at Ronda's famous Tragabuches restaurant and has carried on to acquire considerable fame here, as well as at his chain of smart tapas bars: La Moraga. Dishes are based on contrasts and have tantalising names like 'egg without an egg' and lychees and roses popcorn. The open-plan dining space is all steely grey and chrome. Seafood is his forte.

El Estrecho
TAPAS €€

(Calle San Lázaro; tapas €1.50, raciones €5-8) Always crammed, elbow your way to a space in the small back dining room and order from a massive menu that includes tapas such as *salmorejo*. This is one of several great tapas bars on this narrow pedestrian street.

Loving Hut
VEGAN €

(http://marbella.lovinghut.es; Calle Miguel Cano 11; mains €8-10) Part of a global chain of vegan restaurants run by followers of the Buddhist spiritual leader, Ching Hai, the menu includes some Asian dishes, including sushi, teriyaki wraps, as well as curries, pasta dishes, quiches and salads.

Santiago
SEAFOOD €€€

(☑952 77 00 78; www.restaurantesantiago.com; Paseo Marítimo 5; mains €22-28; ⊙closed Nov) Push the boat out and dine at this fine seafood restaurant with elegant time-tested surroundings and superb dishes, including an exemplary paella and lobster *termidor*. It gets packed to the gills at weekends; grab a pew on the outside terrace overlooking palm-studded Playa de Venus.

🍷 Drinking

For the most spirited bars and nightlife, head to Puerto Banús, 6km west of Marbella. In town, the best area is around the small Puerto Deportivo. There are also some holiday-in-the-sun-style beach clubs open only in summer.

Buddha
CLUB

(Avenida del Mar; ⊙7pm-late) In the shadow of Buddhist statues overlooking the heathens on the dance floor, the DJ spins everything from funk and acid jazz to hip hop and rock. The interior is all plush fabrics and suitably posh with moody lighting and comfortable sofas. There are regular theme nights.

Nikki Beach
CLUB

(www.nikkibeach.com; Don Carlos Hotel; ⊙noon-late Apr-Sep) Sprawl out on white sofas overlooking the surf as you nibble on haute tapas and enjoy the live music or DJ playing a riveting mix of music. Nikki Beach is a fixture on the glam clubbing scene; don your best party garb, shine those shoes and assume some attitude – it's that kind of place.

ℹ Information

Tourist office (www.marbella.es; Plaza de los Naranjos 1; ⊙9.30am-9pm Mon-Fri) Has plenty of leaflets and a good town map.

ℹ Getting There & Away

BUS Buses to Fuengirola (€3.20, one hour), Puerto Banús (€1.50, 20 minutes) and Estepona (€2.80, one hour) leave about every 30 minutes from Avenida Ricardo Soriano.

CAR Marbella's streets are clogged with traffic and street parking is notoriously difficult to find. The most central underground car park is on Avenida del Mar (per hour €1.75).

MÁLAGA PROVINCE MARBELLA

LOCAL KNOWLEDGE

MICHELLE CHAPLOW: PROFESSIONAL PHOTOGRAPHER

Michelle Chaplow (www.michellechaplow.com) is a professional photographer who has photographed Andalucía for international media and corporate clients for over 20 years.

Your favourite Andalucian scenes? If you are planning a trip to Andalucía there are so many photographic hot spots, such as the white villages of Gaucín, Frigiliana, Comares and, of course, Ronda.

That perfect shot? I was en route to Seville at 5.30 one morning and could barely see for the thick mist, so stopped at the car park of a bar from where I witnessed the old town of Ronda slowly revealing its beauty as the mist gently wafted away from the historic spires and towers to commence rolling down the hill. Nature doesn't hang around! I ran for my tripod and took at least 50 pictures of the scene.

What do you like to do on your day off? I have been photographing Andalucía for the last 20 years and I never tire of heading off into the hills or driving along the coast in search of new images, especially if there is a fiesta taking place.

Your secret spot? Whenever I return home from a trip, I pop out to the no-frills Estepona restaurant, La Escollera (p162), where they serve up, right on the beach, what I consider to be the finest *calamares* (squid) and fresh fish in the world.

Estepona

POP 66,500

Estepona was one of the first resorts to attract foreign residents and tourists some 40 years ago and, despite the surrounding development, the centre of the town still has a cosy old-fashioned feel – for good reason; the town's roots date back to the 4th century. Centuries later during the Moorish era, Estepona was an important and prosperous town, due to its strategic proximity to the Straits of Gibraltar.

Estepona has a wide promenade overlooking the sandy Playa de la Rada beach; the Puerto Deportivo is the heart and soul of the nightlife, especially at weekends and is also excellent for water sports, as well as bars and restaurants.

◎ Sights & Activities

Selwo Aventura WILDLIFE RESERVE
(www.selwo.es; Carretera A7 Km162.5; adult/child €24.50/17; ⊙10am-6pm) This popular safari park has over 200 exotic animal species. You can tour the park by 4WD or on foot and enjoy various adventure activities. It is home to the only Asian elephant born in Spain and there is even a lodge if you fancy an overnight stay in – erm – Africa.

FREE Aloe Vera Finca FARM
(☑952 80 83 43; www.santaverde.es; Camino Cala Bujeo; ⊙9am-2pm & 4-6.30pm) If you are an aloe vera fan or intrigued about its curative properties, head to this dedicated farm where you can learn about the cultivation, harvesting and processing of this ancient medicinal plant. Call ahead to book a tour or just turn up to check out all the products and buy your very own plant.

Buceo Estepona DIVING
(☑645 61 03 74; www.buceoestepona.com; Puerto Deportivo; ⊙10am-2.30pm & 4.30-8pm) A reputable diving outfit that offers a wide range of courses, ranging from Discover Scuba (€45) to a Dive Master–accredited PADI course (€750).

✗ Eating

Estepona has no shortage of good restaurants, particularly in the old town and port.

Venta Garcia MODERN EUROPEAN €€
(☑952 89 41 91; Ma 8300, Km7; mains €12-18) Situated on the road to Casares, around 7km from the centre of town, Venta Garcia specialises in superbly presented and conceived dishes, like wild asparagus stew and Sicilian-style tuna. The countryside views are similarly sublime, but the word is out, so be sure to reserve – especially at weekends.

La Escollera SEAFOOD €
(Puerto Pesquero; mains €6-9; ⊙closed Feb) Locals in the know arrive in shoals to dine on, arguably, the freshest and best seafood in town. Located in the port, the atmosphere is no-frills basic with plastic tables and paper cloths. When the fish tastes this good, who cares?

Tikitano MODERN EUROPEAN €€€
(☑952 79 84 49; www.tikitano.com; Urbanización Guadalmansa, Ctra de Cádiz 340, Km164; mains €20-28) Large picture windows overlook the beach and sea at this top choice for an elegant dining experience. There is plenty of choice and everything is just a tad fancy, like pasta with truffles, mint-infused lobster bisque, and similar. Homesick Brits turn up in droves for the Sunday roast. Regular live music.

La Taberna del Puerto TAPAS €
(Puerto Deportivo, Edificio Puertosol; tapas €1.80; ⊙Wed-Mon) This place has a genuine *pueblo* (village) feel to it, with the flamenco music, dark woody interior, hams over the bar and barrel tables. The tapas are a cut above the average with choices like stuffed vol au vents and tasty *tostas* (toasts) with simple toppings like sweet red pepper and cured Manchego cheese.

☕ Drinking

The Puerto Deportivo is the best place to head for late night bars. Beach clubs also swing into action in the summer. Check flyers around town to see where the action is.

Puro Beach BAR
(www.purobeach.com; Laguna Village; ⊙noon-late Apr-Oct) Laguna Village is an Asian-inspired beachside complex of bars, restaurants and shops set around lush landscaping, tinkling fountains and snaking waterways. This bar enjoys prime position and is the place to luxuriate with its private 'nomad' tents, pool, DJs and overall summer-in-the-sun party setting.

❶ Information

Tourist office (www.estepona.es; Avenida San Lorenzo 1; ⊙9am-8pm Mon-Fri) Has racks of leaflets and information.

ℹ Getting There & Away

BUS There are regular buses to Marbella (€2.80, one hour), and Málaga (€7.20, two hours).

CAR Estepona has several well-signposted car parks on Avenida España (per hour €1.40).

Mijas

POP 76,362 / ELEV 428M

The story of Mijas encapsulates the story of the Costa del Sol. Originally a humble village, it is now the richest town in the province. Since finding favour with discerning bohemian artists and writers in the 1950s and '60s, Mijas has sprawled across the surrounding hills and down to the coast yet managed to retain the picturesque charm of the original *pueblo*.

Mijas has a foreign population of at least 40% and the municipality includes Mijas-Costa, on the coast southwest of Fuengirola. Golf courses abound, and Mijas is a noted area for rock climbing (particularly in winter), with around 100 grade V-7 climbs. Mijas is also famous for its donkey taxis, which have resulted in criticism from animal welfare groups.

◉ Sights

Virgen de la Peña HISTORIC SITE
(Avenida Virgen de la Peña) Keep walking past the *ayuntamiento* (town hall) and you will reach this grotto where the Virgin is said to have appeared to two children who were led here by a dove in 1586. During the annual village procession on 8 September, the effigy of the Virgin is carried 2km up to the **Ermita del Calvario**, a tiny chapel built by Carmelite brothers. Black-iron crosses mark a short walking trail that leads up to the hermitage.

FREE **Casa Museo de Mijas** MUSEUM
(Plaza Libertad 2; ⊙10am-2pm & 5-8pm) Mijas is also home to a quaint folk museum, the Casa Museo de Mijas. It was created and is still run by Carmen Escalona, who specialises in crafting folk-themed models which, together with other artefacts, show perfectly the style and mode of living some 50 years ago.

Plaza de Toros BULLRING
(bullfights €50-90, museum €3; ⊙10am-8pm) This unusual square-shaped bullring is located at the top of the village, surrounded by lush ornamental gardens with wonderful views of the coast. There is a modest museum dedicated to local bullfighting history.

✕ Eating

It's not the most exciting of places to eat, but Mijas has a couple of decent restaurants.

El Padrastro MODERN EUROPEAN €€
(☑952 48 50 00; www.elpadrastro.com; Paseo del Compás; mains €12-27) The haute-Med Padrastro is perched on a cliff above the main plaza, with suitably spectacular views. You don't have to climb the stairs as there is a lift, so it's good for mobility-impaired people. Delicious fare includes a spider-crab-and-guacamole starter, rice with seafood, and plenty of fish dishes.

El Mirlo Blanco SPANISH €€
(☑952 48 57 00; www.mirlo-blanco.es; Paseo Marítimo 29; mains €16-35; ⊙closed Tue Sep-Jun) The Basque-style El Mirlo Blanco is one of Mijas' best restaurants. The menu varies seasonally but roast lamb and hake in a green sauce are good choices. Finish with a Grand Marnier soufflé.

ℹ Information

Mijas Tourist Office (☑958 58 90 34; www .mijas.es; Plaza Virgen de la Peña; ⊙9am-7pm Mon-Fri Oct-Mar, to 8pm Mon-Fri Apr-Sep, 10am-3pm Sat year-round) Has a foreign residents' department, so there's plenty of information on local activities and events.

ℹ Getting There & Away

Frequent buses run from Fuengirola (€1.50, 25 minutes).

THE INTERIOR

The mountainous interior of Málaga province is an area of raw beauty and romantic white villages sprinkled across craggy landscapes. Beyond the mountains, the verdant countryside opens out into a wide chequerboard of floodplains. It's a far cry from the tourist-clogged coast.

Ronda

POP. 37,000 / ELEV 744M

Perched on an inland plateau riven by the 100m fissure of El Tajo gorge, Ronda is Málaga province's most spectacular town. It has a superbly dramatic location, and owes its name ('surrounded' by mountains), to the encircling Serranía de Ronda.

Established in the 9th century BC, Ronda is also one of Spain's oldest towns. Its existing

Ronda

N 0 — 200 m
0 — 0.1 miles

Train Station

C Jerez
C de Sevilla
C José María Castello
Plaza Concepción García Redondo
Av de Andalucía
C de Monterejas
Av de Córdoba
Av Martínez Astein

C Molino
C de Sevilla
C Jerez
Paseo de las Inglesas
C de San José
Av de Andalucía
C Madrid
C Lauria
Plaza del Ahorro

C Pozo
C Doctor Ramón y Cajal
C Infantes
C Setenil

Iglesia de la Merced
C Mariano Soubirón
C Naranja
Carrera del Espinel
C Calvo Asensio
Iglesia de los Descalzos
Plaza de los Descalzos

C Virgen de la Paz
C Borrego Gómez
22
Iglesia de Nuestra Señora del Socorro
C María Cabrera
C Capitán Cortés
C San Vicente de Pauli

Alameda del Tajo
10
C Santa Cecilia
17
Plaza Carmen Abela

Plaza de Toros
19
7
C Pedro Romero
25
23
C las Tiendas
EL MERCADILLO

Plaza Teniente Arce
Regional Tourist Office
24
C Nueva
C Madre Petra
Iglesia de Nuestro Padre Jesús

Municipal Tourist Office
20
C Villanueva
C Real

Plaza de España
C los Remedios
8
C Real

Río Guadalevín
Puente Nuevo
El Tajo Gorge

16
C Santo Domingo
2
La Mina
Puente Viejo
Arroyo

LA CIUDAD
6
Puente Árabe

11
C Tenorio
18
1

Plaza María Auxiliadora
12
9

Plaza del Campillo
C José M Holgado
C de Armiñán
C Marqués de Salvatierra
Hoyo San Miguel

4
Plaza Mondragón
3
5
C Espíritu Santo

Plaza Duquesa de Parcent
21
13
C Imágenes

Puerta de Almocábar
Iglesia del Espírito Santo

Puerta de Carlos V
14
Plaza Arquitecto Pons Sorolla

15
BARRIO DE SAN FRANCISCO

Ronda

old town, La Ciudad (the City), largely dates back to Islamic times, when it was an important cultural centre filled with mosques and palaces. Its wealth as a trading depot made it an attractive prospect for bandits and profiteers and the town has a colourful and romantic past in Spanish folklore.

Ronda was a favourite with the Romantics of the late 19th century, and has attracted an array of international artists and writers, such as David Wilkie, Alexandre Dumas, Rainer Maria Rilke, Ernest Hemingway and Orson Welles.

⊙ Sights & Activities

La Ciudad, the historic old town on the southern side of El Tajo gorge, is an atmospheric area for a stroll with its evocative, stilltangible history and wealth of museums. But don't forget the newer town, which has its distinctive charms and is home to the emblematic bullring, plenty of good tapas bars and restaurants and the leafy Alameda del Tajo gardens. Three bridges cross the gorge.

La Ciudad   NEIGHBOURHOOD
Straddling the dramatic gorge and the Río Guadalevín (deep river) is Ronda's most recognisable sight, the towering Puente Nuevo, best viewed from the Camino de los Molinos, which runs along the bottom of the gorge. The bridge separates the old and new towns.

The old town is surrounded by massive fortress walls pierced by two ancient gates: the Islamic Puerta de Almocábar, which, in the 13th century, was the main gateway to

the castle; and the 16th-century Puerta de Carlos V. Inside, the Islamic layout remains intact, and its maze of narrow streets now takes its character from the Renaissance mansions of powerful families whose predecessors accompanied Fernando el Católico in the taking of the city in 1485.

Casa del Rey Moro   GARDENS
(House of the Moorish King; Map p164; Calle Santo Domingo 17) The terraced gardens here give access to La Mina, an Islamic stairway of over 300 steps that are cut into the rock all the way down to the river at the bottom of the gorge. These steps enabled Ronda to maintain water supplies when it was under attack. It was also the point where Christian troops forced entry in 1485. The steps are not well lit and are steep and wet in places. Take care.

Luckily the historic gardens here have not been primped and prettified within a green shoot of their life; the chipped ancient tiles and overgrown beds somehow add to the atmosphere, although it is a shame that the main building is falling into ruin.

Museo Lara   MUSEUM
(www.museolara.org; Calle de Armiñán 29; adult/child €4/2; ⊙11am-8pm; 🚹) There is something very compelling about private museums, although you may not actually want anyone like Juan Antonio Lara Jurado and his Museo Lara in your immediate family – unless you have a similar-sized family mansion, that is.

Lara Jurado has been a collector since the age of 10. Now in his 70s, he still lives above the museum, but his living space is set to shrink as he wants to expand still further. You name it, it is here: priceless, historic collections of clocks, weapons, radios, gramophones, sewing machines, telephones, opera glasses, Spanish fans, scales, cameras and far, far more.

There is an impressive archaeological section, plus a suitable grisly exhibit on the Inquisition with various torture apparatus, including head crushers and stocks. Then there is the witchcraft room, which kids, in particular, will love. Think pickled toads and the like.

Visiting this museum is a humbling experience for anyone who enjoys collecting, because Juan Antonio seems to have collected just about everything possible – except stamps, that is.

Museo de Ronda   MUSEUM
(Palacio de Mondragón, Plaza Mondragón; admission €3; ☺10am-7pm Mon-Fri, to 3pm Sat & Sun) The city museum has artefacts and information especially related to both Roman and Islamic funerary systems. Of even more interest to some will be the palatial setting. Built for Abomelic, ruler of Ronda in 1314, the palace retains its internal courtyards and fountains, the most impressive of these being the Patio Mudéjar, from which a horseshoe arch leads into a cliff-top garden with splendid views.

Iglesia de Santa María La Mayor   CHURCH
(Calle José M Holgado; adult/child €4/1.50; ☺10am-8pm) The city's original mosque metamorphosed into this elegant church. Just inside the entrance is an arch covered with Arabic inscriptions, which was part of the mosque's *mihrab* (prayer niche indicating the direction of Mecca). The church has been declared a national monument, and its interior is an orgy of decorative styles and ornamentation. A huge, central, cedar choir stall divides the church into two sections: aristocrats to the front, everyone else at the back.

Museo del Bandolero   MUSEUM
(Calle de Armiñán 65; admission €3; ☺10.30am-8pm Apr-Sep, to 6pm Oct-Mar) This small museum is dedicated to the banditry for which central Andalucía was once renowned. Old prints reflect that when the youthful *bandoleros* (bandits) were not being shot, hanged or garrotted by the authorities, they were stabbing each other in the back, literally as much as figuratively. You can pick up your fake pistol or catapult at the gift shop.

Baños Arabes   HISTORIC SITE
(Arab Baths; Hoyo San Miguel; admission €3, Sun free; ☺10am-7pm Mon-Fri, to 3pm Sat & Sun) Enjoy the pleasant walk here from the centre of town. Backing on to Ronda's river, these 13th- and 14th-century Arab baths are in good condition, with horseshoe arches, columns and clearly designated divisions between the hot and cold thermal baths. They're some of the best-preserved Arab baths in Andalucía.

El Mercadillo   NEIGHBOURHOOD
Directly across the Puente Nuevo is the main square, Plaza de España, made famous by Hemingway in his novel *For Whom the Bell Tolls,* where he describes how, early in the civil war, the 'fascists' of a small town were rounded up in the square, clubbed and made to walk the gauntlet between two lines of townspeople before being thrown off the cliff. The episode is based on events that took place here in Plaza de España. What was the *ayuntamiento* is now Ronda's *parador* (luxurious state-owned hotel).

On a lighter note, don't miss a stroll through the delightful Alameda del Tajo Park, especially at the weekend when it is full of local families.

Plaza de Toros   BULLRING
(Calle Virgen de la Paz; admission €5; ☺10am-8pm) Ronda's Plaza de Toros is a mecca for bullfighting aficionados. It has been in existence for more than 200 years, and is one of the oldest and most revered bullrings in Spain. It has also been the site of some of the most important events in the history of bullfighting.

Built by Martín Aldehuela, the bullring is universally admired for its soft sandstone hues and galleried arches. At 66m in diameter, it is also the largest and, therefore, most dangerous bullring, yet it only seats 5000 spectators – a tiny number compared with the huge 50,000-seater bullring in Mexico City. In July the ring is used for a series of fabulous concerts, and opera.

The on-site **Museo Taurino** (Calle Virgen de la Paz; admission €6; ☺10am-8pm Apr-Sep, to 6pm Oct-Mar) is crammed with memorabilia such as blood-spattered costumes worn by Pedro Romero and 1990s star Jesulín de Ubrique. It also includes photos of famous

PARQUE NATURAL SIERRA DE LAS NIEVES

Southeast of Ronda lies the 180-sq-km Parque Natural Sierra de las Nieves, noted for its rare Spanish fir, the *pinsapo*, and fauna including some 1000 ibex and various species of eagle. The *nieve* (snow) after which the mountains are named usually falls between January and March. **El Burgo**, a remote but attractive village 10km north of Yunquera on the A366, makes a good base for visiting the east and northeast of the park. Information is available from Yunquera's **tourist office** (Calle del Pozo 17; ⊙8am-3pm Tue-Fri), or the **ayuntamiento** (town hall; ☑952 16 00 02) in El Burgo.

The most rewarding walk in the Sierra de las Nieves is the ascent of the highest peak in western Andalucía, **Torrecilla** (1918m). Start at the Área Recreativa Los Quejigales, which is 10km east by unpaved road from the A376 Ronda–San Pedro de Alcántara road. The turn-off, 12km from Ronda, is marked by 'Parque Natural Sierra de las Nieves' signs. From Los Quejigales you have a steepish 470m ascent by the **Cañada de los Cuernos gully**, with its tranquil Spanish-fir woods, to the high pass of **Puerto de los Pilones**. After a fairly level section, the final steep 230m to the summit rewards you with marvellous views. The walk takes five to six hours round trip, and is easy to moderate in difficulty. The IGN/Junta de Andalucía *Parque Natural Sierra de las Nieves* map (1:50,000) shows the relevant path and other hikes.

fans such as Orson Welles and Ernest Hemingway, whose novel *Death in the Afternoon* provides in-depth insight into the fear and tension of the bullring.

Behind the Plaza de Toros, spectacular cliff-top views open out from Paseo de Blas Infante and the nearby Alameda del Tajo park.

Barrio de San Francisco   NEIGHBOURHOOD
Outside La Ciudad's city walls is the Barrio de San Francisco, the original Muslim cemetery of the city. A small market was established here in the 15th century, when traders refused to enter the city in order to avoid paying hefty taxes. Some inns and taverns were built and thus began a new quarter. The barrio still has a reputation for down-to-earth tapas bars.

✯ Festivals & Events

Corpus Cristi   RELIGIOUS
On the Thursday after Trinity (usually falling somewhere between May and June) there are bullfights and festivities after the 900kg Station of the Cross is carried 6km through the town.

Feria de Pedro Romero   BULLFIGHTS
An orgy of partying during the first two weeks of September, including the important flamenco event, Festival de Cante Grande. Culminates in the Corridas Goyesca (bullfights in honour of legendary bullfighter Pedro Romero).

✗ Eating

Typical Ronda food is hearty mountain fare, with an emphasis on stews (called *cocido, estofado* or *cazuela*), *trucha* (trout), *rabo de toro* (bull's tail stew) and game such as *conejo* (rabbit), *perdiz* (partridge) and *codorniz* (quail). But, as is the case elsewhere, inspired chefs are trying out new ideas.

TOP CHOICE Bodega San Francisco   TAPAS €
(www.bodegasanfrancisco.com; Calle Ruedo Alameda; raciones €6-10; ☑) With three dining rooms and tables spilling out onto the narrow pedestrian street, this may well be Ronda's top tapas bar. The menu is vast and should suit the fussiest of families, and even vegetarians, with its nine-plus salad choices. Try the *revuelto de patatas* (scrambled eggs with potatoes and peppers). The house wine is good.

Restaurante Tragabuches   CONTEMPORARY SPANISH €€€
(☑952 19 02 91; www.tragabuches.com; Calle José Aparício 1; menus €59-87; ⊙1.30-3.30pm & 8-10.30pm Tue-Sat) Ronda's best and most famous restaurant is a 180-degree turn away from the ubiquitous 'rustic' look and cuisine. Michelin-starred in 1998, Tragabuches is modern and sleek with an innovative menu to match. Choose from the three set menus. People flock to Tragabuches from miles away to taste the food, prepared by its creative chef.

RONDA'S FIGHTING ROMEROS

Ronda can bullishly claim to be the home of bullfighting – and it does. It proudly boasts the Real Maestranza de Ronda equestrian school, founded in 1572 for the Spanish aristocracy to learn to ride and fight. They did this by challenging bulls in an arena, and thus was born the first bullfight.

Legend has it that one of these fights went awry when a nobleman fell from his horse and risked being gored to death. Without hesitation local hero Francisco Romero (b 1698) leapt into the ring and distracted the bull by waving his hat. By the next generation Francisco's son, Juan, had added the *cuadrilla* (the matador's supporting team), consisting of two to three *banderilleros* (who work on foot) and two to three *picadors* (men on horseback with pike poles). This married both the habits of the aristocracy (who previously conducted fights on horseback) and the common, dangerous bullfights that took place during fiestas in the main square of each town.

Juan's son Pedro Romero (1754–1839), whose distinguished career saw the death of over 5000 bulls, invented the rules and graceful ballet-like movements of the modern bullfight, introducing the *muleta* (a variation on his grandfather's hat), a red cape used to attract the bull's attention.

In 1932 Ronda also gave birth to one of Spain's greatest 20th-century bullfighters, the charismatic Antonio Ordóñez, who was immortalised by Hemingway in *The Dangerous Summer*.

It was the Ordóñez family that inaugurated Ronda's Corridas Goyescas, held each year in early September in honour of Pedro Romero, and which attracts Spain's best matadors. During the bullfights the matadors wear the stiff, ornate 19th-century costume that Goya depicted in his paintings of Romero.

Restaurante Albacara INTERNATIONAL €€€
(☏952 16 11 84; www.hotelmontelirio.com; Calle Tenorio 8; mains €14.50-22) One of Ronda's best restaurants, the Albacara is in the old stables of the Montelirio palace and teeters on the edge of the gorge. It serves up delicious meals – try the beef stroganoff or classic magret of duck. Be sure to check out the extensive wine list – and to reserve your table in advance.

Faustino ANDALUCIAN €
(Calle Santa Cecilía; tapas €1.50, raciones €6-8) This is the real deal, a lively, atmospheric tapas bar with plenty of seating space in the open traditional atrium decorated with plants, *feria* posters and bullfighting and religious pictures. Tapas and *raciónes* are generous. Go with the recommendations like *champingnones a la plancha* (grilled mushrooms with lashings of garlic). The only downside is the uncomfortable, if pretty, rustic-style painted chairs. Ouch!

Bar Restaurant Almocábar ANDALUCIAN €
(Calle Ruedo Alameda 5; tapas €1.50, mains €10; ⊙1.30-5pm & 8pm-1am Wed-Mon) Almocábar is little touched by the tourist hordes at the top of town. In fact, the tapas are so good that this spot is normally super-packed and finding a place at the bar can be a challenge.

If that's the case, try reserving the *comedor* (dining room).

Casa Santa Pola ANDALUCIAN €€
(Calle Santo Domingo 3; starters €10-12, mains €17-22) This is an atmospheric restaurant spread over three floors of a historic aristocratic house, a former 8th-century Moorish palace. At night each of the small dining rooms is intimate and candlelit, while during the day there are good views over El Tajo. The roast lamb with honey and rosemary is a popular speciality.

Restaurante Pedro Romero ANDALUCIAN €€
(☏952 87 11 10; www.rpedroromero.com; Calle Virgen de la Paz 18; menú €16, mains €15-18) Opposite the bullring, this celebrated eatery dedicated to bullfighting turns out classic *rondeño* dishes (dishes from Ronda). This is a good place to try the *rabo de toro*. Vegetarians will doubtless prefer the fried goat's cheese starter, which is served with apple sauce.

La Casa del Dulce BAKERY
Calle Tenorio 11; (🖰) Stop by La Casa del Dulce and ogle the trays of freshly-baked *mantecada* biscuits; a delicious crumbly speciality based on almonds and topped with icing

sugar. Don't worry, they can't be that sinful – they're made by nuns.

Drinking

Tragatapas BAR
(Calle Nueva 4; ☺6pm-midnight Mon-Sat) Although a tad too brightly lit (like most bars in Ronda), this place has a contemporary vibe with its background jazz, black beamed ceiling and arty bites like curried-chicken *pinchos* (snacks).

New Baco BAR
(☺7pm-4am) Get here too early and you may be greeted by football on the big screen, but later on – and definitely at weekends – there are DJs as well as plenty of dancing from midnight.

Los Canto BAR
(Espíritu Santo 9; ☺noon-2am) A spacious bar in the Barrio de San Francisco with lovely pastoral views of the natural park from the front terrace. Set against a background of mellow music, the interior is a strange decor mix including a mosaic Miró-style floor. There's a pool table.

Tetería Al Zahra TEAHOUSE
(Calle las Tiendas 17; ☺4.30pm-midnight) Come to this *tetería* and try a pot of herbal, Moroccan, Pakistani or a host of other teas. They're all served in pretty Moroccan ceramic teapots and cups and saucers. There are hookahs for smoking, too, and you can settle in for a few hours of sipping, puffing and gossiping.

☆ Entertainment

Círculo de Artistas FLAMENCO
(Map p164; Plaza del Socorro; admission €23; ☺Mon-Wed May-Sep) Stages flamenco shows in a sumptuous historical building on the square from 10pm, as well as other song and dance performances. Note unconventional weekday timings.

❶ Information

Muncipal Tourist Office (www.turismo deronda.es; Paseo de Blas Infante; ☺10am-7.30pm Mon-Fri, 10.15am-2pm & 3.30-6.30pm Sat, Sun & holidays) Helpful and friendly staff with a wealth of information on the town and region.

Regional Tourist Office (www.andalucia.org; Plaza de España 1; ☺9am-7.30pm Mon-Fri May-Sep, to 6pm Oct-Apr, 10am-2pm Sat year-round)

❶ Getting There & Around

Bus
The bus station is at Plaza Concepción García Redondo 2. **Comes** (www.tgcomes.es) has buses to Arcos de la Frontera (€8.75, two hours, two daily), Jerez de la Frontera (€11.50, three hours, three daily) and Cádiz (€15, two hours, three daily). **Los Amarillos** (www.losamarillos .es) goes to Seville via Algodonales, Grazalema, and to Málaga via Ardales.

Car
There are a number of underground car parks and some hotels have parking deals for guests. Parking charges are about €1.10 per hour, or €15 to €20 for 14 to 24 hours.

MÁLAGA PROVINCE RONDA

SMURFING THE BLUES

You could be forgiven for whipping off the shades and blinking hard if arriving at the historic Moorish village of Júcar for the first time. It's a very strange sight: what should be a traditional *pueblo blanco* (white village) is painted that distinctive more smurf-than-sky blue – even the church. There is only one rebel white house (unfortunately no one was home when we knocked).

The story is that the village was used to promote *Los Pitufos*, the first 3-D box-office smash Smurf film, released in 2011. Sony subsequently dutifully bought the white paint so villagers could revert to, well, anonymity. Unsurprisingly they have voted to stay blue. Just as well as, at the time of research, the word on the street was that a sequel is going to be filmed here.

It is worth visiting Júcar for its novelty value, although only one savvy resident (a New Yorker) who owns Hotel (and restaurant) Bandolero at the village entrance, has seriously cashed in on the camera-slung Spanish visitors. His young waiters wear Smurf hats (not a good chat-up look) and he sells Smurf T-shirts and similar, including blue Smurf *turron* (nougat). Thankfully, there is a more digestible range of tapas and mains available: the latter including a tasty plate of roast lamb with chips (€12).

Train

Ronda's **train station** (📞952 87 16 73; Avenida de Andalucía) is on the line between Bobadilla and Algeciras. Trains run to Algeciras via Gaucín and Jimena de la Frontera. This train ride is incredibly scenic and worth taking just for the views. Other trains depart for Málaga, Córdoba, Madrid, and Granada via Antequera. For Seville change at Bobadilla or Antequera. It's less than 1km from the train station to most accommodation. Supposedly every 30 minutes, town minibuses run to Plaza de España from Avenida Martínez Astein (across the road from the train station), but they're not very reliable. It's not too far to walk to the town centre but, with luggage, you'll need a taxi (€5).

Around Ronda

SERRANÍA DE RONDA

Curving around the south and southeast of the town, the Serranía de Ronda may not be the highest or most dramatic mountain range in Andalucía, but it's certainly among the prettiest. Any of the roads through it between Ronda and southern Cádiz province, Gibraltar or the Costa del Sol make a picturesque route. Cortés de la Frontera, overlooking the Guadiaro Valley, and Gaucín, looking across the Genal Valley to the Sierra Crestellina, are among the most beautiful spots to stop.

To the west and southwest of Ronda stretch the wilder Sierra de Grazalema and Los Alcornocales natural parks. There are plenty of walking and cycling possibilities and Ronda's tourist office can provide details of these as well as maps.

◉ Sights

FREE Ronda la Vieja   ARCHAEOLOGICAL SITE
(📞630 429949; ⊙9am-3pm Tue-Sat, 8am-2pm Sun) To the north of Ronda, off the A374, is the relatively undisturbed Roman site of Acinipo at Ronda la Vieja, with its partially reconstructed theatre. Although completely ruinous, with the exception of the theatre, it is a wonderfully wild site with fantastic views of the surrounding countryside and you can happily while away a few hours wandering through the fallen stones trying to guess the location of various baths and forums.

Ardales & El Chorro

Fifty kilometres northwest of Málaga, the Río Guadalhorce carves its way through the awesome Garganta del Chorro (El Chorro gorge). Also called the Desfiladero de los Gaitanes, the gorge is about 4km long, as much as 400m deep and sometimes just 10m wide. Its sheer walls, and other rock faces nearby, are a major magnet for rock climbers, with hundreds of bolted climbs snaking their way up the limestone cliffs.

Along the gorge runs the main railway into Málaga (with the aid of 12 tunnels and six bridges) and a path called the Camino (or Caminito) del Rey (king's path), so named because Alfonso XIII walked along it when he opened the Guadalhorce hydroelectric dam in 1921. For long stretches the path becomes a concrete catwalk 100m above the

> **DON'T MISS**
>
> ## CUEVA DE LA PILETA
>
> Twenty kilometres southwest of Ronda la Vieja are some of Andalucía's most ancient and fascinating caves: the **Cueva de la Pileta** (📞952 16 73 43; www.cuevadelapileta.org; Benaoján; adult/child €8/4; ⊙hourly tours 10am-1pm & 4-6pm; 🅿). The guided tour, by torchlight, into the dark belly of the cave reveals Palaeolithic paintings of horses, goats and fish from 20,000 to 25,000 years ago. Beautiful stalactites and stalagmites add to the effect. The guided tours are given by members of the Bullón family, who discovered the paintings in 1905 and who speak some English.
>
> The fact that the caves are so uncommercial is a real plus. Although the family are finding the upkeep a battle, they are loathe to give in to pressure from the local authority who would obviously like to exploit the caves for maximum tourist euros.
>
> **Benaoján** village is the nearest that you can get to the Cueva de la Pileta by public transport. The caves are 4km south of the village, about 250m off the Benaoján–Cortés de la Frontera road; there is no transport to the caves, so you will need your own car to get here. The turn-off is signposted. Benaoján is served by two Los Amarillos buses (from Monday to Friday) and up to four daily trains to/from Ronda. Walking trails link Benaoján with Ronda and villages in the Guadiaro Valley.

A WALK BACK IN TIME

Back in the 9th century, the rugged El Chorro area was the redoubt of a kind of Andalucian Robin Hood, Omar ibn Hafsun, who resisted the armies of Córdoba for nearly 40 years from the hill fortress of **Bobastro**. At one stage he controlled territory all the way from Cartagena to the Strait of Gibraltar.

Legend has it that Ibn Hafsun converted to Christianity (thus becoming a Mozarab) and built Bobastro's **Iglesia Mozárabe**, where he was then buried in AD 917. When Bobastro was finally conquered by Córdoba in 927, Ibn Hafsun's remains were taken away for posthumous crucifixion outside Córdoba's *mezquita* (mosque).

Although the small church is now only a ruin, the drive and walk to get to it are delightful. From El Chorro follow the road up the valley from the western side of the dam, and after 3km take the signposted Bobastro turn-off. Nearly 3km up, an 'Iglesia Mozárabe' sign indicates the 500m footpath to the remains of the church. The views are magnificent.

river, clinging to the gorge walls. It has been officially closed since 1992 and has long since fallen into disrepair, although that has not stopped some folk from tackling the hazardous path (take a look on YouTube for some spine-chilling footage). In early 2011 work finally got underway to renovate the path, which is predicted to take at least three years at a cost of some €8.3 billion.

The pleasant, quiet town of Ardales (population 2700) is the main centre of the area and is a good base for exploring further afield. However, most people aim for the climbing mecca of El Chorro, a small village in the midst of a spectacular and surreal landscape of soaring limestone crags. **Andalucia Aventura** (www.andalucia-aventura .com) organises rock climbing and abseiling for various levels of skill, as well as hiking excursions. See the website for full details.

ARDALES & AROUND

At the entrance to Ardales is the **Museo de Ardales** (Avenida de Málaga 1; adult/child €1/0.50; ⊙10am-2pm & 4-6pm Tue-Sat, 10am-2pm Sun), an ethnographic and archaeological museum largely concerned with the **Cueva de Ardales** (admission €5; ⊙Tue, Thu, Sat & Sun), a Palaeolithic cave complex similar to the Cueva de la Pileta. For two-hour guided visits to the Cueva de Ardales itself (4km from the museum), contact the museum two to three weeks in advance. The caves contain 60 Palaeolithic paintings and carvings of animals, done between about 18,000 BC and 14,000 BC, and traces of later occupation and burials from about 8000 BC to after 3000 BC. The museum has copies of the prehistoric rock paintings and carvings, an exhibit of Roman and Islamic artefacts and more.

Six kilometres from Ardales is the picturesque **Embalse del Conde del Guadalhorce** – a huge reservoir that dominates the landscape and is noted for its carp fishing.

Antequera

POP 45,234 / ELEV 577M

Antequera is a fascinating town, both architecturally and historically, yet it has somehow managed to avoid being on the coach-tour circuit – which only serves to add to its charms.

The three major influences in the region – Roman, Moorish and Spanish – have left the town with a rich tapestry of architectural gems. The highlight is the opulent Spanish-baroque style that gives the town its character and which the civic authorities here have worked hard to restore and maintain. There are also an astonishing number of churches in Antequera – over 30, many of them with wonderfully ornate interiors.

And there's more! Some of Europe's largest and oldest dolmens (burial chambers built with huge slabs of rock), from around 2500 BC to 1800 BC, can be found just outside the town's centre.

The flip side to all this antiquity is a vibrant city centre with very few economic signs of *la crisis* in evidence, and some of the best tapas bar this side of Granada.

◉ Sights

The substantial remains of the Alcazaba, a Muslim-built hilltop castle, dominate Antequera's historic quarter and are within easy (if uphill) distance of the town centre.

FREE **Dolmens** ARCHAEOLOGICAL SITE
(Cerro Romeral; ☺9am-6pm Tue-Sat, 9.30am-2.30pm Sun) The **Dolmen de Menga** and **Dolmen de Viera**, both dating from around 2500 BC, are 1km from the town centre in a small, wooded park beside the road that leads northeast to the A45. Head down Calle Encarnación from the central Plaza de San Sebastián and follow the signs.

Prehistoric people of the Copper Age transported dozens of huge slabs from the nearby hills to construct these burial chambers. The stone frames were covered with mounds of earth. The engineering implications for the time are astonishing. Menga, the larger, is 25m long, 4m high and composed of 32 slabs, the largest of which weighs 180 tonnes. In midsummer the sun rising behind the Peña de los Enamorados hill to the northeast shines directly into the chamber mouth.

A third chamber, the **Dolmen del Romeral** (Cerro Romeral; ☺9am-6pm Tue-Sat, 9.30am-2.30pm Sun), is further out of town. It is of later construction (around 1800 BC) and features much use of small stones for its walls. To get there, continue 2.5km past Menga and Viera through an industrial estate, then turn left following 'Córdoba, Seville' signs. After 500m, turn left at a roundabout and follow 'Dolmen del Romeral' signs for 200m.

Alcazaba FORTRESS
(adult/child incl Colegiata de Santa María la Mayor €6/3; ☺10.30am-2pm & 6-8.30pm Tue-Sun) Favoured by the Granada emirs of Islamic times, Antequera's hilltop Moorish fortress has a fascinating history and covers a massive 62,000 sq metres. The main approach to the hilltop is from Plaza de San Sebastián, up the stepped Cuesta de San Judas and then through an impressive archway, the **Arco de los Gigantes**, built in 1585 and formerly bearing huge sculptures of Hercules. All that is left today are the Roman inscriptions on the stones.

Recently re-opened as a dedicated tourist site, the admission price generously includes an audoguide with several language options which sets the historical scene and provides good explanations as you meander along tidy pathways, flanked by shrubs and some archaeological remains of a Gothic church and Roman dwellings from the 6th-century AD.

You can climb the 50 steps of the **Torre del Homenaje**, from where there are great views, especially towards the northeast and the **Peña de los Enamorados** (Rock of the Lovers), about which there are many legends.

Admission to the Colegiata de Santa María la Mayor is included in the price. Don't miss the ruins of **Roman Baths** dating from the 3rd-century AD which can be viewed from Plaza Santa María, outside the church entrance. Although a tad overgrown, the layout can be clearly seen, aided by an explanatory plaque.

Colegiata de Santa María la Mayor CHURCH
(Plaza Santa María; adult/child incl Alcazaba €6/3; ☺10am-2pm & 6-8.30pm) Just below the Alcazaba is the large 16th-century Colegiata de Santa María la Mayor. This church-cum-college played an important part in Andalucía's 16th-century humanist movement, and boasts a beautiful Renaissance facade, lovely fluted stone columns inside, and a Mudéjar *artesonado* (a ceiling of interlaced beams with decorative insertions). It also plays host to some excellent musical events and exhibitions.

Museo Municipal MUSEUM
(Plaza del Coso Viejo; compulsory guided tour €3; ☺10am-1.30pm & 4.30-6.30pm Tue-Fri, 10am-1.30pm Sat, 11am-1.30pm Sun) Located in the town centre, the pride of the Museo Municipal is the elegant and athletic 1.4m bronze statue of a boy, *Efebo*. Discovered on a local farm in the 1950s, it is possibly the finest example of Roman sculpture found in Spain.

The museum also displays some pieces from a Roman villa in Antequera, where a superb group of mosaics was discovered in 1998. The collection includes a treasure trove of religious items, containing so much silver that you can only visit by guided tour on the half-hour.

Museo Conventual de las Descalzas MUSEUM
(Plaza de las Descalzas; compulsory guided tour €3.30; ☺10.30am-1.30pm & 5-6.30pm Tue-Fri, 10am-noon & 5-6.30pm Sat, 10am-noon Sun) The Museo Conventual de Descalzas, in the 17th-century convent of the Carmelitas Descalzas (barefoot Carmelites), approximately 150m east of town's Museo Municipal, displays highlights of Antequera's rich religious-art heritage. Outstanding works include a painting by Lucas Giordano of St Teresa of Ávila (the 16th-century founder of the Carmelitas Descalzas), a bust of the Dolorosa by

Pedro de Mena and a *Virgen de Belén* sculpture by La Roldana.

Iglesia del Carmen · CHURCH
(Plaza del Carmen; admission €2; ☺10.30am-1.30pm & 4.30-6pm Tue-Fri, 11am-1.30pm Sat & Sun) Only the most jaded traveller would fail to be impressed by the Iglesia del Carmen and its marvellous 18th-century Churrigueresque retable. Magnificently carved in red pine by Antequera's own Antonio Primo, it is spangled with statues of angels by Diego Márquez y Vega, and saints, popes and bishops by José de Medina. While the main altar is not painted, the rest of the interior is a dazzle of colour and design, painted to resemble traditional tilework.

✯ Festivals & Events

Semana Santa · HOLY WEEK
One of the most traditional celebrations in Andalucía; items from the town's treasure trove are actually used in the religious processions.

Real Feria de Agosto · FAIR
This festival celebrates the harvest with bullfights, dancing and street parades; held in mid-August.

✗ Eating

Local specialities on almost every Antequera menu include *porra antequerana*; *bienmesabe* (literally 'tastes good to me'), a sponge dessert; and *angelorum,* a dessert incorporating meringue, sponge and egg yolk. Antequera also does a fine breakfast *mollete* (soft bread roll), served with a choice of toppings.

⬛ TOP CHOICE Restaurante
Coso San Francisco · ANDALUCIAN €
(www.cososanfrancisco.com; Calle Calzada 27-29; mains €7-13, tapas €2.50) The *simpática* (friendly) owner of this hotel restaurant has her own garden that provides fresh ingredients for her dishes. Meat, fish, Antequeran specialities, traditional Spanish egg dishes and salads await you. On Thursday and Friday evenings classical musicians provide entertainment. The adjacent tapas bar serves unusual light bites like a *sartén de pisto con huevo* (ratatouille topped with a fried egg).

Restaurante
La Espuela · CONTEMPORY ANDALUCIAN €€
(✆952 70 30 31; Calle San Agustín 1; mains €14-18; ☺1-4pm & 8-11pm Tue-Sun) Located in a pretty restaurant-flanked cul-de-sac off Calle Infante Don Fernando, La Espuela doubles as a cooking school and offers a fine selection of Antequeran specialities, such as oxtail with honey and rosemary, along with some international fare including pasta dishes. The elegant dining room is painted a dark mulberry pink, contrasting with crisp white table linens. The bow-tied waiters complete the dress-for-dinner feel.

Rincon de Lola · TAPAS €
(www.rincondelola.net; Calle Encarnación 7; tapas €2, raciones €7; ☺Tue-Sun) A great place to come for inexpensive varied tapas that can give you a taster of local dishes, like *cochinillo* (suckling pig), or the more unusual (for these parts), like sushi. There are also piled high *tostas* and *raciones* such as tomatoes filled with cheese, salmon, wild mushrooms and prawns.

El Angelote · ANDALUCIAN €€
(Plaza del Carmen 10; tapas €1, raciones €6) This place wins hands down for location on this pretty square, lined with orange trees. Already reliably good, its new owners have boosted the menu with some innovative choices such as swordfish in a red vermouth sauce, along with more traditional steaks and oxtail.

❶ Information

Municipal Tourist Office (✆952 70 25 05; www.antequera.es; Plaza de San Sebastián 7; ☺11am-2pm & 5-8pm Mon-Sat, 11am-2pm Sun)

❶ Getting There & Around

Bus
The **bus station** (Paseo Garcí de Olmo) is found 1km north of the centre. **Alsa** (www.alsa.es) runs buses to Seville (€13, 2½ hours, five daily), Granada (€8, 1½ hours, five daily), Córdoba (€10, two hours 40 minutes, one daily), Almería (€21, six hours, one daily) and Málaga (€4.30, 1½ hours, two daily).

Buses run between Antequera and Fuente de Piedra village (€2, 25 minutes, three daily).

Car
A toll road, opened in 2012 (AP-46) running from Torremolinos to Las Padrizas (€3.05), is located around 21km southeast of Antequera.

There is underground parking on Calle Diego Ponce north of Plaza de San Sebastián (per hour €1.50, 12 to 24 hours, €18).

MÁLAGA PROVINCE ANTEQUERA

Taxis

Taxis (€5 to €6 per 2km to 3km) wait halfway along Calle Infante Don Fernando, or you can call ☎952 84 55 30.

Train

The **train station** (Avenida de la Estación) is 1.5km north of the centre. Trains run to/from Granada (€9.15, 1½ hours, nine daily), and there are regular services to Seville (€31, 1½ hours). Another three run to Málaga or Córdoba, but you'll need to change at Bobadilla.

Around Antequera

PARAJE NATURAL TORCAL DE ANTEQUERA

South of Antequera are the weird and wonderful rock formations of the Paraje Natural Torcal de Antequera. A 12-sq-km area of gnarled, serrated and pillared limestone, it formed as a sea bed 150 million years ago and now rises to 1336m (El Torcal). It's otherworldly out here and the air is pure and fresh. There is an **information centre** (☺10am-5pm) that provides details on walks, and flora and fauna.

Two marked walking trails, the 1.5km Ruta Verde (green route) and the 3km Ruta Amarilla (yellow route) start and end near the information centre. More dramatic views are along the restricted Ruta Rojo (red route), for which guided tours are organised; contact the Antequera tourist office for details. Wear shoes with good tread as the trails are rocky.

To get to El Torcal, you will need your own car or a taxi. By car, leave central Antequera along Calle Picadero, which soon joins the Zalea road. After 1km or so you'll see signs on the left to Villanueva de la Concepción. Take this road and, after about 11km, a turn uphill to the right leads 4km to the information centre. A return taxi costs €32, with one hour at El Torcal. The tourist office in Antequera will arrange a taxi for you.

LAGUNA DE FUENTE DE PIEDRA

About 20km northwest of Antequera, just off the A92 *autovía* (toll-free dual carriageway), is the Laguna de Fuente de Piedra. When it's not dried up by drought, this is Andalucía's biggest natural lake and one of Europe's two main breeding grounds for the greater flamingo (the other is in the Camargue region of southwest France). After a wet winter as many as 20,000 pairs of flamingos will breed at the lake.

The birds arrive in January or February, with the chicks hatching in April and May. The flamingos stay till about August, when the lake, which is rarely more than 1m deep, no longer contains enough water to support them. They share the lake with thousands of other birds of some 170 species.

The **Centro de Información Fuente de Piedra** (☺10am-2pm & 4-6pm) is at the lakeside and can advise on the best spots for birdwatching. It also sells a range of good maps and hires out binoculars (an essential).

Near the lake is the the well-regarded **Caserío de San Benito** (☎952 11 11 03; www.caseriodesanbenito.com; Km108 Carretera Córdoba-Málaga; menú €15; ☺noon-5pm & 8pm-midnight Tue-Sun), which is a good place to stop for a quality lunch. A beautifully converted farmhouse, San Benito is stuffed with antiques and serves up exquisitely prepared traditional dishes.

EAST OF MÁLAGA

The coast east of Málaga, sometimes described as the Costa del Sol Oriental, is less developed than the coast to the west. The suburban sprawl of Málaga extends east into a series of unmemorable and unremarkable seaside towns – Rincón de la Victoria, Torre del Mar, Torrox Costa – which pass in a concrete high-rise blur, before culminating in more attractive Nerja, which has a large population of Brits and Scandinavians.

The area's main redeeming feature is the rugged region of La Axarquía, just as stunning as Granada's Las Alpujarras yet, as well as being even more difficult to pronounce, is hardly known. (Think of taking a chopper to one of those infuriating Scandinavian flatpack stores: *Axe – Ikea*). The area is full of great walks, which are less discovered than those in the northwest of the province around Ronda. A 406-sq-km area of these mountains was declared the Parque Natural Sierras de Tejeda, Almijara y Alhama in 1999.

La Axarquía

The Axarquía region is riven by deep valleys lined with terraces and irrigation channels that date to Islamic times. Nearly all the villages, dotted around hillsides planted with olives, almonds and vines, date from this era. The wild inaccessible landscapes, especially around the Sierra de Tejeda, made it a stronghold of *bandoleros* (bandits) who roamed the mountains without fear or favour. Nowadays, its chief attractions include fantastic scenery; pretty white villages; strong, sweet, local wine made from sun-dried grapes; and good walking in spring and autumn.

The 'capital' of La Axarquía, **Vélez Málaga**, 4km north of Torre del Mar, is a busy but unspectacular town, although its restored hilltop castle is worth a look. From Vélez the A335 heads north past the turquoise Embalse de la Viñuela reservoir and up through the **Boquete de Zafarraya** (a dramatic cleft in the mountains) towards Granada. One bus a day makes its way over this road between Torre del Mar and Granada.

The highest mountains in Málaga province stretch east from the Boquete de Zafarraya. Around the Embalse de la Viñuela (reservoir) you'll see plenty of newish homes. Most are occupied by foreigners, especially Brits, and were built illegally. At the time of writing, a decree was being implemented that would legalise most of these homes although in some cases, the properties cannot be sold or used to obtain a mortgage, creating a real catch-22 situation for some homeowners. One positive outcome of this foreign concentration has been the creation of a good Tuesday **farmers market**, where organic food and handicrafts are sold, at Puente de Don Manuel on the Vélez–Boquete de Zafarraya road.

Some of the most dramatic La Axarquía scenery is up around the highest villages of **Alfarnate** (925m) and **Alfarnatejo** (858m), with towering, rugged crags such as Tajo de Gomer and Tajo de Doña Ana rising to their south.

You can pick up information on La Axarquía at the tourist offices in Málaga, Nerja, Torre del Mar or Cómpeta. Prospective walkers should ask for the leaflet on walks in the Parque Natural Sierras de Tejeda, Almijara y Alhama. Good maps for walkers are M*apa Topográfico de Sierra Tejeda* and M*apa Topográfico de Sierra Almijara* by Miguel Ángel Torres Delgado, both at 1:25,000. Useful guides include *Walk! Axarquía* published by **Discovery Walking Guides** (www .walking.demon.co.uk).

COMARES

Comares sits like a snowdrift atop its lofty hill. The adventure really is in getting there. You see it for kilometre after kilometre before a final twist in an endlessly winding road lands you below the hanging garden of its cliff. From a little car park you can climb steep, winding steps to the village. Look for ceramic footprints underfoot and simply follow them through a web of narrow, twisting lanes past the **Iglesia de la Encarnación** and eventually to the ruins of Comares' **castle** and a remarkable summit **cemetery**.

The village has a history of rebellion, having been a stronghold of Omar ibn Hafsun, but today there is a tangible sense of contented isolation, enjoyed by locals and many newcomers. The views across the Axarquía are stunning.

Have lunch at **El Molino de los Abuelos** (☑952 50 93 09; mains €7-16, menú €8), a converted olive mill on the main plaza which serves typical cuisine and doubles as a as a delightful small hotel. There are a couple of friendly bars at the heart of the village.

On weekdays only, a bus leaves Málaga for Comares at 6pm and starts back at 7am the next morning (€2.90, 1½ hours).

CÓMPETA

This picturesque village with its panoramic views, steep winding streets and central, bar-lined plaza, overlooking the 16th-century church, has long attracted a large mixed foreign population. Not only has this contributed to an active cultural scene but Cómpeta is also home to one or two above-*pueblo*-average restaurants serving contemporary cuisine, as well as a couple of charity shops (rare in Spain) and a foreign-language bookshop. The village makes a good base for hiking and other similar adrenalin-fuelled activities.

◉ Sights & Activities

Cómpeta has some of the area's best local wine, and the popular **Noche del Vino** (Night of the Wine) on 15 August features a program of flamenco and *sevillana* (a form of Andalucian folk dance) music and dance in the central and pretty Plaza Almijara, and limitless free wine.

Salamandra   OUTDOORS
(www.Málaga-aventura.com; Avenida de la Constitución 47) This is a one-stop centre that organises a wide range of activities, including guided hikes, potholing, canyoning and kayaking, as well as themed tours, like orchid trips in the spring, mushroom picking and following historical routes. The latter includes the former merchants pathway linking Cómpeta with Játar and covering some 20km (on foot).

MÁLAGA PROVINCE LA AXARQUÍA

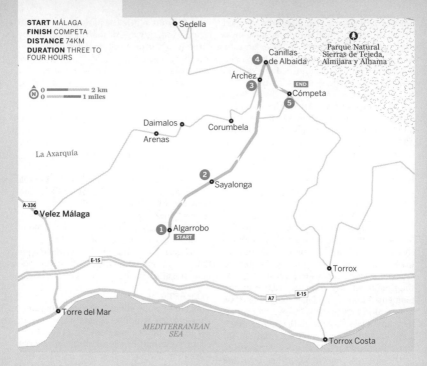

START MÁLAGA
FINISH COMPETA
DISTANCE 74KM
DURATION THREE TO
FOUR HOURS

Driving Tour
Axarquía Villages

› Take the MA-20 highway bypassing Málaga city, direction Motril. Exit at Km277, taking the A706 signposted ❶ **Algarrobo**. Drive into the village, and find a spot next to the leafy park with its jacaranda trees and palms. There is a large municipal pool here (open July to August) if you feel like a dip. Seek out the nearby bakery, Carmen Lupiañez (Calle Blas Infante), famous for its *tortas de algarroba* made with carob, almond and lemon peel. Explore the surrounding winding narrow streets enjoying sights such as the *escalera al cielo* (stairway to heaven), the Río Algorrobo, a Phoenician archaeological site and an exquisite 16th-century church.

The A706 continues its winding mountainous route, flanked by mimosa trees, olives and avocado groves. Next stop is ❷ **Sayalonga**, another exquisite whitewashed *pueblo* with sights including the Fuente el Cid, a fountain dating from Moorish times; the narrowest street in La Axarquía (56cm); an unusual *cementero redondo* (round cemetery); a 16th-century church (formerly a

mosque) – and chairs on the square at Jocavi (Plaza Rafael Alcobi) for a coffee (to accompany those biscuits you bought...).

After around 6km, follow the signs to a scenic road that winds down to the tranquil hamlet of riverside ❸ **Árchez**. Consider stopping en route at Bodega Lopez Martín to buy some local vino then cross over the tiny bridge, surrounded by a thicket of bulrushes, below orchards of orange and lemon trees. Overlooking the river is Bar La Peña, which has a reasonable and tasty *menú del día* for just €7.

Overlooking Árchez is the larger town of ❹ **Canillas de Albaida**, with a labyrinth of flower-filled streets that clearly show their Moorish roots. Head for the delightful Plaza Mayor where Posada La Plaza equals a scenic stop for a postlunch coffee. The owner here has maps and information on local walks.

It is just a short 3.5km to the final stop: ❺ **Cómpeta**, where you can easily while away the rest of the day.

MOUNTAINTOP WALK

Perhaps the most exhilarating walk in La Axarquía region is up the dramatically peaked **El Lucero** (1779m). From its summit on a clear day there are stupendous views as far as Granada in one direction and Morocco in the other. This is a full, demanding day's walking, with an ascent of 1150m from Cómpeta: start by climbing left along the track above Cómpeta's football pitch. About 1½ hours from Cómpeta you pass below and west of a fire observation hut on La Mina hill. Four hundred metres past the turning to the hut, turn right through a gap in the rock (not signed, but fairly obvious). This path leads in about one hour to **Puerto Blanquillo** (1200m), from where a path climbs 200m to **Puerto de Cómpeta**.

One kilometre down from the latter pass, past a quarry, the summit path (1½ hours) diverges to the right across a stream bed, marked by a signboard and map. El Lucero is topped by the ruins of a Guardia Civil post that was built after the civil war to watch for anti-Franco rebels.

It's possible to drive as far up as Puerto Blanquillo on a rough mountain track from Canillas de Albaida, a village 2km northwest of Cómpeta.

Los Caballos del Mosquin
HORSE RIDING
(www.horseriding-andalucia.com; Canillas del Albaida, Cómpeta; half-day trek €65) Guided horseriding treks ranging from one hour to three days (including full board and accommodation) in the surrounding countryside.

✗ Eating & Drinking

El Pilón
INTERNATIONAL €€
(✆952 55 35 12; www.restauranteelpilon.com; Calle Laberinto; mains €11-18.50; ☺7-11pm Mon & Wed-Sat, 1-3.30pm Sun; ✐) This former carpenter's workshop is one of the village's most popular restaurants. Dishes are created using locally-sourced ingredients, whenever possible, and reflect an eclectic range including tandoori chicken, bruschetta and plenty of vegetarian options, as well as more traditional Spanish dishes. There's a cocktail lounge with sweeping views and regular events, including wine tastings and live music.

Alberdini
INTERNATIONAL €€
(www.alberdini.com; Pago La Lomilla 85; mains €9-12; ✐) This place is a kilometre or so out of town, towards Torrox. The terrace has wonderful views of the mountains and sea, while the dining room is equally inviting with its open fireplace and warm stone-and-wood decor. Dishes are reliably well prepared and include pastas, salads, meat and fish dishes and some familiar international choices.

Museo del Vino
ANDALUCIAN €€
(Avenida Constitución; raciones €8-15) Exuding rustic warmth with exposed bricks and beams, this long-time tourist favourite serves excellent ham, cheese and sausage *raciones* and wine from the barrel. It's also something of an Aladdin's cave of regional crafts and produce and Moroccan bits and pieces.

ℹ Information
Tourist office (✆952 55 36 85; Avenida de la Constitución; ☺10am-2pm & 3-6pm Tue-Sat) By the bus stop at the foot of the village.

ℹ Getting There & Away
BUS Three buses travel daily from Málaga to Cómpeta (€4, 1½ hours), stopping via Torre del Mar.

CAR There's a free car park up the hill from the tourist office.

FRIGILIANA
Considered by many as the prettiest village in La Axarquía, Frigiliana is 7km north of Nerja and linked to it by several buses daily (except Sunday). The narrow streets are lined with simple whitewashed houses adorned with pots of blood red geraniums. The **tourist office** (Plaza del Ingenio; ☺9am-8pm Mon-Fri, 10am-1.30pm & 4-8pm Sat & Sun) is helpful.

El Fuerte, the hill that climbs above the village, was the scene of the final bloody defeat of the *moriscos* (converted Muslims) of La Axarquía in their 1569 rebellion, and where they reputedly plunged to their death rather than be killed or captured by the Spanish. You can walk up here if you follow the streets to the top of the town and then continue along the dusty track.

Frigiliana prides itself on its sweet local wine, its local artists, its local honey and by simply being just so sugar-cube perfect and picturesque.

Nerja

POP 22,000

Fifty-six kilometres east of Málaga with the Sierra Almijara rising behind it, the centre of Nerja has succeeded in rebuffing the developers and retained its low-rise village charm, despite the proliferation of souvenir shops and day trippers. At its heart is the perennially beautiful Balcón de Europa, a palm-lined promontory built on the foundations of an old fort with panoramic views of the cobalt-blue sea flanked by honey-coloured coves.

The town is increasingly popular with package holidaymakers and 'residential tourists', which has pushed it far beyond its old confines. There are sizeable urbanisations, especially to the east. The holiday atmosphere, and seawater contamination, can be overwhelming from July to September, but the place is more *tranquilo* and the water cleaner the rest of the year. Made famous in Spain during the '80s by the TV series *Verano Azul* (Blue Summer), a kind of Spanish *Neighbours,* Nerja attracts both national and international visitors.

◉ Sights & Activities

The town centres on the delightful Balcón de Europa, which juts out over the deep blue water and is *the* place for the local *paseo* (promenade) on a languid summer's evening; there are a couple of handy terrace bars here, as well.

There is a lively **market** (Map p179; Calle Almirante Ferrandíz) on Tuesday and a *rastro* (flea market) on Sunday morning north of town in Urbanización Flamingo.

Cueva de Nerja TOP CHOICE / CAVE
(www.cuevadenerja.es; adult/child €8.50/4.50, incl Museo de Nerja €12.50/6.50; ☉10am-2pm & 4-7.30pm) Nerja's major tourist attraction, the Cueva de Nerja, lies 3km north of town, just off the A7, and is extremely busy in summer. The enormous 4km-long cave complex, hollowed out by water around five million years ago and once inhabited by Stone Age hunters, is a theatrical wonderland of extraordinary rock formations, subtle shifting colours and stalactites and stalagmites.

Don't miss the huge central column in 'Cataclysm Hall.' Every July, Spanish and international ballet and music stars perform in the cave as part of the **Festival Cueva de Nerja**. The tourist office has program details.

Museo de Nerja MUSEUM
(Map p179; Plaza de España; adult/child €6/3, incl Cueva de Nerja €12.50/6.50; ☉10am-2pm & 4-6.30pm Tue-Sun) Traces the history of the town from the cave dwellers of Paleolithic times to the tourist boom years of the '60s and is well worth an hour or so of time. Highlights centre on artefacts found in the Cueva de Nerja and range from the thought-provoking skeleton of an adult cave dweller to the fascinatingly mundane prehistoric cheese dish.

Buceo Costa Nerja DIVING
(☏952 52 86 10; www.nerjadiving.com; Playa Burriana) Diving can be especially rewarding here, due to the Atlantic stream, which results in a highly varied marine life. This reputable outfit organises a range of courses for most levels, including a 2½-hour Discover Scuba Diving course for €100 and a PADI open-water course for €450. It also operates snorkelling trips (€30).

Beaches

The picturesque small cove to the east of the Balcón de Europa is **Playa Calahonda**, where you can rent sunbeds and parasols, though it does get busy at the height of summer. To the Balcón's west is another popular sandy stretch, the **Playa el Salón** while, further east, is **Playa Burriana**, which is Nerja's best beach with plenty of towel space on the sand. You can walk here via picturesque Calle Carabeo, continuing down the steps to the beach and along to Burriana.

East of Nerja the coast becomes more rugged and with your own wheels you can head out to some great beaches reached by tracks down from the A7/N340. **Playa de Cantarriján**, just over the border in Granada province, and **Playa del Cañuelo**, immediately before the border, are two of the best, with a couple of summer-only restaurants.

⭑ Festivals & Events

Healing Arts Festival NEW AGE
(www.healingartsinternational.com) Held in early September in Nerja, this is a highly successful New Age gathering.

Noche de San Juan SUMMER SOLSTICE
Every 23 June, Nerja's inhabitants celebrate St John's day and get their barbecue kits out and head for the beach, where they eat sizzling sardines, fish and seafood, drink wine and beer and stay up until the next morning swimming, dancing, partying and, ultimately, flaking out on the sand.

Nerja

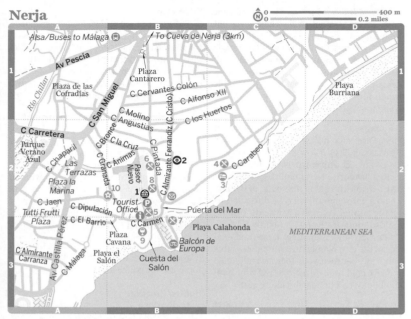

Virgen del Carmen RELIGIOUS

The fishers' feast day is marked with a procession that carries the Virgin in fishing boats; held on 16 July.

✕ Eating

Nerja has an abundance of restaurants and bars, most geared towards undiscerning tourists. In general, avoid any advertising all-day English breakfasts or with sun-bleached posters of the dishes. Playa Burriana, Nerja's best beach, is backed by an animated strip of restaurants and bars.

TOP CHOICE Oliva MODERN EUROPEAN €€

(☎952 52 14 29; www.restauranteoliva.com; Calle Pintada 7; mains €15-19) Single orchids, a drum and bass soundtrack and a charcoal grey-and-green colour scheme. In short, this place has class. The menu is reassuringly brief and changes regularly according to what is fresh in season; typical dishes are grilled scallops in a beetroot sauce and sea bass with wasabi, soy and ginger. The toffee pud with hazelnut cream is appropriately sinful and delicious.

Café Mandarina INTERNATIONAL €

(Plaza Balcón de Europa; mains €6-8; ☑🚼) Tucked into a corner, this tiny place dishes

Nerja

◎ Sights
1 Museo de Nerja B2
2 Tuesday Market B2

⊜ Sleeping
3 Hotel Carabeo C2

✕ Eating
4 A Taste of India C2
5 Café Mandarina B2
6 El Desvan B2
7 El Papagayo B3
8 Oliva B2
 Restaurante 34 .... (see 3)

⊜ Drinking
9 Cochran's Irish Bar B3

✿ Entertainment
10 Centro Cultural Villa de Nerja B2

up well-priced breakfasts, baguettes, tapas and salads; the latter including tasty choices like hummus, goats' cheese and oranges. While the majority of the menu is vegetarian, they are not too pious to include burgers and bacon and eggs. There are regular art exhibitions and several outside tables.

A Taste of India
INDIAN €€

(Calle Carabeo 51; mains €8-13) Though it's not the most obvious choice in Spain, this place is worth visiting for its fantastic Goan-style Indian food, such as a delicious Goan fish curry, biryanis, tandooris and other spicy meals cooked on the spot. The hospitable owners are from a former Portuguese colony in Gujarat.

El Papagayo
SEAFOOD €€

(Playa Calahonda; mains €6-12; ⊙noon-5pm & 10pm-late Jun-Sep) A low-key beach bar and restaurant, El Papagayo is the locals' and visitors' favourite Nerja haunt. You can just have a drink and enjoy the sound of the lapping sea, although this may be difficult during the annual Papagayo Noche de Verano; a midsummer festival with nightly DJs.

Alternatively enjoy good tapas and specials of the day, mainly fish, sitting on a stool with sand between your toes, accompanied by an ice cold *tinto de verano* (red wine with lemonade); real holiday-brochure stuff.

Merendero Ayo
SEAFOOD €€

(Playa Burriana; mains €9-13) At this open-air place you can enjoy paella cooked in sizzling pans over an open fire – and even go back for a free second helping. It's run by Ayo, a delightful local character famed for the discovery of the Cueva de Nerja complex, who throws the rice on the *paellera* (paella dish) in a very spectacular fashion, amusing all his guests.

Restaurante 34
MODERN EUROPEAN €€

(☑952 52 54 44; www.hotelcarabeo.com; Hotel Carabeo, Calle Carabeo 34; mains €15-25) A truly gorgeous setting both indoors and outside in the garden, which is gently stepped to its furthest section overlooking the sea. Delicious and exotic food combinations are served, although the portions may be a tad nouvelle for those with a big appetite.

El Desvan
TAPAS €

(Calle Pintada 23; tapas €1.50-2.30) Surrounded by shops, this narrow tapas bar with its intimate interior and couple of outside tables dishes up inventive generously portioned tapas, such as brie with caramelized onion, dates with bacon and (wait for it) duck with rose petal jelly. Great value.

🍷 Drinking & Entertainment

Cochran's Irish Bar
BAR

(Paseo Balcón de Europa 6) A longstanding Irish bar with a superb blarney atmosphere plus a foot-hopping program of live twanging at weekends. Has a beautifully sited outdoor bar with sweeping sea views and a romantic tropical-island feel which makes it especially perfect at 'locked eyes over cocktails' time.

Tropy Sol
CAFE

(Playa Burriana; ⊙10am-10pm) Playa Burriana's top place for coffee and ice cream.

Centro Cultural
Villa de Nerja
CULTURAL CENTRE

(☑952 52 38 63; Calle Granada 45) This well-run centre organises an ambitious annual program of classical music, theatre, jazz and flamenco, featuring international and Spanish musicians and performers.

ℹ Information

Tourist office (www.nerja.org; Calle Carmen; ⊙10am-2pm & 6-10pm) Plenty of useful leaflets.

ℹ Getting There & Around

BUS Alsa (www.alsa.es) runs regular buses to/from Málaga (€4.15, 1¾ hours, 23 daily), Marbella (€9.50, 1¼ hours, one daily) and Antequera (€8.30, 2¼ hours, two daily). There are also buses to Almería and Granada.

PARKING Follow the signs to the central **underground car park** (1/24hr €1.20/18) in Plaza de España.

Córdoba Province

Best Places to Eat

» Casa Mazal (p194)

» Bar Santos (p194)

» Bodegas Campos (p194)

» Las Camachas (p200)

» Restaurante Zahorí (p199)

Best Places to Stay

» Hotel Zuhayra (p302)

» Casa Baños de la Villa (p302)

» Hotel Caserío de Iznájar (p303)

» Hospedería Alma Andalusí (p301)

» Parador Nacional Arruzafa (p302)

Why Go?

Once the dazzling beacon of Al-Andalus, the city of Córdoba inevitably dominates a visit to its namesake province. Remnants of the caliphate, such as the Great Mosque and the palatial complex of Madinat al-Zahra, hold immense historical and architectural interest. But there's plenty of less trampled territory to explore outside the provincial capital. The Río Guadalquivir divides not just the city but the province. To the north looms the Sierra Morena, a mountainous expanse of protected forest and ruined castles. To the south, rippling terrain is carpeted with olive trees, an agricultural bounty that is transformed into a velvety oil, while Andalucía's signature wines flow sweetly around Montilla and Moriles. Further south, caves and canyons are carved out of the limestone massif of the Sierras Subbéticas, punctuated by the unexpected bustle of Priego de Córdoba and the remote splendor of Zuheros, a perfect base for mountain hiking and cheese noshing.

Driving Distances (km)

	Córdoba	Priego de Córdoba	Almodóvar del Río	Baena
Priego de Córdoba	103			
Almodóvar del Río	30	133		
Baena	60	34	90	
Montilla	46	58	76	37

DON'T MISS

Cool, flower-filled courtyards with fountains and mosaic floors, the *patios cordobeses* (p192) make a delightful retreat from Córdoba's sizzling summers. In May they're on view during the Festival de Los Patios Cordobeses.

Castles of Córdoba

» Castillo de Almodóvar (p200)

» Alcázar de los Reyes Cristianos (p191)

» Castillo de Miramonte (p202)

» Castillo de Zuheros (p196)

Best Walks

» Cañon de Bailón (p197)

» Sendero Botánico (p201)

» Cueva de los Murciélagos (p197)

» Puente Romano (p191)

Resources

» **Info Cordoba** (www .infocordoba.com) Practical info and tips.

» **Córdoba 24** (www .cordoba24.info) What's on in Córdoba.

» **Tourism of Cordoba** (www.turismodecordoba .org) Official tourism board site, featuring themed walking tours.

» **Cordobapedia** (http:// cordobapedia.wikianda .es) Córdoba's very own wiki covering the province's culture and history.

Getting Around

The city of Córdoba is an important crossroads for both highways and railroads, with connections to Spain's major cities and local buses to most towns in the province. Travellers with their own wheels often ply the scenic N-432, which drops down from Extremadura through the Sierra Morena, proceeding through the Sierras Subbéticas on its way to Granada, or the A-431, which hugs the Guadalquivir west to Seville.

THREE PERFECT DAYS

Day 1: Córdoba, a Fusion of Cultures

A day's exploration of Córdoba suitably starts with a visit to the **Torre de la Calahorra**, on the Guadalquivir's south bank, for inside is an exhibit on the fusion of Islam, Judaism and Christianity. Cross the Roman bridge to the **Mezquita** and wander through its miles of archways. Navigate the tortuous lanes of the **Judería** and savor a Sephardic lunch at **Casa Mazal**. To complete the religious trilogy, stroll amid the palms of the **Alcázar de los Reyes Cristianos**. In the evening, do some tapas bar-hopping, then enjoy fiery Flamenco jams at **La Pataita de Antonio**.

Day 2: Castles & Christians

Make a morning of the **Madinat al-Zahra**, ruler Abd ar-Rahman III's own personal city, featuring a superb new museum on Andalucía's Islamic heritage. Skirt the Guadalquivir westward and make for the castle on the horizon; keeping a stern watch over the river, the **Castillo de Almodóvar** sports nine towers. Proceed west to **Hornachuelos**, gateway to a swath of protected forest, and hike amid the cork oaks and wild olives. Celebrate your return to Córdoba with a fino (sherry) at **Bodega Guzmán**.

Day 3: Earthly Delights

Take a day to indulge in the culinary bounty of the province's southern reaches. Head first for the vineyards of **Montilla** and taste the signature wines at the area's bodegas. Next visit **Baena**, where mills produce an olive oil so outstanding it's been granted its own designation of origin; see it made the traditional way at the Núñez de Prado mill. Further south, the hills give way to the limestone cliffs of La Subbética, where the whitewashed village of **Zuheros** nestles. Take a ramble through the dramatic mountain scenery or burrow below to the cave network of the **Cueva de los Murciélagos**.

Accommodation

Córdoba has a wide range of options and makes a good base for exploring the province. Rates are competitive but leap in April and May, during fiesta season. Consider Zuheros, with its supremely situated Hotel Zuhayra (p302), for exploring the southern Subbética range; the western Hornachuelos range is awash in *casas rurales* (country homes). Read all about hotel choices in our dedicated Accommodation chapter (p288).

CÓRDOBA

POP 328.659 / ELEV 110M

Córdoba is ideal for those who like to eat well, explore on foot, dive into old bodegas and relish architectural wonders. The city's heart needs no introduction, for its fame is widespread: the magnificent Mezquita, a symbol of worldly and sophisticated Islamic culture, lords over the town centre and pulls thousands of tourists into its arched interior every day. The streets of the Judería (Jewish quarter) stretch out from the great mosque like capillaries (albeit those nearest the monument are clogged with tourist bric-a-brac), unexpectedly emerging on peaceful plazas. The compact town centre has a more boisterous vibe with some excellent bars and restaurants – some of which have become sights in themselves – while the Islamic ruin of Medinat al-Zahra, west of town, stirs the imagination with its glory and grandeur.

Córdoba is quiet and withdrawn during the winter months but bursts into life from mid-April to mid-June, when the city stages most of its major fiestas. At this time of year the skies are blue, the heat is tolerable and the city's many trees and courtyards drip with foliage and blooms.

The medieval city is immediately north of the Río Guadalquivir, with a warren of narrow streets surrounding the Mezquita. Within the medieval city, the area northwest of the Mezquita was known as the Judería, the Muslim quarter was north and east of the Mezquita, and the Mozarabic (Christian) quarter was further to the northeast. The main square of Córdoba is Plaza de las Tendillas, with the main shopping streets to the plaza's north and west.

History

The Roman colony of Corduba was initially established by the Romans in 152 BC as a strategic provisioning point for troops. After the civil wars between Pompeii and Caesar, the settlement's status changed and Córdoba became the capital of the province of Baetica, ushering in an era of prosperity and cultural ascendancy and bringing the writers Seneca and Lucan to the world. It was during this era that a bridge was built spanning the Guadalquivir as well as a temple dedicated to the emperor, whose remains are still visible east of Plaza de las Tendillas. By the 3rd century the Roman city had fallen into decline and Christianity's expansion reached Córdoba. Visigoths took over in the 5th century but never attained stability, and after continuous rebellions Córdoba fell to Islamic invaders in AD 711. It soon took the role as Islamic capital on the Iberian Peninsula.

It was here in 756 that Abd al-Rahman I set himself up as the independent emir of the Al-Andalus region, founding the Omayyad dynasty, but the town's and region's heyday came under Abd al-Rahman III (AD 912–61). He named himself caliph (the title of the Muslim successors of Mohammed) in 929, sealing Al-Andalus' long-standing de facto independence from Baghdad.

Córdoba was by now the biggest city in Western Europe, with a flourishing economy based on agriculture and skilled artisan products, and a population somewhere between 100,000 and 500,000. The city shone with hundreds of dazzling mosques, public baths, patios, gardens and fountains. Abd ar-Rahman III's court was frequented by Jewish, Arab and Christian scholars, and Córdoba's university, library and observatories made it a centre of learning, the influence of which was still being felt in Christian Europe many centuries later. Córdoba also became a place of pilgrimage for Muslims who could not get to Mecca or Jerusalem.

Towards the end of the 10th century, Al-Mansur (Almanzor), a ruthless general whose northward raids terrified Christian Spain, took the reins of power from the caliphs. But after the death of Al-Mansur's son Abd al-Malik in 1008, the caliphate descended into anarchy. Rival claimants to the title, Berber troops and Christian armies from Castile and Catalonia all fought over the spoils. The Berbers terrorised and looted the city and, in 1031, Omayyad rule ended. Córdoba became a minor part of the Seville *taifa* (small kingdom) in 1069, and has been overshadowed by Seville ever since.

Twelfth-century Córdoba produced the two most celebrated scholars of Al-Andalus – the Muslim philosopher Averroës (1126–98) and the Jewish philosopher Moses ben Maimon (known as Maimónides; 1135–1204). Their philosophical efforts to harmonise religion with Aristotelian reason were met with ignorance and intolerance: the Almohads put Averroës in high office, and persecuted Maimon until he fled to Egypt.

When Córdoba was taken by Castile's Fernando III in 1236, much of its population

CÓRDOBA PROVINCE CÓRDOBA

Córdoba Province Highlights

1 Discovering a scintillating World Heritage Site and glorious fusion of three great cultures in **Córdoba** (p183)

2 Losing yourself amid the arches of the **Mezquita** (p186), a hallucinatory relic of the caliphate

3 Walking through cork oak forest at **Parque Natural Sierra de Hornachuelos** (p200)

4 Pondering the remnants of **Madinat al-Zahra** (p192), city of the caliph, with a splendid new museum

5 Exploring the subterranean caverns of **Parque Natural Sierras Subbéticas** (p196)

6 Admiring the baroque architecture of **Priego de Córdoba** (p198)

7 Surveying the countryside from the monumental castle complex of **Almodóvar del Río** (p200)

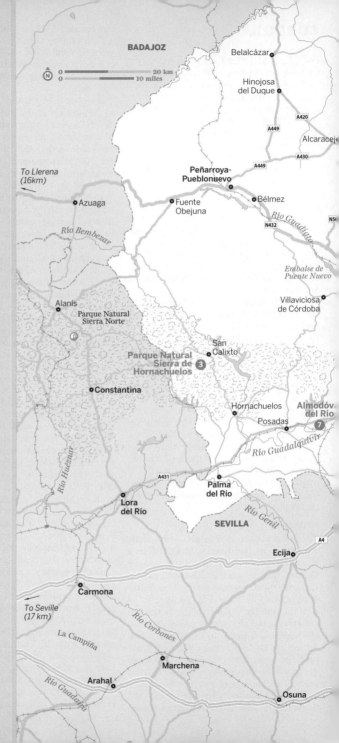

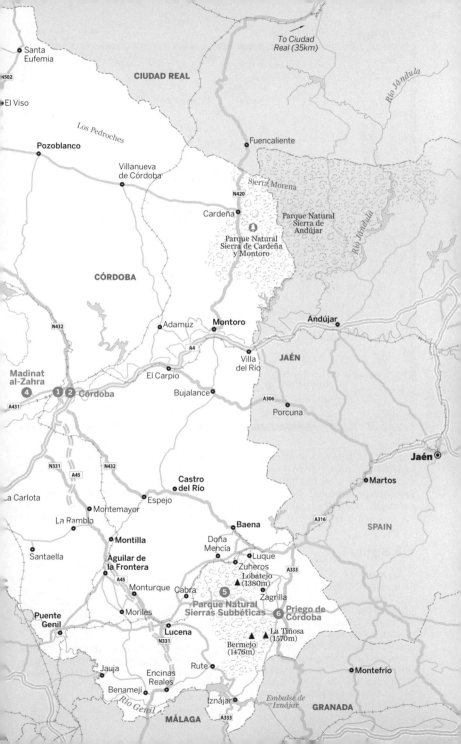

Córdoba

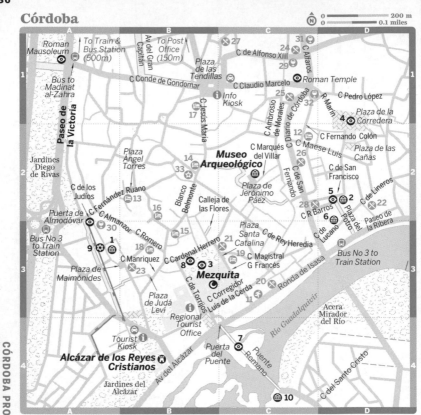

fled. Córdoba became a provincial city and its decline was only reversed through the arrival of industry in the late 19th century. But something of Córdoba's former splendour remained – one of the greatest Spanish poets, Luis de Góngora (1561–1627), was from the city.

◉ Sights

TOP CHOICE **Mezquita**   GREAT MOSQUE

(Mosque; ☎957 47 05 12; www.mezquitadecordoba .org; Calle Cardenal Herrero; adult/child €8/4, 8.30-10am Mon-Sat free ; ⊙10am-7pm Mon-Sat, 8.30-10am & 2-7pm Sun Mar-Oct, 8.30am-6pm Mon-Sat, 8.30-10am & 2-6pm Sun Nov-Feb) It's impossible to overemphasise the beauty of Córdoba's Great Mosque, with its remarkably peaceful and spacious interior. The Mezquita hints, with all its lustrous decoration, at a lavish and refined age when Muslims, Jews and Christians lived side by side

and enriched their city and its surroundings with a heady interaction of diverse and vibrant cultures.

The Visigothic Church of St Vincent was the original building located on the site of the Mezquita, and Arab chronicles recount how Abd ar-Rahman I purchased half of the church for the use of the Muslim community's Friday prayers. However, the rapid growth of that community soon rendered the space too small and in AD 784 he bought the other half to erect a new mosque. Al-Hakim II added the existing mihrab (prayer niche) and, for extra light, built a number of domes with skylights over the area in front of it.

What you see today is the building's final form with one major alteration – a 16th-century cathedral right in the middle (hence the often-used description of 'Mezquita-Cathedral'). The structure was partly dismantled to make way for the cathedral,

Córdoba

which took nearly 250 years to complete (1523–1766). The cathedral thus exhibits a range of changing architectural styles and tastes, from plateresque and late Renaissance to extravagant Spanish baroque.

The main entrance to the Mezquita is the **Puerta del Perdón**, a 14th-century Mudéjar gateway on Calle Cardenal Herrero. There's a ticket office immediately inside on the pretty **Patio de los Naranjos** (Map p186) (Courtyard of the Orange Trees), from where a door leads inside the building itself. Mass is held at 11am, noon and 1pm on weekdays. Entrance is free from 8.30am to 10am Monday to Saturday and groups are not admitted, so weekday morning visits are perfect for appreciating the Mezquita in peace and quiet. Mass is celebrated from 11am to 1pm Sunday in the central cathedral.

The Mesquita-Cathedral
The Mezquita's architectural uniqueness and importance lies in the fact that, structurally speaking, it was a revolutionary building for its time. It defied precedents. The Dome of the Rock in Jerusalem and the Great Mosque in Damascus both had vertical, navelike designs, but the Mezquita's aim was to form an infinitely spacious, democratically horizontal and simple space, where the spirit could be free to roam and communicate easily with God. The original Islamic prayer space (usually the open yard of a desert home) was transformed into a 14,400-sq-m metaphor for the desert itself. Men prayed side by side on the *argamasa*, a floor made of compact, reddish slaked lime and sand. A flat roof, decorated with gold and multicoloured motifs, shaded them from the sun. The orange patio, where the ablution fountains gurgled with water, was the oasis. The terracotta-and-white-striped arches suggested a hallucinogenic forest of date palms, and supported the roof with 1293 columns (of which only 856 remain).

Abd ar-Rahman I's initial mosque was a square split into two rectangular halves – a covered prayer hall and an open ablutions courtyard. The prayer hall was divided into 11 'naves' by lines of two-tier arches striped in red brick and white stone. The columns

Mezquita

TIMELINE

600 Foundation of the Christian Visigothic church of St Vincent on the site of the present Mezquita.

785 Salvaging Visigoth and Roman ruins, Emir Abd ar-Rahman I converts the Mezquita into a mosque.

822-5 Mosque enlarged in reign of Abd ar-Rahman II.

912-961 A new minaret is ordered by Abd ar-Rahman III.

961-6 Mosque enlarged by Al-Hakam II who also enriches the **mihrab 1**.

987 Mosque enlarged for the last time by Al-Mansur Ibn Abi Aamir. With the addition of the **Patio de los Naranjos 2**, the building reaches its current dimensions.

1236 Mosque reconverted into a Christian church after Córdoba is recaptured by Ferdinand III of Castile.

1271 Instead of destroying the mosque, the overawed Christians elect to modify it. Alfonso X orders the construction of the **Capilla de Villaviciosa 3** and **Capilla Real 4**.

1300s Original minaret is replaced by the baroque **Torre del Alminar 5**.

1520s A Renaissance-style cathedral nave is added by Charles V. 'I have destroyed something unique to the world' he laments on seeing the finished work.

2004 Spanish Muslims petition to be able to worship in the Mezquita again. The Vatican doesn't consent.

Capilla de Villaviciosa
Sift through the building's numerous chapels till you find this gem, an early Christian modification added in 1277 which fused existing Moorish features with Gothic arches and pillars. It served as the Capilla Mayor until the 1520s.

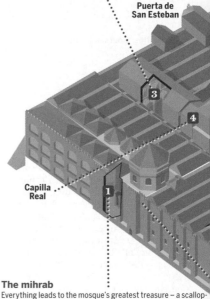

Puerta de San Esteban

Capilla Real

The mihrab
Everything leads to the mosque's greatest treasure – a scallop-shell-shaped prayer niche facing Mecca that was added in the 10th century. Cast your eyes over the gold mosaic cubes crafted by imported Byzantium sculptors.

The cathedral choir

Few ignore the impressive *coro* (choir): a late-Christian addition dating from the 1750s. Once you've admired the skilfully carved mahogany choir stalls depicting scenes from the Bible, look up at the impressive baroque ceiling.

Torre del Alminar

This is the Mezquita's cheapest sight because you don't have to pay to see it. Rising 93m and viewable from much of the city, the baroque-style bell tower was built over the mosque's original minaret.

The Mezquita arches

No, you're not hallucinating. The Mezquita's most defining characteristic is its unique terracotta-and-white striped arches that support 856 pillars salvaged from Roman and Visigoth ruins. Glimpsed through the dull light they're at once spooky and striking.

Puerta del Perdón

Patio de los Naranjos

Abandon architectural preconceptions all ye who enter here. The ablutions area of the former mosque is a shady courtyard embellished with orange trees that acts as the Mezquita's main entry point.

Capilla Mayor

A Christian monument inside an Islamic mosque sounds beautifully ironic, yet here it is: a Gothic church commissioned by Charles V in the 16th century and planted in the middle of the world's third largest mosque.

The maksura

Guiding you towards the mihrab, the maksura is a former royal enclosure where the caliphs and their retinues prayed. Its lavish, elaborate arches were designed to draw the eye of worshippers towards the mihrab and Mecca.

used for the Mezquita were a mishmash of material collected from the Visigothic cathedral that had previously occupied the site, Córdoba's Roman buildings and places as far away as Constantinople. This, predictably, presented problems in keeping the ceiling height consistent and making it high enough to create a sense of openness. Inventive builders came up with the idea of using the tall columns as a base and planting the shorter ones on top in order to create the ceiling arches. Later enlargements of the mosque extended these lines of arches to cover an area of nearly 120 sq metres and create one of the biggest mosques in the world. The arcades are one of the much-loved Islamic architectural motifs. Their simplicity and number give a sense of endlessness to the Mezquita.

Originally there were 19 doors, filling the interior of the mosque with light. Nowadays, only one door sheds its light into the dim interior, dampening the vibrant effect of the red and white voussoirs (wedge-shaped pieces) of the double arches. Christian additions to the building, such as the solid mass of the cathedral in the centre and the 50 or so chapels around the fringes, further enclose and impose on the airy space.

At the furthest point from the entrance door, on the southern wall of the mosque, the aisles draw you towards qibla (the direction of Mecca) and the mosque's greatest treasure, the mihrab built by Al-Hakim II.

Mihrab & Maksura

Like Abd ar-Rahman II a century earlier, Al-Hakim lengthened the naves of the prayer hall, creating a new mihrab at the south end of the central nave. The bay immediately in front of the mihrab and the bays to each side form the *maksura*, the area where the caliphs and their retinues would have prayed. Inside the mihrab a single block of white marble was sculpted into the shape of a scallop shell, a symbol of the Quran. This formed the dome that amplified the voice of the imam (person who leads Islamic worship services) throughout the mosque.

The arches within and around the *maksura* are the mosque's most intricate and sophisticated, forming a forest of interwoven horseshoe shapes. These ingenious curves are subtly interwoven to form the strongest elements of the structure. But they were not only physically functional: their purpose was to seduce the eye of the worshipper with their lavish decorations, leading it up to the

mihrab – to the focus of prayer and the symbolic doorway to heaven. Equally attractive are the skylit domes over the *maksura*, decorated with star-patterned stone vaulting. Each dome was held up by four interlocking pairs of parallel ribs, a highly advanced technique in 10th-century Europe.

The greatest glory of Al-Hakim II's extension was the portal of the mihrab itself – a crescent arch with a rectangular surround known as an *alfiz*, surmounted by a blind arcade. For the decoration of the portal, Al-Hakim asked the emperor of Byzantium, Nicephoras II Phocas, to send him a mosaicist capable of imitating the superb mosaics of the Great Mosque of Damascus, one of the great 8th-century Syrian Omayyad buildings. The Christian emperor sent the Muslim caliph not only a mosaicist but also a gift of 1600kg of gold mosaic cubes. These shimmering cubes, shaped into flower motifs and inscriptions from the Quran, decorated the whole *maksura*.

Patio de los Naranjos & Minaret

Outside the mosque, the leafy, walled courtyard and its fountain were the site of ritual ablutions before prayer. The crowning glory of the whole complex was the minaret, which at its peak towered 48m (only 22m of the minaret still survives). Now encased in its 16th-century shell, the original minaret would have looked something like the Giralda in Seville, which was practically a copy. Córdoba's minaret influenced all the minarets built thereafter throughout the western Islamic world.

The Cathedral

For three centuries following the Reconquista (Christian reconquest) in 1236, the Mezquita remained largely unaltered save for minor modifications such as the Mudéjar tiling added in the 1370s to the Mozarabic and Almohad Capilla Real (located nine bays north and one east of the mihrab, and now part of the cathedral). In the 16th century King Carlos I gave permission (against the wishes of Córdoba's city council) for the centre of the Mezquita to be ripped out to allow construction of the Capilla Mayor (the altar area in the cathedral) and *coro* (choir). However, the king was not enamoured with the results and famously regretted: 'You have built what you or others might have built anywhere, but you have destroyed something that was unique in the world.'

Subsequent additions included a rich 17th-century jasper and red-marble retable (ornamental screenlike structure behind the altar) in the Capilla Mayor, and fine mahogany stalls in the choir, which were carved in the 18th century by Pedro Duque Cornejo.

AROUND THE MEZQUITA

Alcázar de los Reyes Cristianos CASTLE

(Castle of the Christian Monarchs; Campo Santo de Los Mártires; admission €4, Fri free; ☺10am-2pm & 5.30-7.30pm Tue-Sat, 9.30am-2.30pm Sun & holidays) Built by Alfonso XI in the 14th century on the remains of Roman and Arab predecessors, the castle began life as a palace. It hosted both Fernando and Isabel, who made their first acquaintance with Columbus here in 1486. Its terraced gardens – full of fish ponds, fountains, orange trees, flowers and topiary – are a pleasure to stroll and a joy to behold from the tower.

A hall here displays some remarkable Roman mosaics, dug up from the Plaza de la Corredera in the 1950s. Most notable is a portrait of the mythical couple Polyphemus and Galatea, whose story was later retold by the Spanish poet Luis de Góngora.

Puente Romano BRIDGE

Traversing the Río Guadalquivir, the much restored Roman bridge formed part of the ancient Vía Augusta, which extended from Cádiz to Girona. Now it is a favored stroll for *cordobeses*. Around midway a statue of the archangel San Rafael (one of many throughout the city) stands on a parapet.

Torre de la Calahorra MUSEUM

(Map p186; ☎957 29 39 29; Puente Romano; adult/child €4.50/3; ☺10am-6pm Oct-Apr, 10am-2pm & 4.30-8.30pm May-Sep) On the south end of the Puente Romano stands this squat tower, erected under Islamic rule to control access to the bridge. It now houses Museo Vivo de Al-Andalus, an interesting museum highlighting the fusion of Córdoba's three great cultures/religions.

JUDERÍA

The old Jewish quarter is an atmospheric labyrinth of narrow streets and small squares, whitewashed buildings and wrought-iron doorways that allow glimpses of plant-filled patios. The importance of the Jewish community is illustrated by the proximity of the Judería to the Mezquita and the city's centres of power. Spain had one of Europe's biggest Jewish communities, recorded from as early as the 2nd century AD. Persecuted by the Visigoths, they allied themselves with the Muslims following the Arab conquests. By the 10th century they were established as some of the most dynamic members of society, holding posts as administrators, doctors, jurists, philosophers, poets and functionaries. In fact, one of the greatest Jewish theologians, Maimónides, was from Córdoba. He summarised the teachings of Judaism and completed his magnum opus, the *Mishne Torah*, which systemises all of Jewish law, before fleeing persecution to Fès, Morocco, and later to Egypt.

Although somewhat diminished, what remains of the Judería extends west and northwest from the Mezquita, almost to the beginning of Avenida del Gran Capitán. The most famous street in the area is known as Calleja de las Flores (Flower Alley) and gives a picture-postcard view of the Mezquita bell tower framed between the narrow alley walls.

Sinagoga SYNAGOGUE

(Calle de los Judíos 20; admission €0.30; ☺9.30am-2pm & 3.30-5.30pm Tue-Sat, 9.30am-1.30pm Sun & holidays) Built in 1315, this is one of the few testaments to the Jewish presence in Andalucía, though it hasn't actually been used as a place of worship since the expulsion of Jews from Spain in 1492. It is decorated with some extravagant stuccowork that includes Hebrew inscriptions and intricate Mudéjar star and plant patterns.

Casa de Sefarad MUSEUM

(www.casadesefarad.es; Calle Judíos; admission €4; ☺10am-6pm Mon-Sat, 11am-2pm Sun) In the heart of the *Judería*, and once connected by underground tunnel to the Sinagoga, this small museum is devoted to the Sephardic-Judaic tradition in Spain. There is a refreshing focus on music, domestic traditions and on the women intellectuals (poets, singers and thinkers) of Al-Andalus. A program of live-music recitals and storytelling events runs most of the year.

ELSEWHERE IN CORDOBA

Plaza del Potro SQUARE

Córdoba's famous Square of the Colt has in its centre a lovely 16th-century stone fountain topped by a rearing *potro* (colt) that gives the plaza its name. On its western side is the legendary 1435 inn Posada del Potro (Plaza del Potro 10; admission free; ☺5-9pm Tue-Fri, 10am-2pm Sat), described in *Don Quijote* as a 'den of thieves.'

✱ Plaza de la Corredera wonderfull square (eat/drink

CÓRDOBA PROVINCE CÓRDOBA

PATIOS CORDOBESES

Studded with pots of geraniums, threaded with pebbled mosaic paths, bougainvillea cascading down the walls and a trickling fountain in the middle, the famed patios of Córdoba have provided shade during the searing heat of summer for centuries. The origin of these elaborate courtyards probably lies in the ancient Greek megaron and the Roman atrium, but the tradition was continued by the Arabs, for whom the internal courtyard was an area for women to go about family life and household chores. The addition of a central water fountain and multitudes of plants heightened the sensation of coolness.

Beautiful examples of patios can be glimpsed in Córdoba's Judería, as well as on Calle San Basilio, about 400m southwest of the Mezquita, in the Santa Marina district and around the Plaza de la Magdalena. The patios are at their prettiest in spring, when many are entered in an annual competition as part of the Festival de los Patios Cordobeses (p193).

Museo de Bellas Artes — MUSEUM

(Plaza del Potro 1; admission €1.50; 2.30-8.30pm Tue, 9am-8.30pm Wed-Sat, 9am-2.30pm Sun) Occupying the old charity hospital on the Plaza del Potro, the city art museum displays mainly Cordoban masters, with much of the work culled from monasteries around the region. The works of Julio Romero Torres, famed for his portrayals of jealous bullfighters and proud prostitutes, can be viewed here while the adjacent museum dedicated to that local artist is under renovation.

Museo Arqueológico — MUSEUM

(Archaeological Museum; Plaza de Jerónimo Páez 7; admission €1.50; 2.30-8.30pm Tue, 9am-8.30pm Wed-Sat, 9am-2.30pm Sun & public holidays) Recently installed in a new wing while the Renaissance palace that formerly housed the museum is being restored, the exhibit brilliantly covers Córdoba's illustrious history, with an overriding theme of cultural interchange. The building stands upon an archaeological site, the Roman theatre of Colonia Patricia, and the basement level features a walkway through the ruins.

The upper level gives an overview, with major sections on Roman and Islamic Córdoba, featuring many important pieces from those periods, as well as an impressive coin collection. The ground floor displays a fascinating collection of mostly ceramic objects for everyday use, from women's jewellery to funerary urns.

Plaza de la Corredera — PLAZA

This grand 17th-century square has an elaborate history of public entertainment and gory showbiz. It was the site of Córdoba's Roman amphitheatre, and the location for horse races, bullfights and Inquisition burnings. Nowadays the square is ringed by balconied apartments and an assortment of lively pubs, cafes and shops.

Palacio de Viana — MUSEUM

(www.palaciodeviana.com; Plaza de Don Gome 2; admission whole house/patios only €6/3; 10am-7pm Tue-Fri, 10am-3pm Sat & Sun Sep-Jun, 9am-3pm Tue-Sun Jul & Aug) Stunning Renaissance palace set around 12 beautiful patios that are a genuine pleasure to visit in the spring. Occupied by the Marqueses de Viana until a few decades ago, the 6500-sq-metre building is packed with art and antiques. The charge covers a one-hour guided tour of the rooms and access to the patios and garden. It's about 600m northeast of the Plaza de las Tendillas. Or take bus number 6 to Puerta de Sevilla, get off at Plaza de Colón and walk four blocks east.

Madinat al-Zahra — RUINS

(Medina Azahara; 957 32 91 30; Carretera Palma del Río; admission €1.50; 10am-8.30pm Tue-Sat May–mid-Sep, 10am-6.30pm Tue-Sat mid-Sep–Apr, 10am-2pm Sun year-round) West of Córdoba stand the remains of Madinat al-Zahra, the sumptuous palace-city built by Caliph Abd al-Rahman III in the 10th century. Located at the foot of the Sierra Morena, the complex spills down over three terraces with the caliph's palace on the highest terrace overlooking what would have been the court and town. A fascinating new museum has been installed at the base of the site.

Legend has it that Abd al-Rahman III built Madinat al-Zahra for his favourite wife, Az-Zahra. Dismayed by her homesickness and yearning for the snowy mountains of Syria, he surrounded his new city with almond and cherry trees, replacing snowflakes with fluffy white blossoms. More realistically, it was probably the case that Abd al-Rahman's rivalry with the Abbasid dynasty in Baghdad drove him to build an opulent royal complex outside Córdoba. Building started in AD 936 and chroniclers record some staggering construction statistics: 10,000 labourers set 6000 stone blocks a day, with outer walls extending 1518m west to east and 745m north to south.

It is almost inconceivable to think that such a city, built over 40 years, was only to last a mere 30 more before the usurper Al-Mansur transferred the seat of government to a new palace complex of his own in AD 981. Then, between 1010 and 1013, it was wrecked by Berber soldiers. During succeeding centuries its ruins were plundered repeatedly for building materials. Only around one-tenth of the site has been excavated to date.

The visitors' route takes you down through the city's original northern gate to the palatial residence, arranged around several square courtyards, to the administrative sector, presided over by the grand arched Edificio Basilical Superior, and then to the centrepiece of the site, the Salón de Abd al-Rahman III. Inside, the royal reception hall (closed at time of research) has been much restored, and the exquisitely carved stuccowork, a riot of vegetal designs, has been painstakingly repaired to cover most of the wall's surface. It gives just a glimpse of the lavishness of the court, which was said to be decorated with gold and silver tiles, and arches of ivory and ebony that contrasted with walls of multicoloured marble. For special effect, a bowl at the centre of the hall was filled with mercury so that when it was rocked the reflected light flashed and bounced off the gleaming decoration.

The new museum, on the foundation of one of the excavated buildings, blends seamlessly with its surroundings. It takes you through the history of the city, with sections on the origins of its development, its actual planning and construction, the inhabitants and its eventual downfall, illustrated with beautifully displayed pieces taken from the site and some amazing interactive displays, and complemented by flawless English translations.

There are two buses (€7 round trip, 30 minutes) each morning at 9.30am and 10.15am, Tuesday to Sunday, from downtown Córdoba to Madinat Al-Zahra, each returning 3½ hours later. In Córdoba it stops on Paseo de la Victoria by the Cruz Roja Hospital and Roman Mausoleum. The bus stops at the parking lot outside the museum at the Midinat al-Zahra. Another bus (€2.10 round trip) takes you up the hill to the site.

✯✰ Festivals & Events

Spring and early summer are the chief festival times in Córdoba.

Semana Santa   HOLY WEEK
Every evening during the week before Easter Sunday, up to 12 *pasos* (decorated platforms on which statues are carried in a religious procession) and their processions file through the city, passing along the *carrera oficial* (official trail) – Calle Claudio Marcelo, Plaza de las Tendillas, Calle José Cruz Conde – between about 8pm and midnight. The climax is the *madrugá* (dawn) of Good Friday, when six *pasos* pass between 4am and 6am.

Cruces de Mayo   RELIGIOUS
During Crosses of May, crosses decorated with flowers and Manila shawls stand on squares and patios, which become a focus for wine and tapas stalls, music and merrymaking; late April to early May.

Feria de Mayo   FAIR
The May Fair is a massive party dedicated to Nuestra Señora de la Salud takes over the Arenal area near the river with concerts and Sevillana dancing, and the main bullfighting season in Los Califas ring on Gran Via Parque; last week of May.

Festival de Los Patios Cordobeses   PATIOS
The Córdoba Courtyard Festival is a 'best patio' competition with many private courtyards open for public viewing till 10pm nightly (till midnight Friday and Saturday) in the first half of May. A concurrent cultural program has flamenco concerts set appropriately in the city's grandest patios, gardens and plazas. The tourist office provides a map of the contestants along with a program of events.

Festival Internacional de la Guitarra MUSIC
(International Guitar Festival; www.guitarracordoba.com) A two-week celebration of the guitar, with live performances of classical,

flamenco, rock, blues and more; top names play in the city's concert halls and plazas; first half of July.

Eating

Córdoba's culinary legacy is *salmorejo*, a delicious chilled soup of blended tomatoes, garlic, bread, lemon, vinegar and olive oil, sprinkled with crumbled hard-boiled egg and strips of *jamón* (ham). *Rabo de toro* (bull's tail stew) is another favourite. Don't miss the wine from nearby Montilla and Moriles.

TOP CHOICE Casa Mazal   JEWISH €€
(☎957 94 18 88; www.casamazal.com; Calle Tomás Conde 3; Mains €12-15) A meal here makes a fine complement to the nearby Casa de Sefarad museum, as it brings the Sephardic (Judeo-Spanish) tradition to the table. A sort of culinary diaspora, Sephardic dishes contain elements of Andalucian, Turkish, Italian and North African cuisine, with such varied items as Syrian lentil salad, honeyed eggplant fritters and *minas* (a matzo-based vegetarian lasagna) on the menu.

Bar Santos   TAPAS €
(Calle Magistral González Francés 3; tortilla €2.50) The legendary Santos serves the best *tortilla de patata* (potato omelette) in town – and don't the *cordobeses* know it. Thick wedges are deftly cut from giant wheels of the stuff and customarily served with plastic forks on paper plates to take outside and gaze at the Mezquita. Don't miss it.

Bodegas Campos   ANDALUCIAN €€
(☎957 49 75 00; www.bodegascampos.com; Calle de Lineros 32; tapas €5, mains €13-21) One of Córdoba's most atmospheric and famous wine cellar-restaurants, this sprawling hall features dozens of rooms and patios, with oak barrels signed by local and international celebrities stacked up alongside. The bodega produces its own house Montilla, and the restaurant, frequented by swankily dressed *cordobeses*, serves up a delicious array of meals.

La Boca   INTERNATIONAL, FUSION €€
(☎957 47 61 40; www.restaurantelaboca.com; Calle San Fernando 39; mains €11-15; ⊗closed Mon dinner & Tue) Trendy for a reason, this cutting-edge eatery whips up exciting global variations with traditional ingredients, then presents them in eye-catching ways: Iberian pork on

a bed of Thai noodles? Zuheros cheese garnished with sun-dried tomatoes? Why not? Dine in one of the cosy salons or take a table in the courtyard. Reservations are essential on weekends.

Delorean Bar de Tapas   TAPAS €
(Calle de Alfonso XIII; tapas €0.90; ⊗closed Sun) Makes sense that the cheapest tapas in town are amid the alternative club zone – hipsters have to eat too. It's cheap but tasty; beyond the burgers, there's eggplant in vinaigrette sauce, *flamenquín* balls (croquettes of rolled ham and cheese), mushroom quesadillas and more. It's a youthful hang-out but they respect one time-honored tradition: free tapas with every beer.

El Astronauta   HEALTH FOOD €€
(Map p186; ☎957 49 11 23; www.elastronauta. es; Calle Diario de Córdoba 18; menú €9.50, mains €12-15) Located on a busy corner near the Roman temple, the Astronauta whips up zesty salads, sandwiches and meals, with an emphasis on fresh, healthy ingredients. The decor is cosmic, the vibe alternative and the local clientele loyal.

Taberna San Miguel El Pisto   TAPAS €
(Plaza San Miguel 1; tapas €3, media raciones €5-10; ⊗closed Sun & Aug) Brimming with local character, El Pisto is one of Córdoba's best *tabernas* (taverns), both in terms of atmosphere and food. Traditional tapas and *media raciones* (half-rations; smaller tapas servings) are done perfectly, and inexpensive Moriles wine is ready in jugs on the bar. Be sure to try the namesake item, a sort of ratatouille topped with a fried egg.

Taberna Sociedad de Plateros   TAPAS €
(☎957 47 00 42; Calle de San Francisco 6; tapas €3, raciones €8-10) Run by the silversmiths' guild, this well-loved restaurant in a converted convent serves a selection of generous *raciones* (large tapas servings) in its light, glass-roofed patio. The seafood selection is particularly fine, highlighted by such items as *bacalao rebozado* (breaded cod) and *salpicón de mariscos* (shellfish salad).

Amaltea   ORGANIC €€
(☎957 49 19 68; Ronda de Isasa 10; mains €10-16; ⊗closed Sun dinner; ⊘) This intimate riverside spot specialises in organic food and wine, with a serious Middle Eastern influence (Lebanese-style tabbouleh, couscous). There's a good range of vegetarian fare.

🍷 Drinking & Entertainment

For 'what's on' info, consult the daily newspaper *Diario Córdoba* or inquire at the tourist office. Flyers for live music are posted at El Astronauta and music bars like Café Bar Automático. Bands usually start around 10pm and there's rarely a cover charge.

Bodega Guzmán   BAR

(Calle de los Judíos 7; ⊘noon to 4pm & 8pm-midnight, closed Thu) Close to the Sinagoga, this atmospheric drinking spot bedecked with bullfighting memorabilia is frequented by both locals and tourists. Montilla wine is dispensed from three giant barrels behind the bar: don't leave without trying some *amargoso* (bitter).

Bar Correo   BAR

(Calle Jesús María 2; ⊘10am-2pm & 6-10pm) Why does this humble bar just down from Plaza de las Tendillas attract throngs of beer drinkers every afternoon? Hard to say, but it's a local tradition going back to the bar's origins in 1931. If you can manage to squeeze yourself inside the locale you'll be pleased to see the simple tiled room from which all that *cerveza* (beer) flows.

La Pataíta de Antonio   FLAMENCO

(☏957 49 15 44; www.sensesandcolours.com; Calle Barros 3) 'Antonio' is renowned flamenco dancer Antonio Modéjar, and this is his project: a living space for the art where young up-and-comers delight aficionados with their dazzling licks. Performances nightly plus matinees Friday and Saturday.

Bar-Cafetería Soul   MUSIC

(Calle de Alfonso XIII 3; ⊘9am-3am Mon-Fri, 10am-4am Sat & Sun, closed Aug; 🛜) Quirkily furnished with music to match, this DJ bar gets hotter and busier as the evening progresses. The vibe is friendly and funky.

Café Bar Automático   MUSIC BAR

(Calle Alfaros 4; ⊘from 5pm) This is a low-key spot specialising in wacky cocktails and fruit shakes, with alternative rock playing over a good sound system.

Jazz Café   LIVE MUSIC

(Map p186; Calle Espartería; ⊘8am-late) Not just for jazzbos, this long-standing club is as likely to stage electric blues or belly dancing as its namesake style, attracting a varied crowd until the wee hours. Tuesday nights are reserved for jazz jam sessions.

ℹ️ Information

Ambulance (☏957 43 38 78)

Municipal Tourist Office kiosks (☏902 20 17 74; www.turismodecordoba.org) Campo Santo de los Mártires (infoalcazar@turismodecordoba.org; ⊘9am-2pm & 5-7.30pm); Plaza de las Tendillas (infotendillas@turismodecordoba.org; ⊘9am-2pm & 5.30-8pm); train station (infoave@turismodecordoba.org; entry hall; ⊘9am-2pm & 5-7.30pm) The Campo Santo branch is opposite Alcázar de los Reyes Cristianos.

Policía Nacional (☏091; Avenida Doctor Fleming 2) The main police station.

Regional Tourist Office (Calle de Torrijos 10; ⊘9am-7.30pm Mon-Fri, 9.30am-3pm Sat, Sun & holidays) A good source of information about Córdoba province; located inside the Palacio de Congresos y Exposiciones.

ℹ️ Getting There & Away

Bus

The bus station is located 1km northwest of Plaza de las Tendillas, behind the train station. Each bus company has its own terminal.

Alsa (www.alsa.es) Runs services to Seville (€10.40, 1¾ hours, six daily), Granada (€12.50, 2½ hours, seven daily), Málaga (€12.75, 2¾ hours, five daily) and Baeza (€10, three hours, one daily).

Empresa Carrera (www.autocarescarrera.es) Heads south, with several daily buses to Priego de Córdoba (€7.50, 2½ hours), Cabra (€5.75, 1½ hours), Zuheros (€5.75, two hours) and Iznájar (€8.35, 1¾ to 2¼ hours).

Socibus Secorbus (☏902 22 92 92; www.socibus.es) Operates buses to Madrid (€15.80, 4½ hours, six daily)

Train

Córdoba's modern **train station** (Avenida de América) is 1km northwest of Plaza de las Tendillas.

Services include Seville (€11 to €33, 45 to 80 minutes, every half hour until 11.20pm), Málaga (€22 to €45, 45 minutes to one hour, 16 daily), Madrid (€53 to €68, 1¾ to 2¼ hours, roughly every half hour until 10pm) and Barcelona (€138, 4½ hours, four AVEs daily).

ℹ️ Getting Around

Bicycle

Córdoba has installed bicycle lanes throughout town, though they're still little used. Bike hire is available from **Solobici** (☏957 48 57 66; www.solobici.net; María Cristina 5; per day €15), which also offers regional bike tours.

Bus

Bus 3 (€1.20), from Vía Augusta, the street between the train and bus stations, runs to Plaza de las Tendillas and down Calle de San Fernando, east of the Mezquita. For the return trip, you can pick it up on Paseo de la Ribera, just east of Calle de San Fernando.

Car

For drivers, metered street parking around the Mezquita and along the riverside is demarcated by blue lines and is in effect from 9am to 9pm Monday to Friday and 9am to 2pm Saturday. Overnight parking outside these hours is free. There are no meters in the zone west of Avenida de la República Argentina, just west of the Judería. If you can find a spot along Paseo de la Victoria or Avenida de la República Argentina, leave a tip for one of the self-appointed street guards. Charges for hotel parking are from €12 to €15.

Taxi

Taxis from the bus or train stations to the Mezquita cost around €7. In the city centre, taxis congregate at the northeastern corner of Plaza de las Tendillas.

SOUTH OF CÓRDOBA

The south of Córdoba province straddled the Islamic-Christian frontier from the 13th to the 15th centuries, as evidenced by the many towns and villages that cluster around huge, fortified castles. Towards the southeast, the Parque Natural Sierras Subbéticas protects more than 300 sq km of mountains, canyons and wooded valleys as well as a number of towns, of which Zuheros and Priego de Córdoba, in the northern section of the park, are among the most appealing. The southern boundary of the region is demarcated by a long, wriggling reservoir overlooked by the village of Iznájar.

Baena

POP 21,028

This small market town, surrounded by endless serried ranks of olive trees, produces olive oil of such superb quality it's been accredited with its own Denominación de Origen (DO; a designation that indicates the product's unique geographical origins, production processes and quality) label. The periphery of the town is dotted with huge storage tanks.

The best reason for coming to Baena is to experience the working olive-oil mill

of **Núñez de Prado** (☎957 67 01 41; Avenida Cervantes 15; admission free; ⊙9am-2pm & 4-6pm Mon-Fri, 9am-1pm Sat). Overall, the family owns around 100,000 olive trees. Olives are hand-picked to prevent bruising, then crushed in the ancient stone mills. It takes approximately 11kg of olives to yield just 1L of oil. The mill is famous for *flor de aceite,* the oil that seeps naturally from the ground-up olives.

Tours are given during opening hours; it's best to call ahead. (June through to August tours are given mornings only.) Visitors are shown a video about the process of olive-oil production, then taken on a tour of the mill to see traditional olive-pressing techniques and the modern bottling facility. The tour also takes in the old bodega (cellar).

Parque Natural Sierras Subbéticas

With an abundance of springs and streams, this nature reserve is wonderful for hiking among oak, maple, wild olive and mastic trees. Birdwatchers will be able to spot eagles (golden and imperial), falcons and vultures, and wildlife lovers might spot wild cats and boar, though the area prides itself on the presence of the rare cabrera shrew. The park covers an area of 320 sq km and encompasses the towns of Priego de Córdoba, Zuheros, Carcabuey and Iznájar, among others.

Exploring the Parque Natural Sierras Subbéticas is made easier if you have a copy of the *Guía de Senderismo,* a handy guide published by the Mancomunidad de la Subbética, with details of 15 walks; it's available at the tourist office in Priego de Córdoba. The park's visitor center is located 10km east of Cabra.

ZUHEROS & AROUND

POP 746 / ELEV 625M

Rising above low-lying *campiña* (countryside) south of the CO241, Zuheros sits in a dramatic location, crouching in the lee of a craggy mountain. It's approached via a steep road through a series of hairpin bends and provides a beautiful base for exploring the northern portion of the natural park.

◉ Sights

Zuheros Town   VILLAGE

Zuheros has a delightfully relaxed atmosphere. All around the western escarpment on which it perches are miradors (lookouts) with exhilarating views of the dramatic limestone crags that tower over the village and create such a powerful backdrop for Zuheros' castle. The ruined Islamic castle juts out on a pinnacle and has a satisfying patina of age and decay in its rough stonework.

Zuheros is also renowned for its local cheeses and there is a wonderful organic-cheese factory, **Fábrica de Queso Los Balanchares** (☑957 69 47 14; www.losbalanchares .com; Carretera A 318 Km68), along the Baena road.

Cueva de los Murciélagos CAVE
(Cave of the Bats; ☑957 69 45 45; www.cueva delosmurcielagos.com; adult/child €5/4; ☺guided tours 11am, 12.30pm & 2pm year-round, 5pm & 6.30pm Apr-Sep, 4pm & 5.30pm Oct-Mar) Carved out of the limestone massif some 4km above the village is this extraordinary cave. From the vast hall at the start of the tour, it's an almost 500m-long hike through a series of corridors filled with fantastic rock formations. Traces of rock paintings showing abstract figures of goats dating from the Neolithic period can be admired along the way.

Visits to the cave are by guided tour only and can be reserved by phone or via the website. The drive up to the cave is equally exhilarating, as the road twists and turns through the looming mountains with vertiginous views of the town from various lookout points.

Activities
A number of wonderful walks can be done in the vicinity. Hotel Zuhayra (p302) can put you in contact with an English-speaking walking guide, Clive Jarman (clivejarman@ gmail.com), who lives in Zuheros. He has charted a series of walks in the area which are available as handouts from the hotel.

Behind Zuheros village lies a dramatic rocky gorge, the **Cañon de Bailón**, through which there is a pleasant circular walk of just over 4km (taking about two to three hours). To pick up the trail, find the Mirador de Bailón, just below Zuheros on the village's southwestern side, where the approach road from the Doña Mencía junction bends sharply. There is a small car park here and the gorge is right in front of the mirador. From the car park's entrance – with your back to the gorge – take the broad stony track heading up to the left.

Follow the track as it winds uphill and then curves left along the slopes above the gorge. In about 500m the path descends and the valley opens out between rocky walls. The path crosses the stony riverbed to its opposite bank and, in about 1km, a wired-down stone causeway that recrosses the river appears ahead. A few metres before you reach this crossing, bear up left on what is at first a very faint path. It becomes much clearer as it zigzags past a big tree and a twisted rock pinnacle up on the right.

Keep climbing steadily and then, where the path levels off, keep left through trees to reach a superb viewpoint. Continue on an obvious path that passes a couple of parque natural noticeboards and takes you to the road leading up to the Cueva de los Murciélagos. Turn left and follow the road back down to Zuheros.

Eating
Mesón Atalaya ANDALUCIAN €
(☑957 69 46 97; Calle Santo 58) This family-run establishment does good local fare, with a *menú del día* (three-course meal) offered at midday. For an evening meal, it's best to order early in the day. From the castle, head east along Calle Mirador to the bottom of the street, turn right and then left (on Calle Pozo). The restaurant is at the end of this street.

Restaurante Zuhayra ANDALUCIAN €€
(www.zercahoteles.com; Calle Mirador 10; mains €9-14; ☑) The restaurant of the Hotel Zuhayra prepares pretty fine versions of such *cordobés* classics as *salmorejo* and *rabo de toro* and is one of the few places around to offer good vegetarian food. Try the Plato Zuhereño, a sampler of regional specialties, including the highly acclaimed Zuheros sheep's cheeses.

Information
Turismo Zuheros (☑957 69 45 45; www .zuheros.es/zuheros; Plaza de la Paz No 2; ☺10am-2pm & 5-7pm Mon-Fri Apr-Sep, 10am-2pm & 4-6pm Mon-Fri Oct-Mar) operates out of the small archaeology museum.

Getting There & Away
Buses depart from opposite Museo de Costumbres y Artes Populares, on the northeast side of the village.

The best place to park your car is at the base of the road to the Cueva de los Murciélagos, on the east end of the village.

Empresa Carrera (☎957 50 03 02) Runs two to four daily buses to/from Córdoba (€5.75, two hours).

Linesur (☎Seville 954 98 82 22; www.linesur .com) Offers service to/from Seville.

PRIEGO DE CÓRDOBA

POP 23,528 / ELEV 650M

Perched on an outcrop like a big vanilla cake, Priego de Córdoba is a surprisingly bustling market town in a fertile pocket of the Sierras Subbéticas, with two of the province's highest peaks, 1570m La Tiñosa and 1476m Bermejo, rising to the southwest. Inhabited since Roman times, it was a strategically important outpost of the caliphate until its ultimate Christian conquest by Alfonso IX in 1340. Its cavalcade of extravagant baroque churches, fine civic buildings and mansions are the legacy of a centuries-long run of prosperity, cresting with an 18th-century boom in silk and velvet production. It remains an important agricultural centre, particularly for the velvety olive oil that flows from several mills in the area.

◉ Sights

The town's catalogue of elegant architecture has earned it a reputation as the capital of Cordoban baroque. Northeast of the central Plaza de la Constitución, the narrow lanes of the Barrio de La Villa (the old Arab quarter) all converge on the handsome Balcón de Aldarve with its elevated promenade and magnificent views over the Río Salado.

Parroquia de la Asunción　　　　CHURCH
(Plaza Santa Ana 1; admission €3; ⊙10.30am-1.30pm Tue-Sun) At the center of the Barrio de

la Villa stands this church, the chapel and ornate *retablo* (retable) of which represent a high point in Andalucian baroque and are now considered national monuments. Don't miss the chapel of **El Sagrario** (the sacristy), in which a whirl of frothy white stuccowork surges upwards to a beautiful cupola.

Carnicerías Reales　　　　HISTORIC BUILDING
(Royal Slaughterhouses; Calle Santiago; admission incl admission to Castillo €1 ; ⊙11am-1.30pm daily & 4.30-6.30pm Tue-Sat) This well-preserved, 16th-century slaughterhouse has an enclosed patio and a wonderful stone staircase; exhibitions of paintings are often held here.

Castillo de Priego de Córdoba　　　　CASTLE
(Plaza de Abad Palomino; admission incl admission to Carnicerías Reales €1; ⊙11am-1.30pm daily & 4.30-6.30pm Tue-Sat) The rectilinear towers of Priego's castle stand proudly on the northern side of the Plaza de Abad Palomino. Originally an Islamic fortress, it was thoroughly remodeled by the new Christian overlords between the 13th and 15th centuries. Dozens of stone catapult balls from those belligerent times lie scattered around the courtyard.

Clamber up the tower for aerial views of the white city.

Barrio de La Villa　　　　NEIGHBOURHOOD
Potted geraniums stud whitewashed walls along the labyrinthine streets of the Barrio de La Villa, especially along Calles Real, Santiago, Bajondillo and Jazmines. All lanes lead to the Paseo de Adarve, which affords fine views across the rolling countryside and

---

WORTH A TRIP

IZNÁJAR

South of Priego de Córdoba, stranded on a dramatic promontory above a huge reservoir, is the isolated *pueblo* (village) of Iznájar, which is dominated by its Islamic castle. It's a place of outstanding natural beauty and tranquillity, where you can enjoy the beautiful scenery and indulge in a host of outdoor activities such as fishing, birdwatching, swimming and hiking.

The PR-A 234 trail follows the south bank of the reservoir for 15km west, to the point where the Río Genil is dammed to form the reservoir. It takes off from the south end of the Puente Fernández, the bridge that links Iznájar town to the south shore. The trail ascends 2.5km, providing mesmerising views of the reservoir and hilltop village, then skirts the Arroyo de Gata before climbing once again to a lookout point, 7km from the starting point. Here you may spot griffon vultures, peregrine falcons and other raptors with the peaks of the Sierras Subbéticas as a backdrop. One-way the walk will take approximately five hours; it's not especially strenuous but you do have to climb a bit.

mountains. The southern edge of the barrio (district) is bordered by the highly strollable Paseo de Colombia, with fountains, flowerbeds and an elegant pergola.

Fuente del Rey   FOUNTAIN
(Fountain of the King; Calle del Río) West of the centre an entire plaza is reserved for this splendid 19th-century fountain, with its three-tiered basins continuously filled with splashing water from 139 spouts. When the level of the water rises to cover Neptune's modesty, the townsfolk know that it will be a good harvest. Behind it is the less flamboyant Fuente de la Virgen de la Salud.

If you take the stairs to the left of the Fuente de la Virgen de la Salud you can walk to the Ermita del Calvario (Calvary Chapel), from where there are scenic views of the town and surrounding countryside.

FREE Museo Histórico Municipal   MUSEUM
(957 54 09 47; Carrera de las Monjas 16; 10am-1.30pm Tue-Sun & 6-8.30pm Tue-Fri, 5-7.30pm Sat) The city's history museum, just west of Plaza de la Constitución, features three components: an archaeology survey; a gallery devoted to the works of local painter Adolfo Lozano Sidro, who resided here until his death in 1935 and whose realistic illustrations cover the spectrum of social life of his era; and a stylistically varied set of landscape paintings.

Jardín Micológico 'La Trufa'   GARDENS
(off Carretera CP 030; admission free; 10am-6pm Tue-Sun Sep-May, 10am-2pm Tue-Sun Jun-Aug) Located in the outlying village of Zagrilla Alta, 7km northwest of Priego de Córdoba, this botanical garden/museum complex gives perhaps the most comprehensive overview on the continent of the mysterious mushroom. A stroll around the gardens takes you through Andalucía's eight ecosystems, each featuring its trademark toadstools.

✖ Eating & Drinking
Restaurante Zahorí   ANDALUCIAN €
(www.hotelzahori.es; Calle Real 2; mains €10-12) Overseen by Don Custodio with the same rigorous attention he brings to his adjacent guesthouse, the Zahorí prepares traditional sierra fare. With its various stone-walled salons, it's a good place to unwind with a long meal and to sample some signature olive oils and Montilla-Moriles wines. The restaurant

faces the Plaza Santa Ana, just east of the castle in Priego's Barrio de la Villa.

Balcón del Adarve   ANDALUCIAN €€
(957 54 70 75; www.balcondeladarve.com; Paseo de Colombia 36; mains €10-20) Overlooking the valley, with a terrace that takes full advantage of this privileged setting, this excellent restaurant brings a touch of elegance to local favourites like bull's tails and pig's cheeks. It's at the far end of the Paseo de Colombia, a 10-minute walk east of the central Plaza de la Constitución.

Cafetería El Águila   CAFE
(Plaza de Andalucía, cnr Calle Solana; 8am-10pm) Crowds gather most mornings here for conversation over a rich *café con leche* (coffee with milk) and toasted roll drizzled with olive oil. Life-long baristas set 'em up behind a long polished wood bar with vintage espresso machine. A classic!

ℹ Information
The helpful **tourist office** (www.turismode priego.es; Plaza de la Constitución 3; 10am-2pm daily & 4.30-6.30pm exc Sun) is inside the town hall on Plaza de la Constitución.

ℹ Getting There & Around
BUS
Priego's bus station is about 1km west of the centre on Calle Nuestra Señora de los Remedios. Yellow local buses head there from Plaza de la Constitución every half-hour till 2.15pm. **Empresa Carrera** (957 40 44 14) runs buses from the station to Córdoba (€7.50, 2½ hours, some via Baena), Granada (€6.50, 1½ hours, up to four daily), Cabra (€2, 30 minutes, three to four daily) and elsewhere.

CAR
There is a small car park (€1, open 8am to 8pm) near Plaza Palenque along Carrera de las Monjas, the street that runs west from Plaza de la Constitución. Or you can park your vehicle free in a vacant lot on Calle San Luis, about 100m downhill from Carnicerías Reales.

WEST OF CÓRDOBA

Towards Sevilla province unfolds a dramatic, sparsely inhabited landscape cut through by the broad Guadalquivir and dotted with villages and castles, the most formidable one looming over the whitewashed jumble of Almodóvar del Río. Further west, orange groves perfume the lands around Palma del Río at the confluence of the Guadalquivir

MONTILLA

If you fancy getting closer to winemaking country and tasting some of that sweet wine, then Montilla is the place for you. The **tourist information office** (📞957 652 462; Calle Capitán Alonso de Vergas 3; ⊙10am-2pm Mon-Fri, 11am-2pm Sat & Sun) has details of wines and bodegas in the area, as does the **Ruta del Vino** (www.rutadelvinomontillamoriles .com) website. The **Fiesta de la Vendimia Montilla-Moriles**, a vineyard harvest festival, happens on the first weekend in September, to mark the picking of the first grapes.

Some 70,000 barrels of wine are contained by the various wineries in and around Montilla. The following offer tours of their facilities, with the chance to sample some renowned Pedro Ximénez wine.

Bodegas Alvear (📞957 65 01 00; www.alvear.es; María Auxiliadora 1; ⊙tours 12.30pm Mon-Fri) Most renowned of Montilla's winemakers and one of Spain's oldest, with a range of PX vintages. Located just south of Montilla's historic core.

Bodegas Cruz Conde (📞957 65 12 50; www.bodegascruzconde.com; Ronda del Canillo 4; 9am-2pm Sep-Apr, 8am-3pm May-Aug) Over a century old, with the area's only underground cellar. It's a few blocks south of Montilla's historic core.

Bodegas Pérez Barquero (📞957 65 05 00; www.perezbarquero.com; Avenida de Andalucía 27; ⊙tours 11am daily) The vast warehouses here are stacked high with oak barrels of highly acclaimed wines, with tastings in an atmospheric former chapel. Located just off the main road to Montilla from the N-331.

Bodegas Cabriñana (📞957 33 53 86; www.cabrinana.es; Vereda Cerro Macho, Sierra de Montilla) The rustic halls of this country estate are ideal for sampling a a fragrant fino (sherry) or raisiny PX. Located in Sierra de Montilla, southeast of town, about halfway along the road to Cabra.

For food, Montilla's **Las Camachas** (📞957 65 00 04; www.restaurantelascamachas.com; Avenida de Europa 3; mains €12-20) has won prizes for its delicious local specialties, many prepared with the region's signature wines, served in six elegant dining halls.

and Geníl. To the north the pleasant burg of Hornachuelos is the gateway to a remote, mysterious range of forested hills interspersed with pasturelands and populated by deer, wild boar and mongoose.

Almodóvar del Río

Almodóvar's monumental and sinister-looking **castle** (📞957 63 51 16; www.castillodealmodovar.com; Calle del Castillo; adult/child €5/3; ⊙11am-2.30pm & 4-8pm, to 7pm Oct-Mar) dominates the view from miles around. It was built in AD 740 but owes most of its present appearance to post-Reconquista rebuilding. Because the castle had never been taken by force, Pedro I ('the Cruel') used it as a treasure store. Its sense of impregnability is still potent within the massive walls. Most formidable of the nine towers is the Torre del Homenaje (Tower of Homage), where vassals paid tribute to their king, as demonstrated in a scene with mannequins. The rooftop terrace affords panoramic views of the white-washed town and surrounding countryside through which the Río Guadalquivir. Other towers house exhibits on medieval apparel (Torre Redonda), the reconstruction of the castle (Torre Escuela) and other themes.

There is parking below the castle, but you can also drive up the stony approach track (there is no official parking area but you can still park there).

Hornachuelos & Parque Natural Sierra de Hornachuelos

The Parque Natural Sierra de Hornachuelos is a 600-sq-km area of rolling hills in the Sierra Morena, northwest of Almodóvar del Río. The park is densely wooded with a mix of holm oak, cork oak and ash, and is pierced by a number of river valleys that are thick with willow trees. It is renowned for its eagles and other raptors, and harbours the second-largest colony of black vultures in Andalucía.

THE SWEETEST OF WINES

Pedro Ximénez wine is a treat after dinner and its taste will linger on your tongue for hours. For miles and miles across the rolling *campiña* (countryside) its vines grow in soggy, rain-drenched soil under a glaring sun. Such conditions would destroy other vines, but not Pedro Ximénez (sometimes called Pe Equis in Spanish, or PX). This is a tough one, a Rambo of vines: it loves hardship and thrives on extreme weather. In fact it is exactly these conditions that give it the unusual flavours, ranging from a very thin, dry, almost olive taste through to a sweet, dark treacle.

Originally thought to be a type of Riesling, legend has it that the Ximénez grape was imported to the region in the 16th century by a German called Peter Seimens (the Spanish adapted it to Pedro Ximénez). Its intensely sweet wine is endlessly compared to sherry, much to the irritation of the vintners. The fundamental difference between the Jerez sherries and Montilla is the alcoholic potency – alcohol is added to Jerez wine, while Montilla grapes achieve their own high levels of alcohol (15% proof) and sweetness from the intense summer temperatures experienced by the grapes when they are laid out to dry. Left to darken in the sun, the grapes produce a thick, golden must when crushed. What results from this was traditionally racked off into huge terracotta *tinajas*, now steel vats, for ageing. Wine that is clean and well formed goes on to become the pale, strawlike *fino;* darker amber wines with nutty flavours create the *amontillado;* and full-bodied wines become the *oloroso.* The wines are then aged using a *solera* system, where younger vintages are added to older ones in order to 'educate' the young wine.

Hornachuelos makes the ideal base for enjoying the park's quiet charms. The pleasant village stands above a small reservoir and on its banks is a delightful little picnic area. From Plaza de la Constitución, a lane called La Palmera, with a charming palm-tree pebble mosaic underfoot, leads up to the **Iglesia de Santa María de las Flores** and an **observation platform** overlooking the olive-dotted hills.

Heading 1.5km northwest from Hornachuelos on the road to San Calixto will take you to the **Centro de Visitantes Huerta del Rey** (☑957 64 11 40; Carretera Hornachuelos-San Calixto Km1.5; ☉10am-2pm Wed-Sun & 4-6pm Sat & Sun Oct-Jun, 10am-2pm & 6-8pm Fri-Sun Jul-Sep). This visitor centre features interesting displays on the area and its creatures, has information on visiting the Parque Natural Sierra de Hornachuelos and sells local produce. Half a dozen walking trails fan out from the centre. The **Sendero Botánico** climbs a hillside through mossy cork forest, leveling off momentarily, then winds down a narrow dirt trail with excellent views of the surrounding countryside, making for a wonderfully varied 1.2km loop. The easy **Sendero de la Rabilarga** skirts a creek dotted with elms, poplars and brambles. There is a bar-restaurant situated just by the centre car park.

Hornachuelos' most convenient lodging is the motel-style Hostal El Álamo (p302), along the main road between the park and the Córdoba highway. Further down this road you'll find **Bar Casa Alejandro** (Avenida Guadalquivir 4; raciones €5-10), popular with local hunters as the trophies on the walls make clear. A tapa of stewed venison and a glass of fino make a toothsome snack.

The **tourist office** (www.hornachuelosrural .com; Carretera de San Calixto; ☉8am-3pm Mon-Fri, 10am-2pm Sat & Sun) is located in the sports complex on Carretera San Calixto, west of the centre.

Empresa AT San Sebastián runs buses to/from Córdoba (€3.60, one hour, four times daily Monday to Friday, once on Saturday). Buses leave from Carretera San Calixto, just below the police station

NORTH OF CÓRDOBA

Exploring Córdoba's mysterious north, you'll find wild landscapes, dark-green hills and tiny, hard-working *pueblos* (villages) little affected by tourism. The Sierra Morena rises sharply just north of Córdoba city, then rolls back gently over most of the north of the province.

Los Pedroches & Around

The N432 runs northwest into Extremadura, but after 50km, detour onto the N502, which will take you to the far north along some incredible landscapes in the area of **Los Pedroches**. The area is known for being covered with holm oak, and during the era of Al-Andalus it was called 'the Land of Acorns.' Thanks to the acorns, this area is a source of quality *jamón ibérico de bellota*, ham which comes from small black pigs who feast on the October harvest of acorns. The acorns give the meat its slightly sweet, nutty flavour. Salted and cured over a period of six to 12 months, the resulting dark-pink ham is usually served wafer-thin with bread and Montilla wine. And, luckily for you, it can be sampled it in almost every village in this area.

If you enjoy off-the-beaten-track destinations, head to the castles at **Belalcázar** and **Santa Eufemia**. The 15th-century **Castillo de los Sotomayor** looms over remote Bela- lcázar, and is one of the spookiest fortifications in Andalucía. The castle is in private hands so you can't go inside, but it provides a dramatic focus amid the low-lying hills. **Albergue Camino de Santiago** (☎957 14 61 16; caminosantiagobelalcazar@hotmail.com), just below the castle, is a well-managed hostel primarily used by pilgrims on El Camino de Santiago but open to all. Santa Eufemia, 26km east of Belalcázar across empty countryside, is Andalucía's northernmost village. The **Castillo de Miramonte**, on a crag to the north above the village, is a tumbled ruin of Islamic origin, but the 360-degree views are stupendous. To reach the castle, turn west off the N502 at Hostal La Paloma in the village, and after 1km turn right at the 'Camino Servicio RTVE' sign, from which it's a 1.5km drive uphill to the castle.

Jaén Province

POP 670,761

Best Places to Eat

» Casa Vicente (p208)

» Restaurante Antique (p219)

» Parador Condestable Dávalos (p219)

» Zeitúm (p219)

Best Places to Stay

» Parador Castillo de Santa Catalina (p303)

» Palacio de la Rambla (p303)

» Hotel Postigo (p303)

» La Casona del Arco (p303)

Why Go?

Vast plains of chalky-white and rust-red soil neatly striped with olive trees is one of this province's most emblematic and memorable sights. In the towns, the proximity of the nearby region of Castilla-La Mancha is more palpable than in southern Andalucía; medieval castles, Renaissance mansions and flamboyant plateresque facades exude wealth and grandeur, particularly in Baeza and Úbeda, declared Unesco Heritage Sites in 2003. In the provincial capital of Jaén, there is a beguiling, albeit shabbier, historic charm, along with some great tapas bars.

The province is also home to the Parque Natural Sierras de Cazorla, Segura y Las Villas, perhaps the most beautiful of all of Andalucía's mountainous regions and which attracts a number of discerning travellers. Many head for this breathtaking natural scenery to enjoy a wide range of outdoor activities, particularly hiking, with many well-marked trails crossing the mountains and pine-clad valleys.

Driving Distances (km)

	Úbeda	Jaén	Baeza	Cazorla
Jaén	60			
Baeza	16	50		
Cazorla	44	102	58	
Santa Elena	72	79	65	116

DON'T MISS

Driving around the Parque Natural Sierras de Cazorla, Segura y Las Villas with its stunning landscape, tranquil lake and historic towns and castles.

Best Purchases

» Olive oil, La Casa del Aceite (p215)

» Ceramics, Alfarería Tito (p220)

» Black or green olive pâté, Paniaceite (p220)

Best Renaissance Buildings

» Cathedral (p205)

» Sacra Capilla del Salvador (p216)

» Palacio de Jabalquinto (p213)

» Hospital de Santiago (p219)

Resources

» **Ayuntamiento de Jaén** (www.aytojaen.es) The town hall's website.

» **Diputación de Jaén** (www.dipujaen.es) Lots of information about the province.

» **Jaén Online** (www .jaenonline.com) Useful general information.

Getting Around

Even though the distances between cities are short in Jaén province and can be travelled by public transport, having your own car will allow you to reach some of the more remote mountain areas, especially if you want to do some more challenging treks. The area around Parque Natural Sierras de Cazorla, Segura y Las Villas is perfect for driving with excellent scenic roads. Jaén capital is a relatively small city so can be largely explored on foot.

THREE PERFECT DAYS

Day 1: Úbeda - a Renaissance Star

Spend a day exploring and admiring some of Spain's most flamboyant and magnificent **architecture** – the Renaissance work of Valdelvira, Jaén province's grand architect. Delve into this magnificent city's countless aristocratic palaces, simple and elegant squares, and narrow cobbled streets lined with architectural treasures. You can eat well at several superb restaurants and visit the fascinating **pottery workshops** to pick up some distinctive ceramic pieces (or have them shipped home).

Day 2: Sierra Villages

Consider taking a drive and exploring the picturesque villages west of Jaén in the beautiful **Sierra Almadén Mágina**. Or limit yourself to just two stunning mountain top *pueblos* (villages): **Segura de la Sierra** and **Hornos** in the natural park northwest of Úbeda. Both villages have castles, historic churches, panoramic views and a fine selection of homey local bars and restaurants, as well as accommodation if you feel like staying around.

Day 3: Cazorla Outdoors

Jaén province is Andalucía's top area for nature lovers. Choose from Cazorla's easy **day walks** around the town or more exhilarating treks around the mountains by car. Enjoy the views, or head for **Parque Natural Sierra de Andújar** for more demanding hikes. The region's flora and fauna, rugged mountain peaks and rich cultural heritage are bound to get you lacing up those hiking boots and striding out.

Accommodation

Accommodation in Jaén province is moderately priced and sometimes located in some fantastic palaces. You can also get beautiful rural hotels, close to hiking options. Hotels in Jaén are rarely full, although can be in Cazorla, a major destination for city folk at weekends. Read all about hotel choices in our dedicated Accommodation chapter (p288).

JAÉN

POP 116,790 / ELEV 575M

Located in the centre of vast olive groves, upon which its precarious economy depends, Jaén is overshadowed by the beauty of nearby Úbeda and Baeza and is often passed over by visitors to the province. Travel beyond the industrial approach, however, and you will discover a charming, if mildly dilapidated, historic centre with hidden neighbourhoods, excellent tapas bars and a grandiose cathedral.

Although Jaén was the first capital of the kingdom of Granada, after the Muslims were driven out in 1492, the city suffered centuries of decline with many *jiennenses* (locals of Jaén) emigrating to the Spanish colonies, hence the existence of other Jaéns in Peru and the Philippines.

◎ Sights & Activities

Jaén's old Arab quarter, with its narrow, winding streets, huddles around the foot of the Cerro de Santa Catalina. The wooded, castle-crowned hill is above the western side of town, while the city's pride, the monumental cathedral, is near the southern end of the old city. Northwest of here are the city's notable museums.

FREE Cathedral   CATHEDRAL
(Plaza de Santa María; tours adult/child €5/1.50; ◎8.30am-1pm & 5-8pm Mon-Sat, 9am-1pm & 5-7pm Sun) They say one should be able to worship God from anywhere, and that proved to be particularly true in Jaén. The Christians worshipped in an old mosque for over 100 years following the Reconquista, and it wasn't until the 16th century that the ambitious plans for Jaén's huge cathedral were conceived and master architect Andrés de Vandelvira, also responsible for many fabulous buildings in Úbeda and Baeza, was commissioned.

Its size and opulence still dominate and dwarf the entire city, and the cathedral is strikingly visible from the hilltop eyrie of Santa Catalina. The southwestern facade, set back on Plaza de Santa María, was not completed until the 18th century, and it owes more to the late-baroque tradition than to the Renaissance, thanks to its host of statuary by Seville's Pedro Roldán. The overall Renaissance aesthetic is dominant, however, and is particularly evident in the overall size and solidity of the internal and external structures, with huge, rounded arches and clusters of Corinthian columns that lend it great visual strength.

The cult of the Reliquia del Santo Rostro de Cristo – the cloth with which St Veronica is believed to have wiped Christ's face on the road to Calvary – has its home behind the main altar, in the Capilla del Santo Rostro. On Friday at 11.30am and 5pm long queues of the faithful assemble to kiss the cloth.

FREE Palacio de Villardompardo   PALACE
(Plaza de Santa Luisa de Marillac; ◎9am-8pm Tue-Fri, 9.30am-2.30pm Sat & Sun) Undergoing renovation at the time of research (but due to re-open in early 2013), this Renaissance palace houses three excellent attractions: the beautiful 11th-century Baños Árabes (Arab Baths), with a transparent walkway for viewing the excavated baths; the Museo de Artes y Costumbres Populares (Museum of Popular Art & Customs), devoted to the artefacts of the harsh rural lifestyle of preindustrial Jaén province; and the Museo Internacional de Arte Naïf (International Museum of Naïve Art), with a large international collection of colourful and witty naive art. You can spend hours lost in the everyday detail so playfully depicted in these works.

Castillo de Santa Catalina   CASTLE
(Cerro de Santa Catalina; admission €3; ◎10am-2pm & 5-9pm Tue-Sun) Watching the city from atop the cliff-girt Cerro de Santa Catalina is the former Islamic fortress of Castillo de Santa Catalina. It was undergoing renovation when we visited, but the Centro de Interpretacíon (Interpretation Centre), including audiovisual presentations, should have reopened by the time you read this. Past the castle at the end of the ridge stands a large cross, from where there are magnificent views over the city and the olive groves beyond.

If you don't have a vehicle for the circuitous 4km drive up from the city centre, you can take a taxi (€7). You can also walk (about 40 minutes from the city centre) by heading uphill from the cathedral to join Calle de Buenavista. Go up the right-hand branch before crossing over onto the Carretera de Circunvalación; a short distance along to the right, take the path that heads off steeply uphill to the left.

Even if you are not staying at the parador here, try and drop in for a drink to see firsthand the extraordinary vaulted and decorative ceilings in the main salon and dining room.

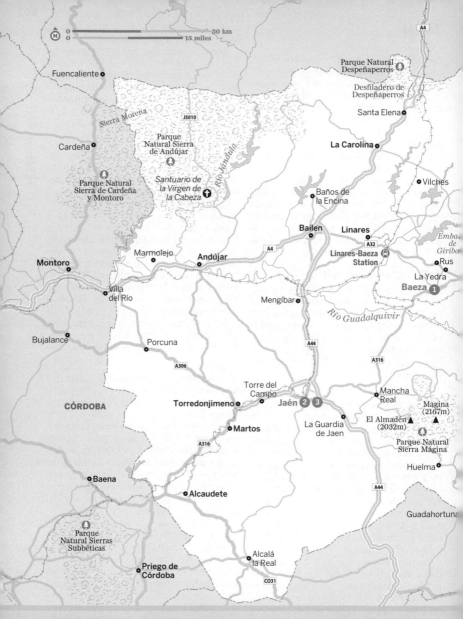

Jaén Province Highlights

1 Visiting the beautiful Renaissance towns of **Úbeda** (p216) and **Baeza** (p212)

2 Exploring the superb backstreet tapas bars in **Jaén** (p205)

3 Stopping for a drink or staying at Jaén's stunning **Parador Castillo de Santa Catalina** (p303)

4 Buying some distinctive green glazed pottery in Úbeda's **Barrio San Millán** (p220)

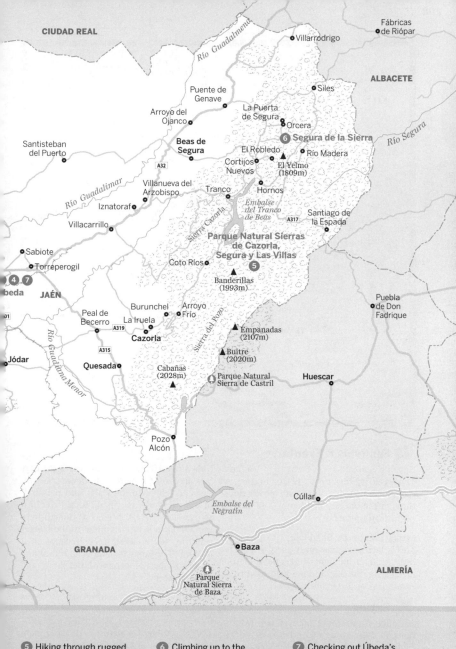

CIUDAD REAL

Fábricas de Riópar

Villarrodrigo

Río Guadalmena

ALBACETE

Puente de Genave

Siles

Arroyo del Ojanco

La Puerta de Segura

Orcera

Beas de Segura

⑥ Segura de la Sierra

Río Segura

A32

El Robledo

Río Madera

Cortijos Nuevos

El Yelmo (1809m)

Villanueva del Arzobispo

Tranco

Hornos

Santisteban del Puerto

Río Guadalimar

Iznatoraf

Embalse del Tranco de Beas

A317

Santiago de la Espada

Villacarrillo

Sierra Cazorla

Parque Natural Sierras de Cazorla, Segura y Las Villas

Sabiote

Coto Ríos

⑤

Torreperogil

④ ⑦

Banderillas (1993m)

beda

JAÉN

Puebla de Don Fadrique

01

Peal de Becerro

Burunchel

Arroyo Frío

La Iruela

A319

Sierra del Pozo

Émpanadas (2107m)

Cazorla

A315

Buitre (2020m)

Jódar

Quesada

Río Guadiana Menor

Cabañas (2028m)

Parque Natural Sierra de Castril

Huescar

Pozo Alcón

Embalse del Negratín

Cúllar

GRANADA

Baza

ALMERÍA

Parque Natural Sierra de Baza

⑤ Hiking through rugged mountains at the **Parque Natural Sierras de Cazorla, Segura y Las Villas** (p222)

⑥ Climbing up to the mountaintop castle at **Segura de la Sierra** (p225)

⑦ Checking out Úbeda's fascinating **Sinagoga del Agua** (p16), a former synagogue and rabbi's home

Jaén

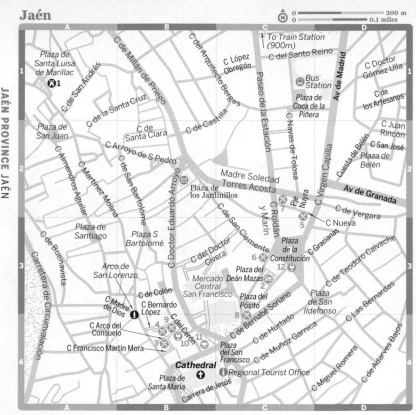

JAÉN PROVINCE JAÉN

★ Festivals & Events

Semana Santa   HOLY WEEK
The week leading up to Easter Sunday is celebrated in a big way, with processions through the old city by members of 13 *cofradías* (brotherhoods).

Feria y Fiestas de San Lucas   RELIGIOUS
This is Jaén's biggest saintly party, with concerts, funfairs, bullfights and general merry-making in the eight days leading up to Saint's Day on 18 October.

✗ Eating

Although there aren't many fancy restaurants in Jaén, some of Andalucía's quirkiest tapas bars are here, and the *jiennenses* cherish and preserve them. For the highest concentration of tapas bars, head for the web of narrow pedestrian streets northwest of the cathedral.

TOP CHOICE **El Gorrión**   ANDALUCIAN €
(Calle Arco del Consuelo 7; tapas from €1.50) Lazy jazz plays on the stereo, old newspaper cuttings are glued to the walls, and paintings of bizarre landscapes hang lopsidedly next to oval oak barrels. It feels as though local punters have been propping up the bar for centuries (or at least since 1888, when it opened). The tapas are simple and traditional, and are best enjoyed with the sherry and wine on offer.

Casa Vicente   CONTEMPORARY SPANISH €€€
(☎953 23 28 16; www.restaurantecasavicente.com; Calle Francisco Martín Mora; menú €32, mains €16-22; ⊙closed Aug) Located in a restored mansion with a patio, Casa Vicente is one of the best restaurants in town. It has a great bar where you can take a tipple with tapas, or head for the patio or interior dining room to enjoy specialities such as the *cordero mozárabe* (lamb with honey and spices).

Jaén

Mazas CONTEMPORARY SPANISH €€
(Calle de la Pescadería 15; mains €10-12) Join the animated young crowd who favour this fashionable bar and restaurant with its charcoal grey interior and striking contemporary artwork. The menu includes risottos and meat and fish dishes, while the soufflé with *turron* (nougat) should round off the evening (as well as your figure) nicely.

Mesón Rio Chico ANDALUCIAN €€
(www.mesonriochico.com; Calle Nueva 12; mains €10-18; ⊘Tue-Sat, lunch only Sun) Calle Nueva, a narrow pedestrian street, is lined with bars and restaurants; this place has the advantage of offering both a great tapas bar for sharing *raciones* (large tapas servings)like partridge pâté and grilled *setas* (oyster mushrooms), plus an elegant white-tableclothed restaurant for more serious dining choices, including oxtail and duck.

Taberna La Manchega ANDALUCIAN €
(www.tabernalamanchegadejaen.com; Calle Bernardo López 12; platos combinados €4-10; ⊘10am-5pm & 8pm-1am Wed-Mon) This place has been in action since the 1880s; apart from enjoying the great, simple tapas here, you can drink wine and watch the local, characterful clientele. La Manchega has entrances on both Calle Arco del Consuelo and Calle Bernardo López.

La Gamba de Oro SEAFOOD €
(Calle Nueva 5; raciones €6-8) Although this brightly lit place has a distinct diner feel, the seafood is some of the best in town – and the freshest, despite being miles from the sea. There are baskets underfoot for discarded shells, and a tank of tentacled lovelies by the bar. A selection of fried fish costs between €6 and €10.

Panaceite CONTEMPORARY SPANISH €
(www.panaceite.com; Calle de Bernabé Soriano 1; tapas from €1.50) Always packed, this corner bar has a broad arc of outside tables just down from the central market and serves some seriously good tapas and *raciones* like black rice with *ali oli* (garlic mayonnaise), as well as salads and organic wines by the glass.

 Drinking

Deán BAR
(Plaza del Deán Mazas; ⊘11am-late) The interior is small and cramped with punters spilling out onto the leafy square, but this place has a pulsating late-night vibe with its exposed industrial steel piping and pumping music. During the day, it is more of a cafe with plenty of chairs on the square and light eats like hummus and topped *tostas* (small pieces of toast).

Café del Consuelo COCKTAIL BAR
(Calle Arco del Consuelo 6; ⊘3pm-late Wed-Sun) Shiny black tiles combined with raspberry-pink paintwork, moody low lights and a drum-and-bass soundtrack create the perfect surround-sound scenery for a little hand-holding time.

Columbia 50 CAFE
(Calle del Cerón 6; ⊘10am-9pm) Wood panelling, wicker chairs, oversized ceiling fans and white-smocked waiters set the scene for catering to any caffeine or chocoholic cravings. The menu includes global coffees and hot chocolates spiked with everything from Irish whiskey to honey and cream. Eats are suitably calorific, including brownies and crêpes.

ⓘ Information
Tourist office (www.andalucia.org; Calle de Valparaiso; ⊘10am-8pm Mon-Fri, to 1pm Sat & Sun) Has helpful, multilingual staff and plenty of information about the city and province.

JAÉN PROVINCE JAÉN

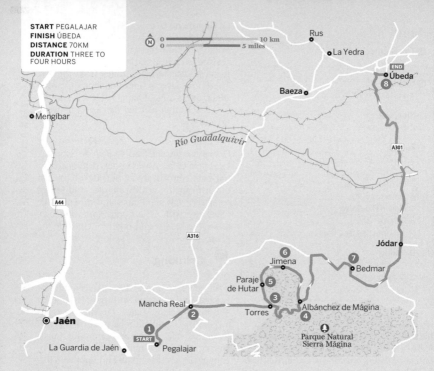

START PEGALAJAR
FINISH ÚBEDA
DISTANCE 70KM
DURATION THREE TO FOUR HOURS

0   10 km
0   5 miles

Rus
La Yedra
END Úbeda 8
Baeza
Mengíbar
Río Guadalquivir
A301
A44
A316
Jódar
Jimena 6
Paraje de Hutar 5   Bedmar 7
Mancha Real   Torres   3
2   Albánchez de Mágina
Jaén   4
START 1   Parque Natural Sierra Mágina
La Guardia de Jaén   Pegalajar

Driving Tour
Sierra Almadén Mágina

❯ This drive links Jaén with Úbeda in a roundabout but justifiably scenic way. From the A44, heading towards Granada, take exit 50 to ❶ **Pegalajar**, via a quiet road surrounded by olive trees and backed by mountains. Stop in the village to look at the medieval 14th-century arch, then follow signs to La Chaca, a large reservoir that essentially replaces the more traditional plaza as being the focal point of town. If you're peckish, stop at waterfront Mesón El Caribe (Calle Baja Fuente) for a *cerveza* (beer) and tapa. Continue towards Mancha Real, passing the Cueva Los Majuelos cave restaurant (open only at weekends). This pretty mountain road overlooks undulating hills covered with olive groves and almond trees.

Anyone interested in ecclesiastical architecture should dip into the attractive market town of ❷ **Mancha Real** for a look at the historic portal of the 16th-century Iglesia de San Juan. After a further 9km, you reach ❸ **Torres**, a picturesque village located in the folds of the mountains, surrounded by

cherry trees. Enjoy the stunning panoramic views stretching beyond traditional terraced gardens.

Follow the signs to Albánchez de Mágina, swinging by the prettily situated Hotel Rural Almoratin for lunch on the terrace. At ❹ **Albánchez de Mágina** you may (or may not) want to take the 365 steps to the spectacularly perched castle which looms high above the whitewashed village houses. At the very least, it is a camera-clicking sight.

Head 2km north out of Albanchez, to signposted ❺ **Paraje de Hutar**, a leafy picnic area complete with waterfall, restaurant and rural hotel. The main attraction of the next town, ❻ **Jimena**, is the Cueva la Granja, signposted at the entrance, with its remnants of Neolithic cave paintings. Your next stop is ❼ **Bedmar**, its fortress comprising impressive ancient castle walls, surrounded by mountains and nestled against the 17th-century church of Iglesia de la Virgen de la Cabeza. Continue north on the A401 to the final destination: ❽ **Úbeda**.

WORTH A TRIP

PARQUE NATURAL SIERRA DE ANDÚJAR

Thirty-one kilometres north of Andújar on the J-5010 is the 13th-century Santuario de la Virgen de la Cabeza. It is tucked away in the secluded Parque Natural Sierra de Andújar, and is home to one of Spain's biggest religious events, the **Romería de la Virgen de la Cabeza**. The original shrine was destroyed during the civil war, when it was seized by 200 pro-Franco troops. The shrine was only 'liberated' in May 1937 after eight months of determined Republican bombardment.

On the last Sunday in April nearly half a million people converge to witness a small statue of the Virgin Mary – known as La Morenita (The Little Brown One) – being carried around the Cerro del Cabezo for about four hours from around 11am. It's a festive, emotive occasion: children and items of clothing are passed over the crowd to priests who touch them to the Virgin's mantle.

The park is said to have the largest expanse of natural vegetation in the Sierra Morena. Full of evergreen and gall oaks, it is home to plenty of bull-breeding ranches, a few wolves, lynx and boars, plus deer, mouflon and various birds of prey. Information is available from the **Centro de Visitantes** (Visitor Centre; 953 54 90 30), at Km12 on the road from Andújar to the Santuario de la Virgen de la Cabeza, and from Andújar's **tourist office** (953 50 49 59; Plaza de Santa María; 8am-2pm Tue-Sat Jul-Sep, 10am-2pm & 5-8pm Tue-Sat Oct-Jun). Buses run daily from Úbeda to Andújar (€6, 1½ hours, three daily) and there are buses from Andújar to the sanctuary on Saturday and Sunday.

❶ Getting There & Around

BUS From the **bus station** (953 25 01 06; Plaza de Coca de la Piñera), **Alsa** (www.alsa.es) runs buses to Granada (€8, 1¼ hours, 12 daily), Baeza (€4, 45 minutes, 11 daily), Úbeda (€5, one hour, 12 daily) and Cazorla (€8.50, 3½ hours, three daily). **Ureña** (www.urena-sa.com) travels up to Córdoba and Seville. Other buses head for Málaga and Almería.

CAR Driving in Jaén can be mighty stressful due to the one-way road system and the weight of traffic. Street parking is hard to find in the centre, but there is convenient underground parking at Plaza de la Constitución and at Parking San Francisco, off Calle de Bernabé Soriano, near the cathedral.

TRAIN Jaén's **train station** (953 27 02 02; www.renfe.com; Paseo de la Estación) is the final stop of a branch line. A train leaves at 8am for Córdoba (€12, 1¾ hours, four daily) and at 7.15am for Seville (€29, 2½ hours, three daily). There are also trains to Madrid (€31.50, four hours, three daily).

NORTH OF JAÉN

The A4 north out of Jaén passes through indifferent countryside until the hills of the Sierra Morena appear on the horizon. Ahead lies the Desfiladero de Despeñaperros (Pass of the Overthrow of the Dogs), so named because the Christian victors of the 1212 battle at nearby Las Navas de Tolosa are said to have tossed many of their Muslim enemies from the cliffs.

The full drama of the pass is not best appreciated until the last minute, when the road from the south descends suddenly and swoops between rocky towers and wooded slopes to slice through tunnels and defiles.

Parque Natural de Despeñaperros & Santa Elena

The **Desfiladero de Despeñaperros** is one of Spain's most beautiful and remote areas, with rolling hills clothed with dense woods. Although road and rail have robbed the region of much of its historic romance, it remains dramatic with protruding cliffs and pinnacles of fluted rock. The area around the pass is now a natural park, home to deer and wild boar, and maybe the occasional wolf and lynx. There are no local buses, so you need your own transport to get the most out of your visit here.

The main visitor centre with information and maps on walking routes in the area is the **Centro de Visitantes Puerta de Andalucía** (Carretera Santa Elena a Miranda del Rey; 10am-2pm & 4-8pm) on the outskirts of **Santa Elena**, the small town just south of the pass with shops, bars and restaurants. The

OLIVE OIL: THE FACTS

In Jaén, the *aceituna* (olive) rules. The pungent smell of *aceite de oliva* (olive oil) perfumes memories of the city and province. The province's olive statistics are pretty staggering: over 40 million olive trees stud a third of the province – more than 4500 sq km. In an average year these trees produce 900,000 tonnes of olives, most of which are turned into approximately 200,000 tonnes of olive oil – meaning that Jaén provides about half of Andalucía's olive oil, one-third of Spain's and 10% of that used in the entire world.

The olives are harvested from late November to January. Despite some mechanisation, much is still done traditionally – by spreading nets beneath the trees, then beating the branches with sticks. The majority of Jaén's (and Andalucía's) olive groves are owned by a handful of large landowners. The dominance of this one crop in the province's economy means that unemployment in Jaén rises from 10% during the harvest to around 45% in summer. An olive picker earns about €30 a day.

Once harvested, olives are taken to oil mills to be mashed into a pulp that is then pressed and filtered. Oil that is considered good enough for immediate consumption is sold as *aceite de oliva virgen* (virgin olive oil), the finest grade, and the best of the best is *virgen extra*. *Aceite de oliva refinado* (refined olive oil) is made from oil that's not quite so good, and plain *aceite de oliva* is a blend of refined and virgin oils. Specialist shops in Jaén, Baeza and Úbeda sell quality oil.

latter includes the sound choice **El Mesón de Despeñaperros** (Avenida Andalucía 91) with its menu of no-fuss local dishes and *raciones* like grilled mushrooms with garlic, or battered fried eggplants drizzled with honey.

EAST OF JAÉN

This part of the region is where most visitors spend their time, drawn in by the allure and Renaissance architecture of Baeza and Úbeda, as well as the leafy hills and hiking trails of Cazorla.

Baeza

POP 16,360 / ELEV 90M

If the Jaén region is known for anything (apart from olives), it's the twin towns of Baeza (ba-*eh*-thah) and Úbeda, two shining examples of Renaissance beauty. Smaller Baeza makes a good day trip from Úbeda, some 9km away. It has a richness of architecture that defies the notion that there is little of architectural interest in Andalucía apart from Moorish buildings. Here a handful of wealthy, fractious families, made rich by the wool trade, left a staggering catalogue of perfectly preserved Renaissance churches and civic buildings.

Baeza was one of the first Andalucian towns to fall to the Christians (in 1227), and

there is little left of its Muslim heritage after so many years of Castilian influence.

◉ Sights

Baeza's sights cluster around the central Plaza de España and along wide Paseo de la Constitución stretching southwest. You can take them all in during a leisurely day's stroll. The opening hours of some of the buildings are unpredictable, so check at the tourist office first.

Plaza del Pópulo   HISTORIC SITE

On Plaza del Pópulo is the old entrance to the city, the **Puerta de Jaén** (Jaén Gate), connected to the huge **Arco de Villalar** (Villalar Arch). The arch was erected by Carlos I in 1526 to commemorate the crushing of a serious insurrection in Castilla that had threatened to overthrow his throne.

The Plaza del Pópulo is also called Plaza de los Leones after the **Fuente de los Leones** (Fountain of the Lions) at its centre. The fountain is made of carvings from the Iberian and Roman village of Cástulo and is topped by a statue reputed to represent Imilce, an Iberian princess and the wife of the notorious Carthaginian general Hannibal.

On the southern side of the square is the lovely 16th-century **Casa del Pópulo**, formerly a courthouse and now Baeza's tourist office. It was built in the plateresque style, an early phase of Renaissance architecture noted for its decorative facades.

On the eastern side of the square stands the **Antigua Carnicería** (Old Butchery), a beautiful building that must rank as the one of the most elegant tanning sheds in the world.

Through the Puerta de Jaén and along to the **Paseo de las Murallas**, a path loops around the old city walls to a point near the cathedral. From here, Baeza's fantastic position on the escarpment can be fully appreciated.

FREE **Cathedral**   CATHEDRAL
(Plaza de Santa María; donations welcome; ◷10.30am-1pm & 4-6pm Oct-Mar, 10.30am-1pm & 5-7pm Apr-Sep) As was the case in much of Andalucía, the Reconquista destroyed the mosque and in its place built the Baeza cathedral. This was the first step towards the town's transformation into a Castilian gem.

The cathedral itself is an aesthetic hotchpotch, although the overall style is 16th-century Renaissance, clearly visible in the **main facade** on Plaza de Santa María. The cathedral's oldest feature is the 13th-century Gothic-Mudéjar **Puerta de la Luna** (Moon Doorway) at its western end, which is topped by a 14th-century rose window.

The cathedral is on Plaza de Santa María; the most typical of all the town's squares, this plaza was designed to be a focus of religious and civic life, and is surrounded by mansions and churches, such as the **Seminario Conciliar de San Felipe Neri** on the square's northern side, a seminary that now houses the Universidad Internacional de Andalucía.

FREE **Palacio de Jabalquinto**   PALACE
(Plaza de Santa Cruz; ◷9am-2pm Mon-Fri) Baeza's most extraordinary palace, the Palacio de Jabalquinto was probably built in the early 16th century for one of the Benavides clan. It has a spectacularly flamboyant facade with pyramidal stone studs that are typical of Isabelline Gothic style, and a patio with Renaissance marble columns, two-tiered arches and an elegant fountain. A magnificent carved baroque stairway ascends from one side.

FREE **Antigua Universidad**   HISTORIC BUILDING
(Old University; Calle del Beato Juan de Ávila; ◷10am-2pm & 4-7pm Wed-Sun) Baeza's historic

university was founded in 1538 and became a fount of progressive ideas that generally conflicted with Baeza's conservative dominant families, often causing scuffles between the highbrows and the well-heeled. It closed in 1824, and since 1875 the building has housed an *instituto de bachillerato* (high school).

The main patio, with its elegant Renaissance arches, is open to the public, as is the classroom of poet Antonio Machado, who taught French at the high school from 1912 to 1919.

Ayuntamiento   HISTORIC BUILDING
(Town Hall; Pasaje del Cardenal Benavides 9) A block north of the Paseo de la Constitución is the Baeza *ayuntamiento* (town hall), with a marvellous plateresque facade. The four finely carved balcony portals on the upper storey are separated by the coats of arms of the town, Felipe II (in the middle) and the magistrate Juan de Borja, who had the town hall built. The building was originally a courthouse and, conveniently, a prison.

FREE **Torre de los Aliatares**   TOWER
(Tower of the Aliatares; Map p214; Plaza de España) The lonely Torre de los Aliatares is one of the few remnants of Muslim Bayyasa (as the town was called by the Muslims), having miraculously survived the destructive Isabel la Católica's 1476 order to demolish the town's fortifications. The order was meant to end the feud between the Benavide and Carvajal noble families.

The tower is located in Plaza de España in the centre of the town and which merges with the sprawling, cafe-lined Paseo de la Constitución, once Baeza's marketplace and bullring.

Convento de San Francisco   CONVENT
(Calle de San Francisco) The ruined Convento de San Francisco is one of Andrés de Vandelvira's masterpieces, conceived as the funerary chapel of the Benavides family. Devastated by an earthquake and sacked by French troops in the early 19th century, it has been completely restored, albeit controversially, its quality deemed inferior to the original.

At the eastern end, a striking arrangement of curved girders traces the outline of its dome over a space adorned with Renaissance carvings. Until early 2012 the convent was home to the Restaurante Van-

Baeza

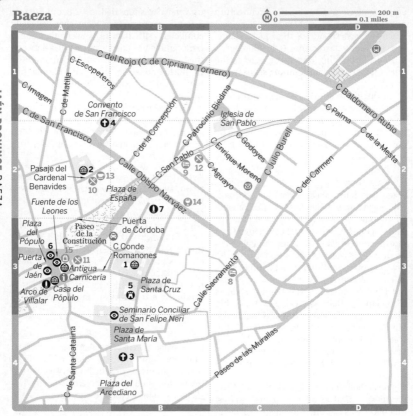

delvira, so was accessible to view. At the time of research, the future of the building was uncertain.

🎊 Festivals & Events

Semana Santa HOLY WEEK
A typically big, raucous celebration complete with devotional processions. Festivities are held during the week before Easter Sunday.

Feria FAIR
Held in mid-August, this is a Castilian carnival procession of *gigantones* (papier mâché giants), along with fireworks and a huge funfair.

🍴 Eating

Baeza has visibly suffered from the global economic downturn, and a number of restaurants (and hotels) have pulled down their shutters for good. *Económicos* (inex-

pensive restaurants) have fared better, with their cut-price daily menus and affordable tapas.

Mesón Restaurante
La Góndola ANDALUCIAN €€
(www.asadorlagondola.com; Portales Carbonería 13, Paseo de la Constitución; mains €8-16) A terrific local, atmospheric restaurant, helped along by the glowing, wood-burning grill behind the bar, cheerful service and good food. Try *patatas baezanas,* a vegetarian delight that mixes a huge helping of sautéed potatoes with mushrooms.

La Campana ANDALUCIAN €€€
(✆953 76 51 42; Hacienda La Laguna, Puente del Opispo; mains €13-17; 🚗) A sizeable hacienda (10 minutes' drive from Baeza, towards Jaén) is home to this excellent restaurant, as well as a cooking school, hotel and olive-oil museum. The menu is classic *jienese* with an emphasis on exquisitely prepared game,

Baeza

◎ Sights

⊜ Sleeping

⊗ Eating

⊜ Drinking

⊜ Shopping

including venison. Naturally enough, olive oil is used lavishly – extending even to the desserts (olive-oil ice cream with tulip-and-tomato jam anyone?).

After lunch consider a 2km stroll around the nearby signposted *laguna verde* surrounded by carob trees and bulrushes; it's a haven for birdlife.

La Almazara ANDALUCIAN €€
(Pasaje del Cardenal Benavides 15; mains €10-17; ◷Tue-Sun) Great terrace position across from the imposing *ayuntamiento*. Serves up lots of fresh fish, a creamy *salmorejo* (thick and garlicky gazpacho) and a veggie *parillada de verduras* (grilled vegetables) for non-meat eaters who have grown weary of *revueltos* (scrambled eggs).

Restaurante Palacio Sánchez Valenzuela ANDALUCIAN €€€
(Calle San Pablo 24; menú €12, mains €10) Also known as the Nueva Casino; dine in the courtyard of this 16th-century palace, although don't get too excited – the chairs are metal and there is no shade. The setting is still pretty impressive, however, while the food is simple local fare with a well-priced daily menu.

🍷 Drinking

TOP CHOICE⁄ Café Teatro Central BAR
(www.cafeteatrocentral.com; Calle Obispo Narváez 19; ◷4pm-3am) Well worth a visit, except possibly on Wednesday – karaoke night. Owner Rafael has put a lot of love into creating a virtual museum piece with his display of family-owned historic instruments, and eclectic decorations ranging from giant stone Buddhas to his own abstract paintings. Once inside, don't miss the open lift with flashing lights (Rafael lives above the club). There is live music every Thursday, playing everything but heavy metal, plus a delightful terrace complete with bubbling fountain and languid goddess statues.

Café da Vinci CAFÉ
(Pasaje del Cardenal Benavides 7; ◷10am-10pm) Take a seat outside on this long pedestrianised plaza that overlooks the sumptuous facade of the historic *ayuntamiento* and enjoy ice creams, cocktails, *cervezas* (beers) or cocktails. Come here for the *churros* (tubular deep-fried doughnuts) in the morning.

🛍 Shopping

La Casa del Aceite FOOD
(www.casadelaceite.com; Paseo de la Constitución 9) For good-quality olive oil visit this shop, which sells a huge selection, along with other products such as soap, ceramics and olive-wood bowls.

ℹ Information

Tourist office (☑953 77 99 82, 953 77 99 83; www.andalucia.org; Plaza del Pópulo; ◷9am-7.30pm Mon-Fri, 9.30am-3pm Sat, Sun & holidays Apr-Sep) Situated just southwest of Paseo de la Constitución in the 16th-century plateresque Casa del Pópulo, a former courthouse.

ℹ Getting There & Around

Bus
Alsa (www.alsa.es) runs to Jaén (€4, one hour, 14 daily), Úbeda (€1.05, 15 minutes, 19 daily) and Granada (€11.75, two hours, 10 daily). There are also buses to Cazorla (€4.40, 1¾ hours, three daily), Córdoba (€10.50, 2½ hours, two daily) and Seville (€39.75, 4½ hours, two daily).

Car
Parking in Baeza is fairly restricted, but there are parking spots around the Paseo de la Constitución and in Pasaje del Cardenal Benavides.

JAÉN PROVINCE BAEZA

Taxi

Taxis wait for fares in Paseo de la Constitución. A taxi to the train station costs €15.

Train

The nearest train station is **Linares–Baeza** (☑953 65 02 02; www.renfe.es), 13km northwest of town, where a few trains a day leave for Granada, Córdoba, Seville, Málaga, Cádiz, Almería, Madrid and Barcelona. Buses connect with most trains from Linares, Monday to Saturday.

Úbeda

POP 36,026 / ELEV 760M

Úbeda (oo-be-dah) is a slightly different proposition to its little sister, Baeza. Aside from the splendour of its architecture, the town has good tapas bars and restaurants, interesting antique shops and is home to some of the finest pottery workshops in Spain.

The city became a Castilian bulwark on the inexorable Christian march south. Following the success of the Reconquista, Úbeda's aristocratic lions lost no time in jockeying for power in the Castilian court. In the 16th century Francisco de los Cobos y Molina secured the post of privy secretary to King Carlos I and was later succeeded by his nephew Juan Vázquez de Molina.

Exposed to the cultural influences of the Italian Renaissance, and benefiting from the wealth and privilege of high office, the Molina family turned their attention to commissioning what are now considered to be some of the purest examples of Renaissance architecture in Spain. As a result Úbeda (along with neighbouring Baeza) is one of the sole places in Andalucía where you can see stunning buildings and architecture that were *not* built by the Moors.

◎ Sights

Most of Úbeda's splendid buildings are in the southeast of the town, among the maze of narrow, winding streets and expansive squares that make up the *casco antiguo* (old quarter). This area is particularly imposing at dusk with its looming plateresque facades floodlit gold against an inky black sky.

The Plaza Vázquez de Molina is a good place to start exploring Úbeda's architectural gems. Just east of the square, 150m along Baja de El Salvador, a mirador (lookout) gives fine views across the olive fields,

overshadowed by the snowcapped Cazorla mountains in the distance. The Plaza de Andalucía marks the boundary between the two parts of town.

Sacra Capilla del Salvador CHAPEL
(Plaza Vázquez de Molina; adult/child €3/1.50; ◎10am-2pm & 4-7.30pm Mon-Sat, 11.15am-2pm & 5-8pm Sun) The purity of Renaissance lines is best expressed in this famous chapel, built in 1525; it is the first of many works executed in Úbeda by celebrated architect Andrés de Vandelvira. A pre-eminent example of the plateresque style, the chapel's main facade is modelled on Diego de Siloé's Puerta del Perdón at Granada's cathedral.

The classic portal is topped by a carving of the transfiguration of Christ, flanked by statues of St Peter and St Paul. The underside of the arch is a veritable orgy of classical sculpture, executed by French sculptor Esteban Jamete, depicting the Greek gods in a Renaissance touch that would have been inconceivable just a few decades earlier.

The church is still privately owned by the Seville-based ducal Medinaceli family, descendants of the Cobos (original owners), and one of Andalucía's major landowning families.

Next door to the *capilla* (chapel) stands the **Palacio del Condestable Dávalos**. Partly remodelled in the 17th century, the mansion is now Úbeda's luxurious parador (see p304).

TOP CHOICE **Casa Museo Arte Andalusí** MUSEUM
(☑953 75 40 14; Calle Narvaez 11; admission €2; ◎11am-2pm & 5-8pm) The Casa Museo Arte Andalusí is a fascinating private museum and the venue for regular flamenco performances. The first glimpse that this is somewhere special is the original 16th-century heavy carved door. Ring the bell if it is closed.

Owner Paco Castro has lovingly restored this former palace without detracting from its crumbling charm (in other words, it has not metamorphosed into just another 'historical' boutique hotel). Ask him to show you the Star of David etched into one of the original columns in the central patio. Above are balconies and painted Mudéjar-style ceiling and eaves. It is the ideal faded grandeur setting for Paco's fascinating collection of antiques which include 19th-century ceramics, a 14th-century well, stained glass, ancient millstones, painted tiles, tapestries,

Úbeda

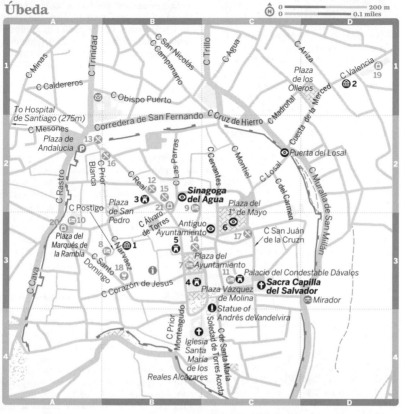

Úbeda

BONO TURÍSTICO

If you plan on visiting the monuments in Baeza and Úbeda, you may want to consider investing in a €19.90 **ticket** (www.bonoturistico.com) that covers not only more than nine sights, but also includes a guided tour of each town and provides discounts on the tourist trains that chug through town. The only downside is that the guided tours are only provided twice daily at 11am and 5pm. Tickets can be purchased at the sights and tourist offices.

intricately carved wooden chests and art work, collected from all over Spain and Morocco.

Downstairs, the former barrel-vaulted bodega is lined with photos of Paco and his flamenco chums, including the famous maestro Paco de Lucía, who has played here in the past. No promises, of course, but the weekly flamenco show at 9.30pm on Saturday is generally of a high foot-stomping standard (€18, includes a drink). Book in advance.

Palacio de Vázquez de Molina PALACE
(Plaza Vázquez de Molina; ⊙10am-2pm & 5-9pm) To the west of Plaza Vázquez de Molina stands this huge palace, now Úbeda's *ayuntamiento* (town hall). It was built by Vandelvira for Juan (Francisco's nephew and successor to the post of privy secretary), whose coat of arms surmounts the doorway. Facing the Palacio de Vázquez de Molina is the site of Úbeda's old mosque, now the location of the **Iglesia Santa María de los Reales Alcázares**.

Sinagoga del Agua HISTORIC SITE
(Calle Roqas 2; admission €4; ⊙10am-8.30pm) There is evidence of a considerable Jewish community in Úbeda dating as far back as the 10th century when they cohabited peacefully with the considerably larger Muslim population. However, it was not until 2006 when this synagogue and former rabbi's house was discovered by a refreshingly ethical realtor who bought the property to knock down and build apartments – only to discover that every swing of the pickaxe revealed some tantalising archaeological piece of a puzzle.

The result is this, the city's latest museum, a sensitive re-creation of a centuries-old synagogue and rabbi's house using original masonry whenever possible, some still bearing Jewish symbols, and including capitals, caliphs and arches. A separate women's gallery was discovered in the excavation, as well as a bodega, the giant urns still in place.

Half-hour tours take place, currently only in Spanish, although there are plans to provide in more languages in the future, according to demand.

Palacio de Vela de los Cobo PALACE
(Plaza del Ayuntamiento; admission €4) A warren of winding streets north of Úbeda's Plaza Vázquez de Molina gives way to a series of elegant squares. The first of these is the broad Plaza del Ayuntamiento, watched over from its northwestern corner by the 16th-century Palacio de Vela de los Cobo. This fascinating, fully furnished palace full of paintings and antiques can only be visited by prior arrangement with the tourist office.

Palacio de los Condes de Guadiana PALACE
(Calle Real) One of the town's most decorative mansions is the 17th-century Palacio de los Condes de Guadiana, located on Calle Real (once Úbeda's main commercial street), with some elegant carving around the windows and balconies. At the time of writing, this palace was being converted into a five-star hotel, due to open in early 2013. For more information, check at the tourist office.

Plaza del 1 de Mayo HISTORIC SITE
This imposing plaza was originally the town's market square and bullring. It was also the grisly site of Inquisition burnings, which the local worthies used to watch from the gallery of the **Antiguo Ayuntamiento** (Old Town Hall) in the southwestern corner.

Leaving no doubt about their political persuasion, locals renamed this square from the former (fascist) Plaza del Generalríssimo several years ago.

Museo de Alfarería MUSEUM
(Calle Valencia 22; ⊙10.30am-2pm & 5-7pm Mon-Fri) The workshop of Paco Tito and his son Pablo (part of a family dynasty of local potters), this museum is located in Barrio San Millán where most of the pottery workshops are located. There is a large exhibition space with explanatory plaques and photographs about all aspects of their craft, including

the historical links to Úbeda, materials used and traditional designs and techniques. Ask to see the 14th-century kiln dating back to when this *barrio* (district) was part of the thriving Jewish quarter.

FREE **Hospital de Santiago** CULTURAL CENTRE (Calle Obispo Cobos; ⊗8am-3pm & 4-10pm Mon-Fri, 11am-3pm & 6-10pm Sat & Sun) Vandelvira's last architectural project was this, the Hospital de Santiago. Completed in 1575, it has often been dubbed the Escorial of Andalucía – a reference to a famous old monastery outside Madrid, which was a precursor to the kind of Renaissance architecture employed by Vandelvira. It now acts as Úbeda's cultural centre, housing a library, municipal dance school and an exhibition hall. To get here, turn left along Calle Mesones from the northwest corner of Plaza de Andalucía. The hospital is a couple of blocks down on your right.

✦ Festivals & Events

Semana Santa HOLY WEEK
Solemn brotherhoods, devotional processions and lots of atmospheric drama can be found in the week leading up to Easter Sunday.

Festival Internacional de Música y Danza Ciudad de Úbeda MUSIC FESTIVAL
(www.festivaldeubeda.com) This festival concentrates on classical music, but includes jazz, flamenco and ethnic music concerts, held at various venues throughout the month of May.

Fiesta de San Miguel FESTIVAL
Celebrates the capture of the town in 1233 by Fernando III, with firework shows, parades, concerts, a flamenco festival, a bullfighting season and more. It's held from 27 September to 4 October.

✗ Eating

Úbeda has some good places to eat. Calle Real, in the old town, is the best place for tapas bars.

TOP CHOICE **Zeitúm** EUROPEAN €€
(www.zeitum.com; Calle San Juán de la Cruz 10; mains €14-20; ⊗Tue-Sat, lunch only Sun) This restaurant is housed in a headily historic building, dating from the 14th century, in the former Jewish quarter. Ask the owner to show you the original well and stonework and beams bearing Jewish symbols.

MASTER BUILDER

Most of what you see in Úbeda, Baeza and Jaén is the work of one man: Andrés de Vandelvira. Born in 1509 in Alcaraz (in Castilla-La Mancha), 150km northeast of Úbeda, Vandelvira almost single-handedly brought the Renaissance to Jaén province. Influenced by the pioneering Renaissance architect Diego de Siloé, Vandelvira designed numerous marvellous buildings and, astonishingly, his work spanned all three main phases of Spanish Renaissance architecture: the ornamental early Renaissance phase known as plateresque, as seen in the Capilla del Salvador del Mundo; the much purer lines and classic proportions, which emerged in the later Palacio de Vázquez de Molina; and the austere late-Renaissance style called Herreresque, as shown in his last building, the Hospital de Santiago. With all these achievements, Vandelvira's was certainly a life well spent.

It's fascinating stuff and sure makes a change from the cookie-cutter sameness of modern restaurant chains. Olive-oil tastings are taken seriously here, along with the superb preparation of diverse dishes like steak tartare and a local favourite: partridge salad.

Parador Condestable Dávalos ANDALUCIAN €€€
(☎953 75 03 45; Plaza Vázquez de Molina; mains €13-18, menú €27) This deservedly popular restaurant serves up delicious, elegant dishes. While a tad pricier than most, this is definitely *the* place to eat in Úbeda and the dining room buzzes well into the evening, even in low season. Try the local specialities: *carruécano* (green peppers stuffed with partridge) or *cabrito guisado con piñones* (stewed kid – the four-legged variety – with pine nuts).

Restaurante Antique CONTEMPORARY ANDALUCIAN €€€
(☎953 75 76 18; www.restauranteantique.com; Calle Real 25; mains €12-26; ⊗Mon-Sat) This place plays on twisting traditional recipes with modern, high-quality cuisine – try the partridge pâté with quinoa and olive-oil marmalade or wild salmon with a creamy

leek sauce. The decor is fittingly understated and elegant with simple, stylish decor.

Taberna La Imprenta
CONTEMPORARY ANDALUCIAN €€

(Plaza del Doctor Quesada 1; mains €10-13; ⊘Wed-Mon) This wonderful old print shop, done stylishly and frequented by Úbeda's posh noshers, provides delicious free tapas with your drinks. You can also sit down and eat lobster salad, excellent meat dishes and saucy little desserts like green apple sorbet with gin on crushed ice.

Mesón Restaurante Navarro
ANDALUCIAN €€

(Plaza del Ayuntamiento 2; menú €15, raciones €4-12) Always crammed and noisy, the Navarro is a cherished local favourite. Eat your tapas at the bar, or in summer sit out on the sunny plaza. There is also a daily menu with gamey choices like venison and rosemary. Note that the sign just says 'Mesón Restaurante.'

La Taberna
ANDALUCIAN €

(Calle Real 7; mains €6-10; 🐾) Children run around screaming, their parents clink glasses and scoff tapas, and bar people sweat and work like crazy – this is a typical Spanish evening scene at this popular tapas bar. Order a drink, get your tapa and join in. It's good for breakfasts too.

Lope
CAFE €

(Calle Real 1; cakes from €1.20; ⊘9.30am-8pm Mon-Fri, 10am-6pm Sat & Sun; 🐾) This old-school cafe and cake shop is perfect for breakfasts and cake fixes. Try its *yemas* (soft, crumbly biscuit cakes), *bollos* (sweet rolls stuffed with cream) and other sweets with a good *café con leche* (coffee with milk).

ÚBEDA'S POTTERY

The typical emerald green glaze on Úbeda's attractive pottery remains from Islamic times. The potters' quarter still has three original kilns from this period (there are only six left in the whole of Spain).

Several workshops sell pottery in Barrio San Millán, northeast of the old town, and the potters are often willing to explain some of the ancient techniques they use. These include adding olive stones to the fire to intensify the heat, which results in a more brilliant glaze.

Drinking

Most of the drinking takes place in the tapas bars, with a more vigorous younger scene taking place in the newer part of town.

Beltraneja
BAR

(Calle Alcolea 6; cocktails €4.50; ⊘4pm-3am Sun-Thu, to 4am Fri-Sat) Hidden away in the backstreets of the historic centre, this place combines a cavernous interior – with exposed stone, dark-pink walls, graffiti-style murals and a fireplace – and a sprawling terrace where there is occasional live music, plus storytelling and other off-beat delights.

Shopping

The main high-street style shopping streets are Calle Mesones and Calle Obispo Cobos, between Plaza de Andalucía and the Hospital de Santiago, with everything from ubiquitous international chains to independent local shops. If you are interested in purchasing pottery, head through the impressive Puerta de Losal and down into the Barrio San Millán, Úbeda's famous potters' quarter, with pottery workshops located on Calle Valencia, along with the Museo de Alfarería.

Alfarería Tito
CERAMICS

(Calle Valencia 32) Juan Tito has a distinctive style which veers away from the classic green glaze with intricate patterns and bright colours. He has won several national awards. The pieces are a little pricier than the norm (think €25 for a jug) but are well worth it for the originality, dazzling designs and craftsmanship.

Artesur
ARTS & CRAFTS

(Plaza del Marqués de la Rambla 2) A rambling shop with a vast choice of ceramics, Tiffany-style stained glass lights, wicker, brass and wrought-iron decorative items. Everything is handcrafted locally. Ask owner Victor to show you the cave accessed by steep steps from the main showroom which was used as a hideout during Moorish times and later for food storage: the giant urns still remain.

Paniaceite
FOOD

(Calle Real 19) The place to come for artisanal handily packaged biscuits with several shelves of choice, plus hot paprika-spiked breadsticks and pâtés, including partridge and green or black olives.

ℹ Information

Regional Tourist Office (☑953 75 08 97; otubeda@andalucia.org; Calle Baja del Marqués 4; ◷9am-2.45pm & 4-7pm Mon-Fri, 10am-2pm Sat) Located in the 18th-century Palacio Marqués de Contadero.

ℹ Getting There & Around

BUS The **bus station** (☑953 75 21 57; Calle San José 6) is located around 1.5km to the northwest in the new part of town. **Alsa** (www .alsa.es) runs to Baeza (€1.05, 15 minutes, 19 daily), Jaén (€5, one hour, 15 daily), Cazorla (€3.85, one hour, five daily), Granada (€11.85, three hours, 10 daily) and Córdoba (€11, 2½ hours, five daily).

CAR There is a convenient underground car park in Plaza de Andalucía (one hour €1.20, 12 hours €14; open 7.30am to 11.30pm).

TRAIN The nearest station (see www.renfe .es) is Linares–Baeza, 21km northwest of town, which you can reach on Linares-bound buses. Trains depart from here daily for Granada, Córdoba, Seville, Málaga, Cádiz, Almería, Madrid and Barcelona.

Cazorla

POP 8104 / ELEV 836M

Huffing and puffing up the steep streets of this attractive rural town is perfect for those who want to continue huffing and puffing in the Parque Natural Sierras de Cazorla, Segura y Las Villas, which begins dramatically amid the cliffs of Peña de los Halcones (Falcon Crag), towering above the town. From here, you can see the passive landscape of the plains, and the rugged swathe of mountains and valleys that unfolds enticingly to the north and east.

◉ Sights

Here, as in the rest of Jaén province, local history has been shaped by the rich land-owning classes, and the town's *palacios* (palaces) belong to a few wealthy families. The central square, Plaza de la Corredera, is the civic centre of the town, and the elegant *ayuntamiento* dominates the square with its landmark clock tower.

Canyonlike streets radiate south of the plaza to the Balcón de Zabaleta. This little mirador is like a sudden window in a blank wall – it has stunning views over the town and up to the Castillo de la Yedra.

The shortest way up to the castle is from the attractive Plaza de Santa María, starting along the street to the right of the ruined

---

WILD THINGS

If you're a wildlife enthusiast, you have to get yourself to Cazorla. Apart from the excellent hiking here, this is the place with better prospects of spotting wildlife than almost anywhere else in Andalucía. Creatures such as red and fallow deer, wild boar, mouflon and ibex are all here in good numbers, as well as some 140 bird species, including eagles, vultures and falcons. Efforts are also being made to reintroduce the majestic lammergeyer (bearded vulture). In short, get walking and keep those binoculars at the ready...

JAÉN PROVINCE CAZORLA

Iglesia de Santa María. The devastated church – now being restored – was built by Vandelvira and was wrecked by Napoleonic troops in reprisal for Cazorla's tenacious resistance. It is now used for occasional open-air concerts.

Castillo de la Yedra CASTLE
(Castle of the Ivy; ◷2.30-8pm Tue, 9am-8pm Wed-Sat, 9am-2pm Sun) The dramatic Castle of the Ivy is of Roman origin, though it was largely built by the Muslims, then restored in the 15th century after the Reconquista. Much money has been spent on a modern restoration. There are superb panoramic views from here. The castle is home to a museum.

Museo del Alto Guadalquivir MUSEUM
(Castillo de la Yedra; admission €1.50; ◷2.30-8pm Tue, 9am-8pm Wed-Sat, 9am-2pm Sun) Housed in Castillo de la Yedra, this interesting museum comprises art; antiques and crafts, including 17th-century baroque tapestries; ceramics; and a small chapel featuring a life-sized Romanesque-Byzantine Crucifixion sculpture.

✯ Festivals & Events

La Caracolá RELIGIOUS
The image of Cazorla's patron saint, San Isicio (a Christian apostle supposedly stoned to death at Cazorla in Roman times) gets carried from the Ermita de San Isicio to the Iglesia de San José on 14 May.

Fiesta de Cristo del Consuelo FESTIVAL
Fireworks and fairgrounds mark Cazorla's annual fiesta, celebrated between 17 and 21 September.

✗ Eating

There are some good bars on Cazorla's three main squares, where you can choose tapas as well as *raciones*.

La Cueva de Juan Pedro ANDALUCIAN €€
(Plaza de Santa María; raciones €9, menú €10-12) An ancient, wood-beamed place with dangling *jamónes* (hams) and clumps of garlic and drying peppers. Taste the traditional Cazorla *conejo* (rabbit), *trucha* (trout), *rin-rán* (a mix of salted cod, potato and dried red peppers), *jabalí* (wild boar), *venado* (venison) and even mouflon. The *menú* includes rabbit in vinaigrette. There are two branches of La Cueva on this square, so if one is full, head to the other across the way.

Mesón Don Chema ANDALUCIAN €€
(Calle Escaleras; mains €10-17) Under the mounted antlers, dine on game, pork and a variety of meaty mains, as well as such sizzling local fare as *huevos cazorleña* (a mixed stew of sliced boiled eggs and chorizo with vegetables).

Bar Las Vegas TAPAS €
(Plaza de la Corredera 17; raciones €6) The best of Cazorla's bars, this spot has barrel tables outside (but little atmosphere within). You can try the tasty prawn-and-capsicum *revuelto* (scrambled eggs), as well as the town's top breakfast, *tostadas* (toasted bread) with various toppings, including the classic crushed tomatoes with garlic and olive oil.

❶ Information

Tourist Office (Paseo del Santo Cristo 17; ☺10am-1pm & 5.30-8pm) Located 200m north of Plaza de la Constitución, this tourist office provides useful information on the park and town, including some walks around the town.

❶ Getting There & Around

BUS **Alsa** (www.alsa.es) runs buses to Úbeda (€3.85, one hour, five daily), Jaén (€4.40, 1¾ hours, three daily) and Granada (€16, 3¾ hours, three daily). The main stop in Cazorla is Plaza de la Constitución. A few buses run from Cazorla to Coto Ríos in the park with stops at Arroyo Frío and Torre del Vinagre.

CAR There is a convenient car park in Plaza del Mercado, located below Plaza de la Constitución.

Parque Natural Sierras de Cazorla, Segura y Las Villas

One of the biggest drawcards in the whole of Jaén province is the lushly wooded, 2143-sq-km Parque Natural Sierras de Cazorla, Segura y Las Villas. It is the largest protected area in Spain, and its corrugated, craggy mountain ranges are memorably beautiful, as is the huge, snaking 20km reservoir in its midst.

This park is also the origin of the Río Guadalquivir, Andalucía's longest river, which rises between the Sierra de Cazorla and Sierra del Pozo in the south of the park and flows northwards into the reservoir, before heading west towards the Atlantic Ocean.

The best times to visit the park are in the shoulder seasons of spring and autumn, when the vegetation is at its most colourful and the temperatures are mild.

Exploring the park is a lot easier if you have a vehicle, but some bus services exist and there are plenty of places to stay within the park. If you don't have a vehicle to get to the more remote regions, you do have the option of taking guided excursions to those areas. The tourist office in Cazorla can provide you with a list of tour operators.

The park is hugely popular with Spanish tourists and attracts an estimated 600,000 visitors a year – some 50,000 of those coming during Semana Santa. The other peak periods are July and August, and weekends from April to October.

❶ Information

The main park information centre, the **Centro de Interpretación Torre del Vinagre** (☺10am-2pm & 4-7pm), is at Torre del Vinagre. It has a rather dry display on the park's ecology.

❶ BE PREPARED

When walking, be sure to equip yourself properly, with enough water and appropriate clothes. Temperatures up in the hills are generally several degrees lower than down in the valleys, and the wind can be cutting at any time. In winter the park is often blanketed in snow.

Sierra de Cazorla

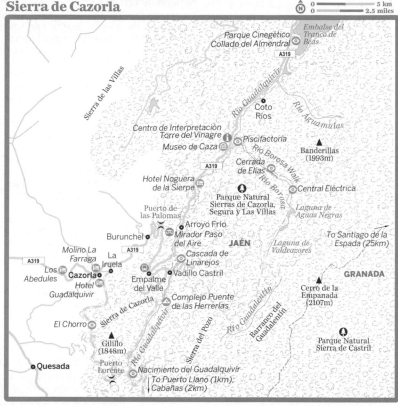

ℹ Getting There & Away

BUS

Carcesa (📞953 72 11 42) Runs two buses daily (except Sunday) from Cazorla's Plaza de la Constitución to Empalme del Valle, Arroyo Frío, Torre del Vinagre and Coto Ríos. Pick up the latest timetable from the tourist office. No buses link the northern part of the park with the centre or south, and there are no buses to Segura de la Sierra or Hornos.

Alsa (www.alsa.es) Runs a bus from Jaén, Baeza or Úbeda to La Puerta de Segura (€12, three hours, three daily).

CAR

If you're driving, approaches to the park include the A319 from Cazorla, roads into the north from Villanueva del Arzobispo and Puente de Génave on the A32, and the A317 to Santiago de la Espada from Puebla de Don Fadrique in northern Granada province. There are at least seven petrol stations in the park.

SOUTH OF THE PARK

The park begins just a few hundred metres up the hill east of Cazorla town. The footpaths and dirt roads working their way between the pine forests, meadowlands, crags and valleys of the park's mountains offer plenty of scope for day walks or drives, with fine panoramas. The park's abrupt geography, rising to 2107m at the summit of the **Cerro de la Empanada**, and descending to 460m, makes for rapid and dramatic changes in landscape.

The A319, east from Cazorla, doesn't enter the park until it reaches Burunchel, 7km from Cazorla. From Burunchel it winds 5km up to the 1200m Puerto de las Palomas, with the breezy **Mirador Paso del Aire** a little further on.

Five twisting kilometres downhill from here is Empalme del Valle, a junction where the A319 turns north towards the park's first major centre, **Arroyo Frío**. From here the road follows the north-flowing Río Guadalquivir.

An interesting detour from Empalme del Valle will take you to the river's source (Nacimento del Guadalquivir). From here you can continue a further 8km south to Cabañas, which at 2028m is one of the highest peaks in the park.

Further good walks in the south of the park are to be had in the Sierra del Pozo, which rises above the eastern side of the upper Guadalquivir Valley, and in the Barranco del Guadalentín, a deep river valley further east. The latter is particularly rich in wildlife, but you will need your own vehicle, or a guide with one, to reach these areas.

Continuing along the A319 from Arroyo Frío, the road continues down the Guadalquivir Valley to Torre del Vinagre, where you will find the park's Centro de Interpretación Torre del Vinagre (p222). Beyond Torre del Vinagre is Coto Ríos and the beginning of the Embalse del Tranco de Beas. The bus from Cazorla only goes this far and to explore the park further you will need your own transport.

NORTH OF THE PARK

From Coto Ríos the road follows the western edge of the huge, wide reservoir, with tantalising glimpses of the water through the trees. Just 7km north of Coto Ríos, on a spur of land between the A319 and the reservoir, you will find the Parque Cinegético Collado del Almendral, a large enclosed game park where ibex, mouflon and deer are kept.

A kilometre-long footpath leads from the parking area to three miradors (lookouts) where you might see animals – your chances are best at dawn and at dusk. Fifteen kilometres further north from here, the A319 crosses the dam that holds back the reservoir near the small village of Tranco.

Twelve kilometres north of the dam at Tranco, the A319 runs into a T-junction from which the A317 winds 4km up to Hornos. About 10km northeast of Hornos on the A317 is the Puerto de Horno de Peguera junction.

One kilometre up the road to the north (towards Siles), a dirt road turns left at some ruined houses to the top of El Yelmo

THE PARK'S BEST-LOVED WALK

The most popular walk in the Parque Natural Sierras de Cazorla, Segura y Las Villas follows the Río Borosa upstream. It goes through scenery that progresses from the pretty to the majestic, via a gorge and two tunnels (a torch is useful) to two beautiful mountain lakes – an ascent of 500m. This is a 24km, seven-hour walk (return; not counting stops).

A road signed 'Central Eléctrica,' east of the A319 opposite the Centro de Interpretación Torre del Vinagre (p222), crosses the Guadalquivir after about 500m. Within 1km of the river, the road reaches a piscifactoría (fish farm), with parking areas close by. The marked start of the walk is on your right, shortly past the fish farm.

The first section is an unpaved road crisscrossing the tumbling, trout-rich river over bridges. After about 4km, where the road starts climbing to the left, take a path forking right. This takes you through a beautiful 1.5km section where the valley narrows to a gorge, Cerrada de Elías, and the path changes to a wooden walkway. You re-emerge on the dirt road and continue for 3km to the Central Eléctrica, a small hydroelectric station.

The path passes between the power station and the river, and crosses a footbridge, where a 'Nacimiento de Aguas Negras, Laguna de Valdeazores' sign directs you ahead. About 1.5km from the station, the path turns left and zigzags up into a tunnel cut into the cliff. This tunnel allows water to flow to the power station. A narrow path, separated from the watercourse by a fence, runs through the tunnel, which takes about five minutes to walk through. There's a short section in the open air before you enter a second tunnel, which takes about one minute to get through. You emerge just below the dam of Laguna de Aguas Negras, a picturesque little reservoir surrounded by hills and trees. Cross the dam to the other side of the lake then walk about 1km south to reach a similar-sized natural lake, the Laguna de Valdeazores.

You can do this walk as a day trip from Cazorla if you take the bus to Torre del Vinagre. Be sure to carry plenty of water with you.

HORNOS

Like better-known Segura de la Sierra, Hornos is fabulously located – atop a crag backed by a sweep of nearby mountains, and with even better views over the shimmering blue waters of the Embalse del Tranco reservoir. The surroundings are lush and green, richly patterned with olive trees, pines and almond trees with the occasional tossed dice of a farmhouse.

Hornos dates back to the Bronze Age when there was a settlement here, while the castle with its distinctive four towers was built in the early 13th century. At the time of research it was undergoing restoration, with plans to build an observatory.

Don't expect colour-coordinated geraniums, souvenir shops or even a tourist office – Hornos' charms lie in exploring the narrow winding streets, climbing the ramparts and wondering at the magnificent view from several strategically placed miradors (lookouts).

Seek out the early-16th-century Iglesia de Nuestra Señora de la Asunción, which has the oldest, albeit crumbling, plateresque (highly decorated) portal in the province, plus a vibrant and colourful *retablo* (altar) of six 'saintly' painted panels dating from 1589.

There are a couple of good restaurants, plus places to stay. If you want to stride out beyond the village, study the large plaque at the entrance where maps outline five trails of varying distances and levels of difficulty.

(1809m), one of the most distinctive mountains in the northern part of the park. It's 5km to the top – an ascent of 360m. At a fork after 1.75km, go right (the left fork goes down to El Robledo and Cortijos Nuevos).

The climb affords superb long-distance views and gliding griffon vultures. The road is fine for cars, if narrow, but this is also a good walk (about six to seven hours round trip).

SEGURA DE LA SIERRA

Segura de la Sierra sits perched on a 1000m-high hill that is crowned by an Islamic castle. It's 20km north of Hornos; turn east off the A317 4km after Cortijos Nuevos.

Characterised largely by its Islamic heritage, the village actually dates all the way back to Phoenician times and ultimately became part of the Christian defensive front line when it was taken from the Muslims in 1214.

As you approach the upper, older part of the village, you'll find a tourist office (Calle Cortijos Nuevos; ☺10.30am-2pm & 6.30-8.30pm) beside the Puerta Nueva, an arch that was once one of four gates of Islamic Saqura.

☉ Sights & Activities

The village's main sight – aside from what you'll see if you just wander around the picturesque cobbled streets – is the magnifi-

cent castle, perched at the top of the *pueblo*. You can walk or drive here – if you're walking, take the narrow Calle de las Ordenanzas del Común to the right after passing the Iglesia de Nuestra Señora del Collado, the parish church.

After a few minutes you'll emerge alongside Segura's tiny bullring (which has seen famous fighters such as Enrique Ponce during the October festival), with the castle track heading up to the right.

Near the signposted Baño Moro is the Puerta Catena, the best preserved of Segura's four Islamic gates; from here you can pick up the waymarked GR-147 footpath to the splendidly isolated village of Río Madera (a 15km downhill hike).

Segura Castle   CASTLE
(adult/child €4/2; ☺10.30am-2pm Wed-Sun; ♿) Extensively restored in the 1960s, this lofty three-storey castle dates back to Moorish times, but it was virtually destroyed during the 15th-century Christian conquest and was later rebuilt, complete with a chapel.

The Centro de Interpretación (Interpretation Centre) incorporates 3D audiovisual presentations about the history and landscape. You can also see the chapel and theoriginal Arab steam baths, and climb the tower to get a bird's-eye view across to El Yelmo, about 5km to the south-south-west.

FREE **Baño Moro**   BATHHOUSE

(Calle Baños Moro 1; ☺10.30am-2pm Wed-Sun)
Built around 1150, probably for the local
ruler Ibn ben Hamusk, the Baño Moroit,
just off the central Plaza Mayor, has three
elegant rooms (for cold, temperate and hot
baths), with horseshoe arches and barrel
vaults studded with skylights.

✗ Eating

Mirador de Peñalta   ANDALUCIAN €

(Calle San Vicente 29; mains €8-10; ☒) Situated
on the right at the approach to the village,
this place caters to hungry hikers with a
meaty menu that includes steaks, lamb
chops and pork, as well as some sierra specialties like *ajo atao*, a belly-filling fry-up of
potatoes, garlic and eggs.

Granada Province

POP 918,072

Best Places to Eat

» Oliver (p246)

» Ruta del Azafrán (p243)

» Bodegas Castañeda (p247)

» Baraka (p257)

Best Places to Stay

» Hotel Posada del Toro (p305)

» Santa Isabel la Real (p306)

» Apartamentos Turísticos San Matías (p305)

Why Go?

Granada has it all: the looks, the jewels, the sense of fun, a streetwise edge and, while the magnificent Alhambra continues to count among the country's 'do before you die' sights, there is so much more to this Andalucian star city. The old Islamic quarter of the Albayzín is another of Granada's gems; its whitewashed houses and steep narrow streets wind up the hill of the former Islamic quarter like a tangled string of pearls. City-wide, discover evocative architecture, traditional (and innovative) bars and restaurants and the youthful vivacity of a university city, along with some of the best nightlife in the province.

And the province of Granada offers more surprises; there's skiing and climbing in the snowy Sierra Nevada, and walking in the amazing Las Alpujarras. You can check out cave life on the Altiplano (high plain) or forget it all and go swimming and sunbathing on the Costa Tropical on Granada's Mediterranean coastline.

Driving Distances (km)

	Granada	Guadix	Almuñécar	Trevélez
Guadix	52			
Almuñécar	80	132		
Trevélez	74	76	65	
Pampaneira	58	92	49	16

DON'T MISS

The Palacios Nazaríes, the stunning highlight of the city's fabled Alhambra.

Best Flamenco Venues

» Le Chien Andalou (p249)

» Eshavira (p249)

» Al Sur de Granada (p248)

Best for Quality Souvenirs

» Tienda Librería de la Alhambra (p249)

» Artesanías González (p249)

» Nade Taller del Telar (p259)

Resources

» **Turismo de Granada** (www.turismodegranada.org) Provincial tourist office.

» **Walking in the Alpujarras** (www.walking.demon.co.uk) Invaluable guide to trails.

» **Ayuntamiento de Granada** (www.granada.org) Government website with good maps; click on 'La Ciudad.'

» **Granada Information** (www.granadainfo.com/english) General guide to Granada.

Getting Around

Buses connect even the tiniest villages with the city of Granada, but a car enables flexibility and some dramatic drives. Yet a car can be a liability in the city, with its gnarled mess of unsigned streets, many closed to all but taxis and buses. Ideally, plan your trip so you're car-free for your Granada stay, or leave your car in a (costly) underground car park for the duration. Trains are of limited help – the only stops are Granada and Guadix.

THREE PERFECT DAYS

Day 1: Granada's Islamic Heritage

Start your sightseeing early, with a morning visit to the Moorish palaces of the Alhambra. For lunch, sample Spanish–Middle East fusion at **Ruta del Azafrán**, then retire for a well-deserved siesta. In the late afternoon, head uphill again, this time to the winding streets of the Albayzín district and the fantastic sunset vistas from the **Mirador San Nicolás**, followed by tapas at **El Ají** and other bars on this plaza.

Day 2: City Pleasures

Pay your respects to Fernando and Isabel at their final resting place in Granada's **Capilla Real**, then treat yourself to ice cream at **Los Italianos** and a bit of shoe shopping around Plaza Bib-Rambla. Elbow up to the bar for a seafood lunch at **Oliver** or **Los Diamantes**. After a siesta, you might need just one more small ice cream... Later, it's off for tapas at iconic bars such as **Bodegas Castañeda**. If you're still feeling lively, drop by **Eshavira** for a late-night flamenco session.

Day 3: Alpujarran Idyll

In the mountains south of Granada, get into the slow groove of village life in Pitres, then set out on foot for the villages just downhill, descending all the way to a centuries-old bridge over a rushing river. After your hike back up, you'll have an appetite for the delectable food at **L'Atelier**. Crawl into bed and enjoy the silence, broken only by the occasional goat bell.

Accommodation

Unsurprisingly, Granada has no shortage of hotels, as well as a good range in all categories, including less expensive options. Elsewhere, Las Alpujarras has a solid choice of rustic-style small hotels and apartments which get booked up fast at holiday time, particularly Easter. Read all about hotel choices in our dedicated Accommodation chapter (p288).

GRANADA

POP 258,000 / ELEV 738M

Seville may have the *pasión* and Córdoba a medieval charm, but Granada has an edge. Most visitors concentrate solely on the magnificent Alhambra, but if you explore further, you'll find Andalucía's hippest, most youthful city, with a 'free tapas' culture, innovative bars and intimate flamenco haunts.

Here the Islamic past feels recent, as Muslim North Africans make up some 10% of the population; there's even a modern mosque in the medieval district of the Albayzín. And though Granada looks alpine, with the white-capped Sierra Nevada peaks startlingly close, you could just as easily go swimming down on the coast for the day and be back in time to enjoy the city's nightlife.

History

As lively as Granada is today, it's hardly what it was five centuries ago. The city came into its own late in Spain's Islamic era. As Córdoba and Seville fell to the Catholics in the mid-13th century, a minor potentate called Mohammed ibn Yusuf ibn Nasr established an independent state based in Granada. The town was soon flooded with Muslim refugees, and the Nasrid emirate became the last bastion of Al-Andalus.

The Alhambra was developed as royal court, palace, fortress and miniature city, and the Nasrids ruled from this increasingly lavish complex for 250 years. During this time, Granada became one of the richest cities in Europe, with a population of more than 350,000. Under emirs Yusuf I (r 1333–54) and Mohammed V (r 1354–59 and 1362–91), traders did booming business, and artisans perfected such crafts as wood inlay.

As usual, though, decadent palace life bred a violent rivalry over succession. One faction supported the emir Abu al-Hasan and his Christian concubine, Zoraya, while the other backed Boabdil (Abu Abdullah), Abu al-Hasan's son by his wife Aixa – even though Boabdil was still just a child. In 1482 Boabdil started a civil war and, following Abu al-Hasan's death in 1485, won control of the city. With the emirate weakened by infighting, the Catholics pounced in 1491. Queen Isabel in particular had been smitten by Granada – so fittingly named for the jewel-like pomegranate, she thought, its buildings clustered like seeds along the hillsides – and she wanted it for herself. After an eight-month siege, Boabdil agreed to surrender the city in return for the Alpujarras valleys, 30,000 gold coins and political and religious freedom for his subjects. Boabdil hiked out of town – letting out the proverbial 'Moor's last sigh' as he looked over his shoulder in regret – and on 2 January 1492, Isabel and Fernando entered the city ceremonially in Muslim dress, to set up court in the Alhambra.

Their promises didn't last. They soon divided the populace, relegating the Jews to the Realejo and containing the Muslims in the Albayzín. Subsequent rulers called for full-scale expulsion, first in 1570 and again in 1610. It is said that there are families in Morocco who, still today, sentimentally keep the keys to their long-lost homes.

This brutal expulsion backfired, however, and Granada – once the Catholic Monarchs' prize jewel – became a backwater. In 1828 American writer Washington Irving visited the ruined palace and decided to move in. His *Tales of the Alhambra,* published in 1832, brought tourists from all over the world to marvel at the city's Islamic heritage; they helped give the city a little push into the modern age. Now Granada thrives on a culture that mixes Spanish, Moroccan, *gitano* (Roma) and student, plus tourist life.

◉ Sights

Most major sights are an easy walk within the city centre, and there are buses for when the hills wear you out.

TOP CHOICE Alhambra   PALACE

(Map p232; ☎902 44 12 21; www.alhambra -tickets.es; adult/EU senior/EU student/under 8yr €13/9/9/free, Generalife only €6; ⊙8.30am-8pm 16 Mar-31 Oct, to 6pm 1 Nov-14 Mar, night visits 10-11.30pm Tue-Sat Mar-Oct, 8-9.30pm Fri & Sat Nov-Feb) The sheer red walls of the Alhambra rise from woods of cypress and elm. Inside is one of the more splendid sights of Europe, a network of lavishly decorated palaces and irrigated gardens, a World Heritage Site and the subject of scores of legends and fantasies.

But at the height of summer, some 6000 visitors tramp through daily, making it difficult to pause to inspect a pretty detail, much less mentally transport yourself to the 14th century. Schedule a visit in quieter months, if possible; if not, then book in advance for the very earliest or latest time slot.

The Alhambra takes its name from the Arabic *al-qala'a al-hamra* (the Red Castle).

Granada Province Highlights

1 Sample some of Spain's best succulent ham in **Trevélez** (p260)

2 Drive through open plains where dinosaurs once roamed in **Orce** (p253)

3 Enjoy the castanet-clicking authenticity of Granada city's **flamenco bars** (p249)

ALBACETE

Barranda

MURCIA

Parque Natural Sierras
de Cazorla,
Segura y las Villas

Peal de
Becerro

Puebla
de Don
Fadrique

Almaciles

Empanadas
(2107m)

Río Guadiana Menor

Quesada

Buitre
(2020m)

Parque Natural Sierra
de Castril

La Cañada
de Cañepla

Huescar

Castril

Galera

María

Orce

Parque Natural
Sierra de María-
Los Vélez

Pozo
Alcón

A330

Embalse
del Negratín

Cúllar

A92N

Velez
Rubio

Zújar

GRANADA

A92N

Baza

Caniles

Huercal-
Overa

Santa
Bárbara
(2271m)

Albox

Purulfena

Parque
Natural Sierra
de Baza

Macael

Guadix

Río Almanzora

Córdbar

Antas

rez del
arquesado

A92

La Calahorra

Doña
María
Ocaña

ALMERÍA

Puerto de
la Ragua

Huenija

Sorbas

Paraje Natural
de Karst en
Yesos

an Juan
(2786m)

Abla

Gergal

Chullo
(2612m)

Sierra
Nevada

A337

Parque
Natural
Sierra
Nevada

Canjáyar

Tabernas

Laroles

Ugijar

Cherin

Cádiar

Fondón

Rioja

Las Alpujarras

Berja

Huercal de
Almería

Parque Natural
de Cabo de
Gata-Níjar

Albondón

Almería

Retamar

Albuñol

Santa María
del Águila

Adra

Roquetas
de Mar

Golfo de
Almería

Cabo de
Gata

San Jose

a Rábita

Almerimar

MEDITERRANEAN
SEA

④ Hike surrounded by
breathtaking scenery in **Las
Alpujarras** (p256)

⑤ Walk or ski in the snowy
Sierra Nevada (p254)

⑥ Check out Granada's
scintillating student-driven
nightlife (p248)

⑦ Enjoy freshly caught
seafood at a beachside
chiringuito (small open-air
eatery) in **La Herradura** (p263)

Alhambra

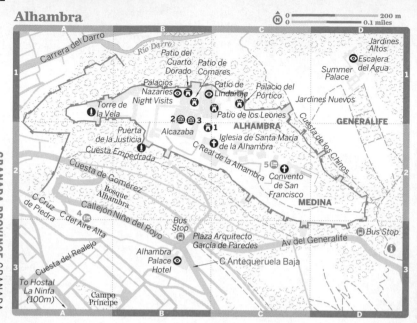

Alhambra

⊙ **Sights**

🛏 **Sleeping**

✕ **Eating**

The first palace on the site was built by Samuel Ha-Nagid, the Jewish grand vizier of one of Granada's 11th-century Zirid sultans. In the 13th and 14th centuries, the Nasrid emirs turned the area into a fortress-palace complex, adjoined by a village of which only ruins remain. After the Reconquista (Christian reconquest), the Alhambra's mosque was replaced with a church, and the Convento de San Francisco (now the Parador de Granada) was built. Carlos I (also known as the Habsburg emperor Charles V), grandson of the Catholic Monarchs, had a wing of the palaces destroyed to make space for his huge Renaissance work, the Palacio de Carlos V.

During the Napoleonic occupation, the Alhambra was used as a barracks and nearly blown up. What you see today has been heavily but respectfully restored.

Palacios Nazaríes

The central palace complex is the pinnacle of the Alhambra's design. Though the Nasrid Palaces were erected late in Spain's Islamic era, when the empire was already well in decline (and architects had switched from stone to more expedient, cheaper brick), they make up one of the finest Islamic structures in Europe, a harmonious synthesis of space, light, shade, water and greenery that sought to conjure the gardens of paradise for the rulers who dwelt here. Expanses of tile, *muqarnas* (honeycomb) vaulting and wood trim survive, but most mesmerising is the intricate stucco work that adorns the walls. The Arabic inscription *'Wa la ghaliba illa Allah'* (There is no conqueror but God) covers nearly every surface in various calligraphy styles, transforming the words from ritual praise into geometric pattern. But virtually no documents confirm the functions of the palaces, built in two main phases – about the only certainty is that the niches in the walls held water pitchers. So the rooms are now largely a blank slate for visitors' imaginations.

Entrance is through the 14th-century **Mexuar**, perhaps an antechamber for those awaiting audiences with the emir. Two centuries later, it was converted to a chapel, with a prayer room at the far end. Look up here and elsewhere to appreciate the geometrically carved wood ceilings. From the Mexuar, you pass into the **Patio del Cuarto Dorado**. It appears to be a forecourt to the main palace, with the symmetrical doorways to the right, framed with glazed tiles and stucco, setting a cunning trap: the right-hand door leads nowhere but out, but the left passes through a dogleg hall (a common strategy in Islamic domestic architecture to keep interior rooms private) into the **Patio de Comares**, the centre of a palace built in the mid-14th century as Emir Yusuf I's private residence.

Rooms (likely used for lounging and sleeping) look onto the rectangular pool edged in myrtles, and traces of cobalt blue paint cling to the *muqarnas* vaults in the side niches on the north end. Originally, all the walls were lavishly coloured; with paint on the stucco-trimmed walls in the adjacent **Sala de la Barca**, the effect would have resembled flocked wallpaper. Yusuf I's visitors would have passed through this annex room to meet him in the **Salón de Comares**, where the marvellous domed marquetry ceiling uses more than 8000 cedar pieces to create its intricate star pattern representing the seven heavens.

Adjacent is the recently restored **Patio de los Leones** (Courtyard of the Lions), built in the second half of the 14th century under Muhammad V, at the political and artistic peak of Granada's emirate. But the centrepiece, a fountain that channelled water through the mouths of 12 marble lions, dates from the 11th century. The courtyard layout, using the proportions of the golden ratio, demonstrates the complexity of Islamic geometric design – the varied columns are placed in such a way that they are symmetrical on numerous axes. The porticoes jutting into the centre are uncommon – this is effectively the previous patio built inside-out, creating complex shadows by day and moonlit night. The stucco work, too, hits its apex here, with almost lacelike detail.

If you walk counterclockwise around the patio, you will first pass the **Sala de Abencerrajes**. The Abencerraje family supported the young Boabdil in the palace power struggle between him and his own father, who was the reigning sultan.

GRANADA PROVINCE GRANADA

ALHAMBRA PRACTICALITIES

Tickets are timed for either morning (from 8.30am) or afternoon (after 2pm) entry to the grounds, and, more important, for admission to the Palacios Nazaríes within a 30-minute period (you can stay as long as you like). Allow three hours or more to see the whole complex, and at least 10 minutes to walk from the Generalife to the Palacios Nazaríes. Guards allow absolutely no late entries; in high season, be in the queue at the palaces at the start of your time slot.

Same-day tickets sell out early, so it's more convenient to buy tickets up to three months ahead. Pick up phone or internet orders at the yellow machines to the right of the **ticket office**, using the credit card with which you made the purchase. When full-access tickets are sold out, you can still buy a ticket to the Generalife and gardens (€7). The Palacios Nazaríes are open for **night visits** (☉10-11.30pm Tue-Sat Mar-Oct, 8-9.30pm Fri & Sat Nov-Feb), good for atmosphere rather than detail.

There is no explanatory signage in the complex; an average-quality audioguide is available for €4. No outside food is allowed, but there is a slightly pricey cafeteria at the Parador de Granada (p246), plus vending machines by the ticket office and the Alcazaba. Outside the complex, no restaurants are notable, but the bar at the **Alhambra Palace Hotel** (☎958 22 14 68; Plaza Arquitecto García de Paredes 1; drinks €4-6) has stunning views.

Walk up one of three ways: Cuesta de Gomérez, through woods to the **Puerta de la Justicia** (enter here if you already have your ticket) or, further along, to the ticket office; Cuesta de los Chinos, to the east end of the complex; or up Cuesta de Realejo via the Alhambra Palace Hotel.

Buses 30, 32 and (less directly) 34 run from near Plaza Nueva from 7am to 11pm, stopping at the ticket office and in front of the Alhambra Palace. By car, follow 'Alhambra' signs from the highway to the car park, just uphill from the ticket office.

Alhambra

TIMELINE

900 The first reference to *al-qala'at al-hamra* (red castle) atop Granada's Sabika Hill.

1237 Founder of the Nasrid dynasty, Muhammad I, moves his court to Granada. Threatened by belligerent Christian armies he builds a new defensive fort, the **Alcazaba 1**.

1302-09 Designed as a summer palace-cum-country estate for Granada's foppish rulers, the bucolic **Generalife 2** is begun by Muhammad III.

1333-54 Yusuf I initiates the construction of the **Palacio Nazaríes 3**, still considered the highpoint of Islamic culture in Europe.

1350-60 Up goes the **Palacio de Comares 4**, taking Nasrid lavishness to a whole new level.

1362-91 The second coming of Muhammad V ushers in even greater architectural brilliance exemplified by the construction of the **Patio de los Leones 5**.

1527 The Christians add the **Palacio de Carlos V 6**. Inspired Renaissance palace or incongruous crime against Moorish art? You decide.

1829 The languishing, half-forgotten Alhambra is 'rediscovered' by American writer Washington Irving during a protracted sleep-over.

1954 The Generalife gardens are extended southwards to accommodate an outdoor theatre.

TOP TIPS

» **Queue-dodger** Reserve tickets in advance online at www.alhambra-tickets.es

» **Money-saver** You can visit the general areas of the palace free of charge any time by entering through the Puerta de Justica

» **Stay over** Two fine hotels are encased in the grounds: Parador de Granada (expensive) and Hotel América (more economical)

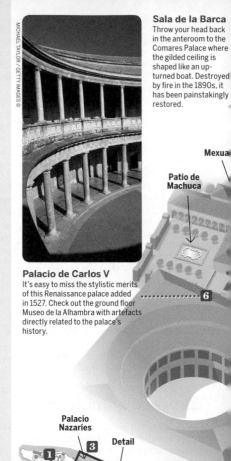

Sala de la Barca
Throw your head back in the anteroom to the Comares Palace where the gilded ceiling is shaped like an upturned boat. Destroyed by fire in the 1890s, it has been painstakingly restored.

Mexua

Patio de Machuca

Palacio de Carlos V
It's easy to miss the stylistic merits of this Renaissance palace added in 1527. Check out the ground floor Museo de la Alhambra with artefacts directly related to the palace's history.

Palacio Nazaríes

Detail

Puerta de Justica

MICHAEL TAYLOR / GETTY IMAGES ©

Alcazaba
Find time to explore the towers of the original citadel, the most important of which – the Torre de la Vela – takes you, via a winding staircase, to the Alhambra's best viewpoint.

DAVID TOMLINSON / GETTY IMAGES ©

Patio de Arrayanes

f only you could linger longer beside the rows of myrtle bushes *(arrayanes)* that border this calming rectangular pool. Shaded porticos with seven harmonious arches invite further contemplation.

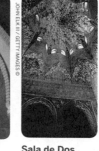

Palacio de Comares

The neck-ache continues in the largest room in the Comares Palace renowned for its rich geometric ceiling. A negotiating room for the emirs, the Salón de los Embajadores is a masterpiece of Moorish design.

Sala de Dos Hermanas

Focus on the *dos hermanas* – two marble slabs either side of the fountain – before enjoying the intricate cupola embellished with 5000 tiny moulded stalactites. Poetic calligraphy decorates the walls.

Torre de Comares

4

Patio de Arrayanes

Baños Reales

Washington Irving Apartments

Jardín de Lindaraja

5

Sala de los Abencerrajes

Jardines del Partal

Palacio del Partal

Generalife

coda to most people's visits, the 'architect's garden' is no afterthought. While Nasrid in origin, e horticulture is relatively new: the pools and cades were added in the early 20th century.

Patio de los Leones

Count the 12 lions sculpted from marble, holding up a gurgling fountain. Then pan back and take in the delicate columns and arches built to signify an Islamic vision of paradise.

Granada

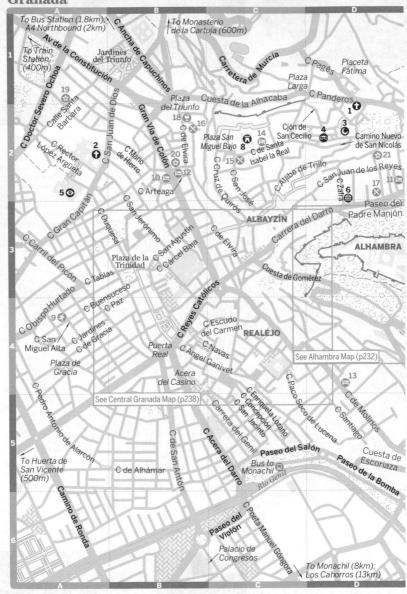

The legend has it that the sultan had the traitors killed in this room, and the rusty stains in the fountain are the victims' indelible blood – but the multicoloured tiles on the walls and the great octagonal ceiling are far more eye-catching. In the **Sala de** **los Reyes** (Hall of the Kings), at the east end of the patio, the painted leather ceilings depict 10 Nasrid emirs. The European style (the artists were probably Genoans) indicates the cross-cultural foment of the 14th century.

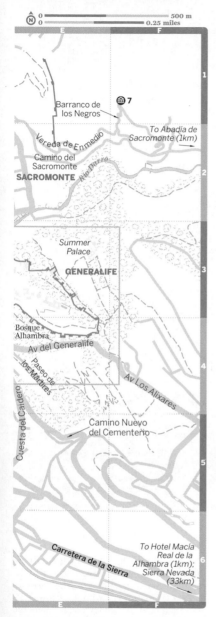

Granada

and acorns – and the band of calligraphy at eye level, just above the tiles, is a poem praising Muhammad V for his victory in Algeciras in 1369, a rare triumph this late in the Islamic game. The dizzying ceiling is a fantastic *muqarnas* dome with some 5000 tiny cells. The carved wood screens in the upper level enabled women (and perhaps others involved in palace intrigue) to peer down from hallways above without being seen. At the far end, the tile-trimmed **Mirador de Lindaraja** was a lovely place for palace denizens to look onto the garden below. Traces of paint still cling to the window frames, and a few panels of coloured glass set in the wood ceiling cast a warm glow.

From the Sala de Dos Hermanas, a passageway leads past the domed roofs of the baths on the level below and into rooms built for Carlos I in the 1520s and later used by Washington Irving. From here you

On the patio's north side, doors once covered the entrance to the **Sala de Dos Hermanas** (Hall of Two Sisters) – look for the holes on either side of the frame where they would have been anchored. The walls are adorned with local flora – pine cones

Central Granada

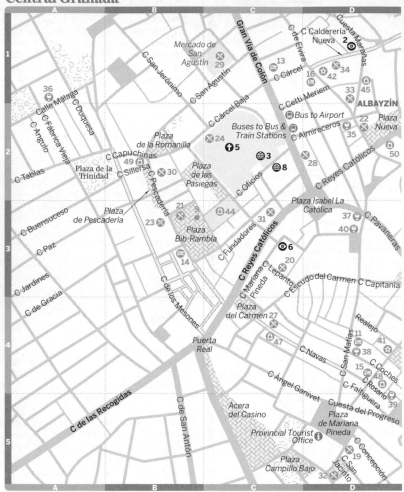

descend to the pretty **Patio de Lindaraja**. In the southwest corner is the bathhouse – you can't enter, but you can peer in at the rooms lit by star-shaped skylights.

You emerge into an area of terraced gardens created in the early 20th century, and the reflecting pool in front of the small **Palacio del Pórtico** (Palace of the Portico), the oldest surviving palace in the Alhambra, from the time of Mohammed III (r 1302–09). You can leave the gardens by a gate facing the Palacio de Carlos V or continue along a path to the Generalife.

Alcazaba, Christian Buildings & Museums

The west end of the Alhambra grounds are the remnants of the **Alcazaba**, chiefly its ramparts and several towers. The **Torre de la Vela** (Watchtower), with a narrow staircase leading to the top terrace, is where the cross and banners of the Reconquista were raised in January 1492.

By the Palacios Nazaríes, the hulking **Palacio de Carlos V** clashes spectacularly with its surroundings. In a different setting its merits might be more readily appreciated – it is the only example in Spain of the

⊘9am-2pm Mon-Fri) displays paintings and sculptures from Granada's Christian history.

Further along, the 16th-century **Iglesia de Santa María de la Alhambra** sits on the site of the palace mosque, and at the crest of the hill the **Convento de San Francisco**, now the Parador de Granada hotel, is where Isabel and Fernando were laid to rest while their tombs in the Capilla Real were being built.

Generalife

From the Arabic *jinan al-'arif* (the overseer's gardens), the Generalife is a soothing arrangement of pathways, patios, pools, fountains, tall trees and, in season, flowers of every imaginable hue. To reach the complex you must pass through the Alhambra walls on the east side, then head back northwest. You approach through topiary gardens on the south end, which were once grazing land for the royal herds. At the north end is the emirs' **summer palace**, a whitewashed structure on the hillside facing the Alhambra. The courtyards here are particularly graceful; in the second courtyard, the trunk of a 700-year-old cypress tree suggests what delicate shade once graced the patio. Climb the steps outside the courtyard to the **Escalera del Agua**, a delightful bit of garden engineering where water flows along a shaded staircase.

Capilla Real   HISTORIC BUILDING
(Map p238; www.capillareal.granada.com; Calle Oficios; admission €3.50; ⊘10.30am-1.30pm & 4-7.30pm Mon-Sat, 11am-1.30pm & 4-7pm Sun Apr-Oct) The **Royal Chapel** adjoins Granada's cathedral and is an outstanding Christian building. Catholic Monarchs Isabella and Ferdinand commissioned this elaborate Isabelline Gothic-style mausoleum. It was not completed until 1521; they were temporarily interred in the Convento de San Francisco.

The monarchs lie in simple lead coffins in the crypt beneath their marble monuments in the chancel, enclosed by a stunning gilded wrought-iron screen created in 1520 by Bartolomé de Jaén. Also here are the coffins of Isabella and Ferdinand's unfortunate daughter, Juana the Mad, and her husband, Philip of Flanders. There is some doubt as to whether Juana was mad at all. She was Charles V's mother and the rightful heir to the Spanish throne. When Charles arrived in 1517 from Flanders, she was forced to sign papers of abdication and then locked up in a windowless cell for the last 40 years of her life. The film *Mad Love* by Juana la Loca

Renaissance-era circle-in-a-square ground plan. Begun in 1527 by Pedro Machuca, a Toledo architect who studied under Michelangelo, it was financed, perversely, from taxes on Granada's *morisco* (converted Muslim) population but never finished because funds dried up after the *morisco* rebellion.

Inside, the **Museo de la Alhambra** (Map p232; admission free; ⊘9am-2.30pm Tue-Sat) has a collection of Alhambra artefacts, including the door from the Sala de Dos Hermanas, and the **Museo de Bellas Artes** (Fine Arts Museum; Map p232; non-EU/EU citizen €1.50/free;

Central Granada

depicts the story to dramatic effect and won three Goya awards (the Spanish equivalent to the Oscars) back in 2001.

The sacristy contains a small but impressive **museum** with Ferdinand's sword and Isabella's sceptre, silver crown and personal art collection, which is mainly Flemish but also includes Botticelli's *Prayer in the Garden of Olives*. Felipe de Vigarni's two fine early-16th-century statues of the Catholic Monarchs at prayer are also here.

La Madraza   HISTORIC BUILDING

(Map p238; Calle Oficios; admission free; ⊙8am-10pm) La Madraza was founded in 1349 by Sultan Yusuf I as a school and university. You can gaze into the splendid prayer hall with its elaborate mihrab, where the light has a special mellow quality. The building was closed for renovations at the time of research.

Cathedral   CATHEDRAL

(Map p238; ☑958 22 29 59; admission €3.50; ⊙10.45am-1.30pm & 4-8pm Mon-Sat, 4-8pm Sun, to 7pm daily Nov-Mar) Granada's cavernous cathedral was another Isabel commission, but construction began only after her death, and didn't finish until 1704. The result is a mishmash of styles: baroque outside, by the 17th-century master Alonso Cano, and Renaissance inside, where the Spanish pioneer in this style, Diego de Siloé, directed operations to construct huge piers, white as meringue, a black-and-white tile floor and the gilded and painted chapel. Even more odd, the roof vaults are distinctly Gothic.

Casa de los Pisa HISTORIC BUILDING
(Archivo Museo San Juan de Díos; Map p238; Calle de la Convalecencia 1; suggested donation €2.50, admission only by guided tour in Spanish; ☉10am-1.30pm Mon-Sat) Granada's most famous resident saint, San Juan Robles (San Juan de Díos), dedicated his life to healing the destitute and inspired a medical fraternity. He died in 1550, at the age of 55, in the Casa de los Pisa.

The mansion of the wealthy Pisa family, who took the saint off the streets when he fell ill, now displays a treasure trove of liturgical art, as well as secular oddities such as boa skins and even a shrunken head. Tours take about 45 minutes, ending in the very room where the saint expired.

FREE **Iglesia de San Juan de Díos** CHURCH
(Map p236; Calle San Juan de Díos; ☉10am-1pm & 4-7pm) The humble San Juan Robles's death in a mansion is odd enough; it's even stranger to see his final resting place, this stunningly gaudy church. The saint's remains are set deep in a niche surrounded by gold, gold and more gold.

Monasterio de San Jerónimo MONASTERY
(Map p236; Calle Rector López Argüeta 9; admission €3.50; ☉10am-2.30pm & 4-7.30pm) One of the most stunning Catholic buildings in Granada is a little out of the centre. At the 16th-century Monasterio de San Jerónimo, where nuns still sing vespers, every surface of the church has been painted – the stained glass literally pales in comparison.

Gonzalo Fernández de Córdoba, known as El Gran Capitán and the Catholic Monarchs' military man, is entombed here, at the foot of the steps, and figures of him and his wife stand on either side of the enormous gilt retablo, which rises eight levels. Almond cookies, baked by the nuns, are for sale at the front desk, to stop your head from spinning.

Monasterio de la Cartuja MONASTERY
(Paseo de la Cartuja; admission €3.50; ☉10am-1pm & 4-8pm Mon-Sat, 10am-noon Sun) Built between the 16th and 18th centuries by the Carthusian monks themselves, this 16th-century monastery has an imposing sand-coloured stone exterior, but it is the lavish baroque monastery church that people come to see, especially the *sagrario* (sanctuary) behind the main altar, a confection of red, black, white and grey-blue marble,

columns with golden capitals, profuse sculpture and a beautiful frescoed cupola.

To the left of the main altar lies the *sacristía* (sacristy), the ultimate expression of Spanish late baroque, in effusive 'wedding-cake' stucco and brown-and-white Lanjarón marble (resembling a melange of chocolate mousse and cream). The *sacristía's* cabinets, veneered and inlaid with mahogany, ebony, ivory, shell and silver in the 18th century, represent a high point of Granada's marquetry art.

San Bruno, founder of the Carthusian order, can be seen everywhere, looking wan and contemplating a skull; a few of his bones are embedded in the gilt and mirrored altar.

From the centre, catch bus 8, C or U north from Gran Vía de Colón. On school days, get off at Paseo de la Cartuja I; on weekends, the bus stops directly in front of the monastery.

Corral del Carbón HISTORIC SITE
(Map p238; Calle Mariana Pineda) Across Calle Reyes Católicos, you can't miss the elaborate horseshoe arch of the Corral del Carbón, which began as a 14th-century merchants' inn. It has since been used as an inn for coal dealers (hence its modern name, Coal Yard) and later a theatre. It is home to government offices and hosts occasional concerts.

ALBAYZÍN

A walk in the Albayzín is recommended in the late afternoon, when you can enjoy stunning Alhambra views at sunset. Granada at dusk, when the Alhambra is bathed in hues of pink and gold, is one of the most breathtaking sights in the world; join the scene at Mirador San Nicolás for the best views of the Alhambra with its Sierra Nevada backdrop. (Don't let the vista distract you from your wallet, however; this is prime pickpocket territory.)

The best route through the tangled maze of streets is whichever one you take. That said, it's easiest to start along the Río Darro.

Iglesia de Santa Ana CHURCH
(Map p238; Plaza Santa Ana) Plaza Nueva extends northeast into Plaza Santa Ana, where the Iglesia de Santa Ana incorporates a mosque's minaret in its belltower.

Baños Árabes El Bañuelo BATHHOUSE
(Map p238) A simple yet well-preserved 11th-century Islamic bathhouse, located along narrow Carrera del Darro.

Museo Arqueológico   MUSEUM
(Archaeological Museum; Map p236; ☑58 57 54
08; Carrera del Darro 43; non-EU/EU citizen €1.50/
free; ⏱2.30-8.30pm Tue, 9am-8.30pm Wed-
Sat, 9am-2.30pm Sun) Housed in a Renaissance
mansion, Museo Arqueológico displays finds
from Granada province including ancient
tools, mammoth molars and astrolabes.

Colegiata del Salvador   CHURCH
(Map p236) Plaza del Salvador, near the top
of the Albayzín, is dominated by the Colegiata del Salvador, a 16th-century church
on the site of the Albayzín's former main
mosque, the patio of which still survives at
the church's western end.

Palacio de Dar-al-Horra   PALACE
(Map p236) Down a short lane is the 15th-century
Palacio de Dar-al-Horra, a romantically di-
shevelled mini-Alhambra that was home to
the mother of Boabdil, Granada's last Muslim ruler.

Mirador San Nicolás   LOOKOUT
(Map p236; Callejón de San Cecilio) Callejón
de San Cecilio leads to the Mirador San
Nicolás, a lookout with unbeatable views
of the Alhambra and Sierra Nevada. Come
back here later for sunset (you can't miss
the trail then!). At any time of day take
care: skilful, well-organised wallet-lifters
and bag-snatchers operate here. Don't be
put off; it is still a terrific atmosphere with
buskers and local students intermingling
with the camera-touting tourists.

Mezquita Mayor de Granada   MOSQUE
(Map p236) Off Cuesta de las Cabras, the
Albayzín's first new mosque in 500 years,
opened in 2003, has been built to serve
modern Granada's growing Muslim population. Members of the public can enter the
gardens, but the mosque itself is open only
to Muslims.

Calle Calderería Nueva   STREET
(Map p238) Centre of the city's modern Muslim community. The touristy shops brim
with hookahs, slippers and scarves, but the
mellow teahouses, such as **Tetería As-Sirat**
(Calle Calderería Nueva 4), are popular with non-
drinking Muslim youth.

🏃 Activities

Granada has three *baños árabes* (Arab-
style baths), though none is historic – nor
much like a Middle Eastern *hammam*.
Here the emphasis is on lazy lounging in

pools, rather than getting scrubbed clean.
But the dim, tiled rooms are suitably syba-
ritic and a relaxing end to a long sightseeing day. All offer pool access in two-hour
sessions, with the option of a 15-minute or
30-minute massage for a bit more; reservations are required. Swimwear is obligatory
(you can rent it), a towel is provided and all
sessions are mixed.

Hammams de Al Andalus   HAMMAM
(Map p238; ☑902 33 33 34; www.granada.hammam
spain.com; Calle Santa Ana 16; bath/bath & massage €22/32) The best option is Hammams
de Al Andalus, with three pools of different
temperatures, plus a steam room and the
option of a proper skin-scrubbing massage
(*masaje tradicional* €39).

Baños de Elvira   HAMMAM
(Map p236; ☑958 20 26 53; www.banosdeelvira
.com; Calle Arteaga 3; bath/bath & massage
€18/25) Smaller than the other *hammams* is
Baños de Elvira; the first and third Tuesday
of the month are clothing optional.

Aljibe San Miguel Baños Árabes   HAMMAM
(Map p236; ☑958 52 28 67; www.aljibesanmigue
.es; Calle San Miguel Alta 41; bath/bath & massage
€21/30) The largest hammam in Granada,
with seven pools, but no steam room and no
scrubbing. Although the massages include
cherry mousse and *chocolate* so possibly
compensate....

👣 Tours

Cicerone Cultura y Ocio   WALKING TOUR
(Map p238; ☑650 541669; www.ciceronegranada
.com; tour €15) Informative walking tours of
central Granada and the Albayzín leave daily
from Plaza Bib-Rambla at 10.30am, or 11am
in winter.

Alhambra Night Tour   CULTURAL TOUR
(☑902 44 12 21; www.alhambra-patronato.es;
adult/under 12yr €13/free; ⏱10-11.30pm Tue-Sat)
The Palacios Nazaríes are romantically lit in
the evening and are truly heart-flutteringly
beautiful. You won't get to see as much as on
a day visit, but you won't have to deal with
the same crowds either.

Secret Granada   WALKING TOUR
(☑958 20 19 39; www.granadaunderground.blog
spot.com.es; tours €15-30; ⏱9.30am-midday &
4-6.30pm) Explore the tunnels and dungeons
that lie under the city (including the Alhambra). Dug out by the Moors or by Christian
prisoners (no one is certain), they were used

until relatively recently, as many link various residences and therefore enabled the great and the good to lead secret lives. Reserve via the website.

City Sightseeing Tour   BUS TOUR

(☎902 10 10 81; www.city-sightseeing.com; adult/child €18/9; 📷) Granada's double-decker city tour bus has 20 stops including the main sights, like the cathedral and the Alhambra. Hop on and off where you like; the ticket is valid for 24 hours.

✯ Festivals & Events

Semana Santa   HOLY WEEK

The two most striking events in Granada's Easter week are Los Gitanos (Wednesday), when the *fraternidad* (brotherhood) toils to the Abadía de Sacromonte, lit by bonfires, and El Silencio (Thursday), when the streetlights are turned off for a silent, candlelit march.

Feria del Corpus Cristi   RELIGIOUS

(Corpus Christi Fair) The big annual fair, which starts 60 days after Easter Sunday, is a week of bullfights, dancing and street puppets; most of the action is at fairgrounds by the bus station.

Día de la Cruz   RELIGIOUS

On 3 May, squares, patios and balconies are adorned with floral crosses, beginning three days of revelry.

Festival Internacional
de Música y Danza   MUSIC

(www.granadafestival.org) For three weeks in June and July, first-class classical and modern performance takes over the Alhambra and other historic sites.

✕ Eating

Granada's a place where gastronomy remains reassuringly down to earth. What it lacks in flashy *alta cocina* (haute cuisine) it makes up for in generous portions of Andalucian standards. The city also has a wealth of places serving decent tapas and *raciones* (large tapas servings).

Ruta del Azafrán   FUSION €€

(Map p236; www.rutadelazafran.es; Paseo del Padre Manjón 1; mains €13-20) One of the few high-concept restaurants in Granada, this sleek spot with its steely-modern interior has an eclectic menu which ranges from Asian-inspired tempuras to broccoli-based pesto, lamb couscous and roasted pork. The terrace

outside on the Río Darro is a great place for a snack, but you'll get better service inside.

Paprika   VEGETARIAN €€

(Map p236; www.paprika-granada.com; Cuesta de Abarqueros 3; mains €10-12, menu €12; 📷) Ecological wines, vegetarian and vegan cuisine and a brightly coloured Mexican-inspired interior combine to make this an inviting alternative eating option. The American chef whips up some healthy south-of-the-border dishes, as well as veggie Thai curries and tofu and seitan specialities.

El Ají   MODERN SPANISH €€

(Map p236; Plaza San Miguel Bajo 9; mains €12-20; 📷) Up in the Albayzín, this chic but cosy neighbourhood restaurant is no bigger than a shoebox but serves from breakfast right through to the evening. Chatty staff at the tiny marble bar can point out some of the highlights of the creative menu (such as prawns with tequila and honey). But even the simple items, like the tortilla, are done with special care. It's a good place to get out of the sun and rest up, especially if you are hiking up from Plaza Nueva.

Café Futbol   CAFE €

(Map p238; www.cafefutbol.com; Plaza de Mariana Pineda 6; churros €2; 📷) This three-storey cafe with its butter-coloured walls and gaudy chandeliers dates from 1910 and is generally packed with coiffured señoras, foreign students and families. Elderly white-shirted waiters attend to the morning rush with hot chocolate, fat *churros* and delectable cakes like the chocolate and custard *tarta san cecilio*. Sit upstairs for views of the square. Savoury snacks also available.

Restaurante Chikito   ANDALUCIAN €€

(Map p238; ☎958 22 33 64; www.restaurantechikito.com; Plaza Campillo Bajo 9; mains €17-20; ⊙Thu-Tue) One of the city's most historic restaurants was apparently a favourite of Lorca's (his table is in the corner) and is perennially popular with the smart local set; its walls are plastered with local celeb pics. The tapas bar specialty is snails (€5). The adjacent restaurant concentrates on hearty dishes like oxtail stew and pork medallions, which it has spent many years getting right. Reservations recommended for the restaurant.

Los Diamantes   SEAFOOD €

(Map p238; Calle Navas 26; racionés €8-10) This corner bar-restaurant near Plaza del Carmen shows off the Andalucian penchant for

Teterías & Hammams

It's 500 years since the Moor uttered his last sigh, but the civilised habits of Al-Andalus' erstwhile rulers live on in many Andalucian cities, in dark, atmospheric *teterías* (tearooms) and elaborate *hammams* (bathhouses). While away lazy evenings in shadowy Moorish leisure facilities embellished with puffed cushions, stuccoed arches and winking lanterns.

Tetería Almedina

1 Liquid refreshment in this Almería establishment (p273) could include anything from an aromatic tea-tray of global brews. Try the Moroccan mint or Indian chai accompanied by a plate of delicate Arabic sweets.

Hammam Andalusi

2 Underrated in almost every department, Jerez harbours plenty of Moorish exoticism, including the Hammam Andalusi (p119) with its unusual 'chocolate bath'.

Tetería Nazarí

3 A Granada tearoom popular among students and bohemians, who huddle in the dark corners sharing furtive puffs on the ubiquitous *shishas* (water-pipes).

La Tetería

4 Unbeknownst to many, Málaga remained Moorish almost as long as Granada did, meaning that its revitalised *teterías* can claim equal authenticity. You'll find stand-out brews and cakes at the rather unadventurously named La Tetería (p155), near the Museu Picasso Málaga.

Hammams de Al Andalus

5 Moroccan *hammams* often resemble one-sided wrestling tournaments, but in Andalucía they're a shade more relaxing. Sample the hot baths at Hammams de Al Andalus (p242) before cooling down with a glass of mint tea.

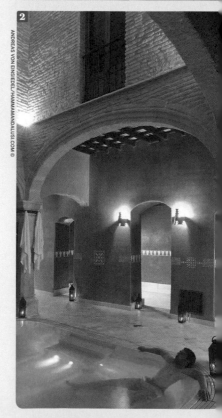

Right
1. Tea in a *tetería* **2.** Hammam Andalusi (p119)

National & Natural Parks

Andalucía's national and natural parks provide visitors with much-needed 'breathing space' between heavy doses of art, culture and history. They also act as important bulwarks against the encroaching development that plagues much of Spain's Mediterranean coast.

Parque Nacional Sierra Nevada

1 Peak-baggers can make for the easily accessible summits of Veleta and Mulhacén (p256), the Spanish mainland's highest peak. The less height-obsessed can ski, cycle, horse-ride, canyon or trek from park access points in Pradollano (p254) and Capileira (p259).

Parque Natural de Cabo de Gata-Níjar

2 Remember Spain before mass tourism? No? Then come to Almería's undeveloped littoral (p279) and reacquaint yourself with deserted coastlines and sleepy fishing villages.

Parque Nacional de Doñana

3 A World Heritage–listed rare European wetland, the 542-sq-km Doñana National Park (p82) features copious bird species, large coastal sand dunes and vital water-based ecosystems.

Parque Natural Sierra de Grazalema

4 You can debate all day about Andalucía's finest park, or you can vote with your feet and get up onto the dreamy hiking trails and craggy mountains of this one (p126).

Parque Natural Sierra de Aracena y Picos de Aroche

5 Northern Huelva's *dehesa* ecosystems are the bastion of its finest cured hams, produced in the bucolic oak pastures of one of Andalucía's least-known parks (p90).

Left
1. Sierra Nevada (p254) 2. Cabo de Gata-Níjar (p279)

GRANADA'S SACRED MOUNTAIN

Sacramonte, the primarily *gitano* (Roma) neighbourhood northeast of the Albayzín, is renowned for its flamenco traditions, drawing tourists to nightclubs and aficionados to music schools. But it still feels like the fringes of the city, literally and figuratively, as the homes dug out of the hillside alternate between flashy and highly extemporaneous, despite some of the caves having been established since the 14th century.

The area is good for an idle stroll, yielding great views (especially from an ad hoc cafe on Vereda de Enmedio). For some insight into the area, the **Museo Cuevas del Sacromonte** (Map p236; www.sacromontegranada.com; Barranco de los Negros; admission €5; ☉10am-2pm & 5-9pm Tue-Sun) provides an excellent display of local folk art. This wideranging ethnographic and environmental museum and arts centre is set in large herb gardens and hosts art exhibitions, as well as flamenco and films at 10pm on Wednesday and Friday from June to September. Some caves on or near Sacromonte's main street, Camino del Sacromonte, are venues for expensive tourist-orientated flamenco shows. Be discerning so that you don't get ripped off.

The diligent can press on to the **Abadía de Sacromonte** (admission €3; ☉11am-1pm & 4-6pm, closed Tue), at the very top of the hill, where you can squeeze into underground cave chapels.

Wander up from the Albayzín, or take bus 34 to the Venta El Gallo Flamenco School, 250m along the road from El Camborio cave disco, and follow the signs up Barranco de los Negros to the museum. For the abbey, take the bus two more stops, then walk up through the arch. (Several times a day, the bus goes all the way to the abbey.) If you're feeling like it's a long walk up, imagine what it's like in the fifth hour of a Semana Santa procession.

---

frying, particularly seafood. The plates are heaped with an amazing mix of *pescado frito* (fried fish) and succulent prawns. A *caña* (small glass of beer) makes the perfect accompaniment. It attracts a tide of hungry diners, especially around midday, so try to get here early.

Los Italianos   ICE CREAM €€
(Map p238; Gran Vía de Colón 4; ice cream €1.10-4; ☉9am-1am Apr-Oct; ⊕) Stretched along a long zinc bar, a battalion of white-jacketed women stands ready to scoop up a *barquillo* (cone) or *terrana* (cup) of the ice cream of your choice. Our local informant swears by pistachio and raspberry, but the orange is equally divine. If the crowd at the front looks too daunting, try the back entrance in Calle Abenamar. Alas, this *helado* heaven is closed in winter.

Mercado de San Agustín   MARKET €
(Map p238; Calle San Agustín; ☉closed Sun) For fresh fruit and veg, and a general feast for the eyes, head for the large, covered market a block west of the cathedral. As a bonus, **herb and spice stalls** are set up along the Calle Cárcel Baja side of the cathedral, dealing medicinal and culinary herbs out of bulging sacks. (It goes without saying,

though, that the stuff labelled 'saffron' is nothing of the sort.)

Oliver   SEAFOOD €€
(Map p238; www.restauranteoliver.com; Calle Pescadería 12; mains €12-18; ☉closed Sun) The seafood bars on this square are a Granada institution, and Oliver is one of the best for food and unflappable service in the midst of the lunch rush. Sleek business types pack in alongside street-sweepers to devour *raciones* of garlicky fried treats at the mobbed bar, which can be ankle deep in crumpled napkins and shrimp shells come 4pm. The only place for any peace is the back dining room or the terrace tables, which fill up early.

Greens & Berries   INTERNATIONAL €
(Map p238; Plaza Nueva 1; snacks from €2.50; ⊕) Conveniently located for benches in the square, this is a great choice if you want to pick up something healthy, fast and filling. Sandwiches include tasty choices like salmon, avocado and lemon, and goat's cheese and caramelised onion, plus there are soups of the day, fresh fruit smoothies and a wickedly delicious New York cheesecake.

Parador de Granada   INTERNATIONAL €€
(Map p232; ☎958 22 14 40; Calle Real de la Alhambra; mains €19-22; ☉8am-11pm) On one side,

the Parador de Granada is a hushed, swanky dinner experience, with a Moroccan/Spanish/French menu that also features local goat and venison. On the other, it's a stylish little canteen for sightseers, where even your *bocadillo de jamón* tastes special – and it ought to, considering its €12 price tag. Overall, a bit inflated, but a lovely treat for the location.

Pastelería López-Mezquita BAKERY €
(Map p238; www.pastelerialopezmezquita.com; Calle Reyes Católicos 39; pastries €2-6; ⊙9am-6.30pm Mon-Sat; ⊛) This venerable pastry shop provides great on-the-go snacks – a flaky *empanadilla* filled with bacon and dates, for instance, or a piece of cinnamon-rich *pastela moruna,* a Moorish-style chicken pie. Take a number to order at the counter, or sit down and rest your feet in the back room.

Samarkanda LEBANESE €€
(Map p238; Calle Calderería Vieja 3; mains €8-12; ⊅) Despite the rather tired decor, this longstanding Lebanese restaurant is a sound choice, particularly for vegetarian fare. The lentil soup spiked with lemon and cumin is delicious, along with mainstays hummus, *mutabal* (aubergine and tahini-based dip) and falafel. A finale of *mugle* (cinnamon cream with nuts and orange blossom) should put a smile on your face.

Hicuri VEGETARIAN €€
(Map p238; Plaza de los Girones 3; mains €7-12; ⊅) Colourful Lantino-inspired murals cover the walls at this spacious restaurant that specialises in vegetarian food with a few dishes for diehard carnivores, including pork tenderloin and chicken salad. Tofu and seitan are liberally used in dishes, and classic Spanish puds are given the eco treatment with organic eggs and soy milk.

Bodegas Castañeda BAR
(Map p238; Calle Almireceros; tapas €2-3, raciónes €6-8) An institution among locals and tourists alike, this buzzing bar doles out hearty portions of food (try a hot or cold *tabla,* or platter; a half order, €6, is ample for two) and dispenses drinks from big casks mounted in the walls. The best choice is a lively, herbaceous *vermut* (vermouth) topped with soda. Don't confuse this place with Antigua Bodega Castañeda around the corner, which is not as enticing.

Cisco y Tierra TAPAS €
(Map p238; Calle Lepanto 3; tapas €1.50-3.50) All the tapas here come from cans, or are preserved in some other way – but that's nowhere near as dismal as it sounds. Try the special cheese, a super-aged *manchego* with a caramel-like richness, or the aged hams. The ceiling is decorated with policemen's hats, siphon bottles and other knick-knacks, while romantic tunes crackle from a vintage-look radio behind the bar.

Gran Café Bib-Rambla CAFE €
(Map p238; Plaza Bib-Rambla 3; chocolate & churros €4; ⊛) Granada's oldest cafe dates back to 1907 when the coffee beans were roasted in the square outside and the milk was brought in daily from surrounding farms. Today, the hot chocolate and *churros* keep locals coming back.

La Candela ANDALUCIAN €
(Map p238; Calle Santa Escolástica 9; montaditos €1.10-2.50) For a taste of hip Realejo, stop in at this golden-lit bar where the house speciality is the *montaditos,* slices of bread topped with all manner of meats, veggies and cheese. Pick one or two from the epic list to round out your tapa allotment. They're artfully (slowly) constructed one by one, but you can pass the time checking out concert posters and fellow drinkers' tattoos.

GRANADA PROVINCE GRANADA

GRANADA'S PLAZAS

Built on the site of one of the old city gates, the large **Plaza Bib-Rambla** is jammed with cafes, flower stalls and ice-cream shops. Its proximity to major sights makes it a bit of a tourist haunt, but the chocolate and *churros* at the historic Gran Café Bib-Rambla (above) are excellent, as is the ice cream at **Heladería Tiggiani** (Map p238; Plaza Bib-Rambla 11) – you might need these restoratives after a bout of shoe shopping in the surrounding streets.

Northwest out of Bib-Rambla, pedestrianised **Calle Pescadería** forms its own small plaza, edged with fish restaurants. This connects almost directly with **Plaza de la Romanilla**, with several chic bars. Heading the other direction off Calle Pescadería, you reach the delightful shady **Plaza de la Trinidad**, surrounded by traditional neighbourhood shops, with good inexpensive bars in the surrounding streets.

YOUR PERSONAL CHEF

Francisco Lillo, owner of La Oliva (p250), is also an accomplished chef and passionate about local produce and ingredients. With advance warning of just a day, he will whip up a feast comprising around 13 'taster'-size dishes, along with a variety of accompanying wines. A superb host, he will also clue you up on the traditional Andalucian ingredients, and, if you opt for lunch instead of dinner, will invite you along to the local market to help him select the seasonal produce.

Don't expect gourmet but do expect tasty food like partridge paté, hake with saffron sauce, Granada salad with citrus and cod, potatoes and chorizo (spicy salami) and fresh grilled asparagus. Space is limited to around 14 people and the cost is €35 a head. For more information, check the www.laolivagourmet.com website.

 Drinking

The city – in fact, the whole province – proudly carries on the tradition of free tapas, with each round of drinks earning you a slightly better bite. But these are seldom a bar's best, so you'll want to order a little something off the menu as well. Most bars are open for lunch too. Also try the bars around the Plaza de Toros, a 15-minute walk northwest from the Gran Vía, which are renowned for their food.

La Budinka   WINE BAR
(Map p238; www.labudinka.com; Calle San Matías 14; ☺6pm-late Mon-Sat) This is a seriously chic place. Think buckets of dry ice, walls of pastel-coloured bottles, shiny steel furniture and black and burgundy walls. Superb wines are available by the glass and there are wine tastings every Wednesday at 3.30pm (€5 for four wines), no reservations necessary. Classy tapas, like fried goat's cheese with fig jam and spring rolls with mango and mint are on the menu, as are plates to share.

Cafe Bar Manila   BAR
(Map p238; www.mundomanila.org; Placeta de las Descalzas 3; ☺8am-1am; ☎) Cafe Bar Manila is the first bar in Granada to have a zero emissions impact, due to an EU-certified reforestation program it is involved with in Costa Rica and Madagascar. It also recycles just about everything and serves organic products as far as possible, including wines and beers.

There is a regular program of art exhibitions, audiovisual presentations and talks. And let's not forget the food, which includes vegan dishes, sweet and savoury crepes and breakfast *tostadas* (toasts) with toppings ranging from chestnut puree to classic tomato and olive oil. The interior is all comfy sofas, cluttered walls and world music.

There is free wi-fi so people tend to hang out here for a while.

La Tana   BAR
(Map p238; Calle Rosario; ☺11am-late Mon-Sat) The walls lined with wine bottles at this Realejo bar can be a little intimidating, but you can always start with one of the featured 'wines of the month', or give the bartender a little idea what you like – a *suave* (smooth) red, or something more *fuerte* (strong). The tapas are generous and very meaty, and the place feels intimate and pleasantly old – but not old-fashioned.

Al Sur de Granada   BAR
(Map p236; ☎958 27 02 45; Calle de Elvira 150; ☺10.30am-3.30pm & 6.30-11.30pm) This delicatessen, dedicated to the best food and wine from around Granada province, doubles as a bar. A downstairs room often hosts flamenco concerts, and there are wine tastings every Thursday at 7pm (€10). Get a sampler cheese platter, and try some of the various mountain liqueurs. If you want to visit the source, the friendly owners can even arrange lodging. Also a great place to pick up some local products to take home.

Botánico   BAR
(Map p238; www.botanicocafe.es; Calle Málaga 3; ☺1pm-1am) This eco-chic bar and restaurant dishes up healthy Med-inspired cuisine during the day and morphs into a bar and club at dusk with DJs or live music, mainly jazz and blues, after dark. Named after the peaceful botanical garden across the way, which is worth a stroll around if you are here during the day.

Mundra   BAR
(Map p238; Plaza de la Trinidad; platters €10; ☺8.30pm-2am Mon-Thu, 8.30pm-3am Fri & Sat) Overlooking the leafy square, this place

has a global-chic feel with its black barrel tables, Buddha statues and chill-out soundracks. There are platters to share for the peckish, including fresh prawns which comes from Motril and provolone cheese – which doesn't.

☆ Entertainment

Granada buzzes with flamenco devotees, footloose travellers and grooving students. The latter congregate on Calle de Elvira, while the Realejo draws a hipper crowd (Calle Navas is a good place to start), and the centre, near Plaza Nueva, has some excellent vintage bars. Cave clubs in Sacromonte are known for flamenco shows, but these are largely spectacles staged for tour groups. Given the scores of music students in town, there are usually far more enthusiastic shows to be seen in more casual venues, as well as live music. Start with these reliable spots and look out for posters and leaflets.

Boogaclub DJ
(Map p236; www.boogaclub.com; Calle Santa Barbara 3; ⊘2pm-6am Mon-Thu, 11pm-7am Fri-Sun) Chill to soulful house, funk, electro and Chicago house then kick up your (high) heels to the international DJs hitting the decks with funk, soul, reggae and tribute sessions (to Amy Winehouse, and alike), plus karaoke nights, jam sessions and live music. Check the website for the current line-up.

Le Chien Andalou FLAMENCO
(Map p238; www.lechienandalou.com; Carrera del Darro 7; admission €8; ⊘shows 9pm) This is one of Granada's most atmospheric venues to enjoy some vigorous castanet-clicking flamenco with a varied and professional line-up of musicians and dancers throughout the week. The cave-like surroundings of a renovated *aljibe* (well) create a fittingly moody setting and the whole place has a more genuine feel to it than the Sacromonte coach-tour traps. Book through the website.

Eshavira LIVE MUSIC
(Map p236; Postigo de la Cuna 2; ⊘from 10pm) Just off Calle Azacayas, duck down the spooky alley, cross the small patio and battle with the hefty door to slip into one of the best jazz and flamenco haunts in town, with musicians coming down from Sacromonte to jam. The party doesn't get rolling till at least 1am, and that's on weeknights. There's a good formal show (earlier) on Sunday nights, if you can't stick it out till the wee hours.

Peña de la Platería FLAMENCO
(Map p236; Placeta de Toqueros 7) Buried in the Albayzín warren, Peña La Platería claims to be the oldest flamenco aficionados' club in Spain. It's a private affair, though, and not always open to nonmembers. Performances are usually Thursday and Saturday at 10.30pm – look presentable, and speak a little Spanish at the door, if you can.

Café Picaro LIVE MUSIC
(Map p238; www.picarojazz.com; Calle Varela 10; ⊘live jazz 10pm Thu) Enjoy a bohemian vibe coupled with live jazz at this corner bar tucked away in a backstreet off Calle San Matías in the heart of the spirited Realejo nightlife quarter. Not a lot of elbow room but a great atmosphere. Best night is Thursday with regular live bands.

Granada 10 CLUB
(Map p238; www.granadaten.com; Calle Calderería Nueva 11; admission €10; ⊘from midnight) A glittery converted cinema is now Granada's top club for the glam crowd, who recline on the gold sofas and get hip-swivelling to cheesy Spanish pop tunes.

🛍 Shopping

Granada's craft specialities include *taracea* (marquetry) – the best work has shell, silver or mother-of-pearl inlay, applied to boxes, tables, chess sets and more.

Artesanías González ARTS & CRAFTS
(Map p238; Cuesta de Gomérez 2) Specialises in exceptionally fine examples of marquetry, ranging from small easy-to-pack boxes to larger pay-the-overweight-allowance chess sets.

Daniel Gil de Avalle MUSIC
(Map p238; Plaza del Realejo 15; ⊘closed afternoon Sat) This longstanding music store specialises in exquisite, handmade guitars. Step inside and you may well see the *guitarrero* (guitar maker) at work. Sheet music is also available, with an obvious emphasis on flamenco.

Marie FLAMENCO
(Map p238; Calle Pescadería 15) Come here for your flamenco frills, together with all the accessories you could possibly need to complete that authentic polka-dot look, including bangles, shawls, hoop earrings and fans.

Tienda Librería de la Alhambra SOUVENIRS
(Map p238; Calle Reyes Católicos 40) This is a fabulous shop for Alhambra aficionados,

GRANADA'S BONO TURÍSTICO

Valid for five days, the **Bono Turístico Granada** (€32) is a card that gives admission to the city's major sights, plus 10 rides on city buses, use of the sightseeing bus for a day and discounts on the Cicerone Cultura y Ocio walking tour and a city audioguide. When you add it all up, the savings are significant only if you visit virtually all of the sights.

You can buy the Bono at **this.is: granada**, an orange kiosk opposite Plaza Nueva, where the bus to the Albazyín stops. For a €2.50 surcharge, you can pre-order by phone from the **Bono information line** (☎902 10 00 95; English spoken) or on the internet (www.caja-granada.es, in Spanish), then pick it up at the **CajaGranada** (Plaza Isabel La Católica 6; ☉8.30am-2.15pm Mon-Fri) bank. Buying in advance gives you the advantage of choosing your Alhambra entrance time, rather than being assigned one.

with a tasteful selection of quality gifts including excellent coffee table–style tomes, children's art books, hand-painted fans, arty stationery and stunning photographic prints which you select from a vast digital library (from €14 for A4 size).

Alquímia Pervane   PERFUME
(Map p238; Calderería Nueva) A fragrant hole-in-the-wall place near the top of this Moroccan-themed street with its teashops and hookah pipes, selling a wide choice of wonderful oils in pretty bottles, plus rose water and similar.

Granada Vinos   WINE
(Map p238; Calle Navas 29) This small wineshop has an excellent selection of vintages from around Granada and Andalucía, as well as the rest of Spain and further afield, including Argentina and Chile. The owner holds wine-tasting courses and one-off tasting sessions.

Alcaicería   SOUVENIRS
(Map p238; Calle Alcaicería) Formerly a grand Moorish bazaar where silk was made and sold, the stalls are now taken up with souvenir shops. The setting is still very reminiscent of the past, however, especially in the early

morning, before the coach tours descend. You can still see where the gates once stood at the entrances, there to guard against looting and closed at night. The narrow streets inside were then patrolled by watchmen.

La Oliva   FOOD
(Map p238; Calle Rosario 9) For a superb range of quality deli items with an emphasis on fine wines and olive oil (see p248).

ℹ Information

Provincial tourist office (www.turismode granada.org; Plaza de Mariana Pineda 10; ☉9am-10pm Mon-Fri, 10am-7pm Sat)
Regional tourist office (☎958 22 10 22; Calle Santa Ana 1; ☉9am-7pm Mon-Sat, 10am-2pm Sun & holidays) Plaza Santa Ana.

ℹ Getting There & Away

AIR Aeropuerto Federico García Lorca (www .aena.es) is 17km west of the city, near the A92. **Autocares J González** (www.autocaresjose gonzalez.com) runs buses (one way €3) to Gran Vía de Colón opposite the cathedral. Departures from the airport are timed with each flight; from the centre, they leave virtually hourly between 5.20am and 8pm. A taxi costs about €22.

BUS Granada's **bus station** (Carretera de Jaén) is 3km northwest of the city centre. Take city bus 3 to the centre or a taxi for €7. **Alsa** (www .alsa.es) handles buses in the province and across the region, plus a night bus direct to Madrid's Barajas airport (€24.50, six hours).

TO	COST (€)	DURATION	FREQUENCY
Almería	13.50	2¼-4hr	9 daily
Córdoba	13.50	2¾hr	8 daily
Guadix	9	1hr	9 daily
Jaén	8	1¼	12 daily
Málaga	10.50	2hr	18 daily
Mojácar	19	4hr	2 daily
Seville	20.50	3-4hr	10 daily

CAR Granada is at the junction of the A44 and the A92. The Alhambra has easy car access from the A395 spur. Parking:
  Alhambra Parking (Avenida Los Alixares; per hr/day €2.50/16.75)
Parking San Agustín (Calle San Agustín; per hr/day €1.75/20)
  Parking Plaza Puerta Real (Acera del Darro; per hr/day €1.45/17).
LOCAL BUS Individual tickets are €1.20, or pay €2 for a refillable pass card, then add at least €5, for rides as low as €0.80. Both can be bought with notes or coins from the bus driver.

Most lines stop on Gran Vía de Colón; the tourist office dispenses maps and schedules.

TAXI Pick up at Plaza Nueva or call **Teleradio taxi** (☑958 28 06 54).

TRAIN The **train station** (☑958 24 02 02; Avenida de Andaluces) is 1.5km northwest of the centre, off Avenida de la Constitución. For the centre, walk straight ahead to Avenida de la Constitución and turn right to pick up buses 1, 3, 5, 7 or 33 to Gran Vía de Colón; taxis cost about €5.

TO	COST(€)	DURATION	FREQUENCY
Algeciras	25	4¼hr	3 daily
Almería	16.50	2½hr	4 daily
Barcelona	58	11¼hr	1 daily
Córdoba	35.50	2½hr	2 daily
Linares-Baeza	15	2½hr	2 daily
Madrid	68	4¾hr	2 daily
Seville	25	3hr	4 daily

LA VEGA & EL ALTIPLANO

Surrounding Granada is a swathe of fertile land known as La Vega, planted with shimmering poplar groves, as well as food crops. Heading northeast, the A92 passes through the hilly Parque Natural Sierra de Huétor before entering an increasingly arid landscape, made all the more dramatic by the white peaks of the Sierra Nevada looming to the south. Up close, the terrain around the town of Guadix is also fascinating, with the largest concentration of cave houses in Spain, and possibly in Europe.

Outside Guadix, the A92 veers southeast towards Almería, crossing the Marquesado de Zenete district below the northern flank of the Sierra Nevada, while the A92N heads northeast across the Altiplano, Granada's 'High Plain', which breaks out into mountains here and there and affords superb long-distance views all the way to northern Almería province.

Guadix

POP 20,400

Guadix (gwah-*deeks*), 55km from Granada near the foothills of the Sierra Nevada, is famous for its cave dwellings – not prehistoric remnants, but the homes of at least 3000 present-day townsfolk, carved into the heavy clay of the hills. Cave hotels, which are wonderfully cool in summer and cosy in winter, let you try the lifestyle. The *accitanos* (from the town's Moorish name, Wadi Acci) also enjoy some excellent, tourist-free tapas bars. The **tourist office** (☑958 66 26 65; Avenida Mariana Pineda; ⊙9am-1.30pm & 4-6pm Mon-Fri) is on the road leaving the town centre towards Granada.

◉ Sights

Most visitors make a beeline to the cave district, but the town's old quarter has its own distinctive architecture, much of it rendered in warm sandstone. At the centre is a fine **cathedral** (Calle Santa María del Buen Aire; admission €3; ⊙10.30am-1pm & 2-7pm Mon-Sat, 9.30am-1pm Sun), built between the 16th and 18th centuries on the site of the town's former main mosque in a mix of Gothic, Renaissance and baroque styles.

Near Guadix Cathedral, the **Plaza de la Constitución** feels almost fortified, edged with porticos and gracefully worn brick steps.

GRANADA PROVINCE GUADIX

LORCA'S LEGACY

The great writer Federico García Lorca was born just outside Granada and died here, shot in an open field by Nationalists at the beginning of the civil war. His summer house, **Huerta de San Vicente** (☑958 25 84 66; Calle Virgen Blanca; admission only by guided tour in Spanish €3, Wed free; ⊙10am-12.30pm & 5-7.30pm Tue-Sun), is a museum in a tidy park, a 15-minute walk from Puerta Real; head 700m down Calle de las Recogidas, turn right on Calle del Arabial, and the park entrance is ahead on the left.

In Lorca's birthplace, the village of Fuente Vaqueros, 17km west of Granada, the **Museo Casa Natal Federico García Lorca** (☑958 51 64 53; www.museogarcialorca.org; Calle Poeta Federico García Lorca 4; admission €2; ⊙guided visits hourly 10am-2pm & 5-7pm Tue-Sat) displays photos, posters and costumes for the writer's plays. Buses (€2, 20 minutes) operated by **Ureña** (☑958 45 41 54) leave from Avenida de Andaluces in front of Granada train station roughly hourly between 9am and 8pm weekdays, and every two hours till 5pm on weekends. Lorca's remains – and those of thousands of others – lie in mass graves between Víznar and Alfacar, northeast of the city off the A92. It's now a memorial park.

Just up the hill, look for the off-kilter tile Mudéjar tower of the 16th-century **Iglesía y Monasterio de Santiago** (Placeta de Santiago), with an elaborate plateresque facade by Diego Siloé. Only open when services are on.

Just to the west of the Iglesía y Monasterio de Santiago, you'll find the 10th- and 11th-century Islamic castle, the **Alcazaba** (Calle Barradas 3; admission €1.20; ⊙11am-2pm & 4-6.30pm Tue-Sat, 10am-2pm Sun), from where there are fine views across town and into the main cave quarter, the Barriada de las Cuevas, some 700m south.

Barriada de las Cuevas   CAVES
Up in the hills on the south side of town is Guadix's largest cave district, some 2000 whitewashed dwellings nestled among rolling hills, with spindly chimneys, satellite dishes and full connections to the town's power and water lines. You can walk or drive a route past some rather splendid homes, as well as some more ramshackle ones.

Cueva Museo   MUSEUM
(Plaza de Padre Poveda; admission €2.50; ⊙10am-2pm & 5-7pm Mon-Fri, 10am-2pm Sat) Re-creates cave life of years past with audiovisual presentations and traditional housewares and furnishings including ox yokes, clay water pots, woven esparto grass, and wooden furniture painted in bright primary colours. The museum was closed for refurbishment at research time but should have reopened by the time you read this.

For more insight, stop into the **Ermita Nueva**, across the plaza, and have a beer at **Mesón Virgen de Gracia** (Plaza Ermita Nueva), a family-friendly neighbourhood bar – that just happens to be in the cave neighbourhood (with your back to the museum, head to the right).

🍴 Eating & Drinking
No need for a sit-down meal in Guadix – you can feed yourself well, and meet the locals, at the exceptional bars around town. At every place, you'll pay less than €1.50 for a beer, and *raciones* cost about €5.

La Bodeguilla   TAPAS €
(Calle Doctor Pulido 4; drink & tapa €1.70, ración €6) Between Avenida Medina Olmos and the river, La Bodeguilla is one of the best traditional bars in town – and the oldest, dating from 1904. Here, old men in flat caps line the bar tucking into delicious tapas, like *habas y jamon* (broad beans and ham), accompanied by wine, vermouth, muscatel or *fino* (sherry) direct from one of the stacked-up barrels lining the far wall of the room.

Bodega Calatrava   TAPAS €
(Calle La Tribuna; drink & tapa €1.70, raciones €6) An atmospheric traditional bar tucked down a side street in the centre of town and specialising in simple tapa treats like juicy fried prawns and wedges of crumbly well-aged Manchego cheese, as well as more substantial *raciones*.

Cafetería Versalles   CAFÉ €
(Calle Medina Olmos 1; churros & chocolate €3.50; 🖫) Located across from the municipal park, this time-tested cafe is *the* place in town for breakfast including, reputedly, the best *churros con chocolate* (tubular deep-fried doughnuts and thick hot chocolate) in town.

Café Jazz   BAR
(📞958 66 05 00; Hotel Comercio, Calle Mira de Amezcua) Part of a tastefully reformed hotel, this elegant small bar has an intimate sophisticated vibe and hosts occasional live jazz.

ℹ️ Getting There & Away
BUS Buses run to Granada (€5, one hour, 12 daily), Almería (€8.50, two hours, three daily), Málaga (€6, 2¾ hours, four daily) and Mojácar (€14.30, 3½ hours, two daily). The **bus station** (📞958 66 06 57; Calle Concepción Arenal) is off Avenida Medina Olmos, about 700m southeast of the centre.

TRAIN There are four trains daily to either Granada (€8, one hour) or Almería (€9, 1¼ hours). The station is off the Murcia road, about 2km northeast of the town centre – walkable, but dusty and drab; a cab costs €5 to the centre, and about €9 to the cave district.

La Calahorra

Castillo de La Calahorra   CASTLE
(📞958 67 70 98; admission €3; ⊙10am-12.30pm & 4-5.30pm Wed) During the Reconquista, the flatlands between Guadix and the mountains fell under the command of Marqués Rodrigo de Mendoza, whose tempestuous life included a spell in Italy unsuccessfully wooing Lucrezia Borgia. About 20km southeast of Guadix, his forbidding Castillo de La Calahorra looms on a hilltop, guarding the pass over the Sierra Nevada.

Built between 1509 and 1512, the domed corner towers and blank walls enclose an elegant Renaissance courtyard with a staircase of Carrara marble. Guided tours (in Spanish) take about 30 minutes, and if you arrive while one is going on, you'll have to wait for the door to be opened.

For guided tours outside of regular hours, contact the caretaker Antonio Trivaldo on the castle phone number to arrange a time. To drive up to the castle, turn onto the dirt road opposite La Hospedería del Zenete in La Calahorra and take the winding route uphill, or park in the town plaza and walk up the stone footpath.

Baza

POP 22,581

The market town of Baza, 44km northeast of Guadix, dates back to Iberian times. It has an attractive historic centre and its own small cave-dwelling district, and while there's not enough sightseeing for a long stay, it's a good place to stop for a few hours to break up a day's drive. The **tourist office** (☑958 86 13 25; Plaza Mayor 2; ☺10am-2pm & 4-6.30pm, closed holidays) is on the plaza, south of the main road through town.

◉ Sights

Iglesia Concatedral de la Encarnación   CATHEDRAL

(Plaza Mayor) The Plaza Mayor, several blocks south from Baza's main road through town, is dominated by the 16th-century Iglesia Concatedral de la Encarnación, its stone fa-

cade weathered and worn. Inside, the pulpit drips with intricate carvings.

Museo Municipal   MUSEUM

(Plaza Mayor 1; admission €1.20; ☺9.30am-1.30pm Tue, 9.30am-1.30pm & 5-6.30pm Wed-Fri, 11am-2pm Sat & Sun) Adjacent to the Baza cathedral on Plaza Mayor is the excellent Museo Municipal, fittingly housed in a 16th-century Renaissance building. The exhibits concentrate on finds from nearby archaeological sites; the most remarkable item is a copy of the *Dama de Baza,* a person-sized Iberian goddess statue unearthed in 1971 (the original is in Madrid's Museo Arqueológico Nacional).

✖ Eating

La Curva   ANDALUCIAN €€

(Carretera de Granada; menú €10, mains €12-18) Perched on a sharp curve on the main street through town, La Curva is a popular local option for a large meal, despite its admittedly drab frontage. Dapper waiters in white shirts dole out local wines and platters of perfectly fresh clams, oysters and whole fish, some fried, some doused in vinegary *escabeche.* Note that much of the fish is priced per kilo.

❶ Getting There & Away

BUS The **bus station** (☑958 70 21 03; Calle Reyes Católicos) is 200m north of Plaza Mayor. Between six and eight buses per day run to and from Guadix (€4.50, one hour) and Granada (€9, 1¾ hours), and three run to Vélez Rubio (€5.50, one hour) in Almería province.

GRANADA PROVINCE BAZA

WORTH A TRIP

PREHISTORIC ORCE

A dusty Altiplano village, **Orce** is the centre of a debate about humanity's ancient history. The town and the surrounding rolling, empty plains, studded with crumbling farmhouses, makes an interesting, scenic detour on a drive between Granada and Almería's Los Vélez area.

Near Orce in 1982, archaeologist Josep Gilbert found a fossilised bone fragment that he believed was from a *Homo erectus* skull, some 1.7 million years old – substantially older than any similar fragment yet found in Europe. Sceptics, however, have since said the fragment is more likely from a horse and is not nearly so old. Regardless, Orce can still claim Spain's oldest evidence of human presence, in the form of stone tools that are 1.3 million years old. And further digging has unearthed bones of mammoths, sabretooth tigers and other beasts that met their end at the lake that once filled this basin.

The finds are on show in Orce's **Museo de Prehistoria y de Paleontología** (☑958 74 61 01; admission €1.50; ☺10am-2pm & 5-9pm Tue-Sun Jun-Sep; ⊞), in a castle just off the village's central square.

To reach Orce from the A92N, turn north 18km east of Baza onto the A330 towards Huéscar. After 23km, turn east along the GR9104 for Orce (6km away). Continuing east from Orce it's a further 30km to María, the first village in Los Vélez.

SIERRA NEVADA & LAS ALPUJARRAS

Granada's dramatic alpine backdrop is the Sierra Nevada range, which extends about 75km from west to east and into Almería province. Its wild snow-capped peaks include the highest point in mainland Spain, while the lower reaches of the range, known as Las Alpujarras (sometimes just La Alpujarra), are dotted with tiny scenic villages. From July to early September, the higher elevations offer wonderful multi-day trekking and day hikes. Outside of this period, there's risk of seriously inclement weather, but the lower Alpujarras are always welcoming, with most snow melting away by May.

The 862-sq-km Parque Nacional Sierra Nevada, Spain's largest national park, is home to 2100 of Spain's 7000 plant species, among them unique types of crocus, narcissus, thistle, clover, poppy and gentian. Andalucía's largest ibex population (about 5000) is here, too, frolicking above 2800m. Surrounding the national park at lower altitudes is the Parque Natural Sierra Nevada, with a lesser degree of protection.

Along the southern edge of the protected area, the Alpujarras is a 70km-long jumble of valleys along the southern flank of the Sierra Nevada. It is a beautiful, diverse and even slightly strange place, heavenly in its landscape of arid slopes, deep crags and egg-white villages that look as if they were spilled onto the mountainside. The towns on the mountain's lower belts simmer with spiritual seekers, long-term travellers and rat-race dropouts, while the higher villages have a disorienting timelessness.

Even the most visited Alpujarran towns are appealing, as the villages' Berber-style flat-roofed houses and the winding lanes between them look out on hillsides that have been carefully terraced and irrigated since the earliest Moorish times. With well-trod footpaths connecting each settlement, it's a delightful area to explore on foot.

ℹ Information

Las Alpujarras Website (www.turismoalpujarras.es)

Órgiva tourist office (⊘9am-2pm & 5-7pm Mon-Fri, 10am-2pm Sat)

Pampaneira tourist office (Punto de Información Parque Nacional de Sierra Nevada; Plaza de la Libertad; ⊘10am-2pm & 5-7pm Tue-Sat)

Sierra Nevada tourist office (Centro de Visitantes El Dornajo; ⊘10am-2pm & 4.30-7.30pm Oct-Mar) Information centre for the Sierra Nevada, about 10km before the ski station. Stocks maps and guides.

Sierra Nevada Website (www.sierranevada.es)

ℹ Getting There & Away

BUS Alsa (www.alsa.es) operates local buses. From Granada, it runs on two routes: one twice daily on the low road through Cádiar and Válor; the other three times daily to the higher villages and ending in Trevélez or Bérchules. Return buses start before 6am and mid-afternoon. There is a bus that runs from Málaga to Órgiva (€11, 3¾ hours, one daily except Sunday), and a bus from Almería runs to Cádiar (€8.30, three hours, daily).

CAR To reach the higher elevations of the Sierra Nevada, and the ski area, take the A395 from the eastern edge of Granada. The main road into Las Alpujarras from the west is the A348, which leaves the A44 about 34km south of Granada to pass through the relative lowlands. Just west of Órgiva, the A4132 turns off to the north to wind along the mountain slopes and pass through many of the higher villages; it merges with the A4130 and then rejoins the A348 a few kilometres north of Cádiar, via the A4127. Most villages have a municipal parking lot near the edge of town.

Sierra Nevada

LOS CAHORROS

A short drive southeast of Granada, not far from the village of Monachil, the area known as Los Cahorros is good for short walks, with trails running through dramatic gorges alongside the Río Monachil. The most popular route – the **Cahorros Altos**, heading upstream – passes over a suspension bridge and alongside waterfalls. Look for the start of the 5km route just east of Monachil.

You can also take a bus from Granada to Monachil (€3, 30 minutes), from Paseo del Salón in Granada; buses run nearly hourly from 8.10am to 11.10pm, except Saturday afternoon and Sunday.

PRADOLLANO

The ski station **Sierra Nevada Ski** (☎902 70 80 90; www.sierranevadaski.com), at Pradollano, 33km from Granada on the A395, often has better snow conditions and weather than northern Spanish ski resorts, so it can get very crowded on weekends and holidays in season. A few of the 85 marked runs start

Sierra Nevada & Las Alpujarras

Río Baúarcal
Río de Laroles
A337
Bayárcal
Laroles
Cherín
To Laujar de
Andarax (9km);
Almería (86km)
Lucainena
Darrical
Embalse de
Beninar
A337
Mairena
Cojáyar
Ugíjar
Nechite
Válor
Parque Natural
Sierra Nevada
San Juan
(2786m)
To Puerto de la
Ragua (4km)
10 km
5 miles
Peñón del
Puerto
(2750m)
Río de Mecina
Yegen
Yátor
A348
Jorairátar
Río Grande
GR-7
Foot
path
Golco
Mecina-Bombarón
A4130
Narila
Cádiar
A127
Cerro Trevélez
(287m)
Puerto de
Trevélez
(2800m)
Río Chico
Mecina-Bombarón
Bérchules
Alcútar
A4130
Timar
A345
Horcajo
(3182m)
To Jerez del
Marquesado
(10km)
Sierra Nevada
Juviles
Lobras
La Atalaya
(3107m)
El Cuervo
(3152m)
Puntal de
Vacares ▲
(3129m)
Alcazaba ▲
(3966m)
Cañada
de Siete
Lagunas
Río Culo de Perro
El Chorrillo
(2727m)
Trevélez
Río Trevélez
Portichuelo
de Cástaras
A4132
Busquístar
Cástaras
Notáez
Río Guadalfeo
LAS
ALPUJARRAS
Mulhacén
(3479m)
Refugio
Poqueira
Mirador de
Trevélez
Puerto
Molina
Pórtugos
Atalbéitar
Ferreirola
Almegíjar
Río Valdecasillas
Río Mulhacén
Capileira
Pampaneira
Pitres
Mecina
Fondales
Mecinilla
A4132
Hoya de
la Mora
Las Posiciones
del Veleta
Veleta
(3395m)
Central de
Poqueira
La Cebadilla
Río Poqueira
Bubión
Pradollano (Sierra
Nevada Ski)
Borreguiles
(2645m)
Tosal del
Cartujo
(3152m)
Sierra
Nevada
Barranco de
Poqueira
Sel·Ling Buddhist
Monastery
Soportújar
Carataunas
Bayacas
Órgiva
Río Dílar
Parque
Nacional Sierra
Nevada
Caballo
(3010m)
Río Lanjarón
Parque Natural
Sierra Nevada
Cáñar
GR-7
Foot
path
A348
Lanjarón

ALPUJARRAN SPECIALITIES

In addition to the ubiquitous and incredibly hearty *plato alpujarreño* (a platter of eggs fried in olive oil, potatoes, spicy sausage and mellow, oniony blood sausage, or *morcilla*), try these local culinary standards:

» **Patatas a lo pobre** Potatoes pan-fried in olive oil with green peppers, onions and garlic.

» **Perdiz en escabeche** Partridge in a vinegary onion broth, an ages-old treatment brought by the Arabs.

» **Garbanzos and lentejas** Chickpeas and lentils, made into hearty stews, usually a daily special at restaurants.

» **Migas** Another crossover dish from Moorish times, which probably originally translated as couscous but is made from fried breadcrumbs with bacon, onions and sometimes some fruit, like melon.

» **Solpllllos** Literally 'little breaths' of crumbly almond based meringues.

» **Vino de costa** The local rosé, raw and bright, and very refreshing on a hot day

almost at the top of 3395m-high Veleta. There are cross-country routes, too, and a dedicated snowboard area, plus a whole raft of other activities for non-skiers. In summer you can mountain-bike, ride horses and more.

In winter Tocina (☎958 46 50 22) operates three daily buses (four on the weekend) to the resort from Granada's bus station (€5/8 one way/return, one hour). Outside the ski season there's just one daily bus (9am from Granada, 5pm from the ski station). A taxi from Granada costs about €50.

MULHACÉN & VELETA

The Sierra Nevada's two highest peaks are Mulhacén (3479m) and Veleta (3395m). Two of three known as Los Tresmiles, because they rise above 3000m, they're on the western end of the range, close to Granada. From the ski station on the mountains' north flank, a road climbs up and over to Capileira, the highest village in the Barranco de Poqueira in the Alpujarras on the south side, but it's closed to motor vehicles on the highest stretch. From late June to the end of October (depending on snow cover), the national park operates two shuttle buses to give walkers access to the upper reaches of the range – or just a scenic guided drive.

One bus runs up from 3km above the ski station, starting at the national park information post at Hoya de la Mora (☉during bus-service season approx 8.30am-2.30pm & 3.30-7.30pm). The other leaves from the town of Capileira in Las Alpujarras. Tickets are €5 one way or €9 return.

From the end of the bus route on the north side, it's about 4km up Veleta, an ascent of about 370m with 1½ hours' walking (plus stops); or 14km to the top of Mulhacén, with four to five hours' walking; or about 15km (five or six hours) all the way over to Mirador de Trevélez (avoiding the summits). From the Mirador de Trevélez (the end stop on the Capileira side), it's around three hours to the top of Mulhacén (6km, 800m ascent).

If you want to make it an overnight trip, you can bunk down for the night at the Refugio Poqueira (☎958 34 33 49, 659 55 42 24; refugiopoqueira@hotmail.com), which sits at 2500m below the southwestern face of Mulhacén. Although it is spacious, with room for 84 people, it is advisable to book in advance.

Las Alpujarras

The alternating ridges and valleys of Las Alpujarras are criss-crossed with a network of mule paths, irrigation ditches and hiking routes, for a near-infinite number of good walks between villages or into the wild. The best time for walking in Las Alpujarras is April to mid-June, and also mid-September to early November, when the temperatures are just right and the vegetation is at its most colourful.

The villages in the beautiful Barranco de Poqueira are the most popular starting point, but even there, you'll rarely pass another hiker on the trail. Colour-coded routes ranging from 4km to 23km (two to eight hours) run up and down the gorge, and you can also hike to Mulhacén from here. Get maps and advice at Pampaneira's Punto de Información Parque Nacional de Sierra Nevada in the central Plaza de la Libertad. Or you can make do with the Editorial Alpina map, which shows most of the trails in the gorge.

Of the long-distance footpaths that traverse Las Alpujarras, the GR-7 (which runs all the way to Greece) follows the most scenic route; you could walk it from Lanjarón to Laroles in one week. From Bubión, you can follow it over the ridgeline to Pitres, in the next valley, and catch a bus back in the late afternoon (4.30pm or 6pm).

For road-trippers looking to stretch their legs, Pampaneira's well-marked La Atalaya trail is a good option, with green-flagged posts leading down to the roaring river and up to a ruined building on the opposite hillside, about two hours' round trip.

LANJARÓN

The closest of Las Alpujarras villages to Granada, leafy Lanjarón often bustles with tourists. Second only to Trevélez in ham production, it's also packed with shops selling the stuff. And that bottled water you've been drinking? It's from here as well. The therapeutic waters have been harnessed at the large Balneario de Lanjarón (958 77 01 37; www.balneariodelanjaron.com; Avenida de la Constitución; 1hr bath €30), a spa on the west edge of town, just opposite the tourist office.

If you'd rather snack than swim, wander down the main street to the middle of town, to Arco de Noé (Jamones Gustavo Rubio; Avenida de Andalucía 38), one of the better ham shops, where you can stock up on supplies or order a tasting tray and have a swig of sherry out the back. A little further down the street are two bakeries for completing your picnic purchases, if need be.

ÓRGIVA

The main town of the western Alpujarras, Órgiva is probably most well known as the home of Chris Stewart, British author of *Driving Over Lemons* and other entertaining books about his life here as a sheep farmer. It's a bit scruffier and considerably larger than neighbouring villages, but makes a convenient base. The landmark 16th-century twin-towered church stands beside Órgiva's central traffic lights, and the plaza in front is one of town's main gathering spots.

Eating & Drinking

Baraka INTERNATIONAL €
(Calle Estación 12; closed Fri) This place has a laid back vibe and an eclectic menu that includes Moroccan dishes, tofu burgers, *shwarmas*, delicious brownies and natural juices. There are also preserves, spices and teas for sale, plus bakery items to take away. Located beside the municipal car park in the upper part of town.

Mesón Casa Santiago ANDALUCIAN €
(Plaza García Moreno; mains €6-12; closed Sun) The best of the bars on the plaza, with outside tables and a bricks-and-beams rustic interior. The menu includes solidly traditional dishes like *migas* (fried breadcrumbs with ham, garlic and onions) and *sopa de ajo* (garlic soup topped with a poached egg), plus tortilla.

GRANADA PROVINCE LAS ALPUJARRAS

BUSES FROM GRANADA TO LAS ALPUJARRAS

DESTINATION	COST (€)	DURATION	FREQUENCY
Bérchules	9	3hr	2 daily
Bubión	6.50	2¼hr	3 daily
Cádiar	8	3hr	2 daily
Capileira	6.50	2½hr	3 daily
Lanjarón	4.50	1hr	6-9 daily
Órgiva	5	1¾hr	6-9 daily
Pampaneira	6	2hr	3 daily
Pitres	6.50	2¾hr	3 daily
Trevélez	7	3¼hr	3 daily
Válor	9.50	3¾hr	2 daily
Yegen	9	3½hr	2 daily

THE MOOR'S SIGH

A spectacular alternative to the A44 from the coast to Granada is the **Carretera del Suspiro del Moro**. Straight through, the drive takes about two hours, but you can stop for a good walk en route. From the N340 in Almuñécar, turn northwest out of the main roundabout (McDonald's is off to the south side), where a small sign points towards Otívar.

In Otívar, note your car's odometer reading. The road ascends sharply here, with breathtaking panoramas. Where it finally levels off, after 13km, the landscape is barren limestone studded with pine trees. Just over 16km from Otívar, the trailhead for **Sendero Río Verde** starts on the left side of the road. This trail descends nearly 400m into the deep valley of the Río Verde, with a good chance of sighting ibex as you go. The full loop is 7.4km (about 3½ hours), but requires walking back to your car along the road, so when you reach the Fuente de las Cabrerizas, a water pump near the bottom of the gorge, you may prefer to turn around and head back the way you came.

Back on your way, and descending the other side of the mountain, 43.5km from Otívar you'll see a road signed 'Suspiro del Moro' heading to the left. Follow this, and in five minutes you emerge in front of the Suspiro del Moro tourist restaurant, a modern marker of the pass where, legend has it, the emir of Granada, Boabdil, looked back and let out a last regretful sigh as he left the city in 1492. Follow the 'Granada' signs to continue to the city, 12km further.

Shopping

The town attracts numbers of New Age and dreadlocked folk who gather to buy and sell everything from vegetables and cheese to bead necklaces at the Thursday-morning market held in the centre of town.

Angel Vera CERAMICS
(www.angelveraceramica.com; Órgiva-Pampaneira) Situated 4km out of Órgiva, this workshop displays the exquisite ceramics and woodwork of Angel Vera with vases, tables, lamps and ornamental plates included in the display. Ceramic workshops also available.

Nara ETHNIC HANDICRAFTS
(Mercado Municipal, Calle Ramon y Cajal 4) Fancy a Mongolian yurt, a string of Tibetan flags, curative incense, minerals, jewellery or ethnic clothes (new and secondhand)? Then this is your place.

PAMPANEIRA

When seen from the bottom of the **Barranco de Poqueira**, the three villages of Pampaneira, Bubión and Capileira, 14km to 20km northeast of Órgiva, look like splatters of white paint, Jackson Pollock–style, against the grey stone behind. They're the most beautiful villages of the Alpujarras, and the most visited – but don't let their popularity deter you. Even the scores of craft shops are tastefully done, and the villages are linked by hiking trails that are perfectly doable in a day.

The best-stocked tourist office is in Pampaneira. The lowest village in the gorge has a lively plaza, and ham-curing operations lurking in its back streets. It is also the most obviously tourist-driven of the villages, the small streets flanked by shop frontages displaying the famous Alpujarran coarsely woven colourful rugs.

Sights

O Sel Ling MONASTERY
(958 34 31 34; www.oseling.com; 3.30-6pm) Opposite the village, 2km up the western side of the gorge, you can just make out the stupa of the small stone Buddhist monastery established in 1982 by a Tibetan monk. It makes a good destination for a hike.

Eating & Drinking

Restaurante Casa Diego ANDALUCIAN €
(Plaza de la Libertad 3; menú €9, mains €6.50-13.50) Sit on the upstairs terrace here across from the magnificent 16th-century stone church and dine on traditional meals like *conejo a lo cortijero* (rabbit stewed with garlic) and *papas a lo pobre* (fried potatoes, peppers and onions).

Bodega El Lagar ANDALUCIAN €
(Calle Silencio; raciones €6-8) Located on one of the prettiest winding sidestreets to be found here, this tiny place sells local products, including preserves, and some funky clothing, plus it has an attractive tucked-away terrace for trying *raciones* like chick-

en and garlic. It doubles as a bodega too, so ask to taste the wine; it costs less than €3 a litre and it's surprisingly fruity and palatable.

🛍 Shopping

El Chocolate de la Alpujarra   CHOCOLATE
(www.abuelailichocolate.com; Plaza Romanilla 13) First, you get to taste loads of samples here. Second, the chocolate is just fabulous. It is made right here and includes some wonderful and unusual sweet and savoury flavours ranging from mango to mustard (yes, that's right!). It's Argentinian-run; check the website for more chocolaty background.

BUBIÓN

Bubión is a delightful village with a tangible feel of its Moorish roots in its picturesque backstreets with their arches, squares and flat-roofed houses.

◉ Sights

Casa Alpujarreña   MUSEUM
(Calle Real; admission €2; ⊘11am-2pm Sun-Thu, 11am-2pm & 5-7pm Sat & holidays) Located in the lower village beside the church, this folk museum set in a village house gives a glimpse of bygone Alpujarran life, both good and bad – a washboard is dedicated to the women of Bubión who have endured this 'cruel instrument'.

🍴 Eating

Teide   ANDALUCIAN €
(Carretera de Sierra Nevada; menú €8.50; mains €7-9; ⊘closed Tue) A good restaurant on the main road, frequented by a local clientele of characters stopping in for the reasonable daily menu or a hearty *ración* of *jamón* and wine. The dishes are mainly local with a few international additions like onion soup and spaghetti with pesto.

BEST MAPS

The best maps for the Sierra Nevada and Las Alpujarras are Editorial Alpina's *Sierra Nevada, La Alpujarra* (1:40,000) and Editorial Penibética's *Sierra Nevada* (1:40,000). Both come with booklets describing walking, cycling and skiing routes. Available at the Centro de Visitantes El Dornajo, near the ski station, and at the tourist office in Pampaneira.

Estación 4   INTERNATIONAL €
(Calle Estación 4; mains €7-12; ⊘closed Mon; 🖋) Wind your way down below the main road to find this superb and elegant restaurant with its minimalist dining room and varied menu that includes international bites like hummus and vegetarian croquettes, plus some wonderful innovative salads, and some more traditional local fare.

Poco Picante   ASIAN €€
(🖉669 090582; Calle Alcalde Juan Peréz; mains €7-10; ⊘closed Mon; 🖋) You somehow don't expect to find Thai and Indian food in a tiny mountainside *pueblo* – such is Las Alpujarras! It's Scottish run; come here for Thai and Indian curries and vegetarian dishes, plus an open buffet on Sunday with live music. Reserve ahead of time.

🛍 Shopping

Nade Taller del Telar   HOMEWARES
(www.tallerdeltelar.com; Calle Trinidad 11; ⊘11am-2.30pm & 5-8.30pm) For a glimpse of the past, visit the French-owned weaving workshop, with its historic enormous looms that come from the Albayzín in Granada. Nade only uses natural fabrics in her weaving, like alpaca wool, silk and mohair. The shawls are beautiful, starting at around €65 and well worth the investment. She also produces some original wall-hangings and similar, as well as sofa throws and blankets.

CAPILEIRA

Most people arrive at this village with their hiking shoes well laced up and primed for action. There are several well-signposted walks around the village. One recommended walk is the Sulayr circular trail, which is well marked and runs between Capileira and Travélez.

🍴 Eating

Bar El Tilo   ANDALUCIAN €
(Plaza Calvario; raciones €8) Capileira's village tavern enjoys prime position on a lovely whitewashed square with a terrace. *Raciones* such as *albóndigas* (meatballs in a tomato sauce) are enormous. There are also daily-made cakes and pies.

El Corral del Castaño   INTERNATIONAL €€
(Plaza del Calvario 16; menú €10, mains €8.50-14) Enjoy the gastronomic take on local dishes like a starter of mushrooms stuffed with Iberian ham and mango or *bacalao* (cod) on sautéed wild rice. There is also an Italian

menu with risottos, pastas and pizzas and a memorable tiramisú.

🛍 Shopping

J Brown ACCESSORIES
(Calle Doctor Castilla) Don't miss the excellent leatherwork here, including bags, belts and Western-style hats, all handmade, at very reasonable prices. And J Brown is not a Brit, but José Manuel Moreno (*moreno* meaning 'brown' in Spanish…) and you can watch him at work at the back of the shop.

LA TAHÁ

In the next valley east from Poqueira, life gets substantially more tourist-free. Still called by the Arabic term for the administrative districts into which the Islamic caliphate divided the Alpujarras, this region consists of the town of **Pitres** and a cluster of lovely small villages – **Mecina, Mecinilla, Fondales, Ferreirola** and **Atalbéitar** – in the valley just below. Day-trippers are few, and the expat residents have nearly blended in with the scenery.

Ancient paths between these hamlets (marked with signposts labelled 'Sendero Local Pitres-Ferreirola') wend their way through lush woods and orchards, while the tinkle of running water provides the soundtrack. About 15 minutes' walk below Fondales, an old Moorish-era bridge spans the deep gorge of the Río Trevélez. Park at

the top of the town and follow the signs saying 'Camino de Órgiva' and 'Camino del Campuzano'.

Like the rest of Las Alpujarras, this area attracts artists and craftspeople. For exquisite handmade tiles with a definite Moorish influence, check out **Alizares Fatima** (☑958 76 61 07; Calle Paseo Marítimo 19), on the edge of Pitres, which does beautiful work.

TREVÉLEZ

In a gash in the mountainside almost as impressive as the Poqueira gorge, Trevélez claims to be the highest village in Spain, located at 1476m; it's a starting point for routes into the high Sierra Nevada. It also produces some of Spain's best *jamón serrano*, with hams trucked in from far and wide for curing in the dry mountain air. Along the main road you're confronted by a welter of ham and souvenir shops, but the upper part is a lively, typically Alpujarran village, where you're just as likely to hear the clip-clop of a donkey as the buzz of a motorbike. A small information kiosk by the bus stop dispenses trail advice, snacks, gear and maps.

If you're staying in the middle or upper villages, you can drive up past the hard right turn to the *barrio medio*. There's a very small car park here, by Café Bar Rosales, but if it's full, you'll likely have to backtrack to the larger car park just by the turn.

🍴 Eating

Restaurante La Fragua ANDALUCIAN €€
(Barrio Alto; mains €8-13; ☑) Located at the very top of the village – a deterrent unless you're staying at the neighbouring hotel – but worth the hike up for partridge in walnut sauce, and the fig ice cream. There are some superb salads here, as well, and great views from the glassed-in top-floor terrace.

Café Bar Los Rosales TAPAS €
(Plaza Rosales; tapas €1.50) Offers an array of tapas surprisingly light on the ham – you might even get a succulent garlic shrimp or two. There are a few outside tables.

Mesón Joaquín ANDALUCIAN €
(Carretera Laujar, Órgiva Km22; mains €8-12) One of the town's better restaurants is just west of the main junction. White-coated *jamón* technicians slice up transparent sheets of the local product, and the trout comes from the wholesaler just behind. Ask about the day's special stew.

DON'T MISS

L'ATELIER

Vegetarians, vegans and anyone with a bent for local and organic produce shouldn't miss **L'Atelier** (☑958 85 75 01; www.ivu.org/atelier; Calle Alberca 21, Mecina; s/d incl breakfast €35/50; ☺Mar-Nov), a snug, candlelit restaurant where the globetrotting meatless dishes (Burma curry, Moroccan soup) are exceptional. There are also a few rooms available. French owner Jean-Claude Juston has a suitably pro-veggie background, winning several awards for his London-based restaurants, including the 'City Limits Award' for Best Vegetarian Restaurant in London (Milwards Vegetarian Restaurant). Jean-Claude moved to this atmospheric 350-year-old house in 1994 and runs regular vegetarian and vegan cookery courses; check out the website for specifics.

ALPUJARRAS ITINERARIES

Although it's rarely more than 30 minutes' drive between villages, don't spread yourself too thin, or they'll all start to look alike. Better to settle in one or two spots and appreciate the quiet and local specialities.

» **One day** Pick up fixings for a picnic at a ham shop in Lanjarón, then head to Yegen for a short hike. Have dinner in Válor.

» **Two days** Base yourself in Capileira or Pampaneira for day hikes: one down to Pampaneira and back, and another over to Pitres, catching the bus back.

» **Four days** Spend two nights in Mairena, with day hikes or drives to neighbouring villages. Drive over the Puerto de la Ragua pass for a night in Guadix, then loop back across to Granada the next morning.

Shopping

Jamones González   FOOD
(Calle Nueva) The place to come if you fancy buying some of the famed Trevélez cured ham to take home. Also sells other local gourmet products.

EASTERN ALPUJARRAS

Seven kilometres south of Trevélez, the A4132 crosses the Portichuelo de Cástaras pass and turns east into a harsher, barer landscape, yet still with oases of greenery around the villages. Significantly fewer tourists make it this far from Granada, and those who do are often on long, solitary walking excursions. Many of the pleasures here are in eating: fresh, local products are the focus at the casual restaurants and inns.

BÉRCHULES

In a green valley back in the hills, this village is a walkers' waypoint. **Hotel Los Bérchules** ([J]958 85 25 30; mains €10-14), at the crossroads at the bottom of the village, has an excellent restaurant, with such local specialities as rabbit in an almond sauce. **Cuatro Vientos** ([J]958 76 90 39; Calle Carretera 4; tapas from €1.50; ⊘closed Mon), the unassuming bar just down the hill, dishes out equally tasty meaty tapas.

CÁDIAR

Eight kilometres south of Bérchules, Cádiar is one of the bigger Alpujarras villages, down in the lowlands by the Río Guadalfeo. It hosts an all-purpose market on the 28th of each month, and the wonderful Alquería de Morayma (p307) is a fine rural inn nearby.

YEGEN

East of Bérchules, the 400-strong village of Yegen is best known as the home of writer Gerald Brenan, a peripheral Bloomsbury Group member whose *South from Granada*

depicted life here in the 1920s. A plaque marks **Brenan's house**, just off the fountain plaza below the main road. Walkers can explore the dramatically eroded red landscape on the **Sendero Gerald Brenan**, a 1.9km loop (one hour) – look for a map of the route on the main plaza. On the eastern edge of the village, the excellent restaurant at **El Rincón de Yegen** ([J]958 85 12 70; mains €14-20; ⊘closed Mon) offers treats such as pears in Contraviesa wine and hot chocolate.

On the road midway between Yegen and Mecina-Bombarón, there's a public swimming pool with amazing views of the valley; it's open July to September.

VÁLOR

Válor, 5km northeast of Yegen, was the birthplace of Aben Humeya, a *morisco* (converted Muslim) who led a 1568 rebellion against Felipe II's repressive policies banning Arabic names, dress and even language. The two years of guerrilla war throughout the mountains ended only after Don Juan of Austria, Felipe's half-brother, was brought in to quash the insurrection and Aben Humeya was assassinated by his cousin Aben Aboo. To re-create the historical clash, Válor musters a large **Moros y Cristianos** (Moors and Christians) festival on 14 and 15 September, with colourfully costumed 'armies' battling it out.

The village is known for its olive oil, goats cheese and partridge, all of which you can sample at the notable **Restaurante Aben Humeya** ([J]958 85 18 10; Calle Los Bolos; mains €8-12), downhill off the main road. Its menu features seasonal treats, such as local mushrooms, along with standards like baby kid in a garlic-spiked sauce and delicate *croquetas* (croquettes). For dessert, there's the deadly rich *tocino del cielo* (egg-yolk custard), or soft cheese with honey, washed down with *vino rosado* from Albuñol.

MAIRENA

Up a very winding road just 6km from Válor, Mairena feels much further away, with fine views from its elevated position. The restaurant at British-run **Las Chimeneas** (958 76 00 89; Calle Amargura 6; menú €20), a good guesthouse, serves excellent dinners using largely organic produce from the owners' own 5-hectare *finca*.

Just east of Mairena is easy access to the Sierra Nevada, via the A337 and the 2000m **Puerto de la Ragua** pass. The road then heads down to La Calahorra.

COSTA TROPICAL

The coast of Granada may look typically Mediterranean, with barren hills and wiry pomegranate trees, but it's warm enough to grow tropical crops like custard apples, avocados, mangoes and sugarcane; there's even a rum distiller in Motril. This stretch of the coast is as built up as the Costa del Sol, west of Málaga and, with a frequent bus service, makes an easy beach getaway from Granada.

Salobreña

POP 12,000

Between the N340 and the sea, Salobreña's huddle of white houses rises on a crag, topped with an impressive Islamic castle. The dark-sand beach isn't breathtaking, but it is wide, and the distance from the centre of town (about 1km) has kept the place from getting overbuilt. It's a low-key place for most of the year but jumps in August. The **tourist office** (958 61 03 14; Plaza de Goya; 9am-3pm Mon-Thu & Sat, 9am-3pm & 4.30-6.30pm Fri) is on a small roundabout near the eastern exit from the N340.

◉ Sights & Activities

Castillo Árabe   CASTLE
(Arab Castle; admission incl Museo Histórico €3; 10am-2pm & 6-9pm) At the top of the hill and visible from afar, the Castillo Árabe dates from the 12th century, though the site was fortified as early as the 10th century. The castle was a summer residence for the Granada emirs, but legend has it that Emir Muhammad IX had his three daughters, Zaida, Zoraida and Zorahaida, held captive here.

Washington Irving relates the story in *Tales of the Alhambra*. The inner *alcazaba*, a setting for cultural events, retains much of its Nasrid structure. You can walk along parts of the parapets and take in views over the surf and the sugarcane fields. A zigzagging walkway leads from the beach to the castle, and a town bus runs to the church.

Museo Histórico   MUSEUM
(Plaza del Ayuntamiento; admission incl Castillo Árabe €3; 10am-2pm & 6-9pm) The Museo Histórico is located close to the Castillo Árabe and below the Iglesia de Nuestra Señora del Rosario church and has a striking 16th-century archway. The museum comprises two main exhibition halls; one concentrating on archaeological history with exhibits dating from the Neolithic and Bronze Age. The second gallery has more contemporary photos and artwork, as well as a model of the castle.

Beaches

About 1km from the centre of town along Avenida del Mediterráneo, Salobreña's beach is divided by a rocky outcrop, El Peñón. **Playa de la Charca**, the eastern part, is grey sand; the western **Playa de la Guardia** is more pebbly. There are loads of restaurants, beachside *chiringuitos* (small open-air eateries) and bars, and a spot of nightlife, on and near the sand. **Restaurante El Peñón** (Paseo Marítimo; mains €6-12; closed Mon) is probably better for its position, almost on top of the waves, than for its average seafood – the setting is particularly dramatic at night.

✖ Eating

La Bodega   ANDALUCIAN €€
(Plaza de Goya; menú €9, mains €17-24) It's not all fish and more fish at the beach: Salobreña has two good restaurants that also look inland for inspiration. La Bodega, near the tourist office, conjures country life, with farm tools on the walls and hanging meats, and you can mix a bit of the sea (excellent clams) with a steak and a glug of sherry from the barrel.

Mesón de la Villa   ANDALUCIAN €€
(Plaza Francisco Ramírez de Madrid; mains €11-16; closed Wed;) Hidden away on a quiet palm-filled plaza, locals come here for standards like broad beans with ham served in a warm, candlelit room – ideal if you're in town before the full heat of summer arrives. There are plenty of vegetarian dishes, including a rare eight-plus salad choice.

❶ Getting There & Away

BUS Alsa (📞958 61 25 21; www.alsa.es) runs buses to Almuñécar (€1.17, 15 minutes, 17 daily), to Granada (€6, one hour, nine daily), to Nerja (€3.50, one hour, 11 daily) and to Málaga (€7, 2¼ hours, five daily). There are also buses to Almería (€9, three hours, two daily) and one at 4.45pm (except Sunday) to Órgiva (€2.80, one hour).

CAR Steep streets make parking very difficult. Stick to the flatlands or ask the tourist office about the municipal car parks on the hill.

LOCAL BUS The number 1 bus (€1.10) runs a circular route through town and up to the Castillo Árabe roughly every hour 9am to 1.35pm and 4pm to 6.45pm Monday to Friday, and 9am to 1.35pm Saturday. If you are heading for the beaches, catch the number 2 bus from the centre of town near the tourist office (€1.10, hourly)

Almuñécar & La Herradura

POP 27,754

Dedicated to beach fun, Almuñécar is not too expensive, a little rough around the edges and very relaxed. Many of the tourists on its pebbly beaches are Spanish, and its old city centre is a scenic maze below a 16th-century castle, albeit surrounded by dreary high-rises. The next-door village of La Herradura handles some of the overflow, but maintains a more castaway feel as it caters to a younger crowd of windsurfers. The N340 runs across the northern part of both towns.

◎ Sights & Activities

Castillo de San Miguel   CASTLE
(Santa Adela Explanada, Almuñécar; adult/child €2.35/1.60; ◷10.30am-1.30pm & 4-6.30pm Tue-Sat, 10.30am-2pm Sun) At the top of a hill overlooking the sea, the Castillo de San Miguel was built by the conquering Christians over Islamic and Roman fortifications. The sweaty, circuitous climb up to the entrance rewards with excellent views and an informative little museum. Don't forget to peer into the dungeon at the skeleton; a reproduction of human remains discovered here.

FREE **Museo Arqueológico**   MUSEUM
(Calle San Joaquín, Almuñécar) The Museo Arqueológico is set in 1st-century underground stone cellars called the Cueva de Siete Palacios, built when the Romans called the port town Sexi. The museum displays finds from local Phoenician, Roman and Islamic sites plus a 3500-year-old Egyptian amphora.

Beaches
The beachfront is divided by a rocky outcrop, the Peñón del Santo. **Playa de San Cristóbal** – the best beach (grey sand and small pebbles) – stretches to its west, and **Playa Puerta del Mar** is to the east, backed by a strip of cool cafes.

If you're craving a more remote beach, or more activity, consider heading 7km west to the small, horseshoe-shaped bay at **La Herradura**, where windsurfers and paragliders congregate. **Windsurf La Herradura** (📞958 64 01 43; www.windsurflaherradura.com; Paseo Andrés Segovia 34) is one good operator for these, as well as less extreme water sports, including kayaking. The *chiringuitos* here have a good reputation.

Parks
Just behind the Peñón del Santo is a tropical bird aviary, **Parque Ornitológico Loro-Sexi** (adult/child €4/2; ◷11am-2pm & 6-9pm; 🚻), full of squawking parrots. Beyond that spreads the **Parque Botánico**

LAURIE LEE

The English writer Laurie Lee loved Spain, and in particular Almuñécar, where he spent a considerable amount of time, both before the Spanish Civil War in 1935 and then again in the '50s. He refers to the town as El Castillo in *As I Walked Out One Midsummer Morning* and these early accounts make fascinating reading, providing real historical insight in excerpts like the following:

'Almuñécar itself, built of stone steps from the delta, was grey, almost gloomily Welsh. The streets were steep, roughly paved, and crossed by crude little arches, while the square was like a cobbled farmyard. Part of the castle was a cemetery, part of the Town Hall a jail, but past glories were eroding fast.'

Some 30 years later, the writer returned and wrote the following about the resort's coastline: '[It is] a concrete cliff of filing cabinets for tourists. It's one of the worst things that could have happened, next to a nuclear war...!'

El **Majuelo** (admission free; ⊙9am-10pm), a ramshackle park built around the remains of a Carthaginian and Roman fish-salting workshop, where the sauce called *garum* was produced and then shipped to kitchens across the empire. The park hosts the international **Jazz en la Costa** (www.jazzgranada.es) festival in mid-July.

Eating

Plaza Kelibia in Almuñécar is a good start for tapas.

El Arbol Blanco   ANDALUCIAN €€
(Urbanización Costa Banana; www.elarbolblanco.es; Avenida de la Costa del Sol, Almuñécar; mains €8-19; ⊙closed Wed; 🌐) Run by friendly brothers Jorge and Nacho Rodriguez, the cuisine here includes some creative options, as well as traditional Andalucian dishes, such as the earthy and rich *paletilla de cordero asado* (roast shoulder of lamb). The dining room is airy and light, plus there's a terrace for al fresco dining.

La Yerbabuena   ANDALUCIAN €€
(Calle Puerta del Mar 4-6, Almuñécar; mains €9-18; ⊙closed Tue) Pass through the front bar to the adjacent dining room with plush cushions, low candles and little pots of mint *(yerba buena)* on every table. The menu of Spanish standards reflects attention to detail, with the best-quality ingredients employed in dishes such as grilled baby lamb and rich asparagus gratin with shrimps. Service is attentive and helpful, with wine recommendations.

El Barco   SEAFOOD €€
(Puerto Deportivo, Marina del Este, La Herradura; mains €8-12) The best of a short strip of restaurants overlooking the boats in this tiny harbour. Come here for a drink at sunset or go for the seafood, more specifically the fish dish of the day which you can guarantee has been caught that morning.

La Jardina   SEAFOOD €€
(Paseo Andrés Segovia, La Herradura; mains €8-12) Sit with your toes scuffing the sand at this beachside *chiringuito* with its menu of predominantly seafood. The paella is a good choice, best washed down with a long cold glass of *tinto de verano* (red wine with ice and lemonade) to set you up for another bout of sunbathing and swimming.

❶ Information

Information Kiosk (Avenida Fenicia, Almuñécar; ⊙10am-2pm & 5-8pm) Just north of the bus station near the N340 roundabout.

Information Kiosk (Paseo Andrés Segovia, La Herradura; ⊙10am-7pm Jun-Sep) Located on the coastal road.

Main Tourist Office (www.almunecar.info; Avenida Europa; ⊙10am-2pm & 6-9pm) A few blocks back from Playa de San Cristóbal on the east side, in a pink neo-Moorish mansion.

❶ Getting There & Away

Bus

The **Almuñécar bus station** (📞958 63 01 40; Avenida Juan Carlos I 1) is just south of the N340. At least six buses a day go to Almería (€10, two hours) and Málaga (€6.50, 1¾ hours), eight to Granada (€7.50, 1½ hours), 11 to La Herradura (€1, 10 minutes), and 13 to Nerja (€2.50, 30 minutes) and Salobreña (€1.50, 15 minutes). A bus goes to Órgiva (€4, 1¼ hours) at 4.30pm Monday to Saturday.

La Herradura's bus stop is at the top of Calle Acera del Pilar, by the N340; services from here are slightly more limited.

Car

On the N340, three intersections access the main town. One-way streets create a loop through town and the central beaches.

Park wherever you can, or follow signs to an underground car park at the beach in Almuñécar, or another near the market, on the northwest side.

GRANADA PROVINCE ALMUÑÉCAR & LA HERRADURA

Almería Province

POP 695,560

Best Places to Eat

» Casa Joaquín (p271)

» Casa Puga (p273)

» Restaurante La Villa (p281)

» La Cantina (p284)

» Mesón El Molino (p287)

Best Places to Stay

» Plaza Vieja Alejandro (p308)

» Hotel Nuevo Torrelux (p308)

» MiKasa (p309)

» Hotel Velad Al-Abyadh (p310)

Why Go?

Almería's main draw is the weather, 3000 hours of sunshine a year. It is also famous for being the garden of Europe: a top area for greenhouse production of fruit and vegetables, sold throughout the EU. The downside of this agriculture-driven prosperity is the blight of plastic greenhouses in a province that already suffers serious one-upmanship from Granada and Seville. But to those in the know, Almería has plenty of appeal: it is famously home to a stunning desert landscape with subtly shifting colours and dramatic rock formations. The unspoiled beaches and volcanic basins in the Parque Natural de Cabo de Gata-Níjar are other top destinations, as are the Sorbas caves and the remote Los Vélez region. But don't skip Almería city, an earthy Mediterranean port with monumental sights, like the cathedral and Alcazaba, and memorable experiences, like discovering superb tapas bars and luxuriating at the fabulous *hammam* (Arab bath).

Driving Distances (km)

	Almería	Mojácar	Vélez Rubio	Níjar
Mojácar	81			
Vélez Rubio	138	74		
Níjar	33	54	108	
San José	38	77	131	26

DON'T MISS

Almería's tapas bars are some of the best in the province, serving up generous portions of delicious small dishes, a couple of which can easily equal lunch. Add another for dinner.

Best Beaches

» Playa del Playazo (p280)

» Playa de los Genoveses (p280)

» Playa San Pedro (p280)

» Cala de Enmedio (p280)

Best Historic Sights

» Alcazaba (p267), Almería

» Arab Medina (p274), Almería

» Refugios de la Guerra Civil (p267)

» Los Millares (p278)

Resources

» **Andalucia.com** (www.andalucia.com) Several pages dedicated to Almería.

» **Turismo de Almería** (www.turismodealmeria.org) Municipal tourist office.

» **Los Vélez** (www.losvelezturismo.org) Local tourism board.

» **Editorial Alpina** (www.editorialalpina.com) Best map of Cabo de Gata.

Getting Around

This is a challenging province to explore without a car. Almería city is an exception and can easily be covered on foot or via short taxi hops. Direct bus routes connect the capital with various towns and resorts, including Níjar, Sorbas, Vera, Vélez Blanco and Mójacar. Smaller rural villages will necessitate a further connection. Exploring the desert region around Tabernas is best by car, allowing you to get off the beaten track and really appreciate the drama of the scenery.

THREE PERFECT DAYS

Day 1: City Strolling

Join the locals for breakfast at Almería's bustling **Habana Cristal**, check out the colourful **Mercado Central**, then enjoy a bout of shopping on pedestrian Calle de las Tiendas. Lunch on tapas at historic **Casa Puga** before enjoying a leisurely stroll to the **Alcazaba**, with a mint tea at **Tetería Almedina** en route. Wind up with a luxurious *hammam* bath then a seafood dinner at **Casa Joaquín**.

Day 2: Desert & Mountains

Travel out to a western movie set among the dramatic canyons and rocks of the **Desierto de Tabernas**, then have lunch at olive-oil mill **Los Albardinales**. In the afternoon head for the cooler elevations of the **Alpujarras** for some leisurely wine-tasting, a hike in the mountains or flaking out by the waterfalls at **El Nacimiento** with its handy barbecue pits; bring your own *carne* (meat).

Day 3: Checking out the Coast

Head up the coast to **San José** and explore secluded coves southwest of town. Enjoy a seafood lunch at **Casa Miguel**, then travel north, stopping at the **Mirador de la Amatista** for stunning views, then the botanical gardens and ruined gold mines in the village of **Rodalquilar**. Refresh with a swim at nearby **Playa del Playazo** then travel to **Mójacar** for dinner, or back to Almería for a tapas tour.

Accommodation

Almería province has an adequate number of hotels, although it's sparse in the top-end category. You will rarely have a problem finding a room in the capital, while hotels in the main coastal resorts, like Mójacar and San José, tend to be seasonal. Read all about hotel choices in our dedicated Accommodation chapter (p288).

ALMERÍA

POP 190,349

Almería is something like the Marseilles of Spain, a rough-around-the-edges port with a large migrant population. Much of the architecture seems stuck in the '60s, the palm trees along the boulevards are a bit dusty and relics of an industrial past lie rusting in the salt air. But as the capital of a province that, since the 1980s, has been dramatically enriched by industrial agriculture, it has recently gained fresh momentum, and the streets have a palpable energy and sense of optimism.

The name Almería comes from the Arabic *al-mariyya* (the watchtower), in reference to the grand Alcazaba; the only remaining Islamic monument in town. At the peak of the Andalucian caliphate, the streets thronged with merchants from Egypt, Syria, France and Italy, as this was the largest, richest port in Moorish Spain and the headquarters of the Omayyad fleet. Following the Reconquista (Christian reconquest), the city began a long, slow decline, exacerbated by the shifting of naval interests – and money – to the Atlantic ports and the Americas. A 1658 census revealed the city had only 500 inhabitants, thanks to a devastating earthquake and persistent attacks by Barbary pirates. Fortunes have only recently turned, with the booming, controversial *plasticultura* industry – the vast sea of plastic greenhouses that extends from the city limits.

◎ Sights

Almería's main sights are the Alcazaba and the cathedral, both of which can be explored in a morning, but there are plenty of interesting additional distractions in the city's meandering streets, particularly around the upper city, which still has a tangible Moorish feel.

Alcazaba   FORTRESS

(Calle Almanzor; adult/EU citizen €1.50/free; ◎9am-8.30pm Tue-Sun Apr-Oct, to 6.30pm Tue-Sun Nov-Mar) A looming fortification with great curtain-like walls rising from the cliffs, the Alcazaba was built in the 10th century by Abd ar-Rahman III, the greatest caliphate of Al-Andalus, and was the most powerful Moorish fortress in Spain. It lacks the intricate decoration of Granada's Alhambra, but it is nonetheless a compelling monument; allow a couple of hours to see everything.

Passing through a grand horseshoe arch, the interior is divided into three distinct sections. The lowest area, the **Primer Recinto**, was the civic centre, with houses, baths and other necessities – now replaced by lush gardens and water channels. From the battlements you can see the **Muralla de Jayrán**, a fortified wall built in the 11th century, as well as stunning city and coastal views.

In the **Segundo Recinto** you'll find the ruins of the Muslim rulers' palace, built by Almotacín (r 1051–91), under whom medieval Almería reached its peak. Within the compound is a chapel, the **Ermita de San Juan**, once a mosque. The highest part, the **Tercer Recinto**, is a fortress added by the Catholic Monarchs. Its keep is used as a **gallery** for painting, photography and similar exhibitions.

Almería Cathedral   CATHEDRAL

(Plaza de la Catedral; admission €3; ◎10am-2pm & 4-5pm Mon-Fri, 10am-2pm Sat) Almería's fortresslike cathedral is built on the site of a former mosque destroyed by an earthquake. It was solidly constructed to withstand pirate raids and is shaded by tall palms and fronted by a peaceful square. The vast interior, trimmed in jasper, marble and carved walnut, is impressive. On the eastern wall you can just make out Almería province's *indalo* symbol, discovered in a cave in 1868 and dating from 2500 BC.

The most notable exterior feature is on the eastern (Calle del Cubo) end of the building: the exuberant **Sol de Portocarrero**, a 16th-century relief of the sun which now serves as the city's symbol.

Guided tours in Spanish are available.

Refugios de la Guerra Civil   HISTORIC SITE

(☑reservations 950 280 207; Plaza de Manuel Pérez García; admission €2; ◎guided tours 9am-3pm Tue-Thu, 9am-3pm & 5-7pm Fri, 10am-2pm & 5-7pm Sat, 10am-2pm Sun) During the civil war, Almería was the Republicans' last holdout province in Andalucía, and was repeatedly and mercilessly bombed. In one raid by German fighters, 40 civilians were killed. This prompted a group of engineers to design and build the Refugios, a 4.5km-long network of concrete shelters under the city, containing storerooms and an operating theatre.

Visitors can see more than 1km of the tunnels, though tours are in Spanish only and must be reserved in advance.

Almería Province Highlights

1 Kicking back on the rugged sandy beaches along the **Parque Natural de Cabo de Gata-Níjar** (p279)

2 Lasso twirling with the cowboys at the Wild West sets of **Desierto de Tabernas** (p275)

3 Exploring Almería's largest Islamic monument, the **Alcazaba** (p267)

4 De-stressing in the steamy surroundings of Almería's luxurious **hammam baths** (p275)

5 Caving at the **Cuevas de Sorbas** (p277); a fascinating underground cave complex

6 Basking in the sweeping views from **Mojácar Pueblo** (p282)

7 Enjoying superb tapas at Almería's classic **Casa Puga** (p273)

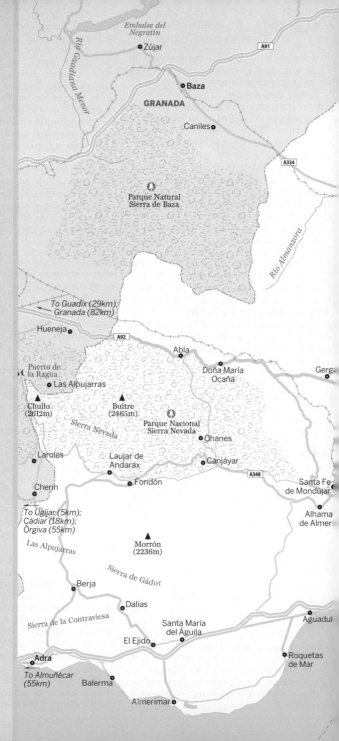

Embalse del Negratín

Río Guadiana Menor

Zújar

A91

Baza

GRANADA

Caniles

A334

Río Almanzora

Parque Natural Sierra de Baza

To Guadix (29km); Granada (82km)

Huéneja

A92

Abla

Gerg

Puerto de la Ragua

Las Alpujarras

Doña María Ocaña

Chullo (2612m)

Buitre (2465m)

Sierra Nevada

Parque Nacional Sierra Nevada

Ohanes

Laroles

Laujar de Andarax

Canjáyar

A348

Santa Fe de Mondújar

Cherín

Fondón

To Ugíjar (5km); Cádiar (18km); Órgiva (55km)

Las Alpujarras

Alhama de Almer

Morrón (2236m)

Sierra de Gádor

Aguadul

Berja

Dalías

Sierra de la Contraviesa

Santa María del Águila

Adra

El Ejido

Roquetas de Mar

To Almuñécar (55km)

Balerma

Almerimar

Almería

Museo Arqueológico MUSEUM
(Carretera de Ronda 91; non-EU/EU citizen €1.50/
free; ☺2.30-8.30pm Tue, 9am-8.30pm Wed-Sat,
9am-2.30pm Sun) Almería's modern Museo Arqueológico presents finds from Los
Millares and other ancient settlements in
the region, as well as Roman and Islamic
traces. Even if pot shards and bone frag-
ments normally make you yawn, don't skip
this – it's a rare example of multimedia
technology deployed to excellent effect,
touched with a uniquely Spanish flair for
the macabre.

FREE **Centro Andaluz
de la Fotografía** GALLERY
(www.centroandaluzdelafotografia.es; Calle Pintor
Díaz Molina 9; ☺11am-2pm & 5.30-9.30pm) Anyone remotely interested in camera snapping
should visit this excellent cultural centre
dedicated to world-class photography. Established in 2007 with extensive facilities

that include a screening space, library and
shop, its temporary exhibitions vary dramatically in theme.

Typical past topics have included Lebanese photographer, Dalia Khamissy's poignant show entitled 'Invaded and Abandoned
Spaces', recording the Israeli attack on Lebanon in 2006, and the 'Poetry of Every Day
Life' by French photographer and humanist
Eduouard Boubat.

FREE **Centro de Arte –
Museo de Almería** MUSEUM
(www.almeriacultura.com; Plaza de la Estación;
☺6-9pm Mon, 11am-2pm & 6-9pm Tue-Sat, 11am-
2pm Sun) Housed in a striking neo-Mudéjar
building dating from the 1920s, with large
light-filled galleries, the city's art museum
has generally excellent exhibitions by contemporary Spanish artists, including such
masters as Juan Miró.

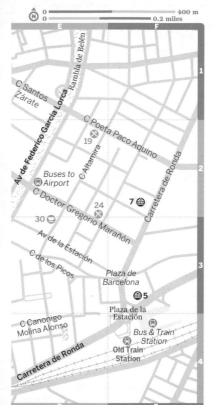

🎭 Festivals & Events

Ciclo Municipal de
Divulgaci'on de Flamenco   FLAMENCO

(www.flamencoenalmeria.blogspot.com) Kicked off with a flourish in 2003, this annual flamenco festival takes place in February and March at the Teatro Apolo with a month-long program of flamenco dancing and singing. Check the website for more information.

Noche de San Juan   SUMMER SOLSTICE

Carousing and enormous bonfires on the beach here, and in every small town along the coast, on 23 June.

Feria de Almería   FAIR

Ten days and nights of live music, bullfights, fairground rides, exhibitions and full-on partying held in late August.

🍴 Eating

For the highest concentration of the city's renowned tapas bars, head for the area around Calle de las Tiendas and east of the cathedral.

Casa Joaquín   SEAFOOD €€

(📞950 264 359; Calle Real 111; mains €14-21; ⊙closed Sat evening, Sun & Sep) Reserve one of the few tables for lunch if you're really serious about your seafood. If you don't mind standing, you can jostle at the bar for platters of baby clams swimming in garlic, delicately fried pieces of monkfish liver and other briny treats. There is no menu.

Aljaima   MOROCCAN €€

(www.restauranteajaima.es; Calle Jovellanos 12; tapas €2.10, tagines €14-18) The interior here resembles a *riad* in the medina with traditional tiling (even on the ceiling) richly patterned fabrics, and Moroccan-themed artwork and photographs. The food is deeply traditional. Go for one of the tagines, like chicken and lemon.

Mesa España   ANDALUCIAN €

(Calle Mendez Nuñez 19; menú €10, fondues €6-18) Owner Antonio will give you a warm welcome at this busy bar and restaurant, which has a comfortable old-fashioned feel. There is a good-value daily menu and some interesting dishes, including several fondues, including meat, cheese and (if you must) chocolate.

FREE **Iglesia de San Juan**   CHURCH

(Calle San Juan; ⊙6pm) Remains of Almería's Islamic past are evident throughout the city, including at this landmark church, the city's old mosque, which still has its 11th-century mihrab marking the direction of Mecca. The church is only open during daily Mass.

FREE **Aljibes de Jayrán**   HISTORIC SITE

(📞950 27 30 39; Calle Tenor Iribarne; ⊙10am-2pm Mon-Fri) North of Plaza de las Flores, the Aljibes de Jayrán were built in the early 11th century to supply the city's water. This underground historic well system is well preserved, and is the venue for regular exhibitions and for the **Peña El Taranto** (www.eltaranto.net), the city's top (but sadly private) club of flamenco *aficionados*. There are occasional concerts open to the public.

Almería

El Mesón de Altamira
SEAFOOD €€
(Calle Altamira 35; mains €11-17) This seafood restaurant east of Avenida Lorca is a no-frills affair. In the evening, the pavement is packed with rickety tables piled high with platters of golden, crispy fried fish or paper-thin slices of fried aubergine, surrounded by happily chomping families. Go early to snag an outside table.

Lamarca
ANDALUCIAN €€
(Calle Doctor Gregorio Marañón 33; raciones €6-12; ☺8am-midnight Mon-Sat, 10am-5pm Sun) Head to the back dining room here to eat under a ceiling of hanging hams. This is the place to sample wine, sausages and cheeses from all over Spain, in tapas sizes or *raciones* to share. There's live jazz every Wednesday from 9.30pm.

Café Barea
CAFE €
(Calle Granada 2; tostadas €2.25-3; ☺8am-11pm Mon-Fri, to midnight Sat & Sun; 🖪) One asset of this bustling, old-fashioned *cafetería* is the great terrace overlooking bustling Plaza San Sebastián, so perfect to watch the world go by. Another is the fact that all the standard menu items, particularly the *tostadas*, are fresher and tastier than at the pavement cafes on Paseo de Almería and have a wider choice of toppings, including anchovies, tomatoes with tuna and *tortilla* (potato omelette).

La Coquette
FRENCH €
(Paseo de Almería 34; coffee & cake from €4, ice cream from €1.80; ☺8.30am-1am; 🖪) Owner Tesni has imported a classic French patisserie to Almería, selling cakes, quiches, *paninis*, traditional French bread, mouth-watering *viennoiseries* (croissants, brioche and similar) and fruit-filled tarts. She also sells creamily authentic Italian *gelati*. There are a few tables in her candy-pink and sunny-yellow interior for those who prefer not to eat on the go.

Mercado Central
MARKET
(Circunvalación Ulpiano Díaz; ☺8am-2pm Mon-Sat) Almería's central market is in a grand old building near the top of Paseo de Almería and was aesthetically renovated in 2012. Go early in the morning to see squid so fresh they're still changing colour, as well as a profusion of vegetables from the

surrounding greenhouses, including some very odd-looking varieties of tomato.

 Drinking

If you are seeking some animated, youthful nightlife, head for Calle Antonio Gonález Egea, where a short but spirited stretch of clubs and discos includes the Latino-themed **Galeon** (www.galeonlatino.com; Calle Antonio Gonález Egea), **Pub Guarapo** (with outside terrace), and the mildly more sophisticated **La Chica de Ayer**, **Ginger** and **De Bianco**, all located within staggering distance of each other. The clubs are generally open from around 10pm until very late from Monday to Saturday.

TOP CHOICE **Tetería Almedina**   TEAHOUSE
(www.restauranteteteriaalmedina.com; Calle Paz 2, off Calle de la Almedina; teas €3, mains €7-12; ⊙11am-11pm Tue-Sun) This lovely little cafe in the old city serves a fascinating range of teas, delectable sweets and good couscous. It's run by a group dedicated to restoring and revitalising the old city, and functions as a sort of casual Islamic cultural centre. There's usually live music on Sunday, in addition to art shows and similar.

Tetería Almeraya   TEAHOUSE
(Calle Perea 9; cocktails €5.50; ⊙Wed-Mon) All warm burgundies and olive greens, this inviting *tetería* has a sexy intimate vibe and plays suitably gentle mood music to keep the romancing couples content. Aside from all the teas you could possibly think of, including spiked with Baileys, cocktails are served.

C Bar   BAR
(www.hotelcatedral.net; Plaza de la Catedral 8; ⊙noon-midnight) Part of the Hotel Catedral, this slick bar has a young fashionable vibe with its giant blackboards, minimalist furniture and innovative tapas like raspberry, gin and basil sorbet.

TAPAS TOURS

Along with Granada, Almería maintains the tradition of free tapas. But it does its neighbour one better: all tapas are *al elegir*, meaning you choose what you want from a list. Portions are so generous that you can easily make a meal over a few drinks, and most places are open for lunch as well. Note that on weeknights many of these bars don't open till 8.30pm or 9pm, then shut by 11pm (Thursday nights roll on until midnight, weekends to 1am).

Casa Puga (www.barcasapuga.es; Calle Jovellanos 7; drink & tapa €2.20) The undisputed tapas champ (since it opened in 1870); it should be your first stop, as it fills up fast. Shelves of ancient wine bottles, and walls plastered with everything from lottery tickets to old maps, are the backdrop for a tiny cooking station that churns out small saucers of stews, griddled goodies like mushrooms, and savoury *hueva de maruca* (smoked fish roe).

Plaza de Cañas (www.plazadecanas.com; Calle Martín 20; drink & tapa €2.20) Presents traditional combos such as *remojón* (salt cod, orange and potatoes) with style.

La Encina (www.restaurantelaencina.es; Calle Marín 16; drink & tapa €1.70) At the legendary Encina, photos attest to all the gastro-prizes these folks have won. Go for the *patatas a lo pobre* with peppers and a fried egg, or one of the marginally more expensive tastebud treats, like prawn fritters.

La Charka (Calle Trajano 8; drink & tapa €2.15) Closer to Paseo de Almería, La Charka is at the centre of the densest concentration of tapas bars, most catering to a youngish crowd. It's raucous with the clatter of dishes and shouted orders for tapas such as fried eggs with chorizo, or stuffed baked potatoes.

Taberna Postigo (Calle Guzman; drink & tapa €2.20) The main appeal of this *taberna* is that the sprawl of tables is shaded by rows of leafy trees. Locals go for the bacon with *pimientos* (peppers) and *morcilla* (blood sausage) in a big way.

El Candil (Calle La Unión 7) Lighten up at this longtime favourite place with its chairs on the square and a long list of tapas, including aubergine *gratin* or toasts with savoury toppings, plus a good selection of wines by the glass.

El Quinto Toro (Calle de los Reyes Católicos; drink & tapa €2) A good place to wind up. The 'Fifth Bull' rivals Casa Puga in old-fashioned charm, with the obligatory bull's head over the bar. Treats include *pulpo en alioli* (octopus in garlic mayo) and rich *albóndigas* (meatballs) in a wine sauce.

Habana Cristal   CAFE
(Calle Altamira 6; cocktails €3.80; ☺7am-10pm)
One of Almería's most emblematic and
well-known cafes with a vast choice of coffees, including the winter-warming Habana Negra with Swiss chocolate, Tia Maria
and Cointreau. There's a large outside
terrace.

Alejandro   BAR
(Plaza de la Constitución; ☺7am-10pm) Adjacent
to the sumptuous Hammam Aíre de Almería, this sophisticated bar (and restaurant)
has shiny black and sunny yellow decor with
exposed steel piping and a well-thought-out
menu of wines by the glass. There are classy
bites, like fresh oysters, and an outside terrace overlooking the city's most beautiful,
historic square.

☆ Entertainment

Teatro Apolo   THEATRE
(☎950 26 92 68; www.almeriacultura.com; Rambla
del Obispo Orbera 25) This relatively new theatre brings a welcome injection of culture
into Almería's predominant (and justifiably
animated) bar scene. Concerts include flamenco, particularly in February and March
with the annual festival.

🔒 Shopping

The main shopping street for national and
international chains is the broad sweep of
the Paseo de Almeria. For smaller shops,
including some intriguingly old-fashioned
places, head for Calle de las Tiendas with
its beguiling combination of haberdasher-
ies, for buttons and bows; hat shops, specialising in flat tweed caps; wedding shops;
healthfood stores; pink-and-blue traditional
babywear shops, and a handy small market,
Mercado La Llonja (Calle Jovellanos; ☺10am-
2pm & 5-7.30pm Mon-Sat), selling everything
you may need for a picnic.

ℹ Information

Municipal Tourist Office (Ayuntamiento, Plaza
de la Constitución 1; ☺10am-1pm & 5.30-
7.30pm Mon-Fri, 10am-noon Sat)
Regional Tourist Office (Parque de Nicolás
Salmerón; ☺9am-7pm Mon-Fri, 10am-2pm Sat
& Sun) Provides free leaflets and brochures.

ℹ Getting There & Away

AIR Almería's small **airport** (☎950 21 37 00) is
10km east of the city. City bus 20 (www.surbus
.com; €1, 30 minutes) runs to the centre, near
Avenida de Federico García Lorca, on weekdays
approximately every 50 minutes from 7.33am
to 10.33pm, and on Saturday and Sunday every
1½ hours between 7.25am and 10.25pm. A taxi
costs about €22.

BOAT For Morocco, **Acciona Trasmediterránea**
(www.trasmediterranea.es), **Ferrimaroc** (☎950
27 48 00; www.ferrimaroc.com) and **Comarit**
(☎950 23 61 55; www.comarit.es) sail from the
passenger port to Melilla and/or Nador (eight
hours). Prices start at €55 for a one-way adult
fare.

BUS The combined bus and train station is just
east of the centre; at the **information desk**
(☺6.45am-10.45pm) ask for the appropriate
ticket window. **Alsa** (☎902 42 22 42; www.alsa
.es) provides the main services across the region.

TO	FARE (€)	DURATION	FREQUENCY
Córdoba	26	5hr	1 daily
Granada	13	2hr	8 daily
Guadix	15	2hr	2 daily
Jaén	18	4hr	1 daily
Madrid	44	10hr	3 daily
Málaga	17	4¾hr	8 daily
Murcia	18	3hr	7 daily
Seville	33	5¾hr	3 daily

TRAIN Direct trains run to/from Granada
(€16.50, 2¼ hours, four daily), Seville (€40, 5½
hours, four daily) and Madrid (€45.50, 6¼ hours,
one daily). Trains leave from the combined bus
and train station.

THE OLD MEDINA

After visiting the Alcazaba, be sure to descend into the maze-like streets of the former
Arab medina. One good destination is Tetería Almedina (p273) teahouse. If it's the
weekend, seek out the market (9am to 2pm) at Plaza de Pavia, a rowdy mix of produce, cheap shoes and *churros* (delicious, fat, tubular doughnuts). To the north and
west is the district called La Chanca, where the houses are dug into the Alcazaba hill
and painted in bright colours. This atmospheric area is gradually being aesthetically
restored; the owners of Tetería Almedina are actively involved in the fundraising and also
organise cultural programs for the local Moroccan immigrants, particularly the children.

HEAVENLY HAMMAMS

Almería has two superb *hammam baños Árabes* (Arab baths). The sumptuous **Hammam Aíre de Almería** (www.airedealmeria.com; Plaza de la Constitución 5; entry incl 15min massage €35; ⊙10am-10pm) opened in 2011. It occupies a wonderful setting on the Plaza de la Constitución (also known as Plaza Vieja), a 17th-century arcaded square with graceful colonnades and sculpted pines, which was, fittingly, the one-time site of the city's main Arab souq (marketplace). Housed in a suitably historic building, this luxurious and spacious *hammam* exudes a feeling of tranquillity throughout its marble and warm brick interior, and offers three baths: the *frigidarium* (16°C), the *tepidarium* (36°C) and the *caldarium* (40°C), as well as a range of aromatherapy massages. The *hammam* also incorporates a hotel, Plaza Vieja Alejandro (p308), and an enticing bar.

The city's second and smaller *hammam*, **Hammam Almeraya** (www.almeraya .info; Calle Perea 9; incl 15min massage €24; ⊙4-10pm), has hot and cold baths, beautiful marble and tiled surroundings and also offers massages, as well as a relaxing *tetería* (p273).

For other destinations in Almería province, see the respective Getting There & Away sections.

ℹ Getting Around

CAR The A7/E15 runs a large ring around Almería; the easiest access to the centre is along the seafront, on the Carretera de Málaga from the west and the AL12 (Autovía del Aeropuerto) from the east.

PARKING Street parking is scarce. Large underground car parks below the Rambla de Belén are €16 per day.

TAXI Catch a taxi at ranks on Paseo de Almería, or call ☎950 22 61 61 or ☎950 25 11 11.

NORTH OF ALMERÍA

Desierto de Tabernas

To the northeast of the city is a stretch of barren landscape that looks as if it has been transplanted from the Mojave desert. Although it has, thankfully, been largely untouched by greenhouses, that doesn't mean the land hasn't been prosperous. Clint Eastwood and Charles Bronson once walked these badlands in westerns such as *The Magnificent Seven* and *Once Upon a Time in the West*, as well as David Lean's *Lawrence of Arabia*. More recently, Spanish director Alex de la Iglesia made the film *800 Bullets* here, and an episode of the popular BBC series *Doctor Who* was filmed here in March 2012, featuring a half-human, half-robot fighting with cowboys (who are usually busy staging shoot-outs and stunts on horseback, then scrambling around the back of the sets to serve paella to the tourists).

◉ Sights

Oasys/Mini Hollywood   AMUSEMENT PARK (www.oasysparquetematico.com; adult/child €20/ 10; ⊙10am-9pm, weekends only Oct-Apr) This is the best-known and most expensive of the Wild West shows and provides some good down-home family entertainment. Although the actual set is looking a bit scuffed, the zoo has grown to a considerable size with some 800 animals at last count, including lions, panthers, tigers and hippos.

There are also a couple of modest museums, with stagecoaches and similar, plus a pool and restaurant (think overpriced burgers and chips). Children should enjoy the (albeit brief) 20-minute daily shoot-out (resulting in an unceremonious hanging), while adults may prefer the clichéd can-can show (or at least the beer) in the saloon. While this is not Hollywood by any stretch of the imagination, it still offers a family-fun few hours out. It is located on the N340 just southwest of Tabernas. Take sunscreen and a hat: there is little shade.

Cinema Studios Fort Bravo   AMUSEMENT PARK (www.fort-bravo.com; adult/child €12/6.50; ⊙10am-10pm, weekends only Oct-Apr) This place has a certain dusty charm. There is a Wild West show and a saloon where David Beckham shot a recent Pepsi ad (may make up for the lack of can-can girls for some). Stagecoach rides, horse-riding treks and overnight stays in log cabins are also available. Fort Bravo is located on the N340.

TWO WAYS TO GROW A TOMATO

In Almería's unprotected flatlands, *invernaderos* (greenhouses) sprawl like some kind of extra-terrestrial colony. The tomatoes produced here have brought wealth to a previously dirt-poor corner of Spain. But water quality has suffered due to pesticide run-off, and exploitation of immigrant labour has been a constant issue.

Meanwhile, mountain-dwellers lament the spoiled view over the valleys and stick with the complex system of *huertas* (terraces) and *acequias* (water channels) installed by the Arabs when they came to Spain more than a millennium ago. No room for hypermodern agriculture here – the old way is the only way to eke a living out of the steep mountainsides.

But the real test is, how do the tomatoes taste? In summer, mountain-grown, sun-ripened tomatoes are delectable. But surprisingly, the *tomate RAF*, a greenish heirloom variety, does very well in the hothouses – and ripens in winter, through to March or April. It's the province's pride and is destined to earn its very own *denominación original*; look for it on Almería menus or at the markets. Expect to pay at least €6 a kilo – if it is less, then it is not the real Raf.

Níjar

POP 29,284

This small town in the foothills of the Sierra Alhamilla, northeast of Almería, is known for producing some of Andalucía's most attractive glazed pottery. At the top of Avenida Lorca, the road bends and leads up into the heart of old Níjar, with delightful **Plaza La Glorieta**, surrounded by trees and overlooked by the church of **Santa María de la Anunciación** and, further still, the tranquil **Plaza del Mercado**. Hiking up even further, following signs, you eventually reach the **Atalaya**, a ruined tower above the village that takes in the whole valley below. There is a small **tourist office** (Plaza Ayuntamiento; ☺10am-9pm) which also sells souvenirs.

✖ Eating & Drinking

La Glorieta SPANISH €

(Plaza La Glorieta; tapas €1.50, menú €9) Enjoy a peaceful view from the terrace overlooking this delightful leafy square. Choices include a long list of tapas, plus a reasonable daily menu. Some unusual dishes, for these parts, like traditional Greek *moussaka*. Locals pack the place out; always a good sign.

Cafetería Pastelería
Virgen de Fátima CAFE €

(Avenida Federico García Lorca 14; pastries €1-2; 🏃) Easy to find on the approach to town, this place should satisfy your sweet tooth with delicious typical local cakes and pastries, including tangy lemon-peel-flecked doughnuts. Cool down with a refreshing lemon *granizado*.

🛍 Shopping

The town has seriously cashed in on its ceramics' fame and the main street running uphill, Avenida Federico García Lorca, is lined with shops selling pottery, woven rugs and the local *higo chumbo* liquor, produced using the cactus plant. For a more specialised pottery selection, head just to the west and the charming Barrio Alfarero (Potters' Quarter).

 La Tienda de los Milagros CERAMICS

(www.latiendadelosmilagros.com; Callejón de los Artesanos) This is the workshop of British ceramicist Matthew Weir and his Spanish wife Isabel Hernandez, who produces quality *jarapa* rugs. As well as ceramics, Matthew produces woodblock prints and works with stoneware and porcelain. The workshop is distinctive for its playful exterior murals and is located midway down the hill, before the jarringly modern craft centre.

❶ Getting There & Away

BUS Níjar is served by just two buses from Almería Monday to Saturday, and one on Sunday (€2.75, 45 minutes to 1¼ hours).

CAR Níjar is 4km north of the A7, 31km northeast of Almería. There are parking bays all the way up Avenida Federico García Lorca.

Sorbas

POP 2905

A prosperous pottery town, Sorbas lies about 34km by road from Níjar and can be reached by a scenic drive through the compact mountains of the Sierra de Alhamilla, passing the old mining town of Lucainena de las Torres. It's located on the edge of a dramatic limestone gorge in the Paraje Natural de Karst en Yesos, where millions of years of water erosion have resulted in fascinating cave complexes.

◉ Sights & Activities

This attractive small town is well worth a wander around. Try and time your visit for a Thursday when a bustling market takes over the central Plaza de la Constitución and the surrounding streets.

Cuevas de Sorbas   CAVE
(www.cuevasdesorbas.com; adult/child €13/9; ☉guided tours 10am-8pm; 🚻) These caves are a rare gypsum karst geosite, created by the erosion of river water and the dissolution that occurs on some rocks. Because of the speed of the latter, degradation is generally quite rapid, which is why there are so few gypsum karsts in the world. The lack of rain in Almería has slowed down this process dramatically, resulting in these rare and spectacular cave tunnels stretching some 50km into the rock face.

There are several tours and routes available where you can see glittering gypsum crystals, tranquil ponds and dark otherworldly tunnels. Tours need to be reserved at least one day ahead.

Juan Simón Ceramics   CERAMICS
(Alfarerías 25; ☉9.30am-8pm) Follow the *alfarería* signs from the Plaza de la Constitución to this vast ceramics workshop at the bottom of a hill (just to the right of the 17th-century Iglesia San Roque), where you can watch the potters and painters at work. It's been in the same family for several generations; have a peek round the back at the 14th-century kiln dating from Moorish times.

Sendero de Los Molinos de Río Aguas   WALKING
This lovely 7km trail follows a river through a gypsum-flecked canyon. It begins 5km along the A1102, past the entrance to Cuevas de Sorbas. You can pick up a guide at the Centro de Visitantes Los Yesares at the entrance to the village. Allow around two hours; the walk is relatively easy and there are descriptive plaques along the route.

✖ Eating

Cafetería Caymar   TAPAS €
(Plaza de la Constitución; tapas €1.80; 🚻) Located on the central plaza, this is a reasonable option. Although a fairly basic place, it is good for tapas and *bocadillos* (sandwiches) and also has chairs on the square in summer.

❶ Information

Centro de Visitantes Los Yesares (☎950 36 45 63; Calle Terraplén; ☉11am-2pm & 4-6pm Tue-Sun Oct-Jun, daily Jul-Sep) Situated at the entrance to Sorbas. It has informative displays on the Sorbas cave system and the odd flora and fauna that thrive there.

❶ Getting There & Away

BUS Buses run from Almería to Sorbas (€4.75, one hour); there are four on weekdays, three on Saturday and two on Sunday. Returning, there are four daily Monday to Saturday, three on Sunday.

LAS ALPUJARRAS DE ALMERÍA

Less visited than their Granada counterpart, Las Alpujarras (as the lower reaches of the Sierra Nevada are known) in Almería province are notably more arid. The landscape

OHANES

Detour off the A348 onto the winding route up to Ohanes. The tiny village specialises in *vino rosado* (rosé wine), and while that's as good a reason to visit as any, it's really the drive here and down that's remarkable. On the 9km road, you wind up through stark red rock along the south-facing side of the valley. When you finally curve around the ridge to the more protected mountain face, the scenery changes completely, to green terrace fields and flourishing vineyards. To explore the village, park at the top and walk down. When leaving, continue along the top of town, then bear left (downhill) where the road splits. This route to the valley is shorter than the ascent, but slightly more nerve-racking, dwindling to one lane as it zigzags down through the fields. It comes out just west of Canjáyar.

is at first relentlessly barren, with serrated ridges stretching to infinity. But it gradually becomes more lush, with lemon and orange orchards, as you approach Fondón. Many of the towns winding along the Río Andarax specialise in grape-growing.

Los Millares ARCHAEOLOGICAL SITE
(◎10am-2pm Wed-Sun) Just before ascending into the mountains, by the Río Andarax, is this archaeological site. The Copper Age culture that thrived here, from around 2700 BC to 1800 BC, built successive lines of defensive walls as the population expanded; outlines of these remain, as do ruined stone houses and some reconstructions of distinctive domed graves.

A small interpretation centre with a model of the site sheds some light on the background, as does the Museo Arqueológico (p270) in Almería, which exhibits the best finds from the area such as pottery with the distinctive goggle-eyes motif. Signs indicate the Los Millares turn-off from the A348, shortly before Alhama de Almería.

Laujar de Andarax

POP 1819
This pleasant 'capital' of the Almería Alpujarras is where Boabdil, the last emir of Granada, settled briefly after losing Granada. It was also the headquarters of Aben Humeya, the first leader of the 1568-70 Morisco uprising. Today the town produces a great deal of Almería's wine. Although it boasts few sights, there's a handsome three-tiered **town hall** on the central Plaza Mayor crowned by a distinctive belfry, and the 17th-century brick **Iglesia de la Encarnación** with a minaret-like tower and lavish golden altar.

◎ Sights & Activities

El Nacimiento Waterfalls WATERFALL
Just east of the main plaza in Laujar de Andarax, a signposted road leads 1km north to El Nacimiento, a series of waterfalls in a deep valley, with a couple of restaurants nearby. On weekends, it's packed with families out for a barbecue

Sendero del Aguadero WALKING
Continuing up the road around 2km from the El Nacimiento waterfalls, you'll reach the start of Sendero del Aguadero, signed as PR-37, a lovely walk up through fragrant pines. The whole trail is 8km (3½ hours),

WORTH A TRIP

LOS ALBARDINALES

East of Tabernas, the terrain gets a little more lush – enough to support the olive groves maintained by organic oil producer **Los Albardinales** (📞950 61 17 07; www.losarbardinales.com; N340, Tabernas; mains €8-10; ◎9am-7pm Fri-Wed), a little more than 2km out of town. Visitors can tour the facilities to see how the oil is pressed and bottled, as well as sample the stuff – just a small taste, or in the form of lunch or dinner at the restaurant which emphasises local artisanal food, including organic wines. A shop is stocked with the oil, as well as organic wines, soaps, vinegars and other local products.

but you can, of course, double back sooner. Look out for wild boar and the abubilla (a black-and-white bird with an elaborate orange crest).

FREE Bodega Valle de Laujar WINERY
(www.bodegasvallelaujar.es; ◎8.30am-2pm & 3.30-7pm Mon-Sat) Located on the access road into town from the A348, this well-established bodega is a good choice for sampling the local wines and *digestifs,* and watching the bottling operations.

Cortijo El Cura WINERY
(www.cortijoelcura.com; ◎8am-8pm) This is a rare organic vineyard and a small family operation, producing some excellent wines that are increasingly gaining national recognition: in 2010 the young red wine, Sierra de Gádor, and the Oroel Llano white wine both won gold medals in the Eco Racimos national awards for wine produced by organic grapes.

The bodega has a beautiful old farmhouse setting. Look for the signs pointing south off the A348, just west of Laujar.

✖ Eating & Drinking

Almirez ANDALUCIAN €
(Calle Almirez 14; mains €8-10, menú €13) Part of a hotel of the same name, this bar and restaurant has a hearty *menu del día* which specialises in local Alpujarran dishes, including *potajes* (soups and stews) and *migas* (fried breadcrumbs with onions, garlic and ham).

ALMERÍA PROVINCE LAUJAR DE ANDARAX

Fonda Nuevo Andarax ANDALUCIAN €
(Calle General Mola 4; mains €6-10) A popular restaurant and bar (with rooms) just off the pretty main square, Plaza Mayor de la Alpujarra. You can fill up fast with tapas from the bar, or grab a chair in the dining room and tuck into typical heart-warming Alpujarran cuisine.

❶ Information

For information on walking routes in the area, visit the **Centro de Visitantes Laujar de** (⊙10am-2pm & 6-8pm Wed-Sun, 10am-2pm Sat), on the access road just west of Laujar de Andarax.

❶ Getting There & Away

BUS The bus from Almería to Laujar (€6, two hours) leaves at 9am daily and returns at 3.50pm. From Laujar, to continue on to the Granada Alpujarras, take a bus to Berja (€2.75, 30 minutes to one hour, two on weekdays, one Saturday and Sunday), then another to Ugíjar or beyond.

COSTA DE ALMERÍA

Parque Natural de Cabo de Gata-Níjar

Some of Spain's most flawless and least crowded beaches are strung like pearls between the rugged cliffs of the Parque Natural de Cabo de Gata-Níjar. The stark terrain, formed by volcanic activity, is studded with agave plants and other desert succulents, interrupted by only a few small settlements of whitewashed flat-roofed houses.

With just 100mm of rain in an average year, Cabo de Gata is the driest place in Europe, yet more than 1000 varieties of animal and plant wildlife thrive in the arid, salty environment. It's also a bonanza of bizarre rock formations and is part of the European Geoparks network. The largest town in the park is San José, a second home for many Almería city folk.

ALMERÍA PROVINCE PARQUE NATURAL DE CABO DE GATA-NÍJAR

Parque Natural de Cabo de Gata-Níjar

HIKING AROUND THE CAPE

A network of roads and trails leads about 60km around the cape, from the town of Cabo de Gata up to **Agua Amarga**, a boho-chic beach getaway for the Madrid jet set. The full hike takes three leisurely days and should be attempted only in spring or, better, autumn, when the sea is warm, as the summer heat is deadly and there is no shade. You can embark on sections of the walk for a day or afternoon, visiting beaches that are otherwise inaccessible.

From San José northeast to Los Escullos, it's a 2½-hour mostly level walk, partially on old mining roads. North of Los Escullos, you can walk to quiet rocky coves; another 45 minutes brings you to La Isleta del Moro.

Another good stretch is from Rodalquilar across the valley to **Playa del Playazo**, then up the coast along scenic cliff edges to the town of **Las Negras** (about two hours from Rodalquilar). It's another 1½ hours to the real prize: **Playa San Pedro**, an abandoned village that supports a small crew of boho-travellers. The beach has some of the finest sand on the coast, with clear water and medium waves. You can, of course, also drive to Las Negras, then make the hike to Playa San Pedro from there.

Cala del Plomo, accessible by road north of Playa San Pedro, is a somewhat uninviting grey-sand beach, but **Cala de Enmedio**, just up the coast, is prettier and very private. About five minutes' walk inland from the Cala del Plomo parking area, look for a trail leading off to the right. Follow this up and over a low ridge for 20 minutes, then bear right down a dry streambed to Cala de Enmedio.

⊙ Sights & Activities

Beaches

Some of the most beautiful *playas* (beaches) are near **San José**, particularly southwest of town. A dirt road runs behind several beaches; to reach it follow the 'Playas' signs pointing southwest at the inland edge of San José. Along the road, the first you reach is **Playa de los Genoveses**, a 1km-long stretch where the Genoan navy landed in 1147 to aid in the attack on Almería. Getting there calls for a bit of a walk from the parking area.

Further along, from the nude beach **Playa del Barronal** – not visible from the road (thankfully!) – you can clamber over the rocks to a series of small coves, the **Calas del Barronal**. Nearer the end of the road is **Playa de Mónsul** (you may recognise the rock overhang from *Indiana Jones and the Last Crusade*), which is busier than the others because the car park is close to the water, and the quieter **Cala de la Media Luna** and **Cala Carbón**. From about mid-July to mid-September, the beach road is closed to cars after about 10am – you must park in the lot by the roundabout at the entrance to town, then take a bus which stops at each beach parking lot.

Other good beaches include the wide **Playa del Playazo**, the closest beach to Rodalquilar, between two headlands; **Los Escullos**, a blip on the map with a few houses and a couple of hotels nearby; and the grey-sand beach at the fishing village of **La Isleta del Moro**, which is quiet on weekdays. The latter two are convenient if you prefer less of a wilderness experience – there are restaurants and bars steps away.

Cabo de Gata

When people dreamily talk of Cabo de Gata, they're usually referring to the whole park, not the village itself. The coarse-sand beach gets crowded with Almería day-trippers, but is windswept and deserted outside of July and August.

Driving on past the prominent lighthouse, you pass several access trails to small, isolated beaches, an easy way to stretch your legs. After about 3km, at an 18th-century watchtower, the Torre de Vigía Vela Blanca, the coast road is blocked to cars; the track, popular with walkers and cyclists, runs on about 5km to San José.

Salinas de Cabo de Gata   SALT FLATS

Southeast of the town are some of the last functioning salt flats in Spain, drawing flocks of flamingos starting in spring and peaking in autumn. An 11km trail loops around the flats, with bird hides placed strategically along the way. At the far end of the lagoons, the collected salt is piled up in great heaps at the desolate village of La Almadraba de Monteleva, where the semi-ruined **Iglesia de las Salinas** dominates the area for miles around.

Faro de Cabo de Gata   LIGHTHOUSE
At the southernmost point of the cape, the Faro de Cabo de Gata is a lighthouse overlooking the jagged volcanic reefs of the **Arrecife de las Sirenas** (Reef of the Mermaids), named for the monk seals that used to lounge here. The view into the water is fantastically clear.

El Cabo a Fondo   BOAT TOUR
(☑637 449170; www.elcaboafondo.es; 1hr tour €20) You can get a different perspective of the lighthouse on a boat trip with this outfit; it's a wonderful way to see the dramatic coastline. Boats leave from a kiosk in La Fabriquilla, a tiny settlement back west along the coast, near the salt flats; reserving ahead is essential.

Caboteando   BOATING
(☑615 396225; info@caboteando.com) If you would like to captain a boat yourself, contact Caboteando where 3.7m-plus size boats cost from €140 for four hours from the nearby harbour at San José.

Rodalquilar

Northeast of La Isleta del Moro, the road climbs to the breathtaking viewpoint Mirador de la Amatista, before heading down into the basin of the Rodalquilar valley, a vast caldera. It's here, among the time-worn lava, that the complexity of Cabo de Gata's flora is most evident, especially after the very brief spring rains, when delicate plants, some with a lifespan of only a few days, flourish.

The village of Rodalquilar, in the centre of the valley, was until very recently a ghost town, with just a few residents among the shells of a gold-mining industry abandoned in the 1970s. Although there are still graffiti-daubed ruined houses on the outskirts, nowadays it's a popular getaway spot, with a cluster of whitewashed holiday homes and some bohemian-chic hang-outs.

Film buffs may want to pass by the **El Cortijo de los Frailes**, the true-life setting for the tragic revenge story related in Federico García Lorca's best-known play, *Blood Wedding*. The romantically ruined farmhouse is in the wilderness midway between Rodalquilar and Los Albaricoques; it can be a bit hard to find, so ask for directions at any of the local tourist offices.

Jardín Botánico El Albardinal   GARDENS
(Calle Fundición; ⊙10am-1pm & 6-9pm Tue-Sun) This is a vast, well-planned botanical garden on the edge of town where every plant, tree and shrub is identified. There is also a charming traditional *huerta* (vegetable garden), complete with scarecrow, plus educational exhibits.

Gold Mines   RUINS
There is something very evocative about these ruined gold mines; a fascinating bit of crumbling industrial wreckage in a barren red-rock landscape. You can follow a rugged road back up behind the main structures. At the entrance to the mines, **La Casa de los Volcanes** (⊙11am-2pm Tue-Fri, 10am-2pm & 4-6.30pm Sat) has an interesting display on the area's geological history.

🍴 Eating

The main tourist resort, San José, has the largest choice of restaurants in the area and the fish restaurants along the marina here (north end of the beach) stay open through the afternoon. Elsewhere, there are some excellent restaurants scattered around the villages and resorts, particularly in and around classy Agua Amarga.

TOP CHOICE Casa Café de la Loma   VEGETARIAN €
(☑950 38 98 31; www.degata.com/laloma; La Isleta del Moro; mains €7-16; ⊙7pm-1am Jul & Aug; 🌿) A Mediterranean heaven with great sea views, this old *cortijo* (country property) runs a summer-only restaurant. The creative menu of crêpes, salads and more is veggie-friendly, and there are regular jazz and flamenco concerts in the garden, by candlelight. Look for the turn off the main road just north of La Isleta del Moro.

Restaurante La Villa   ANDALUCIAN €€
(☑950 13 80 73; Agua Amarga; mains €10-18; ⊙closed Nov-Mar) Appropriately located next to the best hotel in town, this is a time-tested, sophisticated restaurant with a romantic, moodily-lit dining room and a pretty outside terrace. The dishes try just hard enough to be original, but stop short of being slaves to drizzle and tower building. Reservations essential.

La Gallineta   CONTEMPORARY EUROPEAN €€
(☑950 38 05 01; Pozo de los Frailes; mains €14-24; ⊙Tue-Sun, closed mid-Oct-Mar) This small elegant restaurant 4km north of San José is where urbanites on weekend escapes come

for inventive food with an international twist, served in a homey dining room with original tiles in a building that used to be a village shop. Try the ravioli in a walnut and black truffle sauce or go with a rice dish – they are the speciality.

Casa Miguel
SEAFOOD €€
(📞950 38 03 29; www.restaurantecasamiguel.es; Avenida de San José 43-45, San José; mains €18-22) The best seafood restaurant in San José has pavement seating and good service. Skip the pallid paella, however, in favour of the rich *arroz negro* (mixed seafood and rice, black from squid ink). Or pick and mix with the daily fish specials. The bar does good tapas. Reservations recommended at weekends.

Acá Charles
INTERNATIONAL €€
(Avenida de San José 51, San José; mains €14-19) Opened in 2012, this place has all the locals enthusing about the sophisticated menu where seafood doesn't necessarily take central stage. Dishes include truffles, crispy Serrano ham, fresh green asparagus with polenta, and similar. There are just two homemade desserts (and neither is flan).

Costamarga
SEAFOOD €€€
(Playa de Aguamarga, Agua Amarga; mains €11-16; 🕐) One of several restaurants along Agua Amarga's beach, this place does fish, of course, but it also has a considerable menu section devoted to seasonal vegetables, such as artichoke hearts with ham. From the fryer, *chipirones* (thimble-sized squid) and *croquetas* (croquettes) are recommended.

❶ Information

Centro de Visitantes Las Amoladeras (Km 7 Carretera Cabo de Gata-Almería; ⊙10am-2pm & 6-9pm) Main park information centre, on the main road from Almería about 1.1km before (west of) the turn to Cabo de Gata.
San José Visitor Centre (Avenida San José 27; ⊙10am-2pm & 5-8pm) On the left-hand side of main street, midway through town.

❶ Getting There & Away
Bus

There is no bus service connecting towns within the park.
Alsa (📞902 42 22 42; www.alsa.es) Connects Almería to El Cabo de Gata (€3, one hour, six daily) and Las Negras (€5, 1¼ hours, one daily Monday to Saturday).
Autocares Bernardo (www.autocaresbernardo.com) Runs buses from Almería to San José (€2.65, 1¼ hours, four Monday to Satur-

day, two Sunday). It also runs one bus to La Isleta del Moro (€2.65, 1¼ hours) on Monday and Saturday.
Autocares Frahermar (www.frahermar.com) In Almería, runs to/from Agua Amarga (€5.50, 1¼ hour) once on Monday, Wednesday, Friday, Saturday and Sunday; service increases to daily in July and August.

Taxi
Taxi de Gata (📞669 071442; www.taxidegata.com) In Níjar.
Taxi Ramón Ruíz López (📞950 13 00 08, 606 414724) In Carboneras.

Mojácar
POP 7745
There are two Mojácars: old Mojácar Pueblo, a multilevel wedding cake melting down the cliff, with its jumble of white cube houses 2km inland. Then there is Mojácar Playa, a typical modern resort along a broad beach. As recently as the 1960s, the *pueblo* (village) was decaying and almost abandoned. A savvy mayor lured artists and others with bargain property offers, which set a distinct bohemian tone that is still palpable, despite an overlay of more generic tourism. In the winding streets of the *pueblo*, there are mellow bars, galleries and intriguing small shops.

◉ Sights & Activities
The main sight is the *pueblo* itself. To reach the *pueblo* from the *playa* (beach), turn inland at the roundabout by Parque Comercial, a large shopping centre; regular buses connect the two.

El Mirador del Castillo
LOOKOUT
(⊙11am-11pm or later) A byproduct of Mojácar's revival as an arts colony, the bohemian retreat called El Mirador del Castillo occupies the very top of the hill, a mirador (lookout) to end all miradors. From here, you can appreciate the area's weird geology – the sea is off to one side, while the inland vista is studded with volcanic cones just like the one Mojácar occupies.

A cafe-bar here provides sustenance after the hike up, along with jazz on the stereo and plenty of space to relax over a coffee or tapa.

Fuente Mora
FOUNTAIN
(Moorish Fountain) Near the foot of the village, the large rectangular Fuente Mora is a village landmark. A plaque above

Mojácar Pueblo

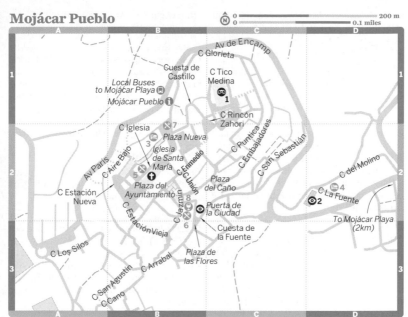

ALMERÍA PROVINCE MOJÁCAR

it is inscribed with the words of the last Muslim governor, Alabez y Garcilaso, who retorted to the Catholic Monarchs' order to leave the village in 1488: 'I am as Spanish as you are... I have not taken up arms against the Christians... I believe it is only just we are treated as brothers, not as enemies.'

Beaches

Stretching some 7km, Mojácar Playa has enough sand for everyone. Distinct stretches of beach are known by different names, though in the central part, there's not much to distinguish the character of each patch of sand. Of the many *chiringuitos* (beach restaurants), **Neptuno** (Playa del Descargador; mains €12-16) is well regarded, especially for its wood-fire sardine feasts. It's just north of the intersection of the beach and the road to the *pueblo*.

A few kilometres further south of Mojácar Playa, the beaches are quieter, and once you get to the fringes of town there are a number of more secluded areas. Several of the beaches beyond the Torre de Macenas, an 18th-century fortification right on the sand, are naturist beaches. There is a pleasant wide promenade that stretches for around 3km north from the Hotel Best Indalo.

Mojácar Pueblo

◎ Sights
1	El Mirador del Castillo	C1
2	Fuente Mora	D2

⌂ Sleeping
	El Mirador del Castillo	(see 1)
3	Hostal Arco Plaza	B2
4	Hotel Simon	D2

✕ Eating
5	El Reclamo	B2
6	La Taberna	B2
7	Pulcinella	B2

☕ Drinking
8	La Tahona	B2

🎊 Festivals & Events

Moros y Cristianos　　　　　　FESTIVAL
Locals don costumes to re-enact the Christian conquest. Dances, processions and festivities are held on the weekend nearest to 10 June.

Noche de San Juan　　SUMMER SOLSTICE
This is basically a fiesta-spirited party on beaches around Spain that takes place on 23 June, to coincide with the summer

solstice. Expect bonfires, dancing and drinking from dusk until dawn.

Eating

La Cantina TOP CHOICE MEXICAN €
(www.lacantinamojacar.com; Complejo Tito's, Playa Las Ventanicas; P✳🐾) La Cantina is the real deal – Tito is from LA so knows his 'south of the border' Tex-Mex cuisine. It is part of the Tito combo of beach bar and restaurant with live music in the summer. The menu includes all the familiar burritos, quesadillas and guacamole, plus there's a huge selection of tequilas and Mexican beers to make sure you are in suitable *ay caramba* mood.

El Reclamo ANDALUCIAN €
(Calle Alcalde Jacinto, Mojácar Pueblo; mains €7-10) With a big TV and fluorescent lights, you're not coming to this bare-bones place for the atmosphere. But the honest home cooking that comes out of the kitchen – rabbit in mustard sauce, chicken pie and the like – more than makes up for the lack of elegance. Unfortunately the place is suffering from the major construction going on outside (a new underground car park), which is scheduled for completion in 2013. Let's just hope they keep going until then....

La Taberna TAPAS €
(Plaza del Caño 1, Mojácar Pueblo; tapas & platos combinados from €4) Good tapas and tasty vegetarian bites get everyone cramming into this thriving little restaurant inside a warren of intimate rooms, full of chatter and belly-full diners. It's located next to an evocative 11th-century Moorish arch; to get here, head downhill and pass through the old city gate – just on the right, you'll see the tiny tapas *plancha* (griddle) in action.

Pulcinella ITALIAN €
(www.pulcinellamojacar.com; Plaza Nueva, Mojácar Pueblo; ⊘Tue-Sun;) Good Italian food and even better views from the terrace here. Plenty of pizza choice including the vegetarian Green Peace variety with lots of greens, plus pastas and some meat dishes, like down-to-earth grilled chicken.

🍷 Drinking

In summer, Mojácar Pueblo has a hopping nightlife, with a number of friendly bars tucked into small houses.

La Tahona BAR
(Plaza de las Flores, Mojácar Pueblo; ⊘Sat & Sun only Oct-Apr) This is the place in town to come for a buzzy good-time atmosphere, shaken up with great mojitos and music. Find it just down from the popular La Taberna tapas bar, through the ancient Moorish arch.

Teatro Bar BAR
(Paseo del Mediterráneo 8, Mojácar Playa; ⊘noon-late) This is a rare Spanish-run music bar (and restaurant) among this energetic strip of British-style pubs and music bars of the 'Dusty Springfield tribute act' ilk. Open all year, with live acts varying from rock 'n' roll to Cuban. There are also plans to have Sunday afternoon music sessions for those seeking to do a little hip swaying in between their sunbathing.

ℹ Information

Mojácar Playa (www.turismomojacar.com; Avenida del Mediterráneo; ⊘9am-4pm Mon-Fri, 9.30am-2pm Sat) Kiosk opposite the Parque Comercial.

MOJÁCAR'S MOORISH HERITAGE

In the 16th century, aggressive campaigns resumed against the population of Andalucía (by then mostly *moriscos*, converted Muslims, under threat of the Inquisitions), and in 1609 there was a final push, with refugees marched to port cities with only the belongings they could carry, and often without their young children, who were taken to Catholic orphanages.

But no matter how thorough the Inquisition claimed to be, a certain percentage of the Muslim population remained, especially in this fringe of Spain. Polish photographer Kurt Hielscher visited Mojácar in the early 20th century and his images document women dressed in black, with veils over their faces. At the entrance to the village, a sign reads 'Mojácar, Kingdom of Granada', as though the last 500 years had never happened.

TITO DEL AMO

Tito del Amo moved to Mojácar from Los Angeles in 1964. He has recently co-produced a documentary about Walt Disney, who he (along with many locals) believes was born in the village and subsequently adopted in the USA. He also runs **Tito's** (☎950 61 50 30; www.elbeachbar.com; Playa de las Ventanicas; ☺Apr-Oct) beach restaurant and bar at Mojácar Playa.

Why did you choose Mojácar? When I came here in the '60s, there were just three cars in the village (remember I came from LA!), then there was the hilltop, the light and the coastal setting. I couldn't resist.

Your favourite place? Aside from La Coquette (p272), which has simply the best French pastries and Italian ice cream in the province, I also enjoy Agua Amarga and the beautiful Cabo de Gata natural park.

Where do you like to go on your day off? I love the rugged rural scenery and just enjoy the simple pleasure of taking long walks in the surrounding countryside, especially in the foothills near the coast.

If you didn't live in Mojácar, where else would you choose to live in Andalucía, and why? I could live in Granada too, for several reasons, but if only to be near the Alhambra!

Mojácar Pueblo (www.mojacar.es; Calle Glorieta; ☺10am-2pm & 5-7pm Mon-Fri, 10.30am-1.30pm Sat)

❶ Getting There & Away

Bus

There is a bus stop at the foot of Mojácar Pueblo (p285) and another at the Parque Comercial in Mojácar Playa.

Enatcar/Alsa (www.alsa.es) runs buses to/from Almería (€7, 1¼ hours, four on weekdays, two on weekends), Granada (€19, four hours, two daily), Madrid (€38, eight hours, two daily), Madrid Barajas (€38, 8½ hours, one daily at 8.55pm) and Málaga (€25, 7½ hours, one daily).

Buses to Alicante, Valencia and Barcelona go from Vera, 16km north, which is served by buses from Mojácar (€1.50, 50 minutes, nine daily).

A local bus (€1) runs a circuit from Mojácar Pueblo down along the full length of the beach, roughly every half-hour from 9am to 11.30pm, April to September, till 7.30pm October to March.

Car

Follow the main road through town to reach two large parking lots on the far edge. Do not leave your car overnight on Tuesday in the upper lot, as it's used for a market on Wednesday morning.

Taxi

Taxis wait in the Plaza Nueva, or call ☎950 47 81 84.

LOS VÉLEZ

The beautiful, sparse landscape of the remote district of Los Vélez, in the northernmost part of Almería, lies 55km inland from Mojácar. In contrast with the rest of the province, parts of it are quite lush and forested. Three small towns – **Vélez Rubio**, **Vélez Blanco** and **María** – nestle in the shadow of the stark Sierra de María range, part of a natural park. Cave paintings here are the source of the prehistoric symbol that's seen everywhere in Almería.

Vélez Rubio is the largest town, with an enormous 18th-century baroque church, but Vélez Blanco has more charm with its scramble of houses with red-tile roofs, overshadowed by a dramatic castle. At 1070m, it's often up above the clouds – you can watch the valley below fill with fog and by afternoon the streets are wreathed in mist. Try and time your visit for a Wednesday morning when there is a lively street market on the main Calle Corredera.

◉ Sights & Activities

Cuevas del Almanzora TOWN
On the drive up from the coast, in the foothills 6km north of Vera, you pass by Cuevas del Almanzora, a busy agricultural town. The handsome **Castillo Marqués de Los Vélez** lords over the town from a hilltop, housing a small archaeology museum and a gallery of Goya lithographs (with a bullfighting theme) as well as the **Museo Antonio**

PARQUE NATURAL SIERRA DE MARÍA-LOS VÉLEZ

If you go walking in the arid mountains of this natural park, a refuge for many birds of prey, foxes and mountain goats, you will almost certainly have the trails to yourself. A visit in spring or autumn is best, as shade can be hard to come by on some trails. Vélez Blanco makes a good base, as does the tiny upland town of **María**, in a fine position against the awesome backdrop of the Sierra de María. The park visitor centres in either town have information on walking trails.

Just west of María on the A317 is the **Jardín Botánico Umbría de la Virgen** (☉10am-2pm & 6-8pm Tue-Sun). Stop in here if you're going hiking – the gardens highlight the unique flora in the mountains.

About 6km west of María, the A317 heads north onto a high plateau towards the lonely village of **La Cañada de Cañepla**, from where it continues, by a superbly scenic road, into the Parque Natural Sierras de Cazorla, Segura y Las Villas.

Manuel Campoy (☎950 45 80 63; Plaza de la Libertad; admission €2; ☉10am-1pm & 5-8pm Tue-Sat, 10am-1pm Sun).

The latter exhibits a large and fascinating selection of paintings and sculpture, mainly of Spanish painters, including works by Picasso and Miró, from the outstanding private collection of Campoy, one of Spain's greatest 20th-century art critics. Among other outstanding works are the sensitive pencil drawings by the Malagueño painter Revello de Toro.

Museo Cueva   MUSEUM
(admission €1; ☉10am-1pm & 5-8pm Tue-Sat) The caves after which the town is named, Cuevas del Almanzora, can be spied from the road (follow the *cuevas* sign) but are no longer open to the public; a couple are still inhabited. If you want to see a typical cave dwelling, a short stroll west of the castle leads you to the Museo Cueva. This cave housed a family with eight children up until the 1960s and the helpful woman at the desk was born in a cave herself so can tell you everything you want to know about cave life – providing you speak some Spanish, that is.

Castillo de Vélez Blanco   CASTLE
(Vélez Blanco; adult/child €1/0.50; ☉10am-2pm & 6-8pm Fri-Mon) The 16th-century castle at the top of the village seems to spring naturally from its rocky pinnacle. It confronts the great sphinx-like butte dubbed **La Muela** (The Tooth) across the tiled roofs of the village, as if in a bizarre duel.

From the outside, the structure is a pure feudal fortress, built in the early 16th century to establish Catholic control over this region filled with Muslim and *morisco* refugees. But the inside is pure Renaissance

palace – or it was until 1904, when the marble details were picked off, save for one lone gargoyle, and sold as a lot by the impoverished owners. American millionaire George Blumenthal bought the entire marble patio and later donated it to the Metropolitan Museum of Art in New York, where it is on permanent display. There is an ongoing project to make a copy of the patio and reinstall it.

A stroll around Vélez Blanco is rewarding, not least for its delightful maze of streets and its many attractive houses, which display a particularly stylish domestic architecture, with overhanging roof tiles, wooden box-framed windows and handsome wrought-iron balconies.

Cueva de los Letreros   HISTORIC SITE
(☎950 61 48 00; A317; admission free; ☉noon-6pm) Just south of Vélez Blanco, signs point to the Cueva de los Letreros, off the west side of the road opposite the Pinar del Rey camping ground. Of several collections of cave paintings in the area, this has the most outstanding examples. The reddish drawings were made sometime between 6000 BC and 3500 BC and depict what appear to be interconnected people – a sort of family tree, goes one theory.

More important is the now ubiquitous *indalo*, a stick figure with arms connected by an arc. It's seen all over the province, on walls and pendants and government letterhead, and there's enough evidence of its use in earlier centuries (and millennia) that ethnologists surmise it may be one of the longest continually used symbols in human culture.

From the A317, it's 600m along the signposted tarmacked road, then a right turn on a steep uphill track. This turns to dirt again and winds its way up to a parking area. A set of stone stairs leads to the cave – more like a rock overhang. From the turn off, it is 700m and will take you around 25 minutes of relatively easy walking. The caves are open to visitors but only by prior appointment. Head for the Centro de Visitantes Almacén del Trigo information office in Vélez Blanco at the far end of the town where, in return for depositing your passport, you will be given the key.

Eating

Mesón El Molino ANDALUCIAN €€
(☎950 41 50 70; Calle Curtidores 1, Vélez Blanco; mains €17-22; ⊘closed dinner Tue-Thu) Tucked away up a narrow lane near the centre of Vélez Blanco, this grand, old-fashioned restaurant places a real emphasis on quality products from all over Spain, proudly displayed at the entrance: aged beef, perfect tomatoes, obscure cheeses and, of course, luscious hams. The menu also includes game birds such as partridge and duck. In warm weather you can dine on the patio with its gurgling fountains and stream passing below.

La Gatera ANDALUCIAN €
(Calle Corredera 12, Vélez Blanco; mains €5-7; ⊘closed Mon evening) This small economical restaurant with lots of pine and bright lights has just a couple of dishes on the menu each day (aside from tapas) that are generally centred on local game, meat or poultry – *conejo al ajillo* (rabbit with garlic) is typical. The food is well prepared and hearty; a good choice for walkers on a budget.

ℹ Information

Centro de Visitantes Almacén del Trigo (Avenida del Marqués de Los Vélez; ⊘10am-2pm Tue, Thu & Sun, 10am-2pm & 4-6pm Fri & Sat) On the northern edge of Vélez Blanco with a small exhibition including models of the Cueva de los Letreros and the castle in Vélez Blanco.

Centro de Visitantes Mirador Umbría de María (⊘10am-2pm Tue, Thu & Sun, 10am-2pm & 4-6pm Fri & Sat) Two kilometres west of María off the A317.

ℹ Getting There & Away

BUS Alsa (www.alsa.es) runs buses from Vélez Rubio to Granada (€13, 2¼ hours, five daily), Guadix (€8.50, 1¾ hours, three daily) and Murcia (€8, 1½ to 2¼ hours, five daily). For Almería (€13, 3½ hours), there's a bus every day but Sunday. The bus stop in Vélez Rubio is on Avenida de Andalucía at the junction by Hostal Zurich.

CAR A bypass runs along the top of Vélez Blanco. Coming from Vélez Rubio, the first turn into town takes you to a stretch of road where you can park and continue on foot. The second turn leads directly to the castle (where there is parking). The third turn takes you into the far side of the village, near the information office.

ALMERÍA PROVINCE LOS VÉLEZ

Accommodation

Best Places to Stay

Where to Stay

Accommodation in Spain is incredibly varied. You can enjoy historical immersion by staying in a sympathetically restored former monastery or palace, or join the backpacker brigade in a cheap but comfortable hostel. In between you can run the price gamut from economical, no-thrills family-run *hostales* to fancy boutique hotels. The state-run *parador* chain is a nationwide collection of luxury hotels which usually inhabit old historic buildings. Boutique hotels are on the rise in Andalucía and they often cleverly combine historic features with dynamic modern design accents. Seville and Granada have plenty of accommodation options to choose from, but a number of the smaller white towns are also sprouting some spectacular places to stay.

Guesthouses are more common in rural areas (where they are often called *casas rurales*). These days, they are sometimes foreign-owned and run. In smaller towns you're more likely to encounter *hostales*. They often offer excellent value for money. Similar to *hostales* in price and nature are *pensiones* (pensions) and *posadas* (inns). These places often also offer apartments and/or family rooms.

Some hotels allow young children to stay in rooms with their parents for no extra charge if they share a bed. An additional bed usually costs from €15 to €30. Always specify beforehand when booking.

Pricing

The following is a guide to our pricing system. Unless stated otherwise, prices given are for a double room with private bathroom.

CATEGORY	COST
€	> €65
€€	€65-€140
€€€	< €140

Hostels & Hostales

In Spain, it is important to make a distinction between hostels and *hostales*. Hostels offer standard backpacker accommodation with dorm beds, kitchen facilities, communal lounges, shared bathrooms and bags of local information on hand for budget travellers. Prices vary according to room size and, to a lesser extent, season, but they start at around €16 for a shared-dorm bed before heading north. Dorms can be four-bed, six-bed, eight-bed or 10-bed, and many hostels offer double rooms and/or family rooms as well, usually with shared bathrooms. *Hostales* are small family-run hotels where basic but adequate facilities are provided in single, double or triple rooms rather than dorms. Double rooms rarely go for more than €60. Travellers can usually expect private bathrooms and more personal service.

In Andalucía, hostels are normally confined to the main cities such as Seville, Granada and Málaga, although there are a handful of Hostelling International (HI) hostels in smaller villages such as El Bosque (in the Parque Natural Sierra de Grazalema), Cortes de la Frontera and Cazorla. The privately run Oasis Hostels (www.hosteloasis .com) is an excellent non-HI bet. It runs hostels in Granada and Málaga, as well as two in Seville (one of which is in an old palace).

All are centrally located and offer heaps of hidden freebies such as tapas tours, drink vouchers, bike hire and pancake breakfasts. Casa Caracol (956 26 11 66; www.caracolcasa .com; Calle Suárez de Salazar 4; hammock/dm incl breakfast €10/16;) in Cádiz is another superfriendly private place in the old Santa María quarter. Melting Pot (956 68 29 06; www.meltingpothostels.com; Calle Turriano Gracil 5; dm/d incl breakfast from €13/35;) in Tarifa is a mega-laid-back option of equal quality.

For more information on hostels or to make online bookings, see www.hostelworld .com or www.hostelbookers.com.

Camping Grounds

Andalucía has approximately 150 camping grounds accommodating both caravans and tents. Cádiz province leads the way with 33 facilities, while Seville province has a select five. Rural areas offer the most idyllic camping spots. Highlights include the Costa de la Luz with over 20 camping grounds, the areas abutting the Parque Nacional de Doñana marshes, the steep Las Alpujarras valleys in the Sierra Nevada, the Cazorla mountains and the Cabo de Gata coastline. Camping grounds in Spain are graded first class, second class or third class, and facilities are generally very good. Even a third-class camping ground will have hot showers, electrical hook-ups and a cafe; top-notch

ACCOMMODATION

PARADORES: HISTORIC LUXURY

The state-run *parador* hotels were founded by King Alfonso XIII in the 1920s. There are 16 of them in Andalucía, all rated either three or four stars. Prices range from €100 to €370 depending on the season and location. Occupying some astounding locations, these are possibly the best accommodation options around if you're up for a splurge. The following all occupy fine historical buildings:

» **Parador Casa del Corregidor** (p297; Arcos de la Frontera) Andalucía's smallest *parador* inhabits a former palace (the Casa del Corregidor) in Arcos' main square. The cliff-top views are stunning.

» **Parador de Granada** (p306; Granada) Andalucía's and Spain's most celebrated (and expensive) *parador* inhabits a 15th-century convent inside the Alhambra.

» **Parador Castillo de Santa Catalina** (p303; Jaén) Situated in a 13th-century Moorish castle atop a hill overlooking the city of Jaén and the surrounding Sierra Morena.

» **Parador Málaga Gibralfaro** (p299; Málaga) On a hill next to the 14th-century Castillo de Gibralfaro and adjacent Alcazaba, this *parador* overlooks the whole spread of the city centre.

» **Parador de Antequera** (p301; Antequera) Encased in the former town hall next to Ronda's gaping gorge, and location of a real-life civil-war massacre fictionalised by Hemingway in *For Whom the Bell Tolls*.

» **Parador Condestable Dávalos** (p304; Úbeda) A luxury *parador* in one of Úbeda's trademark 16th-century Renaissance palaces.

places, meanwhile, often have minimarkets and swimming pools.

Camping grounds normally charge separately per adult, child and car. Average prices are rarely higher than €7.50, €6 and €5 respectively. Many facilties also rent cabins or bungalows from approximately €50 a night depending on size and season.

The **Federación Española de Clubes Campistas** (FECC; www.guiacampingfecc.com) is Spain's main camping club. Its website is an excellent information resource; you can access the websites of individual campsites, most of which allow you to make reservations online and also provide further contact info. It also publishes an annual *Guía Camping,* which is available in bookshops in Spain.

Self-Catering Apartments & Casas Rurales

Self-catering apartments and houses are relatively easy to procure in Andalucía and are particularly popular in coastal resort areas. Basic one-bedroom apartments start at around €30 per night, while a luxury pad with a swimming pool somewhere like Marbella will set you back up to €400 a night for four people.

Casas rurales are usually old renovated farmhouses run as B&Bs or as more independent short-term holiday lets, and they exist predominantly in smaller towns and villages. Prices for double rooms run from about €50 to €100 though many people opt for longer-term bookings, thus saving money.

The agencies listed below all deal with online bookings. In the peak summer months (June to August) and around holiday periods (Semana Santa and Easter), it is best to book at least a month in advance.

Apartments Spain (www.apartments-spain .com) Budget-oriented apartments and rentals throughout Spain.

Atlas Rural (www.atlasrural.com) All forms of rural accommodation in Spain from small *casas rurales* to *paradores.*

Owners Direct (www.ownersdirect.co.uk) Lists all number of privately owned holiday accommodation.

Secret Destinations (www.secretdestina tions.com) Specialises in holiday villas in Mediterranean destinations.

Secret Places (www.secretplaces.com) Guide and agency for more upmarket accommodation including boutique hotels.

SEVILLE

Barrio de Santa Cruz

TOP CHOICE **Hotel Casa 1800**   LUXURY HOTEL €€€
(Map p50; ☎954 56 18 00; www.hotelcasa1800 sevilla.com; Calle Rodrigo Caro 6; d €145-198; ❄@☎) Straight in at number one as Seville's favourite hotel is this newly revived Santa Cruz jewel where the word *casa* (house) is taken seriously. This really is your home away from home (albeit a posh one!), with charming staff catering for your every need. Highlights include a sweet afternoon-tea buffet, plus a quartet of penthouse garden suites with Giralda views.

It's also one of the only places in the city that doesn't hike its Semana Santa (Holy Week) rates up to ridiculous levels.

Hotel Amadeus   HOTEL €€
(Map p60; ☎954 50 14 43; www.hotelamadeus sevilla.com; Calle Farnesio 6; s/d €85/95; P❄☎) Just when you thought you could never find hotels with pianos in the rooms anymore, along came Hotel Amadeus. It's run by an engaging musical family in the old *judería* (Jewish quarter) and several of the astutely decorated rooms come complete with soundproofed walls and upright pianos, ensuring you don't miss out on your daily practice.

Other perks include in-room classical CDs, wall-mounted violins and a rooftop terrace with a jacuzzi. Composers and Mozart lovers, look no further.

Hotel Puerta de Sevilla   HOTEL €€
(Map p50; ☎954 98 72 70; www.hotelpuertadese villa.com; Calle Puerta de la Carne 2; s/d €66/86; P❄@☎) This superfriendly – and superpositioned – hotel is a great mix of the chintz and the stylish. In the lobby there's an indoor water feature lined with superb Seville tile work. The rooms are all flower-patterned textiles, wrought-iron beds and pastel wallpaper. It also features an unbeatable people-watching roof terrace.

Pensión San Pancracio   PENSIÓN €
(Map p50; ☎954 41 31 04; Plaza de las Cruces 9; d €50, s/d shared bathroom €25/35) An ideal budget option in Santa Cruz, this old, rambling family house has plenty of different room options (all cheap) and a pleasant flower-bedizened patio/lobby. Friendly staff make up for the lack of luxury.

Hotel Palacio Alcázar BOUTIQUE HOTEL €€
(Map p50; ☎954 50 21 90; www.hotelpalacio
alcazar.com; Plaza de Alianza 12; s €65, d €76-108;
❄@⚛) Fresh, white minimalism in the lush
barrio (district) of Santa Cruz, Palacio Alcázar is new on the block with 12 lovely rooms
and an equally lovely roof terrace tapas bar
where you call the waiter by ringing a bell
on your table.

Un Patio en Santa Cruz HOTEL €€
(Map p50; ☎954 53 94 13; www.patiosantacruz
.com; Calle Doncellas 15; s €65-85, d €65-125;
❄⚛) Feeling more like an art gallery than
a hotel, this place has starched white walls
hung with loud works of art, as well as
strange sculptures and preserved plants.
The rooms are immensely comfortable, the
staff are friendly, and there's a cool rooftop
terrace with mosaic Moroccan tables. It's
easily one of the hippest and best-value hotels in town.

El Arenal & Triana

Hotel Simón HOTEL €€
(Map p50; ☎954 22 66 60; www.hotelsimon
sevilla.com; Calle García de Vinuesa 19; s €60-70,
d €95-110; ❄⚛) This typically grand 18th-
century Sevillan house in El Arenal, with
an ornate patio and spotless and comfortable rooms, gleams way above its two-star
rating. Some of the rooms are embellished
with rich *azulejos* tilework.

Hotel Puerta de Triana HOTEL €€
(Map p60; ☎954 21 54 04; www.confortel
hoteles.com; Calle Reyes Católicos 5; s/d €71/85;
❄⚛⚛) The exterior of this hotel is all
about old-fashioned Andalucian style, but
what you see isn't what you get here, as the
interior – with small, minimalist and fully
colour coordinated, technology-crammed
rooms – has been completely revamped to
feel more like a cool, cutting-edge Tokyo
hotel.

El Centro

EME Catedral Hotel LUXURY HOTEL €€€
(Map p50; ☎954 56 00 00; www.emecatedral
hotel.com; Calle de los Alemanes 27; d €187-348;
❄@⚛⚛) Take 14 fine old Sevillan houses
and knock them into one hotel. Bring in
a top designer and Spain's most decorated
chef. Carve out a *hammam,* rooftop pool,
four restaurants, including Santo Restau-

rante, and slick, striking rooms with red
colour accents. Then stick it all nose-to-
nose with the largest Gothic cathedral in
the world.

The result: EME Catedral Hotel, the city's
most talked-about new accommodation,
where ancient Seville has been fused with
something a bit more cutting edge. Does it
work? Cough up the 200-euros-plus a night
and find out.

Hotel Almínar HOTEL €€
(Map p60; ☎954 29 39 13; www.hotelalminar
.com; Calle Álvarez Quintero 52; s/d €95/125; ❄⚛)
Disguised inside a dusky yellow townhouse
is this slick and stylish hotel. The blinding-
white rooms are bright and airy and full of
technology, and the bathrooms have glass
sinks and giant showers. All up it feels a
bit like one of those swish New York apartments you see on glamorous TV shows. It's
currently leading the crop as the most popular hotel in Seville.

Patio al Sur HOTEL €€
(Map p60; ☎954 22 10 35; www.patioalsur.es;
Calle de Fernán Caballero 7; s/d €58/68; ❄⚛)
The Patio al Sur is a pleasing clash of
crazy-coloured paintings, a riot of plant life
and ancient inscriptions carved into the
stone. The rooms are simple but they feel
very exclusive and arty. The bright-pink
bougainvilleas surrounding the entrance
seem to be in competition to try to out-
pink the pink building that contains the
hotel.

Hotel San Francisco HOTEL €€
(Map p60; ☎954 50 15 41; www.sanfranciscoh.com;
Calle Álvarez Quintero 38; s/d €55/68; ⊙Aug;
❄⚛) A well-positioned place on a pedestrianised street, the San Francisco is definitely
one-star territory, with variable service,
dark but clean rooms, and wi-fi in the reception only. Note that the hotel is closed
in August.

Alameda de Hércules, Macarena & Isla de la Cartuja

Hotel Sacristía de Santa Ana
BOUTIQUE HOTEL €€

(Map p62; ☎954 91 57 22; www.hotelsacristia. com; Alameda de Hércules 22; d from €79; ❋🛜) Possibly the best deal in Seville, this utterly delightful hotel is located on the Alameda. It's great for visiting the neighbouring bars and restaurants and the hotel itself is a heavenly place with a small fountain surrounded by bonsai trees greeting you in the central courtyard. Away from the courtyard are old-fashioned rooms with big arty bedheads, circular baths and cascading showers. Service is equally excellent.

Hotel San Gil
HOTEL €€

(Map p62; ☎954 90 68 11; www.hotelsangil.com; Calle Parras 28; r from €88; ❋🛜❋) Shoehorned at the northern end of the Macarena neighbourhood, San Gil's slightly out-of-the-way location is balanced by its proximity to the nightlife of the Alameda de Hércules. The nearby web of bike lanes provides a good excuse to get acquainted with the Sevici bike-sharing scheme. A tiled lobby fronts more modern rooms with large beds and ample space.

Hostal Doña Feli
PENSIÓN €

(Map p62; ☎954 90 10 48; www.hostaldonafeli.com; Calle Jesús del Gran Poder 130; s/d €35/45; ❋) If you're looking for somewhere smart and with real Spanish character close to the nightlife of the Alameda de Hércules, then you can't do much better than this spotless, well-run *pensión* with rooms piled around a plant-crammed courtyard. Some of the rooms have baths as well as showers.

HUELVA & SEVILLA PROVINCES

Huelva

Albergue Juvenil de Huelva
HOSTEL €

(☎959 65 00 10; www.inturjoven.com; Avenida Marchena Colombo 14; adult/child incl breakfast €27/16; ❋@🛜; 🚍6) This is a good, modern youth hostel, with 53 rooms around a bright and pleasant courtyard. There are two to six beds per room, all with bathrooms. Bike hire is available. It's 2km north of the bus station: city bus 6 from the station stops just around the corner from the hostel, on Calle JS Elcano.

Hotel Familia Condes
BUSINESS HOTEL €€

(Map p79; ☎959 28 24 00; www.hotelfamilia conde.com; Alameda Sundheim 14; s/d incl breakfast €50/65; 🅿❋@🛜) True, it's housed in a rather soulless block, but this business-class operation is efficiently run with cordial service, and the fresh-smelling rooms have plenty of space and gleaming orange-toned bathrooms. The convenient location is a short stroll from the cafe-lined Gran Vía.

Hotel Costa de la Luz
HOTEL €

(Map p79; ☎959 25 64 22; www.hotelcosta luzhuelva.com; Calle José María Amo 8 & 10; s/d €31/47; ❋🛜) Located on a quiet pedestrian mall near the main shopping district, this is a perfectly good and central option. Well-maintained, spacious rooms have large bath-tubs, nice tiles and super TVs with hundreds of channels. Skip the free breakfast and head for one of the vintage cafes off the nearby parking lot and plaza. There's a slight discount on Friday and Saturday nights.

Around Huelva

Accommodation in El Rocío during the Romería is booked as much as a year in advance so be sure to make reservations – or be prepared to sleep on the sand.

Hotel Plaza Escribano
HOTEL €

(☎959 37 30 63; www.hotelplazaescribano.com; Plaza Escribano 5, Moguer; s/d/ste €41/56/71; 🅿❋🛜) This hotel is incentive enough to stay in Moguer. Near the centre of the historic core, it sports large rooms splashed in pastels that complement the bright bedspreads. There's a small library for guest use, a sunny courtyard and lots of bright tilework.

Casa Miguel
HOSTAL €

(☎959 44 84 72; www.casamiguel.biz; Parque Dunar, Matalascañas; s/d €40/50; 🅿❋) This fine, simple *hostal* is brilliantly situated at the edge of the Parque Dunar, a swath of protected dunes that's ideal for a morning hike. It also happens to have an outstanding seafood restaurant. Rooms are *hostal* classic, with terracotta tile floors and faux antique furniture. Bonus: it's steps from the bus stop.

Hotel Doñana Blues HOTEL €€
(☎959 44 98 17; www.donanablues.com; Sector I, Parcela 129, Matalascañas; s/d from €92/105; ❄@❋) Not blue but mustard yellow (it's named after a tune the owner composed), this enclosed compound is in the suburban maze of central Matalascañas. Decor is standard rural kitsch but you get your own terrace or balcony amid the petunias, bougainvillea, wisteria and dahlias. There's a cool blue pool out back and a cafe inside.

⟨TOP CHOICE⟩ Hotel Sol y Mar HOTEL €€
(☎959 33 20 99; www.hotelsolymar.org; Playa Central, Isla Cristina; s/d €70/114; P❄❋) Possibly the best-value hotel on this coast. Perfect balconies overlook a broad swath of beach and not much else. Though not a luxury hotel, it has plenty of style – see the stunning brass-tile designs on the staircase – and welcome extras like rain shower fixtures. The on-site restaurant serves meals on a wonderful beachfront terrace. Another plus is the friendly, communicative staff.

Hotel La Malvasia HOTEL €€
(☎959 44 38 70; www.lamalvasiahotel.com; Calle Sanlúcar 38, El Rocío; s/d incl breakfast €75/90; P❄❋) Overlooking the marshes, this idyllic hotel is inside a truly magisterial building. Rooms include rustic tiled floors, vintage photos of the town and iron bedsteads in floral designs. Top-level units make great bird-viewing perches. Bilingual owner Enrique is glad to share his voluminous knowledge of the Parque Nacional de Doñana.

Hotel Toruño HOTEL €€
(☎959 44 23 23; www.toruno.es; Plaza Acebuchal 22, El Rocío; s/d incl breakfast €59/80; P❄❋) This blindingly white villa stands right by the *marismas* (wetlands), where flamingos can be glimpsed running through their morning beauty routine. Inside, the ornithological theme continues with tile murals and prints of the local bird life. Rooms are quite cosy, though unfortunately only a few actually overlook the marsh. The hotel arranges horse buggy tours of the national park.

Pensión Cristina PENSIÓN €
(☎959 44 24 13; Calle El Real 58, El Rocío; s/d €40/60; P❄❋) Just east of the Ermita, the Cristina has reasonably comfortable rooms facing a pleasant patio with lots of plants (though, sadly, no marsh views). There's a popular restaurant (mains €10 to €12) serving paella, venison, seafood and more.

Molino Río Alájar RURAL HOTEL €€
(☎959 50 12 82; www.molinorioalajar.com; Finca Cabezo del Molino, Alájar; d cottage for weekend from €225; P❄❋) Beautifully located beside a stream at the bottom of a hidden valley, the modern stone cottages here are made, successfully, to look like old farmhouses and are surrounded by big gardens with tennis courts and a pool. Kids will love all the farm animals. Two-night minimum. The cottages are about 1km south of Alájar as the crow flies. From Alájar, take the HU-8105 west towards Santa Ana la Real; between Km20 and 19, turn left. Cross the river, take the first right and follow the signs.

Casa García HOTEL €
(☎959 14 31 09; Avenida San Martín 2, Almonaster la Real; s/d €39/54; ❄❋) It may lack historic character and its proximity to the main road is disappointing, but this is Almonaster la Real's only in-town lodging. On the plus side, the balconies afford views toward the *mezquita* (mosque) and allow you to pick oranges off the nearby trees. And the restaurant, with a pleasant covered terrace, serves gourmet versions of local fare.

Posada El Camino HOTEL €
(☎959 50 32 40; www.posadaelcamino.es; Carretera Cortegana-Aracena Km6.8, Almonaster la Real; s/d €36/50; P❄❋) Popular with families, this motel-style lodging stands at the bottom of a hill of cork trees, with trails heading off nearby. Good regional fare (wild mushrooms, ham-stuffed chard) is served in the country-style dining hall with fireplace or on the adjacent terrace. It's half a kilometre east of Almonaster on the Alájar road.

Posada del Castaño COUNTRY HOUSE €
(☎959 46 55 02; www.posadadelcastano.com; Calle José Sánchez Calvo 33, Castaño del Robledo; s/d incl breakfast €40/50) This converted old village house, with its bendy roof beams that smell of the forest, has walkers foremost in mind. The young British owners (experienced travellers and hikers) are full of information and tips, and offer self-guided walking tours and horse-riding holidays. Weather permitting, breakfast is served on the sunny rear terrace overlooking a courtyard and garden.

La Casa Noble BOUTIQUE HOTEL €€€
(Map p88; ☎959 12 77 78; www.lacasanoble.net; Calle Campito 35, Aracena; s/d incl breakfast from €165/185; ❄❋) Merely describing this as a boutique hotel does it a disservice. It's actually a divine palace to luxury, filled with

antiques, over-the-top tilework and beds as thick and bouncy as something out of 'The Princess and the Pea'. The dining room has to be seen to be believed! Access is limited to guests 16 years and older.

Molino del Bombo
BOUTIQUE HOTEL €
(Map p88; ☎959 12 84 78; www.molinodelbombo .com; Calle Ancha 4, Aracena; s/d €36/60; ✻🖤) Though of recent vintage, this lodging at the top of the town has a rustic style that blends in with Aracena's time-worn architecture. Bright rooms feature frescos and exposed stonework and brickwork as design features, and bathrooms are done up as picturesque grottoes. You'll likely want to linger in the salon or courtyard with trickling fountain.

Hospedería Reina de los Ángeles
HOTEL €
(Map p88; ☎959 12 83 67; www.hospederiareina delosangeles.com; Avenida Reina de los Ángeles, Aracena; s/d incl breakfast €24/42; P🖤) On the west edge of town, this uncharacteristically hulking structure has an institutional vibe left over from its former role as a student residence hall. Nonetheless, the 90 utilitarian rooms with TV and phone are spotless and surround a placid courtyard. There's a convivial cafe-bar and, for those inclined, a full-on chapel. Staff members are extremely friendly and helpful.

Hostal Atalaya
HOSTAL €
(☎959 59 28 54; www.hostalrestauranteatalaya.es; Avenida de la Esquila, Minas de Ríotinto; s/d €38/48; P@) This newish lodging, just down from the excellent mining museum, is a fine sleeping option, with attractive mineral-hued tile floors, sky-blue bedspreads and views over the town or woods. The popular restaurant features a sunny terrace and offers a set lunch (€9). The hotel's inverted design has the reception area on the top level, parking below.

Sevilla Province

Casa de Carmona
HISTORIC HOTEL €€€
(☎954 14 41 51; www.casadecarmona.com; Plaza de Lasso 1, Carmona; s/d/tr incl breakfast €120/150/210; P✻🖤) This 16th-century palace was once owned by an aristocratic family and has been creatively renovated by a distant descendant. Rooms are furnished in country-manor style, beds are laid with soft white-lace pillows, and bathrooms have old-fashioned fixtures. A lavish breakfast is served in the loggia beside a tropically festooned pool. Everything exudes a sense of comfort.

Las Navezuelas
COUNTRY HOUSE €€
(☎954 88 47 64; www.lasnavezuelas.com; Cazalla de la Sierra; s/d/ste incl breakfast €54/67/85, 4-person apt from €130; ⊘closed Jan & Feb; P☒) Everybody dreams of living in an old farmhouse in the southern sun and this 16th-century *cortijo* (country property) royally fits the bill. From the dusty, olive tree–lined track to the vines clambering up your balcony, it's an ideal rural retreat. It's signposted 3km south of Cazalla on the Seville road.

Italian owner Luca and family prepare wonderful meals using organically grown ingredients from the garden and their recyclable energy centre is fueled by chips from dead trees. The airy, simply furnished rooms occupy an old farmhouse and outlying cottages. You could stay here for weeks lounging in the pool and exploring the sunburnt hills and never feel less than content.

Posada San Fernando
BOUTIQUE HOTEL €€
(Map p94; ☎954 14 14 08; www.posadasanfer nando.com; Plaza de San Fernando 6, Carmona; s/d/tr €55/65/100; ✻🖤) This excellent-value hotel stands on Carmona's liveliest square. Each room in the 16th-century structure is uniquely appointed, with thoughtfully chosen furniture, fittings and wallpaper, down to the hand-painted tiles in the bathrooms, some with claw-foot tubs. All feature modern art, flat-screen TVs and little balconies overlooking the palm-studded plaza.

Hostal Comercio
HOSTAL €
(Map p94; ☎954 14 00 18; hostalcomercio@hotmail .com; Calle Torre del Oro 56, Carmona; s/d €35/50) Just inside the Puerta de Sevilla, this old-fashioned lodging provides 14 spiffy, simple rooms set around a plant-filled patio with Mudéjar-style arches. The unpretentious decor is matched by the cordial service, cultivated over generations.

Five Gates Hostal
HOSTAL €
(☎626 620717; www.fivegates.es; Calle Carrera 79, Osuna; s/d incl breakfast €35/55; ✻🖤) A simple establishment with a bit of colour and flair, the 14 rooms here are compact but stylishly decorated, with cheery bedspreads, retro lampshades and massage showers. The common facilities are great too: there's a big living room with games and DVDs, a terrific guest kitchen and a roof deck. The Five Gates staff can arrange birding tours.

It's 350m north of Osuna's main square along the main thoroughfare.

Hotel Palacio

Marqués de la Gomera HISTORIC HOTEL €€

(☑954 81 22 23; www.hotelpalaciodelmarques
.es; Calle San Pedro 20, Osuna; r/ste €89/139;
P❄@🛜) Occupying one of Osuna's finest
baroque mansions, this is an exceptionally handsome place to stay, with rooms of
princely proportions and quiet luxury. It
even boasts its own ornate private chapel
located off a sumptuous arched courtyard.

From the main square, head 300m up
Calle Carrera and turn left on Calle San
Pedro. It's a block west, facing the Plaza del
Marqués.

Hotel Palacio

de los Granados HISTORIC HOTEL €€

(☑955 90 53 44; www.palaciogranados.com; Calle
Emilio Castelar 42, Écija; s/d/ste 81/108/165;
P❄🛜🅿) This small palace has been carefully restored by its architect owner, with
lavishly furnished chambers of varying design around a small patio. Rates come tumbling down outside peak season.

From the central Plaza de España, go
south on Avenida Miguel de Cervantes, then
turn left on Calle de Emilio Castelar and go
about 450m east.

La Plazuela RURAL HOTEL €

(☑954 42 14 96; www.casarural-laplazuela.es;
Calle Caridad 2, Cazalla de la Sierra; s/d €45/60;
❄🛜) This handsomely converted old house
stands on a pedestrian lane in Cazalla's
historic core. Each of the nine rooms has
been uniquely renovated with colourful
bedspreads and quaint to modern furnishings. Aimed at weekenders from Seville, it
also features a jacuzzi on the rooftop. The
ground-level cafe is a popular meeting place.

CÁDIZ PROVINCE

Cádiz

Hotel Argantonio HOTEL €€

(Map p106; ☑956 21 16 40; www.hotelargantonio
.com; Calle Argantonio 3; s/d incl breakfast €90/107;
❄@🛜) Welcome to a characterful, small-is-beautiful hotel in Cádiz' old quarter. The
stand-out features here are the hand-painted
doors, beautifully tiled floors that adorn both
bedrooms and bathrooms, and the intricate
Moorish arch in the lobby. The hotel has
three themes: the 1st floor is Mudéjar, the
2nd floor is colonial, and the 3rd floor, a mix.

Hospedería Las Cortes de Cádiz HOTEL €€€

(Map p106; ☑956 21 26 68; www.hotellascortes.com;
Calle San Francisco 9; s/d incl breakfast €107/148;
P❄@🛜) This excellent hotel occupies a remodelled 1850s mansion. The 36 rooms are
each themed around a figure, place or event
associated with the Cortes de Cádiz, and they
sport classical furnishings and modern comforts. The hotel also has a rooftop terrace, a
jacuzzi and small gym.

Hotel Patagonia Sur HOTEL €€

(Map p106; ☑856 17 46 47; www.hotelpatagoniasur
.es; Calle Cobos 11; d €80-130; ❄@🛜) The newest establishment in Cádiz' old town, this
sleek gem opened in 2009 and offers clean-lined modernity just steps from the 18th-century cathedral. Bonuses include its sun-filled attic rooms on the 5th floor with cathedral views and a glass-fronted minimalist
cafet-eria at street level.

Hostal Fantoni HOSTAL €€

(Map p106; ☑956 28 27 04; www.hostalfantoni.es;
Calle Flamenco 5; s/d €45/65; ❄@) The pleasant courtyard makes up for more basic
(sometimes windowless) rooms, but Fantoni
is all about its central location – and you're
never going to spend much time in your
room in Cádiz anyway.

The Sherry Triangle

TOP
CHOICE **Palacio San**

Bartolomé LUXURY HOTEL €€€

(Map p114; ☑956 85 09 46; www.palaciosanbarto
lome.com; Calle San Bartolomé 21, El Puerto de Santa María; r €80-175; ❄@🛜🅿) Every now and
again along comes a new hotel that blows
even the most jaded hotel reviewer out of
the water. Fancy a room with its own mini
swimming pool, sauna, jacuzzi, towelling
bathrobes and deckchairs? It's all yours for
€175 at the deftly designed San Bart, opened
in a former palace in 2010.

If you don't bag the pool room, the others
are equally luxurious. Count on four-poster
beds, giant showers and a shared on-site
gym and spa.

TOP
CHOICE **Hotel Posada**

de Palacio HISTORIC HOTEL €€

(☑956 36 48 40; www.posadadepalacio.com; Calle
Caballeros 11, Sanlúcar de Barrameda; s/d from
€88/109; P❄@🛜) Plant-filled patios, gracious historical charm and 18th-century luxury add up to one of the best places to stay

in this part of Andalucía. There's antique furniture, but it's rarely overdone and never weighs heavily on the surrounds thanks to the high ceilings and abundance of light.

To get there from central Plaza Cabildo, cross Calle Ancha to Plaza San Roque and head up Calle Bretones, which becomes Calle Cuesta de Belén. The hotel is at the top of the hill.

Hotel Duques de Medinaceli
HISTORIC HOTEL €€€

(Map p114; 956 86 07 77; www.duquesdemedina celihotel.net; Plaza de los Jazmines 2, El Puerto de Santa María; s/d €179/218; [P][✳][@][≋]) This is El Puerto's premier address. Converted from an 18th-century mansion (it's the former home of the Terry Irish sherry family), this place overflows with antiques and extravagant architectural signposts to the past, not to mention expansive manicured gardens. The 28 gorgeous rooms are equipped with every comfort, including four-poster beds in some.

Hotel Casa Grande
HOTEL €€

(Map p120; 956 34 50 70; www.casagrande.com .es; Plaza de las Angustias 3, Jerez de la Frontera; r €85-105, ste €115-125; [P][✳][@]) This brilliant hotel occupies a carefully restored 1920s mansion. Rooms are spread over three floors and set around a patio, or beside the roof terrace, which has views of Jerez' roof line. All is overseen by the congenial Monika Schroeder, who is a mine of information about Jerez.

El Baobab Hostel
HOSTEL €

(Map p114; 956 54 21 23; www.casabaobab. es; Calle Pagador 37, El Puerto de Santa María; dm €22.50, s/d incl breakfast €28/55; [P][✳][≋]) Just across from the Plaza de Toros in a converted 19th-century building, this small, six-room hostel is the best budget choice in El Puerto with a homely friendly feel. The interior renovations have been tastefully done and the shared bathrooms are spotless.

Hospedería Duques de Medina Sidonia
HISTORIC HOTEL €€

(956 36 01 61; www.hotelpalaciosanlucar.com; Plaza Condes de Niebla 1, Sanlúcar de Barrameda; d incl breakfast €70-120; [P][✳]) Baronial top-end luxury and town views dominate this aristocratic palace in the upper part of the old town. Old World Spain unfolds before your eyes: the place has 800 years of history and is brimming with swish furnishings and decorations. The hotel is situated next door to the Iglesia de Nuestra Señora de la O.

Hotel Barrameda
HOTEL €

(956 38 58 78; www.hotelbarrameda.com; Calle Ancha 10, Sanlúcar de Barrameda; d incl breakfast €45-65; [✳][≋]) Looking out over the tapas bar action of Plaza Cabildo, this 30-room central hotel has added some stylish modern rooms to its newer wing with no big price hikes. Throw in a ground-floor patio, marble floors, decent art and a roof terrace, and you've nabbed a bargain.

🖊 Hotel Chancilleria
HOTEL €€

(Map p120; 956 30 10 38; www.hotelchanc illeria.com; Calle Chancilleria 21, Jerez de la Frontera; s €55-140, d €80-180; [✳][@][≋]) Opened in January 2008, this stunning renovation of two 17th-century homes is a discreet temple to good taste. There are many highlights: African art, an original 17th-century wall, a lovely garden, stylish and spacious rooms, a delightful rooftop terrace and one of Jerez' best restaurants, Sabores (p122).

Hostal Fenix
HOSTAL €

(Map p120; 956 34 52 91; www.hostalfenix.com; Calle Cazón 7, Jerez de la Frontera; d incl breakfast from €30; [✳][≋]) There's nothing flash about the Fenix which is part of its charm. Simple rooms are well maintained by ultrafriendly owners who'll bring you breakfast on a tray to your room. The impressive art adorning the walls is painted by the *dueña* (owner) and her cousin.

Nuevo Hotel
HOTEL €

(Map p120; 956 33 16 00; www.nuevohotel.com; Calle Caballeros 23, Jerez de la Frontera; s/d incl breakfast €27/42; [✳][@][≋]) One of the most pleasant family-run hotels in Anadalucía, the Nuevo's comfortable rooms are complemented by spectacular *habitación* (room) 208, replete with Islamic-style stuccowork and *azulejos* tiles. You'll wake up thinking you've taken up residence in the Alhambra.

Hotel Bellas Artes
HOTEL €€

(Map p120; 956 34 84 30; www.hotelbellasartes .com; Plaza del Arroyo 45, Jerez de la Frontera; d €69-99; [✳][@][≋]) A top-notch palace conversion, the Bellas Artes overlooks the Cathedral de San Salvador from its main terrace and suites. An exquisite carved stone corner pillar graces the sand-coloured neoclassical exterior. Strong interior colours contrast with white marble floors. Free-standing bath-tubs further contribute to an olde-worlde ambience, though rooms have all the mod cons.

The White Towns

TOP CHOICE Parador Casa
del Corregidor HISTORIC HOTEL €€€

(Map p130; ☑956 70 05 00; www.parador.es; Plaza del Cabildo, Arcos de la Frontera; r from €155; ❋@☎) This rebuilt 16th-century magistrate's residence combines typical *parador* luxury with a magnificent cliffside setting. Eight of the 24 rooms have balconies with sweeping cliff-top views. Otherwise, most of the other rooms look out onto the pretty Plaza del Cabildo.

Hotel Arco de la Villa HOTEL €

(☑956 12 32 30; www.tugasa.com; Paseo Nazarí, Zahara de la Sierra; s/d €36/60; P❋☎) The Arco de la Villa is a sparkling-clean, modern hotel with a spectacular cliffside setting at the foot of the castle in Zahara de la Sierra. All 17 rooms and the on-site restaurant are endowed with jaw-dropping views.

Hotel Sierra y Cal HOTEL €

(☑956 13 03 03; www.tugasa.com; Olvera; s/d €36/60; P❋☎⚌) This simple but effective hotel in the untouristed 'white town' of Olvera delivers a few surprises including small-town-friendly rooms, a swimming pool and a decent cafe/restaurant that pulls in locals, especially on football nights.

Casa Campana GUESTHOUSE €€

(Map p130; ☑956 70 47 87; www.casacampana.com; Calle Nuñez de Prado 4, Arcos de la Frontera; d/apt €50/65; ❋@☎) In the heart of old Arcos, and run by the superfriendly Emma and Jim, who are extremely knowledgable about the local area, Casa Campana has two simple doubles and a massive apartment that's filled with character. The quiet rooftop terrace is a fine place to relax with good views and a real sense of privacy. A cafe and ice-cream window has recently been added downstairs.

La Casa Grande HISTORIC HOTEL €€

(Map p130; ☑956 70 39 30; www.lacasagrande.net; Calle Maldonado 10, Arcos de la Frontera; s €59-84, d €70-110, ste €91-120; ⊙closed 7 Jan-6 Feb; ❋☎) A gorgeous, rambling, cliffside mansion that dates back to 1729, La Casa Grande once belonged to the great flamenco dancer Antonio Ruiz Soler. With each of the seven rooms done in different but always tasteful styles, it feels more like a home-cum–artists' retreat than a hotel. Great breakfasts, a good library, a terrific rooftop terrace, and massage

and yoga round out an outstanding package. Closed early January to early February.

Casa de las Piedras HOTEL €

(☑956 13 20 14; www.casadelaspiedras.net; Calle de las Piedras 32, Grazalema; s/d/apt €42/48/65; ❋☎) Mountain air and a homely feel go together like Ferdinand and Isabella at the Casa de la Piedra, a 16-room rustic-style hotel with a snug downstairs lounge and bags of information on park activities. The blankets in the simple but cozy rooms are made in Grazalema village. The hotel is 200m west of the Plaza de España, the main square in the village of Grazalema.

Costa de la Luz & the Southeast

TOP CHOICE V... BOUTIQUE HOTEL €€€

(☑956 45 17 57; www.hotelv-vejer.com; Calle Rosario 11-13, Vejer de la Frontera; d €139-199; ❋@) V... (that's V for Vejer not V for five, and, yes, the three dots are part of the name) is one of Andalucía's most exquisite creations. It's an old-world boutique hotel where trendy, modern design features (luxurious open-plan bathrooms with huge tubs) mix with antique artefacts (antique pre-Columbus doors). The 12 fine rooms all require double takes, and the communal areas include comfy sofas in interesting nooks and a waterfall – wait for it – on a vista-laden roof terrace next to a bubbling jacuzzi.

TOP CHOICE La Casa
de la Favorita HOTEL, APARTMENT €€

(Map p134; ☑690 180253; www.lacasadelafavorita.com; Plaza de San Hiscio 4, Tarifa; d €60-125; ❋☎) A quick internet search will reveal that La Favorita is a lot of people's favourite. It must be something to do with the creamy furnishings, the surgical indoor cleanliness, the kitchenettes in every room, the small library, the roof terrace, and the dynamic, colourful art.

Hotel La Casa del Califa HOTEL €€

(☑956 44 77 30; www.lacasadelcalifa.com; Plaza de España 16, Vejer de la Frontera; s/d incl breakfast €73/86; ❋@) Rambling over several floors, this gorgeous hotel oozes character. Rooms are peaceful and very comfortable, with Islamic decorative touches. Special 'emir' service (€43) also bags you fresh flowers, chocolates and champagne. Downstairs there's a superb Middle Eastern restaurant, El Jardín del Califa (mains €8-16; 🖉).

Hostal El Mirador   HOSTAL €
(🖉956 45 17 13; www.elmiradordevejer.com; Cañada de San Lázaro 39, Vejer de la Frontera; d from €40; ❋🛜) Mirador means 'lookout' in Spanish and you get one for a very cheap rate at this simple family-run establishment, located handily close to the bus stop, with expansive views over the surrounding countryside. Ask for a room at the front for the best views.

Hostal Mini-Golf   HOTEL €€
(🖉956 43 70 83; www.hostalminigolf.com; Avenida Trafalgar 251, Los Caños de Meca; s €35-60, d €45-70; P❋🛜🏊) If you can get past the misleading name (there's no golf or even minigolf here), this well-positioned hotel, located where the road forks to Cabo Trafalgar, is probably Caños' best midrange crash pad. It has an on-site restaurant and kiteboarding central is just 400m down the road.

Posada La Sacristía   BOUTIQUE HOTEL €€
(Map p134; 🖉956 68 17 59; www.lasacristia.net; Calle San Donato 8, Tarifa; r incl breakfast €115-135; ❋@🛜) Tarifa's most elegant boutique accommodation is in a beautifully renovated 17th-century townhouse. Attention to detail is impeccable with 10 stylish rooms, tasteful colour schemes, large comfortable beds and rooms on several levels around a central courtyard. Best of all, it maintains the same prices year-round. Its restaurant is similarly excellent.

Hotel Convento Tarifa   HOTEL €€
(Map p134; 🖉956 68 33 75; www.hotelconvento tarifa.es; Calle de la Batalla del Salado, Tarifa; d €75-125; ❋🛜) White and bright are the themes in Tarifa's spanking-new offering built around the ruined walls of an ancient convent. Bank on power showers, enormous flat-screen TVs, vases of flowers in rooms, and a garden out back for drinks and sporadic live music. The new on-site restaurant promises great things.

Hostal Africa   HOSTAL €€
(Map p134; 🖉956 68 02 20; www.hostalafrica.com; Calle María Antonia Toledo 12, Tarifa; s/d €50/65, with shared bathroom €35/50; ⊘closed Dec & Jan; 🛜) This revamped 19th-century house close to the Puerta de Jerez is one of the best *hostales* along the Costa de la Luz. The owners are hospitable and the rooms sparkle with bright and attractive colours and plenty of

space. There's a lovely, expansive roof terrace with an exotic cabana and views of Africa.

Posada La Casa Grande   APARTMENT, INN €
(🖉956 64 11 20; www.posadalacasagrande.es; Calle Fuente Nueva 42, Jimena de la Frontera; d shared/private bathroom €30/40, apt €70; ❋@🛜) All you need for a pleasant Jimena stay is available at La Casa Grande, including agreeably rustic rooms, affable staff, plenty of hiking info, a library/painting studio with wrap-around views and, well, that's all you need, right?

Gibraltar

Hotel Bristol   HOTEL €€
(Map p142; 🖉20076800; www.bristolhotel.gi; 10 Cathedral Sq; s/d/tr £68/87/99; P❋🛜🏊) Veterans of bucket-and-spade British seaside holidays can wax nostalgic at the stuck-in-the-'70s Bristol with its creaking floorboards, red patterned carpets and *Hi-de-Hi!* reception staff. Arrivals from other climes will enjoy the attractive walled garden, small swimming pool and prime locations just off Main St.

Rock Hotel   HOTEL €€€
(Map p142; 🖉20073000; www.rockhotelgibraltar .com; 3 Europa Rd; d/ste £160/195; P❋@🛜🏊) As Gibraltan as the famous wild monkeys, the Rock is more grand dame than chic young newcomer these days, though it's not lacking in facilties. Tick off sea-view rooms, gym, pool, welcome drink, bathrobes and that all-important trouser press you'll never use. Mingle among the conference delegates and retired naval captains and rekindle the empire spirit.

MÁLAGA PROVINCE

Málaga

Hostal Larios   HOSTAL €
(Map p152; 🖉952 22 54 90; www.hostallarios .com; Calle Marqués de Larios 9; s/d €50/60, with shared bathroom €41/51; ❋) This small hotel may have only one star but it enjoys a veritable five-star location on Málaga's sophisticated main shopping street. There are just 11 rooms, all washed in dark ochre with original antique double doors, high ceilings, colourful bedcovers and flat-screen TVs. Some rooms have shared bathrooms,

which, while small, are clean and adequately equipped. There are maps and brochures available for guests.

El Hotel del Pintor
HOTEL €€

(Map p152; ☑952 06 09 81; www.hoteldelpintor.com; Calle Álamos 27; r from €75; ✳@🛜) The red, black and white colour scheme of this friendly, small hotel echoes the abstract artwork of *malagueño* (person from Málaga) artist Pepe Bornov, whose paintings are on permanent display throughout the public areas and rooms. Although convenient for most of the city's main sights, the rooms in the front can be noisy, especially on a Saturday night.

El Riad Andaluz
GUESTHOUSE €€

(Map p150; ☑952 21 36 40; www.elriadandaluz.com; Calle Hinestrosa 24; s/d €70/86; ✳@🛜) This French-run guesthouse, in the historic part of town, has eight rooms set around the kind of atmospheric patio that's known as a *riad* in Morocco. The decoration is Moroccan but each room is different, including colourful tiled bathrooms. Breakfast is available.

Room Mate Larios
HOTEL €€

(Map p152; ☑952 22 22 00; www.room-matehotels.com; Calle Marqués de Larios 2; s/d €80/100; ✳@🛜) Located on the central Plaza de la Constitución, this hotel is housed in a 19th-century building that has been elegantly restored. Rooms are luxuriously furnished with king-size beds and carpeting throughout; several rooms have balconies overlooking the sophisticated strut of shops and boutiques along Calle Marqués de Larios. The rooftop terrace bar is separately owned but easily accessible and boasts stunning views of the cathedral.

Feel Málaga Hostel
HOSTEL €

(Map p150; ☑952 22 28 32; www.feelmalagahostel.com; Calle Vendeja 25; shared r per person from €16, d €45, with shared bathroom €35; @🛜) This sparkling new hostel opened in October 2011 and is a welcome addition to Málaga's budget sleeping scene. Located within a suitcase trundle of the city-centre train station, the accommodation is clean and well equipped with a choice of doubles and shared rooms. Bathrooms sport classy mosaic tiles and the top-floor kitchen has all the essentials necessary to whip up a decent meal.

Parador Málaga Gibralfaro
HISTORIC HOTEL €€€

(Map p150; ☑952 22 19 02; www.parador.es; Castillo de Gibralfaro; r €160-171; P✳🛜🏊) With an unbeatable location perched on the pine-forested Gibralfaro, Málaga's stone-built *parador* is a popular choice, although rooms are fairly standard. Most have spectacular views from their terraces, however, and you can dine at the excellent terrace restaurant even if you are not a guest at the hotel.

Costa del Sol

In the resorts of the Costa del Sol, you'll find an abundance of hotels with an international flavour and bilingual staff. These will include some of the more well-known chains. Torremolinos alone sports over 80 accommodation options.

🔝CHOICE Claude
BOUTIQUE HOTEL €€€

(☑952 90 08 40; www.hotelclaudemarbella.com; Calle San Francisco 5, Marbella; s/d €225/250; ✳🛜) Situated in the quieter upper part of town, this sumptuous hotel is housed in a 17th-century mansion of some historical significance – it was the former summer home of Napoleon's third wife. The decor successfully marries contemporary flourishes with the original architecture, while claw-foot tubs and crystal chandeliers add to the classic historical feel. There are superb views from the rooftop terrace.

Hotel Tropicana
HOTEL €€

(☑952 38 66 00; www.hoteltropicana.es; Calle Tropico 6, La Carihuela; s/d €95/120; P✳🛜🏊) A thong's throw from the beach, this pleasant low-rise hotel has attractive, homey rooms with warm colour schemes and dazzling white fabrics, a garden of lofty palms and a decent restaurant. It is also perfectly positioned for strolling along the promenade that links Benalmádena Port with Torremolinos.

Riu Marina Hotel
HOTEL €€

(☑952 96 16 96; www.riu.es; Avenida del Puerto Deportivo, Benalmádena Port; r €100; P✳🛜🏊) This slick, modern hotel has a dazzling white facade and spacious, comfortably furnished rooms with bold fabrics contrasting with arty prints and pastel paintwork. Most terraces have sea views. The breakfast buffet is more generous than most.

Casa El Escudo de Mijas
GUESTHOUSE €€

(☑952 59 11 00; www.el-escudo.com; Calle Trocha de los Pescadores 7, Mijas; s/d €70/80; ✳) A tidy midrange option with pretty colour washes, wrought-iron furnishings and tiled bathrooms. Conveniently located in the centre of the village, it has plenty of bars and restaurants within easy strolling distance.

TRH Mijas
HOTEL €€

(☎952 48 58 00; www.trhhoteles.com; Plaza de la Constitución, Mijas; s/d €102/125; P❋❀❃❄) This tastefully furnished Andalucian-style hotel has excellent facilities including horse riding, tennis and hydromassage. The exquisitely landscaped gardens have views stretching down to the coast. On the downside – you're a long way from the beach...

Hotel Lima
HOTEL €€

(☎952 77 05 00; www.hotellimamarbella.com; Avenida Antonio Belón, Marbella; s/d €60/75; ❋❃) Although this hotel does not have a lot of character, it does provide a good central base near the beach. The rooms have dark wood furnishings and floral bedspreads; several have balconies overlooking the leafy street below.

Hostal El Pilar
HOSTAL €

(☎952 80 00 18; www.hostalelpilar.es; Plaza de las Flores 10, Estepona; s/d €35/50; ❋) This is a charming old-fashioned *hostal* with original tilework and a central courtyard. Wedding photos, plants and antiques contribute to the homey feel. The position is ideal, right on the town's most historic square.

The Interior

Ronda has some of the best atmospheric and well-priced accommodation in Málaga province. In the first half of May and from July to September, you definitely need to book ahead. Antequera hotel prices are refreshingly moderate.

El Molino del Santo
TOP CHOICE   RURAL HOTEL €€

(☎952 16 71 51; www.molinodelsanto.com; Estación de Benaoján, Benaoján, Ronda; s/d incl breakfast €72/110; ☉closed mid-Dec–mid-Feb P❋❃) Located near the well-signposted Banaoján train station, this British-owned hotel has a stunning setting next to a rushing stream; the main building was a former olive mill. The rooms are set amid the pretty gardens and have private terraces or balconies. The restaurant is popular with local residents and serves contemporary international cuisine. Management can provide maps of local walks and the village

of Benaoján is nearby (around 15km southwest of Ronda). There are no TVs.

Hotel Alavera de los Baños
HOTEL €€

(Map p164; ☎952 87 91 43; www.alaveradelosbanos.com; Hoyo San Miguel, Ronda; s/d incl breakfast €70/95; ❋❃) Taking its cue from the Arab baths next door, the Alavera de los Baños continues the Hispano-Islamic theme throughout, with oriental decor and tasty North African–inspired cuisine using predominantly organic foods. Ask for a room on the terrace, as they open out onto a small, lush garden.

Enfrente Arte
HOTEL €€

(Map p164; ☎952 87 90 88; www.enfrentearte.com; Calle Real 40, Ronda; r incl breakfast €80-90; ❋@❃) On an old cobblestoned street, the Belgian-owned Enfrente offers a huge range of facilities and funky modern/oriental decor. It has a bar, pool, sauna, recreation room, flowery patio with black bamboo, film room and fantastic views out to the Sierra de las Nieves. What's more, the room price includes all drinks, to which you help yourself, and a sumptuous buffet breakfast.

Hotel Montelirio
HOTEL €€€

(Map p164; ☎952 87 38 55; www.hotelmontelirio.com; Calle Tenorio 8, Ronda; s/d €100/150; ❋❃) Hugging El Tajo gorge, the Montelirio has magical views. The converted *palacio* (palace) has been sensitively refurbished, with sumptuous suites. The lounge retains its gorgeous Mudéjar ceiling and opens out onto a terrace complete with plunge pool. The restaurant is similarly excellent.

Hotel San Gabriel
HOTEL €€

(Map p164; ☎952 19 03 92; www.hotelsangabriel.com; Calle José M Holgado 19, Ronda; s/d incl breakfast €66/82; ❋❃) This charming hotel is filled with antiques and photographs that offer an insight into Ronda's history – bullfighting, celebrities and all. Ferns hang down the huge mahogany staircase and there is a billiard room and a cosy living room stacked with books. There's also a DVD screening room with 10 velvet-covered seats rescued from Ronda's theatre and autographed photos of several actors, including Bob Hoskins and Isabella Rossellini, who were in town to film *Don Quixote* back in 2000.

Jardín de la Muralla
HISTORIC HOTEL €€

(Map p164; ☎952 87 27 64; www.jardindelamuralla.com; Calle Espiritu Santo 13, Ronda; s/d incl breakfast €80/91; ❋@❃) José María has ensured that his historic family home retains plenty of evocative atmosphere with antiques, chandeliers, ancestral portraits and wonderful claw-foot bath-tubs. The terraced gardens lead to the 15th-century city walls. Pets allowed.

Hotel Coso Viejo HOTEL €€
(☎952 70 50 45; www.hotelcosoviejo.es; Calle Encarnación 9, Antequera; s/d incl breakfast €62/78; P❋) This converted 17th-century neoclassical palace is right in the heart of Antequera, opposite Plaza Coso Viejo and the town museum. The comfortable, simply furnished rooms are set around a handsome patio with a fountain and there's an excellent tapas bar and restaurant.

Parador de Antequera HISTORIC HOTEL €€€
(☎952 84 02 61; www.parador.es; Paseo García del Olmo, Antequera; s/d €120/145; P❋🛜🏊) This *parador* is in a quiet area of parkland north of the bullring and near the bus station. It's comfortably furnished and set in pleasant gardens with wonderful views, especially at sunset.

Hotel Hermanos Macias HOTEL €
(Map p164; ☎952 87 42 38; www.hermanosmacias.com; Calle Pedro Romero 3; s/d €35/48; P❋) Located above a popular restaurant and bar, the rooms here are excellent value; rustically styled and simply furnished, several overlook the bustling pedestrian street.

East of Málaga

Nerja has a huge range of accommodation, but for the summer period rooms in the better hotels tend to be booked at least two months in advance.

El Molino de los Abuelos RURAL HOTEL €
(☎952 50 93 09; www.hotelmolinodelosabuelos.com; Plaza del Generalísimo 2, Comares; d incl breakfast from €55) Situated on the main plaza beside the mirador, this converted olive mill has five double rooms and one apartment, the latter complete with jacuzzi. There are traditional Spanish furnishings throughout, including impressive carved-wood beds, plus magnificent views across the valley. The owners are Dutch and Colombian and organise regular flamenco and salsa nights in the restaurant.

Torrox Townhouse APARTMENT €€
(☎952 53 95 05; www.thetorroxtownhouse.co.uk; Calle Baja 38, Torrox; 4-person apt per week from €275; 🛜) Located in a tangle of backstreets, this fascinating 16th-century building is believed to have been the former home of Luis de Torres, the Jewish convert who sailed with Christopher Columbus, as his translator, on Columbus' first voyage to America. Two self-contained apartments surround a central traditional patio and are spacious, comfortable and homey with antiques, books and Scrabble. Each has its own terrace with superb panoramic views. The owners also run a book scheme on Monday, Wednesday and Friday mornings with books available free of charge and in several languages, in exchange for a charitable donation.

Hotel Carabeo HOTEL €€
(Map p179; ☎952 52 54 44; www.hotelcarabeo.com; Calle Carabeo 34, Nerja; d/ste incl breakfast €85/180; ⊗closed Nov-Mar ❋@🛜🏊) Full of stylish antiques, this small, family-run, seafront hotel is set above manicured terraced gardens. There's also a good restaurant and the pool is on a terrace overlooking the sea. The building is an old school house and located on one of the prettiest pedestrian streets in town, festooned with colourful bougainvillea.

CÓRDOBA PROVINCE

Córdoba

The town centre's many accommodation options traverse the budget spectrum, and even some of the lower-end places offer simple, elegant style and spacious rooms, while others are laden with antiques and history. Booking ahead during the main festivals is essential.

Casa de los Azulejos HOTEL €€
(Map p186; ☎957 47 00 00; www.casadelosazulejos.com; Calle Fernando Colón 5; s/d incl breakfast from €85/107; ❋@🛜) Mexican and Andalucian styles converge in this stylish hotel, where the patio is all banana trees, ferns and potted palms bathed in sunlight. Colonial-style rooms feature tall antique doors, massive beds, walls in lilac and sky blues, and floors adorned with the beautiful old *azulejos* tiles that give the place its name.

Hospedería Alma Andalusí BOUTIQUE HOTEL €€
(Map p186; ☎957 76 08 88; www.almaandalusi.com; Calle Fernández Ruano 5; s/d €45/100; ❋🛜) The builders of this guesthouse in a quiet

section of the Judería (Jewish quarter) have brilliantly converted an ancient structure into a stylish, modern establishment while keeping the rates down. Thoughtfully chosen furnishings, polished wood floors and solid colours make for a comfortable base. Check email and enjoy an espresso in the delightful cobbled courtyard.

Hostal Séneca
HOSTEL €

(Map p186; ☎/fax 957 47 32 34; www.cordoba-hostalseneca.com; Calle Conde y Luque 7; dm/s/d incl breakfast from €15/30/50; ☎) An upgraded version of a long-time backpackers' haunt, the Séneca occupies a rambling house with typical Moorish elements. A small cafe-bar supplies breakfast and drinks on a marvelous pebbled patio that's filled with greenery, and there's a kitchen available for guest use. Rooms vary widely – and some share a bathroom – so have a look around before checking in. Hostal Séneca is closed for one week in August and over Christmas.

Hotel Albucasis
HOTEL €€

(Map p186; ☎/fax 957 47 86 25; Calle Buen Pastor 11; s/d €50/70; P ☀ @) The decor here is austere and restful, with modest rooms decorated primarily in white and pale green. The ivy-festooned patio is a great spot for breakfast. It's just 200m north of the Mezquita in a tranquil section of the Judería.

Hotel Hesperia Córdoba
HOTEL €€

(☎957 42 10 42; www.hesperia.com; Avenida Fray Albino 1; r €89-109; P ☀ ☎ ☀) The chief advantage of staying at this luxury franchise, situated across the river near the Puente Romano, is the brilliant view from some of the rooms. Those in the the hotel's new wing are larger and more modern but lack the views.

Hospedería Añil
HOSTEL €

(Map p186; ☎957 49 15 44; www.sensesandcolours.com; Calle Barroso 4; dm/s/d from €12/30/42; ☎) This vibrant, superfriendly establishment is aimed at the backpacker set, though it cuts no corners in the style and comfort departments. Primary colours and fanciful murals maintain an upbeat vibe. It's a skip and a jump to either the Mezquita or Plaza de las Tendillas, and there's a terrific flamenco club just across the way.

Hotel Córdoba Centro
BUSINESS HOTEL €€

(Map p186; ☎957 49 78 50; www.hotel-cordobacentro.es; Jesús y María 8; s/d €97/108; P ☀ ☎) This business-oriented place may lack charm but the comfort level is what matters here.

Standing on one of the main pedestrian thoroughfares, just south of the Plaza de las Tendillas, it puts you more in touch with the contemporary *cordobés* experience than the tourist trail.

Hotel Lola
HOTEL €€

(Map p186; ☎957 20 03 05; www.hotellola.es; Calle Romero 3; r incl breakfast €129; ☀ @ ☎) Individualism and a quirky style are the prime ingredients here. Each room, named after an Arab princess, is decorated with large antique beds and covetable items that you will wish you could take home with you. What's more, you can eat your breakfast on the roof terrace overlooking the Mezquita's bell tower.

Hotel Mezquita
HOTEL €€

(Map p186; ☎957 47 55 85; www.hotelmezquita.com; Plaza Santa Catalina 1; s/d €42/74; ☀) One of the best deals in town, Hotel Mezquita stands right opposite its namesake monument, amid the bric-a-brac of the tourism zone. The 16th-century mansion has large, elegant rooms with marble floors, tall doors and balconies, some affording views of the Great Mosque.

Parador Nacional Arruzafa
HISTORIC HOTEL €€€

(☎957 27 59 00; www.parador.es; Avenida de la Arruzafa; r €161; P ☀ ☎ ☀) This *parador* is 3km north of the city centre, fabulously situated on the site of Abd ar-Rahman I's summer palace. It's a modern affair set amid lush gardens where Europe's first palm trees were planted.

West of Córdoba

Hostal El Álamo
HOSTAL €

(☎957 64 04 76; www.elalamohostal.com; Carretera Comaracal 141 Km7.5, Hornachuelos; s/d €48/60; ☀ ☎ ☀) This motel-style lodging along the main road of Hornachuelos sports a faux *cortijo* style, with tiled roofs and wagon wheels strewn about. Gregarious owner Enrique can arrange various activities such as walking, horse riding or hunting. The cafe is a popular gathering place and football-viewing venue.

South of Córdoba

Hotel Zuhayra
HOTEL €€

(☎957 69 46 93; www.zercahoteles.com; Calle Mirador 10, Zuheros; s/d €55/70; ☀ ☎) A short distance below Zuheros' castle, this hotel holds a privileged perch with breathtaking views of the countryside from every room. Featuring a good restaurant, it makes an excellent base for exploring the cliffs and caves. The friendly proprietors, the Ábalos brothers (who speak English), offer copious information on walking routes and can set you up with a local guide.

Hotel Caserío de Iznájar
RURAL HOTEL €€

(☑957 50 80 11; www.zercahoteles.com; Calle El Remolino, Iznájar; s/d €53/66; P❋🖝🛇) A unique hotel in an amazing setting, the Caserío (Spanish for farmhouse) stands on a promontory that juts into a reservoir, just below the bridge from the hilltop town of Iznájar. The 20 rooms are cheerily furnished and have balconies to appreciate the splendid setting, but the real attraction is the blissfully secluded pool nearer the reservoir.

Casa Baños de la Villa
BOUTIQUE HOTEL €€

(☑957 54 72 74; www.casabanosdelavilla.com; Calle Real 63, Priego de Córdoba; s/d/ste €71/93/175; ❋🖝🛇) The chief draw of this unique hotel in the heart of the Barrio de la Villa is that it has its very own *hammam*, a Moorish fantasy of baths and arches with optional massage and aromatherapy. Each room is distinctly designed with plenty of homey bric-a-brac, and there's ample space for lounging, including a brilliant roof deck.

Hospedería Zahorí
HOSTAL €

(☑957 54 72 92; www.hotelzahori.es; Calle Real 2, Priego de Córdoba; s/d €38/55; ❋) Standing on a little plaza opposite the Iglesia de la Asunción, this is a highly appealing small hotel. All rooms have been lovingly restored by affable owner Custodio Aguilera, with many original elements kept intact. Equal care is lavished on the little restaurant with fine local fare and a celebratory atmosphere.

JAÉN PROVINCE

Jaén

Parador Castillo de Santa Catalina
HISTORIC HOTEL €€€

(☑953 23 00 00; www.parador.es; Cerro de Santa Catalina; r incl breakfast €142; P❋❋🖝🛇) Next to the castle at the top of the Cerro de Santa Catalina, this hotel has an incomparable setting and theatrically vaulted halls. Rooms are luxuriously dignified with plush furnishings, some with four-poster beds. There is

also an excellent restaurant and a bar with terrace seating to maximise the sweeping panoramic views.

Hotel Xauen
HOTEL €

(Map p208; ☑953 24 07 89; www.hotelxauenjaen.com; Plaza del Deán Mazas; s/d incl breakfast €50/60; P❋🖝) This hotel has a superb position in the centre of the historic quarter. Communal areas are decorated with large photos of colourful local scenes while the rooms are a study in beige but good sized. The rooftop bar and solarium have stunning cathedral views.

East of Jaén

This part of the region is where most visitors spend their time, drawn in by the allure and Renaissance architecture of Baeza and Úbeda, as well as the leafy hills and hiking trails of Cazorla.

Palacio de la Rambla
HISTORIC HOTEL €€

(Map p217; ☑953 75 01 96; www.palaciodelarambla.com; Plaza del Marqués de la Rambla 1, Úbeda; d/ste incl breakfast €96/120; ❋🖝) Úbeda's loveliest converted palace has eight gorgeous rooms in the home of the Marquesa de la Rambla. It's not an overstatement to call this one of Andalucía's most stunning places to stay. The ivy-clad patio is wonderfully romantic and entry is restricted to guests only. Each room is clad in precious antiques and has its own salon so that it feels like you're staying with aristocrat friends rather than in a hotel. Breakfast can be enjoyed in the former bodega or served in your room. This hotel is closed for part of July and August.

Hotel Postigo
HOTEL €

(Map p217; ☑953 75 00 00; www.hotelelpostigo.com; Calle Postigo 5, Úbeda; s/d €40/50; 🖝🛇) This appealing small hotel is charmingly situated on a cobbled backstreet with plenty of easy parking nearby. The rooms are spacious and modern with parquet floors and shiny black furnishings. There is a pleasant outside terrace and a large public sitting room with a log fire in winter.

La Casona del Arco
BOUTIQUE HOTEL €€

(Map p214; ☑953 74 72 08; www.lacasonadelarco.com; Calle Sacramento 3, Baeza; r €70; ❋🖝🛇) This tastefully renovated 16th-century palace in the historic centre has modern comforts, including a spa, and delightful rooms with parquet floors, pale stonework, ochre-washed walls and pitched ceilings (or beams). There's a large garden, plus a small pool. The whole place has a tasteful exclusive feel – at an unexclusive price.

Parador Condestable Dávalos
HISTORIC HOTEL €€€

(Map p217; ☑953 75 03 45; www.parador.es; Plaza Vázquez de Molina, Úbeda; r €160; P✸❄) As *paradores* always get the town's best location and building, Úbeda has surrendered its prime spot, looking out over the wonderful Plaza Vázquez de Molina, and has housed the hotel inside an historic monument: the Palacio del Deán Ortega. It has, of course, been comfortably modernised and is appropriately luxurious. It also has the best restaurant (p219) in town.

Palacio de los Salcedo
HOTEL €

(Map p214; ☑953 74 72 00; www.palaciodelossalcedo.com; Calle San Pablo 8, Baeza; r €60; ✸❄) The only part of this 16th-century palace that is genuine is the facade – the rest is authentic-looking faux, ranging from the intricate carved and painted ceilings to the murals, the columns and the arches. Its '80s-style rag-rolled paintwork looks dated and some of the gilt furniture is pretty kitsch but, overall, the atmosphere is fittingly historic.

Finca Amoratín
RURAL HOTEL €

(☑953 33 31 00; www.almoratin.com; Carretera Torres-Albanchez de Mágina; s/d €45/55; P✸❄❄) If you're seeking utter tranquillity or you are a keen hiker, this rural hotel surrounded by olive groves is worth considering. Rooms surround a central circular patio and are pleasant, if unremarkable, with standard pine furniture and pale yellow paintwork. The views are superb and the management have detailed maps of surrounding walks. There is also a spa. The hotel is located around 28km southwest of Jódar on the A320. See the driving tour on p210 for directions.

Hotel Hacienda La Laguna
RURAL HOTEL €€

(☑953 76 51 42; www.ehlaguna.com/hotel; Puente del Obispo, Baeza; s/d €53/79; P✸@❄❄) If you love olive oil, stay at this enormous hacienda (10 minutes' drive from Baeza), where there's a museum of olive oil – the Museo de la Cultura del Olivo (☑953 76 51 42; Puente del Obispo, Complejo Hacienda la Laguna; adult/child €2.50/€1.50; ◷10:30am-1:30pm & 4:30-7pm Tue-Sun) – and 18 stylishly furnished rooms set around a central patio and

fountain. There is an adjacent horse-riding stable and a spa.

Hotel Maria de Molina
HISTORIC HOTEL €€

(Map p217; ☑953 79 53 56; Plaza del Ayuntamiento, Úbeda; s/d €50/70; ❄✸) This is an attractive hotel housed in a 16th-century *palacio* on the picturesque Plaza del Ayuntamiento. The well-appointed rooms are arranged around a central patio decorated with historic tapestries and leafy plants.

Hotel Rosaleda de Don Pedro
HOTEL €€

(Map p217; ☑953 79 61 11; www.hotelrosaledaubeda.es; Calle Obispo Toral 2, Úbeda; s/d €60/70; P❄✸) King-size beds, dark-wood furniture and walls washed with cool pale blue and yellow create a relaxing ambience at this centrally located hotel. There is a large terrace with a small raised pool, plus a spa with Turkish bath, sauna, jacuzzi and massages on request.

Molino La Farraga
RURAL HOTEL €€

(Map p223; ☑953 72 12 49; www.molinolafarraga.com; Calle Camino de la Hoz, Cazorla; s/d €50/70; ✸) Just up the valley from the Plaza de Santa María is the tranquil old mill of La Farraga, nestling in a bucolic idyll of forested slopes criss-crossed by rivers. Inside, the decor is understated comfort, with lots of dark mahogany colours; outside, the wild, lush garden is heavenly.

Hotel Noguera de la Sierpe
RURAL HOTEL €€

(Map p223; ☑953 71 30 21; www.hotelnoguerade lasierpe.com; Carretera del Tranco Km44.5, Parque Natural de las Sierras de Cazorla, Segura y Las Villas; s/d €60/90, 4-person chalet €120; P✸❄) A paradise for hunting aficionados, run by an equally fanatical proprietor who has decorated the place with stuffed animals and suitably proud photos of his exploits. The hotel is housed in a converted *cortijo* and overlooks a picturesque lake. You can arrange riding sessions at the hotel's stables.

Los Abedules
APARTMENT €

(Map p223; ☑953 12 43 08; www.losabedules -cazorla.com; Los Peralejos, Aptdo. 44, Parque Natural de las Sierras de Cazorla, Segura y Las Villas; 2-/4-person apt €50/70; P❄) Surrounded by olive groves, this is an ideal spot for walkers, with fully furnished, comfortable apartments and a saltwater pool for cooling down after a long day's hike. The apartments are run by an English couple; Diane is a qualified therapist in a number of alternative therapies, including reflexology and Reiki. Pets welcome.

Hotel Guadalquivir HOTEL €
(Map p223; ☑953 72 02 68; www.hguadalquivir.com; Calle Nueva 6, Cazorla; s/d €40/50; ✳) Cheap and cheerful, the Guadalquivir has comfortable, blue-hued rooms with pine furniture, TV and heating, though no memorable views. The singles can be a bit cramped, but the hotel is in a central location and equals good value for money.

GRANADA PROVINCE

Granada

Central Granada – the level ground from the Realejo across to Plaza de la Trinidad – is very compact, so hotel location doesn't matter much. The prettiest lodgings are the Albayzín courtyard houses, though these call for some hill-walking, and many aren't accessible by taxi. The handful of hotels up by the Alhambra are scenic but a hassle for sightseeing further afield. Rates are highest in spring and autumn, spiking over Easter. Parking, where offered, costs €15 to €20 per day, and is usually at a municipal parking lot, not on the hotel grounds.

TOP CHOICE Apartamentos Turisticos San Matías APARTMENT €€
(Map p238; ☑958 21 50 29; www.apartamentossanmatias.com; Calle San Matías 17; 2-person apt €70; ✳☎) Located in the buzzy Realejo quarter, these apartments offer well-priced, spacious accommodation. The sitting rooms are furnished with homey prints, comfy sofas and pine furniture and the kitchens are similarly well equipped and include washing machines – a bonus for families. Cots are available upon request.

Hotel Posada del Toro BOUTIQUE HOTEL €€
(Map p238; ☑958 22 73 33; www.posadadeltoro.com; Calle de Elvira 25; d/ste €70/108; ✳☎) A lovely small hotel with rooms set around a tranquil central patio. Walls are washed in a delectable combination of pale pistachio, peach and cream, and the rooms are similarly enticing with parquet floors, stucco detailing Alhambra-style, rustic-style furniture and small but perfectly equipped bathrooms with double sinks and hydromassage

showers. The restaurant dishes up Spanish dishes like Galician octopus, as well as pastas and pizza.

Hotel Palacio de Los Navas HISTORIC HOTEL €€
(Map p238; ☑958 21 57 60; www.palaciodelosnavas.com; Calle Navas 1; d/ste €86/135; ✳☎) Sumptuous 16th-century building with individually furnished rooms with lots of cool creams and whites, original columns and doors, terracotta tiled floors and desks. The rooms surround a traditional columned patio. Convenient for nightlife and tapas bars, and around a 10-minutes walk from the cathedral.

Hostal Venecia HOSTAL €
(Map p238; ☑958 22 39 87; www.veneciahostal.es; Cuesta de Gomérez 2; d €42, with shared bathroom €34; ☎) The house-proud hosts here are as sweet as the flower- and-picture-filled turquoise corridors. The nine rooms overflow with character, and each is different: some have private bathrooms, while others share facilities, and many have small balconies. There's ample heat as well as piles of blankets in the winter, and ceiling fans keep rooms cool in the summer months.

Hotel Fontecruz HOTEL €€
(Map p238; ☑958 21 78 10; www.fontecruz.com; Gran Vía de Colón 20; d/ste €120/370; ✳@☎) The Fontecruz features large rooms that mix sleek and sumptuous, with black-and-white carpeting, dark-wood antique-look writing desks and lovely beds. All have at least one shallow balcony. Windows are double-glazed, but rooms overlooking the side street instead of the Gran Vía are noticeably quieter. A rooftop bar yields great views.

Hotel Los Tilos HOTEL €€
(Map p238; ☑958 26 67 12; www.hotellostilos.com; Plaza Bib-Rambla 4; s/d €55/80; ✳) The spacious rooms, clean and renovated in 2008, overlook Plaza Bib-Rambla, and there are double-glazed windows to shut out the hubbub at night. There's a small but panoramic rooftop terrace if you don't get your own Alhambra view from your room.

Hotel Puerta de las Granadas HOTEL €€
(Map p238; ☑958 21 62 30; www.hotelpuertadelasgranadas.com; Cuesta de Gomérez 14; r €130; ✳@☎) This small hotel has a prime location just off the Plaza Nueva and halfway up the hill to the Alhambra. The red and dark-wood rooms overlook either a back garden

(quiet) or the street (a little larger). Two top-floor rooms have grand views. Extra perks include a lift – rare in a hotel this size – and extremely helpful staff.

Santa Isabel La Real   BOUTIQUE HOTEL €€

(Map p236; ☑958 29 46 58; www.hotelsantaisabella
real.com; Calle de Santa Isabel La Real 19; r €105;
❄@⊛) Ideally situated between the Plaza San Miguel Bajo and Mirador San Nicolas (Plaza de San Nicolás), this gorgeous 16th-century building has been tastefully restored into an exquisite small hotel. Many of the original architectural features are still here, including the marble columns. Rooms are set around a central patio and are individually decorated with lacy bedspreads, embroidered pictures and hand-woven rugs. If you can, go for room 11 with its stunning Alhambra views.

Casa Morisca Hotel   HISTORIC HOTEL €€€

(Map p236; ☑958 22 11 00; www.hotelcasamorisca
.com; Cuesta de la Victoria 9; d €118-48; ❄@⊛) This late-15th-century mansion perfectly captures the spirit of the Albayzín. A heavy wooden door shuts out city noise, and rooms are soothing, with lofty ceilings, fluffy white beds and flat-weave rugs over brick floors. The least expensive ones look only onto the central patio with its fountain – cosily authentic, but potentially claustrophobic for some. The hotel is accessible by taxi.

AC Palacio de Santa Paula   LUXURY HOTEL €€€

(Map p236; ☑902 29 22 93; www.ac-hotels.com; Gran Vía de Colón; r from €170; ℗❄@⊛) The most luxurious hotel in this area, between the centre and the Albayzín, this five-star operation occupies a former 16th-century convent, some 14th-century houses with patios and wooden balconies, and a 19th-century aristocratic house, all with a contemporary overlay. The rooms sport every top-end luxury you might desire, and the hotel also has a fitness centre, sauna and Turkish bath.

Hotel Zaguán del Darro   HISTORIC HOTEL €€

(Map p238; ☑958 21 57 30; www.hotelzaguan.com; Carrera del Darro 23; s/d €55/70; ❄@) This place offers excellent value for the Albayzín. The 16th-century house has been tastefully restored, with sparing use of antiques. Its 13 rooms are all different; some look out over the Río Darro. There's a good bar-restaurant below, and the main street in front means easy taxi access – but also a bit of evening noise.

Hostal Arteaga   HOSTAL €

(Map p236; ☑958 20 88 41; www.hostalarteaga
.com; Calle Arteaga 3; s/d €40/49; ❄@⊛) A charming bargain option just off the Gran Vía de Colón, inching into the Albayzín. The rooms are spruced up with lavender walls, striped bedspreads and chequered blue bathroom tiles for a tidy, modern feel. Stay three nights and you get a free session, including the baths, sauna and jacuzzi, at the adjacent Baños de Elvira spa.

Hotel Macía Real de la Alhambra   HOTEL €€

(☑958 21 66 93; www.maciahoteles.com; Mirador del Genil 2; r €100; ℗❄@⊛⊛) Great if you're dropping into Granada just to see the Alhambra, this comfortable hotel on the edge of the city is an easy 10-minute drive to the monument, and city bus 33 goes right by too. Rooms are chic, in shades of grey, and there are steam baths (extra charge) downstairs.

Hostal La Ninfa   HOSTAL €

(Map p236; ☑958 22 79 85; www.hostallaninfa
.net; Plaza Campo Príncipe; s/d €45/50; ❄⊛) The show-stopping facade of this hotel, with its walls covered with ceramic plaques, sets the scene for the interior, which is artistically cluttered and charming. The rooms are brightly decorated (think turquoise painted beams) with tiled bedheads and pretty tiled bathrooms. It is a 30-minute uphill trek to the Alhambra from here or you can hop on the number 30 bus, which stops virtually outside the door.

Carmen de la Alcubilla   HISTORIC HOTEL €€

(Map p232; ☑958 21 55 51; www.alcubilladelcaracol
.com; Calle del Aire Alta 12; s/d €100/120; ❄@⊛) This exquisitely decorated place is located on the slopes of the Alhambra. Rooms are washed in pale pastel colours contrasting with cool cream and antiques. There are fabulous views and a pretty terraced garden. Ask for the room in the tower for a truly heady experience.

Parador de Granada   HISTORIC HOTEL €€€

(Map p232; ☑958 22 14 40; www.parador.es; Calle Real de la Alhambra; r €315; ℗❄@⊛) This is the most luxurious and highly priced of Spain's *paradores*. Head here if you are looking for romance and history – it's in a converted 15th-century convent located in the Alhambra grounds. Be sure to book well ahead; it is a popular choice.

El Altiplano

Hotel Comercio
HOTEL €€

(☎958 66 05 00; www.hotelcomercio.com; Calle Mira de Amezcua, Guadix; s/d €50/65; ❋🛜) The elegant ochre-washed facade with wrought-iron balconies reflects the superb restoration of this early 20th-century hotel. The public spaces are similarly tastefully furnished with traditional tilework, exposed brickwork and plenty of leafy plants. Rooms are spacious and comfortable and there is a spa with Turkish bath, solarium, jacuzzi, sauna and massage parlour for ultimate self-pampering. In short – a bargain.

Sierra Nevada & Las Alpujarras

It's advisable to book ahead during Semana Santa, from July to September, and in spring and autumn for hotels that cater to walkers.

Refugio Poqueira
REFUGE €

(☎958 34 33 49; Mulhacén, Sierra Nevada; per person €15) This modern, 87-bunk refuge has a restaurant (breakfast €5, dinner €14) and hot showers, a just reward after a day of trekking the Sierra Nevada. You get here by walking 4km from the Mirador de Trevélez (about one hour), or following the Río Mulhacén for 2.3km down from the road beneath the western side of Mulhacén, then veering 750m southeast along a path to the refuge. Phone ahead, if possible. The refuge is open year-round.

Casa Rural Jazmín
GUESTHOUSE €

(☎958 78 47 95; www.casaruraljazmin.com; Calle Ladera de la Ermita, Órgiva; r €48-65; ❋🗷) A sanctuary in the upper town, Casa Jazmín is a French-run house with four rooms, each decorated in a different style (Asian and Alpujarran rooms are smaller; French and African, larger). There's a communal terrace and a pool set in a dense garden. On a cul-de-sac, it has space for parking, once you make it up the winding street.

Sierra y Mar
RURAL HOTEL €

(☎958 76 61 71; www.sierraymar.com; Calle Albaicín, Ferreirola; s/d incl breakfast €42/62; ⊙closed Jan & Feb 🅿🛜) This complex of several small houses, run by a Danish-Italian couple, has been seeing guests since 1985. The rustic rooms have writing desks positioned just so for staring idly out the window at the mountain view – though you could also do this from your terrace, or the wild, grassy garden. Stays of more than one night are preferred.

Hotel La Fragua
HOTEL €

(☎958 85 86 26; www.hotellafragua.com; Calle San Antonio 4, Treveléz; s/d €33/45; ⊙closed early Jan-early Feb) The rooms at La Fragua are typical mountain-village style: pine-furnished, simple and clean. Some have balconies, and there's a large rooftop deck. Early-rising walking groups can be noisy, though. The hotel is at the top of town, a 200m walk (signposted) from the highest plaza. A second more modern property nearby (doubles for €55) has a pool and great views.

Hotel Los Bérchules
RURAL HOTEL €

(☎958 85 25 30; www.hotelberchules.com; Carretera de Granada 20, Bérchules; s/d €47/52; 🅿🛜🗷) By the main road at the bottom of Bérchules, this comfortable hotel has good rooms (all with bath-tubs); singles are a bit small, but doubles all have balconies. The helpful English-speaking hosts can help set up all manner of activities, and there's a large pool, a good restaurant and a cosy lounge stocked with books on Spain. The owners regularly organise painting and walking holidays.

Alquería de Morayma
RURAL HOTEL €

(☎958 34 32 21; www.alqueriamorayma.com; Carretera A348, Km50, Cádiar; d €62, 4-person apt €95; 🅿🗷) One of the better places to stay in Las Alpujarras, with a bit of a New Age bent but still distinctly Spanish. It's an old farmstead lovingly renovated and expanded to provide 20 comfortable rooms and apartments. The restaurant serves very good food with locally made ingredients, and there's fine walking along the nearby Río Guadalfeo.

The hotel is located 3km outside the village on the A348 due south. If you are travelling light you can walk here by following the banks of the river downstream for around 2km. Both the routes are well signposted.

Las Chimeneas
RURAL HOTEL €€

(☎958 76 03 52; www.alpujarra-tours.com; Calle Amargura 6, Mairena; d incl breakfast €85; ❋@🗷) An institution among walkers, this village house is run by a British couple who are extremely well informed about local history, ecology and tradition. They can arrange hikes, painting excursions, cooking classes, children's activities and more. They also have fine taste: the expansive rooms have an antique yet uncluttered style, and the restaurant uses organic produce from the owners' *finca* (farm).

Estrella de las Nieves RURAL HOTEL €€
(📞958 76 39 81; www.estrelladelasnieves.com; Calle Huerto 21, Pampaneira; s/d €60/70; P🗗🛰) Opened in 2010, this dazzling white complex just above the town has airy light and modern rooms with terraces overlooking the rooftops and mountains, plus pleasant gardens and the definite perks of a car park and pool. The hotel is located just outside the village on the A-4132, towards Lanjarón.

Costa Tropical

Rates spike about €10 higher during August.

Hostal San Juan HOSTAL €
(📞958 61 17 29; www.hostalsanjuan.com; Calle Jardines 1, Salobreña; s/d €36/45, 3-person apt €54; ⊙closed Nov-Feb; 🌣@🛰) A lovely tiled and plant-filled patio-lounge welcomes you at this long-established *hostal* on a quiet street about 400m southwest of the tourist office. The rooms have wrought-iron bedsteads and red-and-white bathroom tiling, and many can accommodate families, as can two apartments with kitchenettes. A large rooftop terrace takes in the sunset.

Hotel Al Najarra HOTEL €
(📞958 63 08 73; www.hotelnajarra.com; Calle Guadix 12, Almuñécar; d/tr €58/81; 🌣@🛰🛰) This modern hotel isn't bursting with character but it represents excellent value in Almuñécar, where many properties are a bit tired. The large rooms all open onto terraces or balconies overlooking a back garden and pool (filled only in the summer). It's a couple of blocks walk from the beach.

ALMERÍA PROVINCE

Almería

Plaza Vieja Alejandro HOTEL €€
(Map p270; 📞950 28 20 96; www.plazaviejahl.com; Plaza de la Constitución 5; r €80-110; P🌣🛰) This is, arguably, the most stylish accommodation in the city. It's perfectly situated on the beautiful and tranquil Plaza de la Constitución, yet a few steps away from some of the city's top tapas bars. Part of the stunning Hammam Aire de Almería, the rooms are

spacious and modern with high ceilings, lots of glass and shiny wood, soft natural colours and vast photo-friezes of local sights like the Cabo de Gato.

Hotel Nuevo Torreluz HOTEL €
(Map p270; 📞950 23 43 99; www.torreluz.es; Plaza de las Flores 10; r €54; P🌣🛰) Opened in 2012, this reformed four-star hotel enjoys a superb position on a small square in the heart of the historic centre. Rooms are on the small size but well equipped and comfortable with warm colour schemes, parquet floors, minibars, safes, hair dryers and high-pressure showers. A statue of John Lennon in the centre of the plaza is apparently in recognition of the several months he lived in Almería back in the '60s and was said to have loved the place. Parking costs €11 a day.

Hotel Catedral HOTEL €€
(Map p270; 📞950 27 81 78; www.hotelcatedral.net; Plaza de la Catedral 8; r €70; @🛰) Cozied up to the Almería Cathedral and built with the same warm honey-coloured stone, the hotel building dates from 1850 and has been sensitively restored. Rooms are large with luxury touches and the sun terrace has heady cathedral views.

North of Almería

Cortijo El Saltador RURAL HOTEL €
(📞676 437128; www.elsaltador.com; Rambla Honda, Lucainena de las Torres; s/d €40/60; P) Beautiful and remote, this farmhouse enjoys almost complete silence except for the chatter of birds. The rooms are whitewashed and spare (no TVs), and guests have the run of the main house with a huge kitchen. Excellent dinners are an option, as are yoga classes, massages and other activities. Walking trails head off in all directions – including to an armchair on a mountain top, the only spot nearby that has mobile-phone reception.

To reach here, follow signs to Lucainena de las Torres (12km southwest of Sorbas). The hotel is located around a kilometre southwest of the centre of town.

Hostal Montelés HOSTAL €
(📞950 36 46 35; Calle Calvo Sotelo 4, Sorbas; r €60; 🌣@) A great base for exploring the terrain around Sorbas, this old house located in the centre of town has beautiful tiled floors, high ceilings and grand staircases. The 12 rooms are furnished in a simple, modern style, and

guests have access to a kitchen, lounge and back garden with a whirlpool tub. A friendly cat makes the place extra homey.

Las Alpujarras de Almería

Hotel Almirez
RURAL HOTEL €

(☑950 51 35 14; www.hotelalmirez.es; Laujar de Andarax; s/d €36/47; P ❋ @ 🛜) Where else does a budget room come with a free bottle of wine but in the Alpujarras? The vino is best enjoyed on your terrace, taking in the mountain view. Rooms have gleaming tile floors and groovy striped bedspreads, and the restaurant downstairs serves tasty food. It's on Carretera Laujar-Orgiva, the road leading into the west edge of town.

Costa de Almería

MiKasa
HOTEL €€

(☑950 13 80 73; www.mikasasuites.com; Carretera Carboneras, Agua Amarga; r incl breakfast €55-85; ❋ 🛜 🏊) Want to stay in a villa? An apartment? Or a regular (albeit luxurious) hotel? MiKasa has all options covered. The hotel is the year-round option, located in the centre of town, and a delight with stunning pink Italian-style marble (from Galicia) and lovely rooms – all are different: one has a large circular bath, another a view of the sea, another a large private terrace… There are two pools and an excellent spa, as well as a restaurant, although most guests slink off to the Michelin-starred Restaurante La Villa next door.

Hostal Aloha
HOSTAL €

(☑950 38 04 61; www.hostalaloha.com; Calle Cala Higuera, San José; r €55; ❋ 🏊) White walls, firm beds and gleaming bathrooms make this an appealing budget hotel to start with. Then throw in the enormous pool on the back terrace, and it's one of the best deals in San José. It's a few blocks back from the beach; to reach it, turn left off the main street at the tourist office.

El Jardín de los Sueños
RURAL HOTEL €€

(☑669 184118, 950 38 98 43; www.eljardindelos suenos.es; Calle de los Riscos de las Águilas, Rodalquilar; d/ste incl breakfast €96/116; P ❋ 🏊) Just off the highway opposite Rodalquilar, this expanded old farmhouse is surrounded by lush gardens and fruit trees – some of which contribute to the tasty breakfasts. Bright colours, abstract art and the occa-

sional chandelier distinguish the rooms. Suites with terraces look out onto the desert valley and tubs with skylights are worth the extra euros. Pets welcome.

Atalaya Hotel
HOTEL €€

(☑950 38 00 85; www.atalayahotel.net; Avenida de San José, San José; r incl breakfast €75; ❋ 🛜) This central hotel, situated over a bustling restaurant and bar, has rooms set around small terraces. At the time of research, the owners were in the throes of giving the rooms a Moroccan-style update with warm burgundy-painted walls, low beds and sparkling slate grey bathrooms.

MC San Jose
HOTEL €€

(☑950 61 11 11; www.hotelesmcsanjose.com; Carretera El Faro, San José; d incl breakfast €139; ❋ @ 🛜 🏊) The MC is the best of both hotel worlds: it has a chic boutique design with just 32 rooms and plenty of stylish details, but it also has the kind of hospitality that only comes from a local family. Centrally located and open year-round with a reasonable Chinese restaurant on the ground floor.

El Mirador del Castillo
HOSTAL €€

(Map p283; ☑950 47 30 22; www.elcastillomojacar .com; El Mirador del Castillo, Mojácar; d €80, with shared bathroom €60; ❋ 🛜 🏊) Up at the tip-top of Mojácar's hill, this delightful small hotel has colourful rooms displaying paintings from local artists, plus beamed ceilings and rustic-style dark wood furniture. Private terraces lead onto the gardens and pool. It also organises regular culinary courses.

Hostal Arco Plaza
HOSTAL €

(Map p283; ☑950 47 27 77; www.hostalarcoplaza .es; Calle Aire Bajo 1, Mojácar; s/d €40/60; ❋ 🛜) In the centre of the village, this *hostal* has spacious bathrooms, and sky-blue rooms with wrought-iron beds, white sheets and great views of Plaza Nueva and the valley below. The management is friendly and efficient. Some rooms open onto the plaza, which can be noisy in the evening but quietens down after midnight.

Hotel Simon
HOTEL €

(Map p283; ☑950 47 87 69; www.hotelsimon.es; Calle La Fuente 28, Mojácar; s/d incl breakfast €35/45; ❋) The only downside of this spick-and-span small hotel is the 10-minute uphill slog to the village centre. Otherwise it is a good deal with tidy small rooms with pine furniture, small terraces, and tubs as well as showers.

Hotel Río Abajo   HOTEL €

(☎950 47 89 28; www.rioabajomojacar.com; Calle Río Abajo, Mojácar; d €60; 🅿🛜🏖) Nestled amid the trees in a residential cul-de-sac on the edge of the Lagunas del Río Aguas, the Rio Abajo has to be the most tranquil hotel on Mojácar Playa. Nineteen blue-and-white cottages are dotted among the lush gardens, with direct access to the broad, sandy beach. It's a fantastic place for the kids.

Los Vélez

Hotel Velad Al-Abyadh   HOTEL €€

(☎950 41 51 09; www.hotelvelad.com; Calle Balsa Parra 28, Vélez Blanco; s/d incl breakfast €45/70; 🅿❄) A mock hunting lodge with almost medieval rooms and incredible views over the valley, located at the entrance to Vélez Blanco from Vélez Rubio. Rustic artefacts and exposed brickwork give the place an intimate atmosphere. Also has a good restaurant.

Understand Andalucía

population per sq km

ANDALUCÍA   SPAIN   UK

♦ ≈ 95 people

Andalucía Today

Boom

In 2007 Andalucía had never had it so good. A decade-long boom in construction activity and property prices, massive EU subsidies for agriculture, and steady growth in tourism had seen unemployment drop from 35% in 1994 to 13% by 2007 – the lowest in memory for this region, which has historically been the poorest sister in Spain's economy. Instead of Andalucians leaving Andalucía in search of work – which has often been the case in the past – hundreds of thousands of migrants from Africa, Eastern Europe and South America were finding jobs in Andalucía.

The Andalucía of the early 21st century was a different world from the old Andalucía of just one generation earlier. It had fast highways, shiny shopping malls, internet, mobile phones, ATMs, eye-catching modern architecture and dance-till-dawn nightclubs. More Andalucians went to university, fewer went to church. Women had fewer children and more jobs. Gay marriages were now legal, divorce was easier, and religion had been removed from compulsory school curricula.

Bust

In 2008 the property bubble burst, credit was crunched, global recession struck, tourism slumped and building work ground to a halt. With its over-dependence on construction and tourism and a shortage of technologically advanced industry, Andalucía was hit particularly hard. By 2012 unemployment was back up to 33%, the highest in Spain. Among 16- to 24-year-olds, a shocking 58% were jobless. People started to talk of a 'lost generation', and once again Andalucians started leaving home – to less afflicted parts of Spain, to Germany, to Britain – in search of jobs.

No quick or easy way back from this crisis was in sight. The new conservative Partido Popular (PP) national government, elected in November

» Population: 8.4 million (Spain: 47.2 million)

» Area: 87,268 sq km

» Unemployment (2011): 31%

» Highest peak: Mulhacén (3479m)

» Olive trees: 80 million

» Iberian lynx population: 200–300

Top Reads

» **South from Granada** (Gerald Brenan) Village life in Las Alpujarras in the 1920s.

» **The Ornament of the World** (Maria Rosa Menocal) Examines the tolerance and sophistication of Moorish Andalucía.

» **Driving Over Lemon**s (Chris Stewart) An anecdotal bestseller about life on a small Alpujarras farm.

» **Andalus** (Jason Webster) Webster's adventurous travels uncover the modern legacy of the Moorish era.

Best Flamenco

» **Gold** Selection from great guitarist Paco de Lucía.

» **Lágrimas Negras** Flamenco with Cuban rhythms, by Diego El Cigala and Bebo Valdés.

» **Camarón 1969–1992** Passionate songs from legend El Camarón de la Isla.

belief systems
(% of population)

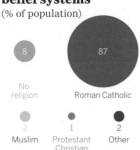

No religion — 8
Roman Catholic — 87
Muslim — 2
Protestant Christian — 1
Other — 2

if Andalucía were 100 people

92 would be Spanish
2 would be Sth American
1 would be British
1 would be Moroccan
1 would be Romanian
3 would be Other

2011, after seven years' rule by the left-of-centre Partido Socialista Obrero Español (PSOE), was slashing public spending drastically in an effort to rein in Spain's budget deficit, and even basic services like health and education were feeling the squeeze.

A Little Good News

At least tourism, after a nasty blip in 2009 and 2010, has showed signs of recovery. In 2011, 8.5 million foreign tourists arrived, up from just over 8 million the two previous years (though still well down on the 2008 record of 9.8 million). From a visitor's point of view, Andalucians are keener than ever to keep their customers happy, and Andalucía still has all the attractions it always had. Indeed, things have got steadily better over the past decade. Accommodation is more comfortable and more stylish, restaurants are more varied and creative, and workers in tourism and information services are increasingly professional. Monuments, museums and historic quarters everywhere have been spruced up. And Andalucía's main airport, at Málaga, has undergone massive expansion and improvement to cope with ever-growing traffic.

Not least, Andalucía's spectacular natural riches are being effectively cared for in 90 national and regional parks and other protected areas, amounting to one-fifth of all Andalucian territory, and have been made infinitely more accessible by excellent information centres, marked walking trails and improved services. Reforestation programs are improving landscapes, and even the iconic Iberian lynx, the world's most endangered feline, shows signs of a comeback following a successful in-captivity breeding program. The number of wild lynxes in Spain, nearly all of them in Andalucía, was estimated at between 200 and 300 in 2011, up from as low as 100 a decade earlier.

The Alhambra in Granada is Spain's most visited monument, with a record 2.3 million visitors clicking through its turnstiles in 2011. May was the busiest month (250,000 visitors), and January the quietest (100,000).

Andalucian Habits

» **Fiestas** There are thousands of them, from week-long summer fairs to one-day religious festivals. And city bar zones become weekend fiestas of their own.

» **Siestas** Most shops and offices close from 2pm to 4 or 5pm, and most Andalucians eat their main meal then. Do they sleep? Depends what they did last night.

Romantic Classics

» **Tales of the Alhambra** Washington Irving's 1832 book established Granada's romantic reputation.

» **Carmen** Bizet's 1874 opera gave Andalucian women an image of fire, guile and flashing beauty.

History

Andalucía's crossroads location at a meeting point of continents and oceans has always been pivotal to its destiny. Four millennia ago Andalucía was the gateway through which the Copper and Bronze Ages entered the Iberian Peninsula. Between two and three millennia ago its resources attracted Phoenician and Greek traders and then the Carthaginian and Roman empires. Andalucía enjoyed several centuries as one of the wealthiest areas of the Roman empire.

In AD 711 Muslim forces invaded from North Africa and rapidly overran the Iberian Peninsula. The Muslims (also known as Moors) were the dominant power on the peninsula for the next four centuries, and a potent force for four centuries after that. Andalucía was always their heartland, with power and culture centred first on Córdoba (756–1031), then Seville (c 1040–1248) and lastly Granada (1249–1492). Between wars and rebellions, Moorish Spain and especially Andalucía developed the most cultured society of medieval Europe.

Northern Spanish Christian kingdoms slowly regained territory in the eight-century Reconquista (Christian reconquest), and the last Moorish kingdom, Granada, fell to the Reyes Católicos (Catholic Monarchs), Isabel of Castilla and Fernando of Aragón, in 1492. The same year, Christopher Columbus found several Caribbean islands on a voyage financed by the Catholic Monarchs, leading to the Spanish conquest of large parts of the Americas and a flood of silver from the new empire. The Andalucian city of Seville boomed as the hub of the American trade. But silver shipments shrank drastically in the 17th century, initiating three centuries of decline in which Andalucía and most of the rest of Spain sank into stagnation and widespread poverty.

The yawning wealth gap between the few rich and the many poor fomented social unrest and political radicalisation in the late 19th and early 20th centuries, eventually leading to the Spanish Civil War (1936–39), in which the right-wing Nationalists, led by General Francisco Franco,

TIMELINE	18,000–14,000 BC	c 1000–800 BC	206 BC
	Palaeolithic (Old Stone Age) hunter-gatherers paint quarry such as aurochs, stags, horses and fish in the Cueva de la Pileta (near Ronda), Cueva de Ardales and Cueva de Nerja.	Olives, grapevines and donkeys arrive in Andalucía with Phoenician traders, who establish coastal colonies such as Gadir (Cádiz) and Onuba (Huelva).	Roman legions under General Scipio Africanus defeat the army of Carthage at Ilipa, near Seville. Itálica, the first Roman town in Spain, is founded near the battlefield.

defeated the left-wing Republicans. Franco then ruled as a dictator until his death in 1975, after which King Juan Carlos I engineered a return to democracy. Three decades of steady economic progress followed, and Andalucía, helped by massive tourism growth and bountiful EU finance, finally emerged after three centuries as a backwater.

Andalucía's Early Immigrants

By the start of the last glacial period (about 100,000 BC), Andalucía, like much of the rest of Europe, was home to Neanderthal humans. Neanderthals began their terminal decline around 35,000 BC as a result of climate change and the arrival of Europe's first *Homo sapiens*, probably from North Africa. Neanderthals may have survived longer in Andalucía than anywhere else. Recent excavations at Gorham's Cave in Gibraltar show that they were probably still hanging on there until at least 26,000 BC.

Like 21st-century tourists, early European *Homo sapiens* gravitated to Andalucía's relatively warm climate, which permitted varied fauna and thick forests to develop, and made hunting and gathering somewhat easier. Between 20,000 and 16,000 years ago they left impressive rock paintings of some of the animals they hunted in Andalucian caves such as the Cueva de Ardales, the Cueva de la Pileta and the Cueva de Nerja.

The Neolithic or New Stone Age reached Spain from Egypt and Mesopotamia around 6000 BC, bringing the revolution of agriculture – the plough, crops, domesticated livestock – and with it pottery, textiles and villages. Some 3500 years later the people of Los Millares, near Almería, learned how to smelt and shape local copper deposits and became Spain's first metalworking culture. Around the same time, Spain's most impressive dolmens (megalithic tombs, constructed of large rocks covered in earth) were erected near Antequera, during the same era as the megalithic age in France, Britain and Ireland.

About 1900 BC the people of El Argar (Almería province) learned to make bronze, an alloy of copper and tin that is stronger than copper – ushering in the Bronze Age on the Iberian Peninsula.

Traders & Invaders

Andalucía's rich resources and settled societies eventually attracted seafaring traders from more sophisticated societies around the Mediterranean. Traders were later replaced by invaders as imperialistic states emerged in the Mediterranean and sought not only to tap local wealth but also to exert political control. All these newcomers – Phoenicians, Greeks, Carthaginians, Romans and Visigoths – left indelible marks on Andalucian life and identity.

Prehistoric Andalucía

» Cueva de la Pileta

» Dolmen de Menga and Dolmen de Viera

» Los Millares

» Orce

» Cueva de Ardales

100 BC–AD 300	AD 98–138	AD 552	711
Andalucía becomes one of the wealthiest, most civilised areas of the Roman empire, with Corduba (Córdoba) its most important city. Christianity arrives in the 3rd century AD.	The Roman empire is ruled by two successive emperors from Itálica in Andalucía: Trajan (AD 98-117) and Hadrian (AD 117–138).	Byzantium, capital of the eastern Roman empire, conquers Andalucía. The Visigoths, a Christian Germanic people now controlling the Iberian Peninsula, drive the Byzantines out in 622.	Muslim forces from North Africa thrash the Visigothic army near the Río Guadalete in Cádiz province. Within a few years, the Muslims overrun almost the whole Iberian Peninsula.

Phoenicians, Greeks & Tartessos

By about 1000 BC, a flourishing culture rich in agriculture, animals and metals arose in western Andalucía. This attracted Phoenician traders, from present-day Lebanon, who arrived to exchange perfumes, ivory, jewellery, oil, wine and textiles for Andalucian silver and bronze. The Phoenicians set up coastal trading settlements at places such as Almuñécar, Cádiz and Huelva. In the 7th century BC Greeks arrived too, trading much the same goods as the Phoenicians. The Phoenicians and Greeks brought with them the potter's wheel, writing and such quintessential elements of the Andalucian landscape as the olive tree, vine and donkey.

The Phoenician- and Greek-influenced culture of western Andalucía in the 8th and 7th centuries BC is known as the Tartessos culture. The Tartessians developed advanced methods of working gold, but it was iron that replaced bronze as the most important metal. Tartessos was described centuries later by Greek, Roman and biblical writers as the source of fabulous riches. Whether it was a city or just a region no one knows. Some argue that it was a trading settlement near Huelva; others believe it may lie beneath the lower Guadalquivir marshes.

Ancient stone tools found near Orce in Granada province reveal the presence of an early version of humanity, possibly *Homo erectus*, cohabiting with mammoths, rhinoceroses, sabre-tooth tigers, hippopotamuses, giant hyenas and elephants about 1.3 million years ago.

Carthage & Rome

From the 6th century BC a former Phoenician colony in modern Tunisia, Carthage, came to dominate trade around the western Mediterranean. Unhappily for the Carthaginians, the next new Mediterranean power was Rome. After losing out to Rome in the First Punic War (264–241 BC), fought for control of Sicily, Carthage conquered southern Spain. The Second Punic War (218–201 BC) saw Carthaginian general Hannibal march his elephants on from here and over the Alps to threaten Rome. But Rome opened a second front by sending legions to fight Carthage in Spain, and its victory at Ilipa (near modern Seville) in 206 BC gave it control of the Iberian Peninsula. The first Roman town in Spain, Itálica, was founded near the battlefield soon afterwards.

As the Roman empire went from strength to strength, Andalucía became one of its most civilised and wealthiest areas. Rome imported Andalucian crops, metals, fish and *garum* (a spicy seasoning derived from fish, made in factories whose remains can be seen at Bolonia and Almuñécar). Rome brought the Iberian Peninsula aqueducts, temples, theatres, amphitheatres, baths, its main languages (Castilian Spanish, Portuguese, Catalan and Galician are all directly descended from the colloquial Latin spoken by Roman colonists and soldiers), a sizeable Jewish population (Jews spread throughout Mediterranean areas of the empire) and, in the 3rd century AD, Christianity.

Phoenician, Greek & Tartessian Andalucía

» Museo Arqueológico, Seville

» Museo de Huelva, Huelva

» Museo de la Ciudad, Carmona

» Museo de Cádiz, Cádiz

» Museo Arqueológico, Almuñécar

756–929	785	929–1031	1091–1140s
The Muslim emirate of Córdoba, under the Omayyad dynasty founded by Abd ar-Rahman I, rules over most of the Iberian Peninsula. The name Al-Andalus is given to Muslim-controlled areas.	The Mezquita (Mosque) of Córdoba, one of the world's wonders of Islamic archiitecture, opens for prayer.	The caliphate of Córdoba: ruler Abd ar-Rahman III declares himself caliph in 929; Al-Andalus attains its greatest power; and Córdoba becomes Western Europe's biggest city.	The strict Muslim rulers of Morocco, the Almoravids, conquer Al-Andalus and rule it as a colony. Their power crumbles in the 1140s.

The Visigoths

When the Huns erupted into Europe from Asia in the late 4th century AD, displaced Germanic peoples moved westwards across the crumbling Roman empire. One group, the Visigoths, took over the Iberian Peninsula in the 6th century, with Toledo, in central Spain, as their capital. The long-haired Visigoths, numbering about 200,000, had little culture of their own and their precarious rule over the relatively sophisticated Hispano-Romans was undermined by strife among their own nobility. Andalucía was an outpost of the Byzantine empire from 552 to 622 but then came under Visigothic sway.

Heartland of Moorish Spain

Following the death of the prophet Mohammed in 632, Arabs carried Islam through the Middle East and North Africa. Legend has it they were ushered onto the Iberian Peninsula by the sexual exploits of the last Visigothic king, Roderic. Chronicles relate how Roderic seduced young Florinda, the daughter of Julian, the Visigothic governor of Ceuta in North Africa; and how Julian sought revenge by approaching the Muslims with a plan to invade Spain. In reality, Roderic's rivals probably just sought support in the endless struggle for the Visigothic throne.

In 711 Tariq ibn Ziyad, the Muslim governor of Tangier, landed at Gibraltar with around 10,000 men, mostly Berbers (indigenous North Africans). Roderic's army was decimated, probably near the Río Guadalete in Cádiz province, and he is thought to have drowned as he fled. Within a few years, the Muslims had taken over the whole Iberian Peninsula except for small areas in the Asturian mountains in the far north. The Muslims were to be the dominant force on the Iberian Peninsula for nearly four centuries and a potent force for a further four. Between wars and rebellions, the Moorish areas of the peninsula developed the most cultured society in medieval Europe. The name given to these territories was Al-Andalus, from which comes the modern name of the region that was always the Moorish heartland – Andalucía.

Al-Andalus' frontiers shifted constantly as the Christians strove to regain territory, but until the mid-11th century the small Christian states developing in northern Spain were too weak to pose much of a threat to Al-Andalus.

In the main cities, the Muslims built beautiful palaces, mosques and gardens, established public bathhouses and bustling *zocos* (markets), and opened universities. The rulers of Al-Andalus allowed freedom of worship to Jews and Christians, but Christians had to pay a special tax, so most either converted to Islam or left for the Christian north. Christians living in Moorish territory were known as Mozarabs (*mozárabes* in Spanish); those who adopted Islam were *muwallads* (*muladíes*).

Roman Andalucía

» Itálica
» Baelo Claudia, Bolonia
» Necrópolis Romana, Carmona
» Museo Municipal, Antequera
» Ronda la Vieja
» Museo Minero, Minas de Riotinto
» Museo Histórico Municipal, Écija

1160–73

The Almoravids' successors in Morocco, the Almohads, in turn take over Al-Andalus, making Seville their capital and promoting arts and learning.

» Torre del Oro (p58)

1212

The armies of three northern Spanish Christian kingdoms, Castilla, Aragón-Catalonia and Navarra, defeat a large Almohad force at Las Navas de Tolosa in northeastern Andalucía; the beginning of the end for Al-Andalus.

1227–48

Castilla's King Fernando III (El Santo, the Saint) conquers the west and north of Andalucía, culminating in the capture of Seville in 1248.

IN MOORISH FOOTSTEPS

The medieval Islamic era left a profound stamp on Andalucía. Great architectural monuments such as Granada's Alhambra and Córdoba's Mezquita are the stars of the Moorish heritage, but the characteristic tangled, narrow street layouts of many a town and village also date from the same period – as do the Andalucian predilections for fountains, running water and decorative plants. Flamenco song, though brought to its modern form by Roma people in post-Moorish times, has obvious Moorish elements. The Muslims developed Spain's Hispano-Roman agricultural base by improving irrigation and introducing new fruits and crops, many of which are still widely grown, often on the same irrigated terracing systems created by the Muslims. The Spanish language still contains many common words of Arabic origin, including the names of some of those new crops – *naranja* (orange), *azúcar* (sugar) and *arroz* (rice).

The Muslim ruling class was composed of various Arab groups prone to factional friction. Below them was a larger group of Berbers, who rebelled on numerous occasions. Before long, Muslim and local blood merged in Spain and many Spaniards today are partly descended from medieval Muslims.

The Cordoban Emirate & Caliphate

In 750 the Omayyad dynasty of caliphs in Damascus, supreme rulers of the Muslim world, was overthrown by a group of revolutionaries, the Abbasids, who shifted the caliphate to Baghdad. One of the Omayyad family, Abd ar-Rahman, escaped the slaughter and somehow made his way to Morocco and then to Córdoba, where in 756 he set himself up as an independent emir (prince). Abd ar-Rahman I's Omayyad dynasty more or less unified Al-Andalus for two and a half centuries.

In 929 Abd ar-Rahman III (r 912–961) gave himself the title caliph to assert his authority in the face of the Fatimids, a growing Muslim power in North Africa. Thus he launched the caliphate of Córdoba, which at its peak encompassed three-quarters of the Iberian Peninsula and some of North Africa. Córdoba became the biggest, most dazzling and most cultured city in Western Europe. Astronomy, medicine, mathematics, philosophy, history and botany flourished, and Abd ar-Rahman III's court was frequented by Jewish, Arabian and Christian scholars.

Later in the 10th century, the fearsome Cordoban general Al-Mansur (or Almanzor) terrorised the Christian north with 50-odd *razzias* (forays) in 20 years. In 997 he destroyed the cathedral at Santiago de Compostela in northwestern Spain – home of the cult of Santiago Matamoros (St James the Moor-Slayer), a key inspiration to Christian warriors. But

1249–1492	1250s–1280s	1350–69	January 1492
The emirate of Granada, ruled by the Nasrid dynasty from the lavish Alhambra palace, sees the final flowering of medieval Muslim culture on the Iberian Peninsula.	Fernando III's son Alfonso X of Castilla, known as El Sabio (the Learned), makes Seville one of his several capitals and launches a cultural revival there.	Castilian king Pedro I 'El Cruel' creates the most magnificent section of Seville'a Alcázar palace, but reputedly has a dozen relatives and friends murdered in his efforts to keep the throne.	After a 10-year war Granada falls to the armies of Castilla and Aragón, which are now united through the marriage of their rulers Isabel and Fernando, the 'Catholic Monarchs'.

after Al-Mansur's death, the caliphate disintegrated into dozens of *tai-fas* (small kingdoms), ruled by local potentates, who were often Berber generals.

The Almoravids & Almohads

Seville, in the wealthy lower Guadalquivir valley, emerged as the strongest *taifa* in Andalucía in the 1040s. By 1078 the writ of its Abbadid dynasty ran all the way from southern Portugal to Murcia (southeast Spain), restoring a measure of peace and prosperity to the south.

Meanwhile, the northern Christian states were starting to raise their game. When one of them, Castilla, captured Toledo in 1085, a scared Seville begged for help from the Almoravids, a strict Muslim sect of Saharan Berbers who had conquered Morocco. The Almoravids came, defeated Castilla's Alfonso VI, and ended up taking over Al-Andalus too, ruling it from Marrakesh as a colony and persecuting Jews and Christians. But the charms of Al-Andalus seemed to relax the Almoravids' austere grip: revolts spread across the territory from 1143 and within a few years it had again split into *taifas*.

In Morocco, the Almoravids were displaced by another strict Muslim Berber sect, the Almohads, who in turn took over Al-Andalus by 1173. Al-Andalus was by now considerably reduced from its 10th-century heyday: the frontier now ran from south of Lisbon to north of Valencia. The Almohads made Seville capital of their whole realm and revived arts and learning in Al-Andalus.

In 1195, the Almohad ruler Yusuf Yakub al-Mansur thrashed Castilla's army at Alarcos, south of Toledo, but this only spurred other Christian kingdoms to join forces with Castilla against him. In 1212 the combined armies of Castilla, Aragón and Navarra routed the Almohads at Las Navas de Tolosa, north of Jaén. With the Almohad state riven by a succession dispute after 1224, Castilla, Aragón and two other Christian kingdoms, Portugal and León, expanded southwards down the Iberian Peninsula. Castilla's Fernando III took strategic Baeza (near Jaén) in 1227, Córdoba in 1236, and Seville, after a two-year siege, in 1248.

The Nasrid Emirate of Granada

The Granada emirate was a wedge of territory carved out of the disintegrating Almohad realm by Mohammed ibn Yusuf ibn Nasr, from whom it's known as the Nasrid emirate. Comprising mainly the modern provinces of Granada, Málaga and Almería, with a population of about 300,000, it held out for nearly 250 years as the last Muslim state on the Iberian Peninsula.

The Nasrids ruled from the lavish Alhambra palace, which witnessed the final flowering of Islamic culture in Spain. Their emirate reached its

Moorish Andalucía

» Alhambra, Granada
» Mezquita, Córdoba
» Albayzín, Granada
» Madinat al-Zahra, Córdoba
» Giralda, Seville
» Castillo de Gibralfaro, Málaga
» Alcazaba, Almería
» Mezquita, Almonaster la Real
» Bobastro

HISTORY HEARTLAND OF MOORISH SPAIN

April 1492	August 1492	1500	1503
Under the influence of Grand Inquisitor Tomás de Torquemada, Isabel and Fernando expel from Spain all Jews who refuse Christian baptism. Some 200,000 Jews leave for other Mediterranean destinations.	Christopher Columbus, funded by Isabel and Fernando, sails from Palos de la Frontera and after 70 days finds the Bahamas, opening up a whole new hemisphere of opportunity for Spain.	Persecution of Muslims in the former Granada emirate sparks rebellion. Afterwards, Muslims are compelled to adopt Christianity or leave. Most, an estimated 300,000, undergo baptism.	Seville is granted a monopoly on Spanish trade with the Americas and becomes the cosmopolitan hub of world trade, with its population jumping from 40,000 to 150,000 by 1600.

PATH OF KNOWLEDGE

Al-Andalus was an important conduit of classical Greek and Roman learning into Christian Europe, where it would exert a profound effect on the Renaissance. The Arabs had absorbed the philosophy of Aristotle, the mathematics of Pythagoras, the astronomy of Ptolemy and the medicine of Hippocrates during their conquests in the eastern Mediterranean and Middle East. Al-Andalus was one of the few places where Islamic and Christian worlds met, enabling this knowledge to find its way northward.

peak in the 14th century under Yusuf I and Mohammed V, authors of the Alhambra's greatest splendours. The Nasrids' final downfall was precipitated by two things: one was Emir Abu al-Hasan's refusal in 1476 to pay any further tribute to Castilla; the other was the unification in 1479 of Castilla and Aragón, Spain's biggest Christian states, through the marriage of their monarchs Isabel and Fernando. The Catholic Monarchs, as the pair are known, launched the final crusade of the Reconquista, against Granada, in 1482.

Harem jealousies and other feuds among Granada's rulers degenerated into a civil war that allowed the Christians to push across the emirate, devastating the countryside. The Christians captured Málaga in 1487, and then Granada itself, after an eight-month siege, on 2 January 1492.

The surrender terms were fairly generous to the last emir, Boabdil, who received the valleys of Las Alpujarras, south of Granada, as a personal fiefdom. He stayed only a year, however, before departing to Africa. The Muslims were promised respect for their religion, culture and property, but this didn't last long.

The Catholic Monarchs, pious Isabel and machiavellian Fernando, united Spain under one rule for the first time since Roman days – a task completed when Fernando annexed Navarra in 1512, eight years after Isabel's death.

Christians in Control

In areas that fell under Christian control in the 13th century, Muslims who stayed on (Mudéjars) initially faced no reprisals. But in 1264 the Mudéjars of Jerez de la Frontera rose up against new taxes and rules that required them to celebrate Christian feasts and live in ghettos. After a five-month siege they were expelled to Granada or North Africa, along with the Mudéjars of Seville, Córdoba and Arcos.

Southern Spain's new Christian rulers handed large tracts of land to nobility and knights who had played important roles in the Reconquista. These landowners turned much of their vast estates over to sheep, and by 1300 rural Christian Andalucía was almost empty. The nobility's preoccupation with wool and politics allowed Jews and foreigners, especially Genoese, to dominate Castilian commerce and finance.

» Statue of Felipe III

1568–70

Persecution of the *moriscos* (converted Muslims) leads to a two-year revolt centred on the Alpujarras valleys, south of Granada. *Moriscos* are eventually thrown out of Spain altogether by Felipe III between 1609 and 1614.

c 1590–1680

Seville plays a leading part in Spain's artistic Siglo de Oro (Golden Century), as a base for artists like Velázquez, Zurbarán and Murillo and sculptors such as Martínez Montañés.

17th Century

The boom engendered by American trade fizzles out as silver shipments slump, and epidemics and bad harvests kill 300,000 Andalucians.

DAVID C TOMLINSON / GETTY IMAGES ©

Fernando III's son Alfonso X (r 1252–84) made Seville one of Castilla's capitals and launched something of a cultural revival there, gathering scholars around him, particularly Jews, who could translate ancient texts into Castilian Spanish. But rivalry within the royal family, and challenges from the nobility, plagued the Castilian monarchy right through till the late 15th century when the Catholic Monarchs took things in hand.

Persecution of the Jews

After the Black Death and several bad harvests in the 14th century, discontent found its scapegoat in the Jews, who were subjected to pogroms around the peninsula in the 1390s. As a result, some Jews converted to Christianity (they became known as *conversos*); others found refuge in Muslim Granada. In the 1480s the *conversos* became the main target of the Spanish Inquisition, founded by the Catholic Monarchs. Many *conversos* were accused of continuing to practise Judaism in secret.

In 1492 Isabel and Fernando ordered the expulsion of every Jew who refused Christian baptism. Around 50,000 to 100,000 converted, but some 200,000, the first Sephardic Jews (Jews of Spanish origin), left for other Mediterranean destinations. A talented middle class was decimated.

Morisco Revolts & Expulsion

The task of converting the Muslims of Granada to Christianity was handed to Cardinal Cisneros, overseer of the Inquisition. He carried out forced mass baptisms, burnt Islamic books and banned the Arabic language. As Muslims found their land being expropriated too, a revolt in Las Alpujarras in 1500 spread right across the former Granada emirate. Afterwards, Muslims were ordered to convert to Christianity or leave. Most converted, becoming known as *moriscos* (converted Muslims), but after the fanatically Catholic King Felipe II (r 1556–98) forbade the Arabic language, Arabic names and *morisco* dress in 1567, a new Alpujarras revolt spread across southern Andalucía and took two years to put down. The *moriscos* were then deported to western Andalucía and more northerly parts of Spain, before being expelled altogether from Spain by Felipe III between 1609 and 1614.

Seville & the Americas: Boom & Bust

In April 1492 the Catholic Monarchs granted the Genoese sailor Christopher Columbus (Cristóbal Colón to Spaniards) funds for a voyage across the Atlantic in search of a new trade route to the Orient. Columbus instead found the Americas and opened up a whole new hemisphere of opportunity for Spain, especially for the river port of Seville.

Recon- quista & Christian Andalucía

» Alcázar, Seville
» Capilla Real, Granada
» Cathedral, Seville
» Úbeda
» Castillo de Guzmán, Tarifa
» Castle, Zahara de la Sierra
» Fuente Mora, Mojácar

The Spanish Inquisition was established by the Catholic Monarchs in 1478. Of the estimated 12,000 deaths for which it was responsible in its three centuries of existence, 2000 took place in the 1480s.

HISTORY SEVILLE & THE AMERICAS: BOOM & BUST

19th Century	1805	1810–12	1850s
Andalucía sinks into economic depression, with landless labourers and their families making up three-quarters of the population.	In the Napoleonic Wars, Spanish sea power is terminated when a combined Spanish–French navy is defeated by the British fleet, under Admiral Nelson, off Cabo de Trafalgar, south of Cádiz.	With most of Spain under Napoleonic occupation, Cádiz survives a two-year siege. In 1812 the Cádiz parliament adopts Spain's first constitution, 'La Pepa', proclaiming sovereignty of the people.	Almería guitar maker Antonio Torres invents the modern acoustic guitar by enlarging the instrument's two bulges and placing the bridge centrally over the lower one, to give extra carrying power.

During the reign of Carlos I (r 1516–56), the first of Spain's new Habsburg dynasty, the ruthless but brilliant conquerors Hernán Cortés and Francisco Pizarro subdued the Aztec and Inca empires respectively with small bands of adventurers, and other Spanish conquerors and colonists occupied vast tracts of the American mainland. The new colonies sent huge quantities of silver, gold and other treasure back to Spain, where the crown was entitled to one-fifth of the bullion (the *quinto real,* or royal fifth).

Seville became the hub of world trade, a cosmopolitan melting pot of money-seekers, and remained the major city in Spain until late in the 17th century, even though a small country town called Madrid was named the national capital in 1561. The prosperity was shared to some extent by Cádiz, and less so by cities such as Jaén, Córdoba and Granada.

But Spain never developed any strategy for utilising the American wealth, spending too much on European wars and opulent palaces, cathedrals and monasteries, while wasting any chance of becoming an early industrial power. Grain had to be imported while sheep and cattle roamed the countryside. The ensuing centuries of neglect and economic mismanagement would turn Andalucía into a backwater, a condition from which it didn't start to emerge until the 1960s.

In the 17th century, silver shipments from the Americas shrank disastrously and the lower Guadalquivir, Seville's lifeline to the Atlantic, became increasingly silted up. In 1717 control of commerce with the Americas was transferred to the seaport of Cádiz, which enjoyed its heyday in the 18th century.

The American Adventure

» Lugares Colombinos, near Huelva

» Columbus' Tomb, Seville Cathedral

» Archivo de Indias, Seville

» Patio de la Montería, Alcázar, Seville

The Great 19th-Century Wealth Gap

The 18th century saw a few economic advances in Andalucía such as the construction of a new road from Madrid to Seville and Cádiz, the opening up of new land for wheat and barley and the arrival of new settlers from elsewhere in Spain, who boosted Andalucía's population to about 1.8 million by 1787. But Spain's loss of its American colonies in the early 19th century was desperate news for the thriving port of Cádiz, which had been totally reliant on trade with them, and as the 19th century wore on, Andalucía declined into one of Europe's most backward, socially polarised regions.

The Disentailments of 1836 and 1855, in which church and municipal lands were auctioned off to reduce the national debt, were a disaster for the peasants, who lost grazing lands. Andalucía's few successful industries, such as the Riotinto mines and the Jerez and Málaga wineries, owed much to British investment and management. At one social extreme were the few bourgeoisie and rich aristocratic landowners; at the other, a very large number of impoverished *jornaleros* – landless agricul-

The epic naval Battle of Trafalgar (1805) is named after a small headland in the town of Los Caños de Meca. A plaque commemorating those who died in the battle was finally erected there on the bicentenary in 2005.

1873	1891–1919	1923–30	1931–36
During Spain's chaotic, short-lived First Republic, numerous cities and towns declare themselves independent states. Seville and the nearby town of Utrera even declare war on each other.	Impoverished Andalucian rural workers launch waves of anarchist strikes and revolts. The powerful anarchist union, the CNT, is founded in Seville in 1910 and gains 93,000 members in Andalucía by 1919.	General Miguel Primo de Rivera, from the Andalucian town of Jerez de la Frontera, rules Spain in a moderate military dictatorship. He is dismissed by King Alfonso XIII in 1930.	The Second Republic: the king goes into exile and Spain is ruled first by the left, then the right, then the left again, with political violence spiralling.

LA PEPA

One of the few places to hold out against the French forces that occupied Spain during the Napoleonic Wars was Cádiz, which withstood a two-year siege from 1810 to 1812. During the siege, the Cortes de Cádiz, a Spanish parliament, convened in the city and on 19 March 1812 it promulgated Spain's first-ever constitution, the Constitución de Cádiz. This was a notably liberal document for its time and it decreed, among other things, universal male suffrage, a constitutional monarchy and freedom of the press. It didn't last long, being abolished by King Fernando VII on his restoration in 1814, but it remained a touchstone for Spaniards of liberal leanings – and was celebrated with great fanfare on its bicentenary in 2012.

Spaniards call the Cádiz Constitution 'La Pepa' – the explanation being that the day of its promulgation, 19 March, is also the Día de San José (St Joseph's Day). None the wiser? The affectionate form of the Spanish name José is Pepe, and since the word *constitución* is of feminine gender, the Cádiz Constitution takes the feminine version of Pepe – hence La Pepa!

tural day labourers who were without work for a good half of the year. Illiteracy, disease and hunger were rife.

Andalucian peasants began to stage uprisings, always brutally quashed. The anarchist ideas of the Russian Mikhail Bakunin, who advocated strikes, sabotage and revolts as the path to spontaneous revolution and a free society governed by voluntary cooperation, gained a big following. The powerful anarchist union, the Confederación Nacional del Trabajo (CNT; National Labour Confederation), was founded in Seville in 1910.

The Civil War

The polarisation of Andalucian society and politics was mirrored in Spain at large. As the 20th century progressed, a large-scale conflagration looked increasingly inevitable.

The Prelude: Dictatorship & Republic

In 1923 an eccentric Andalucian general from Jerez de la Frontera, Miguel Primo de Rivera, launched a comparatively moderate military dictatorship for Spain, with the cooperation of the big socialist union, the Unión General de Trabajadores (UGT; General Union of Workers). Primo was unseated in 1930 as a result of an economic downtown and discontent in the army, and when Spain's republican movement scored sweeping victories in local elections in April 1931, King Alfonso XIII departed for exile in Italy.

Andalucía has always been a hotbed of the controversial activity of bullfighting. Spain's first official bullfighting school, the Escuela de Tauromaquia de Sevilla, was established in Seville by King Fernando VII in the 1830s.

17 July 1936	1936–37	1936–39	1939–75
The Spanish garrison at Melilla (North Africa) revolts against the government, starting the Spanish Civil War. The plot is led by five 'Nationalist' generals, including Francisco Franco.	Western Andalucía falls early in the civil war to the Nationalists, who also take Málaga, with Italian help, in February 1937. Massacres are carried out by both Nationalists and republicans.	Helped by Nazi Germany and fascist Italy, Franco leads the Nationalists to civil-war victory. Much of eastern Andalucía remains in republican hands until the end of the war.	The Franco dictatorship: his opponents continue to be killed and jailed after the civil war; no political opposition is tolerated; the Catholic Church gains a privileged position in society.

The ensuing Second Republic (1931–36) was a tumultuous period of growing confrontation between left and right. National elections in 1931 brought in a mixed government including socialists, centrists and republicans, but the next elections in 1933 were won by the right. By 1934 violence was spiralling out of control, and the left, including the emerging communists, was calling increasingly for revolution. In the February 1936 elections a left-wing coalition narrowly defeated the right-wing National Front. Violence continued on both sides of the political spectrum, the anarchist CNT had over a million members and the peasants were on the verge of revolution.

But when the revolt came, on 17 July 1936, it came from the other end of the political spectrum. On that day the Spanish garrison at Melilla in North Africa revolted against the leftist government, followed the next day by some garrisons on the mainland. The leaders of the plot were five generals. The Spanish Civil War had begun.

The War

The civil war split communities, families and friends. Both sides committed atrocious massacres and reprisals, especially in the early weeks. The rebels, who called themselves Nationalists, shot or hanged tens of thousands of supporters of the republic. Republicans did likewise to those they considered Nationalist sympathisers, including some 7000 priests, monks and nuns.

By most estimates, about 350,000 Spaniards died in the civil war, although some writers put the figure as high as 500,000.

In republican-held areas, anarchists, communists or socialists ended up running many towns and cities. Social revolution followed. In Andalucía this tended to be anarchist-led, with private property abolished and churches and convents often burned and wrecked. Large estates were occupied by the peasants and around 100 agrarian communes were established. The Nationalist campaign, meanwhile, took on overtones of a holy crusade against enemies of God.

The basic battle lines were drawn very early. Cities whose garrisons backed the rebels (most did) often fell immediately into Nationalist hands, as happened at Cádiz, Córdoba and Jerez. Seville was in Nationalist hands within three days and Granada within a few more. The Nationalists killed an estimated 4000 people in and around Granada after they took the city, including the great writer Federico García Lorca. There was slaughter in republican-held areas, too. An estimated 2500 were murdered in a few months in anarchist-controlled Málaga. The Nationalists then executed thousands in reprisals when they and their fascist Italian allies took the city in February 1937. Eastern Andalucía remained in republican hands until the end of the war.

By late 1936 General Francisco Franco emerged as the undisputed Nationalist leader, calling himself Generalísimo (Supreme General).

1950s & 1960s	1975–78	1982–96
Some 1.5 million Andalucians leave to find work elsewhere in Spain or Europe. New mass tourism on Andalucía's Costa del Sol helps to stimulate some economic recovery.	Following Franco's death, King Juan Carlos I and prime minister Adolfo Suárez engineer a transition to democracy. The 1978 constitution makes Spain a parliamentary monarchy with no official religion.	Sevillano Felipe González, of the left-of-centre Partido Socialista Obrero Español (PSOE), enjoys 14 years as Spain's prime minister, presiding over an economic boom after Spain joins the EU in 1986.

BETTMANN / CORBIS ©

» General Francisco Franco

THE DUKES & DUCHESSES OF MEDINA SIDONIA

The Andalucian family that once owned more of Spain than any other traces its lineage back to the Reconquista hero Alonso Pérez de Guzmán, legendary for his heroism while defending Tarifa back in 1294. Guzmán and his descendants acquired vast landholdings in western Andalucía, and the title Duque de Medina Sidonia was conferred on one descendant, Juan Alonso de Guzmán, in 1445. By the early 16th century it was possible to travel right across the provinces of Huelva, Sevilla and Cádiz without leaving Medina Sidonia land.

In 1588 the seventh Duque de Medina Sidonia, despite a tendency to seasickness and lack of naval experience, was appointed by Felipe II to command the Spanish Armada to invade England. Contrary to popular legend, the duke was neither incompetent nor a coward: the Armada's disastrous defeat is now put down chiefly to a flawed strategy ordered by the king. The 15th duke's wife María, Duchess of Alba, reputedly had a fling with the artist Goya and is widely thought to be the subject of Goya's scandalous nude portrait *La Maja Desnuda*.

But few of the dukes' careers match the colour of that of the 21st of the line, Duquesa Luisa Isabel Álvarez de Toledo, who died in 2008. Dubbed the 'Red Duchess', Doña Luisa was a committed republican who spent time in jail and exile during the Franco dictatorship, gave away Medina Sidonia estates to agricultural cooperatives and fell out with her three children. On her deathbed she married, under Spain's recently introduced same-sex marriage laws, her long-time companion and administrator of the huge family archive in Sanlúcar de Barrameda, Liliana Dahlmann.

The scales of the war were tipped in the Nationalists' favour by weapons, planes and 92,000 troops from Nazi Germany and fascist Italy. The republicans had some Soviet planes, tanks, artillery and advisers, and 25,000 or so French soldiers fought with them, along with a similar number of other foreigners in the International Brigades.

The republican government moved from besieged Madrid to Valencia in late 1936, then to Barcelona in 1937. In 1938 Franco swept eastwards, isolating Barcelona, and the USSR withdrew from the war. The Nationalists took Barcelona in January 1939 and Madrid in March. Franco declared the war won on 1 April 1939.

Franco's Spain

After the civil war, instead of reconciliation, more blood-letting ensued and an estimated 100,000 Spaniards were killed or died in prison. Franco ruled absolutely. He was commander of the army and leader of the sole political party, the Movimiento Nacional (National Movement). Army

1982	1992	1996–2004	2000–2010
Under Spain's new regional autonomy system, Andalucía gets its own parliament, dominated ever since by the PSOE. Over 10 years national and regional government eliminates the worst of Andalucian poverty.	Hundreds of thousands of people visit Expo '92 in Seville, and the superfast AVE (Alta Velocidad Española) Madrid–Seville rail link opens. Andalucian roads get a major upgrade, too.	Spain is governed by the right-of-centre Partido Popular (PP). Andalucian unemployment nearly halves (to 16%) thanks to a construction boom, tourism and industrial growth, and EU subsidies.	Hundreds of thousands of northern and eastern Europeans, Africans and Latin Americans migrate to Andalucía. Some are sun-seekers, more are job-seekers. The official foreign population grows to a record 700,000.

FRIGILIANA

garrisons were maintained outside every large city, strikes and divorce were banned and church weddings became compulsory.

Spain stayed out of WWII, but afterwards suffered a UN-sponsored trade boycott that helped turn the late 1940s into the *años de hambre* (years of hunger) – particularly in poor areas such as Andalucía where, at times, peasants subsisted on soup made from wild herbs.

In an effort to relieve Andalucian poverty, mass foreign tourism was launched on the Costa del Sol in the late 1950s. But 1.5 million hungry people still left in the 1950s and '60s to look for work in Madrid, northern Spain and other countries. By the 1970s many Andalucian villages still lacked electricity, reliable water supplies and paved roads, and the education system was pathetically inadequate. Today many rural Andalucians over 50 are still illiterate.

The New Democracy

Franco's chosen successor, Alfonso XIII's grandson Prince Juan Carlos, took the throne, aged 37, two days after Franco's death in 1975. Much of the credit for Spain's ensuing transition to democracy goes to the king and his prime minister, Adolfo Suárez. A new, two-chamber parliamentary system was introduced and in 1977 political parties, trade unions and strikes were all legalised. Spain enjoyed a rapid social liberation too: contraceptives, homosexuality and divorce were legalised, adultery was decriminalised and a wave of hedonism was unleashed.

In 1982 Spain made a final break with the Franco era by voting the left-of-centre Partido Socialista Obrero Español (PSOE; Spanish Socialist Worker Party) into power. The PSOE's leader, Felipe González, a young lawyer from Seville, was to be prime minister for 14 years, and his party's young, educated leadership included several other Andalucians. The PSOE made improvements in education, launched a national health system and basked in an economic boom after Spain joined the European Community (now the EU) in 1986.

The PSOE has also dominated Andalucía's regional government in Seville since it was inaugurated in 1982. PSOE government eradicated the worst of Andalucian poverty in the 1980s and early 1990s with grants, community works schemes and a relatively generous dole system. It also gave Andalucía Spain's biggest network of environmentally protected areas.

The PSOE lost power nationally in 1996 to the centre-right Partido Popular (PP; People's Party), which presided over eight years of economic progress. Andalucía benefited from steady growth in tourism and industry, massive EU subsidies for agriculture, and a long construction boom, with its unemployment rate almost halving in the PP years to 16% (still the highest in Spain).

A few communists and republicans continued their struggle after the civil war in small guerrilla units in Andalucía's mountains and elsewhere. David Baird's book *Between Two Fires* fascinatingly documents the struggle between the guerrillas and the Guardia Civil (Civil Guard) around the village of Frigiliana in the 1940s and '50s.

2003	2004	2008	2008–12
The Museo Picasso opens in Málaga, which joins Barcelona, Paris and New York as cities with major collections of the art of Pablo Picasso, born in Málaga in 1881.	The PSOE wins the Spanish national and Andalucian regional elections, days after the Madrid train bombings by Islamic extremists, which kill 191 people and injure 1800.	A record 9.76 million foreign tourists visit Andalucía, more than one for every Andalucian. They spend an average €706 each and nearly one-third of them come from the UK.	Andalucía, over-dependent on tourism and construction, is savaged by the credit crunch and economic recession; unemployment leaps from 14% to 31%, the highest in Spain.

Andalucian Architecture

Architecturally speaking, Spain – and in particular Andalucía - is different from the rest of Europe. While most of the themes and variations evident elsewhere on the continent have permeated the region at one time or another, they have been diluted by one important invariable: the Moorish factor. The conquering Christian armies may have destroyed Al-Andalus' emirs and government, but tellingly, they didn't have the heart to flatten its most iconic buildings. Córdoba's Mezquita still stands, as does Seville's Giralda, and numerous other noble citadels. As a result, Andalucía's architecture is often a story of layers, hybrids and Christian–Moorish intermixing. Even today, 500 years since the fall of Granada, the impact of Islam is never far from the surface. In villages across the region, and in the heart of cities such as Granada's Albayzín, intricate tangles of streets are redolent of North African medinas, while the Islamic love of ornate, scented gardens – hidden inner sanctums which safeguarded residents from prying eyes – can be seen in patios, courtyards and the carefully manicured greenery of the Generalife. The resulting picture is often complex but never dull. Indeed, one could argue that European architectural design reached a stylistic highpoint in the 1350s on a small hill at the foot of the Sierra Nevada Mountains in a palace complex called the Alhambra. Contemporary architects have struggled to emulate the glories of the Moors, although modernist structures in cities such as Seville have grabbed 21st-century headlines for their unorthodoxy and experimentalism.

Islamic Architecture

The period of Islam's architectural dominance began with the Omayyads, the Moorish invaders who kick-started eight centuries of Islamic rule in 711 and ushered in an architectural era which bequeathed the region, more than anywhere else in Europe, with a strong whiff of the exotic. Elaborate monuments on an unprecedented scale – Granada's Alhambra and Córdoba's Mezquita, for example, which stand like bookends to Islam's reign – were the means through which the Islamic rulers of Al-Andalus brought architectural sophistication to Europe. They remain the most visible legacy of Andalucía's Islamic past.

The Omayyads

The Omayyads of Damascus had been overthrown by the revolutionary Abbasids in 750, forcing their leader Abu'l-Mutarrif Abd ar-Rahman bin Muawiya to escape to Morocco and then Spain. In 756 he set himself up as an independent emir, Abd ar-Rahman I, in Córdoba, launching a dynasty that lasted until 1009 and made Al-Andalus, at the western extremity of the Islamic world, the last outpost of Omayyad culture. But it was

THE HORSESHOE ARCH

The Visigoths are usually classified as Europe's forgotten civilization, inbetweeners who had the historical misfortune of following the more flamboyant Romans. But these erstwhile rulers of an empire larger than the Córdoba caliphate did leave behind one indelible legacy: the horseshoe arch. So called because of their shape (a departure from the earlier semicircle arch), these stylistic arches were recognised and adapted by the Omayyads, who had found them adorning various Visigoth churches: most notably in Córdoba. The Mezquita in Córdoba displays the best early incarnations of horseshoe arches, but the style endured to become the hallmark of Spanish Islamic architecture passed down through Almorávid, Almohad, Nasrid and Mudéjar architects employed by the Christians.

Abd ar-Rahman I's successor, Al Hakim II (r 961–76), who would leave the Omayyads' most enduring architectural mark in Andalucía.

Mezquita of Córdoba

In AD 784 Abd ar-Rahman I was responsible for founding Córdoba's Mezquita, a building that was – and indeed still is – the epitome of Islamic architecture's grace and pleasing unity of form. This sense of harmony – perhaps the Mezquita's most enduring miracle – is all the more remarkable given the significant alterations carried out over the centuries. Zealous Christian architects darkened the original light-filled interior by building thick outer walls, and in the middle of the 16th century an incongruous Christian cathedral was plonked right in the middle of the former mosque.

In its original form, the Mezquita was a square split into two rectangular halves: a covered prayer hall, and an open courtyard where the faithful performed their ritual ablutions before entering the prayer hall. This early structure drew on the essential elements of Omayyad architecture. It maintained, for example, the 'basilical' plan of some early Islamic buildings by having a central 'nave' of arches, broader than the others, leading to the mihrab, the niche indicating the direction of Mecca (and thus of prayer) that is key to the layout of any mosque. But the Mezquita's prayer hall broke away from the verticality of earlier landmark Omayyad buildings, such as the Great Mosque of Damascus and the Dome of the Rock in Jerusalem. Instead it created a broad horizontal space that evoked the yards of desert homes that formed the original Islamic prayer spaces. It also conjured visions of palm groves with mesmerising lines of two-tier, red-and-white-striped arches in the prayer hall.

As Córdoba grew into its role as the increasingly sophisticated capital of Al-Andalus, each emir was desperate to leave his personal stamp on Al-Andalus' landmark building. Later enlargements extended the lines of arches to cover an area of nearly 120 sq m, making it one of the biggest of all mosques. These arcades afford ever-changing perspectives, vistas disappearing into infinity and interplays of light and rhythm that rank among the Mezquita's most mesmerising features.

For all its 8th-century origins and the later extensions, the Mezquita's golden age was the 10th century. It was then, particularly during the 960s under the reign of Al-Hakim II, that the Mezquita came to be considered the highpoint of the splendid 10th-century 'caliphal' phase of Spanish Islamic architecture. Al-Hakim II created a magnificent new mihrab, decorated with superb Byzantine mosaics that imitate those of the Great Mosque of Damascus. In front of the mihrab Al-Hakim II added a new royal prayer enclosure, the *maksura;* its multiple interwoven arches and lavishly decorated domes were much more intricate and

Although strongly associated with Andalucía, Mudéjar architecture originated in Castile and Aragón during the 12th and 13th centuries. The best Andalucian Mudéjar buildings are in Seville.

technically advanced than anything previously seen in Europe. The *maksura* formed part of a second axis to the building, an aisle running along in front of the wall containing the mihrab – known as the qibla wall because it indicates the qibla, the direction of Mecca. This transverse axis creates the T-plan that features strongly in many mosques. In its 'final' 10th-century form the Mezquita's roof was supported by 1293 columns.

The Almoravids & Almohads

As the centuries wore on, power shifted as powerful North African dynasties turned their attention to the glittering prize of Al-Andalus. Some, such as the Almoravids – a Berber dynasty from Morocco from the late 11th to mid-12th centuries – yielded few notable buildings in Spain. But the second wave of Moroccan Berbers to conquer Al-Andalus, the Almohads, more than made up for the Almoravids' lack of architectural imagination.

Late in the 12th century, the Almohads made a priority of building huge Friday mosques in the main cities of their empire, with Seville especially benefiting from their attention. The design of the mosques was simple and purist, with large prayer halls conforming to the T-plan of the Córdoba Mezquita, but the Almohads introduced some important and beautiful decorative innovations. The bays where the naves meet the qibla wall were surmounted by cupolas or stucco *muqarnas* (stalactite or honeycomb vaulting composed of hundreds or thousands of tiny cells or niches), an architectural style with its origins in Iran or Syria. On walls, large brick panels with designs of interwoven lozenges were created. Tall, square, richly decorated minarets were another Almohad trademark.

Seville's cathedral, the city's Great Mosque in Islamic times, is where Almohad architecture is most stunningly on show. The Giralda, the minaret of the Seville mosque, is the masterpiece of surviving Almohad buildings in Spain, with its beautiful brick panels. The mosque's prayer hall was demolished in the 15th century to make way for the city's cathedral, but its ablutions courtyard, Patio de los Naranjos, and its northern gate, the handsome Puerta del Perdón, survive.

With defence a primary preoccupation due to Christian advances in the north, the Almohads went on a fortress-building spree in the 12th and early 13th centuries. Cities with bolstered defences included Córdoba, Seville and Jerez de la Frontera. Seville's primary Almohad creation – aside from its mosque – was the river-guarding Torre del Oro (still standing). Another survivor is Jerez's Alcázar; the tall, austere brick building is based on an unusual octagonal plan inscribed within a square; inside

The Almonaster La Real in Huelva province is like a miniature version of Córdoba's Mezquita, with rows of arches forming five naves, the central one leading to a semicircular mihrab.

MEDINA AZAHARA

The Córdoban caliphate's 'brilliant city', the Medina Azahara was as architecturally lavish as it was ephemeral. The pet project of Abd ar-Rahman III, it was conceived as the caliphate's new capital in AD 936 and laid out from scratch 5km west of the city of Córdoba. Named after his favourite wife, Az-Zahra, the retreat was planned by Rahman as a royal residence, palace and seat of government, set away from the hubbub of the city in the same manner as the Abbasid royal city of Samarra, north of Baghdad. Its chief architect was Abd ar-Rahman III's son, Al-Hakim II, who later embellished the Córdoba Mezquita so superbly. In contrast to Middle Eastern palaces, whose typical reception hall was a domed *iwan* (hall opening to a forecourt), Medina Azahara's reception halls had a 'basilical' plan, each with three or more parallel naves – similar to mosque architecture. Although it was wrecked during the collapse of the Córdoba caliphate less than a century after it was built, the remaining imposing horseshoe arches, exquisite stucco work and extensive gardens suggest that it was a large and lavish place.

its walls the former Almohad mosque was turned into a church while its minaret became a bell-tower. Less heralded Almohad-era creations are Tarifa's Castillo de los Guzmán and the city walls of historic Niebla in Huelva province.

The Nasrids

With the armies of the Reconquista (Christian reconquest) continuing their seemingly inexorable march southwards, the last emirate of Islamic Al-Andalus, the Nasrid emirate of Granada (1249–1492), could have been forgiven for having its mind on nonarchitectural matters. But in a recurring theme that resonates down through Andalucian history, it was the architecture that emerged from this period that best captures the spirit of the age. The Alhambra is at once an expansive fortification that reflected uncertain times and an extraordinary palace of last-days opulence.

THE ALHAMBRA

Granada's magnificent palace-fortress, the Alhambra, is the only surviving large medieval Islamic palace complex in the world. It's a palace-city in the tradition of Medina Azahara but it's also a fortress, with 2km of walls, 23 towers and a fort-within-a-fort, the Alcazaba. Within the Alhambra's walls were seven separate palaces, mosques, garrisons, houses, offices, baths, a summer residence (the Generalife) and exquisite gardens.

The Alhambra's designers were supremely gifted landscape architects, integrating nature and buildings through the use of pools, running water, meticulously clipped trees and bushes, windows framing vistas, carefully placed lookout points, interplays between light and shadow, and contrasts between heat and cool. The juxtaposition of fountains, pools and gardens with domed reception halls reached a degree of perfection suggestive of the paradise described in the Quran. In keeping with the Alhambra's partial role as a sybarite's delight, many of its defensive towers also functioned as miniature summer palaces.

A huge variety of densely ornamented arches adorns the Alhambra. The Nasrid architects refined existing decorative techniques to new peaks of delicacy, elegance and harmony. Their media included sculptured stucco, marble panels, carved and inlaid wood, epigraphy (with endlessly repeated inscriptions of 'There is no God but Allah') and colourful tiles. Plaited star patterns in tile mosaic have since covered walls the length and breadth of the Islamic world, and Nasrid Granada is the dominant artistic influence in the Maghrib (northwest Africa) even today.

Granada's splendour reached its peak under emirs Yusuf I (r 1333–54) and Mohammed V (r 1354–59 and 1362–91). Each was responsible for one of the Alhambra's two main palaces. Yusuf created the Palacio de Comares (Comares Palace), in which the brilliant marquetry ceiling of the Salón de Comares (Comares Hall) represented the seven levels of the Islamic heavens and capped by a cupola symbolising the throne of Allah. This served as the model for Islamic-style ceilings in state rooms for centuries afterwards; the ceiling contains more than 8000 tiny wooden panels. Mohammed V takes credit for the Palacio de los Leones (Palace of the Lions), focused on the famed Patio de los Leones (Patio of the Lions), with its colonnaded gallery and pavilions and a central fountain channelling water through the mouths of 12 stone lions. This palace's Sala de Dos Hermanas (Hall of Two Sisters) features a fantastic *muqarnas* dome of 5000 tiny cells, recalling the constellations.

Roman Footprints

» Itálica

» Baelo Claudia

» Calzada Romana (Roman road), Benaocaz-Ubrique

» Puente Romano, Córdoba

» Roman Ampitheatre, Málaga

» Teatro Romano, Cádiz

Mudéjars & Mozarabics

The days of Islam's rulers may have been numbered in Al-Andalus, but Islam's architectural legacy lived on, even in areas under Christian rule. Gifted Muslim artisans were frequently employed by Christian rulers and the term Mudéjar – from the Arabic *mudayan* (domesticated) – which was given to Muslims who stayed on in areas reconquered by the Christians, came to stick as an architectural label.

One hallmark of Mudéjar style is geometric decorative designs in brick or stucco, often further embellished with tiles. Elaborately carved timber ceilings are also a mark of the Mudéjar hand. *Artesonado* is the word used to describe ceilings with interlaced beams leaving regular spaces for decorative insertions. True Mudéjar *artesonados* generally bear floral or simple geometric patterns.

You'll find Mudéjar or part-Mudéjar churches and monasteries all over Andalucía (Mudéjar is often found side by side with the Christian Gothic style). Andalucía's classic Mudéjar building is the exotic Palacio de Don Pedro, built in the 14th century inside the Alcázar of Seville for the Christian King Pedro I of Castile. Pedro's friend, Mohammed V, the Muslim emir of Granada, sent many of his best artisans to work on Pedro's palace, and, as a result, the Palacio de Don Pedro is effectively a Nasrid building, and one of the best of its kind. Nowhere is this more evident than in the beautiful Patio de las Doncellas at its heart, with its sunken garden surrounded by exquisite arches, tiling and plasterwork.

The term Mozarabic, from *musta'rib* (Arabised), refers to Christians who lived, or had lived, in Muslim-controlled territories in the Iberian Peninsula. Mozarabic architecture was, unsurprisingly, much influenced by Islamic styles and includes, for instance, the horseshoe arch. The majority of Mozarabic architecture is found in northern Spain: the only significant remaining Mozarabic structure in Andalucía is the rock-cut church at Bobastro.

Renaissance Architecture

» Palacio de la Condesa de Lebrija, Seville
» Casa de Pilatos, Seville
» Jaén Cathedral
» Baeza Cathedral
» Palacio de Vázquez de Molina, Úbeda

ANDALUCIAN ARCHITECTURE

Christian Architecture

The churches and monasteries built by the Christian conquerors, and the palaces and mansions of their nobility, are a superb part of Andalucía's heritage. But there is, as always, a uniquely Andalucian twist: after the Christian reconquest of Andalucía (1227–1492), many Islamic buildings were simply repurposed for Christian ends. Many Andalucian churches occupy converted mosques (most famously at Córdoba), many church towers began life as minarets, and the zigzagging streets of many an old town – such as Granada's Albayzín district – originated in labyrinthine Islamic-era street plans.

ANDALUCÍA'S FORMAL GARDENS

Paradise, according to Islamic tradition, is a garden. It's an idea that architects took to heart in Al-Andalus, surrounding some of Andalucía's loveliest buildings with abundant greenery, colour, fragrances and the tinkle of water.

» **Generalife gardens, Alhambra, Granada** Landscaping of near-perfect sophistication.
» **Alcázar gardens, Seville** A classic Islamic palace pleasure garden.
» **Gardens of the Alcázar de los Reyes Cristianos, Córdoba** Lush terrace with abundant water.
» **Parque de María Luisa, Seville** Sprawling greenery in the heart of Seville.
» **Palacio de Viana, Córdoba** Formal gardens with an emphasis on symmetry.

ANDALUCIAN ARCHITECTURE

ALONSO CANO

Andalucian Gothic

Christian architecture reached northern and western Andalucía with the Reconquista during the 13th century. The prevailing architectural style throughout much of Christian Europe at the time was Gothic, with its distinctive pointed arches, ribbed ceilings, flying buttresses and fancy window tracery. Dozens of Gothic or part-Gothic churches, castles and mansions are dotted throughout Andalucía. Some of these buildings combine Gothic with Mudéjar style, while others have Gothic mixed with later styles and so have ended up as a stylistic hotchpotch.

The final flourish of Spanish Gothic was Isabelline Gothic, from the time of Queen Isabel la Católica. Isabelline Gothic features sinuously curved arches and tracery, and facades with lacelike ornament and low-relief sculptures (including lots of heraldic shields).

The Clean Lines of the Renaissance

The Renaissance in architecture was an Italian-originated return to classical ideals of harmony and proportion, dominated by columns and shapes such as the square, circle and triangle. Many Andalucian Renaissance buildings feature elegant interior courtyards lined by two tiers of wide, rounded arcades. Whereas the Gothic period left its most striking mark upon public Christian architecture, the Renaissance period was an era in which the gentry built themselves gorgeous urban palaces with delightful patios surrounded by harmonious arched galleries.

Spanish Renaissance architecture had three phases. First came plateresque, taking its name from the Spanish for silversmith, *platero,* because it was primarily a decorative genre, with effects resembling those of silverware. Round-arched portals were framed by classical columns and stone sculpture. Next came a more purist style, while the last and plainest phase was Herreresque, after Juan de Herrera (1530–97), creator of the austere palace-monastery complex of El Escorial, near Madrid, and Seville's Archivo de Indias.

All three phases of Renaissance architecture were spanned in Jaén province by the legendary master architect Andrés de Vandelvira (1509–75), who gave the town of Úbeda one of the finest ensembles of Renaissance buildings in Spain. Vandelvira was much influenced by Burgos-born Diego de Siloé (1495–1563), who was primarily responsible for the cathedrals of Granada, Málaga and Guadix.

The Baroque Backlash

An inevitable reaction to the Renaissance sobriety that preceded it came in the colours and dramatic sense of motion of baroque. This style really seemed to catch the Andalucian imagination, and this was one of the

Alonso Cano (1601–67) was a sculptor, architect and painter from Granada whose creative talents were as vivid as his famous temper. Sometimes called the Spanish Michelangelo; his most celebrated work is the elaborate baroque facade of Granada cathedral.

ARCHITECTURE BOOKS

» *Moorish Architecture in Andalusia* (Marianne Barrucand and Achim Bednorz; 2002) Wonderfully illustrated with a learned but readable text.

» *Houses & Palaces of Andalucía* (Patricia Espinosa De Los Monteros and Francesco Ventura; 1998) A coffee-table tome full of beautiful photography.

» *The Alhambra* (Robert Irwin; 2004) Challenges the myths that have coalesced around this most famous of Spanish buildings and brings the place to life.

» *Art & Architecture: Andalusia* (Brigitte Hintzen-Bohlen; 2010) A stunning overview of the subject, combining a comprehensive photographic record with informative text.

places where baroque blossomed most brilliantly, reaching its peak of elaboration in the 18th century.

Baroque style was at root classical, but it specialised in ornamental facades crammed with decoration, and interiors chock-full of ornate stucco sculpture and gilt paint. Retables – the large, sculptural altarpieces that adorn many Spanish churches to illustrate Christian stories and teachings – reached extremes of gilded extravagance. The most hyperbolic baroque work is termed *churrigueresco* after a Barcelona family of sculptors and architects named Churriguera.

Before full-blown baroque there was a kind of transitional stage, exemplified by more sober works such as Alonso Cano's 17th-century facade for Granada's cathedral.

Seville has probably more baroque churches per square kilometre than any city in the world. However, the church at Granada's Monasterio de La Cartuja, by Francisco Hurtado Izquierdo (1669–1725), is one of the most lavish baroque creations in all Spain with its multicoloured marble, golden capitals and profuse sculpture. Hurtado's followers also adorned the small town of Priego de Córdoba with seven or eight baroque churches.

Modern Andalucian Architecture

In the 19th century, Andalucía acquired some neo-Gothic and neo-baroque architecture, but most prevalent were neo-Mudéjar and neo-Islamic styles, harking back to an age that was now catching the fancy of the Romantic movement. Mansions such as the Palacio de Orleans y Borbon in Sanlúcar de Barrameda, and public buildings ranging from train stations in Seville to markets in Málaga and Tarifa, were constructed in colourful imitation of past Islamic architectural styles. For the 1929 Exposición Iberoamericana, fancy buildings in almost every past Andalucian style were concocted in Seville, chief among them the gaudy Plaza de España ensemble by local architect Aníbal González.

During the Franco dictatorship, drab Soviet-style blocks of workers' housing were erected in many cities, while Andalucía's decades-long tourism boom spawned, for the most part, architecture that ranged from the forgettable to the kind of concrete eyesores that you wish you could forget. The dawn of the 21st centruy has sparked a little more imagination, most notably in Seville where a trio of big architectural projects – the Metropol Parasol, the Cajasol tower and the Pabellon de la Navegación – have added a little pizzazz to the urban framework.

On a much smaller scale, Andalucía's architects and builders have demonstrated greater flair in restoring older edifices to serve as hotels, museums or other public buildings. Projects such as Málaga's Museo Picasso and Jaén's Palacio de Villardompardo are both 16th-century urban palaces turned into top-class modern museums.

Best Small Towns for Architecture

» Vejer de la Frontera

» Arcos de la Frontera

» Baeza

» Osuna

» Setenil de las Bodegas

Landscape & Wildlife

Andalucía's beautiful wilderness areas protect an important cache of birds, animals and flora. Seeing them might just be your greatest travel experience.

Landscape

Andalucía has mountains in abundance, from the relatively low hills of the geographically distinct Sierra Morena to the dizzying heights of the Sierra Nevada. The Sierra Morena, which rarely surpasses 1000m, rolls across the north of Andalucía like the last outpost of rugged southern Spain before it yields to the sweeping flatlands and empty horizons of central Spain's high *meseta* (plateau). It's more beautiful than dramatic, divided between evergreen oak woodlands, scrub, rough grazing pasture and scattered old stone villages.

Closer to the coast, the Cordillera Bética was pushed up by the pressure of the African tectonic plate on the Iberian subplate 15 to 20 million years ago. This band of jagged mountains widens out from its beginnings in southwest Andalucía to a breadth of 125km or so in the east. The 75km-long Sierra Nevada southeast of Granada, with a series of 3000m-plus peaks (including 3479m Mulhacén, the highest mountain on mainland Spain) forms a subchain of the Cordillera Bética. The cordillera then continues east from Andalucía across Spain's Murcia and Valencia regions, before re-emerging from the Mediterranean as the Balearic Islands of Ibiza and Mallorca. Much of it is composed of limestone, yielding some wonderful karstic rock formations.

Apart from the coastal plain, which varies in width from 50km in the far west to virtually nothing in parts of Granada and Almería provinces, the fertile valley of the 660km-long Río Guadalquivir is Andalucía's other major geographical landmark. Andalucía's longest river rises in the Cazorla mountains of Jaén province, flows westward through Córdoba and Seville and enters the Atlantic at Sanlúcar de Barrameda. Before entering the ocean the river splits into a marshy delta known as Las Marismas del Guadalquivir, which includes the Parque Nacional de Doñana.

Common Species of Tree

» Holly Oak

» Cork Oak

» Spanish Fir

» Eucalyptus

» Poplar

» Olive

Parks & Protected Areas

Andalucía has the biggest environmental protection program in Spain, having set aside more than 90 protected areas covering some 17,000 sq km. This amounts to 20% of Andalucian territory and more than 60% of the total protected area in Spain.

Parques nacionales (national parks) are areas of exceptional importance for their fauna, flora, geomorphology or landscape, and whose conservation is considered to be in the national interest. These are the most strictly controlled protected areas and may include reserve areas closed

ANDALUCÍA'S TOP PARKS & PROTECTED AREAS

Parque Nacional de Doñana
Millions of birds and the Iberian lynx give the park its fame (Doñana is one of the endangered cat's last footholds). Its habitat range is astonishing – wetlands, dunes, beaches and woodlands at the mouth of the Guadalquivir – and supports deer and wild boar. It is best explored by 4WD.

Parque Nacional Sierra Nevada
Spectacular high-mountain wilderness dominates here. Its high peaks are often snow-capped, even as the rest of Andalucía bakes in the sweltering heat, and this *parque nacional* is best explored on foot. Along its many trails you'll find ibex (around 5000 inhabit the park) and high-altitude plants you won't find elsewhere .

Parque Natural de Cabo de Gata-Níjar
Flamingo colonies, volcanic cliffs and sandy beaches make for a combination unlike any other protected area in Andalucía. One of the region's driest corners, the park showcases semidesert and promises a range of activities, including swimming, birdwatching, walking, horse riding, diving and snorkelling.

Parque Natural Los Alcornocales
Some of the most extensive examples of the distinctive southern Spanish phenomenon of *alcornoque* (corn-oak forests) carpet the rolling hill country of this park in Cádiz province, north of Algeciras. It's one of Andalucía's lesser-known protected areas, ensuring that its extensive hiking trails rarely get overwhelmed.

Parque Natural Sierra de Grazalema
Ibex, griffon vultures and other species occupy this beautiful, damp, hilly region that is notable for its vast sweeps of Mediterranean woodlands and stands of Spanish firs. Archetypal white Andalucian villages serve as gateways to fantastic hiking trails, but you can also climb, canyon, paraglide and go caving to your heart's content.

Parque Natural Sierra de las Nieves
Spectacular vistas and deep valleys characterise this mountain region buried deep in the interior of Málaga province. With two iconic examples of Andalucian flora (stands of Spanish firs) and fauna (ibex) and other species, the park is an ideal choice for those looking to hike through the Andalucian wilds.

Parque Natural Sierra Norte
Spring wildflowers carpet the rolling Sierra Morena country of this northern Andalucian park, but its appeal extends further, to ancient villages and expansive panoramas. There's no better way to explore this remote country than hiking or horse riding from village to village.

Parque Natural Sierras de Cazorla, Segura y Las Villas
Abundant, easily visible wildlife, craggy mountains, deep valleys and thick forests – it's difficult to overestimate the charms of this beautiful park, Spain's largest (2143 sq km). Red and fallow deer, wild boar, mouflon and ibex provide the wildlife interest. Hike or explore on horseback or by 4WD.

Paraje Natural Torcal de Antequera
Striking limestone formations are what most visitors remember about this mountainous natural area close to Antequera in Málaga province. It contains some of the strangest landforms in Andalucía and has a handful of walking trails. Not surprisingly given the terrain, it also draws climbers from across Europe.

to the public, or restricted areas that can only be visited with permission. Spain has just 14 *parques nacionales,* and only two of them – Doñana and Sierra Nevada – are in Andalucía.

Parques naturales (natural parks) are intended to protect cultural heritage as well as nature, and to promote economic development that's compatible with conservation. Many include roads, networks of walking trails, villages and even small towns, with accommodation often available within the park. Like national parks, they may include areas that can only be visited with permission. There are 24 *parques naturales* in Andalucía; they account for most of its protected territory and include nearly all of its most spectacular country.

Other types of protected areas in Andalucía include *parajes naturales* (natural areas; there are 31 of these) and *reservas naturales* (nature reserves, numbering 29). These are generally smaller, little-inhabited areas, with much the same goals as natural parks. There are also 37 *monumentos naturales* (natural monuments), protecting specific features such as waterfalls, forests or dunes.

Wildlife

Andalucía is a haven for wildlife that no longer exists elsewhere, and wildlife enthusiasts, if they know where to look, are unlikely to return home disappointed. A terrific source of up-to-date information on Andalucian fauna and flora is the English-language Iberianature (www .iberianature.com).

Signature Mammals

Many large mammal species that once roamed across Western Europe are now confined to small, isolated populations surrounded by an ever-expanding sea of humanity. That they survive at all in Andalucía is thanks to the region's varied, often untamed terrain, but even here they remain at serious risk.

Andalucía's most celebrated mammal, and one of its most endangered, is the Iberian lynx. It's near-on impossible to see in the wild.

The same can be said for the estimated 60 to 80 wolves *(lobos)* that survive in the Sierra Morena, mostly in Parque Natural Sierra de Andújar. Cut off from the rest of Europe's wolves (around 1500 survive in northern Spain), the wolf was, in 1986, declared in danger of extinction in Andalucía. In an effort to protect it from hunters and farmers, farmers are now awarded compensation if their animals are attacked by wolves. The wolf population has nonetheless sunk to levels that are probably fatally low.

Hunting throughout the 20th century is a primary reason why lynx and wolf populations have declined so alarmingly. In order to satisfy rural Andalucians' passion for hunting, and to provide an alternative prey to endangered species, the Andalucian government has introduced the mouflon *(muflón),* a wild sheep that's relatively plentiful, especially in the Parque Natural Sierras de Cazorla, Segura y Las Villas.

In no apparent danger of extinction, and one of the region's most easily viewed mammals, is the ibex *(cabra montés),* a stocky wild mountain goat whose males have distinctive long horns. Around 15,000 ibex live in Andalucía, with the largest populations found in the Sierra Nevada; Parque Natural Sierras de Cazorla, Segura y Las Villas; Sierras de Tejeda y Almijara; and Sierra de las Nieves. The ibex spends its summer hopping with amazing agility around high-altitude precipices; it descends to lower elevations in winter.

One of Spain's most unusual wildlife-watching experiences is the sight of Barbary apes, the only wild primates in Europe, clambering Gibraltar's heights.

Andalucía contains both Spain's wettest region (Grazalema in Cádiz province with up to 200cm annually) and its driest (the Desierto de Tabernas in Almería province with a mere 14cm annually).

Just as the sight of Barbary apes can seem like an apparition of Africa on European soil, whales *(ballenas)* and dolphins *(delfines)* are more often associated in the popular mind with the open waters of the Atlantic than the Mediterranean. Even so, the Bahía de Algeciras and Strait of Gibraltar harbour plenty of common, striped and bottlenose dolphins, as well as some pilot, killer and even sperm whales.

More common, less iconic mammals abound. Although some are nocturnal, those you may come across once you leave behind well-trodden trails include wild boar *(jabalí)*, red deer *(ciervo)*, roe deer *(corzo)*, fallow deer *(gamo)*, genet *(gineta)*, Egyptian mongoose *(meloncillo)*, red squirrel *(ardilla)*, badger *(tejón)* and otter *(nutria)*.

El Parque Natural Sierras de Cazorla, Segura y Las Villas is the largest protected area in Spain and the second largest in Europe.

A Birdwatcher's Paradise

If Andalucía is something of a last refuge for large mammal species, it serves a similar purpose for several highly endangered raptor species. When it comes to migratory bird species, however, Andalucía is a veritable superhighway.

For many in the birdwatching fraternity, raptors (birds of prey) are the soul birds of the avian world. Andalucía has 13 resident raptor species as well as a handful of summer visitors from Africa. Glowering in the almost-sinister manner of its kind, Europe's biggest bird, the rare and endangered black vulture *(buitre negro)* has established a stronghold in the Sierra Morena, with around 230 pairs scattered from Huelva's

MISSING LYNX?

The Iberian (or pardel) lynx (*lince ibérico* to Spaniards, *Lynx pardina* to scientists) is the most endangered cat species in the world. The species once ranged across southern Europe (the Hispanic Legions of the Roman Empire wore breastplates adorned with the Iberian lynx) and a century ago there were still 100,000 Iberian lynx left in the wild. Now there are fewer than 200 confined to an area smaller than a medium-sized European city.

So plentiful was the lynx until 1966 that the Spanish government classed it as 'vermin', encouraging hunters to declare open season on the lynx. By 1973, the species was officially protected. But this has, until recently, done little to slow the lynx's precipitous decline, prompting fears that it would soon be the first cat species to become extinct since the sabre-toothed tiger 10,000 years ago. Until 2007, when the Spanish government confirmed the presence of 15 Iberian lynx in the Montes de Toledo region of Castilla-La Mancha, the only proven breeding populations were in two areas of Andalucía: one is the eastern Sierra Morena, with perhaps 100 adult lynx; the other is the Parque Nacional de Doñana with around 30 adult lynx.

A falling rabbit population, caused by disease and hunting, has played a significant role in the lynx's demise, but human beings are the primary offenders. Of all lynx deaths since 2000, almost 80% were caused directly by humans through a loss of habitat due to new farmland, roads, dams and pine or eucalyptus plantations; illegal traps and snares set for other animals (especially foxes and wolves); and road accidents (33 lynx were run over in the area around the Parque Nacional de Doñana from 1995 to 2006).

But there are tentative signs that the lynx may have turned the corner. An in-captivity breeding program was set up at El Acebuche in Parque Nacional de Doñana in 1992 and it has proved an extraordinary success: 18 lynx were born in the first four months of 2009 alone. Live film of lynxes in the breeding program is displayed on a screen at the Parque Nacional de Doñana's El Acebuche visitor centre, though the breeding centre itself is closed to the public. There are also breeding centres elsewhere in Andalucía, including at Jerez de la Frontera's zoo and in the Sierra de Andújar, Jaén province. In the first half of 2012, 15 captivity-born lynx were released into the wild in the Sierra Morena, suggesting that Europe's emblematic 'big cat' might not be destined to face the same fate as the dodo.

Sierra Pelada to Jaén's Sierra de Andújar. As probably the world's biggest population, the black vulture's survival here is critical to the viability of the species.

Also emblematic and extremely rare is the Spanish imperial eagle (*águila imperial ibérica*), found in no other country. Its total numbers have increased from about 50 pairs in the 1960s to some 200 pairs today, helped by an active government protection plan operative since 2001. About 50 pairs are in Andalucía – mostly in the Sierra Morena, with about eight pairs in the Doñana area. Poisoned bait put out by farmers or hunters is the imperial's greatest enemy.

The mountain La Veleta in the Sierra Nevada sports Europe's highest paved road climbing to within 10m of its summit at 3380m.

LA VELETA

The bearded vulture or lammergeier (*quebrantahuesos*), with its majestic 2m-plus wingspan, disappeared from Andalucía – its last refuge in Spain except for the Pyrenees – in 1986. But all, it seems, is not lost. A breeding centre has been established in the Parque Natural Sierras de Cazorla, Segura y Las Villas and, as a first step, three young bearded vultures were released into the wild in 2006. As of 2012, about a dozen bearded vultures had successfully adapted to life in the wild.

Other large birds of prey in Andalucía include the golden eagle (*águila real*), the griffon vulture (*buitre leonado*) and the Egyptian vulture (*alimoche*), all found in mountain regions.

If Andalucía's raptors lend gravitas to birdwatching here, the waterbirds that visit Andalucía add a scale rarely seen in Europe. Andalucía is a haven for waterbirds, mainly thanks to extensive wetlands along the Atlantic coast, such as those at the mouths of the Guadalquivir and Odiel rivers. Hundreds of thousands of migratory birds, including an estimated 80% of Western Europe's wild ducks, winter in the Doñana wetlands at the mouth of the Guadalquivir, and many more call in during spring and autumn migrations.

Laguna de Fuente de Piedra, near Antequera, sees as many as 20,000 greater flamingo (*flamenco*) pairs rearing chicks in spring and summer. This beautiful pink bird can also be seen in several other places, including Cabo de Gata, Doñana and the Paraje Natural Marismas del Odiel; the last has extensive wetlands that serve as a haven for other waterbirds.

The large, ungainly white stork (*cigüeña blanca*), actually black and white, nests from spring to summer on electricity pylons, trees and towers (sometimes right in the middle of towns) across western Andalucía; the Dehesa de Abajo is home to a large woodland colony of white storks.

For more information on Andalucía's bird life, check out the website of SEO/BirdLife (www.seo.org).

Flamenco

Indian twirls and Jewish chants, Byzantine hymns and anguished Roma laments, Moorish wails and the rhythms of an ancient folk dance resurfacing in a fandango. Listen hard and flamenco, in its numerous guises, can invoke intense feelings of déjà vu, the disparate echoes of the past reconstituted and passed down through the centuries in the cries of the dispossessed.

Lorca called it the 'music of hope and despair', Goethe described its spirit as 'a physical power that all may feel but no philosophy can explain'. Reflective but uplifting, raw but layered, pure yet loaded with historical and emotional complexity, flamenco is far more than just a musical genre; it's a culture unto itself. Shrouded in mystery, its origins remain cloudy and unsubstantiated. Some cite the importance of Spain's Moors, others emphasize the key role of the Roma; almost all agree that the circumstances which sparked its embryonic development were crucially unique. Flamenco couldn't have happened anywhere else. It is proudly and unequivocally a product of Andalucía.

The *sevillana palo* doesn't actually originate in Seville. Rather it is a long-standing folk dance, originally called a *seguidilla*, thought to hail from the Castile region. Since the mid-19th century it has been the de rigueur dance at Seville's Feria de Abril.

The Basics

One of the beauties of flamenco is its lack of any straightforwardness; online searches and historical sleuthing usually throw up more questions than answers. A handful of umbrella points help provide some glue. First, flamenco is an expressive art, incorporating more than just music. In the early days it was a realistic reflection of the daily lives of those who sang it – the oppressed – and they carried it with them everywhere they went: in the fields, at work, at home and in their famed *juergas* (Roma parties). Second, it is very much a 'live' spectacle and – for purists at least – a necessarily spontaneous one. The preserve of the nomadic Roma until the 19th century, performances were never rehearsed or theatrical, and the best ones still aren't. Third, flamenco hinges on the interaction between its four basic elements: the *cante* (song), the *baile* (dance), the *toque* (guitar), and an oft-forgotten fourth element known as the *jaleo* (handclaps, shouts and audience participation/appreciation). The *cante* sits centre stage, the guide which all else follows. Indeed, in its earliest incarnations, flamenco didn't have regular dancers, and guitars weren't added until the 19th century. Some flamenco forms, such as *martinetes* and *carceleras*, remain voice only.

In traditional flamenco performances, players warm up slowly, tuning their guitars and clearing their throats while the gathered crowd talk among themselves. It is up to the dancers and musicians to grab the audience's attention and gradually lure them in.

Flamenco Palos (Musical Forms)

The purist expression of flamenco is known as *cante jondo* (literally 'deep song'), a primitive collection of *palos* that includes *soleares* (quintessential flamenco *palo* with a strong, strict rhythm), *siguiriyas* (tragic and expressive flamenco *palo*), *tientos*, *martinetes* and *carceleras*. *Cante jondo* is considered to be the main building block of flamenco and good singers – whose gravelly operatic voices can sound like a cross between Tom Waits and Pavarotti – are required to 'hurl their song into the air' and

SEEING FLAMENCO

Tablaos

Tablaos are the natural successors to the *cafés cantantes* (erstwhile drinking establishments that offered live flamenco music) that sprung up in Spain in the late 19th century. They are specialised clubs that put on a regular program of flamenco shows using professional artists. Some are top-notch, others lack authenticity. Here are a few of the better ones:

» Casa de la Memoria de Al-Andalus (p70), Seville
» El Lagá Tio Parilla (p123), Jerez de la Frontera
» Los Gallos (p71), Seville

Peñas

Peñas are private clubs run by aficionados. Their repertoire is more spontaneous and esoteric than *tablaos,* and there is less pampering to tourist tastes. Many *peñas* are small, semiprivate affairs. A few open their doors on a regular basis and post a schedule of shows, and include the following:

» Peña de la Platería (p249), Granada
» Peña Flamenca La Perla (p111), Cádiz
» Peña El Taranto (p271), Almería

Festivals

Andalucía is rife with flamenco festivals.

La Bienal de Flamenco (September, even-numbered years) Seville

Festival de Jerez (February/March) Jerez de la Frontera

Potaje Gitano (last Saturday in June) Utrera

Gazpacho Andaluz (July) Morón de la Frontera

Caracolé (July) Lebrija

leave a piece of their soul in every stanza. The raw emotion and almost religious absorption of these powerful performers can be rather unnerving to the uninitiated. The aim is to inspire *duende* – the musical spirit that reaches out and touches your soul during an ecstatic live performance. But *duende* can be elusive. 'There are neither maps nor exercises to help us find the *duende*,' Lorca once opined. Thus, it is up to the singer to summon it up, amalgamating yearning, superstition, anguish and fervour into a force that is both intimate and transcendental.

The other main grouping of flamenco songs is called *cantes chicos* (little songs), *palos* that are more light-hearted and accessible derivatives of *cante jondo*. Popular *cantes chicos* are the upbeat *alegrías* from Cadiz, descended from sailor's jigs; the fast but tongue-in-cheek *bulerías* from Jerez; and the ubiquitous tangos made popular by the great Sevillana singer, La Niña de los Peines.

A third, more nebulous, group of *palos* (sometimes called *cantes andaluzes*) exists outside of what most aficionados would call 'pure' flamenco. This consists mainly of fandangoes which are descended from Spanish folk music with each region broadcasting their own variation. The most famous are the strident Fandangos de Huelva enthusiastically danced during the religious pilgrimage Romería del Rocío. *Verdiales*, an ancient Arabic-style song/dance, are a type of fandango from Málaga, a province that also concocted the freer and easier (and undanced) *malagueñas*. *Granaínas* are an ornamental and introspective fandango offshoot from Granada with no set rhythm; *tarantos* are an earthier, sparser version of the form from the mining communities of the Levante (Almería).

Other, hard-to-classify, *cantes* are *farrucas*, folk dances thought to have originated in Galicia, and *sevillanas*, a quintessential Andalucian fiesta dance best seen at Seville's annual Feria de Abril. A more recent subgenre of flamenco are the *ida y vuelta* (return) *palos,* musical styles that have been sugar-frosted with influences from Latin America before being 'returned' to Spain. The most widely circulated are the *guajira* and *rumba palos* from Cuba and the *columbianas* from Colombia.

Historical Roots

The origins of flamenco are intriguingly vague. The long-time preserve of marginalised and culturally oppressed people (most of whom were illiterate), it was neither written about nor eulogised in its early days. Instead, the music was passed through bloodlines by word of mouth. No published testimonies exist before 1840.

The genesis of the art as we now know it was ignited in Andalucía sometime in the early 15th century among disparate groups of Roma, Jews, Moors and ordinary Spaniards. Anthropological evidence suggests that the nomadic Roma had begun a 400-year-long western migration from the Indian subcontinent in the 11th century, settling all over Europe, with a southern contingent reaching Andalucía in the early 1400s. The Roma brought with them a dynamic form of musical expression – a way of performing that encouraged embellishment, virtuosity and improvisation – and they blended this rich musicality with the songs and melodies of the regions where they settled. In Andalucía, they found natural allies among the Jews and Moors recently disenfranchised by the Reconquista (Christian reconquest). The collision of these three distinct cultures and the subsequent marinating of their music and culture over three or four centuries resulted in what we now know as *cante jondo,* or pure flamenco.

The Ortegas are one of the great Roma families who have produced such flamenco singers as El Fillo (Francisco Ortega Vargas) and El Caracol ('The Snail'; Manuel Ortega Juárez), as well as legendary bullfighters such as Joselito 'El Gallo' ('The Rooster'; José Gómez Ortega)

FLAMENCO

A Tale of Three Cities

Flamenco's documented history begins in the early 19th century and is essentially a tale of three cities in western Andalucía: Seville, Cádiz and Jerez, and their respective Roma neighbourhoods. The first real flamenco singer of note was the mysteriously named El Planeta (Antonio Monge Rivero), a Roma blacksmith born in either Jerez or Cádiz around 1785. El Planeta wasn't a performer in the modern sense, but he soon became well known for his passionate singing voice that rang eloquently out of his forge and gave birth – allegedly – to such early flamenco *palos* as *martinetes* and *livianas*. El Planeta sits at the head of a flamenco 'family tree' of interrelated singers, musicians and dancers which has carried on to the present day. His immediate heir was El Fillo (Francisco Ortega Vargas), whose naturally gravelly voice became the standard to which all others were compared.

Jerez has often been coined the 'cradle of flamenco', primarily because its densely packed Roma quarters of Santiago and San Miguel have produced so many great artists. Today the city is home to Andalucía's main flamenco centre/school and it hosts two major festivals in February and September. Flamenco in Cádiz grew up in the Santa María neighbourhood wedged romantically aside the crashing ocean, while in Seville its font was the riverside Roma district of Triana. Draw a line between these three cities and you'll capture a handful of other towns with strong flamenco traditions including Utrera, Lebrija and Morón de la Frontera, all in Seville province.

Saetas are religious laments that are often placed under the flamenco umbrella. You'll still hear them sung unaccompanied from upper-floor balconies by men and women during Semana Santa (Holy Week) processions as the float passes beneath them.

The Golden Age

Flamenco's so-called 'golden age' began in the late 1840s and lasted until around 1915. In the space of 70 years, the music metamorphosed from an esoteric Roma art practiced spontaneously at raucous *juergas,* into a professional and increasingly popular form of public entertainment that merged *cante jondo* with other forms of Spanish folkloric music. It was during this fertile epoch that the modern musical styles took shape. Other innovations included the more complex choreography of flamenco dance and the emergence of the guitar as the de rigueur accompanying instrument.

The catalysts for change were the famous *cafés cantantes* that took root in many Spanish cities, especially in Andalucía. The first cafe opened in Seville in 1842, and the establishments gradually spread, reaching their apex in the 1880s with prestigious venues such as the Café Silverio in Seville. Decorated with mirrors, bullfighting posters, gilded stages, and tables where patrons could enjoy alcoholic beverages, the cafes were the engine rooms of a dramatic musical cross-fertilisation not dissimilar to the blues-country fusion that later spat out rock and roll. Presiding over this conflation was Silverio Franconetti, proprietor of Seville's Café Silverio and soulful inheritor of El Fillo's *voz afillá* (hoarse, cracked voice in the style of the singer El Fillo). Yet, despite his Roma blood and lifelong penchant for *siguiriyas* and *solerares,* Franconetti couldn't stop the bastardisation of the music he loved as it fled from the *juergas* into the cafes, substituting tragic harshness for tuneful palatability. Unwittingly, he had created the catalyst for flamenco's jump from 'music of the Roma' to popular property.

Slide into Decadence

In 1920, pure flamenco, threatened by changing public tastes and impending political crises, was an endangered species. Fearing oblivion, Andalucian aesthetes Federico Lorca and Manuel de Falla organised a competition in Granada in 1922 to try to save the art – the Concurso de Cante Jondo – but with the civil war approaching, the die was cast. The music entered an era known as *ópera flamenco* when *cante jondo* was diluted further by folk music, greater commercialisation and imported foreign influences from Latin America. The controversial figure of the moment was Pepe Marchena (1903–76), flamenco's first well-paid superstar who broke with tradition by singing lighter fandangos and *cantes de ida y vuelta* often backed by an orchestra. Purists were understandably leery, while others saw it as a natural evolution of a music that had leapt suddenly into the public domain. Just below the radar, *cante jondo* survived, in part because it was still performed by Roma singers such as Manuel Torre and La Niña de los Peines, the greatest male and female voices of their age.

Rebirth

By the 1950s, the re-evaluation of *cante jondo* fell to Antonio Mairena (1909–83), an impassioned Roma *cantaor* (singer) from Seville province and the first real 'flamencologist' to historically decipher the art. Mairena insisted on singing only old forms of *palos,* such as *siguiriyas* and *martinetes,* many of which he rescued from almost certain extinction. Through his stubborn refusal to pamper to commercial tastes, he provided a lifeline between the golden age and the revival that was to come.

By the 1960s, nascent *tablaos* – nightclubs staging professional flamenco shows – had filled the vacuum left by the closure of the *cafés cantantes* in the 1920s. Some *tablaos,* particularly those in the new resort towns on the coast, were fake and insipid, while others played a role in re-establishing *cante jondo* alongside the newer forms of *palos.* But flamenco's ultimate revival was spearheaded not by venues, but by the exciting performers who frequented them. Two in particular stood out: Paco de Lucía from Algeciras was a guitarist so precocious that by age 14 he had absorbed everything any living musician could teach him. His muse and foil was Camarón de la Isla, a Roma singer from San Fernando (La Isla) who by the early 1970s had attained the kind of godlike status normally reserved for rock-stars and bullfighters. Between them Camarón and Lucía took flamenco to a different level, injecting it with new out-of-the box innovations (electric guitars, keyboards etc) while, at the same time, carefully safeguarding its purity. Suddenly the rest of the world was sitting up and taking notice.

Modern Flamenco

In the 1970s musicians began mixing flamenco with jazz, rock, blues, rap and other genres. The purists loathed these changes, but this *nuevo* flamenco (new flamenco) greatly broadened flamenco's appeal. The seminal recording was a 1977 flamenco-folk-rock album, *Veneno* (Poison), by the group of the same name centred on Kiko Veneno and Raimundo Amador, both from Seville.

The group Ketama, whose key members are all from Granada's Montoya flamenco family, mixes flamenco with African, Cuban, Brazilian and other rhythms. Wide-ranging in their search for complementary sounds and rhythms, Ketama's *Songhai* (1987) and *Songhai II* (1995) –

Translated Stage Names

» Camarón de la Isla – Shrimp from the Island

» El Caracol – The Snail

» La Nina de los Peines – Girl of the Combs

» Tomatito – Little Tomato

FLAMENCO

CONCURSO DE CANTE JONDO, 1922

On an ethereal summer's evening in June 1922, a little-known Andalucian poet named Federico García Lorca stood in the Plaza de Aljibes in Granada's Alhambra and welcomed 4000 guests to the Concurso de Cante Jondo (competition of 'deep song'), a flamenco singing contest he had organised in collusion with the distinguished Spanish classical composer Manuel de Falla.

Between them, Spain's two great avant-garde thinkers had struggled relentlessly in their bid to elevate flamenco – and in particular *cante jondo* – into a serious art form; it was a dynamic cultural genre of half-forgotten Andalucian folkloric traditions that was being asphyxiated by a growing penchant for watered-down forms of flamenco 'opera'.

Amassed inside the atmospheric confines of the Alhambra were an impressive array of intellectuals, writers, performers, musicians and flamenco purists. One 72-year-old *cantaor* (singer) named Tio Bermúdez had walked 100km from his home village to be there and stunned the audience with his interpretations of old-style *siguiriyas*. Another, an old blind woman of Roma stock exhaustively hunted down by Lorca, sang an unaccompanied *liviana*, a flamenco form long thought to be dead. A 12-year-old boy named Manolo Ortega Juárez, aka 'El Caracol' ('The Snail'), so impressed the judges that he walked off with first prize. Mesmerised beneath the cypress trees, and heady with the aroma of jasmine and lavender, young men swapped guitar *falsetas* (riffs), ladies stood up and danced *soleares*, while others listened to the virtuosity of established stars such as Ramón Montoya and Manuel Torre. The complex – observers later reported – seemed to be 'alive with spirits'.

Whether the *concurso* ultimately 'saved' flamenco is open to debate. While the music gained some short-lived prestige, and sporadic recordings and revivals ensued, its golden age was well and truly over. An era of decadence followed, hastened by the onset of the civil war and the repressive Franco dictatorship that came after. Flamenco's modern rebirth ultimately had to wait for a second *concurso* in Córdoba in 1956 and the subsequent rise of newer, more ground-breaking innovators such as Camarón de la Isla and Paco de Lucía over a decade later.

Instead, Lorca and Falla's *concurso* has gone down in history as flamenco's 'Woodstock', a beautiful and memorable musical moment, but one that acted more as a coda to the era that preceded it, rather than a portent for what was to come next.

FLAMENCO LEGENDS

» El Planeta (1785–1850) Legendary Roma blacksmith who purportedly invented many unaccompanied *cantes* (songs).

» El Fillo (1829–78) Protégé of El Planeta and famed for his gravelly voice dubbed the *voz afillá*.

» Silverio Franconetti (1831–89) Non-Roma who met El Fillo in Morón de la Frontera. Became an accomplished singer and set up Spain's most famous *café cantante* in Seville.

» Antonio Chacón (1869–1929) Non-Roma singer with a powerful voice. Hired by Franconetti to sing in his Seville *café cantante* in the 1890s.

» Ramón Montoya (1880–1949) Accompanist to Chacón from 1922 onwards – put the guitar centre stage in flamenco.

» La Niña de los Peines (1890–1969) Dynamic Roma singer from Seville who sang with Chacón and provided a vital link between the golden age and the 1950s revivalists.

» El Caracol (1909–1973) Discovered at age 12 at the Concurso de Cante Jondo in 1922. Went on to become one of the greatest yet most self-destructive flamenco singers of all time.

» Camarón de la Isla (1950–1992) Performed in a club owned by El Caracol; this modern flamenco 'god' from San Fernando (La Isla) lived fast, died young and dabbled in bold experimentation.

» Paco de Lucía (1947–) Guitar phenomenon from Algeciras who became Camarón's main accompanist and has successfully crossed over into jazz and classical music.

collaborations with Malian *kora* (harp) player Toumani Diabaté – are among the group's best albums.

Flamenco today is as popular as it has ever been and probably more innovative. While established singers such as Enrique Morente, José Menese and Carmen Linares remain at the top of the profession, new generations continue to broaden flamenco's audience. Among the most popular are José Mercé from Jerez, whose exciting album *Lío* (Entanglement; 2002) was a big seller, and El Barrio, a 21st-century urban poet from Cádiz. Other artists include Cádiz' Niña Pastori, who arrived in the late 1990s singing jazz- and Latin-influenced flamenco. Her albums, such as *Entre dos Puertos* (Between Two Ports; 1997), *María* (2002) and J*oyas Prestadas* (Borrowed Jewels; 2006), are great listening.

Flamenco dance has reached its most adventurous horizons in the person of Joaquín Cortés, born in Córdoba in 1969. Cortés fuses flamenco with contemporary dance, ballet and jazz, to music at rock-concert amplification. He tours frequently both in Spain and all over the world with spectacular solo or ensemble shows.

On the guitar, modern virtuosos include Manolo Sanlúcar from Cádiz, Tomatito from Almería (who used to accompany Camarón de la Isla) and Vicente Amigo from Córdoba; they accompany today's top singers or perform solo.

Andalucian Arts

For significant parts of Spanish history, Andalucía has stood at the forefront of the nation's artistic and cultural life. There has been no *single* high point. Instead, halcyon eras have come and gone, often (though not always) ebbing and flowing with the power of Spain on the world stage: the gilded Córdoba caliphate of the 8th to the 11th centuries, the final flourishing of the Nasrid dynasty in the 1300s and 1400s, the famed Siglo de Oro (Golden Century; actually a 160-year spell that lasted from approximately 1492 to the 1650s); and – more surprising considering Andalucía's economic demise after 1898 – the emergence of the so-called Generación de '27 (a group of poets) in 1927.

Though all the arts are well-represented in Andalucía's cultural pastiche, the region has produced a particularly rich seam of talented painters, including two of the most influential masters to ever grace the world stage: Diego Velázquez and Pablo Picasso.

The Córdoba Caliphate

Today Córdoba is a journeyman city of just over 300,000 people, famous for its ancient Mezquita and left-leaning political inclinations. However, one thousand years ago, it was the most populous and culturally vibrant city in Europe, possibly the world. The Córdoba of the 8th to the 11th centuries was an intellectual powerhouse replete with libraries, schools and a university which competed with the rival caliphate of Damascus to promote the global spread of ideas. Emir Abd ar-Rahman II (r 822–52) was a strong patron of the arts who maintained a close relationship with the influential Arabic poet and musician Ziryab; Abd ar-Rahman III (r 912–61) filled his 'briliant city' Medina Azahara with the finest Islamic art, crafts and mosaics, much of it copied from Byzantium artists; while Al-Hakim II (r 961–76) was an avid reader who collected and catalogued hundreds of thousands of books. Many of the great works of Greek philosophy were later translated and reinterpreted here by scholarly polymaths such as Averroës (1126–98), Maimonides (1135–1204) and Ibn Tufail (1105–85) who dabbled in both the sciences and the arts.

Though Córdoba's influence declined after its reconquest by the Christians in 1236, the invaders from the north subtly absorbed many of the city's work and ideas. It was partly through this intellectual inheritance that western Europe attained the know-how and inspiration that sparked the Renaissance, a movement which ultimately took shape in Italy two centuries later.

The Nasrid Flowering

The Nasrid emirate established in Granada in 1232 was more of a defensive entity than an outward-looking culture-spreader in the mould of Córdoba. However, its foppish rulers were vociferous appreciators of the arts; in particular poetry. Several of the emirate's sultans became acclaimed poets, most notably Yusuf III (r 1408–17), whose yearning,

FRANCISCO PACHECO

Other artists may get more credit, but Andalucian painter Francisco Pacheco (1564–1644), from Sanlúcar de Barrameda, was teacher and mentor to numerous greats, including Diego Velázquez (who married his daughter) and Francisco Zurbarán.

romantic verse acted as a prelude to a Byronic reawakening 400 years later. The highpoint of the Granadian flowering came during the illustrious reigns of Yusuf I (1333–54) and Muhammad V (1354–91), the two great builders of the Alhambra. Both sultans established literary circles in their courts, Yusuf employing Arabic poet and historian Ibn al-Khatib (1313–75), whose verse was set to music and whose lyrical poems remain inscribed on the walls of Alhambra's palaces and fountains. Muhammad V installed al-Khatib as his *vizier* (political advisor), a position that stoked much political controversy at the time and possibly cost al-Khatib his life. In 1375, al-Khatib's student and fellow poet Ibn Zamrak (1333–93) hired assassins to kill him. Ibn Zamrak subsequently became court poet to Muhammad V during an era when poetry and cultural exchange with Morocco and Egypt had created a healthy cross-continental flow of ideas.

Byron first visited Andalucía in 1809. Inspired by the experience, he wrote his mock-epic poetic masterpiece *Don Juan*, based on the famous Spanish fictional hero in the early 1820s.

El Siglo de Oro

Painting

For a brief but glittering 50 years during Spain's Siglo de Oro (Golden Century), ignited in 1492, Andalucian painters pretty much defined world art. The mantle rested on the shoulders of three Seville-based giants: Bartolomé Murillo (1617–82), a baroque master with a delicate touch and a penchant for documentary and religious painting; Francisco de Zurbarán (1598–1664), a more restrained exponent of the Italian art of chiaroscuro (the technique of contrasting light and dark elements in a painting to create a dramatic effect), born in Extremadura but intrinsically linked to the Seville school; and Diego Velázquez (1599–1660), the so-called artist's artist whose exacting methods and subtle use of colour and tone opened up the doors to Impressionism and ultimately made him an aesthetic guru. Velázquez's most celebrated work, *Las Meninas*, is a revolutionary masterpiece of illusion in which the artist depicts himself contemplating his invisible subjects, the king and queen of Spain, whose faces appear reflected in a mirror. Three centuries after his death, an enamoured Picasso made 58 abstract attempts to reinterpret the great work.

Both Velázquez and Zurbarán were employed by the royal court of Philip IV, while Murillo was favoured by the Catholic Church. Murillo painted several works for Seville cathedral, but is best known for his interpretation of the Virgin Mary's Immaculate Conception, executed in 1650 and now displayed in Madrid's El Prado. Velázquez and Zurbarán tackled the same topic in 1618 and 1630, respectively.

JULIO ROMERO DE TORRES

Julio Romero de Torres (1874–1930) was a realist artist from Córdoba born a few years before Picasso, who consequently often fell into the shadow of the Cubist master. He embraced realism and is known for his haunting studies of Spanish women.

Music

Preceding the artistic revolution, and in the days when flamenco was still an esoteric Roma art, Spanish music, soaking up contemporary Italian traditions, gained wider European recognition through Renaissance composers such as Francisco Guerrero (1528–99). Guerrero, the main choir master at Seville cathedral, composed sacred and secular music that was heavy with conservative and Gregorian traditions. His mantle was carried on by his assistant, Alonso Lobo (1555–1617), from Osuna, whose devout works – including hymns, masses and psalms – helped cement Seville as a fermenting ground for sacred music.

Literature

Miguel de Cervantes (1547–1616), the genius creator of *Don Quixote,* was a product of La Mancha region, but his linguistic skills may not have been so exacting had it not been for Antonio de Nebrija (1441–1522), from Lebrija near Seville, who published the Spanish language's first book of grammar in 1492. The book was ceremoniously presented to Catholic

ANDALUCIAN ARTS THE REAWAKENING

TALKIN' BOUT MY GENERATION

From time to time, exceptional circumstances prompt the flowering of exceptional artistic movements. Postwar rigidity in the US led to the rise of the hedonistic Beat poets. In early-20th-century London, the Bloomsbury Set reacted noisily against so-called Victorian values. Spain's great blossoming took place in the small window of serenity between the end of WWI and the onset of the Spanish Civil War. In 1927 in Seville a key group of 10 Spanish poets came together to mark the 300th anniversary of the death of lyrical baroque master Luís de Góngora. The meeting had a strong southern bias. Of the 10, six were born in Andalucía, including the peerless Federico García Lorca (from Granada), the romantic-turned-polemicist poet Rafael Alberti (from El Puerto de Santa María) and the surrealist wordsmith Vicente Aleixandre (from Seville).

Unlike the more pessimistic Generación de '98, which had criticised the conformism of Spain after the restoration of the monarchy in 1868, the 27ers were less damning of what had gone before in their exploration of classic themes such as love, death, destiny and the beauty of images. Obsessed by the work of Góngora, they espoused wider poetic expressionism and free verse, combining elements of the new surrealism with echoes from Spain's ancient folkloric tradition (in particular flamenco). The movement was ultimately shattered and dispersed by the civil war, an event that killed Lorca and sent many of the others into a long exile.

The last surviving member of the Generación de '27, Francisco Ayala from Granada died in 2009 aged 103. Ayala spent many years in exile in Argentina and Puerto Rico after his father and brother were murdered by Nationalists in the Spanish Civil War.

monarch Queen Isabel I, who subsequently discovered its usefulness in subjugating a large Spanish empire in Latin America.

A contemporary of Cervantes, but active primarily in the poetic sphere, Luís de Góngora (1561–1627), from Córdoba, was a baroque wordsmith, as famous for his life-long feud with writing rival (and contemporary) Francisco de Quevedo as for his effortless lyricism. He was ground-breaking enough to have a genre of writing named after him: Gongorismo, a style that stood the test of time and was enthusiastically revived by Federico Lorca and the Generación de '27 three centuries after the master's demise.

The Reawakening

The Andalucian art scene dimmed in the 18th and 19th centuries as Spain lost its overseas empire and position as a global power. Just as the decline looked to be terminal after Spain's humiliation in the Spanish-American war in 1898, a wake-up call was sounded by a group of critical writers known as the Generación de '98. The circle, led by Seville-born social realist poet Antonio Machado (1875–1939) chided the nation for being asleep, adrift in a sea of mediocrity, and their critical works, flecked with rebellion and realism, aimed to offset the cultural malaise and re-establish the nation's literary prominence. Around the same time, classical music found a cohesive Iberian voice in a group of four Spanish composers, two of whom were from Andalucía. Both Manuel de Falla (1876–1946) from Cádiz and Joaquín Turina (1882–1949) from Seville used influences absorbed from the Parisian Impressionists, Debussy and Ravel, to craft operas, songs and chamber music that resonated with echoes of Andalucian folklore. Falla, in particular, was fascinated by flamenco; along with poet Federico Lorca he organised the Concurso de Cante Jondo in 1922.

The 2008 British-Spanish film *Little Ashes* (*Cenicitas*) is based on long-standing rumours of a 1920s love affair between Federico Lorca and Salvador Dalí.

PICASSO RECLAIMED

Ironically for a boy given 23 names at birth, Picasso became famous for signing his paintings with just one. Born in Málaga in 1881 to an artist father, Don José Ruíz y Blasco (also Málaga-born), the young Pablo lived in the city until he was 10. In 1891 he moved with his family to La Coruña in the Galicia region and then, in 1895, to Barcelona where he ultimately established his artistic reputation. Since he never returned permanently to Málaga, Picasso's connection with Andalucía has often been understated; you'll find better expositions of his art in Barcelona and Paris. But, with Málaga undergoing a cultural reawakening in the late 1990s, the city has taken steps to reclaim him. The Picasso Foundation was established in 1988 in his Casa Natal (birth house) in Plaza de la Merced and, in 2003, after 50 years of on-off planning, the Museo Picasso Málaga was opened in a 16th-century palace to honour its most famous native son.

Lorca: A Category of his Own

It is debatable whether you can truly understand modern Anadalucía without at least an inkling of knowledge of Spain's greatest poet and playwright, Federico García Lorca (1898–1936). Lorca epitomised many of Andalucía's potent hallmarks – passion, ambiguity, exuberance and innovation – and brought them skilfully to life in a litany of precocious works. Early popularity was found with *El Romancero Gitano* (Gypsy Ballads), a 1928 collection of verses on Roma themes, full of startling metaphors yet crafted with the simplicity of flamenco song. Between 1933 and 1936 he wrote the three tragic plays for which he is best known: *Bodas de Sangre* (Blood Wedding), *Yerma* (Barren) and *La Casa de Bernarda Alba* (The House of Bernarda Alba) – brooding and dark but dramatic works dealing with themes of entrapment and liberation. Granada produced, inspired and ultimately destroyed Lorca (he was executed by Nationalists there in 1936), and this is the city where his legacy remains most evident.

The 20th Century & Beyond

The huge task for 20th- and 21st-century Andalucian writers and artists has been escaping the shadow left by Picasso and Lorca. Heading the post-Franco literary generation is Antonio Muñoz Molina, a novelist and essayist from Úbeda best known for his book *Sefarad* (2003), an exploration of the Jewish experience from their expulsion from Spain to the Holocaust. António Soler from Málaga added another new voice with his novel *El Camino de los Ingleses* (The Way of the English; 2004), tracking a group of friends' summer of transition from adolescence to adulthood. The book was made into a film starring Antonio Banderas.

In the art world, Madrid's identity-searching Movida movement (the post-Franco cultural awakening) included gay pop artists Enrique Naya and José Carrero from Cádiz. Operating jointly under the name Costus, their Madrid apartment/studio became a metaphoric G-spot for the Movida's main protagonists, including film director Pedro Almodóvar who featured it in his cult movie *Pepi, Luci, Bom* (1980).

Bullfighting

In January 2012, Catalonia bade *adiós* to several hundred years of Spanish tradition and became the first region in mainland Spain to ban bullfighting (it has been banned in the Canary Islands since 1991). Whether other regions will follow suit remains uncertain, though it's unlikely Andalucía will cave into the opposition movement any time soon. Spain's southernmost region has long been considered the heartland of bullfighting; it's where modern bullfighting was invented and it's produced many legendary bullfighters.

For its opponents, bullfighting is intolerably cruel, akin to bear-baiting, and a blight on Spain's conscience in these supposedly more enlightened times. The antibullfighting lobby is bigger and more influential in parts of northern Spain. Spanish antibullfighting organisations include the Barcelona-based **Asociación para la Defensa de los Derechos del Animal** (Association for the Defence of Animal Rights; www .addaong.org) and the Madrid-based **Equanimal** (www.equanimal.org). The British-based **League Against Cruel Sports** (www.league.org.uk), established in 1924, also campaigns against bullfighting. For information about creative protests against bullfighting, visit www.runningofth enudes.com.

History

Culturally speaking, bullfighting shares many similarities with flamenco: its roots are foggy, the practice is distinctively Spanish (and Andalucian) in nature and the inherent skills have traditionally been passed down through bloodlines in various dynasties or families.

Some historical testimonies suggest it was Roman emperor Claudius who introduced bullfighting to Spain. However, it was the Moors who refined what was then an unregulated spectacle by adding ritualistic moves and employing the use of horses. The practice was largely the preserve of the horse-riding nobility until the early 1700s, when an Andalucian from Ronda named Francisco Romero got down from his mount, feinted a few times with a cape and killed the bull with a sword to end the *corrida* (bullfight). Francisco's methods quickly gained popularity and he became the first true professional bullfighter and head of a famous Ronda-Romero dynasty. Francisco's son Juan Romero evolved bullfighting further by adding the cuadrilla (bullfighting team). Despite his dangerous profession, Juan (allegedly) lived until the age of 102. Third in line, Pedro (Francisco's grandson) remains the most celebrated bullfighter of all time, with over 5000 bulls slain in a 60-year career. Pedro introduced theatrics to bullfighting and established it as a serious pursuit. His methods remained commonplace for nearly a century.

Bullfighting's 'golden age' came in the 1910s when it was transformed from an ostentatious 'circus act' into a breathtaking show of aesthetics and technicality with a miniscule margin for error. The change was prompted by a famous rivalry between two matadors: Juan Belmonte and Joselito 'El Gallo.' Regarded as the two greatest bullfighters in history, they were born within three years of each other in Seville province.

Juan Belmonte (1892–1962) had deformed legs. Unable to move like a classic matador, he elected to stand bolt upright and motionless in the ring until the bull was nearly upon him. He once quipped that he went into the ring like a 'mathematician proving a theorem'. This startling new technique kept the audience's hearts in their mouths and resulted in Belmonte getting gored more than 20 times; yet he lived. His rival Joselito (1895–1920) wasn't so lucky. Joselito was a child prodigy who adapted Belmonte's close-quarter methods. The two quickly became rivals and their duels with the *muleta* (the red cloth waved by the matador) between the years 1912 and 1920 are unlikely to be replicated. Joselito was fatally gored in 1920, a sacrificial 'death in the afternoon' that Hemingway – who went on to become a good friend of Belmonte – later wrote about in his famous book of the same name.

Doused in tradition, the essence of bullfighting has changed little since Joselito's demise. Monolete (1917–47), a notoriously serious bullfighter from Córdoba, added some of the short, close passes with the *muleta* that are now common in modern bullfighting, while his fellow Cordoban 'El Cordobés' combined flamboyance inside the ring with equally flamboyant antics outside it. Perhaps the greatest rivalry since the 1910s was between Madrileño Luís Miguel Dominguín and Ronda stalwart Antonio Ordóñez, catalogued once again by Hemingway over the 'dangerous summer' of 1959.

An *espontáneo* is a spectator at a bullfight who illegally jumps into the ring and attempts to fight the bull. The famous matador 'El Cordobes' controversially launched his career this way. Ironically, years later, one of his own fights was interrupted by a less lucky *espontáneo* who was fatally gored.

The Fight

Bullfights usually begin at about 6pm and, as a rule, three different matadors will fight two bulls each. Each fight takes about 15 minutes.

After entering the arena, the bull is first moved about by junior bullfighters, known as *peones,* wielding great capes. The colourfully attired matador then puts in an initial appearance and makes *faenas* (moves) with the bull, such as pivoting before its horns. The more closely and calmly the matador works with the bull, the greater the crowd's appreciation. The matador leaves the stage to the *banderilleros,* who attempt

---

HISTORIC BULLRINGS

There are close to 70 bullfighting rings in Andalucía. The season runs from Easter Sunday to October. The cities with the strongest traditions are Seville and Ronda.

» **Seville** Home to La Maestranza, the so-called 'Catedral del Toreo' (Cathedral of Bullfighting) and the oldest bullfighting venue in the world, dating from 1761. The biggest program runs in tandem with the Feria de Abril.

» **Ronda** The neoclassical Plaza de Toros de Ronda was built in 1784 and was frequented by Pedro Romero and, later, the Ordóñez clan. The Corrida Goyesca festival is held here in September. It is the world's largest ring by size, measuring 66m in diameter.

» **El Puerto de Santa María** A Cádiz province town with a big bullfighting legacy and a 15,000-capacity ring dating from 1880.

» **Antequera** Surrounded by parkland, Antequera's bullring was rebuilt in 1984 to its original 1848 design. It also has a museum on site.

» **Málaga** The famous Malagueta opened in 1878 and was built in neo-Mudéjar style. It holds 14,000 spectators.

» **Córdoba** The Plaza de los Califas, built in 1965, has Andalucía's largest seating capacity with room for nearly 17,000 spectators.

to goad the bull into action by plunging a pair of *banderillas* (short prods with harpoon-style ends) into his withers. Next, the horseback picadors take over, to shove a lance into the withers, greatly weakening the bull. The matador then returns for the final session. When the bull seems tired out and unlikely to give a lot more, the matador chooses the moment for the kill. Facing the animal head-on, the matador aims to sink a sword cleanly into its neck for an instant kill – the *estocada*.

A skilful, daring performance followed by a clean kill will have the crowd on its feet, waving handkerchiefs in appeal to the fight president to award the matador an ear of the animal.

The Spanish king, Juan Carlos (1938–), has been quoted as saying 'the day the EU bans bullfighting is the day that Spain leaves the EU'.

BULLFIGHTING

The Andalucian Kitchen

C'est vrai! Spain is the new France when it comes to creative, out-of-the-box cooking. The driving force of this experimental movement known as *la nueva cocina* is spearheaded by Catalan gastronome Ferran Adriá, whose mercurial restaurant El Bulli near Barcelona was a legend in its own lunchtime before it closed in 2011. Though happier basking in tradition than grabbing at the coat-tails of their precocious northern cousins, Andalucía is no culinary stick-in-the-mud. It won its first Michelin star at Restaurante Tragabuches in Ronda in 1998 courtesy of Dani García, one of Spain's top 10 chefs, and more accolades have followed.

There are nine Michelin-starred restaurants in Andalucía as of 2012, but only one – Calima in Marbella – gets two stars.

MICHELIN

Notwithstanding, Andalucian cuisine still revels in its simplicity. The coast produces fish, a particular speciality being *pescaito frito* (fish deep-fried in olive oil). The mountains nurture meat, especially the Alpujarras and Cazorla regions where game and stews are popular. Olive oil has been a staple in Andalucian cooking since Roman times (the region remains the world's biggest producer), as has wine, the most famous export being sherry. The region's 'caviar' is *jamón ibérico* a much-sought-after, melt-in-your-mouth ham. More importantly, Andalucians also claim that it was they who invented tapas.

The twist in Andalucian cooking is its palpable Moorish inflections. The Moors imported citrus fruits and rice cultivation to Al-Andalus and introduced numerous spices such as cinnamon, nutmeg, coriander and saffron. Equally tangible is the Arabic obsession with almonds, a factor still reflected in many Andalucian desserts.

Fruits of the Sea

That old legend about the Costa del Sol megaresorts once being nothing more than a collection of fishing villages is largely true. Seafood is a way of life all along the Andalucian coast. It is a relationship forged in the days when Andalucía was one of Spain's poorest regions, and fishing fleets almost literally kept the region afloat. Fishing is now the preserve of big business and the smaller fleets are something of an endangered species, surviving most often in nostalgic reminiscences in waterfront bars. But the spirit of that age lives on and the region's daily catch – from both the Mediterranean and Atlantic – is eagerly awaited by restaurant chefs, hungry patrons and *abuelas* (grandmothers) alike.

Andalucians eat fish in a variety of ways, but they are, above all, famous for their *pescaito frito* (fried fish). A particular speciality of Cádiz, El Puerto de Santa María and the Costa de la Luz (although you'll also find it in Granada), fried fish Andalucian-style is an art form with more subtlety than first appears. Just about anything that emerges from the sea is rolled in chickpea and wheat flour, shaken to remove the surplus, then deep-fried ever so briefly in olive oil, just long enough to form a light, golden crust that seals the essential goodness of the fish within. There are few products of the sea that don't get the deep-fry treatment, but the more common ones include *chipirones* or *chopitos* (baby squid), *cazón en adobo* (dogfish or shark that feed on shellfish producing a strong, almost sweet flavour) and *tortilla de camarones*, a delicious, crispy frittata embedded with tiny shrimps.

Other choices you'll encounter again and again include: *boquerones* (anchovies), served either fried or marinated in garlic, olive oil and vinegar; *sardinas a la plancha* (grilled sardines); *gambas* (prawns) and *langostinos* (king prawns) served grilled, fried or cold with a bowl of fresh mayonnaise, with the most sought after coming from Sanlúcar de Barrameda; *chanquetes* (similar to whitebait and served deep-fried), a speciality of Málaga; *ostras* (oysters); *pezespada* (swordfish); and *salmonetes* (red mullet). Stocks of *atún* (tuna) are rapidly depleting, but remain a favourite along the Costa de la Luz, especially in Barbate and Zahara de los Atunes.

Fruits of the Land

Coastal Andalucía is not alone in its devotion to the local produce. Andalucians from the interior make the grand (but by no means unfounded) claim to anyone who will listen that the olive and *jamón* – those mainstays of the Spanish table – produced here are the finest in all of Spain.

But *jamón* is not the only meat that Andalucians get excited about. Throughout the bullfighting season (roughly May to September), bars and restaurants proudly announce '*hay rabo de toro*', which roughly translates as, 'yes, we have bull's tail'.

Andalucians also love cheese, and although most are imported from elsewhere in Spain, there are exceptions. Typical Andalucian cheeses include Grazalema, from the mountains of Cádiz, made from ewes' milk and similar to Manchego; Málaga, a goats' cheese preserved in olive oil; and Cádiz, a strong, fresh goats' cheese made in the countryside around Cádiz.

The region also produces what are arguably the finest fruits and vegetables in Spain due to its generous climate. That's not to say that vegetables dominate most restaurant menus across this most carnivorous of regions – they're there, but usually in the background. The fantastic produce is eaten in season and generally bought fresh in open-air morning markets. Almería province, east of Málaga, is Europe's winter garden, with miles of plastic-covered hothouses of intensively grown vegetables.

Prized Bluefin tuna are still caught on the Costa de la Luz using the ancient *almadraba* method that utilises stretched mazelike nets that are anchored to the sea floor. The technique has been employed for 3000 years and was pioneered by the Phoenicians.

THE ORIGIN OF TAPAS

There are many stories concerning the origins of tapas. One holds that in the 13th century, doctors to King Alfonso X advised him to accompany his small sips of wine between meals with small morsels of food. So enamoured was the monarch with the idea that he passed a law requiring all bars in Castile to follow suit. Another version attributes tapas to bar owners who placed a saucer with a piece of bread on top of a sherry glass either to deter flies or prevent the punter from drinking on an empty stomach and getting too tipsy. As for the name, *tapa* (which means lid) is said to have attained widespread usage in the early 20th century when King Alfonso XIII stopped at a beachside bar in Cádiz province. When a strong gust of wind blew sand in the king's direction, a quick-witted waiter rushed to place a slice of *jamón* (ham) atop the king's glass of sherry. The king so much enjoyed the idea (and the *jamón*) that, wind or no wind, he ordered another and the name stuck.

Jamón

There is no greater taste bud–teasing prospect than a few wafer-thin, succulent slices of *jamón*. Nearly every bar and restaurant in Andalucía has at least one *jamón* on the go at any one time, strapped into a cradle-like frame called a *jamónera*. More often, they have several hams, the skin and hooves still attached, hanging from the walls or ceiling.

Unlike Italian prosciutto, Spanish *jamón* is a bold, deep red, well marbled with buttery fat. At its best, it smells like meat, the forest and the field. Like wines and olive oil, Spanish *jamón* is subject to a strict series of classifications. *Jamón serrano,* which accounts for around 90% of cured ham in Spain, refers to *jamón* made from white-coated pigs introduced to Spain in the 1950s. Once salted and semidried by the cold, dry winds of the Spanish sierra, most now go through a similar process of around a year's curing and drying in a climate-controlled shed.

Jamón ibérico, also called *pata negra* (black leg), is more expensive and comes from a black-coated pig indigenous to the Iberian peninsula and a descendant of the wild boar. Gastronomically, its star appeal is its ability to infiltrate fat into the muscle tissue, thus producing an especially well-marbled meat. Considered to be the best *jamón* of all is the *jamón ibérico* of Jabugo, in Andalucía's Huelva province, which comes from pigs free-ranging in the Sierra Morena oak forests. The best Jabugo hams are graded from one to five *jotas* (Js), and *cinco jotas* (JJJJJ) hams come from pigs that have never eaten anything but *bellotas* (acorns). If the pig gains at least 50% of its body weight during the acorn-eating season, it can be classified as *jamón ibérico de bellota,* the most sought-after designation for *jamón*.

Other much sought-after products from the pig include: *morcilla,* a blood sausage with rice or onions, best eaten lightly grilled; chorizo, a spicy pork sausage with paprika; and *lomo,* another cured pork sausage.

Olive Oil

Spain is the world's largest olive-oil producer and Andalucía's olive statistics are impressive: there are over 100 million olive trees in Andalucía; it is the world's biggest producer of olive oil; a remarkable 10% of the world's olive oil originates in Jaén province, which produces more olive oil than Greece; and Jaén's more than 4500 sq km of olive trees are, it is sometimes claimed, the world's largest human-made forest. The seemingly endless olive groves of Córdoba, Jaén and Sevilla were originally planted by the Romans, but the production of *az-zait* (juice of the olive) – from which the modern generic word for olive oil, *aceite,* is derived – was further developed by the Muslims. Both olives and olive oil continue to be a staple of the Andalucian kitchen.

Olive-oil production is almost as complicated as that of wine, with a range of designations to indicate quality. The best olive oils are those classified as 'virgin' (which must meet 40 criteria for quality and purity) and 'extra virgin' (the best olive oil, where acidity levels can be no higher than 1%). Accredited olive oil–producing regions receive Denominación de Origen (DO; a designation that indicates the unique geographic origins, production processes and quality of the product). Those in Andalucía include Baena and Priego de Córdoba in Córdoba, and Sierra de Segura and Sierra Mágina in Jaén.

The most common type of olive is the full-flavoured and (sometimes) vaguely spicy *picual,* which dominates the olive groves of Jaén province and accounts for 50% of all Spanish olive production. It takes its name from its pointed *pico* (tip) and is considered ideal for olive oil due to its high proportion of vegetable fat, natural antioxidants and polyphenol;

SPAIN'S OLIVE OIL

Spain produces 45% of the world's olive oil and is also responsible for 20% of world consumption.

FOOD & WINE RESOURCES

» *The Flavour of Andalusia* (Pepita Aris; 1998) Recipes and anecdotes.

» *A Late Dinner* (Paul Richardson; 2007) A fascinating Spanish culinary journey.

» *Moro: The Cookbook* (Samuel and Samantha Clark; 2003) From the renowned London-based restaurant of the same name; explores Andalucian cuisine and North African influences on Spanish cooking.

» *Dining Secrets of Andalucía* (Jon Clarke; 2008) A Santana Books guide.

» *World Food Spain* (Richard Sterling, Lonely Planet; 2000) Definitive guide to Spanish food, with a comprehensive culinary dictionary.

» *A Traveller's Wine Guide to Spain* (Harold Heckle; 2012) An authoritative and well-illustrated guide with sections on Andalucía's wine-producing regions.

the latter ensures that the oil keeps well and maintains its essential qualities at a high cooking temperature. Another important type of olive is the *hojiblanca,* which is grown predominantly around Málaga and Sevilla provinces. Its oil, which keeps for less time and should be stored in a cool dark place, is said to have a taste and aroma reminiscent of fruits, grasses and nuts.

Cold Soups

One of the most important influences over Andalucian chefs has always been the region's climate, and the perfect antidote to Andalucía's baking summers is *gazpacho andaluz* (Andalucian gazpacho). This cold soup appears in many manifestations, but its base is almost always a blended mix of tomatoes, peppers, cucumber, garlic, breadcrumbs, oil and (sherry) vinegar. Aside from climate, history played a significant role in its popularity here: it's a legacy of the New World, when Columbus brought back tomatoes and peppers from his travels. The basis for gazpacho developed in Andalucía among the *jornaleros,* agricultural day labourers, who were given rations of oil and (often stale) bread, which they soaked in water to form the basis of a soup, adding the oil, garlic and whatever fresh vegetables were at hand. All of the ingredients were pounded using a mortar and pestle and a refreshing and nourishing dish was made. It is sometimes served in a jug with ice cubes, with side dishes of chopped raw vegetables such as cucumber and onion.

A thicker version of gazpacho is *salmorejo cordobés,* a cold tomato-based soup from Córdoba where soaked bread is essential; it's served with bits of *jamón* and crumbled egg. *Ajo blanco* is a white gazpacho, a North African legacy, made with almonds, garlic and grapes instead of tomatoes.

Drinks

Wine

Vino production in Andalucía was introduced by the Phoenicians, possibly as early as 1100 BC. The Roman colonisers who followed were famous imbibers of wine, while the Moors, whose holy book, the Quran, preached abstinence from alcohol, continued to grow grapes. Andalucía's wine economy skyrocketed in the 16th century, spearheaded by a new British penchant for sherry.

The Montilla-Morales DO in southern Córdoba province produces a wine that is similar to sherry though isn't fortified by the addition of brandy; the fino variety is the most acclaimed. Andalucía's other DO is in Málaga province: sweet, velvety Málaga Dulce pleased palates from

Food & Wine Websites

» www.spaingourmetour.com

» www.andalucia.com/gastronomy

» www.sherry.org

» www.winesfromspain.org

Tejeringos are extralong churros (fried crunchy doughnuts) that have been wrapped into a spiral shape.

Virgil to the ladies of Victorian England, until the vines were blighted around the beginning of the 20th century. Today the Málaga DO area is Andalucía's smallest. You can sample Málaga wine straight from the barrel in some of the city's numerous bars.

Almost every village throughout Andalucía has its own basic wine, known simply as *mosto*. Eight areas in the region produce distinctive, good, non-DO wines that can be sampled locally: Aljarafe and Los Palacios (Sevilla province); Bailén, Lopera and Torreperogil (Jaén province); Costa Albondón (Granada province); Laujar de Andarax (Almería province); and Villaviciosa (Córdoba province).

Wine not only accompanies meals but is also a popular bar drink – and it's cheap: a bottle costing €5 in a supermarket or €12 in a restaurant will be a decent wine. *Vino de mesa* (table wine) may cost less than €1.50 a litre in shops. You can order wine by the *copa* (glass) in bars and restaurants: the *vino de la casa* (house wine) may come from a barrel for about €1. For quality wines, visitors to Andalucía have traditionally opted to play away with Rioja, but new winemakers in regions such as Las Alpujarras have begun experimenting with tempranillo, pinot noir and cabernet sauvignon grapes to produce some fine blends.

Sherry

Sherry, Andalucía's celebrated fortified wine, is produced in the towns of Jerez de la Frontera, El Puerto de Santa María and Sanlúcar de Barrameda, which make up the 'sherry triangle' of Cádiz province. A combination of climate, chalky soils that soak up the sun but retain moisture and a special maturing process called the *solera* process produces these unique wines.

The main distinction in sherry is between fino (dry and straw-coloured) and oloroso (sweet and dark, with a strong bouquet). An amontillado is an amber, moderately dry fino with a nutty flavour and a higher alcohol content. An oloroso combined with a sweet wine results in a cream sherry. A manzanilla is a chamomile-coloured fino produced in Sanlucar de Barrameda; its delicate flavour is reckoned to come from sea breezes wafting into the bodegas.

According to legend, the white Pedro Ximénez grape was brought to Andalucía in the luggage of German/Flemish soldier Peter Siemens in the mid-16th century from the Netherlands. Translated into Spanish, Peter Siemens became Pedro Ximénez; today the moniker of Andalucías finest sweet dessert sherry.

PEDRO XIMÉNEZ

Survival
Guide

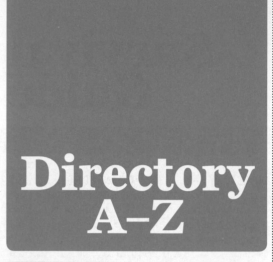

Directory A–Z

Business Hours

The following opening hours have some local and seasonal variations.

» **Banks** Generally open from 8.30am to 2pm Monday to Friday and 9am to 1pm Saturday.

» **Post offices** From 8.30am to 8.30pm Monday to Friday and 9am to 1.30pm Saturday.

» **Restaurants & tapas bars** From around 1pm to around 4pm, and from 8pm or 8.30pm to around midnight. Many are closed one day a week (often Monday). Some bars open for breakfast and stay open throughout the day, while some close up as early as 11pm during the week. Gibraltar follows the same opening hours as the rest of Andalucía.

» **Shops & nongovernment offices (travel agencies, airline offices, tour companies)** From 9am or 10am to 1.30pm or 2pm and 5pm to 8pm or 9pm, Monday to Saturday, though some skip the Saturday-evening session. Large supermarkets, department stores and *centros comerciales* (large, purpose-built shopping

centres) normally stay open all day, from 9am to 9pm, Monday to Saturday.

» **Night-time bars** Generally open in the early evening, but get kicking from between 11pm and midnight to between 2am and 4am – the later in the week, the later they stay open.

Customs Regulations

Duty-free allowances for entering Spain from outside the EU include 2L of wine, 1L of spirits, and 200 cigarettes or 50 cigars. Limits on imports and exports of duty-paid goods between other EU countries and Spain include 110L of beer, 90L of wine, 10L of spirits, 800 cigarettes and 200 cigars.

Dangers & Annoyances

Andalucía is generally a pretty safe place. The main thing you have to be wary of is petty theft (which may not seem so petty if your passport, money or camera go missing).

Most of the safety precautions are simple common sense, but you'd be surprised at how casual some travellers are with their belongings. To safeguard your money, keep a limited amount as cash on hand, and the bulk in more easily replaceable forms such as on plastic cards or as travellers cheques. If your accommodation has a safe, use it. Most risk of theft occurs in tourist resorts and big cities, and when you first arrive in a city and may be unaware of danger signs. Don't draw attention to your money or valuables by waving cameras or large notes around or having a wallet bulging in your pocket. Keep hold of your baggage and watch out for people who touch you or seem to be getting needlessly close. When using ATMs be wary of anyone who offers to help you, even if your card is stuck in the machine. Don't leave anything that even looks valuable visible in a parked car.

If you want to make an insurance claim for anything stolen or lost, you'll need to report it to the police and get a copy of the report. For help replacing a lost or stolen passport, contact your embassy or consulate.

Discount Cards

Student, teacher and youth cards can get you worthwhile discounts on airfares and other travel, as well as reduced prices at some museums, sights and entertainment venues.

The International Student Identity Card (ISIC), for full-time students, and the International Teacher Identity Card (ITIC), for full-time teachers and academics, are issued by colleges and student associations in the country where you're studying. The ISIC gives access to discounted air and train fares, 50% off national museums in Spain and up to

20% off trips with the Alsa bus company.

Anyone under 26 can get a European Youth Card (Euro26 card; Carnét Joven in Spain), which is available in Europe to people of any nationality, or an International Youth Travel Card (IYTC or GO25 card), available worldwide. These give similar discounts to the ISIC and are issued by many of the same organisations. Benefits for European Youth Card holders in Andalucía include 20% or 25% off many train fares, 20% off the cost of some car hire and bus fares with the Socibus company, 10% to 15% off the cost of some accommodation, and discounts at a few museums and tourist attractions.

For more information, including places you can obtain the cards, see www.istc.org and www.euro26.org.

A seniors card, usually for people over 65, generally enables you to obtain similar discounts to those obtained by student-card holders, although some museums will only recognise seniors cards issued in EU countries.

Electricity

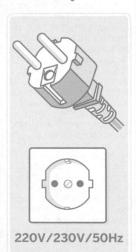

220V/230V/50Hz

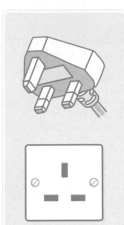

240V/50Hz

Gay & Lesbian Travellers

Andalucía's liveliest gay scenes are in Málaga, Torremolinos, Seville and Granada, but there are gay- and lesbian-friendly bars and clubs in all major cities.

Websites such as www.gayinspain.com, www.guiagay.com (in Spanish) and www.cogailes.org have helpful listings of gay and gay-friendly accommodation, bars, clubs, beaches, cruising areas, health clubs and associations. Gayinspain and Cogailes have message boards too. Cogailes is the site of the Coordinadora Gai-Lesbiana, a gay and lesbian organisation based in Barcelona that operates a free national information telephone line in English, Spanish and Catalan on ☑900 60 16 01, from 6pm to 10pm daily. Other links to gay associations in Andalucía appear on www.orgullogay.org.

The **Asociación Andaluza de Lesbianas y Gais** (Calle Lavadero de las Tablas 15, Granada) runs the **Teléfono Andaluz de Información Homosexual** (☑958 20 06 02).

Even though gay marriage was legalised in Spain in 2005, some hotel receptionists still have difficulty understanding that two people of the same sex might want to share a double bed. One traveller suggested that, for the sake of efficiency, it can be a good idea for one of the pair to do the checking in before the other appears.

Health

For emergency treatment, go straight to the *urgencias* (casualty) section of the nearest hospital, or call ☑061 for an ambulance.

Good health care is readily available and *farmacias* (pharmacies) offer valuable advice and sell over-the-counter medication. In Spain, a system of *farmacias de guardia* (duty pharmacies) operates so that each district has one open all the time. When a pharmacy is closed, it posts the name of the nearest open one on the door.

Tap water is generally safe to drink in Spain, but the city of Málaga is one place where many people prefer to play it safe by drinking bottled water. Do not drink water from rivers or lakes as it may contain harmful bacteria.

Insurance

Medical Insurance

If you're an EU citizen, the free **EHIC** (European Health Insurance Card; ☑in the UK 0845 606 2030; www.ehic.org.uk/Internet/home.do) covers you for most medical care in Spain, including maternity care and care for chronic illnesses such as diabetes (though not for emergency repatriation). However, you will normally have to pay for medicine bought from pharmacies, even if prescribed, and perhaps for some tests and procedures. The EHIC does not cover private medical consultations and treatment in Spain; this includes

PRACTICALITIES

» UK and some other European newspapers are sold at kiosks wherever large numbers of expats and tourists are found.

» The centre-left *El País* (www.elpais.es) is Spain's biggest-selling newspaper. Every sizeable Andalucian city has at least one daily paper of its own.

» For radio stations *El País* publishes province-by-province wavelength guides in its *Cartelera* (What's On) section. Among the several stations of Radio Nacional de España (RNE), RNE3 plays a variety of pop and rock, RNE2 is classical.

» Spain has between six and eight free-to-air TV channels including the state-run TVE1 and TVE2, and a couple of local channels. International satellite channels crop up on some hotel TVs.

» DVDs bought in Spain are region two and may not be compatible with players in North America (region one), Australia (region four) and elsewhere.

» Spain uses the metric system for weights and measures.

nearly all dentists, and some of the better clinics and surgeries. In the UK, you can apply for an EHIC online, by telephone, or by filling out a form available at post offices. Non-EU citizens should find out if there is a reciprocal arrangement for free medical care between their country and Spain.

Travel Insurance

A travel-insurance policy to cover theft, loss and medical problems is a good idea. Travel agents will be able to make recommendations. Check the small print: some policies specifically exclude 'dangerous activities', which can include scuba diving, motorcycling or even trekking. Strongly consider a policy that covers you for the worst possible scenario, such as an accident requiring an ambulance or emergency flight home. Find out in advance if your insurance plan will make payments to doctors or hospitals directly, rather than you having to pay on the spot and claim later. The former option is generally preferable, as it doesn't leave you out of

pocket. If you have to claim later, make sure you keep all documentation.

Buy travel insurance as early as possible. If you buy it in the week before you leave home, you may find, for example, that you are not covered for delays to your trip caused by strikes.

Paying for your airline ticket with a credit card often provides limited travel accident insurance, and you may be able to reclaim payment if the operator doesn't deliver.

Internet Access

There are plenty of internet cafes throughout Andalucía, typically charging around €1.50 per hour. Some are equipped with CD burners, webcams, headphones and so on. But some of the smaller places may not have card readers, so bring your own or a camera-to-USB cable if you plan on burning photos to CD along the way.

For those travelling with a laptop or hand-held computer, a growing number of hotels in Andalucía provide wi-fi access (although often

only in the lobby), or in-room cable connections. Many tourist offices also offer free wi-fi access.

Look for the 🛜 symbol throughout this guide indicating places with wi-fi access.

Legal Matters

Spain has three main types of police.

» The **Policía Nacional** (National Police; ☏091) covers cities and bigger towns, sometimes forming special squads dealing with drugs, terrorism and the like. A further contingent is to be found shuffling paper in bunker-like police stations called *comisarías*.

» The **Policía Local** (Local Police; ☏092), also known as Policía Municipal, are controlled by city and town halls and deal mainly with minor matters such as parking, traffic and bylaws. They wear blue-and-white uniforms.

» The responsibilities of the green-uniformed **Guardia Civil** (☏062; Civil Guard) include roads, the countryside, villages and international borders.

If you need to go to the police (for example, if you're the victim of petty theft), any of them will do, but your best bet is to approach the Policía Nacional or Policía Local. Spain's once-liberal drug laws were severely tightened in 1992. The only legal drug is cannabis, and then only for personal use – which means very small amounts. Public consumption of any drug is illegal. It would be very unwise to smoke cannabis in hotel rooms or guesthouses. Travellers entering Spain from Morocco, especially with a vehicle, should be prepared for intensive drug searches.

Spain's drink-driving laws are relatively strict – the blood-alcohol limit is 0.05%, or 0.01% for new drivers.

Under the Spanish constitution, anyone who is arrested must be informed immediately, in a manner understandable to them, of their rights and the grounds for the arrest. Arrested people are entitled to the assistance of a lawyer (and, where required, an interpreter) during police inquiries or judicial investigations. For many foreign nationalities, including British citizens, the police are also obliged to inform an arrested person's consulate immediately. Arrested people may not be compelled to make a statement. Within 72 hours of arrest, the person must be brought before a judge or released. Further useful information on Spanish legal procedures and lawyers is published on the website of the UK embassy in Madrid (www.ukinspain.com) under the 'Help for British Nationals' section.

Maps

Michelin's 1:400,000 *Andalucía* (No 578) is excellent for overall planning and touring, with an edition published each year. It's widely available in and outside Andalucía; look for it at petrol stations and bookshops.

Maps provided by tourist offices are often adequate for finding your way around cities and towns. For something more comprehensive, most cities are covered by one of the Spanish series such as Telstar, Escudo de Oro, Alpina or Everest, all with street indexes; they're available in bookshops. Be sure to check the publication dates.

Local availability of maps is patchy, so it's a good idea to try to obtain them in advance. **Stanfords** (www.stanfords.co.uk; 12-14 Long Acre, London, UK) has a good range of Spain maps and you can order them online.

Walking Maps

If you're going to do any walking in Andalucía you should arm yourself with the best possible maps, especially as trail-markings can be patchy.

Spain's **Centro Nacional de Información Geográfica** (CNIG; ☎91 755 15 42; www.cnig.es), the publishing arm of the Instituto Geográfico Nacional (IGN), produced a useful *Mapa Guía* series of national and natural parks, mostly at 1:50,000 or 1:100,000, in the 1990s. The CNIG also covers about three-quarters of Andalucía in its 1:25,000 *Mapa Topográfico Nacional* maps, most of which are up to date. Both the CNIG and the **SGE** (Army Geographic Service; ☎ext 6630 915 126 600; Darío Gazapo 8, Madrid; ☺9am-1.30pm) publish 1:50,000 series: the SGE's, called *Serie L*, tends to be more up to date (most of its Andalucía maps have been revised since the mid-1990s). CNIG maps may be labelled CNIG, IGN or both.

The CNIG website lists where you can buy CNIG maps (click on 'Información y Venta') or you can buy online. There are sales offices in Andalucía's eight provincial capitals, including Seville, Granada and Málaga.

Good commercially published series, all usually accompanied by guide booklets, come from **Editorial Alpina** (www.editorialalpina.com), **Editorial Penibética** (www.penibetica.com) and Britain's **Discovery Walking Guides** (www.walking.demon.co.uk).

The **Junta de Andalucía** (www.juntadeandalucia.es), Andalucía's regional government, also publishes a range of Andalucía maps, including a *Mapa Guía* series of natural and national parks. These have been published recently and are widely available, although perhaps better for vehicle touring than for walking, with a scale of 1:75,000. The covers are predominantly green, as opposed to the CNIG *mapas guías* that are mainly red or pink. Other Junta maps include 1:10,000 and 1:20,000 maps covering the whole of Andalucía – they are good maps but sales outlets for them are few.

Money

Spain's currency is the euro (€). The only exception to this is Gibraltar, where the currency is the Gibraltar pound (£).

» Cajeros automáticos (ATMs) are plentiful and easy to find. Make sure the ATM you're using takes international cards – the logos of accepted cards are usually posted alongside.

» Cash and travellers cheques can be exchanged at virtually any bank or exchange office. Banks are plentiful and tend to offer the best rates. Exchange offices, usually indicated by the word *cambio* (exchange), exist mainly in tourist resorts. Generally they offer longer opening hours and quicker service than banks, but worse exchange rates. Widely accepted brands of travellers cheques include Thomas Cook, Visa and American Express (Amex) and all have efficient replacement policies. In some places the more money you change, the better the exchange rate you'll get. Check commissions first, and confirm that posted exchange rates are up to date. A typical commission is 2% to 3%, with a minimum of €4 or €5. Places that advertise 'no commission' usually offer poor exchange rates. In Spain you usually can't use travellers cheques like money to make purchases.

» Visitors from outside the euro zone will get most value for their pound, dollar or whatever by making purchases by credit card or debit card; ATM withdrawals provide second-best value. Obtaining euros by exchanging cash or travellers cheques generally gives less value for your money, after you take into account commissions, handling fees, and exchange-rate differentials.

» Spanish value-added tax (VAT) is called IVA (ee-ba; impuesto sobre el valor añadido). On accommodation and restaurant prices, it's 8% and is usually (but not always) included in the prices that you'll be quoted. On retail goods and car hire, IVA is 18%. To ask 'Is IVA included?', say '¿Está incluido el IVA?' Visitors resident outside the EU are entitled to a refund of the 18% IVA on any purchases costing more than €90.15 from any shop if they are taking them out of the EU within three months. Ask the shop to give you an invoice showing the price and IVA paid for each item and the name and address of the vendor and purchaser. Then you will need to present both the invoice and goods to the customs booth for IVA refunds at the airport, port or border from which you leave the EU. The officer will stamp the invoice and you hand it in at a bank in the airport or port for the reimbursement.

Credit & Debit Cards

You can get by very well in Andalucía with a credit or debit card enabling you to make purchases directly and withdraw cash euros from ATMs.

Not every establishment accepts payment by card, but most do. You should be able to make payments by card in midrange and top-end accommodation and restaurants, and larger shops, but you cannot depend on it elsewhere. When you pay by card, you will be asked for ID such as your passport. Don't forget to memorise your PIN numbers as you may have to key these in as you pay, and do keep a note of phone numbers to call for reporting a lost or stolen card.

American Express (Amex) cards are much less widely accepted than Visa and MasterCard.

Tipping

Spanish law requires menu prices to include the service charge, and tipping is a matter of personal choice – most people leave some small change if they're satisfied, and 5% is usually plenty. Porters will generally be happy with €2. Taxi drivers don't have to be tipped but a little rounding up won't go amiss.

Post

Postage stamps are sold at estancos (tobacconist shops with 'Tabacos' in yellow letters on a maroon background), as well as at oficinas de correos (post offices; www.correos.es). It's quite safe to post mail in the yellow street buzones (postboxes) as well as at post offices. Mail to or from other Western European countries normally arrives within a week; to or from North America within 10 days; and to or from Australia and New Zealand within two weeks.

Public Holidays

Everywhere in Spain has 14 official holidays a year – some are nationwide holidays, some only in one village. The list of holidays in each place may change from year to year. If a holiday date falls on a weekend, sometimes the holiday is moved to the Monday or replaced with another at a different time. If a holiday falls on the second day following a weekend, many Spaniards take the intervening day off too, a practice known as making a puente (bridge).

The two main periods when Spaniards go on holiday are Semana Santa (Holy Week, leading up to Easter Sunday) and the six weeks from mid-July to the end of August. At these times accommodation in resorts can be scarce and transport heavily booked.

There are usually nine official national holidays:
Año Nuevo (New Year's Day) 1 January
Viernes Santo (Good Friday) 29 March 2013, 18 April 2014
Fiesta del Trabajo (Labour Day) 1 May
La Asunción (Feast of the Assumption) 15 August
Fiesta Nacional de España (National Day) 12 October
Todos los Santos (All Saints' Day) 1 November
Día de la Constitución (Constitution Day) 6 December
La Inmaculada Concepción (Feast of the Immaculate Conception) 8 December
Navidad (Christmas) 25 December

In addition, regional governments normally set three holidays, and local councils a further two. The three regional holidays in Andalucía are usually these:
Epifanía (Epiphany) or **Día de los Reyes Magos** (Three Kings' Day) 6 January
Día de Andalucía (Andalucía Day) 28 February
Jueves Santo (Holy Thursday) Easter

The following are often selected as local holidays by town halls:
Corpus Christi Around two months after Easter
Día de San Juan Bautista (Feast of St John the Baptist, King Juan Carlos II's saint's day) 24 June
Día de Santiago Apóstol (Feast of St James the Apostle, Spain's patron saint) 25 July

Telephone

Andalucía is fairly well provided with blue payphones, which are easy to use for both international and domestic calls (as long as they are in working order). They accept coins and/or *tarjetas telefónicas* (phone cards).

Payphone calls are generally 10% to 20% cheaper from 8pm to 8am Monday to Friday, and all day Saturday and Sunday. Coin payphones inside bars and cafes – often green – are normally a little more expensive than street payphones.

Many towns also have cheap-rate call offices known as *locutorios*, where you can make international calls for low rates (eg around €0.20 a minute to the US or €0.30 a minute to Australia), although calls within Spain are generally at similar rates to street payphones. Cheapest of all are internet phone calls, available at some *locutorios* and internet cafes, or on your laptop via sites such as www .skype.com.

Mobile Phones

If you're going to make lots of calls within Spain, it's worth considering buying a Spanish SIM card. Shops on every main street and in every shopping centre sell phones at bargain prices and **Orange** (www.orange.es), **Movistar** (www.movistar.es) and **Vodafone** (www.voda fone.es) are widespread and reputable brands.

If you're considering taking a mobile from your home country to Spain, you should find out from your mobile network provider whether your phone is enabled for international roaming, and what the costs of calls, text and voicemail are likely to be. Don't forget to take a Continental adaptor for your charger plug.

Spanish mobile phones operate on the GSM 900/1800 or 3G 2100 systems.

For more information visit **Ofcom** (www.ofcom.org.uk) or **GSM World** (www.gsmworld .com), which both provide coverage maps, lists of roaming partners and links to phone companies' websites.

Phone Codes & Useful Numbers

Spain has no telephone area codes. Every phone number has nine digits and for any call within Spain you just dial all those nine digits. The first digit of all Spanish fixed-phone numbers is 9. Numbers beginning with 6 are mobile phones. Phone numbers in Gibraltar have eight digits.

Calls to Spanish numbers starting with 900 are free. Numbers starting with 901 to 906 are pay-per-minute numbers and charges vary; a common one is 902, for which you pay about €0.35 for three minutes from a payphone. For a rundown on these numbers, visit www .andalucia.com/travel /telephone/numbers.htm.

Some useful numbers:

International Access Code (☑00)
Country Code (☑34)
Local Operator (☑1009)
English-speaking International Operator (☑Europe 1008, rest of world 1005)
Local Directory Enquiries (☑11822; per second €0.22 plus €0.01)
International Directory Enquiries (☑11825; per minute €1 plus €0.75)

Phone Cards

Phone cards issued by the national phone company Telefónica come in €6 and €12 denominations and are sold at post offices and *estancos*.

Many small grocery stores also sell private-company phone cards (with pin numbers) which can be used from payphones and private phones for much cheaper than the usual rate.

Time

All mainland Spain is on GMT/UTC plus one hour during winter, and GMT/ UTC plus two hours during the country's daylight-saving period, which runs from the last Sunday in March to the last Sunday in October. Most other Western European countries have the same time as Spain year-round, the major exceptions being Britain, Ireland and Portugal. Add one hour to these three countries' times to get Spanish time.

Spanish time is normally US eastern time plus six hours, and US Pacific time plus nine hours. In the Australian winter subtract eight hours from Sydney time to get Spanish time; in the summer subtract 10 hours (the difference is nine hours for a few weeks in March).

Morocco is on GMT/UTC year-round, so is two hours behind Spain during Spanish daylight-saving time, and one hour behind at other times of the year.

Toilets

Public toilets are almost nonexistent; many (but not all) tourist offices are an exception. It's OK to wander into many bars and cafes to use the toilet, although you're usually expected to order something while there. It's worth carrying some toilet paper with you as many toilets lack it.

Tourist Information

All cities and many smaller towns and even villages in Andalucía have at least one *oficina de turismo* (tourist office). Staff are generally knowledgeable and increasingly well versed in foreign languages and can help with everything from town maps and guided tours to opening hours for major sights and, sometimes, bus timetables. Offices are usually well stocked with printed material. Opening hours vary widely.

Tourist offices in Andalucía may be operated by the local town hall, by local district organisations, by the government of whichever province you're in, or by the regional government, the Junta de Andalucía. There may also be more than one tourist office in larger cities: in general, regional tourist offices offer information both on the city and the wider region, while municipal tourist offices deal just with the city and immediate surrounds. The Junta de Andalucía's environmental department, the Consejería de Medio Ambiente, also has visitor centres located in many of the environmentally protected areas (*parques naturales* and so on).

Many tourist offices have Bluetooth information points which allow you to download town maps, guided tours and events listings directly to your mobile phone.

Travellers with Disabilities

Wheelchair accessibility in Andalucía is improving as new buildings (including hotels) meet regulations requiring them to have wheelchair access. Many midrange and top-end hotels are now adapting rooms and creating better access for wheelchair users; accessibility is poorer at some budget accommodation options.

If you call a taxi and ask for a 'eurotaxi', you should be sent one adapted for wheelchair users.

International organisations that can offer advice (sometimes including Andalucía-specific info) include the following:

Access-able Travel Source (☎303-232 2979; www.access-able.com; PO Box 1796, Wheat Ridge, Colorado, USA)

Accessible Travel & Leisure (☎01452-729739; www.accessibletravel.co.uk) Claims

to be the biggest UK travel agent dealing with travel for people with a disability and encourages independent travel.

Mobility International (☎541-343 1284; www.miusa.org; 132 E Broadway, suite 343, Eugene, USA)

Visas

Citizens of EU countries, Switzerland, Norway, Iceland and Liechtenstein need only carry their passport or national identity document in order to enter Spain. Citizens of many other countries, including Australia, Canada, Japan, New Zealand, Singapore and the USA, do not need a visa for visits of up to 90 days, but must carry their passport.

Citizens of other countries should consult a Spanish consulate well in advance of travel if you think you need a visa. The standard tourist visa issued when necessary is the Schengen visa, which is valid not only for Spain but also for all the 24 other countries that are party to the Schengen agreement. You normally have to apply for the visa in person at a consulate in your country of residence.

Remember that Gibraltar is not part of Schengen and if you do not have permission to enter the UK, you may not enter Gibraltar.

Women Travellers

Women travellers in Spain will rarely experience harassment, although women travellers should be ready to ignore any stares, catcalls and comments from time to time. Although far from universal, men under about 40, who have grown up in the post-Franco era, are less prone to gender stereotyping

than their older counterparts whose thinking and behaviour towards women is still directed by machismo.

Skimpy clothes are the norm in many coastal resorts, but people tend to dress more modestly elsewhere. In general, consider avoiding plunging necklines, short skirts and bare shoulders to spare yourself unwanted attention. You can feel rather conspicuous on a Sunday when people take to the plazas and promenades for the afternoon *paseo* (walk) and you're in your casual gear.

Although most places you'll visit are safe, you still need to exercise common sense about where you go solo. Think twice about going alone to isolated stretches of beach or country, or down empty city streets at night. A lone woman, for example, would be better to forget wandering around the uninhabited parts of Granada's Sacromonte area. It's highly inadvisable for a woman to hitchhike alone, and not a great idea even for two women together. Remember the word for help (*socorro*) in case you need to use it. Some women travellers have also reported feeling more comfortable at the front of public transport.

Each province's national police headquarters has a special Servicio de Atención a la Mujer (SAM; literally Service of Attention to Women). The national **Comisión para la Investigación de Malos Tratos a Mujeres** (Commission for Investigation into Abuse of Women; ☎emergency 900 10 00 09; www.malostratos.org; ☉9am-9pm) maintains an emergency line for victims of physical abuse anywhere in Spain. In Andalucía the **Instituto Andaluz de la Mujer** (☎900 20 09 99; ☉24hr) also offers help.

Transport

GETTING THERE & AWAY

Andalucía is a top European holiday destination and is well linked to the rest of Spain and Europe by air, rail and road. Regular hydrofoils and car ferries run to and from Morocco, and there are also ferry links to Algeria. Flights, tours and rail tickets can be booked online at lonelyplanet.com.

Entering the Region

Immigration and customs checks usually involve a minimum of fuss, although there are exceptions. Spanish customs look for contraband duty-free products designed for illegal resale in Spain, in particular on traffic arriving from Morocco. Expect long delays at this border, especially in the summer.

Air

Getting to Andalucía by air from the rest of Europe is easy. Dozens of regular and charter airlines fly into the region's five airports from elsewhere in Europe, especially the UK, and a couple also fly from the UK to Gibraltar. Andalucía's busiest airport, Málaga, also has flights from Morocco. The region is also well connected by domestic flights to other Spanish cities. From outside Europe, you'll need to change planes en route, usually at Madrid or Barcelona or in another European country. However, there are now seasonal charters connecting Málaga with Toronto and Montreal in Canada and Tel Aviv in Israel.

High season generally runs from mid-June to mid-September, although flights can also be fully booked (and prices higher) during Semana Santa (Holy Week).

Airports

Málaga airport (AGP; ☎952 04 88 38; www.aena.es) is the main international airport in Andalucía and Spain's fourth busiest, with almost 60 airlines connecting the city to cities around Spain, Europe and further afield.

Seville (SVQ; ☎954 44 90 00; www.aena.es), **Granada** (GRX; ☎958 24 52 07; www.aena.es), **Jerez de la Frontera** (www.aena.es) and **Almería** (☎950 21 37 00; www.aena.es) also have connections to other Spanish and European cities, although apart from flights to and from Seville, the choices are far more limited. To see which airlines fly into the airport you're hoping to start your journey in, visit www.aena.es, choose the airport from the pull-down menu on the left, then click on 'Airlines' for a full list. The website also has detailed information on facilities at each airport.

Gibraltar (GIB; ☎20 073026) also receives a small number of flights direct from the UK.

Land

Border Crossings

If you're coming from Morocco, journey times are increased by a couple of hours by border formalities, which are notoriously strict at the ferry departure and arrivals terminals. There are usually long queues at customs on both sides of the Strait of Gibraltar.

Bus

Andalucía is well connected by bus with the rest of Spain. Although there are direct bus services from many European countries, it rarely works out cheaper than flying and takes a whole lot longer.

Places from where taking a bus may work out to be more economical include Lisbon and Morocco. There are regular daily services to Seville from Lisbon (seven hours) with **Alsa** (www.alsa.es) and **Anibal** (www.anibal.net). **Eurolines** (www.eurolines.es), a grouping of 32 bus companies from different countries, and Alsa run several weekly buses between Moroccan cities such as Casablanca, Marrakesh and Fès, and Andalucian destinations such as Seville, Marbella, Málaga, Granada, Jerez de la Frontera and Almería, via the Algeciras–Tangier ferries. As an indication of time, the

CLIMATE CHANGE & TRAVEL

Every form of transport that relies on carbon-based fuel generates CO_2, the main cause of human-induced climate change. Modern travel is dependent on aeroplanes, which might use less fuel per kilometre per person than most cars but travel much greater distances. The altitude at which aircraft emit gases (including CO_2) and particles also contributes to their climate change impact. Many websites offer 'carbon calculators' that allow people to estimate the carbon emissions generated by their journey and, for those who wish to do so, to offset the impact of the greenhouse gases emitted with contributions to portfolios of climate-friendly initiatives throughout the world. Lonely Planet offsets the carbon footprint of all staff and author travel.

Málaga–Marrakesh trip takes 19 to 20 hours.

Buses run to most Andalucian cities and medium-sized towns from elsewhere in Spain, with the largest selection leaving from Madrid's **Estación Sur de Autobuses** (☎91 468 42 00; www.estaciondeautobuses.com; Calle de Méndez Álvaro 83; MMéndez Álvaro). The trip from Madrid to Seville, Granada or Málaga takes around six hours. There are also services down the Mediterranean coast from Barcelona, Valencia and Alicante to Almería, Granada, Jaén, Córdoba, Seville, Málaga and the Costa del Sol. The main bus companies serving Andalucía from other parts of Spain are Alsa, **Dainco** (☎902 42 22 42; www.dainco.es), **Damas** (www.damas-sa.es) and **Secorbus/Socibus** (☎902 22 92 92; www.socibus.es).

Car & Motorcycle

Drivers can reach Andalucía from just about anywhere in Spain in a single day on the country's good-quality highways. The main routes run down the centre of the country from Madrid and along the Mediterranean coast from Barcelona. Popular vehicle ferries run from the UK to Bilbao and Santander in northern Spain, from where you can drive to Andalucía via Madrid. Ferry routes also connect Andalucía with Tangier and Nador in Morocco and with Ceuta and Melilla, the Spanish enclaves on the Moroccan coast.

The main highway from Madrid to Andalucía is the A4/AP4 to Córdoba, Seville and Cádiz. For Jaén, Granada, Almería or Málaga, turn off at Bailén. In the east, the AP7/A7 leads all the way down the Mediterranean side of Spain from La Jonquera on the French border as far as Algeciras, except for a couple of stretches in Andalucía where the old, unmodernised N340 remains.

If you just want to drive once you get to Andalucía, it usually works out cheaper (and quicker) to fly and hire a car there. In the UK, further information on driving in Europe is available from the **RAC** (☎0870 572 2722; www.rac.co.uk) or the **AA** (☎European breakdown cover enquiries 0800 085 2840; www.theaa.com).

Train

Renfe (www.renfe.es) is the excellent national Spanish train system which runs services in Andalucía. It has benefited from massive investment in recent years meaning journeys are fast, efficient and comfortable.

IN SPAIN

The fastest way to get into Andalucía by train is on the AVE (Alta Velocidad Española) services from Madrid, operated by Renfe. Travelling at speeds of 280km/h, they connect Madrid to Córdoba (one way from €68.40, 1¾ hours), Seville (from €83.30, around 2½ hours) and Málaga (from €87.70, 2½ hours) in not much more time than

in takes to travel by plane. Work is underway to extend the Madrid–Seville service to Cádiz. From most other parts of Spain you can reach Andalucía by train in one day, usually with a connection in Madrid.

Most long-distance trains have *preferente* (1st-class) and *turista* (2nd-class) carriages. They go under various names indicating standards of comfort and time of travel. An InterCity is a straightforward, limited-stop, daytime train on the Madrid–Córdoba–Málaga route. More comfortable (and more expensive) daytime trains may be called Altaria, Arco, Talgo, Talgo 200 or AVE. Overnight trains are classed as Estrella (with seats, couchettes and sleeping compartments) or the more comfortable Trenhotel. Both types offer seats, couchettes, and single or double compartments with and without shower.

Whichever train you take, it's best to buy your ticket in advance as trains can get fully booked, especially in July and August. You can do so in English by telephone and over the internet. Phonebooked tickets must be collected and paid for at a Renfe ticket office within 72 hours of booking and more than 24 hours before the train's departure from its starting point. Internet tickets can be paid for online. For the first online purchase with any individual credit card, tickets must be picked up at a Renfe ticket office at least one hour before the train's departure from its starting point; for further purchases, tickets can also be printed online.

Return fares on long-distance trains are 20% less than two one-way fares. Children aged under four years travel free; those from four to 11 (to 12 on some trains) get 40% off the cost of seats and couchettes. The European Youth Card (www.euro26.org) gives 20% or 25% off long-distance and regional train fares.

OUTSIDE OF SPAIN

If you're coming from elsewhere in Europe and can afford to take at least a day to arrive, there are rail routes to Andalucía, always involving a change of train in Madrid or Barcelona. Direct trains run from Paris' Gare d'Austerlitz to Madrid's Chamartín (13½ hours). From Chamartín take the cross-town cercanía train service (10 minutes) to Atocha station for onward connections to Andalucian cities. More information is available from **SNCF** (French National Railways; ✆in France 36 35; www.sncf.com).

From London, the simplest and quickest route to Andalucía (about 24 hours) involves **Eurostar** (✆in the UK 0870 518 6186; www.eurostar.com), the Channel Tunnel service from Waterloo to Paris, a change in Paris from the Gare du Nord to the Gare d'Austerlitz, an overnight sleeper-only train to Madrid's Chamartín station, and a change there to Atocha station for a fast train to Andalucía; it's generally cheaper (though less environmentally friendly) to fly. For information and bookings on rail travel from Britain, contact **Rail Europe** (✆in the UK 0870 837 1371; www.raileurope.co.uk) or Eurostar.

No railway crosses from Portugal into Andalucía, but trains run along the Algarve to Vila Real de Santo António, where there's a ferry across the Río Guadiana to Ayamonte in Andalucía. To travel all the way by train from Lisbon (11 hours) to any Andalucian city you need to transfer in Madrid (and change from Chamartín to Atocha station there). Contact Renfe or Caminhos de Ferro Portugueses for more information.

Direct trains run at least three times a week to Barcelona from cities in Switzerland and northern Italy, and daily from Montpellier in southern France. You can transfer to an Andalucía-bound train at Barcelona.

Sea

You can sail to Andalucía from the Moroccan ports of Tangier and Nador, as well as Ceuta or Melilla (Spanish enclaves on the Moroccan coast), and Oran and Ghazaouet (both in Algeria). The routes are: Melilla–Almería, Nador–Almería, Ghazaouet–Almería, Melilla–Málaga, Oran–Almería, Tangier–Gibraltar, Tangier–Algeciras, Ceuta–Algeciras and Tangier–Tarifa.

All routes usually take vehicles as well as passengers and the most frequent sailings are to/from Algeciras. Usually, at least 10 sailings a day ply the routes between Algeciras and Tangier (1¼ to 2½ hours) and 16 between Algeciras and Ceuta (45 minutes). Extra services are added at busy times, especially during the peak summer period (mid-June to mid-September) when hundreds of thousands of Moroccan workers return home from Europe for holidays. If you're taking a car, book well ahead for July, August or Easter travel, and expect long queues and customs formalities.

The following are the main ferry companies; there's little price difference between them.

» **Acciona/Trasmediterránea** (www.trasmediterranea.es)
» **EuroFerrys** (www.euroferrys.com)
» **FRS** (www.frs.es)
» **Balèria** (www.baleria.com)

If you're coming from the UK, **P&O Ferries** (www.poferries.com) operates a service twice-weekly from Portsmouth to Bilbao (29 to 34 hours), while **Brittany Ferries** (www.brittanyferries.com) operates a twice-weekly car ferry from Plymouth or Portsmouth to Santander (19 to 23 hours, March to November). From Bilbao and Santander, there are long-distance road, bus and rail connections to Andalucía.

GETTING AROUND

Andalucía has excellent road and bus networks, although having your own vehicle enables you to make the most of your time as bus services to smaller villages rarely operate more than once a day and there are often no services on weekends. Train services are similarly excellent, although they're not much use for getting around Cádiz province, or between Huelva province and anywhere but Seville.

Bicycle

Andalucía is good biking territory, with wonderful scenery and varied terrain. While some mountain roads (such as those through the Sierra de Grazalema or Sierra Nevada) are best left to professional cyclists in training, there aren't too many corners of Andalucía that keen and reasonably fit cyclists can't reach. Plenty of lightly trafficked country roads, mostly in decent condition, enable riders to avoid the busy main highways. Road biking here is as safe as anywhere in Europe provided you make allowances for some drivers' love of speed. Day rides and touring by bike are particularly enjoyable in spring and autumn, avoiding weather extremes.

If you get tired of pedalling, it's often possible to take your bike on a bus (you'll usually just be asked to remove the front wheel). You can take bikes on overnight sleeper trains (not long-distance daytime trains), and on most regional and suburban trains; check at the train station before buying tickets for any special conditions you'll need to comply with.

Bicycles are quite widely available for hire in main cities, coastal resorts and inland towns and villages that attract tourism. They're often *bicis todo terreno* (mountain bikes). Prices range from €10 to €20 a day.

Bike lanes on main roads are rare, but cyclists are permitted to ride in groups up to two abreast. Helmets are obligatory outside built-up areas.

Boat

The quickest and most enjoyable way to get between Cádiz and El Puerto de Santa María is by catamaran. The 25-minute journey costs €2.35. There are up to 18 departures Monday to Friday and half a dozen at weekends. Tickets can be bought at the Terminal Marítima Metropolitana in Cádiz or on the riverside quay in El Puerto de Santa María.

Bus

Buses in Andalucía are mostly modern, comfortable and inexpensive, and run almost everywhere – including along some unlikely mountain roads – to connect remote villages with their nearest towns. The bigger cities are linked to each other by frequent daily services. On the less busy routes, services may be reduced (or occasionally nonexistent) on Saturday and Sunday.

Larger cities and towns usually have one main

estación de autobuses (bus station) where all out-of-town buses stop. In smaller places, buses tend to operate from a particular street or square, which may be unmarked. Ask around; locals generally know where to go.

During Semana Santa (Holy Week) and July and August it's advisable to buy most bus tickets a day in advance. On a few routes, a return ticket is cheaper than two singles. Travellers aged under 26 should ask about discounts on intercity routes.

Buses on main intercity routes average around 70km/h, for a cost of around €1.20 per 14km.

All of Andalucía's airports are linked to city centres by bus (and, in Málaga's case, also by train). Gibraltar airport is within walking distance of downtown Gibraltar and of the bus station in La Línea de la Concepción, Spain.

Car & Motorcycle

Andalucía's excellent road network and inexpensive rental cars make driving an attractive and practical way of getting around.

Bringing Your Own Vehicle

Bringing your own car to Andalucía is possible. Roads are generally good, although driving and finding parking in cities can be tiresome. Petrol (around €1.30 to €1.40 per litre in Spain) is widely available. In the event of breakdowns, every small town and many villages will have a garage with mechanics on-site.

If the car is from the UK or Ireland, remember to adjust the headlights for driving in mainland Europe (motor accessory shops sell stick-on strips which deflect the beams in the required direction).

Driving Licence & Documentation

All EU countries' licences (pink or pink-and-green) are accepted in Spain. Note, however, that the old-style UK green licence is rarely accepted. Licences from other countries are supposed to be accompanied by an International Driving Permit, but in practice your national licence will suffice for renting cars or dealing with traffic police. The International Driving Permit, valid for 12 months, is available from automobile clubs in your country.

When driving a private vehicle in Europe, proof of ownership (a Vehicle Registration Document for UK-registered vehicles), driving licence, roadworthiness certificate (MOT), and either an insurance certificate or a Green Card should always be carried. Also ask your insurer for a European Accident Statement form, which can greatly simplify matters in the event of an accident.

Hire

If you plan to hire a car in Andalucía, it's a good idea to organise it before you leave. As a rule, local firms at Málaga airport or on the Costa del Sol offer the cheapest deals. You can normally get a four-door air-con economy-class car from local agencies for around €150 a week in August or €120 a week in January. Many local firms offer internet booking and you simply go to their desk in or just outside the airport on arrival. In general, rentals away from the holiday *costas* (coasts) are more expensive.

Well-established local firms with branches at Andalucian airports and/or major rail stations (such as Málaga and Seville) include the following:

Centauro (☎902 10 41 03; www.centauro.net)

Crown Car (☎952 17 64 86; www.crowncarhire.com)

Helle Hollis (☎952 24 55 44, in UK 0871 222 7245; www.hellehollis.com)

MAIN BUS COMPANIES

COMPANY	WEBSITE	TELEPHONE	MAIN DESTINATIONS
Alsa	www.alsa.es	902 42 22 42	Almería, Córdoba, Granada, Jaén, Málaga, Seville
Casal	www.autocarescasal.com	954 99 92 90	Aracena, Carmona, Seville
Comes	www.tgcomes.es	902 19 92 08	Algeciras, Cádiz, Granada, Jerez, Málaga, Ronda, Seville
Damas	www.damas-sa.es	959 25 69 00	Ayamonte, Huelva, Seville
Linesur	www.linesur.com	956 34 10 63	Algeciras, Écija, Jerez, Osuna, Seville
Los Amarillos	www.losamarillos.es	902 21 03 17	Cádiz, Jerez, Málaga, Ronda, Seville
Portillo	www.ctsa-portillo.com	902 14 31 44	Algeciras, Costa del Sol, Málaga, Ronda
Transportes Ureña	-	957 40 45 58	Córdoba, Jaén, Seville

Holiday Car Hire (☎952 24 26 85; www.holidaycarhire.com)

Niza Cars (☎952 23 61 79; www.nizacars.es)

Pepecar.com (☎807 41 42 43; www.pepecar.com)

Major international rental companies are also present at many of the same arrival points and give assuredly high standards of service.

Avis (☎902 13 55 31; www.avis.com)

Europcar (☎913 43 45 12; www.europcar.com)

Hertz (☎917 49 90 69; www.hertz.es)

National/Atesa (☎902 10 01 01, www.atesa.es)

To rent a car you need to be aged at least 21 (23 with some companies) and to have held a driving licence for a minimum of one year (sometimes two years). Under-25s have to pay extra charges with many firms.

It's much easier, and often obligatory, to pay for your rental with a credit card.

As always, check the detail of exactly what you are paying for. Some companies will throw in extras such as child seats and the listing of additional drivers for free; others will charge for them.

Insurance

Third-party motor insurance is a minimum requirement throughout Europe. If you live in the EU, your existing motor insurance will probably provide automatic third-party cover throughout the EU if you're travelling in your own vehicle. But check with your insurer about whether you will also be covered for medical or hospital expenses or accidental damage to your vehicle. You might have to pay an extra premium if you want the same protection abroad as you have at home. A European breakdown assistance policy such as the European Breakdown Cover offered by **AA** (www.theaa.com) or **RAC** (www.rac.co.uk), or the policies offered by **Eurotunnel** (www.eurotunnel.com) and many cross-Channel ferry companies, is also a good investment, providing services such as roadside assistance, towing, emergency repairs and 24-hour telephone assistance in English.

The Green Card is an internationally recognised document showing that you have the minimum insurance cover required by law in the country visited. It is provided free by insurers. If you're carrying an insurance certificate that gives the minimum legal cover, a Green Card is not essential, but it has the advantage of being easily recognised by foreign police and authorities.

If you're renting a vehicle in Andalucía, the routine insurance provided may not go beyond basic third-party requirements. For cover against theft or damage to the vehicle, or injury or death to driver or passengers, you may need to request extra coverage. Always read the fine print and don't be afraid to ask.

Parking

Street parking space can be hard to find in larger cities during working hours (about 9am to 2pm Monday to Saturday and 5pm to 8pm Monday to Friday). You'll often have to use underground or multistorey car parks, which are common enough in cities, and well enough signposted, but not cheap (typically around €1 per hour or €10 to €15 for 24 hours). They are generally more secure than the street. City hotels with their own parking usually charge for the right to use it, at similar or slightly cheaper rates to underground car parks.

Blue lines along the side of the street usually mean you must pay at a nearby meter to park during working hours (typically around €0.50 to €1 an hour). Yellow lines mean no parking. A sign with a red line through a blue backdrop also indicates that parking is prohibited. It's not sensible to park in prohibited zones, even if other drivers have (you risk your car being towed and paying at least €60 to have it released).

Road Rules

As elsewhere in continental Europe, drive on the right and overtake on the left (although the latter is just as often honoured in the breach!). The minimum driving age is 18 years. Rear seat belts, if fitted, must be worn and children under three must sit in child safety seats. The blood-alcohol limit is 0.05% (0.01% for drivers with a licence less than two years old) and breath-testing is carried out on occasion.

The police can – and do – carry out spot checks on drivers so it pays to have all your papers in order. Non-resident foreigners may be fined on the spot for traffic offences. You can appeal in writing (in any language) to the Jefatura Provincial de Tráfico (Provincial Traffic Headquarters) and if your appeal is upheld, you'll get your money back, but don't hold your breath for a favourable result. Contact details for each province's traffic headquarters are given on the website of the **Dirección General de Tráfico** (www .dgt.es). Click on 'Trámites y Multas', then 'Direcciones y Teléfonos', then 'Jefaturas', then select the province you're in.

The speed limit is 50km/h in built-up areas, between 80km/h and 100km/h outside built-up areas, and 120km/h on *autopistas* (toll highways) and *autovías* (toll-free highways).

In Spain it's compulsory to carry two warning triangles (to be placed 100m in front of and 100m behind your vehicle if you have to stop on the carriageway), and a reflective jacket, which must be donned if you get out of your vehicle on the carriageway or hard shoulder outside built-up areas.

It's illegal to use hand-held mobile phones while driving.

Taxi

Taxis are plentiful in larger places and even most villages have a taxi or two. Fares are reasonable – a typical 2km to 3km ride should cost about €3.50 to €4.50, with airport runs costing a bit extra. Intercity runs are around €0.60 per kilometre. You don't have to tip taxi drivers, but rounding up the change is always appreciated.

Train

Renfe (Red Nacional de los Ferrocarriles Españoles; Spanish National Railways; ☎902 24 02 02; www.renfe .es), Spain's national railway company, has an extensive and efficient rail system in Andalucía linking most of the main cities and many smaller places. Trains are at least as convenient, quick and inexpensive as buses on many routes. Remember, however,

Train Routes

Ⓝ 0 _____ 100 km
0 _____ 60 miles

SPAIN

SPAIN

PORTUGAL

Peñarroya-Pueblonuevo

CÓRDOBA
Montoro
Andújar
JAÉN
Úbeda
Baeza

Córdoba

Lora del Río

HUELVA Nerva
Pradollano
Carmona
Montilla
Baena
Jaén
Baza
Huercal-Overa

Lepe Huelva
Seville
Alcalá de Guadaira
Osuna
Lucena
Pinos Puente
Guadix
ALMERÍA

Ayamonte
Utrera
SEVILLA
Puente Genil
Granada
GRANADA

Lebrija
Arcos de la Frontera
Morón de la Frontera
Antequera
Loja

Sanlúcar de Barrameda
Álora
MÁLAGA

Rota
Jerez de la Frontera
Ronda
Cártama
Málaga
Almería

Cádiz
Torremolinos

San Fernando
CÁDIZ
Fuengirola

Algeciras
Gibraltar (UK)

MOROCCO

_____ Train line

that the only services from Huelva go via Seville, while to get elsewhere in Andalucía by train from Cádiz, El Puerto de Santa María or Jerez de la Frontera, you'll need to go via Seville or Utrera.

Some of the long-distance routes linking Andalucía with other parts of Spain are good for journeys within Andalucía as well. These include Córdoba–Málaga, Córdoba–Seville–Cádiz and Córdoba–Ronda–Algeciras.

Generally more frequent services between Andalucian destinations are provided by the cheaper (but slower), one-class *regional* and *cercanía* trains. *Regionales*, some of which are known as Andalucía Exprés, run between Andalucian cities, stopping at many towns en route. *Cercanías* are commuter trains that link Seville, Málaga and Cádiz with their suburbs and nearby towns.

Train tickets can be booked online with Renfe, which also lists full up-to-date timetables. Reservations are usually necessary on high-speed AVE trains, but less important on shorter, slower routes.

Regional trains average around 75km/h, for a cost of around €1 per 15km. Return fares on many routes operated by Renfe (but not its *cercanía* services) are 20% less than two one-way fares.

WANT MORE?
For in-depth language information and handy phrases, check out Lonely Planet's *Spanish Phrasebook*. You'll find it at **shop.lonely planet.com**, or you can buy Lonely Planet's iPhone phrasebooks at the Apple App Store.

Language

Spanish *(español)* – also called Castilian *(castellano)* – is spoken throughout Andalucia.

Most Spanish sounds are pronounced the same as their English counterparts. If you read our coloured pronunciation guides as if they were English, you'll be understood. Note that the kh is a throaty sound (like the 'ch' in Scottish *loch*), r is strongly rolled, ly is pronounced as the 'lli' in 'million' and ny as the 'ni' in 'onion'. If you travel outside the region, you'll also notice that the 'lisped' th sound, which is typical of the pronunciation in the rest of Spain, is pronounced as s in Andalucia. In our pronunciation guides, the stressed syllables are in italics.

Where necessary in this chapter, masculine and feminine forms are marked as 'm/f', while polite and informal options are indicated by the abbreviations 'pol' and 'inf'.

BASICS

Hello.	*Hola.*	o·la
Goodbye.	*Adiós.*	a·*dyos*
How are you?	*¿Qué tal?*	ke tal
Fine, thanks.	*Bien, gracias.*	byen *gra*·syas
Excuse me.	*Perdón.*	per·*don*
Sorry.	*Lo siento.*	lo *syen*·to
Yes.	*Sí.*	see
No.	*No.*	no
Please.	*Por favor.*	por fa·*vor*
Thank you.	*Gracias.*	*gra*·syas
You're welcome.	*De nada.*	de *na*·da

My name is ...
Me llamo ...	me *lya*·mo ...

What's your name?
¿Cómo se llama Usted?	ko·mo se *lya*·ma oo·*ste* (pol)
¿Cómo te llamas?	ko·mo te *lya*·mas (inf)

Do you speak English?
¿Habla inglés?	a·bla een·*gles* (pol)
¿Hablas inglés?	a·blas een·*gles* (inf)

I don't understand.
No entiendo.	no en·*tyen*·do

ACCOMMODATION

hotel	*hotel*	o·*tel*
guesthouse	*pensión*	pen·*syon*
youth hostel	*albergue juvenil*	al·*ber*·ge khoo·ve·*neel*
I'd like a ... room.	*Quisiera una habitación ...*	kee·*sye*·ra oo·na a·bee·ta·*syon* ...
single	*individual*	een·dee·vee·*dwal*
double	*doble*	*do*·ble
air-con	*aire acondicionado*	ai·re a·kon·dee·syo·*na*·do
bathroom	*baño*	*ba*·nyo
bed	*cama*	*ka*·ma
window	*ventana*	ven·*ta*·na

How much is it per night/person?
¿Cuánto cuesta por noche/persona?	kwan·to *kwes*·ta por no·che/per·so·na

Does it include breakfast?
¿Incluye el desayuno?	een·*kloo*·ye el de·sa·*yoo*·no

DIRECTIONS

Where's ...?
¿Dónde está ...?   *don·*de es·*ta ...*

What's the address?
¿Cuál es la dirección?   kwal es la dee·rek·*syon*

Can you please write it down?
¿Puede escribirlo,   pwe·de es·kree·*beer·*lo
por favor?   por fa·*vor*

Can you show me (on the map)?
¿Me lo puede indicar   me lo pwe·de een·dee·*kar*
(en el mapa)?   (en el *ma·*pa)

at the corner	*en la esquina*	en la es·*kee·*na
at the traffic lights	*en el semáforo*	en el se·*ma·*fo·ro
behind ...	*detrás de ...*	de·*tras* de ...
far away	*lejos*	*le·*khos
in front of ...	*enfrente de ...*	en·*fren·*te de ...
left	*izquierda*	ees·*kyer·*da
near	*cerca*	*ser·*ka
next to ...	*al lado de ...*	al *la·*do de ...
opposite ...	*frente a ...*	*fren·*te a ...
right	*derecha*	de·*re·*cha
straight ahead	*todo recto*	*to·*do *rek·*to

EATING & DRINKING

What would you recommend?
¿Qué recomienda?   ke re·ko·*myen·*da

What's in that dish?
¿Que lleva ese plato?   ke *lyo·*va e·se *pla·*to

I don't eat ...
No como ...   no *ko·*mo ...

Cheers!
¡Salud!   sa·*loo*

That was delicious!
¡Estaba buenísimo!   es·*ta·*ba bwe·*nee·*see·mo

Please bring us the bill.
Por favor, nos trae   por fa·*vor* nos *tra·*e
la cuenta.   la *kwen·*ta

I'd like to book a table for ...	*Quisiera reservar una mesa para ...*	kee·*sye·*ra re·ser·*var* oo·na *me·*sa pa·ra ...
(eight) o'clock	*las (ocho)*	las (*o·*cho)
(two) people	*(dos) personas*	(dos) per·*so·*nas

Key Words

appetisers	*aperitivos*	a·pe·ree·*tee·*vos
bar	*bar*	bar
bottle	*botella*	bo·*te·*lya

KEY PATTERNS

To get by in Spanish, mix and match these simple patterns with words of your choice:

When's (the next flight)?
¿Cuándo sale   *kwan·*do sa·le
(el próximo vuelo)?   (el *prok·*see·mo *vwe·*lo)

Where's (the station)?
¿Dónde está   *don·*de es·*ta*
(la estación)?   (la es·ta·*syon*)

Where can I (buy a ticket)?
¿Dónde puedo   *don·*de pwe·do
(comprar   (kom·*prar*
un billete)?   oon bee·*lye·*te)

Do you have (a map)?
¿Tiene (un mapa)?   *tye·*ne (oon *ma·*pa)

Is there (a toilet)?
¿Hay (servicios)?   ai (ser·*vee·*syos)

I'd like (a coffee).
Quisiera (un café).   kee·*sye·*ra (oon ka·*fe*)

I'd like (to hire a car).
Quisiera (alquilar   kee·*sye·*ra (al·kee·*lar*
un coche).   oon *ko·*che)

Can I (enter)?
¿Se puede (entrar)?   se pwe·de (en·*trar*)

Can you please (help me)?
¿Puede (ayudarme),   pwe·de (a·yoo·*dar·*me)
por favor?   por fa·*vor*

Do I have to (get a visa)?
¿Necesito   ne·se·*see·*to
(obtener   (ob·te·*ner*
un visado)?   oon vee·*sa·*do)

bowl	*bol*	bol
breakfast	*desayuno*	de·sa·*yoo·*no
cafe	*café*	ka·*fe*
(too) cold	*(muy) frío*	(mooy) *free·*o
dinner	*cena*	*se·*na
food	*comida*	ko·*mee·*da
fork	*tenedor*	te·ne·*dor*
glass	*vaso*	*va·*so
highchair	*trona*	*tro·*na
hot (warm)	*caliente*	ka·*lyen·*te
knife	*cuchillo*	koo·*chee·*lyo
lunch	*comida*	ko·*mee·*da
main course	*segundo plato*	se·*goon·*do *pla·*to
market	*mercado*	mer·*ka·*do
(children's) menu	*menú (infantil)*	me·*noo* (een·fan·*teel*)
plate	*plato*	*pla·*to
restaurant	*restaurante*	res·tow·*ran·*te

spoon	cuchara	koo·cha·ra
supermarket	supermercado	soo·per·mer·ka·do
vegetarian food	comida vegetariana	ko·mee·da ve·khe·ta·rya·na
with	con	kon
without	sin	seen

Meat & Fish

beef	carne de vaca	kar·ne de va·ka
chicken	pollo	po·lyo
cod	bacalao	ba·ka·la·o
duck	pato	pa·to
lamb	cordero	kor·de·ro
lobster	langosta	lan·gos·ta
pork	cerdo	ser·do
prawns	camarones	ka·ma·ro·nes
salmon	salmón	sal·mon
tuna	atún	a·toon
turkey	pavo	pa·vo
veal	ternera	ter·ne·ra

Fruit & Vegetables

apple	manzana	man·sa·na
apricot	albaricoque	al·ba·ree·ko·ke
artichoke	alcachofa	al·ka·cho·fa
asparagus	espárragos	es·pa·ra·gos
banana	plátano	pla·ta·no
beans	judías	khoo·dee·as
beetroot	remolacha	re·mo·la·cha
cabbage	col	kol
(red/green) capsicum	pimiento (rojo/verde)	pee·myen·to (ro·kho/ver·de)
carrot	zanahoria	sa·na·o·rya
celery	apio	a·pyo
cherry	cereza	se·re·sa
corn	maíz	ma·ees
cucumber	pepino	pe·pee·no
fruit	fruta	froo·ta
grape	uvas	oo·vas
lemon	limón	lee·mon
lentils	lentejas	len·te·khas
lettuce	lechuga	le·choo·ga
mushroom	champiñón	cham·pee·nyon
nuts	nueces	nwe·ses
onion	cebolla	se·bo·lya
orange	naranja	na·ran·kha
peach	melocotón	me·lo·ko·ton

peas	guisantes	gee·san·tes
pineapple	piña	pee·nya
plum	ciruela	seer·we·la
potato	patata	pa·ta·ta
pumpkin	calabaza	ka·la·ba·sa
spinach	espinacas	es·pee·na·kas
strawberry	fresa	fre·sa
tomato	tomate	to·ma·te
vegetable	verdura	ver·doo·ra
watermelon	sandía	san·dee·a

Other

bread	pan	pan
butter	mantequilla	man·te·kee·lya
cheese	queso	ke·so
egg	huevo	we·vo
honey	miel	myel
jam	mermelada	mer·me·la·da
oil	aceite	a·sey·te
pepper	pimienta	pee·myen·ta
rice	arroz	a·ros
salt	sal	sal
sugar	azúcar	a·soo·kar
vinegar	vinagre	vee·na·gre

Drinks

beer	cerveza	ser·ve·sa
coffee	café	ka·fe
(orange) juice	zumo (de naranja)	soo·mo (de na·ran·kha)
milk	leche	le·che
red wine	vino tinto	vee·no teen·to
tea	té	te
(mineral) water	agua (mineral)	a·gwa (mee·ne·ral)
white wine	vino blanco	vee·no blan·ko

Signs	
Abierto	Open
Cerrado	Closed
Entrada	Entrance
Hombres	Men
Mujeres	Women
Prohibido	Prohibited
Salida	Exit
Servicios/Aseos	Toilets

EMERGENCIES

Help!   *¡Socorro!*   so·ko·ro

Go away!   *¡Vete!*   ve·te

Call ...!   *¡Llame a ...!*   lya·me a ...
   a doctor   *un médico*   oon me·dee·ko
   the police   *la policía*   la po·lee·see·a

I'm lost.
Estoy perdido/a.   es·toy per·dee·do/a (m/f)

I'm ill.
Estoy enfermo/a.   es·toy en·fer·mo/a (m/f)

It hurts here.
Me duele aquí.   me dwe·le a·kee

I'm allergic to (antibiotics).
Soy alérgico/a a   soy a·ler·khee·ko/a a
(los antibióticos).   (los an·tee·byo·tee·kos) (m/f)

Where are the toilets?
¿Dónde están los   don·de es·tan los
servicios?   ser·vee·syos

SHOPPING & SERVICES

I'd like to buy ...
Quisiera comprar ...   kee·sye·ra kom·prar ...

I'm just looking.
Sólo estoy mirando.   so·lo es·toy mee·ran·do

Can I look at it?
¿Puedo verlo?   pwe·do ver·lo

I don't like it.
No me gusta.   no me goos·ta

How much is it?
¿Cuánto cuesta?   kwan·to kwes·ta

That's too expensive.
Es muy caro.   es mooy ka·ro

Can you lower the price?
¿Podría bajar un   po·dree·a ba·khar oon
poco el precio?   po·ko el pre·syo

There's a mistake in the bill.
Hay un error en   ai oon e·ror en
la cuenta.   la kwen·ta

ATM   *cajero*   ka·khe·ro
   automático   ow·to·ma·tee·ko

credit card   *tarjeta de*   tar·khe·ta de
   crédito   kre·dee·to

Question Words		
How?	*¿Cómo?*	ko·mo
What?	*¿Qué?*	ke
When?	*¿Cuándo?*	kwan·do
Where?	*¿Dónde?*	don·de
Who?	*¿Quién?*	kyen
Why?	*¿Por qué?*	por ke

internet cafe   *cibercafé*   see·ber·ka·fe

post office   *correos*   ko·re·os

tourist office   *oficina*   o·fee·see·na
   de turismo   de too·rees·mo

TIME & DATES

What time is it?   *¿Qué hora es?*   ke o·ra es

It's (10) o'clock.   *Son (las diez).*   son (las dyes)

Half past (one).   *Es (la una)*   es (la oo·na)
   y media.   ee me·dya

At what time?   *¿A qué hora?*   a ke o·ra

At ...   *A la(s) ...*   a la(s) ...

morning   *mañana*   ma·nya·na

afternoon   *tarde*   tar·de

evening   *noche*   no·che

yesterday   *ayer*   a·yer

today   *hoy*   oy

tomorrow   *mañana*   ma·nya·na

Monday   *lunes*   loo·nes

Tuesday   *martes*   mar·tes

Wednesday   *miércoles*   myer·ko·les

Thursday   *jueves*   khwe·bes

Friday   *viernes*   vyer·nes

Saturday   *sábado*   sa·ba·do

Sunday   *domingo*   do·meen·go

January   *enero*   e·ne·ro

February   *febrero*   fe·bre·ro

March   *marzo*   mar·so

April   *abril*   a·breel

May   *mayo*   ma·yo

June   *junio*   khoo·nyo

July   *julio*   khoo·lyo

August   *agosto*   a·gos·to

September   *septiembre*   sep·tyem·bre

October   *octubre*   ok·too·bre

November   *noviembre*   no·vyem·bre

December   *diciembre*   dee·syem·bre

TRANSPORT

Public Transport

boat   *barco*   bar·ko

bus   *autobús*   ow·to·boos

plane   *avión*   a·vyon

train   *tren*   tren

tram   *tranvía*   tran·vee·a

Numbers

1	uno	oo·no
2	dos	dos
3	tres	tres
4	cuatro	kwa·tro
5	cinco	seen·ko
6	seis	seys
7	siete	sye·te
8	ocho	o·cho
9	nueve	nwe·ve
10	diez	dyes
20	veinte	veyn·te
30	treinta	treyn·ta
40	cuarenta	kwa·ren·ta
50	cincuenta	seen·kwen·ta
60	sesenta	se·sen·ta
70	setenta	se·ten·ta
80	ochenta	o·chen·ta
90	noventa	no·ven·ta
100	cien	syen
1000	mil	meel

first	primer	pree·mer
last	último	ool·tee·mo
next	próximo	prok·see·mo

I want to go to (Córdoba).
Quisiera ir a (Córdoba). kee·sye·ra eer a (kor·do·ba)

At what time does it arrive/leave?
¿A qué hora llega/sale? a ke o·ra lye·ga/sa·le

Is it a direct route?
¿Es un viaje directo? es oon vya·khe dee·rek·to

Does it stop at (Granada)?
¿Para en (Granada)? pa·ra en (gra·na·da)

Which stop is this?
¿Cuál es esta parada? kwal es es·ta pa·ra·da

Please tell me when we get to (Seville).
¿Puede avisarme pwe·de a·vee·sar·me
cuando lleguemos kwan·do lye·ge·mos
a (Sevilla)? a (se·vee·lya)

I want to get off here.
Quiero bajarme aquí. kye·ro ba·khar·me a·kee

a ... ticket	un billete de ...	oon bee·lye·te de ...
1st-class	primera clase	pree·me·ra kla·se
2nd-class	segunda clase	se·goon·da kla·se
one-way	ida	ee·da
return	ida y vuelta	ee·da ee vwel·ta

aisle/window seat	asiento de pasillo/ ventana	a·syen·to de pa·see·lyo/ ven·ta·na
bus/train station	estación de autobuses/ trenes	es·ta·syon de ow·to·boo·ses/ tre·nes
cancelled	cancelado	kan·se·la·do
delayed	retrasado	re·tra·sa·do
platform	plataforma	pla·ta·for·ma
ticket office	taquilla	ta·kee·lya
timetable	horario	o·ra·ryo

Driving & Cycling

I'd like to hire a ...	Quisiera alquilar ...	kee·sye·ra al·kee·lar ...
4WD	un todo-terreno	oon to·do·te·re·no
bicycle	una bicicleta	oo·na bee·see·kle·ta
car	un coche	oon ko·che
motorcycle	una moto	oo·na mo·to

child seat	asiento de seguridad para niños	a·syen·to de se·goo·ree·da pa·ra nee·nyos
diesel	gasóleo	ga·so·le·o
helmet	casco	kas·ko
mechanic	mecánico	me·ka·nee·ko
petrol	gasolina	ga·so·lee·na
service station	gasolinera	ga·so·lee·ne·ra

How much is it per day/hour?
¿Cuánto cuesta por kwan·to kwes·ta por
día/hora? dee·a/o·ra

Is this the road to (Malaga)?
¿Se va a (Málaga) se va a (ma·la·ga)
por esta carretera? por es·ta ka·re·te·ra

(How long) Can I park here?
¿(Por cuánto tiempo) (por kwan·to tyem·po)
Puedo aparcar aquí? pwe·do a·par·kar a·kee

The car has broken down (at Cádiz).
El coche se ha averiado el ko·che se a a·ve·rya·do
(en Cádiz). (en ka·dees)

I have a flat tyre.
Tengo un pinchazo. ten·go oon peen·cha·so

I've run out of petrol.
Me he quedado sin me e ke·da·do seen
gasolina. ga·so·lee·na

Are there cycling paths?
¿Hay carril bicicleta? ai ka·reel bee·see·kle·ta

Is there bicycle parking?
¿Hay aparcamiento ai a·par·ka·myen·to
de bicicletas? de bee·see·kle·tas

GLOSSARY

alameda – *paseo* lined (or originally lined) with *álamo* (poplar) trees
alcázar – Islamic-era fortress
artesonado – ceiling with interlaced beams leaving regular spaces for decorative insertions
autopista – toll highway
autovía – toll-free dual carriageway
AVE – Alta Velocidad Española; the high-speed train between Madrid and Seville
ayuntamiento – city or town hall
azulejo – tile

bahía – bay
bailaor/a – flamenco dancer
bandolero – bandit
barrio – district or quarter (of a town or city)
bodega – winery, wine bar or wine cellar
buceo – scuba diving
bulería – upbeat type of flamenco song
buzón – postbox

cajero automático – automated teller machine (ATM)
calle – street
callejón – lane
cambio – currency exchange
campiña – countryside (usually flat or rolling cultivated countryside)
campo – countryside, field
cantaor/a – flamenco singer
cante jondo – 'deep song', the essence of flamenco
capilla – chapel
capilla mayor – chapel containing the high altar of a church
carnaval – carnival; a pre-Lent period of fancy-dress parades and merrymaking
carretera – road, highway
carta – menu
casa rural – a village house or farmhouse with rooms to let
casco – literally 'helmet'; used to refer to the old part of a city (*casco antiguo*)

castellano – Castilian; the language also called Spanish
castillo – castle
caza – hunting
centro comercial – shopping centre
cercanía – suburban train
cerro – hill
cervecería – beer bar
chiringuito – small, often makeshift bar or eatery, usually in the open air
Churrigueresque – ornate style of baroque architecture named after the brothers Alberto and José Churriguera
cofradía – see *hermandad*
colegiata – collegiate church, a combined church and college
comedor – dining room
comisaría – station of the Policía Nacional (National Police)
converso – Jew who converted to Christianity in medieval Spain
cordillera – mountain chain
coro – choir (part of a church, usually in the middle)
corrida de toros – bullfight
cortes – parliament
cortijo – country property
costa – coast
coto – area where hunting rights are reserved for a specific group of people
cruce – cross
cuenta – bill (check)
cuesta – sloping land, road or street
custodia – monstrance (receptacle for the consecrated Host)

dehesa – woodland pastures with evergreen oaks
Denominación de Origen (DO) – a designation that indicates the unique geographical origins, production processes and quality of wines, olive oil and other products
duende – the spirit or magic possessed by great flamenco performers
duque – duke
duquesa – duchess

embalse – reservoir
ermita – hermitage or chapel
escalada – climbing
estación de autobuses – bus station
estación de esquí – ski station or resort
estación de ferrocarril – train station
estación marítima – passenger port
estanco – tobacconist
estrella – literally 'star'; also class of overnight train with seats, couchettes and sleeping compartments

farmacia – pharmacy
faro – lighthouse
feria – fair; can refer to trade fairs as well as to city, town or village fairs
ferrocarril – railway
fiesta – festival, public holiday or party
finca – country property, farm
flamenco – means flamingo and Flemish as well as flamenco music and dance
frontera – frontier
fuente – fountain, spring

gitano – the Spanish word for Roma people
Guardia Civil – Civil Guard; police responsible for roads, the countryside, villages and international borders. They wear green uniforms. See also *Policía Local, Policía Nacional.*

hammam – Arabic-style bathhouse
hermandad – brotherhood (which may include women), in particular one that takes part in religious processions; also *cofradía*
hospedaje – guesthouse
hostal – simple guesthouse or small place offering budget hotel-like accommodation

infanta – daughter of a monarch but not first in line to the throne

infante – son of a monarch but not first in line to the throne

jardín – garden
judería – Jewish barrio in medieval Spain
Junta de Andalucía – executive government of Andalucía

lavandería – laundry
librería – bookshop
lidia – the modern art of bullfighting on foot
lucio – pond or pool in the Doñana *marismas* (wetlands)

madrugada/madrugá – the 'early hours', from around 3am to dawn; a pretty lively time in some Spanish cities
marismas – wetlands, marshes
marisquería – seafood eatery
marqués – marquis
medina – Arabic word for town or inner city
mercadillo – flea market
mercado – market
mezquita – mosque
mihrab – prayer niche in a mosque indicating the direction of Mecca
mirador – lookout point
morisco – Muslim converted to Christianity in medieval Spain
moro – 'Moor' or Muslim (usually in a medieval context)
movida – the late-night bar and club scene that emerged in Spanish cities and towns after Franco's death; a *zona de movida* or *zona de marcha* is an area of a town where people gather to drink and have a good time
mozárabe – Mozarab; Christian living under Islamic rule in medieval Spain
Mudéjar – Muslim living under Christian rule in medieval Spain; also refers to their decorative style of architecture
muelle – wharf, pier
muladí – Muwallad; Christian who converted to Islam, in medieval Spain

nazareno – penitent taking part in Semana Santa processions
nieve – snow
nuevo – new

oficina de correos – post office
oficina de turismo – tourist office
olivo – olive tree

palacio – palace
palo – literally 'stick'; also refers to the categories of flamenco song
panadería – bakery
papelería – stationery shop
parador – one of the Paradores Nacionales, a state-owned chain of luxurious hotels, often in historic buildings
paraje natural – natural area
parque nacional – national park
parque natural – natural park
paseo – avenue or parklike strip; walk or stroll
paso – literally 'step'; also the platform an image is carried on in a religious procession
peña – a club; usually for supporters of a football club or flamenco enthusiasts *(peña flamenca)*, but sometimes a dining club
pensión – guesthouse
pescadería – fish shop
picadero – riding stable
pícaro – dice trickster and card sharp, rogue, low-life scoundrel
pinsapar – forest of *pinsapo*
pinsapo – Spanish fir
piscina – swimming pool
plateresque – early phase of Renaissance architecture noted for its decorative facades
playa – beach
plaza de toros – bullring
Policía Local – Local Police; also known as Policía Municipal. Controlled by city and town halls, they deal mainly with minor matters such as parking, traffic and bylaws. They wear blue-and-white uniforms. See also *Guardia Civil, Policía Nacional.*

Policía Municipal – Municipal Police; see *Policía Local*
Policía Nacional – National Police; responsible for cities and bigger towns, some of them forming special squads dealing with drugs, terrorism and the like.
preferente – 1st-class carriage on a long-distance train
provincia – province; Spain is divided into 50 of them
pueblo – village, town
puente – bridge
puerta – gate, door
puerto – port, mountain pass
puerto deportivo – marina
puerto pesquero – fishing port
punta – point

rambla – stream
Reconquista – the Christian reconquest of the Iberian Peninsula from the Muslims (8th to 15th centuries)
refugio – shelter or refuge, especially a mountain refuge with basic accommodation for hikers
regional – train running between Andalucian cities
reja – grille; especially a wrought-iron one over a window or dividing a chapel from the rest of a church
Renfe – Red Nacional de los Ferrocarriles Españoles; Spain's national rail network
reserva – reservation, or reserve (eg nature reserve)
reserva nacional de caza – national hunting reserve
reserva natural – nature reserve
retablo – retable (altarpiece)
ría – estuary
río – river
romería – festive pilgrimage or procession
ronda – ring road

sacristía – sacristy, the part of a church in which vestments, sacred objects and other valuables are kept
salina – salt lagoon
Semana Santa – Holy Week; the week leading up to Easter Sunday
sendero – path or track

sevillana – a popular Andalucian dance
sierra – mountain range
Siglo de Oro – Spain's cultural 'Golden Century', beginning in the 16th century and ending in the 17th century

taberna – tavern
tablao – flamenco show
taifa – one of the small kingdoms into which the Muslim-ruled parts of Spain were divided during parts of the 11th and 12th centuries

taquilla – ticket window
taracea – marquetry
tarjeta de crédito – credit card
tarjeta telefónica – phonecard
teléfono móvil – mobile telephone
terraza – terrace; often means an area with outdoor tables at a bar, cafe or restaurant
tetería – Middle Eastern–style teahouse with low seats around low tables
tienda – shop, tent

tocaor/a – flamenco guitarist
torre – tower
trenhotel – sleek, expensive, sleeping car–only train
turismo – means both tourism and saloon car; *el turismo* can also mean the tourist office
turista – second-class carriage on a long-distance train

valle – valley

zoco – large market in Muslim cities

behind the scenes

SEND US YOUR FEEDBACK

We love to hear from travellers – your comments keep us on our toes and help make our books better. Our well-travelled team reads every word on what you loved or loathed about this book. Although we cannot reply individually to postal submissions, we always guarantee that your feedback goes straight to the appropriate authors, in time for the next edition. Each person who sends us information is thanked in the next edition – the most useful submissions are rewarded with a selection of digital PDF chapters.

Visit **lonelyplanet.com/contact** to submit your updates and suggestions or to ask for help. Our award-winning website also features inspirational travel stories, news and discussions.

Note: We may edit, reproduce and incorporate your comments in Lonely Planet products such as guidebooks, websites and digital products, so let us know if you don't want your comments reproduced or your name acknowledged. For a copy of our privacy policy visit lonelyplanet.com/privacy.

OUR READERS

Many thanks to the travellers who used the last edition and wrote to us with helpful hints, useful advice and interesting anecdotes:

Iñaki Arbeloa, Wendy Armstrong, Eric Boucquey, Hayley Dearman, Céline Dewit, Svetlana Efimova, Elaine Farwell, Giulia Gaddi, Michael Glenn, Greg Knittl, Martin Kooiman, Miki Yasha Lentin, Ramon Molier, Julie Pike, Lucy Star, Larry Stein, Michal Tesar, Assen Totin

AUTHOR THANKS

Brendan Sainsbury

Many thanks to all the untold bus drivers, tourist info volunteers, sherry pourers, flamenco singers and innocent bystanders who helped me during my research, particularly to Dora Whitaker for offering me the gig in the first place, and Josephine Quintero, John Noble and Daniel Schechter for their back up. Special thanks to Manon for the help with passports, and to my wife Liz and six-year-old son Kieran for their company in countless bars, buses, flamenco clubs and hotel rooms.

Josephine Quintero

Josephine would like to extend a mighty grand *gracias* to the numerous staff at the various tourist offices. She would also like to thank Robin Chapman for joining her on the road, Paul and Barbara Butler for their Cazorla insight, Miguel and Carmen Guzman for their tips on Granada nightlife and Brendan Sainsbury for his valuable feedback and tips. Thanks, too, to Dora Whitaker for her continued support and guidance on this title.

Daniel C Schechter

Muchas gracias to co-authors John Noble and Josephine Quintero and to Seville blogger Sandra Vallaure for smoothing my arrival and departure, to Tiago Macedo and Paola Zadra for helping out in Córdoba, and to couchsurfing.org pals Juanjo Boullosa and Adolia Romero (Huelva), Pablo Antonio Fontales (Écija), Oscar A Jiménez (Córdoba), Sara Nevado and Juan Erena (Cazalla de la Sierra) and Joanna Wegrzyn (Priego de Córdoba) for their input and friendship. Thanks, too, to Rafael Adamuz for having me on Radio Huelva.

ACKNOWLEDGMENTS

Climate map data adapted from Peel MC, Finlayson BL & McMahon TA (2007) 'Updated World Map of the Köppen-Geiger Climate Classification', *Hydrology and Earth System Sciences*, 11, 163344.

Cover photograph: Montefrio, Andulucía. David Tominson/LPI.

This Book

This guidebook was commissioned in Lonely Planet's London office, and produced by the following:

Commissioning Editor Dora Whitaker

Coordinating Editors Gabrielle Innes, Kate James

Coordinating Cartographer Andrew Smith

Coordinating Layout Designer Adrian Blackburn

Managing Editors Barbara Delissen, Bruce Evans

Senior Editors Andi Jones, Susan Paterson

Managing Cartographers Mark Griffiths, Alison Lyall, Amanda Sierp

Managing Layout Designer Jane Hart

Assisting Editors Jessica Crouch, Carly Hall, Rosie Nicholson, Charlotte Orr, Fionnuala Twomey, Tracy Whitmey

Assisting Cartographer Valentina Kremenchutskaya

Cover Research Naomi Parker

Internal Image Research Aude Vauconsant

Language Content Branislava Vladisavljevic

Thanks to Laura Crawford, Ryan Evans, Larissa Frost, Jouve India, Kate McDonell, Trent Paton, Raphael Richards, Dianne Schallmeiner, Gerard Walker

NOTES

384

index

000 Map pages
000 Photo pages

how to use this book

These symbols will help you find the listings you want:

- ⊙ Sights
- 🏊 Beaches
- 🏃 Activities
- 🛶 Courses
- 👉 Tours
- 🎆 Festivals & Events
- 🛏 Sleeping
- ✕ Eating
- 🍷 Drinking
- ☆ Entertainment
- 🔒 Shopping
- ℹ Information/Transport

These symbols give you the vital information for each listing:

- ☎ Telephone Numbers
- ☉ Opening Hours
- Ⓟ Parking
- ⊖ Nonsmoking
- ❄ Air-Conditioning
- @ Internet Access
- 🛜 Wi-Fi Access
- 🏊 Swimming Pool
- 🥗 Vegetarian Selection
- 📖 English-Language Menu
- 👪 Family-Friendly
- 🐾 Pet-Friendly
- 🚌 Bus
- ⛴ Ferry
- Ⓜ Metro
- Ⓢ Subway
- ⊖ London Tube
- 🚋 Tram
- 🚃 Train

Look out for these icons:

TOP CHOICE — Our author's recommendation

FREE — No payment required

🍃 — A green or sustainable option

Our authors have nominated these places as demonstrating a strong commitment to sustainability – for example by supporting local communities and producers, operating in an environmentally friendly way, or supporting conservation projects.

Reviews are organised by author preference.

Map Legend

Sights
- Beach
- Buddhist
- Castle
- Christian
- Hindu
- Islamic
- Jewish
- Monument
- Museum/Gallery
- Ruin
- Winery/Vineyard
- Zoo
- Other Sight

Activities, Courses & Tours
- Diving/Snorkelling
- Canoeing/Kayaking
- Skiing
- Surfing
- Swimming/Pool
- Walking
- Windsurfing
- Other Activity/Course/Tour

Sleeping
- Sleeping
- Camping

Eating
- Eating

Drinking
- Drinking
- Cafe

Entertainment
- Entertainment

Shopping
- Shopping

Information
- Post Office
- Tourist Information

Transport
- Airport
- Border Crossing
- Bus
- Cable Car/Funicular
- Cycling
- Ferry
- Metro
- Monorail
- Parking
- S-Bahn
- Taxi
- Train/Railway
- Tram
- Tube Station
- U-Bahn
- Other Transport

Routes
- Tollway
- Freeway
- Primary
- Secondary
- Tertiary
- Lane
- Unsealed Road
- Plaza/Mall
- Steps
- Tunnel
- Pedestrian Overpass
- Walking Tour
- Walking Tour Detour
- Path

Boundaries
- International
- State/Province
- Disputed
- Regional/Suburb
- Marine Park
- Cliff
- Wall

Population
- Capital (National)
- Capital (State/Province)
- City/Large Town
- Town/Village

Geographic
- Hut/Shelter
- Lighthouse
- Lookout
- Mountain/Volcano
- Oasis
- Park
- Pass
- Picnic Area
- Waterfall

Hydrography
- River/Creek
- Intermittent River
- Swamp/Mangrove
- Reef
- Canal
- Water
- Dry/Salt/Intermittent Lake
- Glacier

Areas
- Beach/Desert
- Cemetery (Christian)
- Cemetery (Other)
- Park/Forest
- Sportsground
- Sight (Building)
- Top Sight (Building)

OUR STORY

A beat-up old car, a few dollars in the pocket and a sense of adventure. In 1972 that's all Tony and Maureen Wheeler needed for the trip of a lifetime – across Europe and Asia overland to Australia. It took several months, and at the end – broke but inspired – they sat at their kitchen table writing and stapling together their first travel guide, *Across Asia on the Cheap*. Within a week they'd sold 1500 copies. Lonely Planet was born.

Today, Lonely Planet has offices in Melbourne, London and Oakland, with more than 600 staff and writers. We share Tony's belief that 'a great guidebook should do three things: inform, educate and amuse'.

OUR WRITERS

Brendan Sainsbury

Coordinating Author; Seville, Cádiz Province & Gibraltar An expat Brit, now living near Vancouver, Canada, Brendan once worked in Andalucía as a travel guide, leading cultural and hiking trips in the hills of Grazalema and the Sierra del Terril. He fell unashamedly for the region's romantic charms when he met his future wife in a small white village not far from Ronda in 2003. He has been back numerous times since, and has developed a special passion for flamenco guitar and the city of Granada. Brendan has also written for Lonely Planet in Cuba, Italy and the Pacific Northwest.

Read more about Brendan at:
lonelyplanet.com/members/brendansainsbury

John Noble

Andalucía Today, History Originally from England's Ribble Valley, John has lived in the provinces of Cádiz and Málaga since the mid-1990s. He and his late wife Susan Forsyth raised their two children in Andalucía and wrote the first two editions of this guide, also playing a part in every subsequent edition. John has explored Andalucía from end to end but still finds its nooks and crannies endlessly intriguing to investigate, with every little village and valley revealing more about its fascinating story.

Read more about John at:
lonelyplanet.com/members/ewoodrover

Josephine Quintero

Málaga Province, Jaén Province, Granada Province, Almería Province, Travel with Children Josephine moved to Spain after a seven-year stint in Kuwait where she was the editor of the *Kuwaiti Digest* until the Iraq invasion. Some 20 years on, the relaxed way of life in Andalucía continues to appeal and she happily divides her time between a *pueblo* (village) cottage in La Axarquía and a big-city Málaga suburb. Josephine loves escaping the crowds and enjoying tantalising new sights and experiences in her home province. A highlight of this research trip was visiting a recently excavated synagogue in Úbeda and discovering some incredibly talented craftspeople who have set up shop in Las Alpujarras.

Read more about Josephine at:
lonelyplanet.com/members/josephinequintero

Daniel C Schechter

Huelva & Sevilla Provinces, Córdoba Province Daniel C Schechter has lived on the Iberian Peninsula for a total of four years (Lisbon, Barcelona) and returns there often to travel, work or visit old friends or make new ones. As a Lonely Planet author, he has covered five of Spain's autonomous communities and independently explored four more, including the Canary Islands, where he once washed up on a small Dutch yacht. He currently resides and cycles in the Netherlands.

Read more about Daniel at:
netherlandsbikeways.blogspot.com

Published by Lonely Planet Publications Pty Ltd
ABN 36 005 607 983
7th edition – Jan 2013
ISBN 978174 179 848 7
© Lonely Planet 2013   Photographs © as indicated 2013
10 9 8 7 6 5 4 3 2 1
Printed in China